AF707572

The Sustainability Revolution in International Trade Agreements

The Sustainability Revolution in International Trade Agreements

Edited by

GERALDO VIDIGAL
University of Amsterdam

KATHLEEN CLAUSSEN
Georgetown University

OXFORD
UNIVERSITY PRESS

OXFORD
UNIVERSITY PRESS

Great Clarendon Street, Oxford, OX2 6DP,
United Kingdom

Oxford University Press is a department of the University of Oxford.
It furthers the University's objective of excellence in research, scholarship,
and education by publishing worldwide. Oxford is a registered trade mark of
Oxford University Press in the UK and in certain other countries

© The many contributors 2024

The moral rights of the authors have been asserted

All rights reserved. No part of this publication may be reproduced, stored in
a retrieval system, or transmitted, in any form or by any means, without the
prior permission in writing of Oxford University Press, or as expressly permitted
by law, by licence or under terms agreed with the appropriate reprographics
rights organization. Enquiries concerning reproduction outside the scope of the
above should be sent to the Rights Department, Oxford University Press, at the
address above

You must not circulate this work in any other form
and you must impose this same condition on any acquirer

Public sector information reproduced under Open Government Licence v3.0
(http://www.nationalarchives.gov.uk/doc/open-government-licence/open-government-licence.htm)

Published in the United States of America by Oxford University Press
198 Madison Avenue, New York, NY 10016, United States of America

British Library Cataloguing in Publication Data

Data available

Library of Congress Control Number: 2024933330

ISBN 9780198886884

DOI: 10.1093/9780191994470.001.0001

The manufacturer's authorised representative in the EU for product safety is
Oxford University Press España S.A. of El Parque Empresarial San Fernando
de Henares, Avenida de Castilla, 2 – 28830 Madrid (www.oup.es/en or
product.safety@oup.com). OUP España S.A. also acts as importer into Spain
of products made by the manufacturer.

Acknowledgements

This volume began taking shape in our minds in 2021, when a series of developments in policy and treaty-making prompted us to gather a group of experts to engage in a comprehensive review of the turn to sustainability commitments in international trade law. We were pleased to begin the conversation with those experts at a workshop held under the auspices of the International Economic Law Interest Group of the American Society of International Law. Our first thanks go to the hosts and collaborators in organizing the workshop, which took place in March 2022 at the University of Arizona: David Gantz, Sergio Puig, and Julian Arato.

As we developed the Arizona workshop, we identified the scope for a volume-length treatment of the rapidly expanding array of such provisions in trade agreements. We are grateful to Fay Gibbons from Oxford University Press, who found the project promising and agreed to take it on board.

First drafts of the chapters were presented and discussed at an authors' workshop at the University of Amsterdam in November 2023, generously sponsored by the Amsterdam Centre for European Studies and the Amsterdam Center for International Law. Marie-Claire Cordonier Segger offered a valuable keynote speech at the gathering. We thank Jonathan Zeitlin and Ingo Venzke for believing in the project, and Marie Coffey, Dachi Shanidze, and Ellysia van der Werf for the logistical support. Amsterdam LLM researcher Zoé Baize provided significant help and research assistance.

For proofreading the various chapters, we received inestimable help from Betsy Kuhn and Jennifer Lane at Georgetown University Law Center. We also benefitted from research and editorial assistance from LLM researcher Sara Del Grosso at Amsterdam. We are thankful also to Lindsay Glick from Oxford University Press and Shenbagarajan Subramani from Newgen Knowledge Works for coordinating the hard work of turning our text into a physical volume. Noreen Tareque at Georgetown was extremely helpful throughout the process.

Our final thanks go to the contributors. The concept of sustainability in international law has expanded to include a host of issues with multiple variations in dozens of international trade agreements. No one person (or two) could be familiar with all the underlying nuances. Only by benefitting from the contributors' outstanding experiences and diverse viewpoints could this volume emerge as the longstanding repository of knowledge and expertise in this field that we hope it can be and will remain.

The Editors

Contents

List of Abbreviations

AA	Association Agreement
AASHE	Association for the Advancement of Sustainability in Higher Education
ACCTS	Agreement on Climate Change, Trade, and Sustainability
ACP	African, Caribbean and Pacific Group of States
AfCFTA	Agreement Establishing the African Continental Free Trade Area
AFS	Agreement on Fisheries Subsidies
ANZTEC	Agreement between New Zealand and the Separate Customs Territory of Taiwan, Penghu, Kinmen, and Matsu on Economic Cooperation
APEC	Asia-Pacific Economic Cooperation
BIT	bilateral investment treaty
CAFTA–DR	Dominican Republic–Central America–United States Free Trade Agreement
CARICOM	Caribbean Community
CBAM	Carbon Border Adjustment Mechanism
CBD	Convention on Biological Diversity
CBDR	common but differentiated responsibilities
CBDR-RC	common but differentiated responsibilities and respective capabilities
CEPA	comprehensive economic partnership agreement
CETA	Comprehensive Economic and Trade Agreement between Canada and the European Union
CITES	Convention on International Trade in Endangered Species of Wild Fauna and Flora
CJEU	Court of Justice of the European Union
CPTPP	Comprehensive and Progressive Agreement for Trans-Pacific Partnership
CRPD	Convention on the Rights of Persons with Disabilities
CTD	WTO Committee on Trade and Development
CTE	WTO Committee on Trade and Environment
CUSFTA	Canada–United States Free Trade Agreement
CUSMA	Agreement between Canada, the United States of America, and the United Mexican States
DAG	Domestic Advisory Group
DCFTA	Deep and Comprehensive Free Trade Agreement
DSU	Dispute Settlement Understanding
EAC	East African Community
ECA	economic cooperation arrangement
ECLI	European Case Law Identifier
EFTA	European Free Trade Association
EGA	Environmental Goods Agreement
EPA	Economic Partnership Agreement

FCDO	UK Foreign, Commonwealth and Development Office
FDI	foreign direct investment
FFSR	Fossil Fuel Subsidy Reform
FPIC	free, prior and informed consent
FTA	free trade agreement
G7	Group of Seven
G20	Group of Twenty
GASSA	Global Arrangement on Sustainable Steel and Aluminium
GATS	General Agreement on Trade in Services
GATT	General Agreement on Tariffs and Trade
GDP	gross domestic product
GHG	greenhouse gases
GI	geographical indication
GPA	Government Procurement Agreement
GSP	Generalized System of Preferences
GTAGA	Global Trade and Gender Arrangement
GVC	global value chain
IEL	international economic law
IIA	international investment agreement
ILC	International Law Commission
IMF	International Monetary Fund
IPEF	Indo-Pacific Economic Framework for Prosperity
IPETCA	Indigenous Peoples Economic and Trade Cooperation Arrangement
IRA	US Inflation Reduction Act
ISPO	Indonesia Sustainable Palm Oil
ITAG	Inclusive Trade Action Group
IUU	illegal, unreported, and unregulated
IWG	Informal Working Group on Trade and Gender
LABPTA	dataset on labor provisions in trade agreements
LCR	local content requirements
LDC	least developed country
MARPOL	International Convention for the Prevention of Pollution from Ships
MC12	12th Ministerial Conference of the World Trade Organization
MC13	13th Ministerial Conference of the World Trade Organization
MEA	multilateral environment agreement
MLC	Maritime Labour Convention
MOU	memorandum of understanding
MTEC	Māori Trade and Economic Cooperation
NAAEC	North American Agreement on Environmental Cooperation
NAALC	North American Agreement on Labour Cooperation
NAFTA	North American Free Trade Agreement
NCP	non-compliance procedures
NDC	nationally determined contribution
NGO	non-governmental organization
NIEO	New International Economic Order

OCOF	overcapacity and overfishing
OECD	Organization for Economic Co-operation and Development
OECS	Organisation of Eastern Caribbean States
OSINFOR	Organismo Superivor de los Recursos Forestales Maderables/Agency for Supervision of Forest Resources and Wildlife
POIG	Palm Oil Innovation Group
PTA	preferential trade agreement
RCEP	Regional Comprehensive Economic Partnership
RRLM	Rapid Response Labor Mechanism
RRM	Rapid Response Mechanism
RTA	regional trade agreement
SACU	Southern African Customs Union
SCM	Subsidies and Countervailing Measures
SDGs	Sustainable Development Goals
SDT	special and differential treatment
SIA	sustainability impact assessment
SIDS	Small Island Developing States
STARS	Sustainability Tracking, Assessment & Rating System
SVE	small vulnerable economy
TA	trade agreement
TCA	trade and cooperation agreement
TESSD	Trade and Environmental Sustainability Structured Discussions
TFA	Trade Facilitation Agreement
TNA	technical needs assessment
TPP	Trans-Pacific Partnership
TPR	Trade Policy Review
TRIPS	Trade-Related Aspects of Intellectual Property Rights
TSD	trade and sustainable development
UNCTAD	UN Conference on Trade and Development
UNICEF	United Nations International Children's Emergency Fund
UNEP	United Nations Environment Programme
UNFCCC	United Nations Framework Convention on Climate Change
UNGA	United Nations General Assembly
USD	US Dollar
USMCA	Agreement between the United States, the United Mexican States, and Canada
USTR	Office of the US Trade Representative
VCLT	Vienna Convention on the Law of Treaties
WTO	World Trade Organization

List of Contributors

Amrita Bahri, PhD is Associate Professor of Law and Co-Chair for Mexico, WTO Chair Program, ITAM, Mexico City, Mexico

Kevin Banks, BA, LLB, SJD is Associate Professor of Law, Faculty of Law, Queen's University, Kingston, Canada

Kathleen Claussen is Professor of Law, Georgetown University, United States

Ilaria Espa is Associate Professor, Law Institute, USI Lugano, Switzerland, and Senior Research Fellow, World Trade Institute, Bern, Switzerland

Yuka Fukunaga is Professor, Waseda University, Tokyo, Japan

Frank J Garcia is Professor of Law and Dean's Distinguished Scholar, Boston College Law School, United States

Giovanni Gruni, PhD is Director, Department of International, European Union and Comparative Law, Esade Law School, Barcelona, Spain

James Harrison is Professor, School of Law, University of Warwick, Coventry, United Kingdom

Caroline Henckels is Associate Professor, Faculty of Law, Monash University, Melbourne, Australia

Desirée LeClercq is Assistant Professor, School of Law, University of Georgia, Athens, United States

Jaemin Lee is Professor of Law, School of Law, Seoul National University, Korea

Emily Lydgate is Professor of Law, University of Sussex, Brighton, United Kingdom

Gregory Messenger is Associate Professor in Law, University of Bristol, United Kingdom

Timothy Meyer is Richard Allen/Cravath Distinguished Professor in International Business Law, Duke University School of Law, Durham, United States

James J Nedumpara, PhD is Professor and Head, Centre for Trade and Investment Law/ Jindal Global Law School (on leave), Indian Institution of Foreign Trade, New Delhi, India

Mario R Osorio Hernandez is Senior Fellow, Georgetown University Law Center, Washington, DC, United States

Maria Panezi, LLM, PhD is Associate Professor of Law, University of New Brunswick, Fredericton, Canada

Jan Yves Remy is Director, Shridath Ramphal Centre for International Trade Law, Policy and Services, University of the West Indies, Cave Hill, Barbados

Sonia E. Rolland is Professor of Law, Northeastern University School of Law, Boston, United States

Risa Schwartz, LLB, LLM is sole practitioner, Risa Schwartz International Law, Toronto, Canada

Regis Y Simo is Lecturer, School of Law, Queen's University Belfast, United Kingdom

Carrie Stoddart-Smith, LLM (Hons), PG Cert MIL, LLB, BA is Director and Principal Indigenous Trade and Economies Consultant, OpinioNative, Auckland, New Zealand

Joel Trachtman, BA, JD is Professor of International Law and Henry J Braker Professor of Commercial Law, and directs the Center for International Law and Governance, Fletcher School of Law and Diplomacy, Medford, United States

Sanvid Tuljapurkar, LLM is Consultant, TULIP Consulting, Geneva, Switzerland

Anne van Aaken is Professor for Law and Economics, Legal Theory, Public International Law and European Law, Faculty of Law, Director, Institute of Law and Economics, University of Hamburg, Germany

Geraldo Vidigal is Assistant Professor, Amsterdam Law School, University of Amsterdam, the Netherlands

1

A Sustainability Revolution? The Role of Trade Agreements

Geraldo Vidigal and Kathleen Claussen

I. The Sustainability Revolution

Revolution is a powerful word. From its modest astronomical beginnings—where it designates the motion of planets and other celestial bodies[1]—'revolution' has come to mean a fundamental change in a social order, so that the order's previous rules and norms cease to apply and are replaced by new ones. The modern imaginary is populated with events that fundamentally changed the social and political order of societies. Sudden societal changes in England in 1688, the United States in 1776, France in 1789, Haiti in 1804, Mexico in 1910, Russia in 1917, China in 1949, Cuba in 1959, Iran and Nicaragua in 1979, and, in the twenty-first century, the various 'colour revolutions' in Eastern Europe and movements of the Arab Spring, among others, inspire hope and generate concern. Readers will also be familiar with the Industrial Revolution, which, from its emergence in Europe in the late eighteenth century, has produced 'the greatest transformation in human history since the remote times when men invented agriculture and metallurgy, writing, the city and the state'.[2] In modern parlance, 'revolution' has come to designate the replacement of a formerly dominant order with a new one, whether in a society as a whole or in a specific domain.

Demands for a revolution in global production systems now have the political backing of the United Nations General Assembly.[3] Human use of our surrounding environment and consumption of its resources, though identifiable since 'our ancestors hunted, polluted and outcompeted hundreds of species to extinction',[4] can now deplete resources and modify natural cycles on a planetary scale. The astounding increase in human ability to produce, and the matching voraciousness

[1] See eg Nicolaus Copernicus, *On the Revolutions of Heavenly Spheres* (first published 1543, Prometheus 1995). On the different pre-modern uses of the word, see Arthur Hatto, '"Revolution": An Enquiry into the Usefulness of an Historical Term' (1949) 58 Mind 495.

[2] Eric Hobsbawm, *The Age of Revolution, 1789–1848* (first published 1962, Vintage 1996), 1.

[3] United Nations General Assembly (UNGA), 'Transforming Our World: The 2030 Agenda for Sustainable Development', A/RES/70/1, 25 September 2015, esp Goal 12 ('Ensure sustainable consumption and production patterns').

[4] Beth Shapiro, *Life as We Made It: How 50,000 Years of Human Innovation Refined—and Redefined—Nature* (Basic Books 2021), 3.

Geraldo Vidigal and Kathleen Claussen, *A Sustainability Revolution? The Role of Trade Agreements* In: *The Sustainability Revolution in International Trade Agreements*. Edited by: Geraldo Vidigal and Kathleen Claussen, Oxford University Press. © Geraldo Vidigal and Kathleen Claussen 2024. DOI: 10.1093/9780191994470.003.0001

to consume, have meant that global economic activity not only threatens Earth's climate, the relative stability of which has made human life as we know it possible, but also tests the limits of all nine 'planetary boundaries'—Earth's complex of physical, chemical, and biological processes and cycles that ensure a 'safe operating space for humanity'.[5] A less species-threatening but equally challenging aspect of the economic system brought about by the scientific and industrial revolution is its tendency not only to produce wealth but also to concentrate it in the hands of a few. The mobility of capital and, increasingly, of workers with skills and characteristics considered desirable in the global marketplace has hampered the ability of societies to impose, individually, rules to constrain their activities and secure an equitable distribution of resources.

Accordingly, any useful revolution in global production systems must fulfil three parallel imperatives. Production must become environmentally sustainable, in the sense of not compromising the ability of Earth to sustain life. At the same time, it must be socially sustainable. This imperative embodies the need both to *produce* the goods and services that contemporary citizens have come to expect to be available and to secure *distribution* to those that need those goods and services to meet their basic needs and allow them to pursue meaningful lives. The third imperative, that production must be economically sustainable, increasingly depends on ensuring environmental and social sustainability. This interdependence is most visible with regard to climate change. However, governmental efforts to improve environmental sustainability without considering their impacts on citizens' lives and livelihoods can backfire, leading to social unrest and putting the entire enterprise of environmental sustainability at risk.[6]

These imperatives are captured in the notion of 'sustainable development' provided in 1987 by the World Commission on Environment and Development: to seek 'to meet the needs and aspirations of the present without compromising the ability to meet those of the future'.[7] Recent reports and proposals, including the 2015 UN Sustainable Development Goals, have sought to offer concrete paths to ensuring sustainable development by setting specific targets and proposing indicators to assess the steps taken towards achieving them.[8]

[5] Johan Rockström and others, 'A Safe Operating Space for Humanity' (2009) 461 Nature 472. See also Johan Rockström and Owen Gaffney, *Breaking Boundaries: The Science of Our Planet* (DK 2021).

[6] See eg recent events in France and Sri Lanka. James McAuley, 'France's Climate Change Commitments Trigger Rising Diesel Prices and Street Protests', *The Washington Post* (17 November 2018). Ted Nordhaus, 'In Sri Lanka, Organic Farming Went Catastrophically Wrong', *Foreign Policy* (5 March 2022).

[7] World Commission on Environment and Development, *Our Common Future* (OUP 1987, reprinted 2009), 40.

[8] UNGA, 'Transforming Our World' (n 3). See also eg Kate Raworth, *Doughnut Economics—Seven Ways to Think Like a 21st-Century Economist* (Penguin 2017).

II. The Role of International Trade Agreements

International trade agreements (TAs) have traditionally been considered an unlikely vehicle for promoting global sustainability. The prevailing perception of these agreements is that they have a primary liberalization purpose: to reduce barriers to trade, and barriers to economic exchange more broadly, between states. Under this view, TAs tend or ought to limit states' abilities to adopt domestic regulation that would interfere with that primary purpose, including when that regulation might enhance or promote sustainability objectives.

And yet, an empirical analysis of TAs signed over the past thirty years offers a somewhat different picture. Although their attractiveness in most jurisdictions remains significantly tied to the economic gains they may provide by lowering barriers to trade, TAs serve as vehicles for commitments in a variety of areas, including many previously thought to be reserved to domestic policymaking. Among these, many twenty-first century TAs dedicate entire sections to an area that has been labelled 'sustainability': either a single chapter, entitled 'Trade and Sustainable Development' or simply 'Sustainable Development', or two chapters, one for 'Trade and Labour' or 'Labour', the other for 'Trade and Environment' or 'Environment'. These agreements impose on their parties positive obligations in the fields of labour standards and environmental conservation. Increasingly, they also feature detailed mechanisms and procedures to make these obligations enforceable, through adjudication, trade restrictions, and specific compliance control mechanisms.

Observers from multiple fields have sought to explain this expansion of the coverage of TAs. Many have been sceptical, however, of states' capacity to use (or of their interest in using) such provisions to induce a change in conduct. Some civil society actors have considered these chapters to be political bargaining chips and have remained unconvinced that these agreements can achieve sustainability goals. The fact that, in many early TAs, sustainability obligations were not subject to the same trade retaliation remedies as the conventional trade obligations led some to assume that these were second-class commitments rather than meaningful changes in orientation for TAs.

Recent practice in enforcing these obligations appears to contradict this assumption. In 2017, the first panel to address a dispute arising under a sustainability obligation issued its report. This dispute between the United States and Guatemala under the Dominican Republic–Central America–United States Free Trade Agreement concerned Guatemala's failure to effectively enforce its labour laws. Frustration with this panel's approach, which imposed on the complainant the burden to demonstrate a robust connection between the violation of labour obligations and bilateral trade, prompted even greater attention to these provisions. The 2020 Agreement between the United States, the United Mexican States, and Canada (USMCA) includes specific language to shift to the responding party the burden of demonstrating the absence of connection between the violation and trade or investment.[9] And, in 2021, the second panel to adjudicate a sustainability matter—this time concerning the European Union's challenge of South Korea's compliance with labour obligations under the EU–South Korea free trade agreement (FTA)—concluded that the link between labour standards and trade was inherent in the concept of trade enshrined in the TA. The panel stated that, given the 'strong connection between the promotion and attainment of fundamental labour principles and rights and trade ... national measures implementing such rights are therefore *inherently related to trade* as it is conceived in the EU–Korea FTA'.[10]

This ruling reflects a revolution in the discourse concerning the relationship between trade commitments and sustainability demands, which began with the establishment of the World Trade Organization (WTO) in 1995. Under the 1947 General Agreement on Tariffs and Trade (GATT), the dominant understanding of this relationship followed the approach laid down by the 1952 panel in *Belgian Family Allowances*. This panel stated that a trade restriction based on societal objectives 'was difficult to reconcile with the spirit of the General Agreement'.[11] This view was reaffirmed by the 1994 *US—Tuna* panel, which asserted that, if the GATT were interpreted 'to permit contracting parties to take trade measures so as to force other contracting parties to change their policies within their jurisdiction, including their conservation policies', it 'could no longer serve as a multilateral framework for trade among contracting parties'.[12]

The WTO Appellate Body disavowed this perspective in its report in *US—Shrimp*, a dispute concerning a US policy that made importation of shrimp into the United States conditional on the adoption of conservation measures by other WTO Members. The panel in *US—Shrimp* had stated that the US measures, 'irrespective of their environmental purpose, were clearly a threat to the multilateral trading system'.[13] The Appellate Body reversed this finding and the reasoning underlying it. The WTO Agreements, the Appellate Body found, safeguard the right of WTO Members to adopt certain domestic policies, deviating from their regular trade commitments, because the 'domestic policies embodied in such measures have been recognized as important and legitimate in character'. Rules such as GATT Article XX give effect to this right, permitting Members to 'condition[] access to a Member's domestic market on whether exporting Members comply with, or adopt, a policy or policies unilaterally prescribed by the importing Member' that pursue legitimate objectives.[14] Article XX provides that such measures may

[9] USMCA art 23.3(1), fnn 4 and 5 (Labour); art 24.4(1), fnn 4 and 5 (Environment).

[10] Panel of Experts Proceeding Constituted Under Article 13.15 of the EU–Korea Free Trade Agreement, *Report of the Panel of Experts*, 20 January 2021, para 95 (emphasis added).

[11] GATT Panel Report, *Belgian Family Allowances*, adopted 7 November 1952, BISD 1S/59, para 8.

[12] GATT Panel Report, *United States—Restrictions on Imports of Tuna*, 16 June 1994, DS29/R (not adopted), para 5.26.

[13] WTO Panel Report, *US—Shrimp*, adopted 6 November 1998, WT/DS58/R, para 7.61.

[14] Appellate Body Report, *US—Shrimp*, adopted 6 November 1998, WT/DS58/AB/R, para 121.

not result in 'arbitrary or unjustifiable discrimination between countries where the same conditions prevail'.[15] However, so long as regulations are non-discriminatory, 'conditioning market access on the adoption of a programme *comparable in effectiveness*' in the pursuit of a legitimate objective 'allows for sufficient flexibility in the application of the measure so as to avoid "arbitrary or unjustifiable discrimination"'.[16]

Recent TAs continue to permit, through exceptions, the adoption by individual parties of trade-restrictive sustainability measures. Additionally, they increasingly impose positive sustainability commitments on the parties, sometimes using language that, as the panel in *Korea—Labour Commitments* found, suggests sustainability objectives are not a mere add-on to a trade liberalization agreement but inform the decision of the parties to reciprocally liberalize their trade. And, in addition to substantive commitments, these sustainability-oriented TAs increasingly establish dedicated procedures and mechanisms to promote and control compliance with sustainability standards, not only by states but also by producers.

In some TAs, these sustainability-promoting arrangements respond to growing calls for increased enforceability of labour, environmental, and other socio-economic commitments, and specific institutional frameworks dedicated to pursuing these aims. Most recently, these calls have led to detailed revisions to old models of agreements. First, two TAs—the USMCA and the European Union–United Kingdom Trade and Cooperation Agreement—set up original sanctions mechanisms to address sustainability concerns.[17] Similarly, the recent European Free Trade Association–Indonesia Comprehensive Economic Partnership Agreement conditions tariff preferences on palm oil to sustainable harvesting;[18] and the EU–Mercosur Association Agreement employs a similar mechanism to condition tariff preferences on the fulfilment of animal welfare standards.[19]

Second, inter-state enforcement mechanisms can be effective without a final report. Significant inter-state engagement takes place within Domestic Advisory Groups and through their interplay with bilateral Trade and Sustainable Development committees.[20] Between 2018 and 2020, the United States twice

[15] ibid para 120 (quoting GATT art XX).

[16] Appellate Body Report, *US—Shrimp* (art 21.5), adopted 21 November 2001, WT/DS58/AB/RW, para 144.

[17] Kathleen Claussen, 'Trade's Experimental Compliance Mechanisms' in Manfred Elsig, Rodrigo Polanco, and Peter van den Bossche (eds), *International Economic Dispute Settlement: Demise or Transformation?* (CUP 2021), 350, 353.

[18] Comprehensive Economic Partnership Agreement between the Republic of Indonesia and the EFTA States, signed 16 December 2018, in force 1 November 2021, art 8.10 and Annexes III, IV, and V (fn on last page of each annex).

[19] The tariff benefit requires compliance with Council Directive 1999/74/EC of 19 July 1999 laying down minimum standards for the protection of laying hens (OJ L 203, 3.8.1999, 53–57) 'or any equivalent animal welfare official standards . . . verified either by official certification or by third party certification'. EU–Mercosur Association Agreement (agreed in principle 15 July 2021, not signed), Annex 2-A (Tariff Elimination Schedule—General Provisions), para 5(l).

[20] These mechanisms also operate in tandem with more legalised dispute settlement. See eg the discussions in the aftermath of the *Korea—Labour Commitments* panel. EU–Korea Free Trade

invoked the US–Peru Trade Promotion Agreement (which features a Forest Sector Governance Annex) to address illegal logging in Peru,[21] and requested consultations under the United States–Korea Free Trade Agreement to demand meaningful sanctioning of illegal fishing activities by Korean fishers.[22] Outside the purview of inter-state dispute settlement, sustainability obligations may provide the basis for political demands for compliance within TA institutional structures as well as in other fora.[23]

Finally, the inclusion of sustainability obligations within TAs may lead to normative developments beyond the bilateral relations between parties to the agreement, both by reshaping the expectations of states as to what content is fitting for newly negotiated TAs and through legal mechanisms that require existing agreements and trading relationships to be interpreted in light of their broader contexts. Thus, interpreters gauging the legitimacy of a trade restriction justified on grounds of environmental conservation or protection of workers' rights may find in widely adopted sustainability obligations reasons to deem a certain unilaterally determined requirement legitimate (or, conversely, to deem it excessive if unsupported by the broader normative environment as expressed in other agreements).[24]

III. Argument of the Book

The introduction of obligations in the areas of environmental conservation, labour standards, and increasingly in areas such as human rights or animal welfare challenges the assumption that TAs should be characterized by regulatory neutrality.

Under the 'sustainability revolution', the relationship between TAs and sustainability policies—understood broadly as limits to economic freedom aimed at pursuing other societal objectives—can be thought of in three stages. Prior to the 1990s, states entered into TAs under the assumption that sustainability decisions remained within each state's sphere of domestic regulatory freedom. In the 1990s, the emergence of environmental sustainability as a global concern led to a reconsideration of this relationship. In North America, the three major economies signed two agreements, one on labour (the North American Agreement on Labor

Agreement Committee on Trade and Sustainable Development, Joint Minutes of the 8th Session (15 and 16 September 2022), 2–3.

[21] See Claussen, 'Trade's Experimental Compliance Mechanisms' (n 17), 357.

[22] Geraldo Vidigal, 'Regional Trade Adjudication and the Rise of Sustainability Disputes: Korea—Labor Commitments and Ukraine—Wood Export Bans' (2022) 116 American Journal of International Law 567, 570.

[23] Kathleen Claussen, 'Reimagining Trade-Plus Compliance: The Labor Story' (2020) 23 Journal of International Economic Law 25.

[24] Geraldo Vidigal, 'From Bilateral to Multilateral Law-making: Legislation, Practice, Evolution and the Future of Inter Se Agreements in the WTO' (2013) 24 European Journal of International Law 1027.

Cooperation) and the other on the environment (the North American Agreement on Environmental Cooperation). Despite their status as side agreements and their limited enforceability, they provided a path and a textual basis for future agreements. At the WTO, the reinterpretation of trade exceptions permitted Members to condition importation of goods on the adoption of environmentally sustainable production standards, subject to non-discrimination requirements.

A further development since 2000 has been the addition to TAs of positive sustainability obligations. This addition meant that the balance between economic freedom and sustainability policies was no longer left to individual parties and their regulatory decisions but rather such policies would be inscribed into TAs. To an extent, the latter development is a consequence of some parties' understanding that international trade does not take place in a neutral regulatory space but actively shapes the incentives of trade partners and their ability to adopt regulatory standards. At the same time, by requiring states to adhere to agreed regulatory standards—some defined by each party, some by reference to international norms and standards, and some designed to evolve as shared standards change—TAs increasingly reach beyond bilateral economic relations to other areas of international regulatory governance.

This volume is dedicated to examining the legal, political, and economic effects of the incorporation of sustainability provisions as standard elements in TAs, recent advances surrounding such provisions, and the future outlook for TAs as sustainability tools. While other works have taken on elements of the trade and sustainability agenda, this book takes a general view of the broader practice, the linkages among these goals and mechanisms, and the conceptual debates surrounding their impact for trade and sustainability practices and literatures. Much of the prior work done on these issues is limited to individual sectors or regions—and for good reason: many of these innovations are difficult to identify and suffer from transparency challenges. The chapters that follow draw on expertise from different parts of the world and engage experts familiar with those nuances not only to underscore the importance and prevalence of these trends but also to unpack and analyse their significance in broader strokes for these intersecting fields.

This volume is divided into three parts. Part I features chapters that provide overall context and analysis of this 'sustainability revolution': whether it means a real change in approach, what assumptions ground the pursuit of sustainability through TAs, and how it can be expected to affect outcomes on the ground. The chapters in Part II zoom in on the various components of the sustainability revolution. Some chapters examine how TAs translate social and environmental concerns into legal commitments; other chapters explore the legal mechanisms and procedures and institutional arrangements developed to ensure enforceability of these commitments. Part III considers core challenges for the 'sustainability revolution' to go beyond producing a change in conceptual approach to trade and induce a sustainability revolution in real-life practices in production and trade. The chapters in that Part examine legal, political, and economic challenges to the fulfilment of the promise of a more sustainable production system through TAs.

TAs, just as other international agreements—and all legal instruments—are documents in writing. Legal instruments do not in themselves affect outcomes in the real world. They establish grounds for behaviour, produce language to guide expectations, and set up institutional structures for interaction. It falls upon those advocates seeking to produce a sustainability revolution in global production patterns to pursue it, through legal and other instruments, within available institutions—states, companies, intergovernmental and non-governmental organizations. Many stakeholders remain attached to the idea that TAs are obstacles to the attainment of sustainability goals. The chapters ahead show that TAs should at least be considered seriously as instruments that can actively promote, support, and enforce sustainability objectives.

PART I

SUSTAINABILITY IN INTERNATIONAL TRADE AGREEMENTS: CONFLICT OR COMPLEMENTARITY

2

Embedding Sustainable Development in Trade

Joel P Trachtman[*]

I. Introduction

The world is in the grips of a struggle for survival. The focus of that struggle is on preserving a liveable climate and biodiversity. Other components of sustainability and sustainable development, including poverty alleviation, also present great challenges.

Individual national action to make life on Earth sustainable seems ineffective. Although some leading states may act unilaterally, it is unlikely that unilateral action will be sufficient, given the nature of the public good needed and related incentive problems. Collective action is limited by free-rider problems and problems of different national goals. Even if some leading states may aspire to launch an extraterritorial cascade of positive action, through carbon border adjustments or climate clubs, these unilateral acts will likely fail to respect the agency of other states and can be seen as acts of imperialism, possibly leading to backlash that may destroy the trade system.[1]

Trade is a tool that is used to increase human welfare. It is not an end in itself. Sustainable development, on the other hand, in the sense used herein, is a broad term that includes both tools to increase human welfare and several other values that are ends in themselves, such as planetary preservation and reduction of poverty. Even the goal of increasing human welfare is qualified by a need to distribute human welfare in an appropriate (and politically sustainable) way. Appropriate distribution is both a desideratum and a necessity for political stability and support.

* This chapter was prepared in connection with the Society of International Economic Law (SIEL) Tucson Sustainability and Trade Agreements Workshop in March 2022, and the SIEL Amsterdam Sustainability and Trade Agreements Workshop in November 2022. I am grateful for comments by participants in those workshops. Thanks also to Adelle Blackett, Jeff Dunoff, Dan Esty, Andrew Lang, and Jan Yves Remy, who provided valuable comments.

[1] See Regulation (EU) 2023/956 of the European Parliament and of the Council of 10 May 2023 establishing a carbon border adjustment mechanism.

Joel P Trachtman, *Embedding Sustainable Development in Trade* In: *The Sustainability Revolution in International Trade Agreements.* Edited by: Geraldo Vidigal and Kathleen Claussen, Oxford University Press. © Joel P Trachtman 2024. DOI: 10.1093/9780191994470.003.0002

II. Sustainable Trade Calls for the Reinvention of Embedded Liberalism

'There are four dimensions to sustainable development—society, environment, culture and economy—which are intertwined, not separate.'[2] Holistic integration of these dimensions is at the centre of sustainable development. Focusing on the 2015 UN Sustainable Development Goals, we might consider two broad categories of goals: (i) those regarding environmental and social goals, and (ii) more economic goals relating to poverty, inequality, and growth. These all have to do with a broad measure of human welfare, in the economic but certainly not just in the monetary sense, and a concern for how that welfare is distributed.

With regard to environmental goals, the 'trade and environment' interface first came to broad public attention in 1991 with the first *Tuna—Dolphin* case under the General Agreement on Tariffs and Trade (GATT).[3] While a Committee on Trade and Environment within the World Trade Organization (WTO) was created in 1994, and, in 2020, the WTO commenced Trade and Environmental Sustainability Structured Discussions (TESSD), little has been done at the political level to manage this interface. For example, it has taken years to reach a limited agreement regarding certain fisheries subsidies, or even to begin discussions on the scourge of fossil fuel subsidies.[4] The December 2021 TESSD statement reads like a satire of diplomats: 'intensify our work', 'launch discussions', 'explore opportunities', 'identify best practices', etc. So the trade system has so far done little to contribute directly to sustainability.

On the other hand, trade agreements (TAs) are largely an innocent bystander in relation to the problem of sustainability. The WTO and preferential TAs do little that is directly positive or negative for environmental sustainability, unless we are thinking of the possible positive effect of an environmental Kuznets curve whereby growth is expected to result in greater environmental protection, or the negative effect of increased consumption that accompanies increased wealth.[5] The anti-discrimination, subsidies or even proportionality regimes of TAs do little to restrict environmental protection per se.

However, there are three main areas that seem to require reform. First, it is likely, but not certain enough, that even-handed climate border adjustments are permissible under WTO law. Second, subsidies for sustainability may be countervailable or otherwise actionable. Third, it is true that the anti-discrimination rules limit the ability to utilize discrimination or other protectionism to secure domestic

[2] Eila Kyllikki Jeronen, 'Sustainability and Sustainable Development' in Samuel O Idowu and others (eds), *Encyclopedia of Corporate Social Responsibility* (Springer 2013).

[3] *United States—Restrictions on Imports of Tuna* (3 September 1991) GATT Doc DS21/R.

[4] WTO Agreement on Fisheries Subsidies (17 June 2022) WT/MIN(22)/33 WT/L/1144.

[5] Jose Antonio Monteiro and Joel P Trachtman, 'Environmental Laws' in Aaditya Mattoo, Nadia Rocha, and Michele Ruta (eds), *Handbook of Deep Trade Agreements* (WTO 2020).

political support for environmental protection measures, and that there may be circumstances in which the trade detriment is less than the environmental benefit of securing support for these measures.[6]

Rodrik makes what is in effect a regulatory competition argument to the effect that what he calls 'hyperglobalization'—more complete economic integration—by allowing states with lesser environmental regulation to compete through exports with states with greater environmental protection, disrupts political regulatory bargains in importing states, undermining environmental protection in those states.[7] However, there is still very little evidence of an environmental regulatory competition or a race to the bottom.[8]

Trade agreements are largely focused on maximization of monetary welfare. While monetary welfare does not directly promote sustainability, to the extent that an environmental Kuznets curve is operative, it may at some point promote environmental protection. In addition, liberalized trade in environmental goods and services would enhance environmental protection. Finally, depending on how the increases in monetary welfare are distributed, they may well promote the development component of sustainable development. Indeed, at the same time that globalization has grown, *international* inequality has ebbed:

> China was the primary engine, but around 2000, India began to play an important role. Currently, global inequality is about 63 Gini points, which is some 7 Gini points (or 10%) less than in the 1980s. The level however is still extremely high: the world is about as unequal as South Africa, which is the most unequal country in the world.[9]

As Karl Polanyi wrote in 1944,[10] and as quoted by John Ruggie in 1982,[11] 'normally, the economic order is merely a function of the social, in which it is

[6] Timothy Meyer, 'How Local Discrimination Can Promote Global Public Goods' (2015) 95 Boston University Law Review 1937.

[7] See most recently Dani Rodrik, 'A Better Globalization Might Rise from Hyperglobalization's Ashes' (*Project Syndicate*, 9 May 2022) <https://www.project-syndicate.org/commentary/after-hyperglobalization-national-interests-open-economy-by-dani-rodrik-2022-05> accessed 19 November 2022.

[8] However, for some empirical evidence of regulatory arbitrage, see Shinsuke Tanaka, Kensuke Teshima, and Eric Verhoogen, 'North–South Displacement Effects of Environmental Regulation: The Case of Battery Recycling' (2021) NBER Working Paper 29146 <https://www.nber.org/papers/w29146> accessed 19 November 2022. See also Florian Misch and Philippe Wingender, 'Revisiting Carbon Leakage' (2021) IMF Working Paper WP21/207 <https://www.imf.org/en/Publications/WP/Issues/2021/08/06/Revisiting-Carbon-Leakage-462148> accessed 19 November 2022.

[9] Branko Milanovic, 'Notes on Global Income Inequality: A Non-Technical Summary' (*Global Policy*, 20 May 2021) <https://www.globalpolicyjournal.com/blog/20/05/2021/notes-global-income-inequality-non-technical-summary> accessed 19 November 2022; Karl Polyani, *The Great Transformation* (Farrar & Rinehart 1944).

[10] ibid.

[11] John Ruggie, 'International Regimes, Transactions and Change: Embedded Liberalism in the Postwar Economic Order' (1982) 36 International Organization 2, 379. See also, John Ruggie, 'Embedded Liberalism Revisited: Institutions and Progress in International Economic Relations'

contained. Under neither tribal, nor feudal, nor mercantile conditions was there, as we have shown, a separate economic system in society'. Normally, economic orders are embedded in social orders. Ruggie and Polanyi were thinking of economic disruptions, and domestic redistribution, but the critique of an image of trade separate from other social functions is still applicable, at least domestically, and can be extended to the international system.

In 1999, Jeffrey Dunoff explored the ways in which WTO law might 'undermine the domestic policy tolerance central to the "embedded liberalism" compromise'.[12] In 2002, Rob Howse expressed nostalgia for 'a GATT system that was embedded within a political commitment, broadly shared among the major players in the trading system of that era, to the progressive, interventionist welfare state'.[13] The GATT system neither supported nor restricted a progressive, interventionist welfare state and if there were a reversion to GATT, it would do little to solve today's sustainable development problems.

The proposal in the 1940s for an 'International Trade Organization', which was never formed, and for which the 1947 GATT was established as a placeholder, contained provisions for labour protection and anticipated greater state intervention in the economy. However, while neither the GATT nor the WTO involved much integration of trade policies with other areas of public policy, both are reasonably permissive with respect to industrial and social policy. In 2006, Andrew Lang took stock of the embedded liberalism discourse, including Jeff Dunoff's important work,[14] explaining that Ruggie's work 'shows us that we should also be debating what "social purpose" we want the trade regime to embody [in addition to monetary welfare]'.[15] He explains that 'we need to reinvent embedded liberalism for the global age by finding new ways and new forms through which to combine social protection with a continuing commitment to liberal trade'.[16]

The embedded liberalism literature did not take account of the need for *international* cooperation concerning regulatory issues, as now seems necessary to address global warming and biodiversity loss. International cooperation also seems necessary to avoid unilateral action by large trading powers, or even some standard-setting action by private entities, without sufficiently considering the potential adverse effects on market access for developing countries. And yet the

in Emanuel Adler and Beverly Crawford (eds), *Progress in Postwar Economic Relations* (Columbia University Press 1991).

[12] Jeffrey L Dunoff, 'The Death of the Trade Regime' (1999) 10 European Journal of International Law 733.

[13] Robert Howse, 'From Politics to Technocracy—and Back Again: The Fate of the Multilateral Trading Regime' (2002) 96 American Journal of International Law 94, 97.

[14] Dunoff, 'The Death of the Trade Regime' (n 12).

[15] Andrew Lang, 'Reconstructing Embedded Liberalism: John Gerard Ruggie and Constructivist Approaches to the Study of the International Trade Regime' (2006) 9 Journal of International Economic Law 1, 84.

[16] ibid 98.

example of the EU single market suggests that the only way to responsibly diminish the trade-impeding effects of divergent non-discriminatory regulation is to engage in international agreements for either harmonization or recognition, or a combination of the two. Any deregulation at the local level must be accompanied by re-regulation, or at least opportunities for re-regulation, at the international level.

Ruggie's concept of embedded liberalism depends on two ideas, which may well have been historically apt when he expressed them in 1982: first, that international regimes are functionally isolated projects, and second, that they have discrete social purposes. Much has changed in forty years, perhaps based on the illumination of this literature, or maybe because of broader multifaceted globalization. We can now see clearly that the trade regime is descriptively and normatively part of a broader international society, and that, as the US federation and the European Union found, commerce and the goal of avoiding inefficient impediments to commerce is not functionally separate from regulation, including regulation to promote sustainability. Avoiding impediments to commerce is not itself a social purpose but a tool of achieving the broader social purpose of enhanced welfare.

Recall that Polanyi's original idea was purely domestic: the domestic market needs domestic *redistribution* for stability. The embedded liberalism literature made two moves.

First, Ruggie assumed purely domestic intervention on the one hand, but for him this *domestic* redistribution balances *international* trade, perhaps in addition to balancing the domestic market and economic dislocation caused by competition. While the domestic market, and technological change, cause most of the economic dislocation we observe today, international trade, because of its susceptibility to scapegoating, needed special attention. Rodrik explains that trade itself is not different from the problem of market competition generally:

> Some suggest trade is problematic because it redistributes income. The basis for that claim is true, but trivial. Pretty much everything else that happens in a market economy redistributes income somehow. Technology and market competition are the source of endless churn in an economy. Moreover, plenty of other things, including skill-based innovation and minimum wage laws, have vastly greater effects on income distribution than trade per se.

The problem here is that trade makes the scope of the market global, while redistribution is assumed to be purely domestic. Adelle Blackett, in her work on international labour law, terms the focus on national redistribution as 'methodological nationalism'.[17] Methodological nationalism limits the scope of management of the

[17] Adelle Blackett, 'Toward Social Regionalism in the Americas', (2002) Comparative Labor Law and Policy Journal 901, 591. Methodological nationalism is a concept developed in Andreas Wimmer and Nina Glick Schiller, 'Methodological Nationalism and Beyond: Nation-State Building, Migration and the Social Sciences' (2002) 2 Global Networks 4, 301.

social. Lang points out that the Bretton Woods formulation of embedded liberalism for maintaining stability involved domestic interventions (such as subsidies), provided that they would not impose disproportionate international externalities.[18]

Second, the literature moved from a wealth redistribution focus to a broader social and regulatory focus on environment and other values that are not linked in the same pecuniary sense. Polanyi's idea was monetary, not social. It is suggested that existing TAs do not positively or directly promote non-monetary welfare. This is focused on domestic rather than international regulation. So, in connection with both redistribution and regulation, the embedded liberalism literature has contained a discontinuity: it prescribes domestic instruments to 'embed' a global market.

Compare the WTO to a federation, like the United States or the European Union. Inside those mature federations, internal trade law is not a leading or even very contentious area of law.[19] Internal free trade is assumed, but the US and EU single markets depend on centralized regulation in non-trade areas, subject in the United States to the limits of the Commerce Clause in the US Constitution, and subject in the European Union to subsidiarity. The United States or European Union without centralized regulation would be caricatures of a market economy without parallel capacity for regulation: this is the problem that the international trade system encounters today.

The anti-regulatory capitalism fostered by the Chicago School and the Washington Consensus does not work on a national level—we need regulation to internalize externalities where appropriate and to ensure that the benefits of competition reach the citizens. It is also necessary to migrate that approach to regulation to the international level, where the WTO and the world trading system have come to symbolize an unregulated market economy—benefiting those who profit from commerce at the expense of those who bear the externalities.

While trade law may constrain some environmental or social regulatory measures, the more urgent problem is the failure to act positively to address these sustainable development issues. Embedded liberalism took no account of the need for positive international action because it focused on monetary welfare, and because it envisioned the social as purely domestic: methodological nationalism. The WTO and preferential TAs contain practically no significant positive environmental requirements or other sustainability obligations. Some preferential TAs contain obligations to adhere to and comply with certain international environmental agreements or even other obligations, but the overall additionality in environmental protection is not impressive, and generally does not address climate

[18] Lang (n 15), 98.

[19] But see the 2023 US Supreme Court case, *National Pork Producers v Ross*, 598 US ____ (2023) (upholding California's regulation of the conditions in which pigs are raised in other states).

change.[20] For example, there are no requirements to reduce greenhouse gas emissions beyond existing requirements under international environmental law.

It may be unfair to criticize trade treaties for their negligence of non-monetary welfare because regulation and redistribution have not been viewed as their task. Certainly subsidiarity today argues for much greater action at the international level: the international level is the appropriate level at which to address climate change, biodiversity, and many other issues. In addition to methodological nationalism that assumes that these tasks are national, this may be for reasons of subsidiarity or instrument choice: functional isolation or siloing of different international cooperation. That does not mean that these issues are the appropriate domain of the trade system. The instrument choice claim would argue that TAs or organizations lack a formal mandate and also lack the needed expertise to address non-monetary welfare.

As to the subsidiarity and instrument choice issues, as suggested in Wolfgang Friedmann's 1964 classic, *The Changing Structure of International Law*, international law grows in different subjects at different times and in accordance with different dynamics.[21] There is also dynamic feedback from one area to another, especially from trade liberalization law to these environmental and social fields. Regulation follows the market. Thus, reasonably successful economic integration gives rise to the need to cooperate in the environmental and social fields. While there is still little evidence of regulatory competition in environmental regulation, concerns regarding leakage arising from national carbon regulation, and consequent opposition to regulation, seem like a good reason to link the environment to trade. Globalization has intensified the external effects of national policy in many areas.

These are natural linkages, but there are also constructed linkages—linkages that exploit cross-subject matter reciprocity.[22] William Nordhaus proposed climate clubs that would be secured through threats of trade sanctions, and it is evident that working within carbon regulation, without linkage, has not produced sufficient carbon reduction.[23] Nordhaus' assumption is that states advocating greater carbon reduction hold unused bargaining power that they could use to induce other states to comply. Although it might be thought that this assumption is simply wrong—that all bargaining power is fully deployed in equilibrium—bargaining power can be redeployed from one goal to another if there is political

[20] Monteiro and Trachtman, 'Environmental Laws' (n 5).

[21] Wolfgang Friedmann, *The Changing Structure of International Law* (University Presses of California, Columbia, and Princeton 1964).

[22] See generally Giovanni Maggi, 'Issue Linkage' in Kyle Bagwell and Robert W Staiger (eds), *Handbook of Commercial Policy* vol 1, pt B (Elsevier 2016) 513.

[23] William Nordhaus, 'The Climate Club: How to Fix a Failed Global Effort' (*Foreign Affairs*, 10 April 2020) <https://www.foreignaffairs.com/articles/united-states/2020-04-10/climate-club> accessed 19 November 2022.

will to do so. Additional bargaining power may be gained by making additional trade liberalization available.

Today we observe a disequilibrium—in embedded liberalism terms, an instability. Sustainable trade refers to the need to bring these linkages into equilibrium to maximize global welfare. Regardless of the debate about what law is applicable in WTO dispute settlement,[24] it is clear that international society must work holistically, recognizing that no area of public policy is isolated from other areas. This is a task of integrating different functional spheres more effectively, through bureaucratic and institutional cross-functional engagement. The era of siloed regimes with discrete social purposes, identities, and institutional loyalties must end. International organizations must expand their concerns beyond narrow mandates and cooperate with other international organizations to solve problems.

There is a need for more integrated and flexible international lawmaking capabilities. It was always strange that diplomats would block discussion of 'non-trade' issues in the WTO simply on the basis of this categorization. (It is worth noting that this principle was compromised for the WTO Agreement on Trade-Related Aspects of Intellectual Property (TRIPS).) Siloing the making of international law is simply ignorant of the natural, and constructed, linkages between fields.

In order to reach equilibrium, international politics must be integrated, subject to the principle of subsidiarity, in order to better integrate legal regimes: diplomats must negotiate over trade and sustainable development so that legal rules are not developed in functional isolation. This task requires trade-offs among the varying preferences that different states have with respect to different aspects of global welfare. In particular, developing countries may have different preferences with respect to environmental and social action compared to wealthy countries. On the domestic side, there is a need for states to develop the capacity for more integrated diplomacy—they can no longer separate trade from data, environment, labour, competition, taxation, inequality, or other national policies. Diplomats need new mandates to fully address these cross-functional trade-offs. Furthermore, international organizations must be charged with 'inter-functional' mandates. For example, it is no longer enough for the WTO to maximize trade liberalization: it must maximize overall welfare including a focus on trade liberalization but also take into account, and achieve, sustainable development.

Broader linkage may make international legislation easier by facilitating cross-functional bargaining and trade-offs. In addition, international law needs quasi-constitutional reform to enhance the ability to legislate, by reducing veto points whereby small numbers of states can block global collective action, imposing a tyranny of the minority. The move to majority voting, or qualified majority voting,

[24] See eg Joel Trachtman, 'Review of Joost Pauwelyn, Conflict of Norms in Public International Law: How WTO Law Relates to Other Rules of International Law' (2004) 98 American Journal of International Law 855.

could begin in specific areas viewed as less politically sensitive. The experience of the European Union is instructive. Where specific rules are too difficult to create, states need to explicitly delegate the making of these trade-offs to judges under general standards. This would require policy analysis and synthesis of the type that is common in domestic contexts but all too lacking in international fora. This is what is required for sustainable trade: integration of trade with other parts of global law.

III. 'Green Bargain': Achieving Sustainable Development-Based Trade

I turn now to the second major task before the world trading system: the development component of sustainable development. Lang and Blackett critique the failure of embedded liberalism to include a development dimension.[25] [26] Recall that in Ruggie's approach, each state was responsible for its own domestic intervention for political stability. Moreover, Lang points out that embedded liberalism often externalized the costs of adjustment to developing countries.[27]

Trade is a powerful engine of development. Market access for exports, imports of efficiently produced goods and services to give developing countries the benefits of international supply chains and markets, foreign investment, and migration can all help to reduce the separation of economies. This integration into the world economy provides poor people with access to capital to make them more productive and therefore able to command higher wages. This in turn causes convergence of wages and welfare. In this sense, globalization in general and trade in particular are engines of cross-border equality. To the extent that there is an environmental Kuznets curve, this growth causes convergence of preferences for public goods that can help to support sustainability.

In the shorter term, global society must recognize the different preferences of poor people and poor countries. Where global public goods such as carbon reduction, disease control, tax enforcement, or cybersecurity are concerned, poor countries cannot be expected to prioritize these goods at the same level as wealthy countries. Poor countries have demanded accommodations such as common but differentiated responsibilities, or climate finance, in order to join with wealthy countries to provide the wealthy countries' priorities in connection with global public goods. (While reduced emissions may help poor countries even more than wealthy countries, because of their greater vulnerability or because of the costs of mitigation, it still may be too costly for poor countries to act without support.)

[25] Blackett, 'Toward Social Regionalism (n 17), 608.
[26] Lang (n 15), 99–100.
[27] ibid 100.

In this way, development is linked to sustainability. But the development component, like the sustainability component, has not been sufficiently achieved. Sustainable development, like sustainable trade, requires broadening the agenda—more holistic and integrated thinking. And, of course, the choice of topics excluded from trade liberalization or regulation, like indigenous knowledge, migration, and to some extent agricultural goods, is part of this holistic thinking. But it also requires an examination of the role of power. Assuming, as one must, that developing countries will not be able to depend on altruism from wealthy countries, their problem has been a lack of bargaining power.

Recall the Nordhaus idea that there is slack trade bargaining power that can be used to induce countries that would otherwise not do so to reduce carbon emissions. This is in part because the wealthy countries that prioritize reduced emissions are often economically large, while developing countries are economically small: they lack terms of trade power. Some wealthy countries, on the other hand, like the United States and those in the European Union, but perhaps including other economically large countries in connection with certain goods, hold terms of trade power that allow them to extract producer surplus from exporters through tariffs.

It has always been a puzzle why countries that hold terms of trade power make commitments in TAs to countries that do not.[28] The best strategy for countries that do not hold terms of trade power is unilateral and total liberalization. So, why exchange commitments? The solution to this puzzle is not altruism. Instead, powerful countries are extracting concessions from weak countries. This occurs in areas such as intellectual property protection. The inclusion of the TRIPS in the WTO, and TRIPS plus in preferential TAs, can be understood in this way. But it also includes certain services, demands for investment protection, certain concessions demanded in exchange for the Generalized System of Preferences treatment, and the denial of full public services and other rights to migrants from poor countries.

It would be beneficial if the wealthy countries would turn their use of power towards global public goods that benefit all, but while this may achieve sustainable trade, there are two problems. First, they have not done so sufficiently thus far, and second, it would not go as far to achieve sustainable *development*-based trade. How can poor countries increase their terms of trade power? First, they can grow, as China has done, through industrialization and exports. Second, they can band together in customs unions or other mechanisms in order to aggregate economic power: they are stronger together.

But the developing countries have begun to go further. Recognizing the need for global governance for sustainability—as in climate change—developing

[28] See generally Kyle Bagwell and Robert Staiger, *The Economics of the World Trading System* (MIT Press 2004).

countries, like the more dispossessed classes in Polanyi's original domestic vision, can threaten disruption of that governmentality unless interventions are made to compensate them. Indeed, this is one way to look at common but differentiated responsibilities and climate finance. Developing countries can demand greater market access and greater assistance, in exchange for cooperation in producing global public goods. This transactional approach might lead to a 'Green Bargain', that would promote both sustainability and poverty reduction.

IV. Conclusion

To conclude, as we think about 'sustainable development', the sustainability component should be understood as a call holistically to maximize multidimensional aggregate welfare; and adding 'development' to the equation adds the dimension of seeking an attractive—sustainable—distribution of welfare. It is clear that the separation of topics of discussion makes it difficult to organize and negotiate cross-sectoral exchanges between states. This is not the way that domestic legislatures work—they horse trade. Domestic legislatures also have constitutional structures for majority voting that further facilitate action, and link exchanges over time. In order to negotiate sustainable development facilitating trade, developing countries must increase their leverage by making agreements on sustainability issues, in exchange for greater considerations on trade issues.

3

Making Trade Agreements Contribute to Sustainability

The Potential of Behavioural Science

Anne van Aaken[*]

I. Introduction

The interaction between trade and the environment is not a recent phenomenon. The negotiators of the Uruguay Round squarely put sustainable development in the preamble of the Marrakesh Agreement. Yet, on the global level and in regional trade agreements, the intricate relationship between trade and the environment—or more broadly, sustainability—has not been at the centre of trade governance. This is changing now, also on the global level: the World Trade Organization (WTO) is very much interested in addressing the intersection of trade and sustainability.[1] The Agreement on Fisheries Subsidies of 2022[2] is the first WTO agreement 'with environmental sustainability at its heart'.[3] Coalitions of Member States are working on various issues, such as climate, the circular economy, plastic pollution, and trade in environmental goods to align the international trading system with sustainability.[4] What is at the heart of the matter is that while trade relies on bilaterally understood reciprocity,[5] sustainability is characterized by a public good constellation—often making freeriding the preferred option. Thus, thinking about how to integrate sustainability in trade treaties, or combine reciprocity with public goods, needs careful governance mechanisms. This chapter considers these

* I would like to thank Kathleen Claussen, Geraldo Vidigal, and Joel Trachtman for very helpful comments. All remaining errors are mine.

[1] WTO, 'DG Okonjo-Iweala: Trade is critical in global response to climate change' (8 November 2022) <https://www.wto.org/english/news_e/news22_e/cop27_08nov22_e.htm> accessed 12 February 2024.

[2] Agreement on Fisheries Subsidies, WT/MIN(22)/33, adopted at the 12th Ministerial Conference (MC12) on 17 June 2022 (not in force).

[3] Ngozi Okonjo-Iweala, 'MC12 Closing Session', *Speech to WTO Delegates*, 17 June 2022 <https://www.wto.org/english/news_e/spno_e/spno27_e.htm> accessed 12 February 2024.

[4] WTO Trade and Environmental Sustainability Structured Discussions: Informal Working Group Meetings held on 4–5 October 2022, 'Aide-Memoire', INF/TE/SSD/R/13 (21 October 2022).

[5] Joost Pauwelyn, 'A Typology of Multilateral Treaty Obligations: Are WTO Obligations Bilateral or Collective in Nature?' (2003) 14 European Journal of International Law 907.

Anne van Aaken, *Making Trade Agreements Contribute to Sustainability* In: *The Sustainability Revolution in International Trade Agreements*. Edited by: Geraldo Vidigal and Kathleen Claussen, Oxford University Press. © Anne van Aaken 2024.
DOI: 10.1093/9780191994470.003.0003

possible governance models and their implications in greater detail, taking as a starting point a rationalist approach informed by behavioural insights.

The United Nations, specialized UN Agencies, and other international organizations are turning behavioural.[6] The United Nations clearly states that behavioural science should be included in its work to achieve the Sustainable Development Goals (SDGs).[7] Behavioural science broadly refers to 'the evidence-based study of how people behave, make decisions and respond to programmes, policies and incentives'.[8] Numerous initiatives by states, often guided by international organizations, are taking place.[9]

It is highly promising that more realistic behavioural assumptions and insights underpin policies of international organizations, their member states, and international law, including trade law.[10] Yet, the utilization of behavioural sciences to advance sustainability in international trade law remains unexplored. This is likely for two reasons: first, in trade law and policy, the state is typically considered the relevant unit of analysis. Second, trade is regarded as a field based on reciprocity of trade benefits, in which rationally pursued material self-interest is paramount. This chapter challenges these two assumptions and aims to show how behavioural science may be used when attempting to interlink trade and sustainable development, both at the interstate level, for negotiation and treaty drafting, and when connecting sustainable development and economic operators (including consumers). Markets and sustainable development are deeply intertwined, making them pivotal in achieving the SDGs.[11]

[6] World Bank Group, Behavioral Science Around the World Volume II: Profiles of 17 International Organizations (2020) eMBeD report.

[7] A Guterres, UN Secretary-General, UN Behavioural Science Report (2021), 4 <6436c5424b5cb1b634feeac3_UN BeSci Report 2021 vFF.pdf (webflow.com)> accessed 22 April 2024 : 'Behavioural science is a critical tool for the UN to progress on its mandate. It can contribute to combating poverty, improving public health and safety, preventing and managing crisis, promoting gender and economic equality, tackling corruption, strengthening peacebuilding and all the SDGs.... UN entities are strongly encouraged to invest in behavioural science and work in a connected and collaborative interagency community to realize its tremendous potential to achieve impact.' See also Adam Oliver, *The Origins of Behavioural Public Policy* (CUP 2017) 108.

[8] ibid. Behavioural sciences draw mainly from psychology and behavioural economics.

[9] For an overview see Lauren Alyssa Manning and others, *Behavioral Science Around the World: Volume Two—Profiles of 17 International Organizations (English)* (eMBeD brief Washington, DC: World Bank Group) <http://documents.worldbank.org/curated/en/453911601273837739/Behavioral-Science-Around-the-World-Volume-Two-Profiles-of-17-International-Organizations> accessed 22 April 2024.

[10] Behavioural sciences, especially behavioural economics, has been applied to international law for almost ten years, with rapidly growing literature. See, among many, Jean Galbraith, 'Treaty Options: Towards a Behavioral Understanding of Treaty Design' (2013) 53 Virginia Journal of International Law 309; Anne van Aaken, 'Behavioral International Law and Economics' (2014) 55 Harvard International Law Journal 421; Tomer Broude, 'Behavioral International Law' (2015) 163 University of Pennsylvania Law Review 1099' (2015) 163; Anne van Aaken and Tomer Broude (eds), 'The Psychology of International Law' (2019) Special Issue 30(4) European Journal of International Law; Harlan Grant Cohen and Timothy Meyer (eds), *International Law as Behavior* (CUP 2021).

[11] Anne van Aaken, 'Effectuating Public International Law through Market Mechanisms?' (2009) 164 Journal of Institutional and Theoretical Economics 33; van Aaken, 'Trust, Verify, or Incentivize?

Sustainability concerns have slowly entered international economic law, including international trade law, in the substance of preferential trade treaties, in academic discussion and in policymaking.[12] Heeding the *petitum* of the UN Secretary-General to use behavioural sciences to achieve the SDGs, behavioural insights can be instrumental in making trade law sustainable. This chapter provides a roadmap on where behavioural insights can be used and proposes recommendations for implementation. It aims to merge three perspectives: those of international trade law, sustainability, and behavioural sciences.

There are two principal ways in which behavioural insights can be used for introducing sustainability into trade law:[13] first, on the interstate level, in trade negotiations and treaty drafting between states; second, by using behaviourally informed international trade law norms to target economic operators. The use of behavioural insights for the addressees of international trade law, namely economic operators and consumers, has been explored in the context of sustainability, but remains disconnected from trade law. Can trade treaties incorporate those means of regulation? This roadmap will be explored in the following sections.

Section II briefly reviews the application of behavioural sciences to international law alongside different relevant units of analysis (states or business and consumers). Sections III and IV examine the two main ways in which behavioural science could be used in international trade law: first on the interstate level and second on the policymaking level, to target economic operators and consumers. Section V concludes.

II. Behavioural Science for International Law—A Short Primer

This section firstly describes briefly behavioural sciences (section II.A). It then turns to the units of analysis—which actors (could) use behavioural science, where, and for whom (section II.B).

Effectuating Public International Law Regulating Public Goods Through Market Mechanisms' (2010) 104 Proceedings of the ASIL Annual Meeting 153.

[12] For an overview see Jean-Baptiste Velut and others 'Comparative Analysis of Trade and Sustainable Development Provisions in Free Trade Agreements' (*LSE Consulting*, 2022) <https://www.lse.ac.uk/business/consulting/reports/comparative-analysis-of-tsd-provisions-for-identification-of-best-practices> accessed 13 November 2023.

[13] International nudges are regulatory tools used by international actors to influence the behaviour of other actors, 'either by nudging individuals who are vested with political power directly, or by nudging the public at large, which in turn influences policy-makers indirectly', Doron Teichman and Eyal Zamir, 'Normative Aspects of Nudging in the International Sphere' (2021) 115 American Journal of International Law Unbound 263.

A. Behavioural Science in International Law

Behavioural science relies heavily on cognitive science.[14] The latter is the interdisciplinary study of mental processes involved in acquiring and processing information, as well as judgments and decision-making processes. Those cognitive processes include attention, framing, interpretation, memory, language, evaluation, problem-solving, and reasoning. Cognitive studies are also aimed at explaining cases where mental processes work poorly; for example, when people adopt erroneous judgments or are influenced by various biases. Behavioural economics is closely related to cognitive science and combines insights from several disciplines, notably economics and psychological experimental literature. It primarily explores the impact of motivational and cognitive factors on individuals' decision-making, highlighting deviations from the rational choice paradigm ('heuristics' and 'biases') on cognitive and motivational grounds. The United Nations predominantly employs this approach in its policies to achieve, inter alia, the SDGs, targeting citizens and consumers, and it goes under the heading of behavioural science.[15] Bounded rationality as the central concept is the recognition that human cognitive capabilities are neither perfect nor infinite, even when self-regarding.[16] The human brain employs shortcuts in judgment and decision-making that diverge from the rational choice paradigm of expected utility theory.

Numerous cognitive biases and heuristics have been identified in a variety of decision-making contexts,[17] constituting the hard core of the field. Perhaps the single most important insight of psychology in this regard derives from Prospect Theory.[18] Prospect Theory questions the validity of the Coase Theorem, which both expresses and relies upon the idea of perfect rationality and zero transaction costs. In Coasean economics, in the absence of transaction costs, the initial assignment of resources or entitlements is not determinative of their ultimate allocation. Cost–benefit bargaining between rational actors will assign the entitlements efficiently to the actor to whom they hold the most value, regardless of the starting point.[19] This also underpins trade law—many norms in trade treaties are meant

[14] Michael Hallsworth, 'A Manifesto for Applying Behavioural Science' (2023) 7 Nature Human Behaviour 310, 311: 'In its broadest sense, [behavioural science is] a discipline that uses scientific methods to generate and test theories that explain and predict the behaviour of individuals, groups and populations. . . . Behavioural science is different from "the behavioural sciences", which refers to a broader group of any scientific disciplines that study behaviour.'

[15] Guterres (n 7) 1: 'Behavioural science refers to an evidence-based understanding of how people actually behave, make decisions and respond to programmes, policies, and incentives.' The United Nations has established a behavioural insights unit.

[16] See for this section also Anne van Aaken and Tomer Broude, 'The Psychology of International Law: An Introduction' (2020) 30 European Journal of International Law 1225.

[17] For an excellent overview see Eyal Zamir and Doron Teichman, *Behavioral Law and Economics* (OUP 2018) ch II.

[18] Daniel Kahneman and Amos Tversky, 'Prospect Theory: An Analysis of Decision under Risk' (1979) 47 Econometrica 263.

[19] Ronald H Coase, 'The Problem of Social Cost,' (1960) 3 Journal of Law and Economics 1. Both assumptions, perfect rationality and zero transaction costs, are belied by the real world, but that does not

to lower transaction costs (eg the transparency provisions) and create reciprocal opportunities for beneficial market exchange beyond borders on competitive grounds. Nevertheless, experiments have shown repeatedly, in varying circumstances, that initial entitlements matter greatly in influencing actors' decisions, especially their willingness to part with their entitlements, even in situations where the transaction costs are close to zero. In Coasean terms, $10 (or any other thing of value; in international affairs, this could be territory, resources, or other assets of political or symbolic importance) has equal worth, whether gained or lost. Yet, in real life, people do not regard losses and gains of equal size indifferently. For example, they will often invest more in the prevention of loss than in the generation of gains of the same amount. This is the logic that underlies a variety of related terms that derive or are otherwise related to the ideas of Prospect Theory, such as loss aversion, the endowment effect,[20] and framing effects. Those phenomena might impede consent and cooperation, not only in contract law but also in international (trade) law.

The status quo bias describes the phenomenon that, *ceteris paribus*, a state of the world is preferred for no other reason than it is the current state of the world.[21] Changes in the status quo need more justification than maintaining it. This bias is underlying the power of default rules. Under rationalist assumptions, defaults do not matter, but under psychological assumptions, and in reality, they do (caused by the status quo bias). Thus, default options are crucial since people tend not to deviate from them. Depending on how the default is set ('choice architecture'), different choices are made.[22] Organ donation, for example, can be set up as an opt-in (no donation as default) or an opt-out (donation as default) rule. As has been empirically observed in cross-country studies, a no-donation default leads to very few individuals opting in, in comparison with an opt-out design.[23] This same phenomenon also holds for many other instances, including for the consent to jurisdiction of international courts.[24] It thus matters in international treaty design as well. The default might hinder consent in international (trade) law, but it can also be used to foster cooperation.

mean that the theorem is invalid—it simply means that it does not necessarily predict behaviour in any particular circumstance. It is still a valid starting point to think about transactions.

[20] Daniel Kahneman, Jack L Knetsch, and Richard H Thaler, 'Experimental Tests of the Endowment Effect and the Coase Theorem' (1990) 98 Journal of Political Economy 1325; Cass R Sunstein (ed), *Behavioral Law and Economics* (CUP 2000) 211.

[21] Scott Eidelman and Christian S Crandall, 'Bias in Favor of the Status Quo' (2009) 6 Social and Personality Psychology Compass 270.

[22] Richard H Thaler and Cass R Sunstein, *Nudge: Improving Decisions about Health, Wealth, and Happiness* (Yale University Press 2008).

[23] Eric J Johnson and Daniel Goldstein, 'Can Default Rules save Life?' (2003) 302 Science 1338.

[24] Galbraith (n 10).

What, one could ask, does behavioural science have to do with international law? After all, states do not make decisions.[25] Rather, states are legal constructs that have been legally ascribed power and the authority to act. Yet, behind the entity of the 'state' are decision-making individuals who employ cognitive processes to respond to their (legal) environment and changing circumstances.[26] These perceptions of reality by international law's decision-makers (including national policymakers and international adjudicators) affect not only their assessments of and response to factual and normative situations but also how they interpret existing legal rules and develop new rules and institutions.

Public international law scholarship increasingly embraces social sciences, including behavioural sciences, regarding a broad range of questions, such as treaty design, custom, soft law, interpretation, substantive norms, and international legal theory. Rational choice theory applied to states has been largely accepted in law and international relations scholarship, but growingly the implications of behavioural science are also being systematically explored.[27] They have been successfully applied to domestic legal issues and are increasingly used in public policy and regulation.[28] Behavioural insights have been used in international political psychology for a long time;[29] now, international practice, including by international organizations, is also turning to behavioural sciences. The United Nations clearly states that behavioural sciences should be included in its work to achieve the SDGs.[30] It applies behavioural science mainly to citizens and consumers. In international treaty practice behavioural science has been less openly applied to states, that is, their representatives, such as treaty negotiators.

[25] See for a more extensive argument Anne van Aaken and Moshe Hirsch, 'Introduction' in van Aaken and Hirsch (eds), *International Legal Theory and the Cognitive Turn* (OUP forthcoming 2024).

[26] See eg Tamar Megiddo, 'Methodological Individualism' (2019) 60 Harvard International Law Journal 219. Most of the biases can also be found in individuals deciding on behalf of others, see Christoph Engel, 'The Behaviour of Corporate Actors: How Much Can We Learn from the Experimental Literature?' (2020) 6 Journal of Institutional Economics 445.

[27] See literature in (n 10). For the environmental field see Anne van Aaken, 'Behavioral Aspects of the International Law of Global Public Goods and Common Pool Resources' (2018) 112 American Journal of International Law 67.

[28] Among many, see Eyal Zamir and Doron Teichman (eds), *The Oxford Handbook of Behavioral Economics and the Law* (OUP 2014).

[29] Rose McDermott, *Political Psychology in International Relations* (Michigan University Press 2004); James Davis (ed), *Psychology, Strategy and Conflict* (Routledge 2013). International Relations scholarship has revisited the incorporation of behavioural insights, without directly addressing international law, see Emilie M Hafner-Burton and others, 'The Behavioral Revolution and International Relations' (2017) 71, Supplement 2017 International Organization S1.

[30] United Nations (n 7).

B. Units of Analysis Relevant for Using Behavioural Insights for Trade Law and Sustainability

Different actors are involved when using behavioural insights to foster sustainable development in trade. The first category of actors is those using behavioural insights for their policy goals. The actors can be divided between the national (or local) and the international level. At the national level, regulators on all levels of government use behavioural tools that can, but need not, be informed by international policies or norms.[31]

On the international level, actors using behavioural science can be international negotiators and diplomats who use those insights in negotiations,[32] be it with other states or their home states.[33] Behavioural science can also be used in trade treaty design, and it has presumably been used in the WTO 12th Ministerial Conference (MC 12), as further explained in section III of this chapter.

Behavioural insights can also be used by secretariats of international organizations. The use of behavioural insights is often developed and implemented by so-called 'behavioural units' of international organizations. Prominent examples with such units are, inter alia, the Organization for Economic Co-operation and Development (OECD),[34] the European Union,[35] the World Bank,[36] and the United Nations[37] and its agencies, such as the World Health Organization (WHO)[38] and the United Nations International Children's Emergency Fund (UNICEF).[39] Already in 2017, the United Nations Environmental Programme (UNEP) issued a report on the use of behavioural insights for sustainable consumption with examples from food, energy, water, transportation, and mobility as well as waste.[40]

31 Cass R Sunstein, Lucia A Reisch, and Julius Rauber, 'A Worldwide Consensus on Nudging? Not Quite, but Almost' (2018) 12 Regulation & Governance 3.

32 Andrea Caputo, 'A Literature Review of Cognitive Biases in Negotiation Processes' (2013) 24 International Journal of Conflict Management 374; Russell B Korobkin and Chris Guthrie, 'Heuristics and Biases at the Bargaining Table' (2004) 87 Marquette Law Review 795.

33 For a difference of views between negotiators and their home state administration see for trade law: Bernard Hoekman and Robert Wolfe, 'The Geneva Effect: Where Officials Sit Influences Where They Stand on WTO Priorities*' (2023) Review of International Political Economy 1.

34 OECD, 'Behavioural Insights' <https://www.oecd.org/gov/regulatory-policy/behavioural-insights.htm> accessed 22 April 2024.

35 European Commission, 'Competence Centre on Behavioural Insights' <https://knowledge4policy.ec.europa.eu/behavioural-insights_en> accessed 22 April 2024.

36 World Bank, 'The Mind, Behavior, and Development Unit' (eMBeD) <https://www.worldbank.org/en/programs/embed> accessed 22 April 2024.

37 United Nations, 'The Secretary-General's Guidance Note on Behavioural Science' <https://www.un.org/en/content/behaviouralscience/ accessed 22 April 2024.

38 WHO, 'World Health Organization, Technical Advisory Group on Behavioural Insights and Sciences for Health' <https://www.who.int/our-work/science-division/behavioural-insights> accessed 22 April 2024.

39 UNICEF, 'Bringing Behavioural Insights to Scale in the United Nations' (10 December 2018) <https://www.unicef.org/innovation/stories/behavioural-insights-UN> accessed 22 April 2024.

40 UNEP, 'Consuming Differently, Consuming Sustainably: Behavioral Insights for Policymaking' (2017). There is an updated version from 2021.

Similarly, in the same year, the OECD submitted a report highlighting behavioural insights in tackling environmental concerns.[41] These ultimately target consumers and/or business, even if mediated via guidelines to national governmental bodies.

The second category of actors concerns those to whom the behavioural intervention is addressed. Those can be states on the national (or local) level, respectively their governments and administrations. A lot of guidance is given by UN Agencies to states on how to employ behavioural tools to achieve certain policy goals, such as sustainable development. Those tools can also be, and often are, used for businesses[42] or consumers/citizens. At the international level, the addressees can again be states, that is, their negotiators. They can also be other actors, such as when an international secretariat sets agendas or is involved in interstate negotiations. Scholars have discussed the application of behavioural insights in the negotiation of environmental treaties, such as the Paris Agreement.[43] Yet, there is no general discussion on how to use behavioural insights in international trade negotiations.[44]

III. Using Behavioural Insights at the Interstate Level—Treaty Design

According to Joel Trachtman:

> [t]he WTO and preferential TAs contain practically no significant positive environmental law or other sustainability obligations. Some preferential TAs contain

[41] OECD, 'Tackling Environmental Problems with the Help of Behavioural Insights' (2017) <https://www.oecd.org/env/tackling-environmental-problems-with-the-help-of-behavioural-insights-9789264273887-en.htm> accessed 22 April 2024.

[42] Mark Armstrong and Huck Steffen, 'Behavioral Economics as Applied to Firms: A Primer' (2010) 6 Competition Policy International 3; OECD, 'Behavioural Insights and Organisations: Fostering Safety Culture' (2020) <Behavioural Insights and Organisations: Fostering Safety Culture | en | OECD> accessed 22 April 2024; Cass Sunstein, 'Conspiracy Theory: On Certain Misconceptions About the Uses of Behavioral Science in Government' (SSRN 8 January 2023) <https://ssrn.com/abstract=4320348> accessed 22 April 2024, 1: 'Behavioral science has been used, and is being used, to help inform nudges imposed on companies (with such goals as reducing greenhouse gas emissions, improving occupational safety, and protecting personal privacy).'

[43] A Schein and Z Baynham-Herd, 'What if a Behavioural Scientist Redesigned Climate Negotiations?' (*The Behavioral Insights Team Blog* 28 July 2021) <https://www.bi.team/blogs/what-if-a-behavioural-scientist-redesigned-climate-negotiations/> accessed 22 April 2024; Anne van Aaken and Jan-Philip Elm, 'Framing in and Through International Law' in Andrea Bianchi and Moshe Hirsch (eds), *International Law's Invisible Frames—Social Cognition and Knowledge Production in International Legal Processes* (OUP 2022); Scott Barrett and Astrid Dannenberg, 'Sensitivity of Collective Action to Uncertainty About Climate Tipping Points' (2014) 4 Nat Clim Chang 36; Jean A Garrison, 'Overcoming Obstacles in Global Climate Action from Copenhagen to Paris: Issue Framing as a Tool to Understand Opportunities for Policy Change' (2017) KFG Working Paper No 81.

[44] Generally for treaty design see van Aaken (n 10) and Tomer Broude and Shai Moses, 'The Behavioral Dynamics of Positive and Negative Listing in Services Trade Liberalization: A Look at the Trade in Services Agreement (TiSA) Negotiations' in Martin Roy and Pierre Sauvé (eds), *Research Handbook on Trade in Services* (Edward Elgar 2015).

> obligations to adhere to and comply with certain international environmental agreements or even other obligations, but the overall additionality in environmental protection is not impressive, and generally does not address climate change.[45]

Indeed, the integration of sustainability concerns is primarily found in trade agreements with deep economic integration.[46] In the European Union, these mechanisms rely mainly on a cooperative approach for compliance;[47] the lack of provisions on sanctions for non-compliance has been criticized on various grounds.[48]

Are there other ways to make trade law more sustainable? Rationalist approaches to international law oftentimes use economic contract theory when analysing international treaties.[49] The rationalist approach is modified and refined by behavioural insights; the strategic interests at play are not denied but the perception of interests is considered. On the international interstate level, several behavioural insights can be used in both treaty design and negotiations.[50]

First, behavioural insights can be applied to negotiation strategies (departing from rationalist negotiation theories). Experiments have shown repeatedly, in varying circumstances, that initial entitlements matter greatly in influencing an actor's decisions, especially their willingness to part with what they perceive as their entitlement (or any other thing of value). The status quo bias impedes change and acts as a reference point for determining what counts as a loss or gain. But what are the units of losses and gains? In trade negotiations, they used to be market access for economic operators of the respective country—exchanged reciprocally. Yet, once the sustainability dimension comes in, gains and losses should also be measured in environmental values, or contributions to global public

[45] See Joel Trachtman, Chapter 2 in this volume.

[46] Velut (n 12) 237.

[47] 'The diversity of implementation and enforcement approaches included in trade agreements ranges from no dispute settlement for these provisions to state-to-state dispute settlement (CPTPP, EU trade agreements) with some variations, including criminal and civil liability (US), use of dedicated expert panels and civil society monitoring (EU), committees and joint councils (Canada) and penalty fees or sanctions (US and Canada)', ibid 28.

[48] Marco Bronckers, 'The EU's Inconsistent Approach towards Sustainability Treaties: Due Diligence Legislation v. Trade Policy' (*EJIL: Talk!* 9 November 2022) <https://www.ejiltalk.org/the-eus-inconsistent-approach-towards-sustainability-treaties-due-diligence-legislation-v-trade-policy/> accessed 13 November 2023.

[49] Robert E Scott and Paul B Stephan, *The Limits of Leviathan. Contract Theory and the Enforcement of International Law* (CUP 2006); Joel P Trachtman, *The Economic Structure of International Law* (Harvard University Press 2008) 120 et seqq; Eric A Posner and Alan O Sykes, *Economic Foundations of International Law* (Harvard University Press 2013) 24. For an application to WTO law see Simon Schropp, *Trade Policy Flexibility and Enforcement in the WTO. A Law and Economics Analysis* (CUP 2009); for an application to investment law see Anne van Aaken, 'International Investment Law Between Commitment and Flexibility: A Contract Theory Analysis' (2009) 12 Journal of International Economic Law 507.

[50] On how behavioural insights can and are used between countries see Doron Teichman and Eyal Zamir, 'Nudge Goes International' (2020) 30 European Journal of International Law 1263.

goods, such as the reduction of plastic pollution or climate change. This would need a reframing of negotiations, extending the dimensions within which states negotiate their trade treaties and hence what the units of loss and gain are. A sustainability dimension can thus change the reference point of gains and losses by making trade treaties more multidimensional. Behavioural science emphasizes the power of framing, including issue framing.[51] Trade treaties can incorporate behavioural insights to frame sustainability as a desirable and socially normative behaviour. By highlighting the positive impact of sustainable trade practices on the environment, human well-being, and future generations, policymakers can foster a sense of collective responsibility and encourage pro-environmental attitudes in negotiations. This can be done in addition to the more rational choice-based frame of highlighting the potential to acquire competitive advantages (eg in green technologies).

An alternative option is to incorporate the use of behavioural insights for the design of the law itself. MC 12 gives two examples of how behavioural insights can be used on the interstate level for treaty design; those can be used not only on the WTO level but also for regional or bilateral trade treaties to enhance sustainability.

First, attention can be paid to the 'ground rules' for negotiation of particular disciplines, such as opt-ins/-outs (positive or negative listing in trade speak)[52] as has been done with respect to acceptance of international jurisdiction more generally.[53] Research demonstrates that states will opt-in significantly less frequently than opting-out;[54] the default thus influences the willingness to commit. Default rules in trade treaties, based on insights concerning the status quo bias, matter. At MC 12, opt-out was used for the Ministerial Decision on the Agreement on the TRIPS Agreement,[55] which states in para 1, fn 1: 'Developing country Members with existing capacity to manufacture COVID-19 vaccines are encouraged to make a binding commitment not to avail themselves of this Decision.' This is the use of an enhanced opt-out mechanism for developing countries with manufacturing capacity, such as India and China. This enhanced opt-out was especially important for reluctant (developed) countries to commit.

Similarly, psychological mechanisms were presumably employed for the Agreement on Fisheries Subsidies.[56] Deadlines have generally been identified as a

[51] For details see van Aaken and Elm (n 43).

[52] Broude and Shai (n 44).

[53] Galbraith (n 10).

[54] ibid.

[55] Ministerial Decision on the TRIPS Agreement, adopted 17 June 2022, WT/MIN(22)/30.

[56] As the WTO puts it on its website: 'The Agreement represents a historic achievement for the membership as the first Sustainable Development Goal (SDG) target to be fully met, the first SDG target met through a multilateral agreement, the first WTO agreement to focus on the environment, the first broad, binding, multilateral agreement on ocean sustainability, and only the second agreement reached at the WTO since its inception' <https://www.wto.org/english/tratop_e/rulesneg_e/fish_e/fish_e.htm> accessed 22 April 2024.

nudge since they can counteract procrastination and forgetfulness.[57] Specifically, a last-minute consensus has been proposed as a possible nudge in negotiations.[58] But deadlines can also be applied to treaty design.[59] The Agreement on Fisheries Subsidies states in Article 12: 'If comprehensive disciplines are not adopted within four years of the entry into force of this Agreement, and unless otherwise decided by the General Council, this Agreement shall stand immediately terminated.' Missing the deadlines means missing the opportunity to capture the gains from the Agreement and is likely perceived as a loss. This looming termination thus induces loss aversion about losing the Agreement, building up pressure to adopt measures within four years. This psychological mechanism of loss aversion can also be used for other sustainability concerns in treaty design. Note that the new reference point from which a loss is perceived is a sustainability goal in the Fisheries Subsidies Agreement. It is thus a public good whose non-provision is a perceived loss.

Trade treaties contain flexibilities. One of those is exceptions. Default rules can also change the perspectives on exceptions.[60] Sustainability measures taken by states have usually had to be justified as exceptions, for instance under Article XX of the General Agreement on Tariffs and Trade (GATT). An exception is, behaviourally speaking, a departure from the legal status quo (the obligation, such as Articles I and III GATT as default) and therefore needs justification. Introducing positive sustainability obligations in trade treaties thus reverses the status quo (sustainability as obligation and thus default). Notwithstanding the legal issue of burden of proof, also reversing the default for sustainability provisions (from exceptions to obligations) strengthens the sustainability dimension from a behavioural perspective as well.

Other flexibility mechanisms included in agreements are reservations and objections to them. These are sometimes used in trade treaties as well (although not hitherto in the WTO)[61] and they may provide for desired flexibility by states, allowing states to exclude some sustainability norms of treaties that they do not like, especially in multilateral trade treaties. Rationalist approaches have been analysing reservations from a game theoretic point of view, using Article 21(1) of the Vienna Convention on the Law of Treaties (VCLT) as an explanation for why states make reservations (or do not).[62] But given the importance of behavioural

[57] Eyal Zamir, Daphna Lewinsohn-Zamir, and Ilana Ritov, 'It's Now or Never! Using Deadlines as Nudges' (2017) 42 Law and Social Inquiry 769.

[58] Zamir and Teichmann (n 28).

[59] And are used in treaty design, ibid.

[60] See Caroline Henckels, Chapter 18 in this volume.

[61] Article XVI:5 prohibits reservations to the Marrakesh Agreement Establishing the World Trade Organization (WTO Agreement) unless specifically permitted.

[62] Francesco Parisi and Catherine Sevcenko, 'Treaty Reservations and the Economics of Article 21 (1) of the Vienna Convention' (2003) 21 Berkeley Journal of International Law 1. A reservation precludes the operation, as between the reserving and other states, of the provision reserved; and an objection thereto leads to the reservation being in operation as between the reserving and objecting state to the extent that it has not been objected to.

insights on defaults, behavioural approaches suggest additional design options for treaty-makers, including for objections to reservations.[63] Not objecting to a reservation can be seen as the default option: states can either explicitly accept a reservation or implicitly consent to it by not issuing an objection within 12 months, explaining the few objections existing generally.[64] Currently, treaties allow reservations on all norms, prohibit reservations on all norms, or allow them for some and not for others in one treaty (cf Article 19 (a) and (b) VCLT).[65] However, a more fine-grained approach would use objections as a decentralized consent-oriented approach. For example, they could change the default option of interpreting the omission of an objection as an implicit consent to the reservation to another default rule where silence is interpreted as an objection (opt-out rule). This would respect the consent of states while taking into account their biases and it would help solve the problem that Article 19 (c) VCLT permits de facto (self-serving) auto-interpretation if there is no court available when deciding on the question of whether a reservation is compatible with the object and purpose of the treaty. The decentralized solution of Article 19 (c) VCLT can thus be used in the reverse: if a certain percentage of states does not explicitly accept a reservation, it might be deemed incompatible with the object and purpose of the treaty. This option could be used in trade treaties, for example, for reservations concerning sustainability and human rights. It would safeguard flexibility for states and thus enhance commitment but still avoid using reservations as diluting sustainability obligations.

Some trade treaties, especially those of the United States,[66] referencing sustainability treaties, be it multilateral environmental treaties, treaties of the International Labour Organization, or human rights treaties, rely on sanctioning if trading partners do not adhere to the referenced sustainability treaties. Other approaches are more cooperative and open to rewarding states with better trade terms when fulfilling those sustainability treaties. Rewarding has many facets and has been shown to be a successful effectuation tool, especially in international environmental treaties. Next to rationalist reasons for using rewarding (eg Pareto efficiency), there are behavioural reasons to revert to rewarding concerning the perception, the reaction of states, and the stability of state relationships.[67] The Fisheries Subsidies Agreement, for example, contains in Article 7 targeted technical assistance and capacity-building assistance to developing country members, which can be qualified as rewards. Additionally, compliance design can benefit

[63] For a behavioural analysis of reservations and objections see van Aaken (n 9) 463–468.

[64] Vienna Convention on the Law of Treaties (Vienna, 23 May 1969) 1155 UNTS 331, entered into force 27 January 1980, art 20 (5).

[65] See eg the total prohibition in art 120 Rome Statute of the International Criminal Court, 2187 UNTS 90, entered into force 1 July 2002.

[66] Velut (n 12) 29, 30; Ida Bastiaens and Evgeny Postnikov, 'Greening Up: The Effects of Environmental Standards in EU and US Trade Agreements' (2017) 26 Environmental Politics 847.

[67] Anne van Aaken and Betül Simsek, 'Rewarding in International Law' (2021) 115 American Journal of International Law 195.

from behavioural insights as they tend to favour rewarding mechanisms more than a rational choice approach.[68] It would be possible to reward trading partners with staggered benefits (eg gradually lowering tariffs) or help in capacity building when certain sustainability measures are adopted. This is one means of interlinking the reciprocity aspect of trade treaties with the public good aspects of sustainability norms. It is also a means to internalize positive externalities created by states when following sustainability policies. Internalizing those positive externalities gives incentives for sustainable trade policies. The WTO has cross-retaliation as a means of effectuating compliance after breach. The reverse could also be used, namely cross-rewarding. Positive externalities could be 'compensated', for example, through cross-rewarding with lower tariffs, even though care needs to be taken to except this from the Most-Favoured Nation clause.

Furthermore, the use of soft law can be considered, and this is especially pertinent for using behavioural insights to achieve the SDGs. International soft law can be surprisingly useful and effective, despite the absence of enforcement mechanisms. The 'practical purchase of soft law'[69] can be attributed to both traditional rational choice explanations (emphasizing the creation of focal points) and cognitive effects, such as status quo bias associated with 'default rules', the difficulty to discount soft rules as information, and anchoring effects associated with (legal) standards. A soft law approach has also been explored for the National Determined Contributions of the Paris Agreement's goal of keeping global temperature change below two degrees Celsius, which sets a psychologically powerful baseline against which future policy failures can be measured.[70]

International (soft) law often targets national law and thus the behaviour of citizens, yet it can also be effectuated in international dispute settlement. The WHO and its members have, for instance, used soft law based on behavioural insights successfully in the WHO Guidelines on packaging and labelling of tobacco products[71] (eg when the WTO Appellate Body upheld a dispute settlement panel's use of non-binding provisions of the Guidelines as evidence of emerging tobacco control practices on plain packaging, thus turning soft law into hard law).[72] In trade treaties, relevant guidelines of international agencies on sustainability issues, such as environmental regulations, may be used—and effectuated as hard law in the relevant dispute settlement mechanisms of trade treaties.

[68] ibid.

[69] Tomer Broude and Yahli Shereshevsky, 'Explaining the Practical Purchase of Soft Law: Competing and Complementary Behavioral Hypotheses' in Harlan Grant Cohen and Timothy Meyer (eds), *International Law as Behavior* (CUP 2021).

[70] Arden Rowell and Josephine van Zeben, 'A New Status Quo? The Psychological Impact of the Paris Agreement on Climate Change' (2016) 7 European Journal of Risk Regulation 49.

[71] WHO, 'Guidelines for Implementation of Article 11 of the WHO Framework Convention on Tobacco Control' (Packaging and labelling of tobacco products) (2011) <https://fctc.who.int/publications/m/item/packaging-and-labelling-of-tobacco-products> accessed 22 April 2024.

[72] Appellate Body reports, *Australia—Tobacco Plain Packaging*, WT/DS435/AB/R, WT/DS441/AB/R, adopted 29 June 2020, para. 6.707.

Furthermore, the WTO secretariat could gather best practices from state practice on sustainability and trade issues and distribute them as an information device (the treaties are anyhow notified under GATT XXIV). This would be a bottom-up approach to international guidance on the use of behavioural insights. This type of approach could promote sustainability by fostering collaboration among countries, businesses, and civil society organizations. By highlighting successful examples of sustainable trade and emphasizing the social norm of environmental stewardship, policymakers can encourage the adoption of sustainable practices across trade networks. A similar approach is used by the UN Behavioural Insights Unit.

IV. Using Behavioural Insights Within Trade Treaties for Economic Operators

Sustainable development is not a top-down project—it needs bottom-up action as well. Ultimately, the SDGs need to be achieved by economic operators and consumers, for example, in energy saving, avoidance of plastic, sustainable production and consumption, and the circular economy (SDG12). And this needs to be integrated in the area of trade, although, given the nature of trade treaties, they will not expressly impose any obligations on private actors. One model is the Rapid Response Labor Mechanisms under the United States–Mexico–Canada–Agreement (USMCA). It is the first of its kind and allows the United States to take enforcement actions against individual factories if they fail to comply with domestic freedom of association and collective bargaining laws. Other treaties could also impose those mechanisms in case certain obligations for certain sectors or certain sustainability norms are not met.[73] These mechanisms seem to be rational choice based. Yet, just as in national law, on the international plane, when regulating business or consumer behaviour, in addition to sanctioning private operators, behavioural insights could be used.

Furthermore, trade agreements may integrate mechanisms for (soft law) guidelines on sustainability developed by UN Agencies using behavioural insights. These mechanisms may indeed be referred to in trade agreements and thus turned into hard law. For example, the Annex on Forest of the United States–Peru Trade Promotion Agreement contains several provisions to prevent illegal logging.[74] These provisions have been used by the United States,[75] and thus may be legally

[73] See Kevin Banks, Chapter 17 in this volume.

[74] United States–Peru Free Trade Agreement (PTPA), entry into force 1 February 2009. Annex 18.3.4 (Annex on Forest Sector Governance) <https://investmentpolicy.unctad.org/international-investment-agreements/treaty-files/2721/download> accessed 22 April 2024.

[75] Yilly Vanessa Pacheco Restrepo, 'Enforcement Practice Under Preferential Trade Agreements: Environmental Consultations and Submissions on Environmental Enforcement Matters in the US–Peru TPA' (2019) Legal Issues of Economic Integration 247.

effective; yet, they have not been deemed effective from an empirical perspective to avoid deforestation.[76] Imposition of sustainability obligations risks being prone to failure unless domestic interests mobilize in their support. It is exactly those interests that are targeted by the behavioural policy of the UN Agencies. Successful sustainability obligations must produce behavioural change on the ground. Change may be better achieved by also considering behavioural insights for the relevant actors than by relying solely on criminal or administrative sanctions, as the Forestry Annex of the US–Peru Trade Promotion Agreement does.

Although transparency provisions play a crucial role in trade law, there is room for enhancement through improved information provisions. Behavioural science emphasizes the importance of clear and accessible information, as in the notification requirements and the Trade Policy Review Mechanism under the WTO. Trade treaties can create platforms for comprehensive and user-friendly information on sustainable trade practices, including the environmental impacts of different products or services. Transparent and incentivizing labelling systems can help consumers make informed choices, facilitating the demand for sustainable products and services. Trade treaties could incorporate by reference, for example, the policies used by UNEP for consumers as well as business to foster change in behaviour, allowing practices to differentiate between sustainable and non-sustainable consumption, using nudges towards consumers, and more. Yet, those nudges and interventions have to be very carefully designed in order to be effective. Empirical evidence on labelling to nudge consumers toward sustainable behaviour has been mixed and more research is clearly needed here.[77]

V. Outlook

Behavioural science insights can play a significant role in making trade treaties more sustainable by addressing behavioural barriers and promoting environmentally conscious behaviours, both at the interstate level and for economic operators. This chapter suggests ways in which behavioural science can be applied to enhance the sustainability of trade treaties; yet it remains explorative. By integrating behavioural science insights into the design and implementation of trade treaties, policymakers can promote sustainable behaviour, incentivize environmentally friendly practices, and align trade policies with broader environmental goals. This can contribute to the transition towards a more sustainable global trading system. Most

[76] Clint Peinhardt, Alisha A Kim, and Viveca Pavon-Harr, 'Deforestation and the United States–Peru Trade Promotion Agreement' (2019) 19 Global Environmental Politics 53.

[77] See eg Maike Gossen and others, 'Nudging Sustainable Consumption: A Large-Scale Data Analysis of Sustainability Labels for Fashion in German Online Retail' (2022) 3 Frontiers in Sustainability; J Vandenbroele and others, 'Nudging to Get Our Food Choices on a Sustainable Track' (2020) 79 Proceedings of the Nutrition Society 133.

importantly, the cooperation of states for sustainability in trade law also concerns public goods in which reciprocity, although important, is not a sufficient factor for their provision. This needs to be considered for the governance of trade treaties. Behavioural insights point to additional factors needed to provide them.[78]

Yet, clearly, strategic and material interests remain important in trade policy, be it at the individual, business, national, or interstate level. Behavioural insights cannot in and of themselves solve complex political and economic problems. Changing the behaviour of all relevant actors towards more sustainable behaviour is a complex enterprise and has normative and scientific limitations.[79] What behavioural science can do is provide insights into how humans, including state representatives, those in charge of economic activity, and consumers, make decisions. This allows both an assessment of situations in which norms and norm design can influence behaviour 'on the ground' and a recognition of the limits of international legal norms in producing the kind of behavioural change desired by their proponents without subsequent or parallel action at the domestic level.

[78] Anne van Aaken, 'Behavioral Aspects of the International Law of Global Public Goods and Common Pool Resources' (2018) 112 American Journal of International Law 67.

[79] Not all nudges are created equal and much depends on the design of the nudge, also for their legality: Anne van Aaken, 'Judge the Nudge: In Search of the Legal Limits of Paternalistic Nudging in the EU' in Alberto Alemanno and Anne Lise Sibony eds, *Nudge and the Law. A European Perspective* (CUP 2015); Pelle G Hansen and Andreas M Jespersen, 'Nudge and the Manipulation of Choice. A Framework for the Responsible Use of the Nudge Approach to Behaviour Change in Public Policy' (2013) 1 European Journal of Risk Regulation 3.

4

Evaluating the Sustainability Agenda in International Trade Agreements

Aims, Effectiveness, Legitimacy, and Importance

James Harrison

I. Introduction

The 'sustainability agenda' in regional and bilateral free trade agreements (FTAs) refers to those legal provisions in international trade agreements that explicitly seek to directly address social and environmental outcomes (eg trade and sustainable development chapters, labour and environmental commitments, etc.). It also refers to processes associated with the trade agreement through which sustainability issues are evaluated (eg impact assessments).[1] This chapter explores a series of issues that, it is argued, are critical to evaluating the sustainability agenda in FTAs. By so doing, it seeks to highlight what is marginalized within, missing from, or contested in legal academic debates about the sustainability agenda at the moment, and what a programme of research that addresses those issues in the future might look like.

The sustainability agenda in FTAs has expanded hugely in recent years. This is true in terms of the number of trade agreements that contain provisions on sustainability and the extent of those sustainability provisions in individual FTAs. More traditional sustainability provisions, such as commitments to international labour rights and multilateral environmental agreements, now appear in far greater numbers of trade agreements than they did 20 years ago.[2] At the same time, the typologies of sustainability provisions are evolving and expanding. For instance, sustainability provisions are expanding into different subject areas (such as gender

[1] See James Harrison, 'Trade Agreements and Sustainability: Exploring the Potential of Global Value Chain (GVC) Obligations' (2023) 26 Journal of International Economic Law 199. See (n 5) for a range of publications utilizing this terminology in an analogous way.

[2] On the growing number of labour provisions in trade agreements see International Labour Organization, 'Labour Provisions in Trade Agreements Hub' (*ILO*, no date) <https://www.ilo.org/LPhub> accessed 13 March 2023.

James Harrison, *Evaluating the Sustainability Agenda in International Trade Agreements* In: *The Sustainability Revolution in International Trade Agreements*. Edited by: Geraldo Vidigal and Kathleen Claussen, Oxford University Press.
© James Harrison 2024. DOI: 10.1093/9780191994470.003.0004

provisions[3]) and new types of provisions, such as those that place obligations directly on corporate entities which benefit from trade under the FTA.[4]

Academic scholarship has charted this rise. A number of studies have mapped out the FTAs containing sustainability provisions and compared and contrasted the way in which they are constructed.[5] This scholarship is important in helping us to understand the extent of the sustainability agenda in FTAs and its varying forms and functions. But the increasing presence and diversity of sustainability provisions in trade agreements is not itself evidence that a significant phenomenon is taking place—significant in the sense that it has important real-world impacts rather than impacts only on the texts of the agreements in question. In fact, one hypothesis for the spread and uptake of such provisions over time is that governments sign up to these provisions precisely because they have realized that they do not in practice require a great deal of action to be taken. According to this critique, their function is primarily one of legitimation and pacification; they allow governments to argue to key stakeholders advocating on sustainability issues (eg civil society organizations, trade unions, members of parliaments) that they have addressed sustainability issues in their trade policymaking processes.[6]

What is therefore required is an evaluation of the significance of the commitments that have been enacted. In the legal scholarship, discussion about the significance of sustainability provisions has sometimes boiled down to consideration of their enforceability;[7] the harder the enforcement process, the more the provisions in question are considered to be serious and meaningful. But I want to suggest that a broader framework of analysis is required that has not yet been fully developed. In pursuit of this, I set out four issues that, I argue, are critical to an evaluation of the real significance of the sustainability agenda in FTAs, and are all marginalized and/or contested, to varying degrees, within current debates.

[3] See World Trade Organization, Database on gender provisions in RTAs (*WTO*, no date) <https://www.wto.org/english/tratop_e/womenandtrade_e/gender_responsive_trade_agreement_db_e.htm> accessed 13 March 2023.

[4] For an analysis of these types of provisions see Harrison, 'Trade Agreements and Sustainability' (n 1).

[5] Eg Sikina Jinnah and Elisa Morgera, 'Environmental Provisions in FTAs' (2013) 22 Review of European Comparative and International Environmental Law324; Jean-Frédéric Morin and Myriam Rochette, 'Transatlantic Convergence of PTAs' Environmental Clauses' (2017) 19(4) Business and Politics 621; Peter Draper, Nkululeko Khumalo, and Faith Tigere 'Sustainability Provisions in Regional Trade Agreements: Can they be Multilateralised?' (*International Centre for Trade and Sustainable Development*, 2017) <https://e15initiative.org/wp-content/uploads/2015/09/RTA-Exchange-Sustainability-Provisions-Draper-Khumalo-Tigere-Final.pdf> accessed 23 November 2023; Jean-Baptiste Velut and others 'Comparative Analysis of Trade and Sustainable Development Provisions in Free Trade Agreements' (*LSE Consulting*, 2022) <https://www.lse.ac.uk/business/consulting/reports/comparative-analysis-of-tsd-provisions-for-identification-of-best-practices> accessed 13 November 2023.

[6] Making this argument with regard to labour rights commitments see James Harrison, 'The Labour Rights Agenda in Free Trade Agreements' (2019) 20(5) Journal of World Investment and Trade 705.

[7] On the dominance of the enforceability issue with discussions about sustainability provisions in the academic scholarship see Velut and others (n 5).

The first issue concerns interrogating the range of aims sustainability provisions seek to achieve. The second is to seek to obtain a better shared understanding of their effects. The third is to consider a range of legitimacy issues associated with the sustainability agenda in FTAs. The fourth and final issue concerns weighing and balancing the relative importance of sustainability provisions in FTAs in comparison to other policy instruments for advancing the sustainability agenda through trade policymaking. Each of these four issues are discussed in the four sections that follow. The chapter then provides some concluding thoughts about the implications of this discussion for future research on the sustainability agenda in FTAs.

II. Aims of the Sustainability Agenda

The sustainability agenda in FTAs has varied proponents. Civil society organizations, trade unions, business groups, and politicians have all pushed for various types of sustainability provisions in trade agreements as well as for processes that will assess and monitor the sustainability impacts of FTAs.[8] It is therefore unsurprising that the sustainability provisions that are finally negotiated in concluded FTAs may be seeking to achieve a range of different sustainability outcomes in a variety of different ways. It is impossible in this limited contribution to chart all the forms that sustainability provisions take, and the differentiated aims that sit behind them. The focus here is on one key factor, which will mean that sustainability provisions have fundamentally different aims—that is, to consider who or what is their target. Three key targets for sustainability provisions are identified: (1) the trade partners; (2) the trade between the parties; and (3) the trade agreement itself.

First, sustainability provisions can target countries that are signatories to the FTA in question. Such provisions seek to impose obligations on governments that are signatories to that FTA; for instance, obligations to sign, ratify, and effectively implement international labour and environmental treaties.[9] These are the types of sustainability provisions that have been most discussed by policymakers and in the academic literature. The assumption here is that trade agreements are perhaps the most powerful international foreign policy instruments that states have at their disposal.[10] They can be utilized to encourage governments of other countries who are party to the FTA to take action to address sustainability issues domestically.

[8] See eg Bart Kerremans and Myriam Martins Gistelinck 'Interest Aggregation, Political Parties, Labour Standards and Trade: Differences in the US and EU Approaches to the Inclusion of Labour Standards in International Trade Agreements' (2009) 14 European Foreign Affairs Review 683.

[9] Eg Evgeny Postnikov and Ida Bastiaens, 'Does Dialogue Work? The Effectiveness of Labor Standards in EU Preferential Trade Agreements' (2014) 21(6) Journal of European Public Policy 923.

[10] Flavia Jurje and Sandra Lavenex 'Trade Agreements as Venues for "Market Power Europe"?' (2014) 52(2) Journal of Common Market Studies 320.

Often it is the more powerful and developed countries that are pushing for these types of governmental commitments in FTAs.[11] Such countries target their trade partners with these provisions with the primary aims of enhancing those countries' commitments on sustainability issues and creating leverage to ensure domestic implementation of commitments they have made.[12]

Second, sustainability provisions can target the trade taking place between the parties under the auspices of relevant FTAs. The primary aim of these types of provisions is to make global value chains (GVCs) more sustainable and to improve social and environmental outcomes in export-oriented industries in the parties to the agreement, or even globally. The justification for trade agreements targeting GVCs in this way is partly that FTAs offer opportunities for such value chains to expand and for corporate actors to benefit from that expanded trade. Does it not therefore appear reasonable that there should also be obligations on those actors to trade in a way that promotes sustainable outcomes?

Traditionally, provisions that targeted the value chain were often limited to vague corporate social responsibility commitments, which have been found to be restricted in scope, vigour, and potential future impact.[13] But value chain provisions have featured more prominently in recent agreements; for instance, enforcement of collective bargaining and freedom of association directly against factories in the United States–Mexico–Canada Agreement (USMCA)[14] and palm oil sustainability standards conditioning market access in the Indonesia–EFTA FTA.[15] These types of provisions can be envisaged as building blocks towards improving the conditions of workers and environmental outcomes in internationally traded goods and services between the parties, and perhaps even beyond.

A third target of sustainability provisions is the trade agreement itself. In this scenario, the aim is to understand what the impacts of a given trade agreement are on sustainability outcomes and in particular to take action where negative impacts are identified. Commercial provisions of trade agreements can have negative environmental and social impacts, which empirical studies are beginning to uncover.

[11] As identified in most of the academic literature, this is an agenda pushed primarily by trading blocs and countries like the European Union and the United States, often at the behest of civil society groups and trade unions.

[12] Although because these types of commitments are often included as a result of external pressure (from NGOs, trade unions, parliamentary bodies, etc.), trade partners that are 'pushing for' the inclusion of such provisions may not in reality be keen to actually drive forward the sustainability agenda in practice. Making this point in relation to EU provisions, see Adrian Smith and others, *Free Trade Agreements and Global Labour Governance: The European Union's Trade-Labour Linkage in a Value Chain World* (Routledge 2020).

[13] James Harrison and others, 'Labour Standards Provisions in EU Free Trade Agreements: Reflections on the European Commission's Reform Agenda' (2019) 18 World Trade Review 635; see also Smith and others (n 12).

[14] Agreement between the United States of America, Mexico, and Canada, in force 1 July 2020.

[15] Comprehensive Economic Partnership Agreement Between the Republic of Indonesia and the EFTA States, in force 1 November 2021. For a discussion of these cases see Harrison, 'Trade Agreements and Sustainability' (n 1).

For instance, on the environment, a study of FTAs in almost 200 countries over an 11-year period from 2001 to 2014 found 'a large and statistically significant increase in deforestation over the 3 years following the enactment of an [F]TA, which coincides with an increase in agricultural land conversion'.[16] This suggests that commitments in FTAs on trade liberalization in the agricultural sector are leading to increased rates of deforestation.

A study of the social impact of FTAs has also sometimes identified problems caused by commercial provisions of those agreements. Qualitative studies have been the key building block of work in this area. One study (in which this author was a contributor) found that in Moldova, as tariff barriers were reduced due to a trade agreement negotiated with the European Union,[17] exports particularly to the United Kingdom and Italy increased. While this stabilized the previously volatile and predominantly female workforce in the apparel sector, pressure from lead firms in the United Kingdom and Italy, combined with weaknesses in the labour protection system in Moldova, also led to the entrenchment of poverty wages and heavy reliance on piece rate payments and other troubling overtime practices and production methods.[18] Other case studies, presented in the same study, identified a range of other labour issues caused, at least in part, by commercial obligations of EU FTAs in the context of the Caribbean and South Korea.[19] This all suggests the need for a more widespread study of the social impacts of commercial provisions in FTAs.

Impact assessment processes are currently the primary mechanisms for assessing the sustainability of FTAs themselves. Most notably the European Union has a process of conducting sustainability impact assessments (SIAs) of trade agreements during the negotiation process, in which the environmental, labour, and human rights impacts of the agreement are assessed and recommendations made about the action required to address some of the negative impacts identified. Many of the trade and sustainable development chapters included in EU FTAs, then, contain an obligation to monitor the impact of the trade agreement itself on sustainable development after it comes into force.[20] These types of monitoring processes recognize that trade agreements may themselves have deleterious

[16] Ryan Abman and Clark Lundberg, 'Does Free Trade Increase Deforestation? The Effects of Regional Trade Agreements' (2020) 7(1) Journal of the Association of Environmental and Resource Economists 35.

[17] Association Agreement between the European Union and the European Atomic Energy Community and their Member States and the Republic of Moldova, in force 1 July 2016 (Moldova–EU Association Agreement).

[18] Smith and others (n 12).

[19] ibid.

[20] Eg see Free Trade Agreement between the European Union and its Member States, of the one part, and the Republic of Korea, in force 13 December 2015, art 13.10; Moldova–EU Association Agreement (n 17), art 374; Economic Partnership Agreement between the CARIFORUM States and the European Community and its Member States, provisionally applied 29 December 2008, art 195.

sustainability impacts and that mechanisms are required to assess where this occurs and take action to address the identified issues.

As yet, there has been little discussion of the relative weight that should be given to these different 'targets' of sustainability provisions, and what the extent of ambition should be in relation to each type of associated aim.[21] Of course, this is not an either/or phenomenon. A sustainability agenda in FTAs can pursue all of these targets and aims at the same time. But we should carefully scrutinize sustainability provisions that are aimed at these different 'targets' to understand the very different ways in which they seek to affect sustainability outcomes, and the differentiated legitimacy and effectiveness issues such provisions raise, as considered in sections III and IV.

III. Effectiveness of the Sustainability Agenda

When it comes to assessing the effectiveness of sustainability provisions in FTAs, traditional legal scholarship has focused on analysing the textual provisions of agreements and the processes by which they are enforced.[22] Such analysis provides important insights about issues such as the degree to which sustainability provisions create soft or hard obligations, whether such provisions conflict with or reinforce other provisions in the FTA, and whether the mechanism for their enforcement is credible.

This legal analysis of the text of provisions is then augmented by analysis of the case law produced by the dispute settlement bodies that are enacted through respective FTAs. There is an increasingly rich case law that has addressed sustainability issues in FTAs.[23] Analysis of this case law is important because it refines our understanding of the sustainability provisions contained in FTAs, and the nature of the obligations they impose on governments and other key actors.

But there is also a broader social sciences literature that has sought to investigate the effects of sustainability provisions in FTAs on sustainability issues *in practice*. This research and its contested conclusions have not been the subject of detailed analysis in the legal scholarship on FTAs and sustainability. Two methodological approaches to researching this issue have come to rather different conclusions about the effectiveness of sustainability provisions in FTAs.

[21] For instance, given the vast environmental and social challenges facing the world as a result of issues like climate change and endemic labour rights abuses in many GVCs, perhaps impact assessment processes should have a more challenging goal? Should they go beyond the identification and prevention of negative impacts and be identifying ways in which trade agreements can make a significant positive impact on sustainability issues as well?

[22] Jinnah and Morgera (n 5).

[23] Geraldo Vidigal, 'Regional Trade Adjudication and the Rise of Sustainability Disputes: Korea—Labor Commitments and Ukraine—Wood Export Bans' (2022) 116(3) American Journal of International Law 567.

First, there have been quantitative studies, which have largely been undertaken by economists and have identified various positive (although bounded) impacts of sustainability provisions. A number of studies have used regression analysis of large-N datasets to establish a statistical relationship between a country's participation in a given trade agreement and the corresponding change in environmental or labour rights protection.

For example, in relation to environmental provisions, one study utilized statistical estimations of EU and US FTAs containing environmental provisions on countries' environmental policy reform (measured by Yale University's index of environmental protection) and the signing of multilateral environmental treaties.[24] It found that EU FTAs with environmental provisions are effective in improving environmental conditions in countries with strong civil societies while US FTAs are effective during the negotiation period in improving the environmental policy environment of partner countries.

Moreover, in relation to labour provisions, the same authors considered all states that have FTAs in force with the European Union prior to 2010. Using the Cingranelli-Richards (CIRI) Human Rights Data Project, they found that the likelihood of a state fully protecting workers' rights rises from 4 per cent to 14 per cent once such an agreement has come into force. They argued that improved labour standards resulted from civil society dialogue that took place under the auspices of the FTAs in question. Another study of labour standards provisions in FTAs used the Labor Provisions in Trade Agreements (LABPTA) dataset covering 487 FTAs signed between 1990 and 2015 and found that FTAs that included specific reference to collective labour rights and featured 'deep cooperation mechanisms' (such as EU FTAs) were effective at improving state compliance with labour law (although this did not necessarily translate to better protection of labour rights in practice).[25] In another study, a team of International Labour Organization (ILO) researchers compared the effects of FTAs with and without labour provisions. They found that labour provisions had a positive impact on (particularly female) labour force participation rates (but not on other labour rights).[26]

Overall then, these studies have tended to find some significant effects occurring as a result of the presence of labour and environmental provisions in FTAs. The strength of these studies is that they have been able to consider labour and environmental provisions across a wide range of agreements, thereby providing highly

[24] Ida Bastiaens and Evgeny Postnikov, 'Greening Up: The Effects of Environmental Standards in EU and US Trade Agreements' (2017) 26(5) Environmental Politics 847.

[25] Céline Carrère, Marcelo Olarreaga, and Damian Raess 'Labor Clauses in Trade Agreements: Worker Protection or Protectionism?' CEPR Discussion Paper No DP12251 (August 2017) <https://ssrn.com/abstract=3031888Presentation+ETUI+event+Raess.pdf> accessed 13 March 2023.

[26] International Labour Office 'Assessment of Labour Provisions in Trade and Investment Agreements' (*ILO* 2016) <https://www.ilo.org/wcmsp5/groups/public/---dgreports/---inst/documents/publication/wcms_498944.pdf> accessed 13 March 2023.

generalizable findings. Weaknesses include limitations of the datasets relied upon and speculative findings about causality.[27] So, sustainability provisions are posited as a likely cause of improvements in environmental and labour protection, but either there is no attempt to substantiate these causal claims or attempts are methodologically very weak.[28]

The second methodological approach is qualitative. Qualitative studies, usually undertaken by political scientists, geographers, and business and socio-legal scholars, paint a different picture. Such studies have generally involved case study methodologies involving process tracing (an analytic tool for drawing descriptive and causal inferences from diagnostic pieces of evidence) and qualitative techniques, such as in-depth interviews, focus groups, and participant observation that allow deep exploration of the causal effects of particular sustainability provisions. Most of the detailed studies have focused on EU trade and sustainable development chapters and the labour standards provisions therein. Case studies on impacts in EU FTAs with the Caribbean Forum (CARIFORUM) countries, Colombia, Korea, Moldova, and Peru have found little or no evidence that the existence of trade and sustainable development chapters led to improvements in labour standards governance, nor that there were significant prospects of longer-term change.[29] Less robust studies of labour standards provisions in individual US agreements have led to similar conclusions, although they have identified more positive impacts in the pre-ratification period as have more recent studies of the EU–Vietnam FTA.[30]

Overall, these qualitative studies have identified very limited impacts of labour provisions in FTAs, particularly once agreements have come into force. On the few occasions where positive changes have occurred, studies have tended to emphasize the importance of the individual dynamics of particular trading relationships and domestic political situations in making those changes happen. This is very much in contrast to the findings of the discussed quantitative studies. Methodological strengths and weaknesses can also be strongly contrasted. Qualitative studies take causality seriously and are able to give detailed answers to the questions of *how* and *why* sustainability provisions have or do not have effects. On the other hand, they are weaker when it comes to generalizability; reliance on individual case studies

[27] For a more detailed critique see Smith and others (n 12) ch 3.

[28] Eg see Postnikov and Bastiaens, 'Does Dialogue Work?' (n 9) where causal analysis is based on only a couple of interviews (one from a trade partner).

[29] Summarizing the findings of many of these studies see Harrison and others, 'Labour Standards Provisions in EU Free Trade Agreements' (n 13).

[30] Free Trade Agreement between the European Union and the Socialist Republic of Viet Nam, in force 1 August 2020. See eg Kristoffer Marslev and Cornelia Staritz, 'Towards a Stronger EU Approach on the Trade–Labor Nexus? The EU-Vietnam Free Trade Agreement, Social Struggles and Labor Reforms in Vietnam' (2022) Review of International Political Economy 1; Jeffrey Vogt, 'The Evolution of Labor Rights and Trade—A Transatlantic Comparison and Lessons for the Transatlantic Trade and Investment Partnership' (2015) 18 Journal of International Economic Law 827.

leaves qualitative studies open to accusations that they have missed the 'bigger picture'.[31]

More research needs to be done to understand the rationale for these different findings and to promote better mutual understanding and discussion between scholars with very different research methods. Legal scholars can both learn from and contribute to these broader conversations about the effectiveness of sustainability provisions. First, they can seek to learn from these studies to better understand when and why sustainability provisions are having real-world effects. They can then utilize this knowledge to consider how provisions should be redesigned to maximize their sustainability impacts.

Second, legal scholars can contribute to these debates by differentiating between different types of sustainability provisions more carefully and demanding that studies of effectiveness become more nuanced as a result. For instance, most of the aforementioned studies assume that the target of sustainability provisions is the domestic policy space of FTA parties. But, as discussed in section II, targets can include internationally traded goods and services and the trade agreement itself. Studies of effectiveness should perhaps start to consider the effectiveness of provisions that aim to address these different targets and understand how well they are performing in relation to their particular aims.[32]

IV. Legitimacy of the Sustainability Agenda

A third important dimension of discussions about sustainability provisions in FTAs is their legitimacy; to what extent is it legitimate for FTAs to contain sustainability provisions? And are some types of sustainability provisions more concerning from a legitimacy perspective than others? Legitimacy questions are raised, first, by the type of international law instrument (trade law) in which sustainability provisions are contained and, second, by the types of actors, who are generally proponents (developed countries) and recipients (developing countries) of the sustainability agenda in FTAs.

In relation to the first set of issues, legal scholars have generally focused on concerns about the inclusion of international labour, human rights, and environmental obligations into the international trade law regime, and how those obligations

[31] Although in some studies, 'most likely' case studies are chosen, which increases their generalizability.

[32] There is some research that has analysed the capacity of EU SIAs to address sustainability issues, particularly from a human rights perspective. It generally finds serious deficiencies. See eg Simon Walker, 'Human Rights in the Trade and Sustainability Impact Assessment of the EU–Tunisia Free Trade Agreement' (2018) 10(1) Journal of Human Rights Practice 103; Nicolás Brando and others, 'The Impact of EU Trade and Development Policies on Human Rights' (*FRAME*, 2015) <https://repository.gchumanrights.org/server/api/core/bitstreams/7d3f237e-9fee-4c75-98e4-780bc151b798/content> accessed 13 March 2023.

might be interpreted as a result.[33] When such obligations are enforced, there are concerns both about the selective application (government officials making decisions about when to bring cases) and adjudication processes involving judges from the trade law regime, rather than those from the international regimes where those norms were originally created (the ILO and UN human rights and environmental bodies).[34] Concerns about adjudication can be assuaged to a certain extent by specifying that it should be labour, human rights, or environmental specialists and not trade specialists who adjudicate such cases. But concerns about the fragmentation of important substantive areas of international law remain, particularly where different trade law tribunals are coming to seemingly very different conclusions about the relative weight of legal obligations from other international legal regimes.[35]

In relation to the second set of issues, concerns are most obviously raised in relation to the fact that it is most often more powerful developed countries that are pushing sustainability provisions in international trade agreements and poorer developing countries that are the recipients of this negotiating agenda. The agenda is therefore prone to accusations of neocolonialism and/or disguised protectionism.[36] It can be seen as neocolonialist if developed countries are utilizing their economic leverage to exert control over less-developed countries and impose their own policy choices on them. It may be considered as protectionist if countries are seeking to restrict international trade in a way that creates advantages for their own domestic producers while justifying their actions by reference to social and environmental concerns. Requiring developing country governments to conform to environmental and social conditions dictated by developed countries, which are sometimes perceived as being primarily concerned about domestic commercial interests, has undermined the legitimacy of this agenda for many years.[37]

While labour and environmental problems can often be more serious in developing country contexts, the focus on developing country performance can partly be a result of the topics that are selected for consideration as part of the FTA sustainability agenda. For instance, many EU FTAs have a focus on issues of deforestation and how that is impacted by agricultural production in developing country trade partners. There is little or no focus on environmental issues associated with

[33] Martti Koskenniemi, 'The Fate of Public International Law: Between Technique and Politics' (2007) 70(1) Modern Law Review 1; Philip Alston, 'Resisting the Merger and Acquisition of Human Rights by Trade Law: A Reply to Petersmann' (2002) 13(4) European Journal of International Law 815.

[34] Koskenniemi (n 33); Desiree LeClercq, 'Rights-Based Sanctions Procedures' (2023) 75(1) Administrative Law Review 1055.

[35] Eg see discussion of panel reports in cases involving (1) the European Union and Korea and (2) the United States and Guatemala as discussed in Vidigal (n 23).

[36] Jan Orbie, 'EU Trade Policy Meets Geopolitics: What About Trade Justice?' (2021) 26(2) EFA Rev 197.

[37] Such debates led to rejection of a social clause in the WTO. See eg Jagdish Bhagwati and 102 Other Signatories, 'Third World Intellectuals and NGOs' Statement against Linkages' (*TWIN-SAL*, 6 September 1999) <https://cuts-citee.org/third-world-intellectuals-and-ngos-statement-against-linkages/> accessed 13 March 2023.

industrial agricultural processes, which are a major environmental problem in most developed countries. Similarly, US and EU FTAs both tend to focus on ILO core labour standards issues but marginalize issues in relation to the treatment of migrant workers, which is where some of the most serious labour rights abuses occur in their own jurisdictions.[38]

While the overall legitimacy of the sustainability agenda in FTAs has been questioned from a development perspective, there has been relatively little fine-grained analysis of the legitimacy of individual sustainability provisions, and where legitimacy deficits are found, how these can be addressed. The target of sustainability provisions may, for instance, affect the legitimacy concerns that are raised. Obligations that focus on the overall conduct of the parties to the FTA may be somewhat more concerning from a legitimacy perspective than those applying to the value chain. The former obligations are often imposed by more powerful developed countries on less powerful developing countries as part of the price for striking a deal. They apply to entire countries and can change, or even circumvent, domestic political decision-making processes for making sustainability commitments.[39] The latter obligations are imposed onto individual corporate actors who directly benefit from the terms of the FTA. But there are still important legitimacy concerns relating to the latter type of obligations that need to be addressed, including the issue of who bears the cost of sustainability initiatives within the value chain. It is often less powerful actors in the value chain, such as producers in developing countries, who are left to pick up the costs of social and environmental upgrading, while often not reaping the economic benefits.[40]

Finally, where the trade agreement itself is the target of sustainability provisions, legitimacy concerns may include whether current SIA processes put appropriate weight on issues such as the social dislocation and environmental degradation that trade agreements can cause. It has been argued that impact assessments should do more to ensure such effects are carefully scrutinized and action taken to address the identified problems.[41]

[38] Although petitioners to the USMCA have argued that the US government has breached its obligations under the trade agreement by allowing systemic gender-based discrimination against migrant worker women. See Centre de los Derechos del Migrante, 'Migrant worker women submit first-ever petition against the US under the USMCA' (no date) < https://cdmigrante.org/migrant-worker-women-usmca/> accessed 17 July 2023. More generally on the complexities of the interlinkages between trade and migration see Jennifer Gordon 'In the Zone: Work at the Intersection of Trade and Migration' (2022) 23(2) Theoretical Inquiries in Law 147.

[39] Most countries have some form of domestic political and legal processes for determining the international labour, environmental, etc. commitments that they sign up to. Introducing those obligations via a bilateral instrument that is an entirely different area of policymaking (trade) can significantly change the actors and processes involved in those decision-making processes.

[40] Stefano Ponte, *Business, Power and Sustainability in a World of Global Value Chains* (Zed Books Ltd 2019) 32.

[41] Making recommendations for how this should happen on the social side see James Harrison, 'The Use of Impact Assessments by Governments and Businesses: Questioning Purpose and Utility' in Gotzmann (ed), *Handbook on Human Rights Impact Assessment* (Edward Elgar 2019) 424; making recommendations on the environmental side see Eline Blot, Antoine Oger, and James Harrison,

V. Importance of the Sustainability Agenda

A final set of issues relates to the ongoing importance of the sustainability agenda in FTAs. To what extent are trade agreements still a critical policy instrument within which to consider sustainability issues? And to what extent are they being superseded by other trade policy instruments as mechanisms for addressing trade sustainability issues?

Legal scholarship has traditionally identified FTAs (where they are in force) as the most important trade-related policy instrument when considering the legal obligations that exist between states that affect their trading relationships.[42] Sustainability provisions in those FTAs have also therefore been at the centre of scrutiny when it comes to understanding how countries deploy trade-related legal obligations to achieve sustainability outcomes. But there has been a recent shift in focus by policymakers and campaigners to other trade policy instruments when it comes to sustainability issues.

Policymakers in the European Union and the United States are increasingly utilizing unilateral measures to pursue sustainability objectives. Existing EU measures include the Regulation on Conflict Minerals, which excludes importers of tantalum, tin, tungsten, and gold from the EU market unless they source from responsible and conflict-free sources.[43] Measures in development include the Carbon Border Adjustment Mechanism (CBAM), a proposed carbon tariff on carbon-intensive products imported into the European Union,[44] and the Regulation on deforestation-free products, which bans trade in various high-risk agricultural products unless it can be proved that those products are not linked to deforestation.[45] The United States has also enacted the US Uyghur Forced Labor Prevention Act, which stops businesses from importing goods into the United States from China's Xinjiang region unless they can prove through due diligence processes that their products were not made with forced labour.[46] The European Union now also has a proposed regulation that will ban products made with forced labour from the EU market.[47]

'Enhancing Sustainability in EU Free Trade Agreements: The Case for a Holistic Approach' (IEEP, 2022) <https://ieep.eu/publications/enhancing-sustainability-in-eu-free-trade-agreements-the-case-for-a-holistic-approach/> accessed 23 March 2023.

[42] Jurje and Lavenex (n 10).

[43] European Union, Conflict Minerals Regulation (EU) 2017/821.

[44] European Commission, Proposal for a Regulation of the European Parliament and of the Council establishing a carbon border adjustment mechanism, COM/2021/564 final.

[45] European Commission, Proposal for a Regulation of the European Parliament and of the Council on the making available on the Union market as well as export from the Union of certain commodities and products associated with deforestation and forest degradation COM(2021) 706 final.

[46] US Uyghur Forced Labor Prevention Act, Public Law 117–178 (23 December 2021).

[47] European Commission, Proposal for a regulation on prohibiting products made with forced labour on the Union market COM(2022) 453 (14 September 2022).

The increasing prevalence of such measures raises questions about whether unilateral measures may be more important policy instruments for addressing sustainability issues than FTAs in the future. From an effectiveness perspective, the unilateral approach has the advantage that a single policy instrument can cover all of the trade with third parties globally rather than having to be negotiated individually with each trading partner, as is the case for an FTA. In addition, unilateral measures aren't likely to be watered down during the negotiation process as trade partners look for concessions such as the price of adopting the measures in question. As such, these instruments look attractive to policymakers and campaigners from countries and trading blocs wanting to take decisive action to enhance the sustainability of goods imported into their territories. However, these strengths are also weaknesses. Such measures are not negotiated between the parties but are rather imposed on trade partners, raising questions about their legitimacy; to what extent do they sufficiently take into account how global standards apply in different national contexts, and who bears the costs of compliance?

Alongside unilateral measures, there is also a shift to addressing sustainability issues through sectoral agreements. While the United States has signalled that it is not negotiating new traditional trade agreements, it has outlined plans with the European Union for a global arrangement on sustainable steel and aluminium, which is being hailed as the world's first carbon-based sectoral arrangement.[48] The EU Forest Law Enforcement, Governance and Trade (FLEGT) scheme is another example of bilateral trading arrangements that take a sectoral approach to addressing sustainability issues.[49] The scheme involves legally binding trade agreements, between the European Union and timber-producing countries outside the European Union, which seek to ensure that timber and timber products exported to the European Union come from legal sources, as well as assisting timber-exporting countries to stop illegal logging by improving regulation and governance of the forest sector. From a sustainability perspective, this sectoral approach allows for priority sectors to be targeted and measures specific to addressing sustainability issues in each sector to be devised, as opposed to provisions in generalized FTAs, which often deal with sustainability issues across multiple sectors at a high level of abstraction.[50]

[48] US White House, 'The United States and European Union To Negotiate World's First Carbon-Based Sectoral Arrangement on Steel and Aluminum Trade' (31 October 2021) <https://www.whitehouse.gov/briefing-room/statements-releases/2021/10/31/fact-sheet-the-united-states-and-european-union-to-negotiate-worlds-first-carbon-based-sectoral-arrangement-on-steel-and-aluminum-trade/> accessed 14 March 2023.

[49] European Union, Council Regulation (EC) No 2173/2005 on the establishment of a FLEGT licensing scheme for imports of timber into the European Community.

[50] Providing a positive evaluation of the sectoral approach of this initiative see Christine Overdevest and Jonathan Zeitlin, 'Experimentalism in Transnational Forest Governance: Implementing European Union Forest Law Enforcement, Governance and Trade (FLEGT) Voluntary Partnership Agreements in Indonesia and Ghana' (2018) 12(1) Regulation and Governance 64; Saskia Ozinga, 'Getting the Incentives Right. Why Partnership Agreements Should Be at the Heart of EU Efforts to End

If trade and sustainability issues are increasingly addressed through unilateral measures and sectoral arrangements, what does this mean for the role that FTAs can and should play in addressing sustainability issues in the future? How can they stay relevant, when more targeted and effective trade policy instruments may be available to address trade and sustainability issues? One answer is to carefully consider the aims of the sustainability agenda in FTAs in light of these new dynamics. For instance, such an agenda may be less well-suited than other policy instruments to enhancing sustainable trade between the parties, but it may still have a role to play in considering sustainability issues within the domestic jurisdiction of the parties or arising from the commercial provisions of the FTA itself. FTAs could also create important spaces for dialogue, whereby trade partners are able to influence how unilateral requirements (as well as sectoral agreements to which they are not a party but that affect their interests) are interpreted and applied within their own legal and political context.

VI. Concluding Thoughts: Future Research on the Sustainability Agenda in FTAs

The primary purpose of this chapter has been to show that evaluating the significance of the sustainability agenda in FTAs is a complex endeavour. It requires a detailed and nuanced understanding of a range of issues associated with its aims, effectiveness, legitimacy, and importance. For the most part, legal academia has not fully engaged with many aspects of the broader debates associated with these issues. To take just a single example from each of the issues discussed in this chapter: the 'target' of the sustainability agenda is mostly assumed to be the national policy space of the less-developed party to the FTA, rather than the trade between the parties or the FTA itself. The effectiveness of sustainability provisions is often evaluated primarily in relation to their potential enforceability rather than their actual effects on social or environmental outcomes in practice. The legitimacy of sustainability provisions, including in terms of how costs of compliance are shared between affected parties, is generally not central to the consideration of how they operate. And the importance of the sustainability agenda in FTAs is not generally assessed in comparison to the range of other trade policy instruments that seek to achieve (at least some of) the same aims and objectives.

How can future scholarship address these deficits? Three suggestions are made here. First, scholars should consider how the four issues discussed in this chapter (aims, effectiveness, legitimacy, and relevance) affect the construction of studies that seek to evaluate particular aspects of the sustainability agenda in the future.

Deforestation', Fern, 23 October 2020 <https://www.fern.org/publications-insight/getting-the-incentives-right-2236> accessed 14 March 2023.

Second, legal scholars should engage with more scholarship from other disciplines (including economics, political science, business studies, geography, etc.) that investigates the sustainability agenda in FTAs and utilizes methods and provides substantive insights that would add extra dimensions to legal debates in the field. A number of these studies have been cited in this chapter. Third, the approaches of the critical legal tradition of scholarship should be brought to bear on future academic study. The contribution of this tradition has largely been to critique the broader constructs on which the trade and sustainability agenda is based (eg to question the whole concept of sustainability in the context of trade governance or to raise questions about the 'disembedding of' trade from society).[51] Its critical eye could also be turned towards studies that investigate particular aspects of the sustainability agenda in FTAs, identifying their deficiencies and making proposals for alternative models. It is through such approaches that ideas may emerge for a more radical trade and sustainability agenda, which has the potential to address fairly and effectively the serious sustainability challenges of our age.

[51] Eg Andreas Bieler and others, 'Conclusion: Towards Transnational Solidarity on "Free Trade" Policy?' (2014) 11(1) Globalizations 155.

5

Sustainable Development and International Economic Law

Intersections or Convergence?

*Sonia E Rolland**

I. Introduction

While it is tempting to view the legal framework for sustainable development as a convergence of development law, environmental law, and international economic law (IEL), the three strands evolved on separate tracks. Sustainable development is a concept that aims to balance economic, social, and environmental development goals for present and future generations.[1] Development emerged as a socio-economic and political concept that encompasses some of the goals of sustainable development but also at times pits long-term management of natural resources with the short-term pressures to generate revenues from domestic resources. At its core was the notion of exclusive sovereignty over natural resources, an essential part of the New International Economic Order's (NIEO) agenda. IEL is a branch of international law that regulates trade, investment, finance, and to some extent taxation among countries. The relationship between sustainable development, IEL, and development is complex and evolving. For instance, international trade can be an engine for inclusive economic growth and poverty reduction, but it can also have negative impacts on the environment and human rights. Likewise, international investment can foster development by providing capital, technology, and jobs, but it can also pose challenges to host countries' regulatory autonomy and their ability to set and implement developmental priorities. International finance can mobilise resources for development by facilitating cross-border flows of capital and credit, but it can also create instability and contribute to entrenching inequalities.

* The author is grateful to Alexander Recher (McGill University) for his outstanding research assistance. Thank you to the participants of the Amsterdam Workshop of November 2022 for their useful feedback and to Kathleen Claussen and Geraldo Vidigal for their inspiring approach to the issues covered in this collective volume.

[1] World Commission on Environment and Development, 'Our Common Future', UN Report, 1987, ch 2, para 1 (defining sustainable development as 'development that meets the needs of the present without compromising the ability of future generations to meet their own needs').

Sonia E Rolland, *Sustainable Development and International Economic Law* In: *The Sustainability Revolution in International Trade Agreements*. Edited by: Geraldo Vidigal and Kathleen Claussen, Oxford University Press. © Sonia E Rolland 2024.
DOI: 10.1093/9780191994470.003.0005

It is clear even from simplistic working definitions that development, IEL, and sustainable development intersect in many ways, but they also diverge in important respects. The limited nature of a book chapter makes it a good testing ground for different mappings of the relationship between development, sustainable development, and IEL, rather than the venue for a full-fledged plaidoyer in favour of a particular theory.

II. Sustainable Development, IEL, and Development: Where from and Where to?

This section provides a schematic introduction to the concepts of development, sustainable development, and IEL for the purpose of highlighting how they compare in their objectives and methodology.

The law of development theorized in the 1960s was intricately linked to the non-aligned movement and the NIEO, themselves artefacts of the Cold War, and the right to self-determination. With the geopolitical changes of the late 1980s and early 1990s, the movement went dormant. Despite valiant efforts by its Senegalese founder Keba Mbaye,[2] the right to development remained largely aspirational, with only limited translation in legal obligations in international instruments. Over time, the understanding of development broadened to include components, such as the right to education, women's rights, the right to health, and myriad other socio-economic rights that did translate into universal and regional human rights instruments.[3] Perhaps most crucially, development became an element of constitutional law in a number of African and Latin American countries. An important feature of development law as it was theorised in the mid to late twentieth century is the emphasis on political and economic autonomy. It posits as a cornerstone a state's sovereign decision to choose a political and socio-economic model for its people.[4] Import substitution and other endogenous industrialisation models pertain to this conceptual framework.[5]

[2] Keba Mbaye, 'Le droit du developpement comme un droit de l'homme' (1972) 5 Revue des droits de l'homme 503. On the emergence of the right to development see generally James Thuo Gathii, 'Africa and the Radical Origins of the Right to Development' (2020) 1 Third Word Approaches to International Law Review 28.

[3] For an expanded conception of development see eg AK Sen, *Development as Freedom* (First Anchor Books 2000); Martha C Nussbaum, *Women and Human Development: The Capabilities Approach* (CUP 2000) 70–96; Philip Alston and Mary Robinson (eds), *Human Rights and Development Towards Mutual Reinforcement* (OUP 2005).

[4] International Covenant on Economic, Social and Cultural Rights, in force 3 January 1976, art 1(1)); African Charter on Human and Peoples' Rights, in force 21 October 1986, art 22(1); and, relatedly, General Assembly resolution 1803 (XVII) of 14 December 1962 on Permanent sovereignty over natural resources. See generally United Nations, *Realizing the Right to Development—Essays in Commemoration of 25 Years of the United Nations Declaration on the Right to Development* (United Nations 2013).

[5] On the theory and history of import substitution as a development strategy, see generally Michael J Trebilcock and Robert Howse, *The Regulation of International Trade* (Routledge 2005) 486, 486–88.

The legacy of development approaches that emphasize self-determination in all its forms endures today. For instance, despite regulatory and economic reforms numbered in the hundreds of thousands in the wake of its World Trade Organization (WTO) accession, China continues to fiercely defend its unique blend of state capitalism and its political system from what it dubs foreign interference. It has also endorsed a discourse of non-interference in its developing country partners' affairs.[6] The African continent offers another example of a strive towards an endogenous 'renaissance',[7] including an 'Africanization' of IEL with the African Continental Free Trade Agreement (AfCFTA)[8] and the draft Pan-African Investment Code.[9] Likewise, Brazil's exclusion of indirect expropriation and most favoured nation from its Cooperation and Facilitation Investment Agreements is motivated by concerns about encroachments on Brazil's regulatory autonomy. More generally, debates are ongoing regarding tensions between the interpretation of bilateral investment treaties and other international investment agreements (IIAs) by arbitrators and demands by states to safeguard their regulatory autonomy, particularly regarding taxation, environmental regulation,[10] and public health regulation. Such contestation may be viewed as a resurgence of concerns for the protection and promotion of political and economic autonomy that were articulated as part of the development rights discourse.

Environmental law, meanwhile, took centre stage from the 1970s onwards with a series of treaties on specific topics and more general declaratory principles.[11] The landmark 1987 Brundtland Report defines sustainable development as 'development that meets the needs of the present without compromising the

[6] See eg People's Republic of China, 'China and Africa in the New Era: A Partnership of Equals', Communiqué from the State Council Information Office, 26 November 2021, <https://www.fmprc.gov.cn/eng/wjdt_665385/2649_665393/202111/t20211126_10453904.html> accessed 28 April 2024; Suresh Moradi, 'Hegemony and the Chinese Non-Interference Policy in Africa—A Friend or Foe?' (2019) 8 Chinese Studies 156; Aparna Raman, 'Partnerships with Asia: China's Role in South-South Development Cooperation' (2019) 3 Jindal Journal of Public Policy 160.

[7] African Union, *Agenda 2063: The Africa We Want* (African Union Commission 2015). This was billed as 'the continent's strategic framework that aims to deliver on its goal of inclusive and sustainable development and is a concrete manifestation of the pan-African drive for unity, self-determination, freedom, progress and collective prosperity pursued under Pan-Africanism and African Renaissance' <https://au.int/en/agenda2063/overview> accessed 28 April 2024; Charter for African Cultural Renaissance, adopted 24 January 2006 (not in force). See also Symposium on Climate Change, Pan Africanism and African Renaissance, Addis Ababa, 16 August 2013 <https://au.int/en/newsevents/20130816/climate-change-pan-africanism-and-african-renaissance-symposium> accessed 28 April 2024.

[8] Agreement Establishing the African Continental Free Trade Agreement, in force 30 May 2019.

[9] African Union Commission, Draft Pan-African Investment Code, December 2016.

[10] See *Eco Oro Minerals Corp v Republic of Colombia*, ICSID Case No ARB/16/41, Decision on jurisdiction, liability, and directions on quantum (9 September 2021); *Rockhopper Exploration Plc, Rockhopper Italia S.p.A. and Rockhopper Mediterranean Ltd v Italian Republic*, ICSID Case No ARB/17/14, Final award (23 August 2022).

[11] For an overview of the emergence of sustainable development and its relationship with environmental law see eg David Freestone (ed), *Sustainable Development and International Environmental Law* (Edward Elgar 2018).

ability of future generations to meet their own needs'.[12] The Rio Declaration on Environment and Development is another significant signpost for the law of sustainable development. Together, they launch a branch of environmental law that is interdisciplinary in nature, reaching out to human rights and economic law. The United Nations' 17 Sustainable Development Goals (SDGs), promulgated in 2015, embody the confluence of development and sustainability principles that originated in international environmental law. While the SDGs do not claim to absorb all of human rights or environmental law, they provide a broad umbrella for a holistic approach to sustainable development, with the multilateral imprimatur of the United Nations. However, in recent years, some environmental law scholars have pivoted more explicitly towards human rights frameworks as a way to operationalise norms such as the right to a clean environment and the right to water, in a move away from the sustainable development discourse.[13]

Sustainable development has taken on a phenomenology of its own, distinct from its forebearers. With their pragmatic approach, the SDGs attempt to sidestep political and scholarly debates about the universality or regionalism of human rights. They aim to transcend North/South disputes about responsibility for historical contributions to climate change. Perhaps most notably, the SDGs seek to permeate both public policymaking and private sector initiatives. In so doing, they hope to bypass disagreements about the role or duty of the state with respect to people's welfare and the protection of the global commons. Indeed, a number of industry standards and certification schemes have emerged to help corporations and private non-profit organizations describe and quantify their contributions to various aspects of the SDGs, with public regulation at times playing catch-up.[14] As articulated in the SDGs, sustainable development therefore de-emphasises development law's state centricity. It posits itself as results-oriented, whereas development law focuses perhaps more on the means of governance.

[12] Commission on the Environment and Development, *Our Common Future—Brundtland Report* (OUP 1987); Edith Brown Weiss, 'Our Rights and Obligations to Future Generations for the Environment' (1990) 84 American Journal of International Law 198.

[13] Dinah Shelton, 'Human Rights, Environmental Rights, and the Right to Environment' (1991–92) 28 Stanford Journal of International Law 103; Hari M Osofsky, 'Learning from Environmental Justice: A New Model for International Environmental Rights' (2005) 24 Stanford Environmental Law Journal 71, 129; Alan E Boyle, 'Human Rights or Environmental Rights? A Reassessment' (2007) 18 Fordham Environmental Law Journal 471; Linda H Leib, *Human Rights and the Environment: Philosophical, Theoretical and Legal Perspectives* (Martinus Nijhoff 2010) 157; Lavanya Rajamani, 'The Increasing Currency and Relevance of Rights-Based Perspectives in the International Negotiations on Climate Change' (2010) 22 Journal of Environmental Law 391; Alan Boyle, 'Human Rights and the Environment: Where Next?' (2012) 23 European Journal of International Law 613; John H Knox and Ramin Pejan (eds) *The Human Right to a Healthy Environment* (CUP 2018); Lavanya Rajamani, 'Integrating Human Rights in the Paris Climate Architecture: Contest, Context, and Consequence' (2019) 9 Climate Law 180.

[14] From climate finance to sustainability labels for products, to city and higher education sustainability assessments, public and private regulation is proliferating. See eg Eric F Lambin and Tannis Thorlakson, 'Sustainability Standards: Interactions Between Private Actors, Civil Society, and Governments' (2018) 43 Annual Review of Environment and Resources 369; Association

IEL, as it was designed after World War II, also intersects with development, but typically as a second-order consideration. The International Trade Organization had envisioned trade governance embedded in a broader context of fighting unemployment, following fair labour standards, and raising standards of living through production.[15] Ultimately, the General Agreement on Tariffs and Trade (GATT), the International Monetary Fund (IMF), and World Bank were designed to fulfil two pressing objectives: boost production to assist in post-war reconstruction and entrench peace by decreasing barriers to economic relations. They have vastly succeeded with respect to the first and likely made a significant contribution towards the second. Although some development-related provisions were added to the GATT in 1964 and in the 1970s, largely in response to pressure from the NIEO movement, they did little to reorient the course of trade integration.

More recently, the developmental role of trade was mentioned in the Marrakesh Agreement establishing the WTO and in numerous other trade agreements, albeit typically in preambles.[16] Yet, the nature and structure of trade commitments continue to operate largely on the same template. Likewise, environmental aspects remain largely addressed through exceptionalism, including GATT Article XX type exceptions and side-agreements.[17] In the literature, the dominant treatment of environmental issues intersecting with trade regulation initially was through the 'trade-and' approach, which by its own terms excludes environmental considerations from the object and purpose of trade regulation, treating it instead as an

for the Advancement of Sustainability in Higher Education (AASHE) provides a comprehensive 'Sustainability Tracking, Assessment & Rating System' (STARS) <https://stars.aashe.org/about-stars> accessed 28 April 2024; SEC Proposes Rules to Enhance and Standardize Climate-Related Disclosures for Investors, *Press Release* (21 March 2022) <https://www.sec.gov/news/press-release/2022-46> accessed 28 April 2024.

[15] Final Act of the United Nations Conference on Trade and Employment, Havana Charter for an International Trade Organization, E/CONF.2/78 (24 March 1948).

[16] Agreement between the United States of America, the United Mexican States, and Canada, in force 1 July 2020, chs 23 (Labor), 24 (Environment); Agreement Establishing the African Continental Free Trade Area (n 8). Several provisions of both the main text and the protocols on goods and services call on states parties to account for levels of development when negotiating trade preferences. Article 3(e) of the main agreement states 'sustainable and inclusive socio-economic development' as a general objective. Article 3(b) of the Protocol on Trade in Services specifically provides promotion of sustainable development in line with the Sustainable Development Goals); Trans-Pacific Partnership Agreement pmbl, chs 20 (Environment), 23 (Development) (incorporated into Comprehensive and Progressive Agreement for Trans-Pacific Partnership, in force 30 December 2018 [hereinafter, TPP, incorporated *mutatis mutandis* by CPTPP]; Trade Agreement Among the Melanesian Spearhead Group Countries, adopted July 2016 (not signed); Agreement establishing an Association between the European Union and its Member States and Central America, in force 1 May 2024, pt I, tit VIII (Trade and Sustainable Development); regarding EU trade agreements, see generally Lorand Bartels, 'Human Rights and Sustainable Development Obligations in EU Free Trade Agreements' (2013) 40 Legal Issues of Economic Integration 297.

[17] GATT 1994, in force 1 January 1995. Harlan Cohen, 'What Is International Trade Law For?' (2019) 113 American Journal of International Law 326, 328, 342 (discussing environmental side agreements); Yuka Fukunaga, Chapter 21 in this volume.

optional add-on. Over the past decade, a growing number of scholars, many of whom are contributors to this volume, have proposed to repurpose IEL for a sustainable development objective. Policymakers' response has varied, particularly in emerging countries. In many instances, linkages between environmental protection and IEL are viewed with suspicion as legal imperialism from rich countries that abided by no such impositions when they industrialised in past centuries.

Even more starkly, investment agreements proliferated in the 1990s without any development or sustainable development agenda, other than the assumption that increased foreign investment in emerging countries would stimulate their economic growth.[18] International tax treaties, also an important part of IEL, are framed as technical allocations of taxation authority, more akin to conflict of law instruments than instruments engaged in the creation of substantive rights and obligations. Not surprisingly, they are not concerned with either development or sustainability.[19] Unlike the SDGs, IEL remains quite state centric. International investment law is currently undergoing reform in a number of emerging countries with a view to reinforcing the state's regulatory power.[20]

From the features of development, sustainable development, and IEL identified in this section, it transpires that those three pillars intersect and converge at times but also diverge in their normative bedrock and their governance method. Seeking harmony in the future projection of sustainable development, IEL, and development could take different pathways. At one end of the analytical spectrum, one could seek a normative convergence, or at least a normative compatibility between all three. Section III explores how IEL could be recast for a sustainable development objective. But it may be that there is no consensus for convergence, and little appetite to form one. At the other end of the spectrum stand fragmented elements of governance leaving public and private actors to navigate gaps, overlaps, and conflicts in their obligations. In such a context, the role of international law could be at least to help coordinate distinct legal regimes. Section IV offers some perspective on these issues.

[18] See generally Deborah L Swenson, 'Why do Developing Countries Sign BITs?' (2005) 12 UC Davis Journal of International Law and Policy 131; Eric Neumayer and Laura Spess, 'Do Bilateral Investment Treaties Increase Foreign Direct Investment?' (2005) 33 World Development 1567; Mary Hallward-Driemeier, 'Do Bilateral Investment Treaties Attract Foreign Direct Investment? Only a Bit, and They Could Bite', World Bank Policy Research, Working Paper Series No 3121 (2003); Kenneth J Vandevelde, 'Investment Liberalization and Economic Development: The Role of Bilateral Investment Treaties' (1998) 36 Columbia Journal of Transnational Law 501.

[19] See eg Eric Neumayer, 'Do Double Taxation Treaties increase Foreign Direct Investment to Developing Countries' in Karl P Sauvant and Lisa E Sachs (eds), *The Effect of Treaties on Foreign Direct Investment: Bilateral Investment Treaties, Double Taxation Treaties, and Investment Flows* (OUP 2009) 659.

[20] See eg Sonia E Rolland and David M Trubek, *Emerging Powers in the International Economic Order—Cooperation, Competition and Transformation* (CUP 2019) 75–128.

III. Shifting from a Producer-Oriented System to a Sustainable Development-Oriented System for I

In a world emphasising sovereign autonomy and even isolationism, seeking a common understanding of what international governance should do seems almost inapposite. Still, even if a grand moment of convergence is not on the agenda, unilateral or mini-lateral shifts in the understanding of how IEL and sustainable development can better serve global public goods may nonetheless have a systemic impact. In this respect at least, it is still worth considering how the very rationale for international economic governance can be better integrated with the goals of sustainable development.

Nearly eight decades on, the economic governance system must pivot to address two existential challenges: preserving a liveable environment in the face of climate change and ensuring a decent standard of living for all human beings. Fostering overproduction, extracting resources regardless of environmental degradation, and leaving domestic governments to deal with equity issues have become untenable legacies that undermine the legitimacy of IEL and its institutions. At the same time, the peace-building objective of interdependency based on open economic exchanges, as it was envisioned after World War II, remains critical and requires reinforcing multilateral institutions.

The trading system was designed primarily to foster production and eliminate obstacles to trade for producers.[21] This producer-oriented trade liberalisation process assumes trickle-down benefits for workers and consumers. It postulates that increased production and access to markets generate growth and that the profits extracted from such growth provide enough benefits to offset the losses to some from changed production patterns. Yet ample evidence from economics research demonstrates that the current design largely fails to reach the most vulnerable segments of the population in least-developed, developing, and other countries.[22]

[21] Eg IMF, 'Global Trade Liberalization and the Developing Countries' (November 2001) <https://www.imf.org/external/np/exr/ib/2001/110801.htm> accessed 28 April 2024; Wilfried P Thalwitz and Oli Havrylyshyn, 'Trade Liberalization: Policy Options from inward-Looking to Outward-Oriented' in Saíd El-Naggar (ed) *Foreign and Intratrade Policies of Arab Countries* (IMF 1992) 27–46; S M. Shafaeddin, 'Trade Liberalization and Economic Reform in Developing Countries: Structural Change of de-Industrialization?' UN Trade and Development (UNCTAD) Discussion Paper No 179 (2005), UNCTAD/OSG/DP/2005/3.

[22] Jagdish Bhagwati, *In Defense of Globalization* (2014); Christoph Lakner and Branko Milanovic, 'Global Income Distribution: From the Fall of the Berlin Wall to the Great Recession' (2016) 30 World Bank Economic Review 203; Dani Rodrik, *Straight Talk on Trade: Ideas for a Sane World Economy* (Princeton University Press 2017); Nina Pavcnik, 'International Trade and Inequality in Developing Economies: Assessing Recent Evidence' in Luís Catão and Maurice Obstfeld (eds) *Meeting Globalization's Challenges: Policies to Make Trade Work for All* (Princeton University Press 2019) 129; Jakob Engel and others, 'The Distributional Impacts of Trade: Empirical Innovations, Analytical Tools, and Policy Responses' (World Bank 2021). For a country case-study see eg Eduardo Bolio and others, 'A Tale of Two Mexicos: Growth and Prosperity in a Two-Speed Economy' (McKinsey Global Institute 2014).

Equally, economics and political science show that governments have largely failed in their role as redistribution agents through trade adjustment and welfare policies to cushion the hardship for those who would lose out in the global trade system.[23] The producer-oriented model of trade liberalization has also fostered overproduction and overconsumption of natural resources at an unsustainable rate.

Just as there are many tools for understanding economic relations (supply-and demand-side models, labour economics, etc.), there is no reason to think that trade must be premised on a producer-centric view of trade relations. It is merely a product of historical narratives—one that has certainly been a powerful driver for trade integration but not one that is necessary and exclusive.[24] Rather, responding to improved understandings of the effects of trade policies and to changed global circumstances, the 'value chain' of trade could be flipped around. Economic governance could be structured firstly to address sustainability in production and equity in allocating wealth—with excess profits then accruing to some producers. In this paradigm, the baseline objective of trade integration would be sustainability and providing a decent standard of living. Domestic governments would deal with equity allocation of excess windfalls to the few after the needs of the many are met, instead of being saddled with the impossible burden of redistribution from the few to the many.

[23] Dani Rodrik, 'A Primer on Trade and Inequality', NBER Working Paper No 29507 (2021); Nita Rudra, Irfan Nooruddin, and Niccolò W Bonifai 'Globalization Backlash in Developing Countries: Broadening the Research Agenda' (2021) 54 Comparative Political Studies 2416; Anne Krueger, 'Globalization, Trade, and Growth' in Luís Catão and Maurice Obstfeld (eds), *Meeting Globalization's Challenges: Policies to Make Trade Work for All* (Princeton University Press 2019) 157; Laura D Tyson, 'Trade and Policy Adjustment to Automation Challenges' in Luís Catão and Maurice Obstfeld (eds) *Meeting Globalization's Challenges: Policies to Make Trade Work for All* (Princeton University Press 2019) 229; Pol Antràs, Alonso de Gortari, and Oleg Itskhoki, 'Globalization, Inequality and Welfare', NBER Working Paper No 22676 (2016); Opoku Agyeman, 'Power, Powerlessness, and Globalization' (2013) 7 African Journal of Political Science and International Relations 252; Ronald D'Amico and Peter Z Schochet, *Evaluation of the Trade Adjustment Assistance Program: A Synthesis of Major Findings* (Mathematica Policy Research 2012).

[24] Harlan Cohen (n 17), 328, 329, 333, 334. Cohen deconstructs the enduring trade narrative of a consensus around trade increasing overall wealth, with questions about the distribution or redistribution of such wealth left to domestic polity, with each country free to make different choices on the latter. After showing the fallacies of both prongs of the dominant discourse (free-er trade is good because it grows the global economic pie and redistribution is the province of domestic policies), he proposes alternative narratives to support international trade regulation. Instead of justifying trade agreements on the basis of an economic efficiency narrative, he argues that trade regulation be driven by a policy consensus around the state's duty to its own people: '[t]ying international trade law to states' human rights obligations to provide for the welfare of their people may be a narrative through which international economic policy can become "re-embedded"' (ibid 338). 'An international economic policy built around protecting the welfare of a state's people would have to defend domestic environmental and worker protections from outside threats' (ibid 342). See also Anna Aseeva, '(Un)Sustainable Development(s) in International Economic Law: A Quest for Sustainability' (2018) 10 Environmental Law for Sustainability 4022.

IV. Increasing Coherence Between IEL and Sustainable Development as Separate Ecosystems

A. Using Interpretative Tools to Increase Coherence

A number of principles, norms, and rules of sustainable development have been coalescing over the past half-century at least. Examples of such norms include the polluter pays principle and the principle of inter-generational equity and common but differentiated responsibilities.[25] Such principles are embodied in soft and hard law. They at times translate into more specific topical obligations such as the Basel Convention on the control of transboundary movements of hazardous wastes and their disposal,[26] and its Protocol on liability and compensation.[27] They pervade global endeavours such as the UN SDGs. They percolate into domestic laws and policies, as illustrated by the 'nationally determined contributions' established pursuant to the 2015 Paris Agreement[28] negotiated under the aegis of the United Nations Framework Convention on Climate Change (UNFCCC).[29]

If such principles were to inform the interpretation of existing trade and investment agreements, and more explicitly to condition the drafting of future instruments, IEL could coexist more harmoniously with the sustainable development ecosystem. At present, environmental policy, inasmuch as it intersects with trade or investment regulation, is constrained by its status as an exception leading to possible derogation from trade and investment rules. Exceptions modelled on Article XX of the GATT have made their way into most preferential trade agreements and are now appearing in some new investment agreements. This approach sets up sustainability policies as potentially clashing with IEL and being weighed against the principles of IEL. By contrast, a more coordinated interpretative approach would be supported by the language often found in preambles of trade agreements, though such provisions are of limited efficacy due to their non-binding status.

B. Reconsidering the Role of Private Actors in Rule-making

Aside from the role of states, the key role of non-state actors poses an additional layer of governance challenges for sustainable development. The Conference of State Parties of the UNFCCC at Glasgow in November 2021 illustrates the issue.

[25] World Commission on Environment and Development (n 1).

[26] Basel Convention on the Control of Transboundary Movements of Hazardous Wastes and their Disposal, in force 5 May 1992.

[27] Basel Protocol on Liability and Compensation for Damage resulting from Transboundary Movements of Hazardous Wastes and their Disposal, adopted 10 December 1999 (not in force).

[28] Paris Agreement, in force 4 November 2016.

[29] United Nations Framework Convention on Climate Change, in force 21 March 1994.

Industry groups and other corporate representatives vastly outnumbered non-governmental organisations and were more vocal than ever before in attempting to shape the outcome of the conference. Yet, the UNFCCC and related instruments do not offer an institutionalised, transparent, and equitable access mechanism to elicit and account for views from the private sector, whether for profit or civil society.

While trade and investment law have defined loci of decision-making (at least formally) and dispute settlement procedures, they suffer from some challenges similar to those evoked above. Out of these shared governance problems could perhaps arise parallel solutions to better account for the role and power of private actors in shaping IEL, development, and sustainable development rules and outcomes.

The assumption remains that the state acts as a filter and arbiter of corporate and civil society interests, even as the empirical evidence shows a different reality. Should a group such as the World Economic Forum be included in a new legal regime for sustainable development? Certainly, the topics this group discusses (including climate change, the ocean, trade and investment, energy, economic progress, energy, financial and monetary systems) pertain squarely to sustainable development. Coordination between the WTO, regional trade organisations, and other IEL and development organisations, including the World Bank Group and the IMF, is growing but remains limited.

The role of dispute settlement in fostering a coherent and converging decision-making system must also be reassessed. In a broader sense, dispute settlement pertains to decision-making not only directly with respect to the judgments, awards, and other binding outcomes but also as a contributor to the legal discourse on sustainable development[30] and IEL. The legal ecosystem for sustainable development lacks a clearly identifiable dispute settlement system. Rather, issues pertaining to sustainable development might come up in a variety of domestic and international dispute-resolution venues. The rise of climate litigation domestically and across borders illustrates the point. Claims and defences have been presented by private entities against states or against private entities in domestic courts. Investor–state arbitration under bilateral investment treaties is increasingly facing climate and sustainable development issues.[31] Some argue that investor–state

[30] Hari M Osofsky, 'Climate Change Litigation as Pluralist Legal Dialogue' (2007) 43 Stanford Journal of International Law 181, 218.

[31] For a brief overview, see eg UNCTAD, 'Treaty-Based Investor-State Dispute Settlement Cases and Climate Action' IIA Issues Note (September 2022, Issue 4); see also Kyla Tienhaara and others, 'InvestorState Dispute Settlement: Obstructing a Just Energy Transition' (2022) 23(9) Climate Policy 1; Sandrine Maljean-Dubois, Hélène Ruiz Fabri, and Stephan W Schill, 'International Investment Law and Climate Change: Introduction to the Special Issue' (2022) 23 Journal of World Investment & Trade 737 (and full special issue); Cara Dowling, 'Climate Change and Sustainable Disputes Between Foreign Investors and States' in C Mark Baker and others, *International Arbitration Report No 17* (Norton Rose Fulbright 2021).

dispute resolution has been a force counter to climate protection.[32] Development arguments have been made in state-to-state dispute settlement proceedings at the WTO, albeit not on climate responsibility.[33] Other claims are grounded in domestic or international human rights rules, failure to implement greenhouse gas emissions reduction commitments, domestic law on consumer and investor fraud, failure of public bodies to adequately plan for and prevent harm resulting from extreme weather events, and more.[34] International processes are also used in climate litigation.[35]

Overall, sustainable development comes up in dispute-resolution processes in many forms, including in IEL disputes. A survey of the field suggests that advocates for climate protection and sustainable development are only able to use IEL dispute-resolution processes defensively (and indirectly since their arguments are mediated by states). Instead, they are turning to human rights claims in international fora, and a range of consumer and corporate disclosure laws domestically. In any case, trade and investment disputes offer uncertain avenues for building coherent interpretative approaches because of limitations on standing, process, and how much or how little trade and investment treaties offer by way of legal basis for a claim or a defence regarding sustainable development. However, there are now climate commitments that create opportunities for debates about interpretative approaches to the relationship between trade commitments and climate change aspects of sustainable development in at least some preferential trade agreements.[36]

C. Breaking Taboos: Policy Coordination for Trade, Investment, and Environmental Commitments

Countries and governments worldwide have different understandings of the implications of sustainable development for the shaping of IEL.

Internally within the sustainable development legal ecosystem, smaller developing countries might prioritise the 'development' aspect in defining their own policies and interests, while pointing to the states that historically or presently account for the greatest consumption of natural resources as being primarily responsible

[32] Eg Kyla Tienhaara, 'Regulatory Chill in a Warming World: The Threat to Climate Policy Posed by InvestorState Dispute Settlement' (2018) 7 Transnational Environmental Law 229, 230.

[33] Sonia E Rolland, *Development at the WTO* (2012) 139–90.

[34] United Nations Environment Programme, *Global Climate Litigation Report—2020 Status Review* (United Nations Environment Programme 2020).

[35] Eg Human Rights Committee, Views adopted by the Committee, *Daniel Billy et al. v Australia*, CCPR/C/135/D/3624/2019 (22 September 2022).

[36] Geraldo Vidigal, 'Regional Trade Adjudication and the Rise of Sustainability Disputes: *Korea—Labor Commitments* and *Ukraine—Wood Export Bans*' (2022) 116 American Journal of International Law 567.

for the 'sustainability' element of sustainable development. Conversely, while acknowledging their historical role, European countries and the United States insist that fast-growing, energy-hungry emerging countries, including India and China, must curb their environmental impact as a matter of urgency, even as they seek to achieve their poverty-reduction and developmental goals domestically. Nationally determined contributions (NDCs) set as part of the Paris Agreement are a case in point: some countries set their emissions reductions and other targets based on when the government expects emissions to peak on the country's current economic trajectory. Others take a more ambitious approach that would require adjusting the economy's current emissions trajectory. Most are not on track to meet their NDC, however they were set, leading to reports that the overall targets to avert the most drastic effects of climate change are now likely unattainable.[37] Beyond the political live wire of emissions commitments, there are critical needs for increased coherence on more specific issues,[38] such as between sustainability and trade in agriculture.[39]

Nonetheless, significant rifts continue to prevail between actors' expectations with respect to sustainable development. This plays out in particular regarding the reluctance of many WTO Members, both developed and developing, to discuss the impact of trade on the environment and to consider how trade disciplines could be reframed to support sustainability objectives more effectively. In the investment arena, some states are redrafting investment agreements with a view to preserving more domestic governmental autonomy, to carve out some regulatory areas either from the disciplines of the treaty or from its dispute settlement processes. However, such carve-outs rarely explicitly cover environmental and sustainability policies.

The African Union illustrates the parallel but separate tracks of environmental initiatives on the one hand, and trade and investment agreements on the other hand. In recent years, the African Union has developed a remarkable number of policies and frameworks for the environmental preservation and revitalisation of the continent. Core documents recognize Africa's tremendous environmental value and the need to actively protect it. Yet, those policy objectives are hardly reflected at all in the trade regime. The draft investment code takes some steps towards protecting environmental policies from challenges by investors. Some African states

[37] United Nations Environment Programme, *Emissions Gap Report 2022* (United Nations Environment Programme 2022).

[38] Clair Gammage and Tonia Novitz (eds), *Sustainable Trade, Investment and Finance—Toward Responsible and Coherent Regulatory Frameworks* (Edward Elgar 2019) (discussing multilevel regulatory coordination in various sectors).

[39] Elisabeth Bürgi Bonanomi, *Sustainable Development in International Law Making and Trade* (Edward Elgar 2015) (sustainable development to increase coherence in international lawmaking, particularly regarding trade rules on agriculture).

have also taken steps away from traditional bilateral investment treaties (BITs). It will be critical to assess whether these provisions or others are incorporated in the investment protocol to the AfCFTA currently under negotiations.[40]

The AfCFTA lists as a general objective 'promot[ing] and attain[ing] sustainable and inclusive socio-economic development, gender equality and structural transformation of the State Parties'.[41] Yet, the Protocol on Trade is closely modelled after the GATT and Article 26 on general exceptions merely reproduces GATT Article XX. The limitations of GATT Article XX as a tool for environmental and climate protection may therefore similarly percolate into the AfCFTA Protocol on Trade.

The 2016 draft Pan-African Investment Code takes a number of steps towards ensuring that investor rights are not exercised at the expense of environmental protection. It recognises states' 'right to regulate all the aspects relating to investments within their territories with a view to meeting national policy objectives and to promoting sustainable development objectives' in its preamble, along with an acknowledgement of the UN SDGs.[42] The localisation of environmental protection within the ambit of domestic policy autonomy is further enshrined in Article 8, providing an exception to most favoured nation treatment and to national treatment for '[a]ny regulatory measure taken by a member state that is designed and applied to protect or enhance legitimate public welfare objectives, such as public health, safety, and the environment'.[43] Non-discriminatory measures deployed for 'legitimate public welfare objectives, such as . . . the environment' are also carved out from disciplines on indirect expropriation.[44] A general exception inspired by GATT Article XX seeks to exempt measures 'relating to the protection of human, animal or plant life or health'.[45] Policy autonomy for development objectives is treated separately in other carve-outs.[46]

Overall, this framework modifies traditional BITs to preserve explicitly domestic regulatory autonomy vis-à-vis certain provisions when it comes to environmental protection of development-oriented policies. Article 23 stands out for addressing the substance of sustainable development more directly: it provides that '1. Investors shall not exploit or use local natural resources to the detriment of the rights and interests of the host State. 2. Investors shall respect the rights of local populations, and avoid land grabbing practices vis-à-vis local communities'. Operationalizing these obligations, however, may prove difficult due to the

[40] Kathleen Mpofu, 'Investment for Sustainable Development: Opportunities and Challenges for the African Continental Free Trade Area Investment Protocol', *AfronomicsLAW* (31 October 2022) <https://www.afronomicslaw.org/category/analysis/investment-sustainable-development-opportunities-and-challenges-african> accessed 14 April 2024.

[41] AfCFTA (n 8), art 3(e).

[42] Draft Pan-African Investment Code (n 9).

[43] ibid arts 8.2 and 10.2.

[44] ibid art 11.3.

[45] ibid art 14.1.

[46] ibid arts 10.3, 10.5, and 10.7 (national treatment carve-out) and art 17 (allowing performance requirements and local content requirements, which also pertain to national treatment).

wording of the provision and its dependence on the host state to enforce it. Host states undertake to provide for environmental protection in their domestic law and not to lower environmental standards in order to attract investment.[47] It also calls for states and investors to conduct environmental impact assessments in relation to investments. However, the draft does not connect these provisions to sustainability initiatives developed within the African Union. Moreover, with respect to other attempts to reword investment treaties, there is some doubt whether new language will result in an evolution in the interpretation of investment agreements in arbitrations.[48]

The topic of fisheries management offers a useful case study of the deleterious effects on the sustainability of separate and uncoordinated trade and environmental regulatory efforts. Fisheries management treaties range from universal treaties such as the United Nations Fish Stocks Agreement,[49] to broader environmental agreements such as the Convention on Biological Diversity[50] and the Convention on Trade in Endangered Species,[51] and to species-specific rules such as the 1946 International Convention for the Regulation of Whaling[52] and the Agreement on the Conservation of Albatrosses and Petrels.[53] Regional agreements include the Inter-American Convention for the Protection and Conservation of Sea Turtles,[54] the Indian Ocean South East Asian Marine Turtle Memorandum of Understanding,[55] the Convention on the Conservation and Management of Pollock Resources in the Central Bering Sea,[56] the Convention on the Conservation and Management of Highly Migratory Fish Stocks in the Western and Central Pacific Ocean,[57] Federated States of Micronesia Arrangement for Regional Fisheries Access,[58] and many more,[59] along with the European Union's

[47] ibid art 37.

[48] See generally Wolfgang Alscher, *Investment Arbitration and State-Driven Reform—New Treaties, Old Outcomes* (OUP 2022).

[49] Agreement for the Implementation of the Provisions of the United Nations Convention on the Law of the Sea of 10 December 1982 relating to the Conservation and Management of Straddling Fish Stocks and Highly Migratory Fish Stocks, in force 11 December 2001.

[50] Convention on Biological Diversity, in force 29 December 1993.

[51] Convention on International Trade in Endangered Species of Wild Fauna and Flora, in force 1 July 1975.

[52] International Convention for the Regulation of Whaling, in force 10 December 1948.

[53] Agreement on the Conservation of Albatrosses and Petrels, in force 1 February 2004.

[54] Inter-American Convention for the Protection and Conservation of Sea Turtles, in force 2 May 2005.

[55] Memorandum of Understanding on the Conservation and Management of Marine Turtles and their Habitats of the Indian Ocean and South-East Asia, in effect 1 September 2001.

[56] Convention on the Conservation and Management of Pollock Resources in the Central Bering Sea, in force 8 December 1995.

[57] Conservation and Management of Highly Migratory Fish Stocks in the Western and Central Pacific Ocean, in force 19 June 2004.

[58] Federated States of Micronesia Arrangement for Regional Fisheries Access, in force 23 September 1995.

[59] For an overview of instruments and institutions charged with fisheries management see <https://www.nyulawglobal.org/globalex/International_Fisheries_Law.html#RFMOs> accessed 14 April 2024.

complex fishing quota system. Specialised commissions and some UN agencies such as the Food and Agriculture Organization have developed extensive processes to prevent overfishing and ensure sustainable stock management while balancing the interests of coastal states, many of which are small developing island states. Yet, this prolific field of regulation has not fully succeeded in ensuring sustainability as it results in fisheries. Meanwhile, the WTO agreements include some general environmental exceptions that have at times been raised in cases involving trade restrictions on fish and other sea products. The Agreement on Subsidies and Countervailing Measures prohibits some subsidies and allows states to offset some domestic economic harm to producers resulting from foreign subsidies.[60] Yet, overfishing due to subsidies across the industry continues, demonstrating that the design for subsidies disciplines at the WTO is not suitable to address this significant and well-documented challenge.

While there is no question that the WTO and the ecosystem of fisheries management have their respective mandates and are not designed for any kind of merging, the co-existence of these regimes does not mean that they should ignore each other. Indeed, they require each other to provide a more effective solution to a global common problem. After years of debates, WTO Members adopted in 2022 an Agreement on Fisheries Subsidies, which will come into force once it is accepted by two-thirds of the membership.[61] The agreement expressly refers to determinations by regional fisheries management organisations as being determinative on the issue of whether a vessel or operator is engaged in inappropriate fishing,[62] which then automatically bars Members from subsidizing that entity.[63] Likewise, subsidies for fishing overfished stocks are prohibited and fisheries management organizations' determinations on overfished stocks are authoritative.[64] Coordination across regimes, with sustainability as a core normative objective, resulted in this unprecedented WTO agreement. The constraints of WTO developing and least-developed Members are also taken into account, albeit in a limited way, with the creation of a voluntary fund in cooperation with the Food and Agriculture Organization and other relevant organizations. If past practice regarding technical assistance funding at the WTO is any indication, contributions are likely to be limited and sporadic. Much more robust funding assistance systems could have been deployed, for instance, conditioning implementation by vulnerable WTO Members upon funding by wealthier Members.

Ensuring coherence between IEL, development, and sustainable development would require IEL to at least adopt a 'do no harm' principle ensuring that it does

[60] Agreement on Subsidies and Countervailing Measures, in force 1 January 1995.

[61] Agreement on Fisheries Subsidies, WT/Min(22)/33, WT/L/1144, adopted 17 June 2022 (not in force). As of April 2024, 46 Members have deposited their instrument of acceptance.

[62] ibid 3.2

[63] ibid art 3.1.

[64] ibid 4.

not operate at cross-purposes with other instruments promoting sustainable development. This could take the form of a conflict of law provision, whereby in the case of a clash between the IEL obligation and a sustainable development obligation or permission, the sustainable development norm prevails. Of course, this assumes that there is a well-defined applicable sustainable development rule, which is problematic in the current state of the law. Nonetheless, increased coordination between agencies and legal systems pertaining to IEL, sustainability, and development can help to improve normative and regulatory coherence. Incorporating conflict of law rules and other tools from private international law into trade and investment agreements may help to ensure that IEL disciplines do not operate at cross-purposes with sustainable development efforts pursued under other agreements.

V. Conclusion

Trade governance and investment regulation cannot take place in isolation from other regulatory regimes, particularly sustainable development. Regardless of how the relationship between IEL and sustainable development evolves, IEL can and must avail itself of the expertise and momentum generated in other institutions with respect to sustainable development. In so doing, trade governance mechanisms will gain legitimacy and efficacy by actually delivering more realistic, sustainable, and equitable benefits to the world's population and preserving a living environment for all.

6

Trade and Environment Negotiations at the WTO

A New Opportunity for SIDS?

Jan Yves Remy and Sanvid Tuljapurkar

I. Introduction

Small island developing states (SIDS) throw up unique challenges, not just in climate change negotiations but in trade fora as well.[1] Despite being the least responsible for greenhouse gas emissions, these countries' tradeable sectors often bear the full brunt of the climate crisis. In terms of their trade profile, SIDS' share of world trade, relatively weak bargaining power, and non-participation in dispute settlement have placed them at the margins of global trade rules and their enforcement.

In this chapter, we argue that the 'trade and environment' or sustainability agenda provides new opportunities for smaller states to move from the periphery to centre stage in World Trade Organization (WTO) negotiations. Perhaps for the first time ever, a common existential threat presented by climate change binds all countries in a common enterprise that will force different kinds of bargains and calculations to be made. Being among the most vulnerable to climate change, but the least blameworthy for it, SIDS are among those countries with the strongest (moral) claims to agitate for global action. Whether these moral claims can translate into tangible negotiating leverage at the WTO remains to be seen. Using a case study of SIDS within the Caribbean Community (CARICOM)[2] in particular, this chapter considers the situation of and possible strategies to be pursued by SIDS at the multilateral level.

[1] SIDS is a distinct group of 39 States and 18 Associate Members of United Nations (UN) regional commissions that face unique social, economic, and environmental vulnerabilities. The three geographical regions in which SIDS are located are: the Caribbean, the Pacific, and the Atlantic, Indian Ocean, and South China Sea. SIDS were recognized as a special case both for their environment and development at the 1992 United Nations Conference on Environment and Development held in Rio de Janeiro, Brazil. (See UN Office of the High Representative for the Least Developed Countries, Landlocked Developing Countries and Small Island Developing States, 'About Small Island Developing States' <https://www.un.org/ohrlls/content/about-small-island-developing-states> accessed 13 February 2024.

[2] The 15 members of CARICOM are Antigua and Barbuda, Bahamas, Barbados, Belize, Commonwealth of Dominica, Grenada, Cooperative Republic of Guyana, Haiti, Jamaica, Montserrat,

Jan Yves Remy and Sanvid Tuljapurkar, *Trade and Environment Negotiations at the WTO* In: *The Sustainability Revolution in International Trade Agreements*. Edited by: Geraldo Vidigal and Kathleen Claussen, Oxford University Press.
© Jan Yves Remy and Sanvid Tuljapurkar 2024. DOI: 10.1093/9780191994470.003.0006

The chapter is organized as follows. In section II, we consider the overall trade profile of SIDS, and in particular the specific challenges associated with their participation in ongoing WTO (environment-related) negotiations. Section III considers their climate priorities and climate-related peculiarities. In section IV, we propose elements of a new trade and climate agenda that SIDS can articulate at the WTO to promote their offensive interests. Section V briefly concludes.

II. Trade-Related Challenges of SIDS

A. The Limited Participation in International Trade, Dispute Settlement, and Ongoing Negotiations

SIDS share common economic characteristics and challenges despite having varied market structures and economies. Merchandise trade involving SIDS is typically small with approximately 0.3 per cent of globally traded goods being exported to SIDS between 2017 and 2019 and only 0.1 per cent imported from them during the same period.[3] Their trade is also characterized by a high dependence on exports, particularly on the export of primary commodities, and their main trading partners continue to be developed countries. For instance, CARICOM countries mainly export outside the region, namely the United States, the European Union, Canada, and increasingly China.[4] Eighteen out of 28 SIDS are primarily raw material exporters.[5]

The participation of SIDS in the WTO dispute settlement mechanism is also limited. For example, CARICOM countries' involvement in the WTO dispute settlement system, as complainants, respondents, and third parties, has also been largely that of a bystander. In the single case where a CARICOM Member State was complainant—the *US—Gambling*[6] dispute—despite winning on the legal merits before a panel, Appellate Body, and compliance panels, Antigua and Barbuda has not achieved tangible results and to date has not been able to negotiate a mutually

Saint Lucia, Saint Kitts and Nevis, Saint Vincent and the Grenadines, Republic of Suriname, and Republic of Trinidad and Tobago.

[3] United Nations Conference on Trade and Development (UNCTAD), '*Development and Globalization: Facts and Figures 2021—Small Island Developing States*' (United Nations 2021) 45.

[4] UNCTAD, *Caribbean Community (CARICOM) Export Potential to the European Union Voluntary Sustainability Standards (VSS): Feasibility Study* (United Nations 2021).

[5] 'Trade in Goods' (Small Island Developing States DGFF 2021) <https://dgff2021.unctad.org/trade-and-economic-vulnerability/trade-in-goods/#:~:text=Source%3A%20UNCTAD%20(2021a).,cent%20were%20imported%20from%20them> accessed 5 August 2023.

[6] Appellate Body Report, *US—Gambling*, WT/DS285/AB/R, adopted 20 April 2005.

acceptable solution and/or retaliate under the dispute settlement system's rules for doing so.[7]

With specific regard to the impact of climate change, the WTO is increasingly recognizing the linkages between trade and the environment and is working to integrate environmental considerations into its negotiations. In recent times, trade and environment have also been driven by initiatives such as the Trade and Environmental Sustainability Structured Discussions (TESSD), the Dialogue on Plastics Pollution and Environmentally Sustainable Plastics Trade, and Fossil Fuel Subsidy Reform (FFSR). The participation of SIDS in these WTO Members-led trade and environment initiatives has been limited, with only 7 SIDS participating in TESSD out of 74 members and 4 SIDS joining the FFSR. The Dialogue on Plastics Pollution has had the largest representation, with ten SIDS participants and Barbados being a co-convenor.

Instead, SIDS seem to have limited most of their negotiating focus to issues related to the impact of natural disasters. In 2017, six WTO Members of the Organisation of Eastern Caribbean States (OECS) brought attention to the devastating impact of natural disasters on SIDS and small vulnerable economies (SVEs) amid an intense cycle of hurricanes and tropical storms and proposed that the multilateral trading system be fully flexible to support disaster recovery and reconstruction. That work resulted in technical work and the issuing of two reports focused on the impact of natural disasters on WTO countries.[8] A 2022 Ministerial Decision instructed the Committee on Trade and Development (CTD) to continue its work in the Dedicated Session on Small Economies.[9] It is difficult to detect a clear negotiating agenda on climate change for SIDS beyond the discussions on trade and natural disasters arising in CTD.[10]

Outside the WTO, there has been some participation. In January 2023, a group of trade Ministers launched the Coalition of Trade Ministers for Climate, the first ministerial-level global forum dedicated to trade and climate and sustainable development issues.[11] Six SIDS are members of this Coalition.[12]

[7] Kara John, Matthew Chin Barnes, and Selisha Gilchrist, 'Tangible and concrete proposals for improving small State participation the context of the reform of the WTO's Dispute Settlement System and Investor-State Dispute Settlement', *TradeLab* (2020) <https://www.tradelab.org/single-post/2020/07/01/tangible-and-concrete-proposals-for-improving-small-state-participation-the-context-of-th> accessed 1 March 2023.

[8] WTO, *Natural Disasters and Trade: Study I* (WTO 2019); Giovanna Adinolfi, *Natural Disasters and Trade: Study II—A Legal Mapping* (WTO 2019).

[9] WTO Ministerial Decision, Work Programme on Small Economies, WT/MIN(22)/25, WT/L/1136 (17 June 2022).

[10] Jan-Yves Remy, *Trade-related Climate Priorities for CARICOM at the World Trade Organization* (Forum on Trade, Environment & the SDGs and Shridath Ramphal Centre 2023).

[11] Members of the Coalition of Trade Ministers on Climate (*Coalition of Trade Ministers for Climate*) <https://www.tradeministersonclimate.org/members> accessed 5 March 2023.

[12] ibid.

III. Climate-Related Challenges for SIDS

A. Climate Priorities in Ongoing Negotiations

SIDS have prioritized addressing climate change through domestic and international policy tools. Their posture in climate change negotiations is reflected inter alia in their commitment to reduce its fossil fuel dependence and transition to zero-carbon economies; the demands for financial assistance by developed countries to support its mitigation, adaptation and loss and damage priorities; and the request for technology transfer to assist with transition to low-carbon economies. Many of these priorities are also reflected in the Nationally Determined Contributions (NDCs). SIDS have distinguished themselves in the international climate change community, not only because of their natural vulnerability to the impacts of climate change as SIDS but also because of their global championing and advocacy. SIDS are parties to the United Nations Framework Convention on Climate Change (UNFCCC)[13] and the Alliance of Small Island States.

Although the region heavily depends on imported fossil fuels, SIDS have prioritized renewable energy with ambitious targets. For instance, Barbados, Antigua and Barbuda, and Belize have declared that they will achieve net-zero emissions by 2030. Despite the commitment to renewables and the abundance of solar, wind, geothermal energy, and hydropower, investment in the development of these renewable technologies is worryingly low.[14] SIDS also suffer due to high debt levels, and the current international financial infrastructure makes it extremely difficult to borrow at affordable rates. In view of this, SIDS have been among the most vocal proponents of greater emphasis in negotiations on adaptation, loss and damages, more climate finance in the form of grants, and holding developed countries to their promise of the $100 billion fund.[15] CARICOM countries in particular have also been very creative in putting forward ideas for financing the green agenda, including through reform of the existing international financial architecture, as well as through creative financial instruments for financing by the private sector. This includes the Bridgetown Initiative, which seeks to reallocate international public and private finance so that adaptation and mitigation priorities of developing countries are met.[16]

[13] United Nations Framework Convention on Climate Change, in force 21 March 1994.

[14] Caribbean Community Secretariat, *Caribbean Community (CARICOM) Climate Change Statistics—2020* (Caribbean Community Secretariat 2020).

[15] UNFCCC, *Decision 2/CP.27, Funding Arrangements for Responding to Loss and Damage Associated with the Adverse Effects of Climate Change, Including a Focus on Addressing Loss and Damage*, FCCC/CP/2022/10/Add 1 (17 March 2023).

[16] Jan Yves Remy, 'Why the Bridgetown Initiative on climate finance is good for trade' (*SRC Trade Blog*, 10 November 2022) <https://shridathramphalcentre.com/why-bridgetown-initiative-good-for-trade> accessed 28 February 2023.

IV. A New Trade and Climate Agenda for SIDS

Trade-related instruments and policies such as restrictions on the imports of energy-inefficient products and promotion of energy-efficient imports, domestic standards, and transfer of technologies are a part of SIDS' NDCs. However, there is no evidence that this has emerged from a concerted or intentional approach between the respective environment and trade policy divisions of SIDS. Their climate-related strategies and the regional entities with responsibility for climate change have not embraced trade and trade negotiations as part of their policy tools for advancing their respective climate agendas. Therefore, it is important for the SIDS to develop a comprehensive trade and climate agenda that identifies both opportunities for the international trade regime to contribute to climate change mitigation and adaptation; and solutions for SIDS' challenges in effectively engaging with the international trade regime. Such an agenda should underscore the need for more differentiated treatment of SIDS in view of their particular circumstances in the context of trade and climate change. The agenda should also assert SIDS' developmental needs in reference to environmental goods and services, technology transfer, financial support, food security and agriculture, just transition, standard setting, and natural disasters.

A. Special and Differential Treatment

The WTO is founded on the principle of formal equality of its Members as each WTO Member has one vote at the General Council and the Ministerial Conference, the highest decision-making bodies of the WTO.[17] However, WTO Members have been classified into three broad groups: developed countries, developing countries, and least-developed countries (LDCs); and the group that a Member belongs to determines their rights and obligations. Considering the relative disadvantage of developing countries and LDCs, WTO agreements provide special and differential treatment (SDT) to them.[18] The SDT provisions provide various flexibilities such as greater flexibility in implementing developing country's obligations, and technical assistance for developing countries to implement their obligations, participate in dispute settlement, and prepare trade policy review reports.[19] Additionally, several SDT provisions provide added flexibility, protections, and assistance to LDCs as compared to other developing countries. For instance, Article 66.1 of the Agreement on Trade-Related Aspects of Intellectual Property Rights

[17] Agreement Establishing the World Trade Organization, in force 1 January 1995, art IX(1).

[18] WTO Secretariat, *Implementation of Special and Differential Treatment: Provisions in WTO Agreements and Decisions*, WT/COMTD/W/77 (25 October 2000).

[19] ibid.

(TRIPS Agreement)[20] granted LDCs an 11-year transition period to implement TRIPS obligations. Article 15.2 of the Agreement on Agriculture exempts LDCs from reduction commitments. These provisions are intended to promote their integration into the global trading system and to ensure that they benefit from trade liberalization.

SIDS as a group includes developing countries and LDCs that are eligible for various forms of SDT under the WTO agreements. However, the classification of developing countries and LDCs does not take into account their current economic and environmental realities, which are a consequence of their specific physical, geographical, economic, and demographic characteristics.[21] The relative lack of economic power of SIDS has made it more difficult for them to insist on other WTO Members prioritizing their concerns. These challenges are even more apparent in the case of trade and climate negotiations. The unique situation of SIDS in the context of climate was acknowledged at the United Nations Conference on Environment and Development in Rio de Janeiro in 1992,[22] and since then, in the UNFCCC.[23] The 1994 Programme of Action for the Sustainable Development of SIDS recognized that development issues and the natural environment, in SIDS, are closely interrelated and interdependent. However, they have not been formally recognized as a group in the WTO.

The recognition of SIDS as a separate group at the WTO will allow their development partners to understand their issues and the basis of their advocacy. Without a proper definition of the group of countries in question, development partners may be reluctant to extend concessions by virtue of recognition of the relevant category, to any of the countries that might claim to belong to that category.[24] In view of this, SIDS should be accepted in ongoing climate-related negotiations as a separate category or sub-category deserving of special treatment just as LDCs, for instance, are.

B. Trade in Environmental Goods and Services

Environmental goods such as electronic vehicles and solar panels, environmental services such as wastewater management services, and sanitation services are

[20] Agreement on Trade-related Aspects of Intellectual Property Rights, in force 1 January 1995.

[21] Barbara von Tigerstrom, 'Small Island Developing States and International Trade: Special Challenges in the Global Partnership for Development' (2005) 6(2) Melbourne Journal of International Law 402.

[22] UNFCCC Secretariat, *Climate Change, Small Island Developing States* (UNFCCC 2005).

[23] UNFCCC (n 13) art 4.8 refers to 'the specific needs and concerns of developing country Parties arising from the adverse effects of climate change . . . especially on: (a) Small Island countries; (b) Countries with low-lying coastal areas; (c). . .'

[24] UNCTAD, *Is a special treatment of small island developing States possible?*, UNCTAD/LDC/2004/1 (United Nations 2004).

necessary for climate change mitigation and adaptation. Environment-related services such as engineering, construction, installation, and maintenance and repair are necessary for the production, installation, maintenance, and efficient use of environmental goods. Promoting and facilitating environmental goods and environmental and related services has been a core component of the global trade and climate agenda. For instance, in 2014, a group of 46 WTO Members launched—but never concluded—negotiations for an Environmental Goods Agreement (EGA). Promotion and facilitation of environmental goods and services has been included as a working group in TESSD.[25] Provisions relating to environmental goods and services are also a part of free trade agreements. For instance, the Agreement between New Zealand and the Separate Customs Territory of Taiwan, Penghu, Kinmen, and Matsu on Economic Cooperation (ANZTEC) includes a separate annex containing a stand-alone list of 132 environmental goods on which tariffs are to be eliminated upon entry into force.[26] New Zealand–UK FTA provides for the immediate elimination of all import tariffs on environmental goods listed in Annex 22A.[27]

Developing countries are often net importers of environmental goods.[28] Due to the relative disadvantage of most developing countries, they are not the *demandeurs* in the environmental goods and services negotiations at the WTO. Nevertheless, NDCs of some SIDS point towards the region's environmental goods and services priorities, which include restrictions on the import of energy-inefficient products and promotion of energy-efficient imports like electronic vehicles and renewable equipment. This highlights their interest in environmental goods and services. Clarifying which goods qualify as 'environmental' would assist SIDS in identifying priorities and market access opportunities. The definition of environmental goods included in FTAs may be used as a reference point to develop a definition at the WTO. For example, the New Zealand–Taiwan FTA (ANZTEC) defines environmental goods as 'those which positively contribute to the green growth and sustainable development objectives of the parties'.[29] The Asia-Pacific Economic Cooperation (APEC) list of environmental goods may also be a helpful reference point while identifying environmental goods.[30]

SIDS should focus on specific goods for which it can develop a competitive advantage. For instance, given the region's rich biodiversity, natural fibres represent a

[25] WTO, *TESSD Work Plan 2022*, INF/TE/SSD/W/17/Rev 1 (18 February 2022).

[26] Agreement between New Zealand and the Separate Customs Territory of Taiwan, Penghu, Kinmen, and Matsu on Economic Cooperation (10 July 2013) Annex 7.

[27] New Zealand–United Kingdom Free Trade Agreement (28 February 2022) art 22.7.

[28] 'Trade Related Indicators' (*IMF Climate Change Dashboard*) <https://climatedata.imf.org/pages/bp-indicators> accessed 15 February 2023.

[29] Agreement between New Zealand and the Separate Customs Territory of Taiwan, Penghu, Kinmen, and Matsu on Economic Cooperation, in force 1 December 2013, art 3-2(a).

[30] APEC, *2012 Leaders' Declaration* (8–9 September 2012), Annex C: APEC List of Environmental Goods.

potential niche for them to exploit, but greater research is needed in this area. They should ensure that the environmental goods in which they have a competitive advantage are included in the definition and list of environmental goods that may be developed at the WTO. SIDS should also explore opportunities to participate in global value chains for the production of renewable goods, whether through patents or raw materials necessary for their use.[31]

Considering SIDS' services-based economy, they are likely to be highly interested in environmental and related services negotiations. They should also focus on ecotourism in view of the region's tourism exports and susceptibility to climate change. The region's abundance of natural resources and rich biodiversity provide natural competitive advantages for the development of ecotourism.[32]

In addition to focusing on market access opportunities for specific goods and services, SIDS may propose the temporary liberalization of the goods and services necessary to recover and rebuild in case of a climate disaster. The greater availability and accessibility of necessary goods and services is important for SIDS considering their susceptibility to climate-related natural disasters. Such temporary liberalization would be similar to the measures undertaken by WTO Members in the case of medical services during the COVID-19 pandemic such as streamlining the granting of visas and work permits by Australia and the United Kingdom and fast-tracked recognition of qualifications by Belgium, Luxembourg, and Spain.[33]

C. Trade-Related Aspects of Technology Transfer

While technology plays a critical role in achieving climate change mitigation and adaptation, it is often owned and developed by developed countries. It is frequently argued that the diffusion and uptake of technology can be catalysed through the liberalization of environmental goods and services. However, critics have pointed out that while environmentally friendly technologies have been transferred through foreign investment and trade, much of this has not reached LDCs due to their lack of integration into the global economy, and their weak absorptive capacity.[34] Therefore, market-based channels like liberalization of environmental goods and services may not be a solution for the needs of developing countries.

[31] Developers in Barbados in the 1970s created solar water heaters, which have become widespread in the country.

[32] Amandine Vaslet and Romain Renoux, *Regional Ecosystem Profile Caribbean* (European Commission 2016).

[33] World Bank and the WTO, *Trade Therapy Deepening Cooperation to Strengthen Pandemic Defenses* (World Bank 2022).

[34] Thomas Cottier, 'Technology Diffusion in the Triangle of China, the West and Developing Countries: The Contribution of Common Concerns of Humankind' in Henry Gao, Damian Raess, and Ka Zeng (eds), *China and the WTO: A Twenty-Year Assessment* CUP 2023) 514–33; Laura Kelly and others, 'Technology Transfer: A New Agenda for LDC Negotiators', *Policy Brief* (Overseas Development Institute 2021).

The importance of the transfer of technology and know-how has been recognized by the UNFCCC,[35] Paris Agreement,[36] and under the WTO TRIPS Agreement. Nonetheless, the trade-related aspects of technology transfer have not been a focus in climate negotiations. Climate technologies have also not been at the centre of trade negotiations on technology transfer.[37]

While environment-related technology transfer and cooperation provisions have been included in FTAs, they are generally merely best endeavour provisions.[38] For instance, Article 19.08 of the Nicaragua–Taiwan FTA provides for cooperation to facilitate technology development and transfer as well as training related to clean production technologies, water protection, conservation and preservation, hazardous and non-hazardous waste management, and the monitoring and management of biodiversity and endangered species.[39] Article 12.5 of the China–Switzerland FTAstates that environmental cooperation between the parties 'should also address the issue of technology cooperation and transfer, especially regarding environmentally friendly technologies'.[40]

In the WTO, general technology transfer-related discussions have largely revolved around Article 66.2 of TRIPS, which creates a general obligation for developed countries to assist with the diffusion of technology by incentivizing national enterprises and institutions to transfer technology. Trade- and climate-related discussions have taken place at the WTO in the CTE and TESSD. The focus of these discussions on climate-related technology transfer has been limited. For instance, Members did not identify technology transfer as one of the four work streams of the TESSD Work Plan for 2022.[41] The slow progress on technology transfer commitments means that developing countries and LDCs have reduced capability to respond to climate change and maintain and expand market access in an era of increasing environmental regulation.[42]

[35] Eg UNFCCC (n 13) art 5 requires developed countries to offer support in the form of promotion, facilitation, and financing of the transfer of and access to environmental technologies and know-how to developing countries. Article 4.9 states that parties take account of the specific needs and special situation of LDCs in funding technology transfers.

[36] Paris Agreement, in force 4 November 2016: art 10 commits countries to strengthen cooperation on technology transfer and, inter alia, develop a mechanism for implementing this obligation, and to provide support, including financial support, to developing countries and achieve overall balance between support for mitigation and adaptation.

[37] Kelly and others (n 34).

[38] Christophe Bellmann and Mahesh Sugathan, *Promoting and Facilitating Trade in Environmental Goods and Services: Lessons From Regional Trade Agreements* (Forum on Trade, Environment & the SDGs 2022).

[39] Free Trade Agreement between the Republic of China (Taiwan) and the Republic of Nicaragua, in force 1 January 2008, denounced 15 December 2021, art 19.08.

[40] Free Trade Agreement between Swiss and the People's Republic of China, in force 1 July 2014, art 12.5.

[41] WTO, *TESSD Work Plan 2022* (n 25).

[42] Sanna Markkanen and others, *On the Borderline: The EU CBAM and its Place in the World of Trade* (University of Cambridge 2021).

CARICOM, for instance, has underscored the importance of rules or policies that encourage the transfer of green technologies from the developed world to CARICOM countries and has expressly referenced their technology needs in NDCs, as well as in technical needs assessments (TNAs) developed under the aegis of the UNFCCC.[43] Priority areas for the region include technologies related to renewable energy generation and improving water and agricultural systems to address the increasing occurrences of droughts and floods in recent years as a result of climate change.

To ensure that their technology needs are met, SIDS could support recommendations made by LDCs to improve the coordination between the WTO and UNFCCC by inter alia building on existing TNAs to identify the technologies needed from developed country partners; and using the WTO as a venue for reiterating the need for the donor community to prioritize resources to support needs assessments and then delivering technologies.[44] Moreover, the TRIPS Council should be engaged to promote climate-friendly technologies in the context of discussions related to the implementation of TRIPS Article 66.2. TESSD discussions should provide a space for the sharing of best practices, especially by countries like India, that have been effective in domesticating developed country technologies.

SIDS should also strongly advocate for environment-related technology transfer provisions that go beyond a nominal best endeavour approach. This can be achieved through a Doha-like waiver under TRIPS Article 31(f) which could be negotiated to grant compulsory import licences for certain climate technologies.[45] Another suggestion is to amend the WTO's Agreement on Subsidies and Countervailing Measures (SCM Agreement) to allow domestic tax reductions to companies investing in LDCs, and that tax revenues generated from carbon tariffs and border tax adjustments be used to fund technology dissemination in LDCs.[46] SIDS could also seek the extension of the special treatment accorded to LDCs for SIDS under Article 66.2.

D. Financial Support

Climate finance has not been sufficiently addressed in the WTO, except, to a limited extent, in the context of the Aid for Trade initiative. The theme of the 2020–2022 Aid for Trade Work Program was 'Empowering Connected, Sustainable Trade'. Of

[43] Between 2009 and 2023, Antigua and Barbuda, Belize, Dominica, Grenada, Guyana, Haiti, Jamaica, Suriname, Trinidad and Tobago, Bahamas, and Saint Kitts and Nevis completed TNAs that together with those of Latin American countries amounted to $542 million for adaptation and $100 million for mitigation.

[44] Kelly and others (n 34).

[45] Clara Brandi, *Trade Elements in Countries' Climate Contributions Under the Paris Agreement* (International Centre for Trade and Sustainable Development 2017).

[46] Cottier (n 34).

the 53 developing countries that responded to the questionnaire circulated for the 2022 Aid for Trade Global Review, 51 countries referenced environmental sustainability as a priority in their development strategies.[47] The report also noted that while donors have pledged to expand funding for low-carbon transition, and that climate finance provided by developed countries has steadily increased, the funds collected have been inadequate to meet the $100 billion annual target.[48] Therefore, a better understanding of the linkages between the UNFCCC and aid for trade programming is required.[49]

The climate finance agenda at the WTO should go beyond aid for trade given the interlinkages between finance and trade for developing countries and LDCs. Finance should be integrated within the core ambit of the WTO negotiations in view of the current momentum for reforming the international financial architecture inherited under Bretton Woods as well as the ongoing WTO reform discussions.

The climate finance agenda can be built on the foundation of past proposals at the WTO. For instance, Jamaica on behalf of the African, Caribbean, and Pacific Group of States (ACP) in its proposal called on the WTO to foster the conversation with private and multilateral institutions to address that issue.[50] Another proposal that suggested creating a Trade and Environment Fund may also be reconsidered under the current circumstances. As per the proposal, the Trade and Environment Fund would have objectives such as:

> facilitating transfer of environmental technologies at reasonable prices by funding the incremental costs of sourcing both proprietary and non-proprietary environmental technologies through licensing and other mechanisms;
> providing grants to developing country Members that intend to import specific environmental technologies;
> financing the cost of change of production practices in existing manufacturing facilities in developing countries by adopting and implementing environmental technologies;
> financing research and development activities;
> financing appropriate environmental technical assistance and capacity-building programmes; and

[47] OECD/WTO, *Aid for Trade at a Glance 2022: Empowering Connected, Sustainable Trade* (OECD 2022), 51.

[48] ibid.

[49] Jodie Keane and others, 'The Climate and Trade Nexus in Africa: Climate Change and the Transformation of African Trade', *Policy Brief* (Overseas Development Institute 2021).

[50] WTO Working Group on Trade, Debt and Finance, Communication from Jamaica, on behalf of the African, Caribbean and Pacific Group of States (ACP), WT/WGTDF/W/101 (6 October 2011).

establishing technology transfer centres/exchanges/mechanisms in consultation and cooperation with the relevant multilateral environmental agreement Secretariats.[51]

E. Food Security and Agriculture

The WTO Agreement on Agriculture was designed to make competition in agricultural trade fairer for countries that cannot or do not subsidize agricultural produce by reducing trade-distorting domestic support and export subsidies. Addressing food security was not its primary agenda. However, some trade-related food security issues such as trade effects of certain public stockholding programmes that involve government procurement of crops at above-market prices and the sale or other disposal of those stocks have been discussed in the context of this agreement.

Faced with rising food prices caused by the Ukraine war, and the dislocations caused by the COVID-19 pandemic, WTO members issued a Ministerial Declaration on the Emergency Response to Food Insecurity at the 12th Ministerial Conference (MC12). The Declaration specifically recognized the needs of net food-importing developing countries and commits to a dedicated work programme in the Committee on Agriculture.[52] In November 2022, that programme was established with four primary themes to guide future discussions, namely access to international food markets, financing food imports, agricultural and production resilience of LDCs and net food-importing developing countries, and a set of horizontal issues to foster collaboration.[53]

Agriculture-related trade and food security is a critical problem for the SIDS as they are net food importers.[54] Moreover, the inordinate level of external dependence increases their vulnerability to food shortages and price hikes during crisis and global disruptions, which will worsen with increasing global temperatures and food production instability.[55] The food security problem is estimated to be further exacerbated due to a general reduction in food production and the displacement of livelihoods of small farmers as a result of climate change.[56]

[51] CTE Special Session, Communication from China and India, *WTO Negotiations on Environmental Goods and Services: Addressing the Developmental Dimension for a 'Triple-Win' Outcome*, TN/TE/W/79 (15 April 2011).

[52] WTO Ministerial Conference, *Ministerial Declaration on the Emergency Response to Food Insecurity*, WT/MIN(22)/28 (17 June 2022) .

[53] WTO Committee on Agriculture, *Work Programme Pursuant to Paragraph 8 of the Ministerial Declaration on the Emergency Response to Food Insecurity*, G/AG/35 (23 November 2022).

[54] Chelcee Brathwaite, 'An Overview of Food Security & Trade Across CARICOM', *Food for Thought Policy Brief Series* (Shridath Ramphal Centre for International Trade Law 2021).

[55] ibid.

[56] Kevon Rhiney and others, 'Assessing the Implications of a 1.5 °C Temperature Limit for the Jamaican Agriculture Sector' (2018) 18 Regional Environmental Change 2313.

SIDS should align their priorities with the multilateral agenda due to their dependence on developed markets for agriculture and food exports, and their need for investments and technologies from the developed countries for agriculture-related climate change mitigation and adaptation. SIDS should also advocate for multilateral rules that guarantee uninterrupted global supply chains where regional sources are unavailable.

F. Enabling the Just Energy Transition

Given the availability of natural resources such as solar, wind, geothermal energy, and, to a lesser extent, hydro and biomass renewables, SIDS could advance discussions on the liberalization of renewable energy goods and related services. This would help in providing security to foreign direct investment. SIDS could also support a carve-out for renewable energy subsidies from the SCM Agreement disciplines.[57] However, SIDS should try to balance their interest in developing their domestic renewable energy sector with the challenges resulting from substantial subsidies being granted by the developed countries with considerable resources as they are unlikely to be able to outcompete these large-scale subsidies.

Another issue relevant to SIDS in the context of renewable energy subsidies is regarding local content requirements as some of their NDCs have included feed-in-tariff schemes to encourage the transition to a low-carbon economy which may include local content requirements. While local content requirements have been held to be inconsistent with the WTO,[58] SIDS should propose an exemption for local content requirements of SIDS. The small size of the SIDS means that such local content requirements are unlikely to distort trade and such an exemption will also provide assurances of the much-needed policy space for SIDS to develop their indigenous renewable energy sectors.

Moreover, given the economic difficulties and climate vulnerabilities of SIDS, they may also argue for allowing SIDS to use subsidies to compensate for disadvantages and make their environmental products more competitive in global markets. In general, export subsidies are prohibited under the SCM Agreement.[59] Developing countries are provided with a transition period within which to phase out these subsidies, while low-income developing countries with a per capita gross national product of less than US$1000 and LDCs are exempt from the prohibition altogether.[60] Those SIDS that are not LDCs or low-income developing countries

[57] See eg Revised Treaty of Chaguaramas Establishing the Caribbean Community Including the CARICOM Single Market and Economy, in force 1 January 2006, art 11.

[58] Appellate Body Report, *Canada—Renewable Energy*, WT/DS412/AB/R and WT/DS426/AB/R, adopted 24 May 2013; Appellate Body Report, *India—Solar Cells*, WT/DS456/AB/R, adopted 14 October 2016>.

[59] SCM Agreement, in force 1 January 1995, art 3.

[60] ibid, art 27.2(a).

are therefore required to gradually eliminate export subsidies.[61] These rules do not provide flexibilities to SIDS that may need to continue providing export subsidies to compensate for the inherent cost disadvantages, climate vulnerabilities, and resource constraints. Therefore, it may be proposed that the SIDS that are not LDCs and low-income developing countries receive the same exemption from export subsidy prohibition.[62]

G. Standard Setting Relating to Climate Change

Environmental and climate standards are a pertinent trade and climate issue for SIDS as standards are increasingly being imposed as a condition for market access, often unilaterally. In the absence of equivalent standards such as carbon tax being imposed on regional products, and considering the limited capacity to measure, verify, and monitor carbon content and emissions from goods, SIDS stand to be negatively impacted by unilateral rules imposed on the basis of carbon content requirements. For instance, such rules are likely to impact Trinidad and Tobago's exports of ammonia to that market. Deforestation policies might affect countries like Guyana and Suriname with substantial forest cover.[63] Therefore, it is advisable that SIDS actively participate in designing standards. Moreover, considering their challenges in designing and implementing standards, they should advocate for mechanisms that facilitate the exchange of information and cooperation in the design and implementation of standards.[64] They should also insist on the information exchange and cooperation obligations being mandatory.

Some SIDS are also developing standards related to certain sectors. For example, CARICOM NDCs focus on domestic environmental and energy standards. The CARICOM Regional Organization for Standards and Quality has been assisting CARICOM Member States by developing a regional energy efficiency building code, energy efficiency labelling standards, and minimum energy performance standards for electrical appliances as well as developing energy efficiency labelling standards and minimum energy performance standards for light industrial appliances. CARICOM has also signalled a desire to enhance its eco-labelling and standards to promote its tourism product. Participation in standard-setting bodies

[61] ibid, art 27.4.

[62] United Nations, *Draft Strategy for the Further Implementation of the Programme of Action for the Sustainable Development of Small Island Developing States* UN Doc A/CONF 207/L 1 (8 November 2004).

[63] Jan Yves Remy and Kaycia Ellis-Bourne, 'The EU's Carbon Border Adjustment Mechanism and CARICOM' (Shridath Ramphal Centre Trading Thoughts, 6 August 2021) <https://shridathramphalcentre.com/the-eus-carbon-border-adjustment-mechanism-and-caricom> accessed 12 March 2023.

[64] Agreement between the United States of America, the United Mexican States, and Canada, in force 1 July 2020, art 12.D.5; Comprehensive and Progressive Agreement for Trans-Pacific Partnership, in force 18 December 2018, Annex 8-G.

and notification of standards in WTO committees would help to augment SIDS' reputation as climate-friendly destinations. Given that some SIDS are developing domestic standards, they should also advocate for mutual acceptance provisions such as those provided for in Article 7.5 of the EU–Singapore FTA.[65]

H. Natural Disasters

Climate change-related natural disasters are an imminent threat to the environment and economy of SIDS and it is not surprising that they have been leading most of the negotiations on trade and natural disasters. In 2017, in the midst of a particularly intense cycle of hurricanes and tropical storms affecting the region, six SIDS tabled a proposal to bring attention to the catastrophic impact of natural disasters on SVEs. They suggested 'full flexibility' of the multilateral trading system to support disaster recovery and reconstruction, a call that catalysed discussions in the WTO CTD and contributed to the launch in 2018 of the WTO's 'Natural Disaster and Trade Project'.[66]

At MC12, the Work Programme on Small Economies received a boost through a Ministerial Decision highlighting the work carried out since 2018,[67] and instructing the CTD to continue its work in the Dedicated Session on Small Economies under the overall responsibility of the General Council. The WTO Secretariat was also instructed to provide relevant information and factual analysis for discussion among Members in the CTD's Dedicated Session on Small Economies.

SIDS should use this Decision to bring greater awareness and support for trade responses to the impact of natural disasters on SVE economies. For instance, the CTD and TESSD discussions could pinpoint specific places in the recent initiatives (such as e-commerce, investment facilitation, domestic regulations) as well as older ones (fisheries subsidies, market access, agriculture, and services) where a specific focus on natural disasters might assist in promoting SIDS' interests.[68] It is already notable that the Fisheries Subsidies Agreement contains a specific reference to disasters[69] and sustainability concerns are already being discussed in the context of investment facilitation negotiations.

[65] Free Trade Agreement between the European Union and the Republic of Singapore, in force 21 November 2019.

[66] See (n 8).

[67] See (n 9).

[68] For specific ideas on negotiating approaches see Jan Yves Remy, Hannes Schloemann, Clémentine Pitard and others, 'Natural Disasters, Trade and Resilience in Commonwealth Countries', in *Enabling Sustainable Trade in the OECS: The Ocean and Digital Economies* (Commonwealth Secretariat 2023).

[69] The Agreement on Fisheries Subsidies, adopted 17 June 2022, WT/Min(22)/33 (not in force), provides in art. 11.1 that 'Except as provided in Articles 3 and 4, nothing in this Agreement shall prevent a Member from granting a subsidy for disaster . . . relief, provided that the subsidy is: (a)limited to the relief of a particular disaster.'

V. Conclusion

SIDS have for a long time been marginalized in international trade, WTO negotiations, and WTO dispute settlement. The trade/environment agenda presents these countries with a key opportunity to reappraise and reframe their position in the WTO through a more intentional approach that involves the incorporation of climate change considerations into WTO rules. Specifically, this should involve a greater focus on their specific acceptance as a grouping for SDT that is linked to their climatic vulnerability; new approaches to the negotiation of environmental goods and services; reappraising the role of technology transfer and the rules relating to them; greater inclusion of finance in WTO discussions; expansion of concerns relating to food security in agriculture discussions; emphasis on the energy transition and related discussions on fossil fuel subsidies; greater inclusiveness in standard-setting bodies; and new impetus to negotiations on natural disasters at the WTO.

PART II

SUSTAINABILITY OBLIGATIONS: CONTENT AND COMPLIANCE

7

Labour Standards in EU Free Trade Agreements

Substantive Issues and Recent Developments Concerning Their Enforcement

Giovanni Gruni

I. Introduction

Free trade agreements (FTAs) have been a traditional instrument used in EU policy to engage with partner countries. Until around 2005, major developments in world trade law happened mainly via the multilateral negotiations in the General Agreement on Tariffs and Trade (GATT) and then in the World Trade Organization (WTO). However, in the last couple of decades, geopolitical divisions and irreconcilable positions caused a stalemate in most of the areas of negotiation in the Doha Round, which prompted countries to look for alternative ways to conclude commercial agreements and advance their interests. This shift triggered a new wave of FTAs. The European Union has been particularly active in the conclusion of FTAs since its renewed Lisbon Strategy, making them a key element of its commercial policy.[1] Today, the European Union has either concluded or is negotiating FTAs with more than 100 countries, with large recent FTAs such as those with Canada[2] and Japan[3] covering big chunks of EU trade flows with non-EU countries.[4]

All recent EU FTAs include binding provisions on a set of labour standards defined as 'core' by the International Labour Organization (ILO). In addition, the European Union developed a set of procedures that can be activated in case of non-compliance with such standards. This chapter reviews the state of the art of the inclusion of labour standards in EU FTAs, identifying the main shortcomings

[1] On the history of the EU policy leading to the conclusion of FTAs outside the WTO, see G Gruni, *The EU, World Trade Law and the Right to Food* (Bloomsbury Hart 2018).

[2] Comprehensive Economic and Trade Agreement (CETA) between Canada and the European Union and its Member States, provisionally applied 21 September 2017.

[3] Agreement between the European Union and Japan for an Economic Partnership, in force 1 February 2019.

[4] For the state of the art of negotiations of EU FTAs, see EU Commission, Negotiations and agreements <https://ec.europa.eu/trade/policy/countries-and-regions/negotiations-and-agreements/>.

Giovanni Gruni, *Labour Standards in EU Free Trade Agreements* In: *The Sustainability Revolution in International Trade Agreements.* Edited by: Geraldo Vidigal and Kathleen Claussen, Oxford University Press. © Giovanni Gruni 2024.
DOI: 10.1093/9780191994470.003.0007

of the present approach. In the summer of 2022, the European Commission with its Communication 409 modified its longstanding 'promotional' approach to the enforcement of labour standards on the basis of which it was refusing to apply the same state-to-state dispute settlement mechanism available to enforce economic obligations and intellectual property rights contained in FTAs.[5] The final part of this chapter assesses this recent change of posture and asks if the European Union is indeed implementing this new approach or not. The conclusion will be that more than a year after Communication 409 there are some signals already in the law that the European Union will change its posture for the enforcement of labour standards. The recent EU–New Zealand[6] and EU–Kenya[7] FTAs in fact already have a uniform dispute settlement system for labour standards, economic clauses, and intellectual property rights. However, there are also strong doubts about the overall impact of this change of posture, at least in the short term. This is because of the numerous FTAs the European Union have concluded already that utilize the older softer approach to the enforcement of labour standards. In addition, the reticence to include the new strong approach to enforcement in the more recent EU–Chile[8] and EU–Mercosur FTAs,[9] even if both FTAs are not in force yet, indicates that the change of approach of Communication 409 will be limited to a very small number of trade partners at least for the time being.

This chapter is structured as follows. Section II introduces how labour standards are dealt with multilaterally in the ILO and in the WTO. Section III looks at the state of the art of the substantive obligations protecting labour standards in the EU FTAs. Section IV assesses the present mechanisms of enforcement of such standards present in most of the EU FTAs. Sections V and VI look at the recent change in the global posture of the European Union with regard to the enforcement of labour standards in its FTAs. Section VII concludes.

II. Labour Standards in the ILO and in the WTO

A. The ILO

ILO Members have adopted numerous Conventions that are open to ratification and implementation. In 1998, ILO Members identified eight Conventions that

[5] Communication from the Commission, 'The power of trade partnerships: together for green and just economic growth' COM(2022) 409 final (22 June 2022).

[6] Free Trade Agreement between the European Union and New Zealand, in force 1 May 2024.

[7] Economic Partnership Agreement Between the European Union and the Republic of Kenya, signed 18 December 2023.

[8] Interim Agreement on Trade between the European Union and the Republic of Chile, signed 13 December 2023.

[9] EU–Mercosur Trade Agreement—Agreement in Principle, 1 July 2019 (not signed).

they labelled as 'core'. These Conventions refer to the four basic labour standards: freedom of association and the prohibitions of forced labour, child labour, and discrimination at work. Each fundamental standard is composed of two 'core' Conventions that have received widespread, even if not universal, ratification. For instance, the backbone of international protection against forced labour are Conventions 29[10] and 105.[11] Under Convention 29, states have an obligation to make forced labour illegal in their territories and support the prohibition with criminal penalties.

In addition to the eight core Conventions, ILO Members have adopted around 180 additional Conventions on various aspects of labour protection. Even when ILO Conventions are ratified, they are subject only to the soft enforcement mechanisms of the ILO, which establishes a forum to discuss alleged violations but does not provide for sanctions and lacks solid instruments of enforcement.[12] This is a notorious weakness of the ILO system that distinguishes it from other areas of international law, especially in the trade and investment spheres, which are endowed with more effective instruments of supervision and enforcement.

B. The WTO

International law today is fragmented into separate legal regimes. This also applies to international organizations that often specialize in specific areas of law and governance and remain separate from other international organizations. This mostly applies to the WTO, which focuses mainly on trade matters and leaves issues like labour standards to the UN system and the ILO. This principle was enshrined in the 1996 Singapore Declaration where WTO Members reaffirmed their commitment to labour standards while agreeing at the same time to keep them outside the WTO. This means that Members of the WTO are not legally required to respect any labour standards to become Members of the organization. However, they maintain the obligations they accepted under the laws of the ILO and the rest of international law.

The only parts of WTO law that refer to a labour issue are the general exceptions of the GATT and GATS (General Agreement on Trade in Services), which contain a reference to prison labour. These articles provide that, subject to a number of

[10] ILO, Convention Concerning Forced or Compulsory Labour (No 29), in force 1 May 1932.

[11] ILO, Convention Concerning the Abolition of Forced Labour (No 105), in force 17 January 1959.

[12] See ILO, 'ILO Supervisory system/mechanism' <https://www.ilo.org/global/about-the-ilo/how-the-ilo-works/ilo-supervisory-system-mechanism/lang--en/index.htm>. Article 33 of the ILO Constitution allows the Governing Body to recommend action to the International Labour Conference to adopt measures to enforce labour standards. This procedure was utilized very rarely. See ILO, 'Practice on the use of Article 33 of the ILO Constitution' <https://guide-supervision.ilo.org/defending/the-governing-body-may-recommend-action-to-the-international-labour-conference-when-a-government-fails-to-implement-recommendations-of-a-coi-or-the-icj>.

conditions, WTO Members are allowed to impose trade restrictions on the products of prison labour, an expression that has been considered to include the different forms of forced labour prohibited by the ILO.[13] Notably, this does not mean that the Members of the WTO are obliged not to trade between themselves products produced with forced labour but only that, when this happens, they can refuse the import or export of such products. This exception has been used for instance by the US Customs Administration to seize and destroy products that in whole or part had been produced via forced labour while remaining compliant with WTO law.[14] On the contrary, the European Union does not have a system in place to utilize customs controls to enforce international labour rules prohibiting forced labour.[15]

C. The Inclusion of Labour Standards in World Trade Law via FTAs

Notwithstanding the state of separation between world trade law and labour protection, a debate has been developing since the 1990s around the necessity of including labour standards in the rules governing world trade. Such debate stemmed from a number of perceived problems emerging from the lack of labour obligations in world trade law, spanning from fears of unfair competition from countries with lower social protection to claims of insufficient international protection of labour standards via the traditional ILO instruments. This debate produced an array of research proposing amendments to the rules regulating world trade to accommodate labour standards. Such academic and political proposals have failed to produce any amendments to the rules of the WTO. However, not all world trade law remained untouched by such proposals of reform. As mentioned in the introduction, States have been increasingly active in negotiating and concluding FTAs outside the WTO directly with partner countries. It is in the context of FTAs that labour standards started permeating into world trade law more boldly. In 1994, the United States pioneered the first side agreement to an FTA on labour standards when it concluded the North American Free Trade Agreement (NAFTA) with Canada and Mexico.[16] After that, it has been a common practice of the United States, Canada, and the European Union to include references to labour standards, albeit with varying degrees of legal significance, in their FTAs. After the failure of the WTO Doha Round, with the rise in prominence of FTAs to regulate international trade

[13] Y Moorman, 'Integration of ILO Core Rights Labour Standards into the WTO' (2001) 39 Columbia Journal of Transnational Law 555.

[14] SL Bell, 'The US Prohibition on Imports Made with Forced Labour: The New Law is a "Force" to be Reckoned With' (2016) 11 Global Trade and Customs Journal 580.

[15] See, however, the recent proposal going towards this direction, COM(2022) 453, Proposal for a regulation on prohibiting products made with forced labour on the Union Market.

[16] North American Agreement on Labour Cooperation (NAALC), in force 1 January 1994.

relations, the labour standards included in them started to be given a higher level of protection too. Following this trend, all recent EU FTAs include binding references to core labour standards. Such obligations on labour standards, however, do not currently have the same level of enforcement provided to economic obligations and intellectual property rights.

III. Substantive Obligations on Labour Standards in EU FTAs

A. Substantive Obligations

EU FTAs concluded after 2010 contain sections dedicated to the protection of core labour standards, often under the label of sustainable development.[17] Such clauses include obligations falling on state parties aimed at promoting the ratification and respect of the eight ILO core Conventions. Such obligations are not exactly the same in all recent EU FTAs but follow common trends so that they can be divided into three different categories.

Firstly, recent EU FTAs encourage the parties to respect and implement existing international commitments.[18] Within this group, one finds hard obligations, such as the one in the Comprehensive Economic and Trade Agreement (CETA) with Canada, for each party to ensure that its labour laws and practices 'embody and provide protection' of listed ILO standards. Other obligations are less definite. Certain FTAs include an obligation for their signatories to make 'continued and sustained efforts towards ratifying' fundamental ILO conventions on forced labour.[19]

[17] There is already a wide amount of scholarship on labour standards in EU FTAs. See eg H Gött, 'Linkages of Trade, Investment and Labour in Preferential Trade Agreements: Between Untapped Potential and Structural Insufficiencies' in M Bungenberg and others (eds), *European Yearbook of International Economic Law* (Springer 2019); H Gött (ed), *Labour Standards in International Economic Law* (Springer 2018); B Melo Araujo, 'Labour Provisions in EU and US Mega-Regional Trade Agreements: Rhetoric and Reality' (2018) 67 International & Comparative Law Quarterly 233; L Bartels, 'Human Rights, Labour Standards and Environmental Standards in CETA' in Vranes, Orator, and Fuhrer (eds), *Mega-Regional Agreements: TTIP, CETA, TiSA: New Orientations for EU External Economic Relations* (OUP 2017); G Gruni, 'Labour standards in the EU-South Korea Free Trade Agreement' (2017) 5 Korean Journal of International and Comparative Law 100; G Gruni, 'Law or Aspiration? The European Union Proposal for a Labour Standard Clause in the Transatlantic Trade and Investment Partnership' (2016) 43 Legal Issues of Economic Integration 399; L Bartels, 'Social Issues: Labour, Environment and Human Rights' in S Lester, B Mercurio, and L Bartels (eds), *Bilateral and Regional Trade Agreements: Commentary, Analysis and Case Studies* (CUP 2015); L Bartels, 'Human Rights and Sustainable Development Obligations in EU Free Trade Agreements' (2013) 40 Legal Issues of Economic Integration 297.

[18] Finding that the FTA with Singapore did not create *new* labour or environmental standards (in para 152) allowed the European Court to say (in para 155) that the FTA's sustainability chapter did not raise concerns regarding the regulatory competence of the EU or the Member States. See Court of Justice of the European Union, Opinion 2/15 [2017] ECLI:EU:C:2017:376.

[19] Free Trade Agreement between the European Union and the Republic of Korea, in force 13 December 2015 (EU–South Korea FTA) art 13.4(3); CETA, art 23.3.4; EU–Japan Economic

Secondly, EU FTAs contain qualified obligations, which are dependent on additional conditions. This is notably the case for obligations not to lower existing levels of protection, or not to fail to enforce domestic labour laws and regulations. Sometimes, they are accompanied by the condition 'in a manner affecting trade'.[20] In other words, these obligations are violated only when trade effects occur. At other times, the condition is formulated as 'an encouragement to trade'.[21] In that case, an intent to affect trade is necessary, but actual trade effects need not be shown to demonstrate that the obligation has been violated.[22] An FTA may also combine both conditions.[23] Such obligations are present in most of the EU FTAs. These make it more difficult to identify when the obligation has been violated.

Finally, EU FTAs contain a plethora of vaguer obligations such as the one to 'promote awareness' of labour obligations.[24] Other agreements such as the EU–South Korea FTA include mere declarations of intent whereby the parties, for instance, 'reconfirm that trade should promote sustainable development'.[25]

Without underestimating the relevance of this development, it must be stressed that this is not a complete innovation in the landscape of world trade law. US FTAs, for instance, included a positive prohibition of forced labour already in the 1990s.[26] This was done first via a side agreement to the NAFTA called North American Agreement on Labor Cooperation (NAALC).[27] Labour provisions then found their way into the main body of the US FTAs.[28] In addition, the present approach of the European Union to labour standards in its FTAs is weakened by substantive and procedural shortcomings and an overall lack of ambition if compared to what the European Union has already achieved with economic obligations and intellectual property rights. Section III.B presents some of these substantive shortcomings.

Partnership Agreement art 16.3(3); Modernisation of the Trade part of the EU–Mexico Global Agreement, agreed in principle 21 April 2018 (not signed) TSD Chapter, art 3.4 ; Free Trade Agreement between the European Union and the Republic of Vietnam, in force 1 August 2020 (EU–Vietnam FTA), art 13.4 (3a).

[20] See eg EU–South Korea FTA, art 13.7; Free Trade Agreement between the European Union and the Republic of Singapore, in force 21 November 2019 (EU–Singapore FTA), art 13.12.

[21] See eg CETA art 23.4; EU–Japan Economic Partnership Agreement art 16.2 (2).

[22] R Zandvliet, *Trade, Investment and Labour: Interactions in International Law* 215 (Leiden PhD Thesis 2019).

[23] The text of the EU–Vietnam FTA finalized in 2018 contains both conditions: 'in a manner affecting trade' regarding the obligation not to derogate from labour laws (art 13.3(2)); and 'as an encouragement to trade' in respect of failures to effectively enforce labour laws (art 13.3(3)). See COM(2018) 691 final (17 October 2018).

[24] CETA art 23.6.

[25] EU–South Korea FTA art 13.6.

[26] FH Bieszcat, 'Labor Provisions in Trade Agreements: From the NAALC to Now' (2008) 83 Chicago Kent Law Review 1387.

[27] North American Agreement on Labor Cooperation (NAALC).

[28] See eg Agreement between the United States and Jordan on the Establishment of a Free Trade Area, in force 17 December 2001.

B. Substantive Shortcomings of Labour Obligations in EU FTAs

The EU FTAs are complex international treaties, which build on existing world trade law to deepen economic integration and cooperation between states. EU FTAs contain a core of economic rules on the free movement of goods and, often, of services and protection of intellectual property rights, besides other issues such as subsidies and public procurement. Many of these rules are built on rules that have been adjudicated in the WTO and GATT system for decades and that are written in a clear and precise legal language, lending itself to legal enforcement. The sections on the free movement of goods and services in the EU FTAs that build on the GATT and the GATS, for instance, are written in such a way as to allow the identification of domestic policies or pieces of legislation (such as a tariff or a domestic tax) that are illegal under the FTA.[29] Similarly, the sections on intellectual property rights contain clear-cut obligations, for instance, on minimum levels of protection that need to be achieved by state parties.[30]

The ILO Conventions referred to in EU FTAs also contain obligations clear enough to identify non-complying practices. For instance, with regard to forced labour, they contain an obligation to suppress the use of forced labour in all its forms and in the 'shortest period of time'[31] and one to create a criminal liability against forced labour at the domestic level.[32] Such obligations are also clear and precise enough to allow the identification of a non-complying practice (eg forced labour happening on the territory of the state party or the absence of criminal liability). However, even if a number of obligations related to forced labour were included in all recent EU FTAs, the way in which this is done often leaves unnecessary doubts about their legal significance. These substantive shortcomings are additional to the procedural ones that will be laid out in section IV.

First, the references to the core ILO Conventions are not always done in the most prescriptive fashion. This is because the FTAs do not always explicitly refer to the core ILO Conventions or do not always mandate to ratify and implement them in domestic laws. CETA for instance, obliges the parties to the FTA to 'embody and provide protection'[33] in domestic law to the principle of effective abolition of forced labour and to effectively implement the relevant ILO Conventions. Most of the other recent EU FTAs, however, are not as clear in setting out the relevant obligations. The common provision to make 'continuous and sustained efforts towards ratifying' has been considered elusive by some commentators.[34] This lack of clarity

[29] See P Van den Bossche and W Zdouc, *The Law and Policy of the World Trade Organization* (CUP 2018) 305.
[30] ibid 993.
[31] ILO Forced Labour Convention , art 1.
[32] ibid art 25.
[33] CETA, art 23.
[34] See Gött, 'Linkages of Trade' (n 10), 45–47.

is leading to doubts on the extent to which such formulas lend themselves to legal enforcement. For instance, in the *Korea—Labour Commitments*[35] dispute with South Korea, the Commission took the position that the failure of Korea to ratify core ILO Conventions almost 10 years after the FTA's entry into force infringed this best-efforts obligation. South Korea was, however, of a different opinion and claimed, during the hearing of October 2020, that under the FTA there is only an obligation 'to refrain from taking measures that would defeat the purpose of moving towards ratifying the key ILO conventions'.[36] The case, which was adjudicated in favour of the European Union, shows that vaguer formulations of references to the ILO Conventions leave space for interpretative doubts as to the extent that the country has to abide by them.

Second, the FTA can enter into force without the protection of core labour standards already in place at the national level and an (indefinite) amount of time is given for the state parties to implement them. This can lead to situations where the FTA stays in place indefinitely without the labour obligations being fulfilled by the domestic legislator. The way to avoid this would be to write the reference to the ILO Conventions in the FTA in more clear, precise, and prescriptive terms stating explicitly at least that state parties have an obligation to ratify, implement, and enforce the relevant ILO Conventions domestically, if not immediately by a clear deadline stated in the FTA. Another more effective alternative could be for the European Union to insist that the European Union's preferential trading partner ratify ILO Conventions and/or amend its labour laws before the FTA can enter into force. This was the approach advocated by the European Parliament in respect of Vietnam.[37] Such pre-ratification conditionality has been the approach adopted by the United States in its FTAs since 2006.[38] In sum, the presence of vague formulations when referencing to the core ILO Conventions on forced labour cripples the legal significance of the FTA with regard to prohibiting and fighting violations of core labour standards.

Third, what I call 'qualified obligations', namely obligations that require an additional legal requirement to be fulfilled—such as that to violate the FTA the labour

[35] Report, Panel of Experts Proceeding Constituted under 13.15 of the EU–Korea Free Trade Agreement, adopted 20 January 2021.

[36] Panel of experts proceeding established under art 13.15 of the Korea–EU Free Trade Agreement, Contents of the hearing of 8 and 9 2020, Question 29, 22.

[37] In 2018, 32 Members of the European Parliament sent a letter to Commissioner Malmström and High Commissioner Mogherini asking for Vietnam's ratification and implementation of ILO Conventions. See <https://www.europarl.europa.eu/RegData/etudes/BRIE/2018/628248/EPRS_BRI(2018)628248_EN.pdf> accessed 29 April 2024. See also European Parliament, non-legislative resolution of 17 December 2015 on the draft Council decision on the conclusion, on behalf of the Union, of the Framework Agreement on Comprehensive Partnership and Cooperation between the European Union and its Member States, of the one part, and the Socialist Republic of Vietnam, of the other part (P8_TA(2015)0468.

[38] On the US practice of labour standard pre-ratification conditionality see ILO, *Social Dimensions of Free Trade Agreements* (ILO 2013) 36.

violation must 'affect trade'—are also of dubious legal significance. Experience has shown in fact that it is very difficult to demonstrate the trade impact of labour rights violations when this is subject to additional conditions that are difficult to prove. Although the European Union has not had experience with litigating this language, the United States has. This is illustrated by the case brought by the United States under the Dominican Republic–Central America Free Trade Agreement (CAFTA–DR)[39] against Guatemala. In this case it was impossible for the United States to demonstrate that the lack of enforcement of the labour standard had happened 'in a manner affecting trade', an additional condition in the CAFTA–DR.[40] This case demonstrates that maintaining a 'trade effects' requirement could pose a formidable obstacle to complaints about labour standards. This issue was recently considered during the renegotiation of the NAFTA/Agreement between the United States, the United Mexican States, and Canada (USMCA) where the relevance of the effect on trade requirements was diminished.[41] In the USMCA, in fact, the burden of proof to demonstrate the existence of the 'effect on trade' requirement was shifted from the complainant to the respondent.[42] The governments adopted these amendments to make it easier to demonstrate an FTA violation without the need to demonstrate burdensome additional legal requirements beyond the failure to effectively enforce labour laws. Whenever referring to a trade effect as an additional condition for a labour obligation, the EU FTAs disregard these lessons from the US experience. The European Union should spend its political capital in the negotiations differently, to achieve obligations that are legally prescriptive and that trigger an FTA violation solely on the basis of the factual existence of practices of forced labour on the territory of the state party or other violations of the obligations contained in the relevant ILO Conventions. This happens already in the context of intellectual property rights, where illicit activity on the territory of a state party or lack of criminal liability whenever required is considered an FTA violation, without the need to demonstrate any effects on trade.

Fourth, EU FTAs contain numerous passages of an exhortatory or purely aspirational nature. Such provisions do not create any obligations on the state parties and have barely any legal significance. An example is the common clause that the parties to the FTA should 'reconfirm that trade should promote sustainable

[39] The Dominican Republic–Central America–United States Free Trade Agreement, in force 1 March 2006.

[40] See *Guatemala—Issues Relating to the Obligations Under Art 16.2.1(a) of the CAFTA-DR* 14 July 2017; S Polaski, 'Twenty Years of Progress at Risk Labor and Environmental Protections in Trade Agreements' GEGI Policy Brief 004 (2017).

[41] Agreement between the United States of America, the United Mexican States, and Canada, in force 1 July 2020.

[42] R Labonte, D Gleeson, and CL McNamara, 'USMCA 2.0: A Few Improvements but far from a 'Healthy' Trade Treaty' (2020) 43 Globalization and Health 16; FE Campos Ortiz, 'Labor Regimes and Free Trade in North America: From the North American Free Trade Agreement to the United States Mexico Canada Agreement' (2019) 10 Latin American Policy 268.

development'.[43] These parts of EU FTAs pollute the text of the treaty and make the sections on labour standards excessively convoluted. This waters down their overall prescriptive content and opens the door to questions on their legal significance. Rather than spending political capital on such aspirational clauses, the European Union should exclude them from its FTAs and concentrate on achieving obligations on labour standards that are clear and precise and that mandate on state parties certain policies, actions, or objectives that can be checked for non-compliance. It is only this type of obligation in fact that provides an additional contribution to the implementation and respect of ILO Conventions on forced labour beyond what already exists in the rules of the ILO. The ILO in fact already makes use of exhortatory and promotional instruments to promote compliance with its Conventions. What the FTA can provide are more legally prescriptive obligations and, as we will see in section IV, mechanisms of enforcement that are as of today unavailable in the ILO context but possible under the FTA.

Finally, EU FTAs refer only to the core ILO Conventions, without considering newer developments and more recent amendments. For example, the FTAs achieve the prohibition of forced labour via the reference to ILO Conventions 29 and 105. These are the two core instruments defining forced labour and including basic obligations; however, they are relatively old conventions (adopted in 1930 and 1957). The ILO adopted a Protocol to Convention 29 in 2014 that updates the Convention adding some additional obligations. The FTAs, however, do not mention the new protocol. Since the Protocol was concluded recently, recent EU FTAs were a missed opportunity to promote its ratification and implementation.

IV. Enforcement Mechanism of Labour Standards in EU FTAs

All recent EU FTAs contain a section dedicated to the enforcement of the labour provisions included in them. These provisions are designed to serve as a dedicated system of enforcement, which is separate from the one used for the rest of the FTA. On the basis of this system, any of the parties to the FTA can request to start consultations with the other party to discuss alleged violations of the labour provisions contained in the FTA. In case consultations do not solve the dispute, there is now the possibility of requiring a panel of independent experts to assess the alleged violation and write a report. Such a report is binding on the parties, even if it cannot lead, just on the basis of the text of the FTA, to any additional enforcement in the form of economic sanctions or withdrawal of the preferences provided by the FTA.[44] This is in line with the approach of the EU Commission with regard to

[43] EU–South Korea FTA art 13.6.

[44] See, however, Opinion 2/15 of the CJEU (n 18) authorizing the European Union to take unilateral action in case of a violation of an FTA obligation.

labour standards, which has been labelled 'promotional' to contrast it with one of the other countries, such as the United States and Canada, which have been more liberal in the use of traditional dispute settlement and sanctions in FTAs to enforce labour standards. In a recent publication with Marco Bronckers, we have proposed a number of amendments to such procedure of enforcement that would give labour standards the same level of enforcement that economic obligations and intellectual property rights already have in EU FTAs. Such proposed amendments refer to both the EU and international levels of enforcement.[45]

A. The EU level of enforcement: The Trade Barrier Regulation and the Single Entry Points

A key dimension of the Bronckers and Gruni proposal was to give access to private parties, like trade unions and non-governmental organizations (NGOs), to the procedure available at the EU level to investigate violations on FTA obligations in third countries. In the European Union, there is in fact a regulation called the Trade Barriers Regulation (TBR) that companies can use to file complaints with the European Commission whenever they are encountering barriers to trade in third countries that are prohibited by world trade law.[46] Such procedure obliges the EU Commission to investigate the alleged violation. In 2019, we proposed to adapt the TBR to accommodate the enforcement of labour and environmental standards. At this date, it is in fact still impossible to use the TBR to ask the EU Commission to investigate alleged violations of labour standards in third countries. Moreover, only companies have legal standing in this procedure and trade unions and NGOs remain excluded.[47]

A recent initiative of the European Commission attempted to accommodate private complaints at the EU level as well as violations of the obligations related to forced labour in EU FTAs. The Chief Trade Enforcement Officer, a new position created within the European Commission responsible for overseeing EU enforcement of international trade obligations, recently created a new internal procedure allowing private parties to flag to the Commission situations of alleged non-compliance of obligations contained in FTAs. The procedure works on the basis of Single Entry Points allowing private stakeholders but also Member States to complain about violations, among other things, of environmental and labour standards contained in EU FTAs. The procedure is not based on secondary

[45] M Bronckers and G Gruni, 'Retooling the Sustainability Standards in the EU Free Trade Agreements' (2021) 24 Journal of International Economic Law 25.

[46] Regulation 2015/1843, OJ 2015 L 272/1.

[47] For an in-depth analysis of the enforcement mechanism of labour standards in EU FTAs and the details of the proposed amendments see M Bronckers and G Gruni, 'Taking the Enforcement of Labour Standards in the EU's Free Trade Agreements Seriously' (2019) 56 Common Market Law Review 1591.

legislation and leaves wide discretion to the European Commission on how to assess alleged violations of the labour standards obligations, including those related to forced labour. In a set of guidelines published in November 2020, the European Commission explains that the complainant will be kept informed of whether the complaint leads to enforcement action by the Commission utilizing the instruments available under international law.[48] This new development attempts to fill a gap in the enforcement of labour standards contained in trade agreements via EU law, even if it lacks the legal guarantees of the TBR, which remains inaccessible for these kinds of complaints.

B. The International Level of Enforcement in the FTA: Consultations, Litigation, and Retaliation

With regard to the dispute settlement contained in EU FTAs, the European Union made the choice not to allow state parties to use the general dispute settlement for violations of labour standards, including those related to core labour standards. Instead, the FTA has a dedicated system of consultations and the possibility to ask for the creation of a panel of labour law experts to assess the alleged violation. Some of the procedures of the dispute settlement system for labour standards are similar to those utilized for the general dispute settlement of the FTA. After dispute settlement, in case of persistent non-compliance by the state party, there are no additional explicit steps that can be taken under EU FTAs. In fact, unlike Canada and the US trade agreements, EU FTAs do not allow economic or trade sanctions with regard to labour standards in case of violations of the obligations on labour standards. This remains one of the main features of the promotional approach of the EU Commission when it comes to the enforcement of labour standards in its FTAs.[49] The Court of Justice of the European Union (CJEU) had already intervened on this approach in Opinion 1/15 authorizing unilateral decisions on retaliation where no procedure for retaliation exists. However, as shown in sections V and VI, this might be about to change in the text of future EU FTAs as well.

[48] EU Commission, 'Operating guidelines for the Single Entry Point and complaints mechanism for the enforcement of EU trade agreements and arrangements' (22 June 2022) <https://trade.ec.europa.eu/access-to-markets/en/form-assets/operational_guidelines.pdf>.

[49] Melo Araujo (n 17), 242; T Fritz, *Analysis and Evaluation of the Comprehensive Economic and Trade Agreement (CETA) between the EU and Canada* (Hans-Böckler-Foundation Project Number 2014-779-1, 26 January 2015) 29.

V. Communication 409/2022 and the New EU FTAs

In the summer of 2022, the EU Commission issued Communication 409 titled 'The power of trade partnerships: together for green and just economic growth'. The Communication makes a U-turn on the longstanding opposition of the EU Commission to use the full range of enforcement instruments available in world trade law in case of non-compliance with the labour obligations in the EU FTAs. Paragraph 3.6 is particularly relevant:

> The Commission now proposes to further align TSD enforcement with the general state-to-state dispute (SSDS) settlement and to extend the compliance stage to disputes under the TSD chapter. [...] The Commission now proposes the possibility of trade sanctions as a matter of last resort, in instances of serious violations of core TSD commitments, namely the ILO fundamental principles and rights at work, and of the Paris Agreement on Climate Change. In such instances, trade sanctions would be appropriate as a means to foster compliance.

With Communication 409 the EU Commission seems to align itself to the position of the EU Parliament, which was requesting, in addition to a part of civil society, the strengthening of the enforcement of sustainability obligations. This Communication clearly breaks with the European Union's past practice in two ways. First, it accepts that the standard state-to-state enforcement of EU FTAs can be used for violations of labour standards. Second, it accepts the possibility of using trade sanctions in case of persistent non-compliance for 'serious violations' such as those concerning labour standards considered 'core' by the ILO. The Communication also suggests that a reform of the Single Entry Points is in order, so as to improve the access of private parties at the EU level, like trade unions, to the mechanisms of enforcement available. However, this does not go as far as suggesting the reform of the TBR or the adoption of an additional legal instrument providing trade unions with petition rights comparable to the TBR Regulation.

This change of posture is already visible in both the EU–New Zealand FTA and EU–Kenya FTA, which contain the new approach to the enforcement of labour standards. These FTAs can be considered a model of how this new vision is implemented and what the future of this area of legislation could look like. Remarkably, the EU–New Zealand FTA and EU–Kenya FTA do not provide a separate softer enforcement mechanism applicable only to labour standards and environmental obligations. Instead, the general state-to-state dispute settlement can be used for economic clauses, intellectual property rights as well as labour and environmental standards. To make this possible, the procedural rules were adapted to accommodate labour and environmental disputes. This, for instance, requires a different choice of panellists for labour and environmental disputes (EU–New Zealand FTA Article 26.5). Article 26.16 of the EU–New Zealand FTA, on temporary remedies, makes them available for violations of core labour standards as well. This takes the form of suspensions of obligations under the FTA, which would generally be done via trade retaliation.

The EU–New Zealand FTA and the EU–Kenya FTA potentially contain a new model of enforcement for the labour obligations contained in EU FTAs that is more similar to what the United States has been doing for some 30 years already. This is a notable development that comes after decades of reticence in the European Union towards the use of the standard state-to-state enforcement with regard to labour (as well as environmental) standards. Section VI reflects on the impact of such development on world trade law. The section will raise a number of doubts on the relevance of this development, at least in the short term.

VI. The Communication 409 Model of Enforcement: A Real Breakthrough or a Drop in the Ocean?

Having considered the state of the art of labour standards in EU FTAs, this section reacts to the recent change of international posture of the EU Commission with regard to their enforcement. This section raises a number of doubts on the relevance of this development, based on two main lines of argumentation. The first one concerns the timing of this development, which comes very much down the road of an EU policy on FTAs that started almost 20 years ago. This means that the European Union already concluded numerous FTAs that contain the older 'promotional approach' to enforcement. The second argument focuses on the petition rights of private parties that have an interest in the enforcement of labour standards. These are, for instance, trade unions or NGOs focusing on labour protection. In fact, all the enforcement mechanisms available at the FTA level become relevant only if the EU Commission decides to activate them. This remains subject to extensive political discretion. To avoid violations going undetected or the Commission not acting upon them, private parties like trade unions need petition rights to ask the Commission to investigate alleged violations. This is the right that companies have with regard to the economic obligations and intellectual property rights under the TBR. This is what members of the public and trade unions have under other systems, like the Rapid Response mechanism on labour standards of the USMCA. A mechanism that provides members of the public with petition rights[50] already led to nine uses in three years of operation (compared to only one case on labour standards in the whole history of the European Union and for all EU FTAs).

[50] See Chapter 17 in this volume.

A. Communication 409: Better Late Than Never?

Communication 409, the EU–New Zealand FTA, and the EU–Kenya FTA are welcome developments. They come, however, when the strategy of the European Union to conclude FTAs is well into its advanced stage. This means that the European Union already concluded numerous FTAs with states around the world that incorporate the older promotional approach with more limited enforcement of labour standards. Since 2008, the European Union concluded FTAs with states with very different characteristics and levels of development. To give some examples, Japan, Canada, Singapore, Vietnam, and Mexico all have FTAs recently negotiated with the European Union or recently amended. These FTAs do not include the enforcement of labour standards described by Communication 409. In addition, since 2008 the European Union concluded FTAs with numerous developing countries in the Caribbean, Pacific, and Sub-Saharan regions. Again, all these FTAs do not contain the more stringent approach to labour protection included in Communication 409.

FTAs already in force are not the only issue. There have been very mixed signals from the EU Commission especially with regard to the inclusion of the new approach in FTAs that were being negotiated at the moment Communication 409 was published or that are awaiting ratification by the EU Parliament. The EU–Chile FTA, politically concluded on 9 December 2022, does not contain the new approach to enforcement and instead, with regard to labour standards, follows the traditional promotional approach. The same can be said of the EU–Mercosur FTA that the European Union concluded 'in principle' in 2019 with Argentina, Paraguay, Uruguay, and Brazil. The EU Parliament has been vocal in demanding that labour and environmental standards included in the FTA are properly enforced. The EU–Mercosur FTA has, at the time of writing, not been signed yet. Notwithstanding this, the EU Commission has taken steps in this direction. The European Union proposed a Joint Instrument to the Mercosur Party. The Joint Instrument clarifies some of the substantive content of the obligations without, however, modifying the approach to the enforcement of labour and environmental obligations. Notwithstanding the soft approach utilized in this case, the proposed instrument has been labelled 'unacceptable' by the Presidents of both Brazil and Argentina, who were particularly vocal in saying they do not want to deal with environmental problems under 'threat'.

If the EU–Mercosur FTA is concluded without an update of its section on dispute settlement, it will be another FTA following the softer promotional approach to the enforcement of labour standards, instead of the one advocated in Communication 409. This means that most of the American continent, several major partners in Asia, plus most of the developing countries in the African, Caribbean, and Pacific Region have FTAs with the European Union that do not enforce labour standards in the way described by Communication 409. In the absence of a dedicated strategy to update those FTAs (and the willingness of the third country to do so), the new approach to the enforcement of labour standards will have an effect on international law only if and when those FTAs are updated. That could be decades away, or never.

B. The Lacklustre Situation of Petition Rights for Private Parties

Even if the European Union provides labour standards with the same enforcement as economic rights and intellectual property in its FTAs, a question remains: will these procedures be used? In the South Korean case, trade unions and NGOs had been asking for action for years before the EU Commission acted upon it. With the establishment of the new Trade Enforcement Officer, the EU Commission also allowed private parties to bring complaints via so-called Single Entry Points. This procedure is not based on a legislative instrument like the TBR and so it is more influenced by the discretion of the EU Commission. However, in the last version of the Guidelines to submit the complaint,[51] the EU Commission put a lot of flesh around the bones of the Single Entry Points. EU-based private parties, including trade unions, can submit complaints for both factual and legal violations of labour obligations in FTAs. The guidelines also include a clear timeline and occasions for the complainant to collaborate with the EU Commission. The results of the investigation are published on a website.

If private parties and trade unions utilize the Single Entry Points properly, this could lead to a wealth of information on violations of labour standards. This would also put pressure on the Commission to start consultations and litigations under the procedures available in the FTAs. This is not a substitute, however, to a legislative instrument providing a procedure to which the EU Commission is legally bound. Moreover, under the Single Entry Points, the complainant cannot appeal the Decision of the EU Commission to the CJEU. The United States is experimenting with a different system of enforcement of labour standards in its USMCA with Mexico and Canada. In that FTA, the Rapid Response Mechanism allows members of the public to file complaints directly with government authorities under a procedure that leads to international enforcement under the USMCA itself. For reasons that require more investigation, that mechanism is proving more effective than the Single Entry Points in enforcing labour standards and produced already eight cases in around two years of operation.

[51] European Commission, Directorate General for Trade, Operating guidelines for the Single Entry Point and complaints mechanism for the enforcement of EU trade agreements and arrangements <https://trade.ec.europa.eu/access-to-markets/en/form-assets/operational_guidelines.pdf>.

VII. Conclusions

The history of labour standards in world trade law is slow and tortuous. Three decades after the conclusion of the Uruguay Round and the creation of the WTO, labour standards are still not given the same protection as economic obligations and intellectual property rights. Undermined by underdeveloped obligations and weaker enforcement procedures, labour standards can still be considered the ugly duckling of world trade law. However, in the last decade, some steps towards better legal protection and enforcement have been made via the FTAs concluded outside the WTO. There, the four ILO core labour standards are given binding protection and some enforcement procedures are emerging. This chapter has provided an overview of existing substantive obligations and procedures of enforcement identifying several substantive and procedural shortcomings concerning labour standards in EU FTAs. From a substantive perspective, labour obligations in FTAs still tend to be less defined than economic obligations and often include expressions or conditions that cast doubts on their legal significance. The chapter delved into some of these weaknesses in how standards are formulated. With regard to enforcement, all EU FTAs, except those with New Zealand and Kenya, do not allow core labour standards to be litigated under the general state-to-state dispute settlement used for economic obligations and intellectual property rights. In the summer of 2022, in its Communication 409, the EU Commission pledged to change this situation. However, this change of posture will take a long time to affect world trade law. For the time being, most of the FTAs the European Union has in place with its trade partners will follow the old promotional approach and not the stronger approach of Communication 409. This chapter also advocated in favour of having procedures in place to allow private parties to file complaints in front of the EU Commission to investigate violations of labour standards happening in third countries. This chapter has explained why the present system of the Single Entry Points does not provide private parties with the same legal guarantees as the Trade Barrier Regulation, which achieves that objective at the EU level with regard to economic obligations and intellectual property rights.

8

Trade Agreements and Disability Inclusion

Looking Beyond Labour and Gender Equality Provisions

*Amrita Bahri**

I. Introduction

A free trade agreement (FTA), broadly speaking, is a contractual arrangement between countries concerning their trade relationships. Generally, the main purpose of a country in negotiating such agreements is to reduce barriers that impede or that restrict its trade with another country and increase market access for its industries in the FTA partner country or countries. Moreover, a country can also use such agreements to achieve non-economic goals such as to enhance the rule of law in its own country or in the FTA partner country or countries, or to rectify a societal problem in these countries.

With a more nuanced understanding of the impacts of trade liberalization, there is a growing acknowledgement that gains from trade liberalization are not automatic and that liberalization has different impacts on different groups.[1] The international community is now recognizing that trade liberalization and trade agreements create both 'losers' as well as 'winners', as they benefit some and leave others without benefits or even with negative ramifications.[2] Acknowledging that trade liberalization has both positive and negative effects strengthens the need to research and better understand the connection between trade agreements and how they interact with different groups of society, as this can help inform trade negotiations on what society-wide impacts of different negotiating options might be. This understanding can help trade negotiators design trade agreements in such a

* The sections of this chapter on trade and disability inclusion are adapted from the following study: Amrita Bahri, 'Making Trade Agreements Work for People with Disabilities: What's Been Achieved and What Remains Undone?' (United Kingdom Foreign, Commonwealth and Development Office and Cowater International Publication 2022). All errors or omissions are the author's own.

[1] Caroline Dommen, 'On How the Human Rights Framework Can Contribute to Inclusive Trade Agreements', (2023) 1(57) Journal of World Trade 157.

[2] Gregory Shaffer and Marc Fleurbaey, 'Social Cohesion, Global Governance and the Future of Politics: Adapting Trade Policy to Social, Environmental, and Development Goals' (*Think 20 Argentina*, 2018) <https://www.g20-insights.org/wp-content/uploads/2018/07/TF8-8.6-Reconceiving-Trade-Agreements-policy-brief-v4-1.pdf> accessed 11 January 2022.

Amrita Bahri, *Trade Agreements and Disability Inclusion* In: *The Sustainability Revolution in International Trade Agreements.* Edited by: Geraldo Vidigal and Kathleen Claussen, Oxford University Press. © Amrita Bahri 2024.
DOI: 10.1093/9780191994470.003.0008

way as to reduce those agreements' adverse impacts and maximize their benefits by including complementary measures in such agreements.

One of the main sentiments behind such inclusion is the increasing attention that countries are now paying to actors that are recognized as having less access to international markets or those that receive disproportionately higher negative consequences from such agreements (such as Indigenous communities, women, and others). Hence, through FTAs, countries are not only endeavouring to reduce trade barriers but also setting standards regarding a range of non-trade issues such as labour standards, environmental protection, and gender equality.[3] For example, Hafner-Burton observes that an increasing number of FTAs now seek to enforce better human rights practices and that these agreements can influence governments to make some improvements in certain human rights behaviours. Moreover, they can enforce the initial compliance that most human rights treaties cannot.[4]

The scope of FTAs has broadened, and they are now looking beyond the mere market access concerns as they cover a number of objectives, including 'importing higher policy standards, strengthening regional policy coordination, locking-in domestic reforms, and even addressing foreign policy issues'.[5] In this sense, FTAs have included a range of concerns including, but not limited to, labour standards, environment protection, women's rights, and rights of Indigenous peoples.[6] In addition, FTAs have also been vocal in addressing inclusivity issues pertaining to the protection or promotion of people with disability; yet, the existing scholarship is silent on this aspect. While discussions on the nexus between international trade agreements and sustainable development have made headlines for the past two decades, there is not much written about people with disabilities and trade agreements.[7]

[3] Jean-Frédéric Morin, Andreas Dür, and Lisa Lechne, 'Mapping the Trade and Environment Nexus: Insights from a New Data Set' (2018) 18(1) Global Environmental Politics 122.

[4] EM Hafner-Burton, 'Trading Human Rights: How Preferential Trade Agreements Influence Government Repression' (2005) 59(3) International Organization 593, 624.

[5] Jean-Pierre Chauffour and Jean-Christophe Maur, *Preferential Trade Agreement Policies for Development: A Handbook* (World Bank 2014).

[6] For more information, see International Labour Organization, 'Labour Provisions in Trade Agreements Don't Hurt Business' (*ILO*, 18 July 2016) <https://www.ilo.org/global/about-the-ilo/newsroom/news/WCMS_499348/lang--en/index.htm> accessed 23 December 2021; Immaculate Martínez-Zarzoso, 'Assessing the Effectiveness of Environmental Provisions in Regional Trade Agreements: An Empirical Analysis', OECD Trade and Environment Working Papers 2018/02; José-Antonio Monteiro, 'The Evolution of Gender-Related Provisions in Regional Trade Agreements' WTO Staff Working Paper (2021) ERSD-2-21-8. Two recent FTAs that include provisions on Indigenous peoples are: Comprehensive and Progressive Agreement for Trans-Pacific Partnership, in force 18 December 2018 (CPTPP) and Free Trade Agreement between the United States of America, the United Mexican States, and Canada, in force 1 July 2020 (USMCA). For more details see Sergio Puig, *At the Margins of Globalization: Indigenous Peoples and International Economic Law* (CUP 2021).

[7] Disability is a combination of individual factors (impairments) and social factors (barriers). See *Base Code Guidance: Disability Inclusion in the Global Supply Chain* (Ethical Trading Initiative 2018); according to art 1 of the UN Convention on the Rights of Persons with Disabilities, in force 3 May 2008 (CRPD), people with disabilities are 'those who have long-term physical, mental, intellectual, or sensory impairments which, in interaction with various barriers, may hinder their full and effective participation in society on an equal basis with others'. For the purpose of this study, the term 'disability

The 2030 United Nations Agenda for Sustainable Development, which recognizes international trade as an engine for inclusive economic growth, commits to leaving no one behind and provides significant importance to disability inclusion and empowerment of people with disability.[8] In fact, the terms 'persons with disabilities' or 'disability' are explicitly mentioned 11 times throughout the 2030 Agenda for Sustainable Development. The 2030 Agenda clearly states that disability cannot be a reason or criterion for lack of access to development and the realization of human rights, and it includes five goals that explicitly refer to persons with disabilities.[9] FTAs can play an important role in achieving these goals by connecting people with disability to opportunities and benefits offered by foreign trade as countries can encourage their trade partners to create laws and procedures that can reduce barriers and create encouraging conditions for people with disability to participate in foreign trade.

Using the author's experience and understanding of working with trade and gender provisions in the previous years, this chapter seeks to spark discussions on how trade agreements can also be made to work for protecting the interests of persons with disabilities. In this sense, the chapter problematizes the way disability concerns are currently included in FTAs and explores the limited scope of the provisions regarding the rights of persons with disabilities. These findings therefore contribute to the understanding of the inclusion of another non-trade issue in international trade agreements and to the place of disability concerns in global trade governance. Moreover, as we are still amidst an ever-growing debate on which interests should or could be added to trade agreements, this chapter provides some food for thought to inform this debate by addressing why trade negotiators could consider taking another issue onboard their templates of trade agreements (ie the issue of disability inclusion) and how these issues can be incorporated.

This chapter is divided as follows. Section II provides a discussion on why trade agreements can accommodate sustainability concerns, and how the current trade agreements are increasingly being vocal on a range of non-trade-germane concerns, including labour protection and gender equality. Section III presents reflections on how disability inclusion is one such non-trade-germane issue that has found a place in current trade agreements, even though there is scant scholarship that examines trade agreements from this dimension. Section IV zooms into the current trade agreements to identify and assess how countries have included in

inclusion' refers to the promotion of participation of people with disabilities in all aspects of society, including employment, on a basis of equality with others.

[8] UN General Assembly (UNGA), 'Transforming Our World: The 2030 Agenda for Sustainable Development', A/RES/70/1 (21 October 2015).

[9] Goals 4, 8, 10, 11, and 17, United Nations, 'Sustainable Development Goals (SDGs) and Disability' (United Nations 2016) <https://www.un.org/development/desa/disabilities/about-us/sustainable-development-goals-sdgs-and-disability.html> accessed 10 January 2022.

their agreements provisions on disability concerns, with a focus on the areas and scope of such provisions. Section V concludes the chapter.

II. How Can Trade Agreements Accommodate Sustainability Concerns?

While many countries have sought to use trade agreements to support inclusive trade, they have mainly focused on two areas of inclusion: workers' rights and gender equality. Less prominent are provisions that concern other marginalized groups, as few trade agreements speak expressly to concerns relating to racial disparities, Indigenous rights, or disability inclusion. This section explains how countries have successfully incorporated labour and gender provisions and that is not the case with other provisions that still remain elusive in current trade agreements.

Sometimes referred to as 'non-trade issues', both workers' rights and gender equality remain largely excluded from the World Trade Organization (WTO) rulebook. Yet, because trade ultimately affects and is affected by labour as well as gender equality concerns, they have found a noteworthy place in existing bilateral and regional FTAs.[10] Moreover, they are closely interconnected as labour provisions (such as workers' rights, reasonable work hours, parental leave or childcare, occupational safety and health, minimum wage, and anti-discrimination) directly impact female employees. For instance, the Canada–Ukraine FTA provides for the elimination of discrimination in respect of employment and occupation based on gender.[11] Likewise, in the Canada–Costa Rica Agreement on Labour Cooperation, the parties confirm that their domestic laws, regulations, procedures, and practices shall reflect labour standards including the elimination of discrimination and equal pay for women and men.[12] These examples show how these concerns intersect and overlap with each other in the trade policy context.[13]

There are, however, differences in the way labour and gender provisions are drafted and incorporated into existing trade agreements. The first difference lies in

[10] The term 'free trade agreements' or 'FTAs' in this chapter is used to refer to all international trade agreements (except the WTO multilateral agreements) and may include regional trade agreements, plurilateral agreements, bilateral agreements, preferential agreements, economic partnership agreements, and such others.

[11] Free Trade Agreement Between Canada and Ukraine, in force 1 August 2017, Annex 13-A (Canada–Ukraine). See also Trade Agreement between Canada and the Republic of Honduras, in force 1 October 2014 (Canada–Honduras); Free Trade Agreement between Canada and the Republic of Colombia, in force 15 August 2011; Free Trade Agreement between Canada and the Republic of Panama, in force 1 April 2013 (Canada–Panama).

[12] Agreement on Labour Cooperation Between the Government of Canada and the Government of the Republic of Costa Rica, in force November 2002 (Canada–Costa Rica).

[13] For more details see Marcus Gustafsson and Amrita Bahri, 'Progressive Trade: Labour and Gender' in Daniel Bethlehem and others (eds), *Oxford Handbook of International Trade Law* (2nd edn, OUP 2022).

the sheer number of existing FTAs that include such provisions. Over 30 per cent of existing agreements include labour provisions, but only around 21 per cent accommodate gender equality concerns.[14] Moreover, the level of commitments assumed by countries in respect of these provisions is very different. While many labour provisions are now drafted as binding legal obligations with the use of 'hard' verb constructions (see eg the labour Chapter in the United States–Mexico–Canada Agreement (USMCA)), most of the gender equality provisions are drafted as mere best endeavours with non-mandatory verbs and 'soft' permissive grammatical constructions.[15] These differences show that, even though trade agreements have accommodated both labour and gender concerns, it seems that they have developed a comparatively larger appetite for labour standards than for gender concerns.[16]

Both gender equality and labour standards form part of the UN human rights framework and they both extend access to social rights.[17] They are also well accommodated in the UN 2030 Sustainable Development Goals (SDGs).[18] So, even though both labour and gender concerns share a blind spot in the WTO rulebook, which fails to adequately address either of them, this has not dissuaded countries from negotiating provisions about them and including them in their FTAs. With such bilateral or regional developments on a rapid increase, there is little doubt that gender, labour, and other potential human rights will continue to expand their presence across FTAs. Another type of provision that manifests a similar movement for trade agreements, that is, going beyond the protection of workers and seeking to protect other marginalized groups faced with vulnerability as a result of trade liberalization, is the one relating to disability inclusion. However, there is not much written about trade agreements and disability inclusion.

III. Building the Conceptual Nexus: International Trade and Disability Inclusion

Persons with disabilities continue to face many barriers that impact their ability to participate in different aspects of their lives, and these barriers impede their

[14] Author's calculations.

[15] Raj Bhala and Cody N Wood, 'Two Dimensional Hard-Soft Law Theory and the Advancement of Women's and LGBTQ+ Rights Through Free Trade Agreements' (2019) 47(2) Georgia Journal of International and Comparative Law (2019) 299, 306 (the authors state that most gender-related commitments in USMCA and CPTPP are aspirational and non-binding, and hence non-enforceable, and that they are sometimes drafted with vagueness and ambiguity, and so they are susceptible to myriad interpretations).

[16] Desirée LeClercq, 'The Disparate Treatment of Rights in Trade' (2021) 90(1) Fordham Law Review 1 (the author notes that this appetite depends largely on whether the non-trade concerns are related to trade and whether they impact production or trade costs).

[17] See eg Universal Declaration of Human Rights, UNGA Res 217 A(III), adopted 10 December 1948 (UDHR).

[18] See UN SDGs 2030, Goals 5 (gender equality) and 8 (decent work and economic growth).

participation in economic activities.[19] Yet, persons with disability and their interests have been at the margins of international economic governance.[20] The wide and long neglect of this issue has allowed for the perpetuation of discrimination against and exclusion of persons with disability from the systems of governance.[21] As a result, persons with disabilities, their problems and concerns, have often been neglected in a number of aspects that include education, employment, access to justice, and health, among others. This neglect is particularly visible in the regulation of international economic and trade issues, and this is the case even though a number of international instruments clarify and reinforce the role that economic governance institutions and regulations can play in this respect.[22] One such instrument is the Marrakesh Agreement Establishing the WTO, which commits its members to sustainable development in its very preamble.[23] Another instrument that subsequently endorses this inter-relationship is the Doha Ministerial Declaration launching the Doha Development Round, where WTO Members reaffirm their commitment to the objective of sustainable development.[24]

Moreover, the UN Convention on the Rights of Persons with Disabilities (CRPD) in 2006, which entered into force in May 2008, is the main international treaty that recognizes and explains the rights of people with disabilities. It is quite universal as it has been ratified by over 90 per cent of UN Member States since its adoption. In this context, the CRPD is frequently seen as a milestone achievement in disability human rights law and disability inclusion activism.[25] This Convention has sought to position persons with disabilities in systems of domestic and international governance, as it recognizes that international cooperation and its promotion, in support of national efforts for the realization of the purpose and objectives of this Convention, partnerships with relevant international and regional organizations and civil society, and concrete actions of governance can help empower people with disabilities.[26] An example of this type of cooperation is the Marrakesh

[19] For more information see Amrita Bahri, 'Making Trade Agreements Work for People with Disabilities: What's been Achieved and What Remains Undone?' (2022) United Kingdom Foreign, Commonwealth and Development Office and Cowater International Publication.

[20] Margrit Shildrick, *Dangerous Discourses of Disability, Subjectivity and Sexuality* (Springer 2009); Felipe Jaramillo Ruiz, Rebecca Nielsen, and Rodrigo Fagundes Cezar, 'The Inclusion of Disability as a Non-Trade Issue in Preferential Trade Agreements' (2023) 23(1) Global Social Policy 148.

[21] Colin Barnes, 'Understanding the Social Model of Disability: Past, Present and Future' in Nick Watson, Alan Roulstone, and Carol Thomas (eds), *Routledge Handbook of Disability Studies* (Routledge 2013) 26–43.

[22] Sondra Faccio, 'Disability in EU trade and investment agreements' in Delia Ferri (ed), *Research Handbook on EU Disability Law* (Edward Elgar 2020).

[23] Agreement Establishing the World Trade Organization, in force 1 January 1995, Preamble, First Recital (hereinafter WTO Agreement).

[24] World Trade Organization, 'Ministerial Declaration' (20 November 2001) WT/MIN(01)/DEC/1, para 6.

[25] There is also an Optional Protocol to the Convention that established a UN Committee on the Rights of Persons with Disabilities: Optional Protocol to the Convention on the Rights of Persons with Disabilities, in force 3 May 2008.

[26] CRPD, in force 3 May 2008 <https://www.un.org/development/desa/disabilities/convention-on-the-rights-of-Persons-with-disabilities.html> accessed 10 April 2024.

Treaty, which entered into force in 2016, as it creates exceptions to copyright laws to facilitate the creation and publication of texts for people with visual impairments.[27] These developments affirm that the efforts relating to disability inclusion are no longer about 'reinventing the wheel'; these commitments have already been agreed to in a universal setting.

As the CRPD and the Marrakesh Treaty call for cooperation between states to protect the rights of persons with disabilities through international cooperation and regulation, trade policy instruments can also be used as a tool to further these interests as they operate on the basis of interstate cooperation. This argument becomes even more plausible given that persons with disabilities face more significant barriers in accessing economic opportunities.[28] Since trade agreements impact a range of economic interests including workplace safety, worker treatment, compensation and work standards, social protection programmes, access to market opportunities, and others, it becomes important to understand how disability is included in the most common instruments of global trade governance, that is, FTAs. Moreover, the relatively recent inclusion of the rights of persons with disabilities in international trade agreements provides an interesting case to study the way in which change and innovation on non-trade objectives in FTAs are being achieved.[29]

IV. Zooming in on the Disability Inclusion Provisions

FTAs can play an important role in connecting persons with disabilities to opportunities and benefits offered by foreign trade for a number of reasons. First, countries can encourage their trade partners to create laws and procedures that can reduce barriers and create encouraging conditions for persons with disabilities to participate in foreign trade. Second, the existing and future trade agreements between countries can increase trade flows and employment opportunities, leading to more business and employment opportunities for all including persons with disabilities. Third, trade agreements can help if countries can negotiate preferential market access commitments that can aid in reducing the cost and increasing the availability of assistive devices in their countries. Increased affordability and accessibility to assistive devices can help people with disabilities fit into a world that is primarily designed for able-bodied people. But the question is: how far can

[27] Marrakesh Treaty to Facilitate Access to Published Works for Persons Who Are Blind, Visually Impaired or Otherwise Print Disabled, in force 30 September 2016.

[28] Articles 27 and 28 CRPD.

[29] Mehraj Ahmad Sheikh, Mushtaq Ahmad Malik, and Rana Zehra Masood, 'Assessing the Effects of Trade Openness on Sustainable Development: Evidence from India' (2020) 5(1) Asian Journal of Sustainability and Social Responsibility 1; Arlo Poletti, Daniela Sicurelli, and Aydin B Yildirim, 'Promoting Sustainable Development Through Trade? EU Trade Agreements and Global Value Chains' (2020) 51(3) Italian Political Science Review/Rivista Italiana di Scienza Politica 339.

trade agreements go, and how willing are countries to achieve this non-economic goal through such international trade policy instruments?

Several countries have sought to incorporate disability inclusion concerns in their trade agreements. However, most of these agreements are negotiated by very few countries, and most countries have yet to consider their first step in this respect. Moreover, the relevant disability-related provisions found in existing trade agreements are heavily heterogeneous, as they are drafted in different styles and with different focus areas and scope.

For a study commissioned by the UK Foreign, Commonwealth and Development Office (UK FCDO), the author of this chapter analysed a total number of 355 FTAs.[30] Out of these 355 FTAs, 98 were found to have at least one disability-explicit provision that focuses on the protection or promotion of persons with disability. In other words, over 27 per cent of trade agreements (in force and notified to the WTO as of 15 February 2022) were found to have at least one disability-explicit provision. If we include in this count the implicit provisions that relate to the interests of persons with disability or somehow have the potential of working to their benefit, the percentage increases to over 66 per cent.[31] However, with very few exceptions, countries that have included commitments relating to the protection or promotion of persons with disabilities in their FTAs so far are all developed countries. There are very few developing countries that have incorporated disability-related concerns in their trade agreements. China, India, and Indonesia, for instance, have no explicit provision that relates to the protection or promotion of persons with disabilities in their FTAs.[32] Yet, the World Health Organization (WHO) has observed that 80 per cent of the 1 billion people worldwide living with a disability live in developing countries.[33] In India, over 2.1 per cent of the population is living with one or the other kind of disability. In the case of China, nearly 6.2 per cent of its population is living with a disability. These examples show that

[30] Only those trade agreements notified to WTO and currently in force (as of 15 February 2022) are included in this assessment. Their text was accessed using the WTO RTA database <https://rtais.wto.org/UI/PublicMaintainRTAHome.aspx> accessed 15 February 2022. For details see Bahri (n 19).

[31] Explicit provisions are those that directly refer to or mention terms relating to disability in the provision in a clear and explicit manner. Terms used in this study to identify such provisions in trade agreements are: disabled, disability, disabilities, differently-abled, handicapped, invalidity, less able-bodied, and persons with disabilities. An implicit provision is one that relates to the interests of people with disabilities or somehow has the potential of working to their benefit without explicitly including an explicit expression or word relating to disability. The keywords used to locate implicit provisions were: labour, social responsibility, non-discrimination, equality, capacity, education, minority, under-represented, vulnerable, equal, capacity-building, skill development, learning, minority, best practices, disadvantaged, and employability.

[32] International Labour Organization, 'Inclusion of People with Disabilities in China' (ILO) <https://www.ilo.org/wcmsp5/groups/public/---asia/---ro-bangkok/---ilo-beijing/documents/publication/wcms_469048.pdf> accessed 10 February 2023.

[33] World Health Organization, 'Disability and Health' (*WHO*, 24 November 2021) <https://www.who.int/en/news-room/fact-sheets/detail/disability-and-health> accessed 27 January 2022.

disability-related provisions have probably not been included in trade agreements by countries where a large section of such populations reside.

On the other hand, very few developing countries have incorporated provisions relating to disability concerns in their trade agreements, and most of these provisions are only indirectly or remotely related to persons with disability. Colombia is a developing country that has added 14 mentions of disability-explicit words in the 15 trade agreements it has signed so far, and Costa Rica has 15 mentions in the 11 FTAs it is currently a party to. However, it is important to note that the FTAs signed by these developing countries that feature a disability-explicit provision are mostly signed with developed countries such as Canada, the United States, and the United Kingdom. The same pattern is seen with the disability-explicit FTAs signed by other developing countries. So, one possible inference could be that the limited numbers of developing countries that have accepted such commitments have done so at the initiative or even insistence of their developed-country partners.

Moreover, a number of trade agreements have vocalized the interests and rights of persons with disability in an implicit manner, as they have featured provisions that relate to the protection of marginalized or disadvantaged groups, which may be read to include women, Indigenous communities, persons with disabilities, and others.[34] In this sense, these provisions are not focused on a particular group or community; rather, they extend to all minority groups that need protection. Most implicit provisions are found either in the agreement's preamble or in its sections on cooperation. Often, countries have included a mention of sustainable development or human rights or protection of labour standards in the very preamble or general objectives clause of their agreements.[35] In some other agreements, implicit commitments can be found in the agreement's labour chapter or the chapter on trade and sustainable development wherein parties reaffirm their commitments to the UN 2030 Agenda.[36] Countries that have included such implicit provisions in their trade agreements have sought to empower or protect the vulnerable sections of society through work in different areas, including access to education, human resource development, access to finance, support measures in respect of foreign investment, trade in services, provision of social security, safety concerns, non-discrimination, and cultural transformations to change the stereotypes.[37]

[34] Agreement Establishing an Association between the European Union and its Member States and Central America, in force 1 May 2024, art 43 (EU–Central America); Free Trade Agreement between Hong Kong, China and Chile, in force 9 October 2014, Annex 11.6 (Hong Kong–Chile).

[35] Free Trade Agreement between the Government of the People's Republic of China and the Government of New Zealand, in force 1 October 2008, Preamble (China–New Zealand); Free Trade Agreement between the Republic of Chile and the Republic of Turkey, in force March 2011, Preamble (Chile–Turkey).

[36] Comprehensive and enhanced Partnership Agreement between the European Union and the European Atomic Energy Community and their Member States and the Republic of Armenia, in force 1 June 2018, art 272 (EU–Armenia); Agreement between the European Union and Japan for an Economic Partnership, in force 1 February 2019, art 16.1 (EU–Japan).

[37] EU–Central America (n 34), art 43; Free Trade Agreement between Australia and the Republic of Peru, in force 11 February 2020, art 22.3 (Australia–Peru).

Countries have also incorporated in trade agreements different kinds of explicit commitments in this respect; most of these explicit commitments are found either in the form of exceptions in chapters on government procurement, reservations in countries' schedules of specific commitments, or provisions on trade and sustainable development.[38] In addition, various agreements have incorporated explicit commitments, in the form of domestic policy commitments, where countries have sought an approximation of domestic laws to certain legal standards or rights mainly with respect to the elimination of discrimination, protection of rights of persons with disabilities, provision of social security benefits, and protection of personal information relating to health or physical conditions.[39]

Most commonly found explicit commitments are drafted in the form of exceptions, wherein countries have excluded from the operation of said agreement measures that relate to the goods or services that are of particular relevance for persons with disabilities.[40] Other provisions are drafted in the form of reservations, wherein countries have reserved with them the right to adopt or maintain any measure that can protect or support economically disadvantaged groups, including persons with disabilities.[41]

In several agreements, countries have assumed commitments to engage in cooperative actions that can lead to the protection and empowerment of persons with disabilities as employees or entrepreneurs. These provisions are mostly included in chapters on social, cultural, and economic cooperation, and they seek to focus on a range of areas, including job creation, education, skill development, and vocational training.[42] Moreover, there are agreements wherein countries have sought to work on other pertinent areas, including political dialogue, rehabilitation matters, promotion of human rights in a socio-professional context, adjustment of economic and social structures, and economic empowerment.[43]

One striking example of a disability-explicit agreement is the EU–UK Trade and Cooperation Agreement, as it benefits from several interesting best practice

[38] Free Trade Agreement between the United States and Chile, in force 1 January 2004, art 9.16 (Chile–US); Free Trade Agreement between the Republic of Korea and the Republic of Colombia, in force 15 July 2016, Annex II (Colombia–Korea); USMCA (n 6), art 23.12.

[39] See eg Interim Agreement with a view to an Economic Partnership Agreement between the European Community and its Member States and the Central Africa Party, in force 4 August 2014, art 63 (EU–Cameroon); Euro-Mediterranean Agreement Establishing an Association between the European Communities and their Member States and Republic of Tunisia, in force 1 March 1998, art 65 (EU–Tunisia).

[40] Economic Partnership Agreement between the CARIFORUM States and the United Kingdom of Great Britain and Northern Ireland, in force 1 January 2021, art 167 (UK–CARIFORUM); Free Trade Agreement between the Republic of Korea and the Republic of Peru, in force 1 August 2011, art 16.2 (Korea–Peru).

[41] Colombia–Korea (n 38) Annex II.

[42] Agreement Establishing an Association between the European Community and its Member States and the Republic of Chile, in force 1 March 2005, art 38 (EU–Chile); see CPTPP (n 6), art 19.10.

[43] Euro-Mediterranean Agreement establishing an Association between the European Community and its Member States and the People's Democratic Republic of Algeria, in force 1 September 2005, art 74.1 (EU–Algeria); EU–Armenia (n 36) art 3.

examples in this respect.[44] In its Chapter on Air Transport, the parties commit to ensuring that effective and non-discriminatory measures are taken to protect the interests of consumers in air transport and that such measures shall include appropriate access to information and assistance, including for persons with disabilities and reduced mobility.[45] This is a first-of-its-kind provision, not seen in other trade agreements that are currently in force. Another striking provision is found in Article 5 with respect to access to information, as the parties in this provision commit to taking appropriate measures to ensure that the information on the terms and conditions of employment is made generally available in a clear, transparent, comprehensive, and easily accessible way and 'in formats and in accordance with web accessibility standards that ensure access to persons with disabilities'. In Annex SSC.7 of the Agreement, parties define the scope and rules for exchanges between their institutions, wherein they confirm that these exchanges between authorities of the States and institutions and persons shall be based on certain principles including accessibility and e-accessibility, in particular for people with disabilities and the elderly. The parties also provide special insurance benefits and invalidity benefits for persons with disabilities in the form of cash payments and financial allowances. Other areas that have received special attention in this Agreement are the protection of personal data, corporate social responsibility (CSR), sustainable development, and non-discrimination. The parties in this agreement also clarify that an important beneficiary group of social security payments is persons with disabilities and that invalidity benefits are covered under the social security scheme provided in the protocol on social security coordination.

Another leading example is the Australia–UK Agreement, as parties in this agreement endeavour to achieve an appropriate balance in their copyright and related rights system in order to give due consideration to legitimate purposes, which includes the facilitation of access to published works for persons with disabilities.[46] Subsequently, in its Chapter on small and medium-sized enterprises (SMEs), the parties recognize the importance of protecting and supporting the interests of SMEs, in particular SMEs owned or led by under-represented groups such as persons with disabilities and other minority groups in international trade.[47]

The discussions in this section have shown that the inclusion of disability-related interests in trade agreements has materialized into several different forms of commitments; yet, the current inclusions are not revolutionary as they do not directly address the challenges that market access commitments can solve such as the ones relating to tariff and non-tariff barriers imposed on, for instance, the

[44] Trade and Cooperation Agreement between the European Union and the European Atomic Energy Community and the United Kingdom of Great Britain and Northern Ireland, in force 1 January 2021 (EU–UK).

[45] ibid art 438.

[46] Australia–United Kingdom Free Trade Agreement, in force 31 May 2023, art 15.63 (Australia–UK).

[47] ibid art 19.1.

goods and services needed for the physical independence of people with disability. The discussions also show that most of these provisions are found in the form of general cooperation-based provisions included in social, cultural, or sustainable development chapters. This shows that countries so far have equated disability concerns to social or cultural matters, and they have stayed away from including such provisions in other important chapters such as the ones on SME, CSR, investment, market access, and digital trade.

Several studies have shown how trade liberalization can possibly have a negative impact on the employment of people with disabilities as consumers, as it reduces their affordability and access to pharmaceutical products or assistive devices.[48] Yet, there is so far no trade agreement wherein countries have included provisions on duty waivers or relaxed intellectual property standards for products and services that people with disabilities majorly consume.[49] For example, countries through these provisions could possibly exempt the assistive technology and devices from customs duty, brokerage fees, and other border taxes, or relax their standards of patent protection to increase their availability as well as affordability. Countries could also consider reducing the restrictions on otherwise prohibited subsidies, for example, as it can allow for the protection and further development of pharmaceutical companies that invest and engage in the development, manufacture, or export of assistive devices. These important issues so far have remained outside the framework of current trade negotiations, showing that there is probably a disconnect between the barriers people with disabilities face, their needs, and the solutions offered by trade agreements currently in place.

V. Concluding Thoughts—The Way Forward

Trade agreements are not an end in themselves; they are rather a means and a vehicle to achieve and further sustainable development. FTAs have started to accommodate several sustainable development goals as countries have sought to ensure through these policy instruments that their economic development goes hand in hand with social justice, human rights, effective labour standards, and environmental protection. These inclusions provide a useful basis for identifying potential effects of negotiated trade rules, for avoiding their undesirable, unintended,

[48] See eg Deborah Stienstra and others, 'Women with Disabilities: Accessing Trade' (2004) <https://www.researchgate.net/publication/228947041_Women_with_disabilities_accessing_trade> accessed 3 November 2022.

[49] One exception is the UK–Japan FTA art 14.3, wherein parties affirm their commitment to comply with the obligations set out in the international agreements relating to intellectual property including the Marrakesh Treaty to Facilitate Access to Published Works for Persons Who Are Blind, Visually Impaired or Otherwise Print Disabled (n 27).

or negative effects, and for designing complementary measures on a range of non-trade issues.

The discussions in this chapter have shown that the current trade agreements have achieved a lot in respect of accommodating non-market-access interests such as the ones relating to disability inclusion. The preliminary inclusions we have discussed in this chapter are a good starting point but a lot more remains undone before we can make trade agreements work for all, including people with disabilities.

One important aspect to consider for future trade negotiations in this respect is to consider drafting and negotiating more targeted provisions that can directly address the barriers that people with disabilities face in accessing economic opportunities and resources. For example, including provisions on preferential market access, duty waivers, or relaxation of intellectual property rights might be measures that could possibly bring about a positive impact. Another recommendation going forward is to define the concept of 'disability' in future agreements, as the broad and undefined scope of 'disability', which could be of many kinds, may allow countries to disguise an illegal protectionist measure and justify it on one of these provisions. Moreover, almost no FTAs so far contemplate how such commitments could be implemented or enforced. The absence of applicable dispute settlement procedures implies that a country's failure to comply with these obligations has no direct consequence. Future trade negotiations need to work towards more meaningful integration of commitments that can actually be enforced or put into effect.

9

Infusing Indigenous Worldviews in Trade and Sustainability Agreements

Risa Schwartz and Carrie Stoddart-Smith

I. Introduction

Indigenous Peoples represent some of the world's earliest traders, having navigated rivers, oceans, and terrain across diverse geographies, where they formed intimate relationships and cultivated distinct worldviews long before settlers arrived.[1] It is upon those lands that settler colonialism stripped away the natural wealth of Indigenous economies through generations of economic exclusion, including through the development of international trade rules. Dr John Borrows (*Anishinaabe/Ojibway*) highlights an inherent dichotomy when it comes to Indigenous Peoples' desire to participate in international trade and investment negotiations, due to the exploitation of Indigenous lands and resources.[2] Indigenous activist and philosopher Ailton Krenak (*Krenaki*) has openly criticized the way that Indigenous Peoples have had to endure the chaotic and predatory practices of colonialism for centuries.[3] These practices, he argues, have no regard for the stabilization of Earth's ecosystems.[4]

Considering the historical context of betrayal and mistrust experienced by Indigenous Peoples, it is understandable that many of their communities approach state-driven efforts towards equity and inclusion in trade with scepticism. Indeed, Jeff Corntassel (*Tsalagi, Cherokee*) warns that 'there is a danger of buying

[1] Angelique EagleWoman (Wambdi A Was'teWinyan), 'Indigenous Historic Trade in the Western Hemisphere' in John Borrows and Risa Schwartz (eds), *Indigenous Peoples and International Trade: Building Equitable and Inclusive International Trade and Investment Agreements* (CUP 2020).

[2] John Borrows, 'Indigenous Diversities in International Investment and Trade' in Borrows and Schwartz (eds) (n 1) 11; Doris Estelle Long, 'The Impact of Foreign Investment on Indigenous Culture: An Intellectual Property Perspective' (1997) 23(2) North Carolina Journal of International and Commercial Regulation 229.

[3] Conectas, Interview with Ailton Krenak <https://www.conectas.org/en/noticias/the-climate-crisis-has-been-foretold-by-native-peoples-from-the-outset-says-ailton-krenak> (23 September 2021) accessed 2 March 2023.

[4] ibid.

Risa Schwartz and Carrie Stoddart-Smith, *Infusing Indigenous Worldviews in Trade and Sustainability Agreements* In: *The Sustainability Revolution in International Trade Agreements*. Edited by: Geraldo Vidigal and Kathleen Claussen, Oxford University Press. © Risa Schwartz and Carrie Stoddart-Smith 2024. DOI: 10.1093/9780191994470.003.0009

into an illusion of inclusion'[5] as legal recognition of Indigenous rights alone is not the panacea for addressing historical grievances or for protecting against future injustices.

However, as a result of Indigenous Peoples' advocacy as well as inclusive trade policies that have the goal of ensuring 'that the benefits of trade and investment are more broadly shared',[6] certain economies are developing trade and economic legal instruments that recognize Indigenous rights and interests, duties, and responsibilities. Unfortunately, much of this work is still being undertaken without the direct participation of Indigenous Peoples. It is crucial for policymakers and trade negotiations to move beyond engagement and work in partnership with Indigenous Peoples. This will provide for future 'Trade and Indigenous Peoples' chapters or agreements to recognize the inherent '*sustainabilities*' embedded in Indigenous worldviews. Doing so would accelerate the vision of sustainable and inclusive trade that is gaining momentum globally.

The protection of Indigenous Peoples' rights and interests in trade will be essential to designing a trade system that works for everyone. As such, the economic rights set out in the United Nations Declaration on the Rights of Indigenous Peoples (the UN Declaration)[7] must be recognized and respected in regional free trade agreements (FTAs) as the minimum standard of rights to achieving Indigenous Peoples' inclusion in international trade.

This chapter explores the recent infusion of Indigenous Peoples' worldviews and concepts of sustainability in the negotiation and text of various FTAs and economic cooperation arrangements (ECAs). Section II provides a brief discussion on the importance of recognizing both the pluralities and commonalities among Indigenous worldviews. It emphasizes the interconnected links they perceive between nature, humanity, and spirituality. Section III probes key contemporary advancements regarding the rights, interests, duties, and responsibilities of Indigenous Peoples at the intersection of trade, economy, and environment. This includes an examination of pivotal instruments like the UN Declaration and specific agreements such as the Agreement between Canada, the United States of America, and the United Mexican States (CUSMA).[8] Section IV focuses on the

[5] Jeff Corntassel, 'Re-envisioning Resurgence: Indigenous Pathways to Decolonization and Sustainable Self-Determination' (2012) 1(1) Decolonization: Indigeneity, Education & Society 92.

[6] Joint Declaration on Fostering Progressive and Inclusive Trade' (Government of Canada 2 March 2018) <https://www.international.gc.ca/trade-commerce/trade-agreements-accords-commerciaux/agr-acc/cptpp-ptpgp/declaration_fpit-pcpi.aspx?lang=eng> accessed 2 March 2023 (hereafter Joint Declaration on Fostering Progressive and Inclusive Trade). It is notable that Canada was simultaneously advocating for Indigenous inclusion in both the Agreement between Canada, the United States of America, and the United Mexican States (CUSMA) and in the subsequent Inclusive Trade Action Group (ITAG).

[7] UNGA, United Nations Declaration on the Rights of Indigenous Peoples, A/RES/61/295 (13 September 2007).

[8] CUSMA, in force 1 July 2020. CUSMA is named the Accord Canada–États-Unis–Mexique in French. In the United States it is named the Agreement between the United States, Mexico, and Canada Agreement (USMCA). In Mexico, it is named the Tratado entre México, Estados Unidos y Canadá.

growing convergence between Indigenous Peoples' worldviews on sustainability and state perspectives on sustainable trade while acknowledging there is still much distance to travel to achieve cohesion. It also briefly discusses the Indigenous Peoples Economic and Trade Cooperation Arrangement (IPETCA),[9] and recent FTAs that incorporate Indigenous concepts such as the New Zealand–United Kingdom Free Trade Agreement (NZ–UK FTA)[10] and the New Zealand–European Union Free Trade Agreement (NZ–EU FTA).[11] Its aim is to explore how FTAs and ECAs can serve as baselines to safeguard the world's ecosystems while fostering economic relationships with and amongst the world's Indigenous Peoples. This section also investigates the opportunities that FTAs and open plurilateral agreements (PAs) may provide. The last part of the chapter operates as a call to action. It outlines some concrete steps and ideas that are already in progress and the ongoing work required to ensure that the efforts to achieve Indigenous Peoples' inclusion in trade continues beyond FTAs and ECAs to plurilateral and multilateral negotiations in the World Trade Organization (WTO).

II. Briefly on Indigenous Worldviews

Indigenous Peoples comprise around 5 per cent of the world's population and manage between 20–25 per cent of Earth's land surface[12] containing '80 percent of the world's remaining biodiversity and 40 percent of all terrestrial protected areas and ecologically intact landscapes'.[13] They also represent as many as 5,000 distinct cultures and speak more than 4,000 of the world's 6,700 languages.[14] Indigenous languages are intrinsic to their territories and the exclusive and complex knowledge systems that they have developed, observed, and validated over thousands

[9] Indigenous Peoples Economic and Trade Cooperation Arrangement (10 December 2021) (Canada–Australia–New Zealand–Chinese Taipei) (hereafter IPETCA); Nanaia Mahuta and Damien O'Connor, 'Arrangement to Forge New Economic Pathways for Indigenous Peoples' (*beehive.govt.nz*, 10 December 2021) <www.beehive.govt.nz/release/arrangement-forge-new-economic-pathways-indigenous-peoples> accessed 1 March 2023. IPETCA was negotiated in the margins of Asia-Pacific Economic Cooperation (APEC). 'The IPETCA is open for any APEC Member economy, WTO Member or any other economy to join.'

[10] Free Trade Agreement between the United Kingdom of Great Britain and Northern Ireland and New, in force 31 May 2023; Chris Hipkins and Damien O'Connor, 'UK FTA Delivers Benefits from Today' (*beehive.govt.nz*, 31 May 2023) <https://www.beehive.govt.nz/release/uk-fta-delivers-benefits-today> accessed 31 May 2023.

[11] Free Trade Agreement between the European Union and New Zealand, in force 1 May 2024 (NZ–EU FTA).

[12] UN Department of Economic and Social Affairs, 'Challenges and Opportunities for Indigenous Peoples' Sustainability', *Policy Brief No 101* (April 2021).

[13] 'Indigenous Peoples' (*World Bank*, 14 April 2022) <https://www.worldbank.org/en/topic/indigenouspeoples> accessed 1 March 2023; UN Permanent Forum on Indigenous Issues Backgrounder, 'Indigenous Languages'.

[14] *UN News* 'UN Launches 10-Year Survival Plan for Endangered Indigenous Languages' (16 December 2022) <https://news.un.org/en/story/2022/12/1131807> accessed 1 March 2023.

of generations in the protection of their cultures, livelihoods, and natural environments.[15] Their worldviews enabled their ancestors to adapt and respond to any new challenges and opportunities they faced in their global migration journeys that began long before the arrival of settlers. It is important then to build a sense of Indigenous worldviews and how Indigenous Peoples have preserved their distinctiveness in the face of dominant Western ideologies.

Indigenous economist Carol Anne Hilton (*Hesquiaht Nation*) describes a worldview as a lens through which we interpret and experience reality.[16] Similarly, Wahinkpe Topa (*Cherokee*) and Darcia Narvaez suggest the formation of an Indigenous worldview is influenced by the fundamental elements of 'experiencing and being'.[17] They go on to assert that 'there are only two worldviews—one considers nature as intelligent and living, and the other perceives nature otherwise'.[18] These perspectives highlight the significance of personal and cultural understandings in the development of Indigenous worldviews. They also align with Paola Velasco-Herrejón and others who studied the worldviews of Indigenous Peoples from South America, South Africa, North America, and India. [19] Their study identified ecocentrism, pluralism, immaterialism, and relational approaches to sustainability as central to Indigenous worldviews.[20] Evidently, the inseparability of nature and spirituality informs the way Indigenous Peoples will conceive of and approach contemporary issues such as climate change, trade, and sustainability policy more broadly. As such, the emphasis on sustainability in Indigenous worldviews, and as a fundamental aspect of the future of trade discourse, presents an opportunity to create trade policies that benefit both people and the planet as well as begin to reconcile relationships between settler states and Indigenous Peoples.

III. Indigenous Rights and International Trade

Considering the plurality of their worldviews, Indigenous Peoples and their allies have strongly advocated for meaningful inclusion in the shaping of global norms and active participation in international rule-making systems. The protection of Indigenous Peoples' rights, responsibilities, duties, and interests in trade will be

[15] ibid.
[16] Carol Anne Hilton, *Indigenomics: Taking a Seat at the Economic Table* (New Society Publishers 2021) 11.
[17] Wahinkpe Topa (Four Arrows) and Darcia Narvaez, *Restoring the Kinship Worldview: Indigenous Voices Introduce 28 Precepts for Rebalancing Life on Planet Earth* (North Atlantic Books 2022) 21.
[18] ibid.
[19] Paola Velasco-Herrejón, Thomas Bauwens, and Martin Calisto Friant, 'Challenging Dominant Sustainability Worldviews on the Energy Transition: Lessons from Indigenous Communities in Mexico and a Plea for Pluriversal Technologies' (2022) World Development 150 [105725]. Note, Buen Vivir (Ecuador), Vivir Bien (Bolivia), Ubuntu (South Africa), Swaraj (India), and Ganigonhich (Haudenosaunee-North America) were the viewpoints used.
[20] ibid.

essential to designing a trade system that works for everyone. As such, the political and economic rights set out in the UN Declaration[21] must be recognized and respected as the minimum standard of rights to achieving Indigenous Peoples' inclusion in international trade. Such provisions would guarantee the participation of Indigenous Peoples in trade and investment through innovative mechanisms to reduce inequalities, inequities, and injustices within and between economies while contributing to greater social and cultural cohesion.

However, there is resistance in most economies to the development of a distinctive set of international trade and investment rights or exceptions for Indigenous Peoples. Despite the widespread acceptance of the UN Declaration,[22] some economies either do not recognize the economic rights held by Indigenous Peoples or bundle them up as part of a broader suite of inclusivity categories, such as 'women, micro, small and medium enterprises (MSMEs), and others with untapped economic potential'.[23] William David (*Mohawks of Akwesasne*) argues that 'the historic approach of treating international trade obligations, international environmental obligations and the rights of Indigenous Peoples as separate and unconnected issues have had a series of negative impacts on Indigenous Peoples' especially in relation to international trade.[24] Sergio Puig explains this is often because of a tendency to distinguish between international human rights and international economic law—where both fields have historically developed around the United Nations and the WTO respectively, creating a disjuncture in discourses. [25] Encouragingly, there is a growing acceptance of the clear parallels between these fields by academics and practitioners alike.

To counter the adverse impacts of trade and investment policy and its direct outcomes, Indigenous leaders, activists, and advocates have consistently challenged laws that erode environmental protections and commercial projects that threatened the survival of their surrounding ecosystems and natural resources.[26]

[21] UNGA (n 7).

[22] The UN Declaration was adopted by over 140 Member States at the General Assembly in 2007. However, four UN Member States—New Zealand, Canada, Australia, and the United States—voted against adoption of the UN Declaration at that time. By the end of 2010, all four settler states had reversed their initial position and supported the UN Declaration.

[23] 'China' (*IWGIA*) <https://www.iwgia.org/en/china.html> accessed 2 March 2023. See also 'Aotearoa Plan of Action' (*APEC* 2021) <https://aotearoaplanofaction.apec.org/> accessed 2 March 2023; APEC 'Putrjaya Vision 2040' (20 November 2020). For example, China, who adopted the UN Declaration, does not recognize the term Indigenous Peoples but instead refers to majority and minority ethnicities within its territories.

[24] William David, 'Recognizing the Rights of Indigenous Peoples in International Trade and Environment' in Borrows and Schwartz (n 1) 135.

[25] Sergio Puig, *At the Margins of Globalization* (CUP 2021) 37.

[26] Jobs and Growth Act [2012] Canada Bill C-45; 'An Indigenous-Led Social Movement' (*Idle No More*) <https://idlenomore.ca/about-the-movement/> accessed 6 March 2023; '#NoDAPL' (*#MoveMe*) <https://moveme.berkeley.edu/project/nodapl/> accessed 6 March 2023. Some examples include Bill C-45: Jobs and Growth Act (Omnibus Bill) in Canada that removed a number of environmental protections subsequently birthing the Idle No More movement, and, in the United States, the Keystone XL Pipeline and Dakota Pipeline projects that led to the creation of the #NoDAPL movement. Both movements garner significant global visibility and support from Indigenous Peoples around the

In some cases, advocacy for nature-centred Indigenous worldviews has influenced domestic legal systems highlighting the impact advocacy can have in shaping global perspectives. Examples can be found in the constitutional protection for the rights of nature enacted by Ecuador in 2008, followed by the Law of the Rights of Mother Earth in Bolivia in 2010.[27] Subsequently, as part of the reconciliation process with specific Māori tribes, New Zealand granted legal personhood to a culturally significant national park in Te Urewera Act 2014[28] and river in Te Awa Tupua (Whanganui River Claims Settlement) Act 2017.[29] Likewise, India also granted legal personhood to the Ganges and the Yamuna rivers.[30]

Many Indigenous Peoples have consistently raised concerns about the role of international trade in the continued expropriation and exploitation of their lands and resources. An early declaration of this concern was issued by Indigenous protestors during the third WTO Ministerial in Seattle in 1999. In that declaration, they condemned the role of trade as 'destroying Mother Earth and the cultural and biological diversity of which we [Indigenous Peoples] are a part', echoing the criticisms discussed earlier that were raised by Krenak.[31]

A recent example of the impact of Indigenous activism concerns the impeded progression of FTAs involving Canada, the European Union, and Brazil as a constituent member of Mercosur. To prevent further destruction of the Amazon and exploitation of Indigenous lands,[32] Sonia Guajajara, the former head of the Association of Indigenous Peoples of Brazil, and now Brazil's Minister of Indigenous Peoples,[33] led a delegation of Indigenous Peoples from Brazil to visit

world. It is precisely the expropriation of lands, resources, and the resulting degradation to life systems that drive Indigenous Peoples' interests in preserving their rights in respect to global sustainability policy in addressing the adverse impacts of international trade and investment.

[27] Lane Neave, 'Legal Personhood for Nature Has Legal Ramifications' (2018) <https://www.laneneave.co.nz/news-events/legal-personhood-for-nature-has-legal-ramifications/> accessed 6 March 2023.

[28] Section 11, the ancestral lands of the Tuhoe people that was declared in law as holding all the rights, powers, duties, and liabilities of a legal person.

[29] Section 12 provides recognition as indivisible and living whole comprising Whanganui River from mountains to sea including all its physical and metaphysical elements.

[30] 'A court in the northern Indian state of Uttarakhand ordered on Monday that the Ganges and its main tributary, the Yamuna, be accorded the status of living human entities'. Michael Safi, 'Ganges and Yamuna Rivers Granted Same Legal Rights as Human Beings' (*The Guardian*, 21 March 2017). <https://www.theguardian.com/world/2017/mar/21/ganges-and-yamuna-rivers-granted-same-legal-rights-as-human-beings> accessed 6 March 2023.

[31] 'Indigenous Peoples' Seattle Declaration' Third Ministerial Meeting of the WTO (Seattle, 30 November—3 December 1999).

[32] Fabio Teixeira, 'Indigenous Leader Pushes EU to Block Brazil Deal Over Native Community Deaths' (*Reuters*, 4 November 2019 <https://www.reuters.com/article/us-brazil-indigenous-guajajara-interview/indigenous-leader-pushes-eu-to-block-brazil-deal-over-native-community-deaths-idUSKBN1XE22V> accessed 4 March 2023; Christian Poirier, 'Everything is at Stake: The Rainforest, the Climate, and Our Survival' (*Amazon Watch*, 22 November 2019) <https://amazonwatch.org/news/2019/1122-everything-is-at-stake-the-rainforest-the-climate-and-our-survival> accessed 4 March 2023.

[33] In January 2023, Sonia Guajajara was appointed as the first ever Minister for Indigenous Peoples for Brazil. An analysis of the challenges and opportunities she will face in her new position noted the

12 EU Member States to convince them not to sign the trade agreement. Guajajara's activism may have influenced France and Germany's refusal to sign the agreement.[34] To address climate, biodiversity loss, deforestation, and Indigenous land rights, the European Union drafted an 'EU–Mercosur Joint Instrument' to serve as an addendum to the proposed agreement.[35] This leaked draft has been criticized[36] as falling short of actions needed to protect biodiversity and stop deforestation as it would be non-binding and therefore lack any trade sanctions. In Brazil, the EU proposal was initially seen as unacceptable.[37] President Luiz Inácio Lula da Silva had signalled his optimism at concluding the EU–Mercosur agreement late in 2023, but as of April 2024 the agreement is still stalled.[38]

In comparison, Canada's Standing Committee on International Trade recommended that during negotiations for an FTA with the Mercosur countries the Government of Canada work towards outcomes that would create economic opportunities for Canada's SMEs and, inter alia, protect the environment and safeguard the rights of Indigenous Peoples.[39] Canadian negotiators reported that the four Mercosur members were supportive of including an Indigenous Peoples Chapter or mainstreaming provisions to benefit Indigenous Peoples in the agreement.

importance of economic development, including the promotion of Indigenous economies as well as partnerships at the global level to increase Indigenous entrepreneurship in Brazil. Edson Krenak, 'Sonia Guajajara Appointed First Minister of Newly Created Ministry of Indigenous Affairs in Brazil' (*Cultural Survival*, 6 January 2023) <https://www.culturalsurvival.org/news/sonia-guajajara-appointed-first-minister-newly-created-ministry-indigenous-affairs-brazil> accessed 4 March 2023. 'That Resolves Nothing' (*Insitut Veblen*, 23 March 2023) https://www.veblen-institute.org/EU-Mercosur-a-draft-interpretative-declaration-that-resolves-nothing.html accessed 29 July 2023.

[34] Sergio Goncalves, Patricia Rua, and David Latona; 'Brazil Says It Cannot Agree to EU's Proposal for Mercosur Trade Deal' (*Reuters*, 23 June 2023) .

[35] 'Submission of the report of the evaluation commission of the draft EU–Mercosur agreement' (*Government France*, 18 September 2020) <https://www.gouvernement.fr/communique/11745-remise-du-rapport-de-la-commission-d-evaluation-du-projet-d-accord-ue-mercosur> accessed 18 June 2023. Although the French government does not specifically mention Indigenous Peoples, the concerns with deforestation in the Amazon and the position that an agreement with Mercosur cannot under any circumstances lead to an increase in deforestation are aligned with the advocacy undertaken by the Association of Indigenous Peoples of Brazil.

[36] Mathilde Dupré and Stéphanie Kpenou, 'EU–Mercosur: A Draft Interpretative Declaration That Resolves Nothing' (*Insitut Veblen*, 23 March 2023) <https://www.veblen-institute.org/EU-Mercosur-a-draft-interpretative-declaration-that-resolves-nothing.html> accessed 29 July 2023.

[37] Sergio Goncalves, Patricia Rua, and David Latona; 'Brazil Says It Cannot Agree to EU's Proposal for Mercosur Trade Deal' (*Reuters*, 23 June 2023).

[38] Catarina Demony and Andrew Gray, 'Brazil's Lula to Issue Counter-Proposal on Mercosur Trade Deal in 2–3 Weeks' (*Reuters*, 19 July 2023); Buenos Aires Times, 'EU Commission Expresses "Frustration" Over Stalled EU–Mercosur Trade Deal' *Buenos Aires Times* (12 April 2024).

[39] Mark Eyking, 'Canada and the Mercosur Countries: A potential agreement to advance trade relations' (Report of the Standing Committee on International Trade, 42nd Parliament, 1st Session, December 2018) <https://www.ourcommons.ca/Content/Committee/421/CIIT/Reports/RP10269416/ciitrp14/ciitrp14-e.pdf> accessed 20 July 2023.

However, members of Canada's trade-focused Indigenous Working Group[40] were concerned that the inclusion of a Trade and Indigenous Peoples Chapter in a Canada–Mercosur FTA would be rightly criticized as a smokescreen to make a controversial FTA more palatable. To address those concerns, Canadian negotiators were urged to secure enforceable provisions to protect the Amazon in the Trade and Indigenous Peoples and Trade and Environment Chapters. Without corresponding environmental protections and respect for Indigenous Peoples' rights over their lands in Brazil and other Mercosur countries, an increase in trade and investment with countries like Canada would contribute to the destruction of the Amazon.[41]

It is within the context of both advocacy and protest that there is an emerging convergence between trade, economic, environmental rights, and the rights, roles, and responsibilities that Indigenous Peoples ascribe to themselves in protecting the planet and its biodiversity. The UN Declaration is the underpinning for much of this formal advocacy.[42]

The articles of the UN Declaration tightly wind together the land and water rights of Indigenous Peoples with sustainability. For example, Article 29 recognizes the right of Indigenous Peoples to protect the environment as well as to manage the productive capacity of their lands, territories, and resources. It also acknowledges how 'Indigenous knowledge, cultures, and traditional practices contribute to sustainable and equitable development and proper management of the environment'.[43] Equally, it provides that there is a responsibility for states to 'provide effective mechanisms for just and fair redress' and 'appropriate measures . . . to mitigate adverse environmental, economic, social, cultural or spiritual impact[s]'.[44] Borrows characterizes the language of the UN Declaration as reflective of an Indigenous international economic agreement.[45] Similarly, Puig suggests that the intersection between Indigenous rights and international economic law becomes evident through the combination of Articles 21, 23, and 31 of the UN Declaration, which address the rights of Indigenous Peoples to politically and economically develop while determining their own priorities.[46] Additionally, Article 26 further

[40] 'International Trade Agreements and Indigenous Peoples: The Canadian Approach' (Government of Canada 17 November 2020) <https://www.international.gc.ca/trade-commerce/indigenous_peoples-peuples_autochtones/approach-approche.aspx?lang=eng> accessed 4 March 2023.

[41] One of the authors of this chapter was a former member of the Indigenous Working Group.

[42] UN Department of Economic and Social Affairs: Indigenous Peoples, 'UNDRIP: Historical Overview'; UN Department of Economic and Social Affairs: Indigenous Peoples, 'United Nations Declaration on the Rights of Indigenous Peoples'. The UN Declaration was initiated in 1982 when the UN 'Economic and Social Council (ECOSOC) established the Working Group on Indigenous Populations with the mandate to develop a set of minimum standards that would protect indigenous Peoples. Today, it represents 'the most comprehensive international instrument on the rights of indigenous peoples' and 'establishes a universal framework of minimum standards for the survival, dignity and well-being of the indigenous peoples of the world'.

[43] UN Declaration (n 7) art 29.

[44] ibid arts 29 and 32.

[45] Borrows (n 1) 11.

[46] Puig (n 25) 41.

reinforces their rights to own, use, develop, and have control over their lands, territories, and resources.[47]

The American Declaration on the Rights of Indigenous Peoples (American Declaration) also emphasizes the connection between sustainability, economy, and Indigenous rights in international economic and environmental law. For instance, Article XIX of the American Declaration guarantees the right of Indigenous Peoples in the Americas to 'live in harmony with nature and to a healthy, safe, and sustainable environment, essential conditions for the full enjoyment of the right to life, to their spirituality, worldview and to collective well-being'.[48] It also sets out Indigenous Peoples' rights to pursue effective measures to mitigate any adverse ecological, economic, social, cultural, or spiritual impacts and provide compensation for development project harms caused by states, private companies, and international financial institutions.[49]

While there is evidently much more work to do, Indigenous Peoples' worldviews are beginning to influence global trade and sustainability dialogues that could serve nature and humanity for generations to come.

IV. Indigenous Trade and Sustainability

The FTAs and ECAs pursued by like-minded economies such as Canada, Chile, New Zealand, Taiwan, and, more recently, Australia, Mexico, and the United States are beginning to express the economic and environmental rights set out in both the UN Declaration and the American Declaration. This is partly to address longstanding and persistent structural barriers arising from centuries of Indigenous economic exclusion. It is also partly due to the increasing recognition globally of the contributions that Indigenous knowledge and worldviews offer towards sustainable development and environmental protection.[50] Therefore, it is not surprising that agreements like IPETCA that provide opportunities for the active participation of Indigenous Peoples, are the very agreements that incorporate Indigenous Peoples' perspectives on sustainability in the final negotiated texts.

The earliest contemporary example of an Indigenous chapter in a trade agreement is found in Chapter 19 of the Agreement between New Zealand and the Separate Customs Territory of Taiwan, Penghu, Kinmen, and Matsu

[47] ibid.

[48] American Declaration on the Rights of Indigenous Peoples, OAS AG/RES.2888 (XLVI-O/16) adopted at the third plenary session (15 June 2016) art XIX.

[49] ibid art XXIX(5) Right to Development.

[50] Puig (n 25) 67. According to Taubman (as cited by Puig) there are at least 33 trade treaties with formal recognition of Indigenous Peoples' rights or other protections, noting that the footnoted list is not exhaustive, as it does not include every NZ FTA since 2001, which includes a Treaty of Waitangi Exception clause and more recently broader references to Indigenous Peoples across multiple chapters within these agreements.

on Economic Cooperation (ANZTEC).[51] The purpose of the Indigenous Cooperation Chapter (Chapter 19) is to 'strengthen the cooperative framework for cultural and people-to-people contacts between [the parties] [I]ndigenous [P]eoples and expand and facilitate trade and economic relations between them'.[52] ANZTEC also includes a Trade and Environment Chapter.[53] Although it does not explicitly mention Indigenous Peoples, there are synergies between the two chapters. For example, Chapter 19, Article 2(b) provides that the parties shall promote and facilitate the exchange of experiences relating to Indigenous Peoples' issues, including natural resource development, agricultural production, culture, land ownership issues, biodiversity, and traditional medicine. Article 3 enables either party to request consultations where any policies or decisions may adversely impact the Indigenous Peoples' aspects of trade of which environmental matters are acknowledged.[54] Despite ANZTEC's achievement as an early adopting milestone for Indigenous inclusion (beyond carve-outs and exceptions) in an economic cooperation agreement, the chapter is not subject to a dispute settlement mechanism, which leaves it unenforceable.[55] This means that there are limits to what it can achieve given that the agreement's commitment to resourcing activities is only on a 'good faith' case-by-case basis.[56] Accountability to commitments made by settler states remains a key priority for Indigenous Peoples in the trade space.

To date, the largest FTA to include provisions specifically related to Indigenous Peoples is the Comprehensive and Progressive Trans-Pacific Partnership Agreement[57]

[51] Agreement between New Zealand and the Separate Customs Territory of Taiwan, Penghu, Kinmen, and Matsu on Economic Cooperation, in force 1 December 2013 (ANZTEC).

[52] ibid 4–5, 199. This is found in the Preamble and reaffirmed in the ch 19 objectives. Note ANZTEC's implementation is coordinated by each economy's Indigenous development agencies, and in practice focuses on promoting and facilitating exchanges of Indigenous Peoples' experiences in tourism, culture, arts, and natural resource development. Activities have included eg participation in Austronesian economic summits, language and culture conferences, placements of tourism students with Māori tourism operators in New Zealand, Māori business students and early career professional exchanges and programmes in Taiwan, and site visits to tourism, horticultural, and geothermal assets in both countries.

[53] ANZTEC (n 51) ch 17, art 6(5)–(6).

[54] ibid ch 19, art 2(2)(b).

[55] ibid ch 19, art 3(2) 'Neither Party shall have recourse to Chapter 21 (Dispute Settlement) in respect of any issue arising from or relating to this Chapter'; and art 2(2)(j) 'The Parties shall, through their coordinating authorities . . . arrange funding for any exchanges facilitated under this Chapter on a case-by-case basis.'

[56] Notably, ANZTEC celebrated its tenth anniversary in 2023. Given Taiwan's IPETCA membership, this convergence could spark a discussion on a substantive upgrade to ch 19. See Stoddart-Smith, 'A Decade of Indigenous Cooperation Between Aotearoa and Taiwan but Where to Next?' (*OpinioNative*, 12 July 2023) <https://opinio-native.com/opinions/a-decade-of-indigenous-cooperation-between-aotearoa-and-taiwan-but-where-to-next> accessed 18 July 2023.

[57] Comprehensive and Progressive Agreement for Trans-Pacific Partnership, in force 30 December 2018 (CPTPP). See also Jeffrey J Schott 'Which Countries are in the CPTPP and RCEP Trade Agreements and Which Want in?' (*PIIE*, 2 March 2023); Fran O'Sullivan, 'New Zealand's Objectives for CPTPP' *New Zealand Herald* (17 January 2023). Parliament of Australia Joint Standing Committee on Foreign Affairs, Defence And Trade, 'Applications to the CPTPP: the United Kingdom, China, Taiwan and South Korea' in the report *Inquiry into Expanding Membership of the Comprehensive and Progressive Trans Pacific Partnership* (10 February 2022).

(formerly TPP,[58] hereafter CPTPP) signed by 11 economies in 2018.[59] Notably, in 2023 the United Kingdom signed the protocol of accession ahead of other CPTPP aspirants located in the region.[60] The CPTPP provisions related to Indigenous rights and sustainability include the Environment Chapter, which recognizes the 'important role of respecting, preserving and maintaining knowledge and practices of Indigenous and local communities embodying traditional lifestyles that contribute to the conservation and sustainable use of biological diversity'.[61] Additionally, the Intellectual Property Chapter sets out areas of cooperation on traditional knowledge related to genetic resources, although this does not explicitly refer to Indigenous Peoples.[62] Under the Exceptions and General Provisions Chapter, the CPTPP also provides scope for each party to take 'appropriate measures to respect, preserve and promote traditional knowledge and traditional cultural expressions'.[63] A preamble statement was also added to the CPTPP, which reaffirms the importance of promoting environmental protection and conservation as well as Indigenous rights and traditional knowledge.[64] Arguably, the preamble language could be used as an interpretative aid where explicit references could be implied as applying to Indigenous Peoples. Despite these positive aspects, the final CPTPP text disappointed many Indigenous groups.[65] For example, at the time, Canada's trade-focused Indigenous Working Group had collaborated with

[58] See also Deborah Elms, 'The Comprehensive and Progressive Trans-Pacific Partnership Policy Innovations and Impacts' (Global Economic Dynamics 2018) <http://aei.pitt.edu/102526/1/MT_Comprehensive_and_Progressive_Trans-Pacific_Partnership.pdf> accessed 3 March 2023. The original Trans-Pacific Partnership agreement was renamed 'comprehensive and progressive' following the withdrawal of the US signature. Besides the rebranding, little was done to make the CPTPP more progressive. Some provisions that were likely initiatives negotiated by the United States were suspended, such as provisions for intellectual property and investment.

[59] CPTPP (n 57). See also Risa Schwartz, 'Developing a Trade and Indigenous Peoples Chapter for International Trade Agreements' in Borrows and Schwartz (n 1) 248.

[60] CPTPP—Joint Ministerial Statement on the Occasion of the Seventh Commission Meeting, CPTPP/JS/2023/001.

[61] CPTPP (n 57) art 20.13.

[62] CPTPP (n 57) ch 18, art 18.16. Note that New Zealand achieved a carveout that enables the government to adopt measures that it deems necessary to fulfil its obligations under the Treaty of Waitangi in respect of indigenous plant species, but it is subject to the chapeau (see Annex 18-A, Annex to art 18.7.2).

[63] ibid art 29.8.

[64] ibid, Preamble; 'APEC Case Study on Inclusive Policies: Advancing Indigenous Peoples' Economic Interests Through Canada's Trade Agreements' (Government of Canada 7 August 2020).

[65] In New Zealand, the TPPA and subsequent CPTPP negotiations caused widespread disharmony and led to several Māori leaders lodging claims in the Waitangi Tribunal. This grouping became the WAI 2522 Claimants, who subsequently entered into a Mediation Agreement with New Zealand's Ministry of Foreign Affairs and Trade that led to the establishment of Nga Toki Whakarururanga—a Tiriti o Waitangi-based advocacy entity that focuses on trade and related policy, and with whom the government is required to engage with during all negotiations in the trade space. See Mediation Agreement (full text): <https://static1.squarespace.com/static/62d0af606076367ebf83b878/t/63968e8f101ed15eb488d69b/1670811289575/%232b+final+mediation+agreement+signed.pdf> accessed 11 July 2023. Note that the WAI2522 claim was also the impetus for the government entering into a Memorandum of Understanding with Māori Trade Advocacy Group Te Taumata, as it attempted to grow the range of Māori voices to engage with on trade and trade related matters: see <https://tetaumata.com/> accessed 3 March 2023.

Global Affairs Canada to develop a Trade and Indigenous Peoples Chapter precedent for the CUSMA, as well as an Indigenous Peoples General Exception, which was not included in the CPTPP. In New Zealand, the legal action taken against the government by Māori became the catalyst for the government to take a more intentional approach concerning Indigenous rights in its trade policy.[66]

The Regional Comprehensive Economic Partnership Agreement (RCEP) surpasses the CPTPP in terms of scale, encompassing 15 countries that collectively represent 30 per cent of global GDP.[67] However, unlike CPTPP, RCEP lacks specific references to Indigenous Peoples except for New Zealand's standard Treaty Exception. This omission may be attributed to political sensitivities among some RCEP parties. Similar to the CPTPP, RCEP appears to favour terminology that encompasses areas of concern for Indigenous Peoples such as genetic resources, traditional knowledge, and Folklore that are commonly associated with Indigenous rights and interests in trade.[68] The New Zealand government suggests that RCEP 'recognizes the importance of prior and informed consent, access and benefit sharing for accessing and using genetic resources, traditional knowledge and folklore (GRTKF)' and considers RCEP an 'important step forward at the international level to reaffirm the region's commitment to the rights and interests of Indigenous peoples in GRTKF'.[69]

Like all New Zealand agreements since 2001, the CPTPP, RCEP, ANZTEC, UK, and EU agreements all include a Treaty of Waitangi Exception Clause (Treaty Exception) for Māori.[70]

When first introduced in 2001 as part of New Zealand's negotiations to secure an economic partnership with Singapore, the Treaty Exception was regarded as an innovative measure.[71] Functioning as a defence, it allows New Zealand to adopt

[66] See n 65.

[67] Regional Comprehensive Economic Partnership Agreement, in force 1 January 2022. India withdrew from RCEP negotiations in November 2019, but there is a fast-track accession process in place should India wish to re-join RCEP in future. See also <https://asean.org/rcep-agreement-enters-into-force> accessed 3 March 2023.

[68] RCEP, ch 11, art 11.53.

[69] 'Māori Interests' (*New Zealand Foreign Affairs and Trade*) <https://www.mfat.govt.nz/en/trade/free-trade-agreements/free-trade-agreements-in-force/regional-comprehensive-economic-partnership-rcep/maori-interests/> accessed 3 March 2023.

[70] Treaty of Waitangi [English Text] 1840 and Te Tiriti o Waitangi [Te Reo Māori text] 1840. In New Zealand there is an unresolved tension around interpretations between the two texts as they are not direct translations of each other. Around 540 Māori chiefs signed the Te Reo Māori version, in which sovereignty was not ceded. However, the Crown rely on the English version, in which sovereignty was said to have been ceded, despite only 39 chiefs signing that version. Many did not sign the Treaty/Tiriti at all. See <https://www.waitangi.org.nz/about/history> accessed 20 July 2023, see also <https://www.dpmc.govt.nz/sites/default/files/2019-10/CO%2019%20%285%29%20Treaty%20of%20Waitangi%20Guidance%20for%20Agencies.pdf> accessed 20 July 2023; Treaty of Waitangi English text <https://nzhistory.govt.nz/politics/treaty/read-the-treaty/english-text>accessed 20 July 2023; Tiriti o Waitangi Māori text <https://nzhistory.govt.nz/politics/treaty/read-the-treaty/maori-text> accessed 20 July 2023; differences between the texts <https://nzhistory.govt.nz/politics/treaty/read-the-Treaty/differences-between-the-texts> accessed 20 July 2023.

[71] Agreement between New Zealand and Singapore on a Closer Economic Partnership, in force 1 January 2001.

measures it deems necessary to accord *more favourable treatment* to Māori in respect of matters covered by the Agreement, including in fulfilment of its obligations under the Treaty of Waitangi. However, the exception cannot be used as a means of arbitrary or unjustified discrimination against persons of the other party or as a disguised restriction on trade (the chapeau).[72]

The expansion of FTAs to areas such as environment, sustainable development, Intellectual Property, and Investor–State Dispute Settlement (ISDS) prompted Māori leaders, researchers, academics, and lawyers to evaluate the effectiveness of this exception and New Zealand's ability to fulfil its obligation to Māori under the Treaty of Waitangi. Primary concerns include the limited scope of the exception, which only protects measures that provide more favourable treatment; failing to address instances where non-implementation of measures would likely result in a Treaty breach; or cases where the government takes alternative measures related to Treaty obligations influenced by a combination of Treaty and other considerations.[73] Moreover, the chapeau language potentially restricts the legitimate public policy space of New Zealand to regulate in the interests of Māori under the Treaty.

The Treaty exception came under fire during the TPP/CPTPP negotiations, when Māori leaders (the Claimants)[74] supported by legal scholars and experts lodged an urgent hearing with the Waitangi Tribunal. The Tribunal is a permanent commission of inquiry established pursuant to the Treaty of Waitangi Act 1975. It makes recommendations on claims brought by Māori relating to legislation, policies, actions, or omissions of the Crown (New Zealand government) that are alleged to breach the promises made in the Treaty of Waitangi.[75] The Claimants questioned whether the exception would provide effective protection under the TPP and called for Māori to be involved in a redraft of the exception, given that it had not been updated since it was first drafted in 2001. Experts also noted that the nature of the CPTPP was broader than earlier trade agreements. [76] The Crown argued that 'changing the exception in [FTAs] would be risky' as it could be seen 'as an attempt to change the scope of the exception, or as conceding a deficiency which could be exploited'.[77] The Waitangi Tribunal also concluded that 'the exception ...

[72] Waitangi Tribunal Report on the Trans Pacific Partnership Agreement (2016) WAI 2522, 1.3 (hereafter Waitangi Tribunal, Report on the CPTPP).

[73] Dr Jane Kelsey conveyed the implications of the standard Treaty of Waitangi exception clause pursued by New Zealand compared with the CUSMA Indigenous Exception (Personal Communication, 9 July 2023).

[74] Waitangi Tribunal *Concerning the Treaty of Waitangi Act 1975 and applications for urgent hearings concerning the Trans-Pacific Partnership Agreement by the claimants for the Wai 2522, 2523, 2530, 2531 and 2532 claims* (31 July 2015) 7. 'This claim was filed on 24 June 2015 by Papaarangi Reid, Moana Jackson, Angeline Greensil, Hone Harawira, Rikirangi Gage and Moana Maniapoto'.

[75] Ministry of Justice, 'About the Waitangi Tribunal' (last updated 5 May 2023) <https://www.waitangitribunal.govt.nz/about/#:~:text=The%20Waitangi%20Tribunal%20is%20a,in%20the%20Treaty%20of%20Waitangi> accessed 20 July 2023.

[76] Waitangi Tribunal (n 72) 5.1.4.

[77] ibid 5.1.5. Crown Counsel argued further that 'it would be unwise to expend limited negotiating capital to seek changes' and that such changes could 'result in other countries imposing changes which might be harmful to Māori interests'.

could be said to offer a reasonable degree of protection to Māori interests affected by the [TPP]'.[78] However, it also suggested that 'adjustment of the Treaty exception may be necessary ... and this could include space for dialogue between the Crown and Māori on this important provision'.[79]

In 2020, the CUSMA introduced a notably broader general exception recognizing the rights of Indigenous Peoples, although it does retain the chapeau. However, unlike the limited focus of more favourable treatment in New Zealand's Treaty Exception,[80] Article 32.5 of the CUSMA provides that the 'Agreement does not preclude a Party from adopting or maintaining a measure it deems necessary to fulfil its legal obligations to indigenous peoples'.[81] The addition of an Indigenous General Exception provides some protections for measures taken by the parties to fulfil legal obligations to Indigenous Peoples. Like New Zealand's Treaty Exception, some have raised concerns about the legal effectiveness of the exception due to the chapeau. However, any potential pitfalls of the language, such as the validity of the legal obligation to Indigenous Peoples or the need to provide a plausible rationale for how the measure is necessary to protect Indigenous rights, will be less of a hurdle if the party whose measure was challenged directly involves the Indigenous Nation or community in the defence. Also, given that the exception covers the entire agreement and applies to all Indigenous Peoples across North America, challenging a measure underpinned by Article 32.5 may be unpalatable, providing for an effective political barrier.[82]

Despite the challenges for both exceptions, they both provide a precedent that can be improved upon in future trade negotiations. A promising development in this area is New Zealand's proposal to include an Indigenous Peoples exception[83] with language more reflective of the CUSMA, but without the chapeau, in the

[78] ibid 5.1.6. 'Overall, we conclude that the exception would be likely to operate in the TPPA substantially as intended. The exception, in our view, could be said to offer a reasonable degree of protection to Māori interests affected by the TPPA.'

[79] ibid 5.2.3.

[80] The CPTPP also includes other exceptions and for Indigenous Peoples associated with more favourable treatment, eg Canada has included a carve out for Aboriginal peoples for procurement of goods and services for state owned enterprises is found in CUSMA Annex IV—State Owned Enterprises Non-Conforming Activities.

[81] USMCA (n 8). Note that the United States has also included a similar Indigenous Rights Exception in its recent arrangement with Taiwan: Agreement between the American Institute in Taiwan and the Taipei Economic and Cultural Representative Office in the United States regarding trade between the United States of America and Taiwan, signed 1 June 2023 (US–Taiwan).

[82] Note, in US–Taiwan (n 81) art 7.5, a Rights of Indigenous Peoples exception reflecting the same language used in the CUSMA. This signals a shift in the US approach that could prove an influential ally in shifting global perspectives on the rights of Indigenous Peoples in a trade context.

[83] WTO, Communication from New Zealand, Joint Statement Initiative on E-Commerce, WTO INF/ECOM/70 (25 November 2022), para 2.3. Proposed text for the Indigenous Exception:

[NZ: Article [x] Indigenous Peoples

1. Nothing in this Agreement shall preclude a Party/Member from adopting or maintaining measures it deems necessary to protect or promote rights, interests, duties, and responsibilities of indigenous peoples in its territory, including in fulfilment of its obligations under its legal, constitutional or Treaty arrangements with those indigenous peoples.
2. The Parties/Members agree that the interpretation of a Party's/Member's legal, constitutional or Treaty arrangements with indigenous peoples in its territory, including as to the nature of its

Joint Statement Initiative on E-Commerce tabled for consideration at the WTO. This bold attempt indicates that New Zealand may indeed see opportunities to continue to test a broader exception in future agreements including at the multilateral level. The language adopted is a testament to the continued resistance and advocacy by Māori and Tiriti o Waitangi experts involved in New Zealand's negotiations and engagement processes. If this new exception language is accepted by WTO Members, it will be a positive step for elevating Indigenous Peoples' rights and interests within WTO dialogue.

Beyond exception clauses, the CUSMA[84] also included new trade rules relevant to Indigenous Peoples and sustainability in several chapters, including environment, small and medium-sized businesses, and a provision in textiles for duty-free treatment of Indigenous handicraft goods.[85] The Environment Chapter highlights the important stewardship role Indigenous Peoples play in the conservation of the environment, and the acknowledgement of this vital role is found throughout the chapter in provisions relating to sustainable fisheries,[86] forestry management,[87] and biodiversity.[88] Arguably, the most pivotal provision in the CUSMA concerning the environmental protection of Indigenous lands is found in Article 24.2. This article states that 'the Parties recognize that the environment plays an important role in the economic, social and cultural well-being of Indigenous Peoples and local communities and acknowledge the importance of engaging with such groups in the long-term conservation of our environment'.[89] This statement highlights the international legal obligations that all three countries share to consult with Indigenous Peoples.[90]

A. Indigenous Rights Convergence with Sustainable Trade

The CUSMA and CPTPP took most of the global spotlight during their respective negotiating periods. During this time, and in the context of a trend towards inclusivity and sustainability, Canada, Chile, and New Zealand also established the

rights and obligations under it, shall not be subject to the dispute settlement provisions in this agreement.]

[84] CUSMA (n 8).
[85] ibid.
[86] ibid art 24.17, para 1.
[87] ibid art 24.23, para 1.
[88] ibid art 24.15, para 3.
[89] ibid art 24.2, para 4.
[90] Each CUSMA party has either adopted or later endorsed the UN Declaration which contain obligations to free prior and informed consent for proposed undertakings on traditional lands, waters, or use of Indigenous Peoples resources. This provision acknowledges the important linkages between the environment, Indigenous rights, and land rights. Mexico is Party to ILO 169, which also contains obligations for free prior informed consent. All three countries are also parties to the American Declaration on the Rights of Indigenous Peoples.

Inclusive Trade Action Group (ITAG) through the Joint Declaration on Fostering Progressive and Inclusive Trade (the Joint Declaration).[91]

The Joint Declaration clarifies the commitments by Canada, Chile, New Zealand, and recently Mexico,[92] Ecuador, and Costa Rica around the role of trade in 'the achievement of sustainable development and solutions for global issues of concern, including with regard to gender equality, Indigenous Peoples, domestic regional economic development, Small and Medium Enterprises (SMEs), labour rights, environment and climate change'.[93] Although ITAG has successfully advanced the gender aspects of the Joint Declaration with the conclusion of the Global Trade and Gender Arrangement (GTAGA), it has made less progress with its proposed work on Indigenous Peoples in trade.

However, leveraging the ITAG relationship, New Zealand led negotiations for the IPETCA during its Asia-Pacific Economic Cooperation (APEC) host year in 2021. A core priority was to develop a trade and economic arrangement for Indigenous Peoples amongst like-minded economies that was similar to but potentially more ambitious than GTAGA. Four APEC member economies, Australia, Canada, Chinese Taipei, and New Zealand, comprise the first signatories to the agreement, which is open for any economy to join.

IPETCA is the first trade arrangement to conceptualize trade and investment through Indigenous perspectives in a definition drafted by Indigenous Peoples from the four member economies.[94] The definition of 'Indigenous Trade and Investment' signalled to the representatives the importance of recognizing and supporting Indigenous Peoples to fulfil their cultural responsibility to 'protect their lands, resources, and the spiritual interrelationship of the human and natural world, as well as the integrity of the natural systems themselves'.[95]

The centrality and prominence of sustainability incorporated in IPETCA are reflective of Indigenous Peoples' participation and the importance they place on

[91] See Global Trade and Gender Arrangement (signed 4 August 2020). Note the Joint Declaration on Fostering Progressive and Inclusive Trade (Joint Declaration) includes a review clause at para 12 stating that 'The first periodic review of this arrangement will take place on a mutually determined basis no later than 3 years after it takes effect'. On 16 July 2023, the ITAG convened in the margins of the CPTPP Commission in Auckland, New Zealand and issued the Tāmaki Makaurau Joint Declaration on Inclusive and Sustainable Trade <https://www.mfat.govt.nz/assets/Trade-agreements/CPTPP/Tamaki-Makaurau-Joint-Declaration-on-Inclusive-and-Sustainable-Trade.pdf> accessed 20 April 2024. Further, in the margins of the WTO 13th Ministerial Conference (MC13) Australia joined ITAG on 26 February 2024 and ITAG released the Abu Dhabi Joint Statement on Sustainable and Inclusive Trade to reiterate their earlier commitments (see New Zealand Foreign Affairs and Trade 27 February 2024. MC13 Abu Dhabi Inclusive Trade Action Group (ITAG) Joint Statement on Sustainable and Inclusive Trade <https://www.mfat.govt.nz/en/media-and-resources/mc13-abu-dhabi-inclusive-trade-action-group-itag-joint-statement-on-sustainable-and-inclusive-trade/> accessed 20 April 2024).

[92] Damien O'Connor, 'New Zealand welcomes Mexico as a new partner on inclusive trade initiatives' (*Beehive.govt.nz*, 7 October 2021) <https://www.beehive.govt.nz/release/new-zealand-welcomes-mexico-new-partner-inclusive-trade-initiatives> accessed 3 March 2023. Mexico joins ITAG and GTAGA.

[93] Joint Declaration (n 91).

[94] IPETCA (n 9) art 2.

[95] ibid art 2(a)(iv).

the interrelationship between people and nature. It also reflects the growing recognition by the signatories that Indigenous Peoples' worldviews provide a rich source of knowledge, experiences, and understanding about the challenges the world is facing. In total, there are ten references to sustainability and related phraseology throughout the arrangement, which are found in the preamble and four separate articles. These references highlight the connections between sustainability, traditional knowledge, environmental management, and innovation. They also establish sustainability and economic inclusion as dual pillars. In terms of environment and sustainability, cooperation encompasses various activities set out in Article 8 of IPETCA. These activities include expanding market opportunities for thriving Indigenous businesses that inherently prioritize environmental sustainability and innovation.[96] Additionally, Article 8 involves empowering Indigenous Peoples to lead climate mitigation and adaptation strategies,[97] as well as exchanging best practices for monitoring progress related to the UN Declaration and the Sustainable Development Goals (SDGs).[98] Article 8(d)(xxiii) also leaves room for the parties and Indigenous representatives to jointly determine any future issues for cooperation that may not be captured by the themes set out in Article 8.

Although it was disappointing that Indigenous Peoples were not permitted to participate in the formal negotiations, the Indigenous participants from each country set up informal negotiating sessions for Indigenous Peoples, with procedural assistance from the signatories. These informal sessions influenced many aspects of the IPETCA, including the establishment of an IPETCA Partnership Council. This innovation enables Indigenous Peoples to govern the implementation of the arrangement in partnership with the signatories and to take the lead in determining the priorities under the arrangement.[99]

In isolation, the unenforceability of IPETCA could give the appearance of a performative arrangement, born as part of New Zealand's aspirations to be seen as a leader of sustainability and economic inclusion during New Zealand's APEC host year in 2021. However, reading IPETCA alongside recent FTAs reveals that the arrangement may be viewed as a precedent for the inclusion of Indigenous Peoples' rights and responsibilities in newly entered into agreements, as well as an interpretive aid to already existing provisions in FTAs. The prominence of sustainability narratives in IPETCA arguably reinforces existing commitments the signatories have made in modern FTAs such as CUSMA or the CPTPP, insofar as it relates to their sustainability and economic inclusion commitments.

Whether intended by the signatories or not, the language in IPETCA is a useful lever for Indigenous Peoples to begin to actively participate in shaping future

[96] ibid art 8(d)(x).
[97] ibid art 8(d)(xi).
[98] ibid art 8(d)(xxi).
[99] ibid art 9.

trade and sustainability dialogue. In consideration of IPETCA within the wider suite of binding agreements among the current signatories, the express connections between Indigenous Peoples and sustainability, traditional knowledge, and active cooperation arguably serve as a signpost for future negotiations. They could also serve as a backstop for the signatories. Given that the commitments are plurilateral, it will be difficult for the parties to walk back from provisions that protect Indigenous Peoples' rights and promote opportunities and benefits in FTAs, even if the domestic political winds change.

As noted earlier, New Zealand went a step further after IPETCA, to infuse Indigenous concepts connected to sustainability throughout both the UK and EU FTAs including in Māori Trade and Economic Cooperation (MTEC) Chapters and preambular language supporting the UN Declaration.[100] The MTEC Chapters provide new opportunities for Māori to engage with these markets, including through a range of cooperation activities. The intention of these cooperation activities is to grow the Māori economy by boosting Māori business participation under these agreements. They recognize that Māori exporters already enjoy the same range of benefits as other New Zealand exporters such as market access and tariff reductions or elimination. However, the MTECs aim to provide a pathway for emerging exporters and micro, small, and medium enterprises and producers, as well as researchers and scientists, to engage with these markets.

The NZ–UK FTA received some positive feedback from Māori, for the inclusion of kaitiakitanga[101] in a side letter to the agreement as it recognized the widespread cultural appropriation and abuses surrounding Haka Ka Mate,[102] as well as the kaitiakitanga responsibilities of Ngāti Toa Rangatira to protect it.[103] This recognition was previously non-existent. However, critics identified several aspects of the NZ–UK FTA that conflicted with the concept of kaitiakitanga. One example was the way that kaitiakitanga was adopted in the Trade and Environment Chapter as its focus on production ignored the duties of care and protection of the environment and failed to address the fact that 'modern trade practices are often toxic to the *mauri* of an eco-system'.[104] A similar criticism was raised regarding the subsequent

[100] NZ–EU FTA (n 10) art 20.4. See eg reference that sets out a range of provisions the negotiators viewed as beneficial to Māori (where there are references to either Māori or Māori concepts).

[101] Kaitiakitanga refers to guardianship for the sky, the sea, and the land. Story: Kaitiakitanga—guardianship and conservation, *Te Ara, the Encyclopedia of New Zealand* <https://teara.govt.nz/en/kaitiakitanga-guardianship-and-conservation> accessed 4 March 2023..

[102] Haka Ka Mate is most well-known to global audiences through the New Zealand All Blacks who have routinely performed this haka internationally before each rugby match.

[103] Ngā Toki Whakarururanga, Te Tiriti o Waitangi Assessment: NZ–UK FTA.

[104] 'Tiriti o Waitangi Assessment NZ–UK FTA: Māori Trade and Economic Chapter' (*Nga Toki Whakarururanga*) <https://static1.squarespace.com/static/62d0af606076367ebf83b878/t/6372e82b6898ca6e49b4aee1/1668474940380/3.+NZ_UK_FTA_Maori+trade+chapter.pdf> accessed 4 March 2023; 'Tiriti o Waitangi Assessment NZ–UK FTA: What it means for Te Taiao' (*Nga Toki Whakarururanga*) <https://static1.squarespace.com/static/62d0af606076367ebf83b878/t/6373068f3e02ee722b8cb6a1/1668482734875/7.+NZ_UK_FTA_Tiriti+assessment+Te+Taiao+.pdf> accessed 4 March 2023. See also NZ–UK FTA (n 8) arts 22.9.1, 22.10.1, and 22.11.1.

NZ–EU FTA where kaitiakitanga was referenced in the MTEC Chapter alone and was not connected to any other parts of the agreement.[105]

Similarly, both agreements were criticized for undermining the cultural significance of mānuka, a specific tree species (*leptospermum scoparium*) exclusive to New Zealand and known as such in Māori language. Mānuka holds great importance for Māori as a multifunctional resource that generations have used in their culinary practices and traditional medicines, thereby embodying the status of a taonga species that necessitates safeguarding through the implementation of Māori principles of kaitiakitanga. Nonetheless, in December 2021, the UK Intellectual Property Office declined New Zealand's appeal for a trademark on Mānuka Honey. The Māori community voiced their discontent with this decision and critically appraised the UK FTA for its inability to effectively address this matter. Instead, the Intellectual Property Chapter (Chapter 17) further cements the pre-existing regulatory framework established by the United Kingdom. In this specific scenario, the Treaty of Waitangi Exception fails to provide a viable solution, as the predicament stems from the application of UK legislation rather than any actions taken by New Zealand.[106]

Although the NZ–EU FTA offered some benefits through tariff reductions for the export of Mānuka honey to the European Union, it lacked safeguards for the term itself, either through trademark protection or as a geographical indication (GI). The sole reference to 'Mānuka' is a definition found in Article 20.1 of the MTEC Chapter.[107] However, this chapter lacks enforceability and provides insufficient interpretive context for the rest of the agreement. Experts in intellectual property highlight that the 'definition appears to allow "Mānuka" to be recognized as something akin to a GI but that has been placed outside of the context of the GIs within the IP chapter' and 'it is not readily apparent from the text how this definition will translate to recognition and protection within the European market'.[108]

Māori also criticized the EU exclusion of the Sámi, Indigenous Peoples whose territories fall within the boundaries of some EU Member States, during the negotiating process.[109] Despite the European Union's work on Indigenous Peoples'

[105] Ngā Toki Whakarururanga, 'Te Tiriti o Waitangi Assessment: New Zealand—European Union Free Trade Agreement' (March 2023) <https://static1.squarespace.com/static/62d0af606076367ebf83b878/t/6463471db83ddc54d78978dc/1684227873906/NZ+EU+FTA+ToW+Assessment.pdf> accessed 11 July 2023.

[106] Note that the Intellectual Property Office New Zealand's decision 'refuses the application to register MANUKA HONEY as a certification mark. It refuses the application on several grounds, including that MANUKA HONEY is descriptive of the goods of the application and is therefore not registrable under the Trade Marks Act 2002', see *Manuka Honey Appellation Society Incorporated v Australian Manuka Honey Association Limited* [2023] NZIPOTM 19 (22 May 2023).

[107] Mānuka is defined as 'the Māori word used exclusively for the tree Leptospermum scoparium grown in Aotearoa NZ and products including honey and oil deriving from that tree', art 20.1.

[108] Kieran O'Connell, 'What New Zealand's Free Trade Agreement with the EU Means for Intellectual Property' (*ajpark.com*, 8 September 2022). <https://www.ajpark.com/insights/what-new-zealands-free-trade-agreement-with-the-eu-means-for-intellectual-property/> accessed on 18 July 2023.

[109] Note that should Māori wish to pursue bilateral relationships with specific EU members, there may be scope to engage with Denmark and the Greenlandic Inuit through this chapter.

issues, there was no reference at all to Sámi rights, interests, duties, and responsibilities across the entire agreement. Had the Sámi been included in the negotiations, the outcome may have been a more inclusive Trade and Indigenous Peoples Chapter, rather than the MTEC, which is applicable to Māori only.

V. Beyond FTAs: Indigenous Peoples, Trade, and Sustainability at the WTO

The advocacy of Indigenous Peoples in international trade negotiations has only recently begun to impact negotiation tables. From the earliest days of the FTAs, such as at the negotiations of the 1988 Canada–United States Free Trade Agreement, Indigenous Peoples paved the way to IPETCA, and Trade and Indigenous Peoples Chapters in recent agreements. As the influence of Indigenous agency in international economic law and FTAs continues to grow,[110] there has been an increased push to bring this conversation to the WTO. Schwartz and Whiteduck (*Algonquin*) proposed a Joint Declaration on Trade and Indigenous Peoples[111] modelled after the WTO's Joint Declaration on Trade and Women's Economic Empowerment, as a means of furthering inclusiveness and equity at the WTO to include Indigenous Peoples. A similar approach was reinforced during a panel led by New Zealand at the WTO Public Forum in 2022, where Māori representatives—Stoddart-Smith and McGregor—called on all WTO Members to endorse the UN Declaration. They also recommended that the WTO establish a representative Indigenous Trade Taskforce or working group that would highlight the plurality of Indigenous perspectives on trade and broaden the economic framing from recovery and resilience towards peaceful co-existence.[112] While a taskforce may be less ambitious, through the leadership of like-minded Members such as Canada and New Zealand, it may still be an effective means of opening the gates of the WTO to Indigenous trade policy. As Schwartz and Whiteduck note in their proposal:

> Modernizing the WTO in a manner that provides for the inclusive distribution of economic benefits is not only consistent with the economic rights of Indigenous

[110] Bruno Pegorari and Sergio Puig, 'Indigenous Peoples as Actors of International Economic law' (2022) Arizona Legal Studies Discussion Paper 22-12. For a summary of both 'upstream' and 'downstream' agency in international economic law, please see referenced article.

[111] Risa Schwartz and Judy Whiteduck, 'A Proposal for a Joint Declaration on Trade and Indigenous Peoples' (*CIGI*, 27 April 2020) <https://www.cigionline.org/articles/proposal-joint-declaration-trade-and-indigenous-peoples/> accessed 4 March 2023.

[112] Indigenous Perspectives on a Sustainable Trade Agenda (29 September 2022) WTO Public Forum (Session 85) <https://www.wto.org/english/res_e/webcas_e/webcas_video_e.htm?webcast_id=355&subject_code=PF22> accessed 6 March 2023. See also Carrie Stoddart-Smith, '#TradeNotes (part 1)' (*OpinioNative*, 14 October 2022) <https://opinio-native.com/opinions/tradenotes-1> accessed 6 March 2023; Carrie Stoddart-Smith '#TradeNotes (part 2)' (*OpinioNative*, 18 October 2022) <https://opinio-native.com/opinions/tradenotes-2> accessed 6 March 2023.

> Peoples in the UN Declaration [on the Right of Indigenous Peoples] but would also be a step toward achieving the goals of the 2030 Agenda on Sustainable Development, so that 'no one will be left behind.'[113]

Another area where the WTO could effectively include the concerns of Indigenous Peoples is the Trade Policy Review (TPR) process, which enables Members to periodically examine and evaluate each other's trade and related policies and their impact on the multilateral trading system. Through the introduction of a mechanism against which to assess trade and related policy adherence to the interlinkages between Indigenous Peoples and sustainability, the TPR would go some way to supporting the WTO to achieve outcomes on sustainability and inclusivity. Some WTO Members have begun to explore how to incorporate gender into the TPR. For example, in the recent TPR of Mexico,[114] New Zealand asked about funding allocations to women and small-scale agricultural producers, while India explored potential barriers that limited women's access to economic opportunities.[115]

Including a review of policies that cause barriers to the inclusion of women and Indigenous Peoples in international trade would be consistent with a shift towards multipurpose trade policy, which 'tasks trade policy with achieving other substantive policy objectives'[116] as it weaves together previously isolated themes to address broader policy objectives. It is also an area that ITAG parties could support to advance their Indigenous objectives in a multilateral forum. As part of the modernization of the TPR, the WTO Secretariat in collaboration with this proposed Indigenous Trade Taskforce/Working Group could prepare template questions concerning each member's efforts to implement the economic requirements of the UN Declaration. It could also consider questions relating to how Member States are meeting the SDGs, given that the vast majority of WTO Members have already endorsed both the UN Declaration and the 2030 Agenda for Sustainable Development.[117] The TPR mechanism could also examine WTO Member policies on technical support and question whether WTO Members are engaging Indigenous Peoples in accordance with Free, Prior and Informed Consent (FPIC),[118] which would also support the dual pillars of sustainability and inclusion.

[113] Schwartz and Whiteduck (n 111) (footnote omitted).

[114] WTO, Trade Policy Review: Mexico (28 November 2022) WT/TPR/M/429/Add 1.

[115] ibid 240, 298. This is for New Zealand and India respectively.

[116] Nicolas Lamp, 'Toward Multipurpose Trade Policy? How Competing Narratives about Globalization are Reshaping International Trade Cooperation' (*IISD*, 15 January 2023) <https://www.iisd.org/articles/policy-analysis/multipurpose-trade-policy> accessed 6 March 2023.

[117] United Nations General Assembly (2015) Transforming Our World: The 2030 Agenda for Sustainable Development, A/RES/70/1, Resolution adopted by the General Assembly on 25 September 2015 <https://undocs.org/en/A/RES/70/1> accessed 3 March 2023.

[118] 'Free, prior and informed consent' (FPIC) is contextualized within the broader right to participate in decision-making. The right to participate in decision-making is widely recognized in international human rights treaties including the International Covenant on Civil and Political Rights,

VI. Conclusion

As like-minded states follow suit, Indigenous Peoples' rights, interests, and recognition in FTAs and at the WTO have the potential to reposition Indigenous Peoples in both regional and multilateral trade dialogues in a manner that can withstand the turning tides of political resistance. Canada is currently negotiating an FTA with Ecuador that includes discussion on the inclusion of a Trade and Indigenous Peoples Chapter. Similarly, Canada and the United Kingdom are negotiating an FTA that could replicate or build upon the MTEC in the NZ–UK FTA. Some other opportunities for further advancing discussion include the CPTPP Commission meeting that Canada will host in 2024 following New Zealand's host year in 2023, the ITAG Review scheduled for 2024, ongoing activities in and adjacent to APEC, potentially the APEC Business Advisory Council,[119] the annual coordination meeting between the Council for Indigenous Peoples (Taiwan) and Te Puni Kōkiri (New Zealand), and opportunities to grow the dialogue during the WTO Public Forum or events at other international meetings, such as the UN Permanent Forum on Indigenous Issues.

Over time, and through the continued advocacy practiced by Indigenous Peoples in the context of trade, institutional arrangements like IPETCA could demonstrate the value of a partnership approach and allay the unfounded fear of Indigenous Peoples' inclusion in decision-making and governance bodies. As Wayne Garnons-Williams (*Cree*) suggests, IPETCA 'could be a model for a world in ecological crisis, because it takes trade in a different direction'.[120] While IPETCA forms no hard or enforceable commitments, it plays an influential and possibly decisive role in the future commitments that its signatories accept or pursue in future agreements. In conclusion, the cumulative effect of everyday acts of resurgence—the introduction of Indigenous worldviews into FTAs and ECAs, provides the potential to broaden the interpretative aids available to advance Indigenous rights

the International Convention on the Elimination of All Forms of Racial Discrimination, and the International Labour Organization's Indigenous and Tribal Peoples Convention 1989 (No 169). The UN Declaration makes 6 specific references to FPIC and at least 20 references to Indigenous Peoples' right to participate in decision-making.

[119] 'Report to APEC Economic Leaders' (ABAC 2021) <https://www.tradeworks.org.nz/wp-content/uploads/2021/10/ABAC-Report-2021-Final.pdf> accessed 6 March 2023, Annex E. In 2021, the APEC Business Advisory Council hosted its first ever Indigenous Business Leaders Dialogue at which a Joint Statement of Priorities was agreed, later endorsed for inclusion in ABAC's Annual Report to Economic Leaders.

[120] Marisa Coulton, 'A New Trade Arrangement Signals the End of the "European" Way of Doing Business' *Financial Post* (8 July 2022).

discourse in international trade. Within this process, IPETCA could be viewed as a catalyst for the transformative process of 'restoring Indigenous landscapes'[121] within the realm of international trade. Through the ongoing advocacy by Indigenous Peoples to revitalizing Indigenous worldviews and practices in trade, incremental steps can contribute to a broader movement of positive change and empowerment.

[121] Jeff Corntassel and Mick Scow, 'Everyday Acts of Resurgence: Indigenous Approaches to Everydayness in Fatherhood' (2017) 19(2) New Diversities. Corntassel discusses Anishinaabe scholar Leanne Simpson on how 'Indigenous stories break through the everyday impositions of jurisprudence and colonial narratives: "Storytelling is an important process for visioning, imagining, critiquing the social space around us, and ultimately challenging the colonial norms fraught in our daily lives" (Simpson 2011, 34). This restorying of Indigenous landscapes occurs in everyday settings to challenge the erasures of ongoing colonization.'

10

The Legal Links between Free Trade Agreements and Multilateral Environmental Agreements

Gregory Messenger

I. Introduction

The relationship between free trade agreements (FTAs) and multilateral environmental agreements (MEAs), and the inclusion of *legal* links in the former to the latter, can be explained through two parallel but distinct stories.[1]

The first, as a result of pressure from civil society and certain political quarters over the perceived dominance of trade policy in international affairs at the expense of environmental policy, FTAs increasingly included specific reference to MEAs.[2] The second is a (principally legal) anxiety over the relationship between two politically asymmetric sets of international obligations that flew in the face of fundamental principles held dear by the legal community: stability, order, and hierarchy.[3] That is, fears over the 'race to the bottom' and the means to counteract it on one hand, and the existential terror of 'fragmentation' of the international legal order on the other. In both cases, formal links between FTAs and MEAs were seen as (one) means to assuage these concerns.

Many of these anxieties also applied to the law of the World Trade Organization (WTO).[4] However, the expansion of WTO Members' trade negotiation

[1] The legal nature of the connections between the two is stressed here—and indeed is the focus of this contribution—as it is not possible to separate trade and environment in any sphere *other* than law. The economics, politics, ideology, and sociology of these concepts are fundamentally merged. It is only through the construction of distinct legal regimes or orders that we (as lawyers) make them different.

[2] For a recent contribution confronting this old discourse in the context of labour rights see Maayan Menashe, 'The Race to the Bottom Revisited: International Labour Law, Global Trade and Evolutionary Game Theory' (2020) 40(1) Oxford Journal of Legal Studies 53–81.

[3] The paradigmatic example: Report of the Study Group of the International Law Commission, 'Fragmentation of International Law: Difficulties Arising from the Diversification and Expansion of International Law' (13 April 2006) Document A/CN4/L682 and Add 1.

[4] Early concerns manifesting themselves in the *US–Gasoline* (WT/DS2) and *US–Shrimp* (WT/DS58) disputes. More recently, the WTO has taken a less confrontational approach to debating such issues preferring 'structured discussions'. See Ministerial Statement on Trade and Environmental Sustainability, WT/MIN(21)/6/Rev 2 (14 December 2021).

Gregory Messenger, *The Legal Links between Free Trade Agreements and Multilateral Environmental Agreements* In: *The Sustainability Revolution in International Trade Agreements*. Edited by: Geraldo Vidigal and Kathleen Claussen, Oxford University Press. © Gregory Messenger 2024. DOI: 10.1093/9780191994470.003.0010

programmes and the subsequent proliferation of FTAs in the early 2000s increased sensitivity to domestic political pressure for the inclusion of environmental provisions in FTAs specifically. This was coupled with a practical difference from the WTO: the negotiating dynamics of an FTA are more conducive to creative experimentation in the drafting of new legal texts given the lower number of negotiating parties involved and the occasional (or indeed, often, especially in the early days of FTA programmes) power asymmetries between the parties, which allows one to table the large part of the legal text.

And so, while meta-principles of accommodation between trade and environment were leveraged to encourage a less confrontational relationship in the multilateral system at the WTO (most notably, the support for 'sustainable development' and encouragement of greater 'mutual supportiveness' between trade and environment objectives), FTAs were breaking (limited) ground in formalizing these concepts in concrete ways.[5] Going beyond the use of sustainable development to interpret obligations,[6] under FTAs some of these principles constituted the inspiration for new *lex lata*.

Though only one part of the trade–environment tale, the use of legal provisions to formally link FTAs to MEAs constitutes an especially important phase. In this chapter, we will explore how the practice of linking FTAs to MEAs developed, and, while noting the limited progress of this strategy since its innovative original use, we will see how more recent practice in FTA–MEA linkage drafting aligns with wider developments in trade law: the possibility of dynamic implementation and adjustment of commitments, sectoral specification, and an increasing recognition of diplomacy's role in the practice of trade law.

II. Innovations in FTA–MEA Linkage: The US Story

If world trade law is to be considered as having been shaped by one actor more than any other, it is the United States.[7] The General Agreement on Tariffs and Trade (GATT) and later the initial WTO agreements all bear the hallmarks of US proposals. And, in many cases, not only 'approaches' but also, in some cases, direct incorporation of text from US legislation.[8] The hegemonic status of the United States

[5] For a cross-cutting account of sustainable development and mutual supportiveness, see International Law Association, *Final Report of the Committee on Sustainable Development and the Green Economy in International Trade Law* (2022) paras 170–15.

[6] Appellate Body Report, *US— Shrimp*, WT/DS58/AB/R, adopted 6 November 1998, para 129ff.

[7] General Agreement on Tariffs and Trade, provisionally applied 1 January 1948. For an overview see John H Jackson† and Gregory Messenger, 'History of The General Agreement on Tariffs and Trade' in Peter-Tobias Stoll and Holger P Hestermeyer (eds), *Commentaries on World Trade Law* vol 2 (Brill forthcoming).

[8] The paradigmatic example is art XIX GATT and the subsequent Agreement on Safeguards, both modelled on US legislation. See Gregory Messenger, *The Development of World Trade Organization Law* (OUP 2016) 90–96.

was clearly a fundamental reason for this, as well as the close ties between the development of US constitutional structures and its trade policy. That is an especially sensitive set of domestic interests with effective means of communicating them and (subsequently) conditioning support for US positions on their accommodation. The relationship between trade and the environment was one, very clear, example of this dynamic whereby attempts to conclude trade agreements from the mid-1990s onwards were bundled with domestic concerns over the level playing field.

A. Early Inclusions

The negotiations of the North American Free Trade Agreement (NAFTA) marked an important moment in the development of North American economic cooperation and intracontinental supply chains.[9] While Canada and the United States had already concluded an FTA,[10] the inclusion of Mexico expanded the potential for economic integration. An important element of Mexico's inclusion was to entrench (through legally binding commitments under the NAFTA) its recent economic reforms,[11] not least through the addition of investor–state dispute settlement under Chapter 11.

For all the perceived benefits of tying Mexico to its new path of liberalization, its inclusion raised concerns both among labour unions and environmental groups (so-called 'blue and green' groups). The environmental implications were of particular sensitivity, reflecting concerns raised by (and around) the long-running GATT-era dispute between Mexico and the United States over measures to avoid the killing of dolphins during yellowfin tuna fishing.[12]

In a clear shift from Article 104 of the Canada–United States Free Trade Agreement (CUSFTA), which provided for a general conflict clause in favour of CUSFTA in relation to obligations under other treaties, under NAFTA the parties agreed to a conflict clause (also art 104) that reversed the provision in relation to a limited list of MEAs: Convention on International Trade in Endangered Species of Wild Fauna and Flora (CITES),[13] the Montreal Protocol,[14] and the Basel Convention.[15] Additionally, two bilateral agreements were included between those parties: an agreement between Canada and the United States on transboundary

[9] North American Free Trade Agreement (NAFTA), in force 1 January 1994.

[10] Free Trade Agreement between Canada and the United States (CUSFTA), in force 1 January 1989.

[11] A programme of internal economic liberalization had begun under President Miguel de la Madrid (1982–88) but increased in speed and depth under the presidency of Salinas de Gortari (1988–94).

[12] Eg Report of the Panel, *US— Tuna I*, DS21/R, 3 September 1991 (not adopted).

[13] Convention on International Trade in Endangered Species of Wild Fauna and Flora (CITES), in force 1 July 1975.

[14] Montreal Protocol on Substances that Deplete the Ozone Layer (Montreal Protocol), in force 1 January 1989.

[15] Basel Convention on the Control of Transboundary Movements of Hazardous Wastes and Their Disposal (Basel Convention), in force 5 May 1992.

movement of hazardous waste,[16] and an agreement between the United States and Mexico on environmental protection across the border.[17] Article 104.2 provided for additional agreements to be added, though none were.[18]

Although NAFTA had been signed during the Bush presidency, the new Clinton administration had to shepherd the agreement through Congress. To secure support from Democrats wary of the implications of NAFTA for labour rights and environmental protection, the Clinton administration negotiated 'side agreements' on those topics with Canada and Mexico.

The North American Agreement on Environmental Cooperation (NAAEC) did not include any dramatic advances beyond the conflict clause in NAFTA. But it did make explicit reference to the parties' 'tradition of environmental cooperation and expressing their desire to support and build on international environmental agreements and existing policies and laws, in order to promote cooperation between them'.[19] A saving clause is also included, excluding NAAEC from influencing the content or application of any other environmental agreements.[20]

B. Later Developments

As noted earlier, the relationship between trade and environment commitments cannot be reduced to the interactions between FTAs and MEAs. And, indeed, the United States continued to expand the inclusion of environmental provisions within its FTAs without necessarily expanding the number or nature of links to MEAs. For example, the later US–Jordan FTA includes no references to MEAs, though it does include limited non-derogation obligations.[21] This focus on domestic environmental law obligations as the hook for the trade–environment nexus would continue to be the focus of future US FTAs.

Yet, MEAs remained part of the expanding environmental conditions for US FTA negotiations. We recall that one of the principal concerns over the accommodation of environmental commitments in trade law came from domestic political constituencies. Here, the ability of the US executive branch to negotiate new FTAs

[16] The Agreement Between the Government of Canada and the Government of the United States of America Concerning the Transboundary Movement of Hazardous Waste, in force 8 November 1986.

[17] The Agreement Between the United States of America and the United Mexican States on Cooperation for the Protection and Improvement of the Environment in the Border Area, in force 16 February 1984.

[18] A minor provision that nonetheless can be seen as the first step towards dynamic implementation in this area. See further section V.

[19] North American Agreement on Environmental Cooperation (NAAEC), in force 1 January 1994, Preamble, 9th recital.

[20] NAAEC (n 19), art 40.

[21] Agreement Between the United States of America and Jordan on the Establishment of a Free Trade Area, in force 17 December 2001, art 5.1.

was conditioned by the US Congress on (inter alia) the inclusion of specific requirements in relation to MEAs.

In the Trade Act of 2002,[22] the US Congress set out conditions for any new US-negotiated FTA, including in relation to environmental commitments. However, these were particularly vague in relation to MEAs and FTA policy: 'to ensure that trade and environmental policies are mutually supportive and to seek to protect and preserve the environment and enhance the international means of doing so, while optimizing the use of the world's resources'.[23]

Thus, agreements such as the US–Chile FTA had only a high-level reference to the parties' recognition of 'the importance of multilateral environmental agreements, including the appropriate use of trade measures in such agreements to achieve specific environmental goals'.[24] A small additional acknowledgement of the Doha Declaration's reference to negotiations that support the mutual relationship between 'WTO rules and specific trade obligations set out in multilateral environmental agreement' was included, and a commitment to consult on the influence of such negotiations on the FTA.[25] As was the case with NAFTA, a separate agreement was concluded (in this instance, mandated by the FTA itself)[26] as the basis of US–Chile environmental cooperation. A central objective of this US–Chile Environmental Cooperation Agreement[27] was to promote 'the understanding and effective implementation of multilateral environmental agreements to which both Parties are party'.[28]

The Dominican Republic–Central America–United States free trade agreement (CAFTA–DR),[29] is similarly circumspect in relation to MEAs: the 'Parties recognize that multilateral environmental agreements to which they are all party play an important role in protecting the environment globally and domestically and that their respective implementation of these agreements is critical to achieving the environmental objectives of these agreements'.[30] As with US–Chile, a separate Environmental Cooperation Agreement was also concluded.[31] These agreements are linked, explicitly acknowledging the importance of enhancing 'the mutual

[22] Trade Act of 2002, United States Public Law 107-210 (6 August 2002).

[23] ibid s 2102(a)(5).

[24] United States–Chile Free Trade Agreement, in force 1 January 2004, art 19.9.

[25] ibid.

[26] US–Chile FTA, art 19.3 (2)(b)(vi).

[27] Agreement between the Government of the United States of America and the Government of the Republic of Chile on Environmental Cooperation, in force 30 April 2004.

[28] US–Chile FTA, art 19.3 (2)(b)(vi).

[29] Dominican Republic–Central America–United States Free Trade Agreement (CAFTA–DR), in force 1 March 2006.

[30] ibid art 17.12(1).

[31] Agreement among the Governments of Costa Rica, the Dominican Republic, El Salvador, Guatemala, Honduras, Nicaragua, and the United States of America on Environmental Cooperation, in force 1 January 2009.

supportiveness of multilateral environmental agreements to which they are all party and trade agreements to which they are all party'.[32]

The major shift in this area is commonly attributed to the later 2015 conditions for fast-track authority under the Bipartisan Congressional Trade Priorities and Accountability Act of 2015 (TPA-2015), once again demonstrating the importance of domestic pressure in shaping international obligations in this space.[33]

TPA-2015 sets out as a negotiating objective the inclusion of *specific* MEAs in FTAs,[34] including the CITES; the Montreal Protocol; the Protocol of 1978 Relating to the International Convention for the Prevention of Pollution from Ships; the Convention on Wetlands of International Importance Especially as Waterfowl Habitat 1971; the Convention on the Conservation of Antarctic Marine Living Resources 1980; the International Convention for the Regulation of Whaling 1946; and the Convention for the Establishment of an Inter-American Tropical Tuna Commission 1949.[35]

In practice, however, these MEAs were *already* being included in a number of US FTAs: the US–Peru and US–Colombia FTAs included them as 'covered agreements' for the purposes of their environmental chapters.[36] The United States–Mexico–Canada Agreement (USMCA), concluded in 2018, as expected, includes this explicit list, requiring the parties to 'adopt, maintain, and implement laws, regulations, and all other measures necessary to fulfill [their] respective obligations under the following multilateral environmental agreements'.[37] This wording brings the application and implementation of the referenced agreements within the wider, more substantive, obligations in relation to effective enforcement. Though these obligations are limited by the additional requirement that such a failure to act be in 'a manner affecting trade or investment' between the parties, this wording nonetheless provides a more effective hook for a limited list of MEAs into the scope of these agreements.[38] Additionally, these obligations are enforceable through dispute settlement, unlike most EU agreements.

[32] CAFTA–DR, art 17.12(1). Annex 17.9 also includes provision for cooperation on MEAs relating to information exchange on ratification and implementation (at art 3(e)).

[33] United States Public Law 114-26 (29 June 2015). For an accessible introductory overview: Congressional Research Service, 'Environmental Provisions in Free Trade Agreements (FTAs)' (updated 28 February 2023) <https://crsreports.congress.gov/product/pdf/IF/IF10166> accessed 1 May 2023.

[34] ibid s 2.10(A)(i) cross referencing specific MEAs under s 11(6)(B).

[35] ibid s 111(6).

[36] Peru Trade Promotion Agreement, in force 1 February 2009, art 18.2 and Annex 18.2; United States–Colombia Trade Promotion Agreement, in force 15 May 2012, art 18.2 and Annex 18.2.

[37] Agreement between the United States of America, the United Mexican States, and Canada, in force 1 July 2020, art 24.8.4.

[38] This is additionally strengthened by the reversal of the assumption in relation to the 'manner affecting trade' test in ibid art 24.4.1, fn 5 'For purposes of dispute settlement, a panel shall presume that a failure is in a manner affecting trade or investment between the Parties, *unless the responding Party demonstrates otherwise*.' Emphasis added.

While USMCA contains additional references to other MEAs (eg in relation to commitments on conservation and trade, and a cross-reference drawing on CITES for the definition of wildlife),[39] it is the older US–Peru FTA that includes a far wider range of MEA linkages at a sectoral level. Unsurprisingly, given the concerns over forest management in Peru, this FTA includes substantial commitments in this sector. Annex 18.3.4 on forest sector governance provides substantive detail on implementation of CITES, including a focus on specific species, and requires the development of strategic management plans. For example, this Annex includes the establishment of export quotas for bigleaf mahogany 'in a manner consistent with Article IV' CITES.[40] The specificity of the forestry commitments under the US–Peru FTA has led to one dispute over US concerns for the independence of Peru's national forestry agency (resolved a few months later).[41]

It is interesting to note two themes that have already begun to develop (to which we will return in section V). First, the increasing specificity in the linkages between US FTAs and a limited list of MEAs. These constitute a more substantive set of linking tools not in the overarching commitments on MEAs but instead at a *sectoral* level as part of the necessary progress of rules on trade liberalization from overarching meta rules (eg on non-discrimination or transparency) to sectoral or product-specific rules to shape government behaviour more effectively. Second, the importance of these ad hoc systems of enforcement as a means not to generate formal legal findings but instead to provide hooks for the resolution of disputes through processes of economic diplomacy in the shadow of legal obligations.[42] Both developments can be seen elsewhere, not least in the European Union's own practice, as we will see next.

[39] ibid art 24.22 fn 35.

[40] US–Peru Annex 18.3.4, art 3(f).

[41] USTR, 'USTR Successfully Resolves Concerns Raised in First-Ever Environment Consultations Under the U.S.–Peru Trade Promotion Agreement (PTPA)' *Press Release* (9 April 2019).

[42] The exact content of the practice of 'economic diplomacy' is largely undefined or contested. For an excellent discussion see Maaike Okano-Heijmans, 'Conceptualizing Economic Diplomacy: The Crossroads of International Relations, Economics, IPE and Diplomatic Studies', in Peter AG Van Bergeijk, Maaike Okano-Heijmans, and Jan Melissen (eds), *Economic Diplomacy: Economic and Political Perspectives* (Brill 2011). For the purposes of this contribution, economic diplomacy is understood to be the diplomatic practice of subjects of public international law in the pursuit of their own economic interests. Such a practice includes trade diplomacy (ie the pursuit of diplomacy through existing or new institutions of international governance including the WTO, FTAs, the G7, G20, ongoing bilateral international relations, and so on), commercial diplomacy (ie the practice of governments supporting the economic interests of private actors by directly engaging with them on a firm- or sector-specific level or on their behalf), and regulatory diplomacy (ie the practice of working through regulatory and super-regulatory bodies to shape the regulatory foundations of the global system).

III. Further Innovations in FTA–MEA Linkage: The EU Story

Just as the content of US FTAs was principally framed as a response to domestic political pressures, the European Union also began to include in its FTAs links to environmental agreements in response to more vocal, and more effective, pressure from civil society and green political parties.[43]

The Treaty of Lisbon had introduced an increased role for the European Parliament in the approval of FTAs.[44] This had an important impact on the structure and dynamic of EU trade policy.[45] Whereas the European Commission (specifically, DG Trade) had historically been highly hostile to any form of 'non-trade' provision in FTAs, it found that it had to make some accommodations in order to placate Member State legislatures and the European Parliament itself. In retrospect, the principal surprise (given that the EU strength in international relations is principally economic) is that it did not incorporate environmental commitments earlier.

A. Early Inclusions

The first real test for the European Union's new, more environmentally-sensitive position, was the EU–Korea FTA.[46] In spite of pressure from civil society, the Commission's wariness over including provisions that would require it to alter or amend its policy positions vis-à-vis key trading partners meant that early incorporations of environmental commitments were largely ornamental.

Thus, in the EU–Korea FTA the parties 'recognise the value of international environmental governance and agreements as a response of the international community to global or regional environmental problems and they commit to consulting and cooperating as appropriate with respect to negotiations on trade-related environmental issues of mutual interest'.[47]

Beyond this largely symbolic commitment to consult or cooperate over negotiations in the trade–environment space, there is specific reference to

[43] For a brief history, see Wybe Th Douma, 'The Promotion of Sustainable Development through EU Trade Instruments' (2017) 28(2) European Business Law Review 197–216; Gracia Marín Durán, 'Sustainable Development Chapters in EU Free Trade Agreements: Emerging Compliance Issues' (2020) 57(4) Common Market Law Review 1031–68.

[44] [2010] OJ C83/344.

[45] See Katharina Meissner, 'Democratizing EU External Relations: The European Parliament's Informal Role in SWIFT, ACTA, and TTIP' (2016) 21(2) European Foreign Affairs Review, 269–88.

[46] Ie substantive commitments: see Marín Durán (n 43) noting that the Economic Partnership Agreement between the Caribbean Forum States and the European Community and its Member States, provisionally applied 29 December 2008, predated the Free Trade Agreement between the European Union and the Republic of Korea (EU–Korea FTA), in force 13 December 2015, with limited commitments.

[47] EU–Korea FTA, art 13.5:1.

MEAs: 'reaffirm[ing] their commitments to the effective implementation in their laws and practices of the multilateral environmental agreements to which they are party'.[48]

This obligation imposes no requirement that the parties commit to any specific MEAs. They merely 'reaffirm' existing international obligations. More specific provision is made for climate policy in relation to the United Nations Framework Convention on Climate Change (UNFCCC).[49] But this too, while more precise in its outcome (to 'commit to cooperating on the development of the future international climate change framework in accordance with the Bali Action Plan') is still largely symbolic given the lack of detail on how cooperation is to be understood, interpreted, or, most importantly, implemented in practice. Annex 13 on co-operation further develops some of these mechanisms but neither concretizes the nature of the obligation to work in MEAs nor gives specific instruction. Instead, it only identifies 'international fora responsible for social or environmental aspects of trade and sustainable development (TSD) including in particular the WTO, the International Labour Organization (ILO), the United Nations Environment Programme and multilateral environmental agreements'.[50]

In relation to dispute settlement under the EU–Korea FTA (consultative procedures in the case of the chapter on TSD), here too the agreement makes a nod to the integrative principles of sustainable development and mutual supportiveness by ensuring that any resolution 'reflects the activities of the . . . relevant multilateral environmental organisations or bodies so as to promote greater cooperation and coherence between the work of the Parties and these organisations'.[51]

Yet, we note the stark contrast between the EU–Korea FTA (signed in 2009) and the contemporaneous US agreements that include *specific* MEAs to which a signature was necessary for the conclusion of the agreement.

B. Later Developments

Subsequent EU agreements with the Andean Community, Canada, Central America, Georgia, Japan, Moldova, Ukraine, and Vietnam all include TSD chapters with explicit provisions on MEAs. This should come as no surprise: the nature of negotiations is to base new negotiations on recent drafts, especially in the case

[48] ibid art 13.5:2.
[49] ibid art 13.5:3.
[50] ibid Annex 13, 1(b). CF Subsequently narrowed greatly in other agreements (eg Association Agreement between the European Union and its Member States and Ukraine, in force 1 September 2017, art 288: 'The Parties will work together on trade-related aspects of labour and environmental policies in order to achieve the objectives of this Agreement.').
[51] EU–Korea FTA (n 47), art 13.14(2).

of considerable power asymmetries (which the European Union enjoyed in all of these negotiations save two partners).

Thus, these agreements demonstrate minor textual shifts from the EU–Korea starting point, providing limited changes and (somewhat) more specific language. For example, the EU–Andean Community FTA maintains the 'reaffirmation' formulation of other agreements but improves its precision. Under Article 270(2) the 'Parties reaffirm their commitment to effectively implement in their laws and practices' the Montreal Protocol, the Basel Convention, the Stockholm Convention on Persistent Organic Pollutants adopted on 22 May 2001, CITES, the Convention on Biological Diversity (CBD), the Cartagena Protocol on Biosafety, the Kyoto Protocol, and the Rotterdam Convention on the Prior Informed Consent Procedure for Certain Hazardous Chemicals and Pesticides in International Trade.

Echoing US practice, this list can be extended by the parties; in this agreement by the Trade Committee following a proposal of the Sub-Committee on Trade and Sustainable Development.[52]

The EU–Central America FTA also adjusts the standard reaffirmation formulation. While it provides for the usual 'reaffirmation' model it also provides an explicit list.[53] Additionally, in line with the approach taken in relation to labour rights (and the fundamental ILO Conventions in particular), the EU–Central America FTA also instructs the parties to ensure ratification of a CITES amendment permitting the accession of regional economic integration organizations.[54] They are also required 'to the extent they have not yet done so, to ratify *and effectively implement*' an additional agreement (the Rotterdam Convention) on hazardous chemicals and pesticides.[55]

Here we see a more formally effective method of conditionality, linking the conclusion and operation of the FTA with existing MEAs. For example, the EU–Singapore FTA requires that 'The Parties *shall effectively implement*, in their respective laws, regulations or other measures and practices in their territories, the multilateral environmental agreements to which they are party.'[56] Not only is the 'effective implementation' formulation included but it is the only of the pre-2020 set of agreements that does not 'reaffirm' but instead simply requires.

Unlike the other agreements discussed thus far, the EU association agreements with Georgia, Moldova, and Ukraine have a different structure. These Deep and

[52] Agreement between the European Union and its Member States and Colombia, Peru and Ecuador (EU–Andean Community FTA), provisionally applied 1 January 2017, art 270(3).

[53] European Union Central American Association Agreement (EU–Central America FTA), provisionally applied 1 August 2013, art 287(2).

[54] ibid art 287(3): 'The Parties undertake to ensure that they have ratified by the date of entry into force of this Agreement, the Amendment to Article XXI of CITES, adopted at Gaborone (Botswana), on 30 April 1983'.

[55] ibid art 287(4). Emphasis added.

[56] Free Trade Agreement between the European Union and the Republic of Singapore (EU–Singapore FTA), in force 21 November 2019, art 12.6(2). Emphasis added.

Comprehensive Free Trade Agreements (DCFTAs) are designed as a bridge between traditional FTA liberalization and accession agreements, whereby the non-EU parties progressively align with the EU *acquis*, and in doing so, correspondingly increase levels of market access.[57] As approximation with EU legislation forms a core part of the underlying method for these agreements, the links to MEAs are less explicit but also tinged with the logic of EU environmental law.

Note, for example, the EU–Ukraine Agreement, where the customary 're-affirmation' model is used together with the expectation of effective implementation.[58] It also includes a specific exception for MEA implementation (found in all other agreements of this tranche save the Canada–EU and EU–Korea FTAs).[59] Additionally, and unusually for EU agreements, it includes an explicit incorporation of precautionary approaches to environmental obligations, stating that '[t]he Parties shall ensure that environmental policy shall be based on the precautionary principle'.[60]

C. The New Wave of EU Agreements

The EU's active FTA programme continues and includes (inter alia): the modernization of the Eastern and Southern Africa (ESA) agreement, a new Mexico agreement, and FTAs with Indonesia, the Philippines, and India.[61] The European Union is still in negotiations with the Southern Common Market (Mercosur) and, while the text is nominally closed,[62] new additions or amendments are nonetheless expected, not least in the face of civil society criticism of rainforest management in Brazil and (perhaps entirely unrelated) vocal anxiety from Ireland and France over agricultural exports. Debate is ongoing as to the precise contours of changes that could or should be made to 'green' this agreement.[63] One change that has been called for is to ensure the Mercosur agreement aligns with the objective set out in the Commission's European Green Deal,[64] to include an MEA (the Paris

[57] This sui generis approach was rejected by the United Kingdom when it 'transitioned' EU FTAs following withdrawal from the European Union. An account of this is provided in 'Explanatory Memorandum on the Political, Free Trade and Strategic Partnership Agreement between the United Kingdom of Great Britain and Northern Ireland and Ukraine.' Command Paper No CP 312 (2020).

[58] Free Trade and Strategic Partnership Agreement between Ukraine and the United Kingdom of Great Britain and Northern Ireland (EU–Ukraine FTA), signed 4 May 2022, art 278.

[59] ibid.

[60] ibid art 278(4).

[61] An updated list is maintained by the European Commission at <https://policy.trade.ec.europa.eu/eu-trade-relationships-country-and-region/negotiations-and-agreements_en> accessed 1 May 2023.

[62] Texts are available at <https://policy.trade.ec.europa.eu/eu-trade-relationships-country-and-region/countries-and-regions/mercosur/eu-mercosur-agreement/text-agreement_en> accessed 1 May 2023.

[63] For a close reading of the draft see Javiera Cáceres and others, 'Environment and Climate Change in the Draft EU–Mercosur Trade Agreement' (CISDL 2021).

[64] Communication from the European Commission, 'The European Green Deal' COM (2019) 640 final.

Agreement) as an essential element for new FTAs. The inclusion of an essential elements clause lists principles or commitments that the parties consider to be a core underlying component of their agreement. Consequently, where an essential element is not met, the other party is able to suspend the agreement in whole or in part.[65] We find this innovation in the Trade and Cooperation Agreement (TCA) with the United Kingdom.[66]

The TCA includes the largest number of environmental commitments of any EU agreement thus far. However, in relation to MEAs, it adds only limited innovations outside of the 'essential elements' development.

Alongside the commitment to 'effectively' implement the MEAs that the parties have ratified,[67] the TCA makes explicit reference to the 'UN Environment Assembly (UNEA), of the UN Environment Programme (UNEP) and multilateral environmental governance and agreements as a response of the international community to global or regional environmental challenges and stress the need to enhance the mutual supportiveness between trade and environment policies, rules and measures'.[68] It also builds on pre-existing commitments to exchange information in relation to MEA ratification and implementation and provides additional details on information exchange in relation to ongoing MEA negotiations and 'each Party's respective views on becoming a party to additional [MEAs]'.[69]

As before, the parties 'reaffirm' their rights to 'adopt or maintain measures to further the objectives of multilateral environmental agreements' to which they are parties and 'recall' that such measures 'may be justified' under the exceptions provisions of the agreement.[70] The reaffirmation model here serves a different purpose than those in relation to existing commitments under MEAs, where the objective is to limit the impact of these 'external' commitments within the FTA—here the parties secure the policy space they expect within the environmental sphere without opening questions as to their position vis-à-vis GATT Articles XX(b) and (g) or their analogues under other FTAs.

The cooperation provisions do, however, develop one of the more interesting trends we have seen already, that is, the increasing sectorization of commitments under FTAs. In the TCA, we see an expansive list of areas where MEAs play a key role and the parties are to cooperate, including forestry management, biodiversity, fisheries, and climate.

The principal innovation is the inclusion, in line with new EU policy, of the 'fight against climate change' as an 'essential element' of the agreement.[71] More

[65] The EU use of 'essential elements' as a strategic device can be traced back to (at least) art 5 Lomé IV Convention 1989.

[66] Trade and Cooperation Agreement between the European Union and the United Kingdom, in force 1 May 2021.

[67] ibid XI, art 8.4(2).

[68] ibid XI, art 8.4(1).

[69] ibid XI, art 8.4(3).

[70] ibid XI, art 8.4(4).

[71] ibid art COMPROV.12.

detail is provided over the content of this 'fight', clarifying that this relates to commitments under the UNFCCC process, and in particular the Paris Agreement.[72] Thus, each party is required to both 'respect' the Paris Agreement and its process as well as 'refrain from acts or omissions that would materially defeat the object and purpose of the Paris Agreement'.[73]

Here we have a specific MEA being granted an enhanced role within the FTA. The practical implications of this are hard to determine. One can question the desirability of 'hardening' commitments under the UNFCCC process. The assumption is that the Paris Agreement system of nationally determined contributions (NDCs), whereby parties decide for themselves how they will meet targets, could be leveraged under an FTA, such as the TCA, in a way that was never envisaged under the Paris system and—one might argue—would never have been made had it been contemplated that NDCs could become hostages to fortune in a trade dispute. The layering of concerns is exacerbated when one applies this framing to a North–South agreement, such as EU–Mercosur.

Further, the extent to which the European Union (or indeed the United Kingdom) would consider suspending the agreement in whole or part because of a violation of this provision, and indeed, the extent of the violation necessary to trigger action under it, are open to discussion. The use of essential elements to suspend an agreement is largely considered academic but it does nonetheless serve a purpose.

First, as a safeguard against future behaviour ('known unknowns') it can be desirable to maintain options. Second, to improve the negotiability of such provisions with future FTA partners where concerns over climate policy may be greater (one imagines the Gulf Cooperation Council as an illustrative example). And third, to return to the origins of our analysis, to placate domestic constituencies, for whom these provisions are principally designed.

This section has flagged the risk that linking MEAs more closely to FTAs may have (not least if the enforcement mechanisms are retaliatory trade measures), especially for developing countries. And it is hard not to note the explicit transatlantic subject of analysis so far. This is in part a reflection of the realities of global FTA negotiations: the more powerful parties customarily table the first drafts, and their drafts are usually based on their last agreements. As such, we see many FTAs shaped by EU and US models. They are not, of course, the only active FTA negotiators.

[72] ibid art COMPROV.5.
[73] ibid.

IV. Developments Beyond the United States and European Union

The influence of the EU and US powers' approaches to drafting trade agreements is widespread. Not least when one party's model becomes regional, as in the case with the Comprehensive and Progressive Trans-Pacific Partnership (CPTPP), which retains its US-dominated textual heritage.

CPTPP includes MEA linkages, albeit somewhat obliquely. The definition of 'environmental law' under CPTPP is expansive and includes measures that implement obligations under MEAs.[74] This brings MEA *implementation* into the scope of the general commitments found in the agreement, including on non-application of environmental laws in a manner affecting trade or investment.[75]

This is coupled with the obligation to implement MEAs under Article 20.4. Thus, read together, these obligations cover both the implementation of an MEA and its subsequent ongoing application within the party (at least at the central government level).

We have noted the use of implicit or oblique references in FTAs to MEAs previously, and CPTPP is the more expansive example of this practice. Here we have a range of policy-specific provisions that either refer to the relevant MEA in the body of the text or, failing that, in a footnote.

For example: on the protection of the ozone a footnote makes cross-references to the Montreal Protocol;[76] on conservation and trade, CITES is explicitly acknowledged (though its scope is limited by the requirement that any violation be 'in a manner affecting trade or investment');[77] on the marine environment and ship pollution the footnotes cross-reference the International Convention for the Prevention of Pollution from Ships (MARPOL) convention;[78] and on sustainable fishing, again there are footnote references to the wider law of the sea and UN Food and Agriculture Organization regimes.[79] The provisions on fishing are of particular interest, given the willingness of the United States to pursue a dispute (subsequently resolved) under its FTA with Korea over the elimination of illegal, unreported, and unregulated (IUU) fishing in Korea.[80] The ongoing development of disciplines on IUU fishing at the WTO,[81] and elsewhere,[82] all speak to the importance of this sectoral concern.

[74] Comprehensive and Progressive Agreement for Trans-Pacific Partnership (CPTPP), in force 18 December 2018, art 20.1.
[75] ibid art 20.4.
[76] ibid art 20.5.
[77] ibid art 20.17.
[78] ibid art 20.6.
[79] ibid art 20.16(3), fn 12.
[80] USTR, 'USTR Welcomes Passage of Amendments to Korea's Distant Water Fisheries Development Act Following First Ever Environment Consultations under the United States–Korea Free Trade Agreement' *Press Release* (1 November 2019) <https://ustr.gov/about-us/policy-offices/press-office/press-releases/2019/november/ustr-welcomes-passage-amendments> accessed 1 May 2023.
[81] Agreement on Fisheries Subsidies (17 June 2022) WT/MIN(22)/W/22.
[82] Eg the FAO Agreement on Port State Measures to Prevent, Deter, and Eliminate Illegal, Unreported, and Unregulated (IUU) Fishing, in force 5 June 2016.

The influence of these key agreements can be seen elsewhere. Two CPTPP parties' (Peru and Australia) recent 2020 FTA follows a similar practice: the expected provisions on 'recognising' and 'reaffirming' implementation of MEAs[83] and more specific commitments made (oftentimes through footnotes for 'clarity') on biodiversity (art 19.4.3), climate (art 19.4.7), and illegal trade in flora/fauna (art 19.4.8). That said, there are some notable exceptions: the Regional Comprehensive Economic Partnership (RCEP) makes no reference to MEAs (or indeed, any other environmental obligations) and includes seven parties that are also parties to the CPTPP.[84]

We have interesting, albeit oblique, examples from South–South agreements. Though conservative expectations would be that these agreements include fewer (if any) links to MEAs, the picture is, in truth, more nuanced. For example, on trade in toxic chemicals the East African Community (EAC) Treaty requires that 'The Partner States undertake to ratify or accede to international environmental conventions that are designed to improve environmental policies and management.'[85] Though no explicit reference is made to a particular MEA, the Basel Convention looms large. Similarly, reference is made under Article 116(e) for the parties to ratify, accede to, and implement 'relevant international conventions' in relation to wildlife management. Again, there may be no explicit reference to an MEA but CITES is all but included.

Finally, when considering the influence of overlapping or different 'models' of FTAs, a special mention must be made of the United Kingdom, which is currently threading the two different EU and US traditions into its own agreements.[86] The United Kingdom 'transitioned' over 30 EU (now UK) FTAs that incorporate the substantive contours of the pre-existing EU agreements (including their approach to MEA linkage). However, with its accession to CPTPP,[87] the United Kingdom has also included CPTPP-like provisions in its new FTAs, most notably with Australia and New Zealand. And when examining new provisions on trade and environment, the UK–New Zealand FTA's chapter on environment (at 28 pages) is not short of either substance or enforceability.[88]

[83] Free Trade Agreement between Australia and the Republic of Peru, in force 11 February 2020, art 19.4.

[84] Regional Comprehensive Economic Partnership, in force 1 January 2022. The parties are Australia, Brunei Darussalam, Japan, Malaysia, New Zealand, Singapore, and Vietnam.

[85] Treaty for the Establishment of the East African Community, in force 7 July 2000, art 113.3.

[86] On the consequences of this tightrope act see Gregory Messenger, 'EU–UK Relations at the WTO: Towards Constructive Creative Competition' in Juan Santos Vara, Ramses A Wessell, and Polly R Pollack (eds), *Research Handbook on the International Dimensions of Brexit* (Routledge 2021) 135–47.

[87] The UK government announced that it had 'substantially' concluded negotiations to accede to CPTPP on 31 March 2023: <https://www.gov.uk/government/publications/comprehensive-and-progressive-agreement-for-trans-pacific-partnershipcptpp-conclusion-of-negotiations/conclusion-of-negotiations-on-the-accession-of-the-united-kingdom-of-great-britain-and-northern-ireland-to-the-comprehensive-and-progressive-trans-pac> accessed 1 May 2023.

[88] Free Trade Agreement between the United Kingdom of Great Britain and Northern Ireland and New Zealand, in force 31 May 2023, ch 22.

As in CPTPP, the UK–New Zealand FTA includes measures that implement MEAs within its definition of 'environmental laws', thus drawing these instruments into the general commitments, which include non-derogation and non-application.[89] Additionally, the parties also 'affirm' their commitment to implement the MEAs to which they are parties.[90] Further detail is given in relation to MEAs concerned with climate change, in particular the Paris Agreement.

The expansive use of MEAs to buttress provisions with the FTA on biological diversity (drawing on CITES) or marine pollution (drawing on MARPOL) continues.[91] Further steps are taken, however. On cooperation in relation to the protection of the ozone layer, the standard reference to the Montreal Protocol is made,[92] but additionally, the parties are instructed to build on these commitments and go further: 'pursue a more ambitious phase-down of hydrofluorocarbons; and endeavour to reduce the use of pre-charged equipment containing hydrofluorocarbons'.[93] This instruction to build on existing MEAs, through an FTA as a link—and hook—is an intriguing development building on the dynamic potential of agreements we have seen previously. This is a way to encourage a more evolutive approach to FTA–MEA linkage, where the FTA is leveraged to support ongoing efforts in areas where the parties share interests.

This is most notable in relation to fossil fuel subsidies, where the parties make commitments to limit the use of such measures,[94] but, most importantly for our purposes, to 'cooperate bilaterally and in relevant international fora such as the WTO, UNFCCC, and G20 in relation to fossil fuel subsidy reform and the transition to clean energy'.[95] This is echoed in relation to policy on fisheries subsidies, where the parties agree to 'cooperate bilaterally, regionally, and in international fora'.[96]

With the proliferation of FTAs, no longer only by the United States and European Union but by other individual WTO Members and blocs, we see an increase in the imaginative use of linkages between MEAs and FTAs. Though the links may be oblique, it appears that interest is not in FTAs 'incorporating' MEAs' obligations, but instead finding ways to divide labour and draw on each other's normative and institutional frameworks.

[89] On definitions see ibid art 22.1; on general commitments see ibid art 22.4.
[90] ibid art 22.5:2.
[91] ibid arts 22.12 and 22.16 respectively.
[92] ibid art 22.14.
[93] ibid art 22.14:2.
[94] ibid art 22.8.
[95] ibid art 22.8:3.
[96] ibid art 22.9:16.

V. Reflecting on Developments: Dynamic Implementation, Sectoral Specialization, and 'Diplomatic' Dispute Settlement

This contribution has examined a cross-section of FTAs, considering the ways in which the legal continents of trade law and international environmental law have been linked over the decades through treaty text—sometimes by an explicit naming, at other times by an oblique reference. There are three themes that merit revisiting here.

The first is the nature of the dynamic elements within FTAs. These are provisions that allow the parties to increase or amend the scope of MEAs that are linked to the FTA. These provisions can be found as far back as NAFTA[97] and as recently as in the EU–Andean Community FTA.[98] The structures of such mechanisms vary, sometimes allowing for considerable delegated decision-making.[99] The point to note here is that, even in the case of older agreements, should the parties wish to, there may well be scope for an imaginative solution to challenges they may face in the existing structures of their agreements, absent the need to renegotiate or 'modernize' their FTAs. It requires will and political capital, but it can be done. The challenge for lawyers is that it is not our domain; this is fundamentally the task of the trade diplomat, leveraging lawyers' skills rather than being led by them.[100]

The second relates to a wider trend in trade law: the sectoral specialization of disciplines. As we move from the comparative successes of rules of general application (such as non-discrimination) and the gains from broad brush liberalization (particularly in relation to tariffs), the drive to focus on specific technical problems has increased. We see how technical barriers to trade increasingly need sectoral or product-specific solutions (and hence the use of annexes on autos or marine equipment in FTAs). Similarly, the challenges faced by the environment are varied and rooted in particular geographies, ecosystems, and practices. So too the linkages with MEAs move away from a general list (as we saw in the early NAFTA models) to disaggregated references that appear in different policy areas, from protection of flora and fauna, to hazardous waste and ozone gas.[101] Sectorization presents specific discrete challenges for trade law, which has in part been able to base itself on general legal principles of common use, rather than the technical challenges found in engaging with regulatory regimes at a granular level. It is here that practices of regulatory diplomacy are key: supporting inter-regulatory dialogues and structures.[102]

[97] NAFTA (n 9).

[98] EU–Andean Community FTA (n 52).

[99] One might note the role of the Trade Committee in the UK–Ukraine FTA (n 58) under art 404, which consolidates a number of roles from the EU–Ukraine DCFTA's Association Council and Association Committee and can make amendments and additions to annexes under art 404(7).

[100] On trade diplomacy see n 42.

[101] See n 94ff.

[102] On regulatory diplomacy see n 42.

The third, and linked, theme is the role of compliance, which necessarily entails an association with the *effective* use of a dispute settlement mechanism. Here we are confronted with a tension, visible throughout the provisions examined here but also across the trade–labour–environment triad: should we seek to use the mechanisms (including remedies or sanctions) of trade law to enforce commitments under other agreements? Litigation is always rare, and TSD commitments under FTAs are no exception.[103] But we do have examples (as we have noted here) of disputes beginning under FTAs. And the filing of the claim, the escalation, is often sufficient to secure compliance or buy-in from policy actors higher up the chain. We should be sensitive to the dynamic that takes place in trade law disputes: in nearly all cases, economic actors petition governments to escalate disputes. It is the art of commercial diplomacy to support those actors in such a way that they can be successful without having to escalate to the inter-state level.[104] But here, in the case of MEAs, while there will be organized economic interests (the traditional fear of the 'race to the bottom'), legitimate civil society voices are also at play. Our traditional systems, linking commitments crudely, patching them into the 'traditional' trade agreement, seem less appropriate.

Given the shift in focus to FTA implementation in many quarters, it is important to consider how we can best use trade agreements to support MEAs to avoid them becoming tools of this crude enforcement. If we look to some of the best examples of what could be done, it is not by formally linking commitments between two treaties (ie at the normative level); it is instead at the socio-institutional level, enabling diplomats and officials to work with regulators, their counterparts, and non-governmental actors, within a framework created by FTAs, to support the aims of each set of agreements.

[103] On their use to date see n 47.
[104] On commercial diplomacy see n 42.

11

Exploring the Nexus of Environmental Sustainability and International Trade

The Significance of Self-Standing Obligations

Maria Panezi[*]

I. Introduction

Trade expansion, strong trade connections, and trade openness exhibit a direct association with environmental degradation,[1] mostly due to the emissions embedded in traded goods. Trade can thus be a key multiplier of environmental degradation.[2] The relationship between trade and environmental policy concerns harbours a fundamental tension: while environmental protection is identified as possibly the most common collectively shared policy preference,[3] the prevalent discourse is not one of ensuring that trade does not cause more harm to the environment, but instead one of the desires for the two regimes to be 'mutually supportive'.[4] The link between trade and the environment is articulated in international trade agreements in the form of preambular and substantive provisions that relate to environmental obligations, environmental policy exceptions to trade rules or trade, and environment chapters. In fact, these provisions have proliferated to such an extent that they can be categorized and catalogued in several different ways.

* The author would like to thank Emily Hepditch for the excellent research assistance and the participants to the Authors' Workshop for the Sustainability Revolution in International Trade Agreements and Geraldo Vidigal and Kathleen Claussen for many helpful comments and suggestions. The usual disclaimer applies.

[1] Thai-Ha Le, Youngho Chang, and Donghyun Park, 'Trade Openness and Environmental Quality: International Evidence' (2016) 92 Energy Policy 45, 55.

[2] Maria Panezi, 'Special and Differential Treatment: The Relationship between Environment, Development and Trade' in Michael Faure (ed), *Elgar Encyclopedia of Environmental Law* (Edward Elgar Publishing 2023) 775, 782.

[3] Pascal Lamy, 'The Slow American Perfectionist Turn' (*CEPR*, 27 March 2023). <https://cepr.org/voxeu/columns/slow-american-protectionist-turn> accessed 22 May 2023.

[4] José-Antonio Monteiro, 'Typology of Environment-Related Provisions in Regional Trade Agreements' (2016) WTO Staff Working Paper <https://www.wto.org/english/res_e/reser_e/ersd201613_e.pdf> accessed 22 May 2023.

Maria Panezi, *Exploring the Nexus of Environmental Sustainability and International Trade* In: *The Sustainability Revolution in International Trade Agreements.* Edited by: Geraldo Vidigal and Kathleen Claussen, Oxford University Press.
© Maria Panezi 2024. DOI: 10.1093/9780191994470.003.0011

This chapter will discuss one type of these obligations, specifically, 'self-standing' environmental obligations in trade agreements. This conversation will centre on comprehending the characterization of self-standing obligations, specifically with respect to their essence and purpose as they are incorporated in trade agreements. These provisions are deemed independent and can function separately from the trade agreement's overall framework, as articulated in the agreement's text or as they operate in practice. The chapter will argue that understanding the nature of self-standing environmental obligations is crucial for effectively assessing their impact on trade and environmental policy.

The proliferation of such provisions in trade agreements can have diverse outcomes, indicating either the consolidation or the diffusion of environmental policy preferences relating to trade. If the inclusion of self-standing obligations in trade agreements leads to trade disputes or triggers legal reforms for one of the involved parties, this result signifies a consolidation of the environmental regime, rather than its diffusion. This meaningful integration or dispute resolution, coupled with the proliferation of such obligations, results in a strengthening and solidifying of the transnational environmental regulatory framework.

Conversely, when self-standing obligations proliferate in trade agreements but remain inactive or dormant for an extended period, they result in a diffusion of the environment regime, leading to fragmentation and weakened environmental governance. The lack of implementation or enforcement of these obligations leads to a dispersed and fragmented landscape, where the intended environmental standards and policies fail to materialize.

To ensure that the inclusion of environmental policies within trade agreements is meaningful, it is essential to strike a balance between their inclusion, enforcement, and timely implementation to foster a consolidated and coherent framework for sustainable trade practices. Pragmatism during negotiations, a combination of rights, duties, and cooperative platforms, and innovation through intersectional approaches in the design and the interpretation of self-standing environmental provisions can contribute to the consolidation of the trade and environment regime.

This chapter will proceed as follows: section II will present an examination of the categories of environmental provisions found within trade agreements, drawing upon pertinent academic literature. Section III will discuss the possible meanings of 'self-standing' environmental obligations in trade agreements. Section IV will then analyse procedural and institutional obligations that can be characterized as 'self-standing'. Section V examines the self-standing nature of provisions as they relate to dispute settlement, enforcement, and trade remedies. Section VI will briefly look at environmental provisions and agreements at the World Trade Organization (WTO). Finally, I will discuss the global governance dimensions of the inclusion of environment provisions in trade agreements, specifically the consolidation and diffusion potential, and offer some concluding thoughts.

II. Typology of Environmental Policy Provisions in Trade Agreements

The relationship between trade and environmental policy is not new. One of the earliest and also cardinal examples of this relationship is the 1947 General Agreement on Tariffs and Trade (GATT), which contains rules that allow for policy space for the environment. The most obvious GATT rule is Article XX(g), which articulates a policy exception for derogation from the main rules for reasons relating to the conservation of exhaustible natural resources.[5] The 1992 European Economic Area agreement included a version of the precautionary principle,[6] while the North American Free Trade Agreement (NAFTA) contained the first robust side agreement on trade and the environment, setting an ambitious threshold at this time that contributed to mainstreaming trade and environment chapters in subsequent bilateral and free trade agreements (FTAs).[7] The ensuing deceleration in multilateral outcomes at the WTO and the proliferation of FTAs outside the multilateral regime have resulted in strengthening the links between trade and the environment, with positive effects on international environmental governance.

One classification[8] identifies three different periods in the evolution of environmental provisions in FTAs. The first period was before 1992, when barely any economic agreements included environmental policy references.[9] The second period was between 1992 and 2005, where the numbers of environmental provisions in trade agreements increased slightly, but the inclusion of such provisions appeared only in preambles or, in a way similar to Article XX(g), as exceptions. An outlier was NAFTA, an early and principal example of the change in the structure of these provisions, including institutional and dispute settlement provisions in the side agreement.[10] Finally, the most recent period, spanning from 2005 to the present, has witnessed a notable trend in the proliferation of FTAs. This surge in FTAs has been accompanied by a quantitative and qualitative increase in environmental provisions, including provisions with rights and obligations for the parties instead of just environmental exceptions like GATT XX(g).[11] As a result, this inclusion

[5] See for a discussion Peter H Sand, 'The Evolution of International Environmental Law' in Daniel Bodansky, Jutta Brunnée, and Ellen Hey (eds), *The Oxford Handbook of International Environmental Law* (OUP 2012).

[6] And even earlier, about the inclusion of the precautionary principle in the 1980s see Philippe Sands, 'The "Greening" of International Law: Emerging Principles and Rules' (1994) Indiana Journal of Global Legal Studies 293.

[7] Interestingly, the 2011 World Trade Report says that NAFTA put environmental considerations on a pedestal. *World Trade Report, 2011: The WTO and Preferential Trade Agreements: From Co-Existence to Coherence* (WTO 2011) 46.

[8] Monteiro (n 4) 6.

[9] See Sands (n 6) 3; Monteiro (n 4) 6.

[10] Jean-Frédéric Morin and Corentin Bialais, 'Strengthening Multilateral Environmental Governance through Bilateral Trade Deals' (2018).

[11] US trade laws throughout the 2000s have required the inclusion of environmental provisions in all FTAs negotiated by the United States, and there are similar trends with the European Union and Canada.

of environmental clauses has resulted in the production of a large volume of academic literature that systematically documents and analyses these provisions.[12]

Environmental provisions within FTAs can be categorized based on their placement within the agreement. Firstly, provisions can be found within the main text of the FTA. In this context, they may appear in the preamble, as part of an article seemingly unrelated to the environment, as a specific article or provision addressing environmental matters, or within a dedicated chapter on environment and trade, or sustainable development and trade. Alternatively, these provisions may be located in the annexes of the FTA. Secondly, environmental provisions can be included as part of a supplementary document or protocol accompanying the agreement. Similar to the previous category, they might be present in the preamble, within an article that does not primarily pertain to the environment, as a specific article or provision dealing explicitly with environmental issues, or as part of a dedicated chapter on the environment. Lastly, environmental provisions can be established through a dedicated trade and environment document that supplements the FTA. These additional documents can take the form of a side letter, joint statement, memorandum of understanding, or side agreement specifically addressing environmental policies.[13]

Environmental provisions can further be classified based on their comprehensiveness in terms of content and their characteristics in relation to their nature, scope, and language. Regarding content, three categories can be identified:

1. Preambular aspirations, objectives, and cooperation: these parts encompass broad language and outline the overall objectives of the agreement, often expressing the commitment to environmental sustainability and conservation. Preambular references can be found in more than 40 per cent of FTAs.[14] Environmental principles can also appear in the first chapter, where the objectives of the FTA are outlined. Their enforcement strength is limited. Cooperation provisions highlight the importance of collaboration between the parties in areas such as scientific research, capacity building, technology transfer, and information sharing, aiming to enhance environmental protection and sustainable development.[15]
2. Substantive provisions: these can include domestic environmental legislation, ensuring that parties have the right to adopt environmental regulations, or instituting a commitment for parties to implement certain regulations.

[12] Such as the TREND database, which identifies nearly 300 different types of environmental provisions in 730 trade agreements, see 'Trade and Environment Database' (*Canada Research Chair in International Political Economy*, 2022) <https://www.chaire-epi.ulaval.ca/en/trend> accessed 20 April 2024; and more generally on FTAs see 'Design of Trade Agreements (DESTA) Database' <https://www.designoftradeagreements.org/> accessed 20 April 2024.

[13] Monteiro (n 4) 9.

[14] ibid 19, 21.

[15] ibid 74, 79.

This includes a wide range of subcategories such as technical barriers to trade, sanitary and phytosanitary measures, environmental impact assessments, voluntary mechanisms, pollution control measures, biodiversity conservation, and ecosystem management. These provisions generally have stronger enforcement potential and contain concrete obligations, due to their specific wording. These can also include multilateral environmental agreements (MEAs) referring to the integration of commitments derived from existing international environmental treaties or agreements into the FTA. These provisions aim to ensure compliance with MEAs, either by reaffirming the commitment to the MEA or by adopting specific implementation obligations, or commitments regarding the accession or ratification of MEAs.[16] The provisions reaffirming a commitment to MEAs, while self-standing, do not have a strong implementation dimension on their own; provisions requiring parties to sign, ratify, or implement MEAs have a stronger enforcement profile. Further subcategories include intellectual property rights;[17] environmental goods and services;[18] and natural resource management.[19] Depending on how substantive provisions are structured and whether each obligation in the agreement is self-standing (ie can be implemented as is, without the need for an additional entry into force of rules external to the agreement to either the domestic legal framework or an MEA), these provisions can be further classified as: a) dependent-based on the incorporation of other mechanisms, or b) self-standing obligations.

3. Institutional, dispute-related, and environmental governance provisions: provisions pertaining to environmental governance address issues related to the establishment of effective environmental institutions, mechanisms, or bodies responsible for overseeing and implementing commitments (including environment and trade commitments) under the FTA[20] and transparency provisions with respect to environmental policy, practices, laws and management, public participation, access to justice, and procedural fairness.[21] These also include mechanisms for consultation and dispute resolution, either specifically related to environmental matters, or general dispute settlement that also applies to the environmental provisions.[22]

Morin and Bialais discuss the normative strength these references acquire in different texts, such as interpretative context, rules of conflict or hierarchy, obligations

[16] ibid 45, 52; see also infra.
[17] ibid 52, 55.
[18] ibid 57, 60.
[19] ibid 60, 68. In this category are also included fisheries and climate change. For Fisheries discussion see section VI.
[20] ibid 79, 86.
[21] ibid 68, 73.
[22] ibid 94, 103; Morin and Bialais (n 10) 3.

in MEAs and trade agreements, and others. Elsewhere,[23] Morin and Nadeau offer another typology of environmental provision in trade agreements: 'those directly addressing the trade and environment interplay; those related to development and fairness; those related to domestic environmental standards; and those related to domestic and international institutions'. They also attempt to locate not just the most prevalent environmental provisions but also the most innovative ones. Elsewhere, Morin and others discuss 'novel' clauses. Lastly, a distinction is made between exception provisions and others characterized as 'affirmative options'.[24]

The observed advancements in environmental provisions within trade agreements can be attributed to the relatively small number of the participating parties. Consensus is much easier to achieve in bilateral and regional fora. Many chapters under 'trade and the environment' titles as well as specific provisions mandating obligations, information exchange, and cooperation commitments have been incorporated into the extensive array of FTAs signed by various countries and will continue to increase in number and scope.

III. What is a 'Self-Standing' Obligation? Terminology and Boundary Conditions

The notion of a 'self-standing' environmental obligation in FTAs is not as straightforward and needs to be further explored to define it and delineate its content. This section outlines the possible interpretations of the term and scenarios that can further nuance the characterization of an environmental provision as 'self-standing'.

One meaning of a 'self-standing' environmental obligation could be that a trade violation does not need to be established for the environmental obligation to be triggered. Put simply, a violation can result in a breach of the FTA, caused by action that substantively does not relate to traditionally understood trade-related activities, rights, and obligations. If this is what is meant by self-standing, then any inclusion of environmental policy as a defence in a 'general exceptions' chapter, or as an exception clause attached to a specific trade obligation, is not self-standing. This is because a violation needs to first be established of the main rule in order to even consider the exception. Thus, an example of the opposite of a self-standing obligation would be Article XX (b) and (g) of the GATT, which can only be invoked defensively once a breach has been established somewhere else in the GATT. This distinction was articulated by the arbitration panel in *Ukraine—Wood Export Ban*. There, the panel said that 'the Arbitration Panel finds that the provisions of

[23] Jean-Frédéric Morin and Rosalie Gauthier Nadeau, 'Environmental Gems in Trade Agreements Little-known Clauses for Progressive Trade Agreements' CIGI Papers No 148 (2017).

[24] Katrin Kuhlmann (ed), *Handbook on Provisions and Options for Inclusive and Sustainable Development in Trade Agreements* (United Nations Publications 2023).

Chapter 13 are *not self-standing or unqualified exceptions* that could justify measures that are per se in breach of Article 35 of the [agreement]'.[25]

A second meaning of a self-standing obligation is that the reference in the FTA is to the internal environmental law of the parties, and an obligation to comply with it or reform domestic legislation, which can be violated without the trade agreement being violated (if parties do not comply with their domestic laws), thus it is independent from any of the trade rights and obligations, yet still referenced in the FTA.[26] Gracia Marin Durán describes 'minimum-level' clauses that are not expressly linked to trade or investment, and thus their violation can be established 'even when there are *no* direct effects on bilateral trade (or investment)'.[27] As an example, she provides the EU–Singapore FTA, Article 12.2 (1), which reads as follows:

> Right to Regulate and Levels of Protection: 1. The Parties recognise the right of each Party to establish its own levels of environmental and labour protection, and to adopt or modify its relevant laws and policies accordingly, consistent with the principles of the internationally recognised standards or agreements to which it is party, referred to in Articles 12.3 (Multilateral Labour Standards and Agreements) and 12.6 (Multilateral Environmental Standards and Agreements).

The language in this and other similar 'minimum-level' clauses, however, appears to be similar, with the wording of the clause found to not be self-standing by the panel in *Ukraine—Wood Export Ban*. Here, the *direct effect on trade* needs to be decoupled from the notion of a 'self-standing' obligation. The key distinguishing factor is in the term 'qualified' that the panel used in *Ukraine—Wood Export Ban*. While a provision may not have a direct effect on trade, if it is contingent, for it to apply, on compliance with MEAs or other external agreements or rules (such as labour or environmental standards, domestic environmental rules), then it is not 'self-standing'.

Similar to the second, the third possible meaning of a free-standing obligation includes a reference made to an MEA, whose breach can also be established regardless of the trade agreement. Depending on the language in the FTA, the violation of

[25] Final Report of the Panel established pursuant to art 307 of the Association Agreement between the European Union and Ukraine, 16 January 2019, para 251, repeated passim. The *Ukraine—Wood Export Ban* case addressed the complainant's claim that 'the "right to regulate" recognised in Article 290(1) of the [Association Agreement] must be exercised in accordance with the requirements of other provisions of the [Agreement] that give expression and operationalise the "right to regulate", including the policy exceptions mentioned in Article 36 of the AA' and thus it is *not self-standing*. ibid, para 75. See also on the case Geraldo Vidigal, 'Regional Trade Adjudication and the Rise of Sustainability Disputes: *Korea—Labor Commitments* and *Ukraine—Wood Export Bans*' (2022) 116(3) American Journal of International Law 567.

[26] Gracia Marín Durán, 'Sustainable Development Chapters in EU Free Trade Agreements: Emerging Compliance Issues' (2020) 57(4) Common Market Law Review, 6–7.

[27] ibid 6.

the MEA may not carry any significant consequences in the MEA framework but can carry consequences based on the FTA language. FTAs can contain obligations that are directly linked to MEAs. Those links can take three forms:

1) the MEA is not affected at all by the FTA (usually articulated in language such as 'nothing in this . . . shall limit the authority of each party to take [action] consistent with/implementing [the MEA]').
2) MEA obligations are included in the exceptions section, or exception clauses of individual articles or chapters. For example, Article 292.3 of the EU–Ukraine FTA under 'MEAs' notes that 'Nothing in this Agreement shall limit the rights of a Party to adopt or maintain measures to implement the MEAs to which it is a Party. Such measures shall not be applied in a manner which would constitute a means of arbitrary or unjustifiable discrimination between the Parties or a disguised restriction on trade.'[28] This wording is arguably different than traditional Article XX GATT-style exceptions.
3) There is explicit language to determine that in cases of conflict or inconsistency between the MEA and the FTA, the MEA shall prevail, such as happened in NAFTA (conflicts clauses).[29]

In cases (1) and (3), the environmental obligations are self-standing. In the first case, the environmental obligations are separate from the FTA itself and continue to operate notwithstanding the trade obligations.[30] In the third case, the two sets of obligations (trade and environment) are generally symbiotic. Absent conflicts, each can be seen as 'self-standing'. However, the FTA provision must be set aside when there is a conflict. The normative strength that the MEA has based on this prioritization leads to its characterization as 'self-standing' that survives after the conflict while the same does not happen for the FTA provision. Under the 'exception' scenario (2), the two provisions are dependent. The MEA compliance is used as an exception, in case of any derogation from the FTA obligation. It is further qualified usually in the way of the Article XX GATT chapeau.

In the pursuit of examining the limitations that define a 'self-standing' obligation, we should consider two more scenarios. The first one is the withdrawal of all FTA parties from the MEA. It is not clear whether the FTA reference and obligation survive the withdrawal. If the content of the MEA rules is re-articulated in the FTA, and reference is made to the MEA, then arguably, the substance of the MEA obligations survive the withdrawal and that can contribute to the characterization of the obligations as 'self-standing'. The MEA obligations can continue inter partes

[28] Association Agreement between the European Union and the European Atomic Energy Community and their Member States and Ukraine, in force 1 September 2017, art 292.3.
[29] Monteiro (n 4) 52, 55.
[30] See Chapter 12 in this volume.

to the FTA. A last hypothetical scenario is that of a provision that contains the obligation of a party (or both) to accede, ratify, or implement the MEA as part of their FTA obligations. Subsequently withdrawing from the MEA, or repealing the national implementation framework, can constitute a breach of the FTA itself.

A more genuine form of a 'self-standing' obligation, without external references to domestic or international environmental law, would be a provision in the trade agreement containing a novel environmental commitment, which can potentially exist elsewhere but does not refer to any external rules. Thus, the provision creates a self-standing commitment whose legitimacy (and legality) stems directly from the trade agreement. Any duplicate external legislation, if it is not referenced in the FTA, can potentially be revoked, but the FTA obligation can continue to be in force. This approach would be related to pacta sunt servanta and the consensus that established the trade agreement. If litigated, then the obligation can exist independently and produce its own results, such as new interpretations.

IV. Procedural and Institutional Self-Standing Obligations

Another set of self-standing provisions discuss cooperation between the parties, and institutional provisions, which set up new environment-related monitoring or cooperation-related committees. Additionally, obligations to ensure transparency, independence of agencies, and other similar rule of law safeguards directly tied to environmental regulations can be fully self-standing if they are only located in the environment chapter or attached to an environmental provision.

One unique example of a self-standing environmental obligation that relates to the independence of an agency established by an FTA was the issue of the Organismo Superivor de los Recursos Forestales Maderables/Agency for Supervision of Forest Resources and Wildlife (OSINFOR) under the US–Peru Trade Promotion Agreement (TPA).[31] A primary policy objective of this agreement was to address and resolve the issue of illegal logging. As a result, Annex 18.3.4 on Forest Sector Governance was adopted. Interestingly, the Annex, as per footnote 13, is subject to dispute settlement, only after the pursuit of consultations under Article 18.12.1–3. Under the Annex, Peru was obligated to establish OSINFOR. OSINFOR 'shall be an independent and separate agency and its mandate shall include supervision of verification of all timber concessions and permits'.[32] In 2018, the Peruvian government approved Supreme Decree No 122-2018 PCM moving OSINFOR from the Presidency of the Council of Ministers to the

[31] United States–Peru Trade Promotion Agreement, in force 1 February 2009.
[32] ibid annex 18.3.4 para 3(h)(iii).

Ministry of Environment.[33] This move made OSINFOR's independence (which included an independent budget) questionable. No other violation seemed to be occurring, other than the potential for the lack of independence of OSINFOR.

Under the US–Peru TPA, there are two types of recourses for violations. One is bilateral, under Article 18.12 1–3. Parties can request consultations to resolve matters arising out of the Environment Chapter. Secondly, under the TPA, the two parties have established a Secretariat for Submissions of Environmental Enforcement Matters under the TPA,[34] where any person or party can file a submission regarding matters that stem from the TPA. In 2019, immediately after OSINFOR's move under the Peruvian Ministry of Environment, the United States requested consultations under Article 18.12.1 and the Kené Institute of Forestry and Environmental Studies, submitted a claim before the Secretariat for Submissions of Environmental Enforcement Matters.[35] The two mechanisms are not mutually exclusive. Eventually, a few months later the matter was resolved through consultations, the legislation by Peru was withdrawn, and OSINFOR remains an independent agency.[36]

It is noteworthy that the OSINFOR case did not relate to any trade violations. The article itself, ensuring the independence of an environmental agency, is an institutional and rule-of-law-related provision that can have spill-over effects. The enforcement of environmental regulations by an independent agency will combat illegal trade in forestry goods, which will be beneficial to all the trading entities that engage in legal trade. But more importantly, regulating the legal trade in lumber can be done in a manner that respects environmental policy and principles. This is a key example of a self-standing environmental obligation.

The US–Peru TPA Secretariat for Submissions of Environmental Enforcement Matters[37] is a key example of a mechanism that promotes such self-standing environmental obligations. There are several types of legal avenues for the enforcement of environmental rules in Peru. These exist under administrative, civil, constitutional, and criminal law. The Secretariat is only one additional mechanism, which can work in parallel with all the aforementioned domestic avenues on the same subject matter.[38] In fact, the Secretariat can work in parallel to the Article 18.12

[33] Yilly Vanessa Pacheco Restrepo, 'Enforcement Practice Under Preferential Trade Agreements: Environmental Consultations and Submissions on Environmental Enforcement Matters in the US-Peru TPA' (2019) 46(3) Legal Issues of Economic Integration 247, 249.

[34] Memorandum of Understanding (MOU) between the Government of the United States of America, The Government of the Republic of Peru, and the General Secretariat of the Organization of American States Regarding a Secretariat for Submissions on Environmental Enforcement Matters under the United States–Peru Trade Promotion Agreement, in force 9 June 2015.

[35] Restrepo (n 33).

[36] Pablo Peña, 'Could a Trade Agreement Strengthen the Enforcement of Domestic Environmental Laws? Envisioning the Impacts of the US–Peru Environmental Submissions Mechanism' (2023) 32(3) Review of European, Comparative & International Environmental Law 1, 6.

[37] Secretariat for Submission on Environmental Enforcement Measures, <https://www.saca-seem.org/en/secretariat/> accessed 20 April 2024.

[38] Peña (n 36) 3.

bilateral state-to-state consultation mechanism. While under Article 18.8 (4) of the TPA, the Secretariat can consider whether domestic legal remedies have been pursued, this fact is only weighed and not a pre-requisite for the pursuit of the Secretariat mechanism, reinforcing the self-standing nature of the mechanism itself.

V. Enforcement, Sanctions, Dispute Settlement, and Self-Standing Obligations

The normative force of the environmental provisions can relate to their nature as 'self-standing'. The type of dispute settlement attached to the environmental provisions, as well as the consequences of breach, or the possibility of suspending trade concessions because of having determined the occurrence of a breach, can each further nuance the provisions' normative force. First, the environmental provisions or chapter can be covered by the dispute settlement provisions without any other qualifications.[39] One such example is the US–Peru TPA where the Dispute Settlement Chapter applies to the Environment Chapter.

Second, an environmental provision is subject to environment-specific dispute settlement provisions (which can be a combination of the dispute settlement chapter and more specific provisions).[40] Tailoring dispute settlements specifically to address trade and environmental concerns indicates a stronger commitment to environmental governance. Administratively, this fine-tuning comes at a higher cost. Parties are more committed to ensuring that decisions relating to trade and the environment are taken by experts in *both* fields. Parties thus make efforts to avoid a narrower trade-oriented interpretation of FTA rules without meaningful engagement with the environmental dimensions of the agreements. An example is the US–Chile FTA where in Article 19.7 the Agreement provides for a specific Environment Roster for disputes that arise under the Environment Chapter.[41] Determining which of the two aforementioned models contributes to the normative strength, independence, and characterization as self-standing of the environment provisions is not straightforward. Each agreement, its context, the national legal frameworks with respect to the environment, and the actual content of specific obligations have a much larger significance in determining normative strength.

The possibility of suspending concessions in cases of non-compliance findings for environmental provisions is another dimension of enforceability. Effective remedies in a trade agreement necessarily include the suspension of concessions.

[39] Monteiro (n 4) 99.
[40] Monteiro (n 4) 99.
[41] United States–Chile Free Trade Agreement, in force 1 January 2004.

While it is reasonable to exclude suspension in cases where the cooperation chapters or articles are not fully implemented, the same does not apply to more substantive environmental obligations. If environmental obligations are subject to dispute settlement but the only outcome is a determination of violation without any meaningful remedies, then the normative strength of the environmental provisions is weak. While the normative strength is not *the* determinative factor of the 'self-standing' nature of the environmental obligations, it must be factored in. Stronger enforcement potential, including remedies in the form of suspension of concessions, contributes to the characterization of an environmental obligation as self-standing.

An additional aspect that highlights the independent or self-standing nature of an environmental obligation within a trade agreement is the potential ramifications that ensue *for the FTA itself* from a violation of such an environmental stance from an international law dimension. If the breach of an environmental obligation is a material breach as it is understood under Article 60 of the Vienna Convention on the Law of Treaties[42] (VCLT) and results in termination or suspension of the operation of a treaty due to that breach alone, then the obligation in question is self-standing.

One critical example of language that references Article 60 of the VCLT is the European New Green Deal. [43] In the EU Green Deal policy, trade sanctions are contemplated in case of non-compliance only as a matter of last resort in instances of *serious* violations of the Paris Agreement.[44] An example of the incorporation of this policy is Article 26.16 of the EU–New Zealand FTA, where temporary remedies become possible if a panel finds that 'the Party complained against failed to refrain from any action or omission that materially defeats the object and purpose of the Paris Agreement'.[45] Furthermore, under the conditions set out in Article 26.16 paragraph 3, it is possible that a party, for violations relating to the object and purpose of the Paris Agreement by the other party, can suspend the application of obligations.

A similar provision establishing a self-standing obligation of a procedural nature appears in Article 2(3) of the Environmental Cooperation Agreement (ECA)[46]

[42] Vienna Convention on the Law of Treaties, in force 27 January 1980.

[43] See also Chapter 12 in this volume.

[44] Commission to the European Parliament, The Council, The European Economic and Social Committee, and the Committee of the Regions, 'The power of trade partnerships: together for green and just economic growth' COM (2022) 409 final 11.

[45] Free Trade Agreement between the European Union and New Zealand, in force 1 May 2024, art 26.16 [2 a(ii)–(b)(ii)]. This can be understood similarly to the notion of 'self-contained' remedies as it articulated in *United States Diplomatic and Consular Staff in Tehran* (*U.S. v. Iran*), 1980 ICJ Reports 3 (24 May) para 83.

[46] Agreement on Environmental Cooperation among the Governments of the United States of America, the United Mexican States, and Canada, in force 1 July 2020.

signed with the United States–Mexico–Canada Agreement (CUSMA).[47] The ECA provides:

> The Commission will continue to operate under the modalities in place as of entry into force of this Agreement [. . .]. If there is an inconsistency between these modalities and the provisions of this Agreement, the provisions of this Agreement shall prevail.

Such language, which in case of conflict prioritizes an environmental agreement that is attached to a trade agreement, further contributes to its characterization as self-standing. CUSMA, just like the US–Peru TPA, in Article 24.27 (3)(c) does not require the exhaustion of domestic private remedies but simply a demonstration of efforts to do so, which arguably contributes to the independent nature of the rights and obligations under the CUSMA's Environment Chapter.

The 'geography' of self-standing obligations can be an interesting dimension with respect to the characterization of rules. Preamble and general objectives chapters are not likely to contain self-standing obligations. Substantive chapters (market access, services, intellectual property, procurement) can all contain self-standing environmental obligations. Carveouts, or the prioritization of MEAs in the case of conflict are also self-standing, while references to the environment in exceptions' chapters, general provisions, or article-specific exceptions are not. Institutional provisions, to the extent that they contain concrete obligations (and can be breached), can also be self-standing. The same applies to rule-of-law-type and transparency provisions. The types of dispute settlement and remedies can contribute to the nature of an obligation as self-standing.

VI. Self-Standing Environmental Obligations and the Multilateral Trading System

Technically, the GATT does not contain any self-standing obligations. Instead, it includes references in its preamble to concepts such as sustainable development, the use of exhaustible natural resources, and the protection of animal, plant, and human life and health. These references serve as defensive provisions (exceptions) to be invoked only in cases where a violation of another article has been established. In contrast, certain recent agreements, such as the Agreement on Fisheries Subsidies, possess a distinct environmental dimension and potentially establish independent and specific environmental obligations.[48] Additionally, the

[47] Agreement between the United States of America, the United Mexican States, and Canada, in force 1 July 2020.

[48] Ngozi Okonjo-Iweala, 'The WTO'S Contribution to the Challenges of Global Commons' (2023) 26(1) Journal of International Economic Law 12, 15.

Government Procurement Agreement (GPA) of 2014 features an article with environmental implications.

The inclusion of an environment-related exception in the GATT in Article XX serves as further evidence that trade was always seen as a regime that is likely to, at the very least, interact with domestic environmental policy. WTO agreements and case law have remained at least in theory sympathetic to the notion of respect for domestic regulatory space when national governments regulate issues related to natural resources and pollution. Article XX policy exceptions have been incorporated in either a similar or verbatim fashion into regional trade agreements. This incorporation may reflect the desire to integrate some parts of the GATT and WTO jurisprudence and the interpretation of Article XX into the FTAs that include those.[49]

WTO panel and Appellate Body reports have made significant attempts to interpret the WTO agreements generally in line with sustainable development. In *US—Gasoline*, the Appellate Body noted that the wording of Article XX changes in emphasis stemming from the inclusion of the policy as a priority in the WTO Agreement preamble and the Decision on Trade and Environment.[50] In *US—Shrimp*, the Appellate Body reflected on the evolutionary nature of substantive policy considerations in Article XX with respect to the environment, acknowledging that the text of Article XX(g) must be interpreted 'in the light of contemporary concerns of the community of nations about the protection and conservation of the environment'.[51] Thus, the Appellate Body found that the content of the term 'natural resources' in Article XX(g) is dynamic and 'evolutionary'.[52] Analogously, *China—Raw Materials* interpreted the phrase 'to develop an integrated, more viable and durable multilateral trading system' as reflecting a balance 'between trade and non-trade-related concerns'[53] in the 'WTO Agreement, *as a whole*'.[54]

In the larger analytical framework of international trade regulation, we can observe the progression from disembedded obligations in a few agreements, to reading a trade agreement 'under the light' of environmental policy concerns, to finally a symbiosis and proliferation of provisions of trade and environment that now produce self-standing obligations that can trigger trade sanctions without any violations of classically understood trade interests. While the GATT does not contain self-standing environmental obligations, this attitudinal shift can affect

[49] Monteiro (n 4) 39.

[50] Appellate Body Report, *United States—Standards for Reformulated and Conventional Gasoline*, 20 May 1996, WT/DS2/AB/R 30.

[51] Appellate Body Report, *United States—Import Prohibition of Certain Shrimp and Shrimp Products*, 6 November 1998, WT/DS58/AB/R 2755 [129].

[52] ibid [130].

[53] Appellate Body Reports, *China Measures Related to the Exportation of Various Raw Materials*, 22 February 2012, WT/DS394/AB/R and WT/DS395/AB/R and WT/DS398/AB/R 3295 [306].

[54] Emphasis added.

negotiations of subsequent agreements in the context of the WTO and produce self-standing obligations as is the case, for example, for the Fisheries Agreement.

The Agreement on Fisheries Subsidies[55] concluded in 2022 during the 12th WTO Ministerial Conference is an agreement whose spirit relates to the environment.[56] Arguably, the whole agreement addresses the major sustainability crisis with respect to fishing, global biodiversity, fisheries subsidies, and their detrimental environmental impact.[57] It is the first WTO agreement that directly relates to Sustainable Development Goal 14.6, as it is focused on environmental sustainability.[58] The link between the agreement and environmental policy appears more pronounced in Article 4 of the Agreement, addressing subsidies in overfished stocks,[59] as well as Article 8. In Article 8.1 (b)(iii) members commit to notify the WTO Subsidies Committee regarding measures adopted for the conservation and management measures for the relevant fish stock. This obligation appears to be both self-standing and related to sustainability in the marine environment. Meanwhile, the WTO has been criticized as lacking the epistemic capacity to address the environmental dimensions of fisheries subsidies.[60]

Finally, the revised GPA, which binds only its Member States, is now the applicable agreement to the procurement relations between the United States and Canada (as now the CUSMA, replacing the NAFTA does not have a procurement chapter that is applicable between the two parties). Article X paragraph 6 of the GPA provides that:

> For greater certainty, a Party, including its procuring entities, may, in accordance with this Article, prepare, adopt, or apply technical specifications to promote the conservation of natural resources or protect the environment.

Article X.6 of the GPA is less strict and can include more measures than those under Article XX(g) GATT. It contains a self-standing provision and not an

[55] Agreement on Fisheries Subsidies, done at Geneva on 17 June 2022, WT/MIN (22)/33/WT/L/1144.

[56] See WTO Rules Division, 'The WTO Agreement on Fisheries Subsidies, What it does and what comes next' <https://www.wto.org/english/news_e/news22_e/fish_29jul22_e.pdf> accessed 20 April 2024; WTO, 'Implementing the WTO Agreement on Fisheries Subsidies, Challenges and Opportunities for Developing and Least-Developed Country Members' 5 citing Sustainable Development Goal 14.6. For critique see Mitchell Lennan and Stephanie Switzer, 'Agreement on Fisheries Subsidies' (2023) 38(1) International Journal of Marine and Coastal Law 161, 175.

[57] Stephanie Switzer, Elisa Morgera, and Elaine Webster, 'Casting the net wider? The transformative potential of integrating human rights into the implementation of the WTO Agreement on Fisheries Subsidies' 31(3) Review of European, Comparative & International Environmental Law 360, 361. See also Lennan and Switzer (n 57) 163.

[58] WTO, *Implementing the WTO Agreement on Fisheries Subsidies, Challenges and Opportunities for Developing and Least-Developed Country Members* (WTO 2022) 4.

[59] See also Benard Hoekman, Petros Mavroidis, and Sunayana Sasmal, 'Managing Externalities in the WTO: The Agreement on Fisheries Subsidies' (2023) 26(2) Journal of International Economic Law 266, 277.

[60] Switzer, Morgera, and Webster (n 58) 371.

exception. This provision was not in the original GPA but was explicitly added in the revised GPA. The parties clearly wanted to allow regulatory space for governments to regulate procurement in a way that protects the environment. It is also critical that the updated GPA also has a general exceptions clause (like Article XX of the GATT).

VII. Concluding Remarks

The self-standing nature of environmental provisions creates domains where rules negotiated and included in trade agreements may appear prima facie to have little to do with trade concerns or market access. Morin and Kim see the proliferation of environmental clauses and trade agreements as forming superclusters.[61] In theory, the consensus that produces the 'superclusters' is easier to achieve and replicate at a bilateral level. Such chapters and provisions can be very ambitious among willing trading partners and include commitments that were impossible to achieve at a multilateral level in either trade negotiations or environmental negotiations.

The idea of a supercluster implies that the trade and environment nexus or the emerging regime from the formal, treaty-based interaction of the two is evolutionary and is resulting in regime formation and progressive consolidation. However, this proliferation of rules can entail a risk of fragmentation of responsibilities that undermine the original purpose of environmental protection. A possible risk includes, for instance, the abuse of implementation mechanisms by interest groups or lobbyists to hinder progress in national environmental law. Another risk is that of inconsistent dispute settlement outcomes, or 'alternative understandings' regarding the relationship of sustainability provisions and trade considerations in FTAs.[62] These risks are present and do not coherently reflect the progress that is hoped for or is presumed to be coupled with regime consolidation.

Further, the mixed normative strength of obligations and the frequently poorly defined concepts relating to sustainability can add uncertainty to a possibly fragmented landscape. Sustainable development can be seen as the normative backdrop or as an overarching concept to the inclusion of trade and environment provisions in FTAs. Sustainable development is not an easily defined concept, yet it is frequently cited as the overarching commitment that gives rise to the emergence of provisions that regularly include labour and the environment. The commitment to sustainable development can be explicit (as it is in the case of the European Union) or implicit by citing various sustainable development principles (as happens with the inclusive trade agenda and gender-based analysis + in Canada). The

[61] Rakhyun E Kim and Jean-Frédéric Morin, 'Massive Institutional Structures in Global Governance' (2021) 21(3) Global Environmental Politics 26.

[62] Vidigal (n 23).

adoption of sustainability as the umbrella framework for trade agreements can be tailored in a way that fits diverse national narratives. In that sense, national implementation frameworks can produce more versions of trade and sustainability.

The resulting normative link between trade and the environment itself may be looser or stronger in an FTA, depending on the provisions themselves. This proliferation of provisions could further result into two larger outcomes: a) the expansion of global environmental governance—the **consolidation effect** (which is synergetic with the 'supercluster' effect) where such terms become standard and are attached to robust dispute settlement resulting in trade remedies; or b) the further fragmentation of trade and environment regimes—the **diffusion effect**, where the regime itself is not strengthened and progress can be observed but it occurs ad hoc.

If the proliferation of environment and trade provisions is linked to climate change, then it is possible that the doctrinal possibilities identified, fragmentation or regime formation, or the diffusion versus the consolidation effect, are indicative of the doctrinal destabilization that law can experience as a result of climate change.[63] 'Climate change—with its disruptive physical environment impacts – challenges our conception of [. . .] longstanding principles',[64] which also applies to global trade governance and the web of FTAs. The two competing effects are observed simultaneously, as it happens, for example, when FTAs adopt similar or identical wording for sustainability policy priorities but dispute settlement produces divergent interpretations of structurally similar rules. This phenomenon further contributes to the possible doctrinal destabilization. The exit strategy from the destabilization could produce a paradigm shift in two equally diverse *loci*: it is possible that in the long term multilateralism will experience a renewed dynamic and integrate and multilateralize the substance of self-standing trade and environment provisions; or, we will begin observing a strong ratchet effect with respect to trade and environment provisions and be able to trace a common baseline in the overwhelming majority of trade agreements for the safeguarding of key environmental concerns.

[63] Mark Nevitt, 'The Legal Crisis Within the Climate Crisis' (2024) 76 Stanford Law Review 5.
[64] ibid 60.

12

Integrating Climate Action into Free Trade Agreements

Emily Lydgate[*]

I. Introduction

As of September 2022, 140 countries, covering 90 per cent of global emissions, have agreed to or are seriously considering net-zero CO_2 emissions targets.[1] Successful implementation of net-zero targets implies significant reform of countries' trade strategies and patterns. Broadly speaking, countries need to increase trade and investment in low-carbon goods and services, and decrease trade and investment in high-carbon goods and services.[2] Free trade agreements (FTAs) have the potential to support this process. For example, they can remove tariffs between parties on goods that support climate change mitigation and adaptation and liberalize services in this area. They can increase regulatory cooperation to overcome trade barriers based on differing regulations and standards, such as energy efficiency standards or approaches to carbon pricing. Or they can address concerns about asymmetric costs of climate regulation between countries and the need to level the playing field between producers.[3]

* I am grateful to Geraldo Vidigal and Kathleen Claussen for very useful comments, which have greatly improved the chapter, as well as Tim Meyer and the other contributors to this volume who provided feedback. This research was supported by the Centre for Inclusive Trade Policy, UK Economic and Social Research Council [grant number ES/W002434/1].

[1] Climate Action Tracker, <https://climateactiontracker.org/global/cat-net-zero-target-evaluations/> accessed 21 October 2022.

[2] For a brief overview of the ways in which trade contributes to, but also can help to address, the climate crisis see: Margaret A Young and Georgina Clough, 'Net Zero Emissions and Free Trade Agreements: Efforts at Integrating Climate Goals by the United Kingdom and Australia' (2023) 72(2) International & Comparative Law Quarterly 393–436.

[3] A number of academic articles and policy briefings have set out these possibilities. See eg Pascal Lamy, Geneviève Pons, and Pierre Leturcq, 'How to "Green" Trade Agreements?' (Jacque Delors Institute 2020) <https://institutdelors.eu/en/publications/greening-eu-trade-4-how-to-green-trade-agreements/> accessed 1 November 22); Jean-Frédéric Morin and Sikina Jinnah 'The Untapped Potential of Preferential Trade Agreements for Climate Governance' (2018) 27(3) Environmental Politics 541–65; Rafael Leal-Arcas, 'Climate Change Mitigation from the Bottom Up: Using Preferential Trade Agreements to Promote Climate Change Mitigation' (2013) 7(1) Carbon & Climate Law Review 34–42.

Emily Lydgate, *Integrating Climate Action into Free Trade Agreements* In: *The Sustainability Revolution in International Trade Agreements*. Edited by: Geraldo Vidigal and Kathleen Claussen, Oxford University Press. © Emily Lydgate 2024.
DOI: 10.1093/9780191994470.003.0012

Globally, alignment between FTAs and climate objectives remains underdeveloped. A 2021 World Trade Organization (WTO) analysis concludes that only 18 per cent of FTAs notified to the WTO refer to climate change, global warming, greenhouse gas emissions, or low-emissions economy. It concluded that 'compared to other environmental topics, such as biodiversity or sustainable fishery or forestry management, specific provisions on climate change are relatively fewer and less detailed'.[4]

Some of the largest FTAs, including the Comprehensive and Progressive Agreement for Trans-Pacific Partnership (CPTPP), the Agreement between the United States of America, the United Mexican States, and Canada (USMCA), and the Regional Comprehensive Economic Partnership, do not mention climate change by name at all. Failure to endorse climate change mitigation or adaptation as an explicit objective does not preclude its inclusion in some form. For example, CPTPP encourages parties to cooperate in support of transition to a low-emissions economy in a way appropriate to their domestic circumstances and capabilities.[5] But the refusal to identify it by name limits an FTA's ability to support climate action as a strategic objective.

The lack of widespread integration of climate objectives into FTAs reflects the fact that some were negotiated before countries agreed to their current levels of commitment to climate action. In this sense, addressing climate objectives through trade agreements is an emerging trend. Also, while almost all countries have agreed in principle on the need to limit global warming to 1.5°C in the context of the Paris Agreement, the speed and the means by which they contribute to this objective vary and are informed by factors including countries' level of development and political leadership.

The limited role of climate provisions also reflects a traditional perception that FTAs support primarily trade and economic objectives. Environmental objectives have increasingly been incorporated into FTAs to provide them with more social legitimacy.[6] Debates about the appropriate role of these provisions are often described in academic literature as 'trade-and' debates, or debates about the role of 'non-trade' objectives.[7] The increasing frequency and depth of climate-related obligations in FTAs form part of a larger trend towards using trade agreements and

[4] WTO, Trade and Climate Brief: Information note 2, 3 November 2021, <https://www.wto.org/english/news_e/news21_e/clim_03nov21-2_e.pdf> accessed 21 October 2022.

[5] Comprehensive and Progressive Agreement for Trans-Pacific Partnership, in force 18 December 2018, art 20.15 (Transition to a Low Emissions and Resilient Economy).

[6] See eg Ingo Borchert and others, 'The Pursuit of Non-Trade Policy Objectives in EU Trade Policy' (2021) 20(5) World Trade Review 623–47. See also Chapter 11 in this volume by Maria Panezi, which provides useful historical context on the evolution of environmental commitments in trade agreements.

[7] Critiquing this conception in the context of the WTO, Lang wrote: 'It is not self-evident, of course, that the major international institution presiding over the global trade system has no business addressing the social and environmental impacts of that system, and that such impacts are not "trade issues"'. Andrew Lang, 'Reflecting on "Linkage": Cognitive and Institutional Change in the International Trading System' (2007) 70(4) Modern Law Review 537.

arrangements to support other geopolitical objectives.[8] Ultimately, such agreements challenge, or even reverse, the traditional hierarchy between 'trade' and 'non-trade' objectives.

To illustrate this evolution, this chapter first identifies three widespread established approaches to integrating climate obligations into FTAs and then codifies three types of innovations revealed in more recent FTAs. The innovative FTAs examined herein include the European Union's and New Zealand's recent FTAs with the United Kingdom, and with each other, the Agreement on Climate Change, Trade, and Sustainability (ACCTS), the Singapore–Australia Green Economy Agreement,[9] the Indo-Pacific Framework for Economic Prosperity (IPEF),[10] and the Global Arrangement on Sustainable Steel and Aluminium (GASSA).[11] While evolution is ongoing, these agreements, some of which are still being negotiated, date from 2020, and that year is used as a demarcation point for this reason. This analysis, while not comprehensive, shows that FTA reform in this area already demands that we reimagine definitions and uses of FTAs.

II. Common FTA Approaches to Addressing Climate Change Before 2020

Up until 2020, governments accommodated climate change in trade agreements through three common means, listed in order of the level of constraint they impose upon parties: expressions of intent to cooperate, exceptions, and commitments to respect and enforce one's own laws (non-regression/non-derogation). It is important to clarify that climate change has not been the focus of any of these obligations. Indeed, only in the case of cooperative provisions have governments actively addressed climate concerns, and then only in a few, more recent agreements. Instead, climate change was presumed included in broader provisions that aimed to address environmental concerns and environmental regulation.

A. Expressions of Intent to Cooperate

Since 2008, environmental goals have been represented in many FTAs, including those of the United States and European Union, through dedicated Trade and

[8] See eg Emily Jones and Christopher Adam, 'New Frontiers of Trade and Trade Policy: Digitalization and Climate Change' (2023) 39(1) Oxford Review of Economic Policy 1–11.

[9] Singapore–Australia Green Economy Agreement, signed 18 October 2022.

[10] Indo-Pacific Economic Framework for Prosperity, parts in force 24 February 2024.

[11] European Commission, 'Press release: Joint EU–US Statement on a Global Arrangement on Sustainable Steel and Aluminium' *Press Release* (31 October 2021) <https://ec.europa.eu/commission/presscorner/detail/en/ip_21_5724> accessed 31 October 2021.

Environment or Trade and Sustainable Development FTA (TSD) chapters.[12] TSD chapters often assert the intention to cooperate on environmental issues of shared concern and affirm the importance of environmental protection through exhortatory proclamations. As an example of the latter, in the EU–Canada Comprehensive Economic and Trade Agreement (CETA), parties 'shall seek to ensure [their] laws and policies provide for and encourage high levels of environmental protection and shall strive to continue to improve such laws and policies and their underlying levels of protection'.[13] While not mentioned directly, climate change is implied. TSD chapters also include reaffirmations of commitment to implement existing multilateral environmental agreements (MEAs) to which both are parties.[14] A few explicitly affirm that parties are committed to effectively implementing the Kyoto Protocol (pre-dating the Paris Agreement), the United Nations Framework Convention on Climate Change (UNFCCC), and later the Paris Agreement. Such commitments date to the EU–Moldova Deep and Comprehensive Free Trade Area, ratified in 2008, and are also included in some non-EU FTAs, such as the Peru–Korea FTA.[15] Another type of cooperative commitment involves identifying thematic areas of mutual interest that are relevant to climate change. This includes, for example, commitment to cooperate on low-emissions economy in the context of CPTPP.

The implementation of TSD chapters takes place through bilateral committees of officials and other stakeholders from both countries. These committees are tasked with implementing such cooperation commitments. But the effective implementation of open-ended language and broad commitments, as opposed to specific targets or actions, is difficult to monitor and verify, and has resulted in criticism of the effectiveness of such cooperative approaches.[16]

B. Exceptions

Many FTAs recognize the pursuit of environmental regulatory objectives as an exception to non-discrimination obligations. Countries are able in some circumstances to maintain trade-restrictive national regulation, but climate action is not positioned as a shared objective. It is common for FTAs to incorporate by reference

[12] See eg Peter Draper, Nkululeko Khumalo, and Faith Tigere, 'Sustainability Provisions in Regional Trade Agreements: Can They be Multilateralized?' Overview Paper, July 2017, Inter-American Development Bank and International Centre for Trade and Sustainable Development.

[13] Comprehensive Economic and Trade Agreement (CETA) between Canada and the European Union and its Member States, provisionally applied 21 September 2017, art 24.3.

[14] See Chapter 10 in this volume by Gregory Messenger, which provides a fuller picture of how MEAs have interacted with FTAs.

[15] WTO (n 4), 7–8.

[16] EU Commission Services, Non-paper, 'Feedback and way forward on improving the implementation and enforcement of Trade and Sustainable Development chapters in EU FTAs', 26 February 2018.

General Agreement on Tariffs and Trade Article XX, which preserves the parties' right to regulate in order to achieve public interest objectives if particular criteria are met.[17] These include regulations that are 'necessary to protect human, animal or plant life or health', and measures 'relating to the conservation of exhaustible natural resources', both of which suggest a route to defending trade-restrictive climate regulation.[18] These exceptions are sometimes expanded or clarified. For example, the USMCA states that the 'Parties understand that the measures referred to in Article XX(b) of the GATT 1994 . . . include *environmental measures* necessary to protect human, animal, or plant life or health'.[19] However, regulations to support climate change mitigation have not formed an explicit exemption prior to 2020.

C. Maintaining Domestic Environmental Regulation

TSD chapters often include so-called non-regression and non-derogation clauses. While the precise wording varies slightly, such provisions commit parties to upholding and enforcing existing domestic environmental laws, which include by default climate legislation.[20]

For example, Article 13.7(2) of the EU–Korea FTA states that:

> A Party shall not weaken or reduce the environmental or labour protections afforded in its laws to encourage trade or investment, by waiving or otherwise derogating from, or offering to waive or otherwise derogate from, its laws, regulations or standards, in a manner affecting trade or investment between the Parties.[21]

As the conditional application of the non-regression requirement makes clear, such provisions do not function as a general guarantee of environmental protection on the part of trade partners. Instead, they aim to prevent competitive deregulation that takes place in order to benefit trade and investment. In this sense, they guard primarily against economic, rather than environmental, harm. In US-model FTAs such as the USMCA, derogation can result in the imposition of trade sanctions.[22] This obligation presents a deeper constraint on domestic environmental

[17] A list of such agreements is included in Lorand Bartels, 'Social Issues in Regional Trade Agreements: Labour, Environment and Human Rights' in Simon Lester, Bryan Mercurio, and Lorand Bartels (eds), *Bilateral and Regional Trade Agreements* (2nd edn, CUP 2015) 5.

[18] ibid.

[19] Agreement between the United States of America, the United Mexican States, and Canada, in force 1 July 2020, art 32(1)3. Emphasis added.

[20] See eg Draper, Khumalo, and Tigere (n 12).

[21] Free Trade Agreement between the European Union and the Republic of Korea, in force 13 December 2015, art 13.7.

[22] USMCA (n 19).

regulatory processes than cooperative provisions, which are exhortatory in nature, or provisions that characterize climate regulation as an exception to the rules, to the extent that they introduce a positive obligation to maintain environmental regulation.

III. Building on FTA Climate Cooperation and Enforcement

Several FTAs entering into force post-2020 strengthen climate provisions, with the European Union and New Zealand in particular emerging as innovators. Recent innovations build on and strengthen the approaches documented in section II, revealing three major trends: enhanced cooperation, enhanced enforcement, and regulatory cooperation with economic sanctions. Enhanced cooperative approaches are specifically focused on climate action. Enforceability of climate commitments is strengthened, both with respect to existing domestic regulation and also the Paris Agreement. Finally, some agreements include obligations that require the negotiation of future, shared regulatory benchmarks or standards, noncompliance with which can lead to economic sanctions.

The European Union has placed a greater emphasis on enhanced enforcement, which relies on its market power to motivate other parties to uphold their climate commitments. New Zealand has relied on more cooperative (soft power) approaches. While their approaches retain distinctive emphases, they are not mutually exclusive: the European Union has also agreed to cooperative provisions and New Zealand employs coercive approaches in the form of non-regression commitments tied to sanctions.

The post-2020 period has also been characterized by the emergence of a new type of agreement that challenges, and in some cases reverses, the hierarchy of traditional FTAs in which climate or environmental aims are included at the margins, if at all. These include the ACCTS, which is currently being negotiated, with little information available in the public domain, the Singapore–Australia Green Economy Agreement, which has been concluded,[23] the IPEF, which is currently being negotiated[24] and the GASSA, which remains a proposal whose status is uncertain.[25] Rather than traditional FTAs, which cover a wide range of issues, these agreements focus more narrowly on sector- and issue-specific climate cooperation to manage regulatory divergence and reinforce geopolitical alliances.

[23] Government of Australia, Singapore–Australia Green Economy Agreement <https://www.dfat.gov.au/geo/singapore/singapore-australia-green-economy-agreement> accessed 1 December 2023.

[24] USTR, Indo-Pacific Economic Framework for Prosperity (IPEF) <https://ustr.gov/trade-agreements/agreements-under-negotiation/indo-pacific-economic-framework-prosperity-ipef> accessed 1 November 2022.

[25] European Commission (n 11).

A. Enhanced Cooperation

1. Deeper Cooperation in Traditional FTAs

New Zealand's FTA climate innovations have focused on introducing cooperative commitments that differ from past FTA climate-related cooperation in their specificity and precision.[26] This soft power approach is illustrated by its recent FTA with the United Kingdom. It commits the parties to pursue efforts to limit warming to 1.5°C above pre-industrial levels, a more specific obligation than the Paris Agreement implementation more generally.[27] This commitment is not tied to dispute settlement.

The UK–New Zealand FTA also contains unprecedented commitments on fossil fuel subsidy reform, including through a dedicated article, in which parties agree to 'take steps to eliminate harmful fossil fuel subsidies where they exist, with limited exceptions in support of legitimate public policy objectives'. It affirms both sides' commitment to the Powering Past Coal Alliance—an alliance of governments and others operating outside the scope of the FTA—and commits to ending both new direct financial support and export credits for fossil fuel energy, except in narrow circumstances.[28]

These agreements are cooperative in that they obligate the two countries to uphold established mutual objectives. But significantly, none of these commitments requires either the United Kingdom or New Zealand to change its current practices. The UK government's self-characterization as a country with no fossil fuel subsidies has been challenged,[29] but the FTA does not establish criteria for defining fossil fuel subsidies, leaving that to the discretion of parties. Further, the commitment contains an implicit proportionality element: countries are able to provide subsidies if they meet unspecified public policy objectives. The United Kingdom

[26] See eg Friends of Fossil Fuel Subsidy Reform, Statement on Global Fossil Fuel Subsidy Reform on the Fifth Anniversary of the Paris Agreement and FFSR Communiqué (December 2020).

[27] Free Trade Agreement between the United Kingdom of Great Britain and Northern Ireland and New Zealand, in force 31 May 2023, art 22.6.

[28] Not surprisingly, the EU–New Zealand FTA, signed less than a year later, contains a hybrid of both parties' approaches. It includes commitments on fossil fuel subsidy reform, but the language is weaker: rather than eliminating, it commits both parties to 'progressively reducing fossil fuel subsidies'. They also 'reaffirm their commitment to work to meet this objective in accordance with national circumstances, while taking fully into account the specific needs of populations affected'. Reflecting the aforementioned EU policy, the EU–New Zealand FTA also affirms the parties' commitments to the Paris Agreement, which is included as an essential element of the FTA.

[29] The United Kingdom adopts a 'price-gap' approach, which examines the difference between a benchmark price and the price offered to consumers. As a result, the UK government asserts that it does not provide any fossil fuel subsidies. The OECD considers the UK fossil fuel tax regime to include subsidies, and a Commission report in 2016, just before the United Kingdom left the European Union, concluded that it was the largest provider of fossil fuel support in the European Union. UK Parliament, Written Questions and Answers <https://questions-statements.parliament.uk/written-questions/detail/2021-12-10/90854> accessed 20 April 2024; Trinomics, *Study on Energy Prices, Costs and Subsidies and their Impact on Industry and Households* (2018) 268.

and New Zealand have also already agreed to phase out export finance for fossil fuel development.[30]

2. Deeper Cooperation Through Trade and Climate Agreements

Trade and climate agreements include more precise commitments than those found in pre-2020 FTAs. An agreement that exemplifies this trend, the ACCTS, is also led by New Zealand. Announced in September 2019, in partnership with Fiji, Iceland, Norway, and Costa Rica, the centrality of climate-related objectives is clear in the name of the FTA itself. In the Joint Leaders' Statement on its launch, prime ministers of ACCTS countries made clear that its purpose is to aid in achieving the aims of the Paris Agreement.[31] Notably in a field led by developed countries, the ACCTS also includes signatories from developing countries. It aims to support the Paris Agreement by identifying areas in which trade-related measures can reinforce climate action. These include three core objectives: removal of tariffs on environmental goods and new binding commitments for environmental services; introducing disciplines to eliminate harmful fossil fuel subsidies; and developing guidelines on voluntary eco-labelling programmes.[32]

The Singapore–Australia Green Economy Agreement, like the ACCTS, is also based on identifying areas for cooperation. These include commitments to reduce trade barriers to goods and services that mitigate greenhouse gas emissions and mobilize public and private investment to support net-zero emissions.[33] These commitments are exhortatory, and do not proscribe specific outcomes, nor is the agreement enforced through a dispute settlement mechanism.

The IPEF, in the early stages of negotiation at the time of writing, dedicates one of its four pillars, the Clean Economy, to 'pursu[ing] concrete, high-ambition targets that will accelerate efforts to tackle the climate crisis, including in the areas of renewable energy, carbon removal, energy efficiency standards, and new measures to combat methane emissions'.[34] Parties have underscored that cooperative outcomes will respect and reflect national differences:

[30] HM Government, 'PM announces the UK will end support for fossil fuel sector overseas' (12 December 2020) <https://www.gov.uk/government/news/pm-announces-the-uk-will-end-support-for-fossil-fuel-sector-overseas> accessed 13 September 2023; New Zealand Treasury, 'New Zealand Export Credit supports the Clean Energy Transition' (8 December 2022) <https://exportcredit.treasury.govt.nz/news/new-zealand-export-credit-supports-clean-energy-transition> accessed 13 September 2023.

[31] Joint Leaders' Statement on the Launch of the 'Agreement on Climate Change, Trade and Sustainability' Initiative (24 September 2019).

[32] New Zealand Foreign Affairs and Trade, Agreement on Climate Change, Trade and Sustainability (ACCTS) negotiations <https://www.mfat.govt.nz/en/trade/free-trade-agreements/trade-and-climate/agreement-on-climate-change-trade-and-sustainability-accts-negotiations> accessed 1 November 2022.

[33] Singapore–Australia Green Economy Agreement, art 9(a)vi(c); 9(c).

[34] The White House, 'Fact Sheet: In Asia, President Biden and a Dozen Indo-Pacific Partners Launch the Indo-Pacific Economic Framework for Prosperity', 23 May 2022.

> the IPEF partners are concurrently identifying and developing initiatives and proposals to advance cooperation in key areas that are critical to realizing their unique pathways towards net zero emission economies, whilst recognizing the unique national circumstances of each IPEF partner, including their development needs.[35]

This makes clear that, while the thematic areas are specific and targeted, cooperation outcomes remain voluntary and aspirational.

B. Enhanced Enforcement of Climate Obligations

1. Upholding the Paris Agreement

The European Union has listed international climate treaties as an area for cooperation in its past FTAs. More recently, it elevated the importance of such compliance. In June 2022 the Commission produced a Communication stating:

> The Commission now proposes the possibility of trade sanctions as a matter of last resort, in instances of serious violations of . . . [the] Paris Agreement on Climate Change. In such instances, trade sanctions would be appropriate as a means to foster compliance. In the case of the Paris Agreement, the intention would be to capture failure to comply with obligations that materially defeats the object and purpose of the agreement. . .. This approach will build on and reinforce the respect of . . . the Paris Agreement as essential elements of our trade agreements. [36]

In the past, the European Union has excluded TSD chapters from state-to-state dispute settlement mechanisms. Instead, disagreements are subject to consultation. If there is no settlement, a panel of experts will be convened, which can examine failure to comply with obligations and make recommendations, but non-compliance with the non-regression requirement cannot be countered with trade sanctions.[37] This reform goes beyond introducing a non-regression requirement tied to sanctions. Including compliance with the Paris Agreement as an essential element means that either party can partly or fully suspend the agreement if it is

[35] IPEF Partners, *Press Statement for the Trade Pillar, Clean Economy Pillar, and Fair Economy Pillar*, 27 May 2023.

[36] European Commission, 'The Power of Trade Partnerships: Together for Green and Just Economic Growth' COM(2022) 409 final (22 June 2022).

[37] See European Commission Non-Paper, 2017, 'Trade and Sustainable Development (TSD) Chapters in EU Free Trade Agreements (FTAs)'.

breached.[38] In so doing, it elevates its status to accompany traditional EU FTA 'essential elements' of democratic principles, the rule of law, and human rights.

The UK–EU Trade and Cooperation Agreement (TCA) (2021) is illustrative. Its Preamble affirms that the 'fight against climate change' is an essential element of the agreement, acting as a guiding principle for the whole agreement. The chapter establishing the 'Basis for Cooperation' for the TCA also affirms that 'climate change represents an existential threat to humanity' and gives this 'fight' a material form as a requirement to 'respect the Paris Agreement and the process set up by the UNFCCC and refrain from acts or omissions that would materially defeat the object and purpose of the Paris Agreement'.[39]

The Paris Agreement relies upon participating countries to define their own contribution to reducing emissions. Being able to establish that either party took actions that would 'materially defeat the object and purpose of the Paris Agreement', short of withdrawal from the Agreement itself, will prove challenging. But the EU elevation of the Paris Agreement conveys a significant message. Gehring writes, 'through the inclusion of climate change as an essential element in trade treaties, the constitutional objective of combating climate change has now transcended the mere environmental context and become an objective of all EU foreign policy'.[40] By making FTAs contingent on Paris Agreement implementation, the European Union embeds a normative view of the importance of climate action. Unlike cooperative approaches, the European Union uses an economic threat, the suspension of a trade agreement, to incentivize compliance.

2. Enhanced Non-Regression

The European Union has agreed to incorporate similar commitments to the Paris Agreement in all future FTAs. But the TCA has some additional, and unique, climate innovations. While it arose in response to the unusual circumstances of the EU–UK negotiation, it is an experiment with wider significance. The TCA moves beyond using existing domestic regulation as a thematically open-ended benchmark for non-regression (referred to in section II.C). Instead, it specifies climate-related regulatory commitments that parties must maintain. If an arbitral tribunal agrees that non-compliance has occurred, either party can apply sanctions.[41] These include a commitment to uphold both parties' 'climate level of protection'

[38] Pursuant to the Vienna Convention on the Law of Treaties, parties can terminate or suspend a treaty in the event of a material breach, which consists of the violation of an 'essential' provision. Vienna Convention on the Law of Treaties, in force 27 January 1980, art 60.

[39] Trade and Cooperation Agreement between the European Union and the European Atomic Energy Community and the United Kingdom of Great Britain and Northern Ireland, in force 1 May 2021, Title II: Basis for cooperation, art 764.

[40] Markus W Gehring, EU Constitutional Aims and External Relations—Legal Consequences of Climate Provisions in EU Trade Accords, University of Cambridge, Legal Studies Research Paper Series 02/23, 22.

[41] TCA Title XI, art 390(3), 391.

as set out in interim greenhouse gas reduction targets. These targets are quantitative in nature, making compliance assessment relatively concrete and objective. Integrating quantitative climate benchmarks into an FTA is novel. The parties also commit to non-regression on upholding an 'effective system of carbon pricing',[42] a requirement that retains significant interpretative complexity but is nonetheless more precise and enforceable than previous cooperative FTA commitments.

IV. Regulatory Cooperation with Economic Sanctions

Non-regression rests on the maintenance of existing climate regulation that domestic governments set. In contrast, the most constraining (or some might say ambitious) type of trade and climate agreement requires that countries agree to keep pace with each other, through negotiating shared standards or dynamically aligning in order to maintain a similar level of protection in the future. Very few agreements contain commitments to cooperate on climate regulation where non-compliance can result in economic sanctions.

The TCA contains elements that fit this model. It requires both parties to keep pace in their level of protection, through a so-called rebalancing mechanism. It specifies that:

> significant divergences . . . can be capable of impacting trade or investment between the Parties in a manner that changes the circumstances that have formed the basis for the conclusion of this Agreement . . . If material impacts on trade or investment between the Parties are arising as a result of significant divergences . . . either Party may take appropriate rebalancing measures to address the situation.[43]

While non-regression requirements typically focus on preventing the diminishment of current environmental standards, rebalancing addresses divergence in future policies and priorities. This provides a mechanism for approximate alignment of environmental ambitions, which functions through the threat of suspension of all or part of the TCA's trade provisions for failure to keep pace.

In 2021 the European Union and United States produced a statement agreeing to work towards an agreement, the GASSA, which among other objectives will 'restrict market access [of steel and aluminium] for non-participants that do not meet standards for low carbon intensity'. This departs from the cooperative approaches in its explicit invocation of market access restrictions on non-participants. In so doing, it aims to reinforce geopolitical alliances. This becomes clear from its objective to 'confer on entering into discussions on global steel and aluminium

[42] ibid art 392.
[43] ibid art 411.

arrangements to address both non-market excess capacity as well as the carbon intensity of the steel and aluminium industries'.[44] The emphasis on non-market excess capacity suggests that the GASSA excludes China, for whom meeting a low carbon requirement would not be a sufficient condition for membership.

V. The Implementation and Influence of FTA Climate Innovations: Evolution Not Revolution

A. Implementation Challenges

In their reconfiguration of traditional FTA structures and objectives, some of the aforementioned agreements are revolutionary. However, much remains to be seen in the implementation of these commitments. This section identifies four challenges to transformative implementation that apply across the agreements examined here: standstill commitments, failure to cooperate, racing (closer) to the bottom, and atomization/exclusion.

First, in bringing FTAs closer to MEAs, some FTA provisions also replicate a common MEA problem: countries only agree to commitments that they believe they have already fulfilled.[45] This applies to Paris Agreement implementation as an essential element of an FTA and commitments to eliminate harmful fossil fuel subsidies. Viewed in terms of existing domestic commitments, their implementation may change nothing, and they could be characterized as standstill commitments.

A second implementation challenge concerns the likelihood of success in an approach led by commitments to cooperate on regulation. Effective implementation of such provisions will require domestic change through bridging the divide between distinct national approaches. A good example of this is fossil fuel subsidies. Establishing a shared definition would aid efforts to benchmark meaningful national action and increase transparency. At the time of writing, the most recent round of negotiations for the ACCTS aims to address this issue and included presentations from the Organization for Economic Co-operation and Development (OECD) and the International Energy Agency on their respective definitions.[46]

Eco-labelling is another example: different standards across countries can act as non-tariff barriers that hinder trade of green goods and services. The OECD

[44] European Commission (n 11). See also Ministerial Statement for Pillar III of the Indo-Pacific Framework for Prosperity, September 2022 <https://www.commerce.gov/sites/default/files/2022-09/Pillar-III-Ministerial-Statement.pdf> accessed 24 March 2023.

[45] See eg Teall E Crossen, 'Multilateral environmental agreements and the compliance continuum' (2004) Georgetown International Environmental Law Review, 16(3), 473–500.

[46] New Zealand Foreign Affairs and Trade, ACCTS negotiating rounds: Round 10 <https://www.mfat.govt.nz/en/trade/free-trade-agreements/trade-and-climate/accts-negotiating-rounds/#bookmark0> accessed 1 November 2022.

estimates that there are over 400 different eco-label schemes across 200 countries in 25 industry sectors.[47] The ACCTS eco-labelling group is attempting to define guidelines for eco-labels to reduce these barriers. Also, negotiations on environmental goods and services have long been stalled at the WTO, in part because of difficulties with drawing boundaries around the categories.[48] The ACCTS negotiations include environmental goods and services working groups identifying a common set of environmental goods and environmental services criteria.[49]

Another challenge that these agreements can help to unlock is the extent to which new climate border measures, notably carbon border adjustment mechanisms (CBAM), can be alleviated through new forms of regulatory coordination. The EU introduction of a CBAM, which extends EU domestic carbon prices to imported products in some trade-exposed sectors,[50] gives new urgency to this question. Both the GASSA and the TCA generate innovations that allow countries who wish to maintain separate climate regulations to establish shared benchmarks.

Alternatively, such discussions could fail to progress. Past experience using trade agreements to overcome regulatory differences shows that countries are reluctant to cede sovereignty over regulation.[51] For example, it took the United States and the European Union four years to grant mutual recognition of pharmaceutical inspections, such that an EU facility could produce a US-approved drug and vice-versa.[52] The European Union has succeeded in concluding so-called Mutual Recognition Agreements in a few sectors with some countries, but many of these have been only partially functional in practice.[53] The effective implementation of climate-related regulatory cooperation provisions that bring about harmonization or mutual recognition of divergent national standards at a reasonable timescale to address the climate crisis will require a marked increase in the ambition and effectiveness of inter-state recognition of the equivalence of foreign government regulation.

[47] OECD, *OECD Work on Trade and the Environment: A Retrospective 2008–2020* (OECD 2020) 58–62.

[48] See eg Trade in Environmental Goods and Services and Sustainable Development, Domestic Considerations and Strategies for WTO Negotiations, December 2007, ICTSD Programme on Trade and Environment <https://egs.apec.org/uploads/docs/ICTSD_TradeInEnvironmentalGoodsAndServices.pdf> accessed 1 November 2022.

[49] New Zealand Foreign Affairs and Trade (n 46).

[50] European Commission, Proposal for a Regulation of the European Parliament and of the Council establishing a carbon border adjustment mechanism COM(2021) 564 final.

[51] Humberto Zuniga Schroder, *Harmonisation, Equivalence and Mutual Recognition of Standards* (Wolters Kluwer 2011) 97–142.

[52] US Food & Drug Administration, 'Mutual Recognition promises new framework for pharmaceutical inspections for United States and European Union' *Press Release* (2 March 2017) <https://www.fda.gov/news-events/press-announcements/mutual-recognition-promises-new-framework-pharmaceutical-inspections-united-states-and-european> accessed 24 March 2023.

[53] Anabela Correia de Brito, Céline Kauffmann, and Jacques Pelkmans, 'The Contribution of Mutual Recognition to International Regulatory Co-operation' OECD Regulatory Policy Working Papers, No 2, 1–91.

If efforts to establish shared or equivalent standards succeed, another risk to effective implementation emerges. These provisions have the potential to be transformative not only by making trade more seamless but also by codifying norms. The absence of an agreed definition may permit a relatively unambitious approach to self-declaration of such subsidies, as described in the example of the UK–New Zealand FTA. But establishing a shared definition of fossil fuel subsidies is not guaranteed to improve global ambition: adoption of a narrow definition could permit much fossil fuel subsidy support to go unidentified. Similarly, agreeing to mandatory minimum standards for emissions embodied in steel and aluminium risks weakening, rather than strengthening, some countries' domestic regulations.

A final risk to effective implementation results from those who are left behind. Almost all of the agreements documented here are led by developed countries. Global decarbonization is not possible unless all countries participate. Divesting from emissions-intensive manufacturing techniques requires investment, and developing countries may be less likely to have the government subsidies, foreign investment, and technology transfer from multinational firms to support their progress. Regulatory cooperation efforts that are restricted to wealthy countries will only exacerbate this problem, particularly if they result in additional barriers to market access that leave developing countries further behind. Such agreements also could increase geopolitical tensions and schisms. The conflation of trade and climate agreements with other geopolitical aims, as in the case of the GASSA, risks undermining their effectiveness in supporting global decarbonization. Clearly, the exclusion of the world's largest emitter is suboptimal.

B. The Influence of FTA Innovation on Broader Trade and Climate Cooperation

Despite these limitations, these agreements seek to contribute to reshaping global expectations about the contents and purposes of FTAs. In leading such efforts, the European Union and New Zealand act as norm entrepreneurs,[54] propelling plurilateral and multilateral initiatives in other fora, including the WTO and Paris Agreement.

While the causal relationship between FTA and plurilateral or multilateral action is difficult to pin down precisely, New Zealand's efforts in each of these areas likely mutually reinforce each other. With respect to the ACCTS, it writes:

[54] Carmen Wunderlich, 'Theoretical Approaches in the Study of Norms' in H Müller and C Wunderlich (eds), *Norm Dynamics in Multilateral Arms Control, Interests, Conflicts, and Justice* (University of Georgia Press 2013) 20–47.

> We consider that there is an important role for plurilateral agreements like ACCTS to play as a pathfinder and template for action. Our vision is that ACCTS will demonstrate in practical terms how trade rules can support climate and broader environmental objectives while generating momentum towards an eventual multilateral set of solutions.[55]

This summarizes well how formulating and testing new trade and climate norms in FTAs informs broader action. Breakthroughs in the ACCTS on guidelines for environmental goods and services or environmental labels could prove useful not only to ACCTS parties but more broadly, including through propelling similar proposals in other FTAs or at the WTO. New Zealand has pursued efforts to promote fossil fuel subsidy reform through multiple channels, and recent FTAs are in dialogue with other international efforts. For example, the ACCTS and UK–New Zealand FTA stipulate that, in order to be eliminated, fossil fuel subsidies must be 'harmful'. Commitments to phase out environmentally harmful subsidies have been discussed in multilateral fora, such as the WTO in the context of fisheries subsidies, so the use of the term 'harmful' may be intended to create continuity with these discussions.[56]

New Zealand has led the Friends of Fossil Fuel Subsidy Reform, which, together with the United Kingdom as host of the COP26 in November 2021, issued a statement calling for 'support for accelerated action to eliminate fossil fuel subsidies'.[57] At COP26, the Glasgow Climate Pact, pursuant to the Paris Agreement, called upon parties to 'accelerate efforts towards the phasedown of unabated coal power and the phase out of inefficient fossil fuels subsidies'.[58] In December 2021, a group of 45 WTO Members proposed a Fossil Fuel Subsidies Ministerial Statement 'seeking the rationalisation and phase out of inefficient fossil fuel subsidies that encourage wasteful consumption along a clear timeline'.[59] Through these initiatives, fossil fuel subsidy reform has become a part of the negotiating agendas of the WTO and Paris Agreement. Inclusion in the Glasgow Climate Pact is particularly significant due to its multilateral scope, with almost 200 signatories, and was considered one of the COP26's most significant accomplishments.[60]

[55] MFAT, 'ACCTS Negotiations' <https://www.mfat.govt.nz/en/trade/free-trade-agreements/trade-and-climate/agreement-on-climate-change-trade-and-sustainability-accts-negotiations/> accessed 1 November 2022.

[56] See eg WTO Implementing the WTO Agreement on Fisheries Subsidies: Challenges and Opportunities for Developing and Least-Developed Country Members (2022) <https://www.wto.org/english/tratop_e/rulesneg_e/fish_e/implementfishagreement22_e.htm> accessed 18 January 2022.

[57] Friends of Fossil Fuel Subsidy Reform, Statement on Global Fossil Fuel Subsidy Reform on the Fifth Anniversary of the Paris Agreement and FFSR Communiqué (December 2020).

[58] UNFCCC, Report of the Conference of the Parties FCCC/CP/2021/12/Add (8 March 2022) para 20.

[59] WTO General Council, Proposed Fossil Fuel Subsidies Ministerial Statement JOB/GC/264/Rev 3 (18 November 2021).

[60] See eg Harro van Asselt, 'Breaking a Taboo: Fossil Fuels at COP26' (*EJIL: Talk!* 26 November 2021) <https://www.ejiltalk.org/breaking-a-taboo-fossil-fuels-at-cop26/> accessed 1 November 2022.

The EU approach positions MEAs as a 'compass' for FTA strategy, and states that EU strategy for TSD commitments in FTAs, including on climate, will be 'anchored' in multilateral agreements and cooperation.[61] It reconfigures MEA compliance as a baseline requirement for FTAs. Through the incorporation of the Paris Agreement as an essential element of FTAs, the European Union uses its negotiating influence to reinforce existing international commitments to address climate change, introducing additional diplomatic and economic pressure for EU trade partners to implement existing decarbonization plans.

Innovative FTA provisions also contribute to broader climate and trade action by testing new models of international treaty making and cooperation. For example, in the EU–UK TCA, the inclusion of a 'keeping pace' requirement is innovative in international trade and also international environmental law. Broadly defined, non-regression in international law encompasses any commitment not to lower existing levels of protection. It is not a widely recognized principle of international law. However, based on its inclusion in the Paris Agreement and the Rio + 20 Declaration, a growing movement of academics and international lawyers has argued that there is a sufficient basis for it to constitute an emerging principle of international environmental law.[62] One critique of non-regression is that it fixes expectations of environmental protection at the point where a treaty was agreed. The TCA addresses this issue through the inclusion of the rebalancing mechanism, which introduces a penalty if parties fail to dynamically update.

The untested nature of TCA provisions makes its impact difficult to predict. But it goes beyond the multilateral and self-determined approach of the Paris Agreement by embedding long-term coordination of high-level domestic climate policy aims, and also departs from the traditional FTA focus on harmonization or mutual recognition of product standards more narrowly.[63]

The GASSA suggests the potential to agree on shared minimum standards for embodied emissions that can apply to countries that employ carbon pricing (the European Union) as well as performance standards (the United States). Though the GASSA involves market access restrictions of an unspecified type, exclusion from such measures will be built on a foundation of regulatory cooperation between heterogeneous climate regulations. As part of the GASSA, countries agree to exchange information on methodologies for calculating steel and aluminium carbon intensity and share relevant data. While, again, this is unspecified, these methods will presumably lead into a shared understanding of the particular 'low carbon intensity standards' with which exporters must comply. Such discussions can also build on, and contribute to, similar discussions in international and

[61] European Commission (n 36).

[62] See eg Michel Prieur 'The Principle of Non-Regression' in L Kramer and E Orlando (eds), *Principles of Environmental Law* (Edward Elgar 2018) 251–59.

[63] Emily Lydgate, 'Climate Equivalence and International Trade' (October 2022), Working Paper, EUI RSC, 2022/64, Global Governance Programme-479 [Global Economics].

regional bodies such as the WTO, OECD, and International Monetary Fund, and the Industrial Deep Decarbonization Initiative's Clean Energy Ministerial, who are also considering how to facilitate cooperation on embodied emissions standards.[64]

This is an important development in the context of existing and prospective CBAMs. Unlike an Emissions Trading Scheme, which applies directly to installations (producer regulation), CBAMs assess emissions embedded within goods (product regulation). Requiring that exporters assess embedded emissions within products in emissions-intensive trade-exposed industries is novel, and there are no widely adopted international standards for doing so. Inevitably, the EU CBAM will build global capacity for embedded emissions assessment among exporters to the European Union, but only the shared market power of the European Union and the United States could ensure that a successful agreement of shared embodied emissions standards would shape global markets and supply chains.

These negotiations implicitly or explicitly inform other efforts to develop shared methods for measuring emissions embodied in products in energy-intensive industries. These include a German G7 proposal for climate clubs, elaborated in most detail in a 2021 position paper, which states that:

> Members will commit to no longer going below a jointly defined minimum price and will agree on a path for the minimum carbon price over time... This can happen by means of emissions trading systems and carbon taxes, but also through implicit mechanisms, if they provide a comparable carbon price signal.[65]

If it results in agreement on a shared approach between the United States and European Union, the GASSA would constitute a transformative breakthrough that would likely influence discussions in other fora.

VI. Conclusion

This chapter began by identifying a failure among many FTAs to integrate climate change objectives, but the lack of integration is also evident in international climate agreements. The Paris Agreement is based on a voluntary, bottom-up approach

[64] See eg WTO, World Trade Report 2022, Climate Change and International Trade, Chapter 4: Carbon Pricing and International Trade, 78–98; OECD, 'Effective Carbon Rates 2021: Pricing Carbon Emissions Through Taxes and Emissions Trading' (May 2021) <https://www.oecd.org/tax/tax-policy/effective-carbon-rates-2021-0e8e24f5-en.htm> accessed 24 March 2023; F Misch and P Wingender, 'Revisiting Carbon Leakage' (2021) International Monetary Fund Working Paper 21/207 <https://www.imf.org/en/Publications/WP/Issues/2021/08/06/Revisiting-Carbon-Leakage-462148> accessed 24 March 2023; UN Industrial Development Organization, Industrial Deep Decarbonization Initiative <https://www.unido.org/IDDI> accessed 24 March 2023.

[65] German Federal Ministry of Finance and others, 'Steps Towards an Alliance for Climate, Competitiveness, and Industry—Building Blocks of a Cooperation and Open Climate Club' (August 2021) 2.

whereby countries determine their own national contributions to mitigating climate change. It lacks guidance on how to address the trade implications of decarbonization. These include the need to cooperate in order to facilitate trade and investment in low-carbon goods and services and the need to address competitiveness concerns that arise when countries with high climate ambitions impose costly regulation on their domestic industry. Avoiding the use of trade measures to support climate action would clearly slow global decarbonization by impeding the dissemination of low-carbon goods, services, and technologies. It would also risk incentivizing exporters to move to locations with lax climate regulation, where they can enjoy a competitive advantage. Yet, countries introducing such measures unilaterally gives rise to the potential for trade conflict and trade restriction.[66]

Trade and climate agreements are needed to address these issues, and those documented here begin to do so. Equally, the failure of these FTAs to achieve their purported aims will provide useful demonstration value for other countries attempting to ensure that trade and trade agreements support their decarbonization efforts. There is potential for more countries to participate in such agreements, and for them to undertake further cooperation on trade and climate regulation on issues such as embodied emissions methodologies, labelling, subsidies, carbon price cooperation, technology transfer, climate finance, and more. The remaining concern is whether even an evolution that is speedy in the context of international law will add up to the more revolutionary action needed to address the climate crisis.

[66] These issues are examined in Susanne Droege and others, 'The Trade System and Climate Action: Ways Forward under the Paris Agreement' (2017) 13 South Carolina Journal of International Law and Business 195.

13

Sustainability Obligations and Developing Countries

Any Scope for Special and Differential Treatment?

Regis Y Simo

I. Introduction

Labour laws of potential host states are central to investment decisions. While literature argues that less worker protection, hence lower wage costs to investors, can be catalysts for foreign direct investment (FDI),[1] another strand establishes a correlation between core labour standards enforcement and increased FDI.[2] In a globalized world, the asymmetry between the global location strategies of transnational corporations and the essentially national states' regulatory capacities often tends to push governments to lower social, environmental, and fiscal standards to attract foreign investors who otherwise may threaten to (re)locate in lax regulated markets.[3]

Besides labour issues, establishing policies that integrate environmental concerns into countries' strategies is becoming the norm. This is the result of the increasing awareness that non-economic values, notably the protection of the environment, are essential in guaranteeing the stability of the regime in place while contributing to the achievement of sustainable development goals. Although the World Trade Organization (WTO) is often criticized for encroaching on its Members' policy autonomy,[4] it has become common for countries to impose or maintain a set of measures to protect their environment.

[1] See Charles Oman, *Policy Competition for Foreign Direct Investment: A Study of Competition Among Governments to Attract FDI* (OECD 2000) 96–99.

[2] See eg David Kucera, 'Core Labour Standards and Foreign Direct Investment' (2002) 141 International Labour Review 31.

[3] Regulatory 'race to the bottom' is sometimes used to describe the phenomenon whereby states compete to attract FDI by lowering their standards. One often utilized tool by governments to attract investments while guaranteeing, or in exchange for, relaxed labour standards, among others, are special economic zones. On this score see Regis Y Simo, 'Special Economic Zones in an Era of Multilateralism Decadence and Struggles for Post-Pandemic Economic Recovery: Perspectives from the Global South' (2023) 24 German Law Journal 199.

[4] Reduced or limited 'policy space' is very often voiced by WTO developing country members who generally claim that by tying their hands to the mast of multilateral commitments, little room is left for

Regis Y Simo, *Sustainability Obligations and Developing Countries* In: *The Sustainability Revolution in International Trade Agreements*. Edited by: Geraldo Vidigal and Kathleen Claussen, Oxford University Press. © Regis Y Simo 2024.
DOI: 10.1093/9780191994470.003.0013

That international trade has social and environmental effects that must be considered is therefore no longer called into question. Recognizing these implications has given rise to codified obligations, dubbed sustainability provisions or clauses, binding on parties to trade agreements. Sustainability obligations are chapters, provisions, or clauses inserted in trade agreements where parties commit to associate trade liberalization commitments to societal concerns. While the category of sustainability obligations is not exhaustive, the current practice has focused on labour, environment, and climate issues. This trend emerged in the early 1990s and is now a nearly permanent feature of modern trade agreements. Today, all new EU trade agreements include chapters on trade and sustainable development, with far-reaching mutually agreed commitments requiring parties to make continuous and sustained efforts towards the ratification of fundamental International Labour Organization (ILO) conventions and the effective implementation of conventions by the ILO and of multilateral environmental agreements (MEAs) that each party has ratified, such as the Paris Agreement on Climate Change and the Convention on Biological Diversity.

Sponsored by developed countries, North–South trade agreements equally increasingly contain sustainability chapters. For instance, the Economic Partnership Agreement (EPA) between Southern African Customs Union (SACU) Member States and Mozambique and the United Kingdom[5] and the EU–Kenya EPA[6] are some of the latest agreements displaying this feature. One distinguishing attribute of these agreements is their dispute settlement mechanism to enforce sustainability obligations. However, the success of regional trade agreements in embracing these issues contrasts sharply with the multilateral defiance of so-called social clauses.

Resistance, as will transpire in this chapter, is generally meant to sustain developing countries' comparative advantage in cheap labour costs, defend their hard-earned special and differential treatment (SDT), and prevent enforcement of sustainability issues through sanctions. In effect, SDT is the WTO tool that addresses developing countries' concerns for a variable geometry in trade rules and the implementation of the ensuing disciplines. The need for this rebalancing mechanism stems from developing countries' feeling that the rules such as non-discrimination and reciprocity, devised when many of them were colonies and could not take part in

their pursuit of policies in their national interest. See eg Jorg Mayer, 'Policy Space: What, For What, and Where?' (2009) 27(4) Development Policy Review 373.

[5] Economic Partnership Agreement between Southern Customs Union Member States and Mozambique and the United Kingdom of Great Britain and Northern Ireland, in force 1 January 2021, pt I and Annex VII.

[6] At the time of this writing, the negotiations concluded on 19 June 2023, but the text is yet to be ratified by the parties. Reports have it that this deal contains 'strong trade and sustainability commitments, including binding provisions on labour matters, gender equality, environment and the fight against climate change'. See EU Commission, 'EU and Kenya Conclude Negotiations for an Ambitious Economic Partnership Agreement with Strong Sustainability Provisions' (19 June 2023) <https://ec.europa.eu/commission/presscorner/detail/en/ip_23_3323> accessed 31 August 2023.

shaping them, did not (sufficiently) reflect the unequal level of development between developed, developing, and least developed countries (LDCs). For this reason, SDT provisions in WTO-covered agreements are of six categories:[7]

(i) Provisions aimed at increasing trade opportunities of developing countries, such as the establishment of Generalized System of Preference (GSP) schemes under the WTO Enabling Clause.
(ii) Provisions requiring WTO developed members to safeguard the interests of developing countries, for instance, by considering the vulnerability of developing countries' economies before imposing any measures that might affect their trade interests, such as anti-dumping measures.
(iii) Provisions permitting developing countries to assume lesser obligations, such as total exemptions from rules otherwise binding on all WTO Members.[8]
(iv) Provisions allowing longer transitional periods to adjust to multilateral commitments, sometimes owing to weaker institutional capacities.[9]
(v) Provisions relating to technical assistance, which developing countries and LDCs can receive from the WTO Secretariat and develop economies to implement their commitments.
(vi) LDC-specific provisions.

While the continued relevance of SDT within the WTO is today contested,[10] developing countries insist that any new WTO rule must be prepared with SDT in mind.[11] Sustainability obligations are no exception to SDT beneficiaries' position, not least because of the international recognition of a differentiated responsibility on developing countries in combatting global environmental degradation.[12]

[7] See WTO Committee on Trade and Development, Special and Differential Treatment Provisions in the WTO Agreements and Decisions, Note by the Secretariat, WTO Doc WT/COMTD/W/239, 12 October 2018.

[8] An example includes the exemption from the general prohibition by the Agreement on Subsidies and Countervailing Measures to grant or maintain subsidies contingent, in law or in fact, upon export performance.

[9] This may also be the WTO Member's own tariff binding as with Cape Verde when it joined the WTO in 2008. See WTO, General Council, Cape Verde—Implementation of the Schedule of Concessions, Decision of 28 July 2009, WTO Doc WT/L/768, 31 July 2009.

[10] See WTO, General Council, An Undifferentiated WTO: Self-declared Development Status Risks Institutional Irrelevance. Communication from the United States, WTO Doc WT/GC/W/757/Rev 1, 14 February 2019.

[11] WTO, General Council, The Continued Relevance of Special and Differential Treatment in Favour of Developing Members to Promote Development and Ensure Inclusiveness, Communication from China, India, South Africa, the Bolivarian Republic of Venezuela, Lao People's Democratic Republic, Plurinational State of Bolivia, Kenya, Cuba, Central African Republic and Pakistan, WTO Doc WT/GC/W/765/Rev 2, 4 March 2019.

[12] See WTO, General Council, Principles Guiding the Development and Implementation of Trade-Related Environmental Measures, Communication from the African Group, WTO Doc WT/GC/W/894, 13 July 2023.

This chapter is structured as follows. Section II tackles sustainability obligations in the multilateral trading system and highlights developing countries' position on these issues. While the WTO forum is characterized by a substantive and ideological division between proponents and critics of the sustainability question, section III addresses the forums where pushing for such values has been relatively more successful, namely, free trade agreements and unilateral trade preference schemes. Section IV provides concluding remarks and outlooks around the role, if any, of SDT in framing the obligations and implementing them.

II. A Developing Countries' Perspective on Sustainability Obligations in the Multilateral Trading System

Developing countries face trade and sustainability challenges at three levels at least. The first is the multilateral level, namely the WTO. The other two levels are regional trade agreements and preferential trade arrangements. While sustainability obligations found a fertile ground in bilateral trade agreements, their inclusion into the multilateral trading system has not been without challenges of varying degrees. Developing countries' main concern is that while pursuing sustainable development may be recognized as a major goal, abuses of standards and obligations to foster what is a common concern for all humankind are always looming, especially against less economically powerful countries. Developed economies' intention to use sanctions to induce compliance with these provisions heightens resistance.[13] This section addresses the WTO framework regarding labour and environment standards.

A. Rejection of Labour Standards

Literature defines labour provisions in trade agreements as:

(i) any principle or standard (including international labour standards) or rule which addresses labour relations, minimum working conditions, terms of employment, and/or other labour issues;
(ii) any framework to promote compliance with standards through cooperative activities, dialogue, and/or monitoring of labour issues; and/or
(iii) any mechanism to ensure compliance with standards, either set under national law or in the trade agreement.[14]

[13] See Clyde Summers, 'The Battle in Seattle: Free Trade, Labor Rights, and Societal Values' (2001) 22 University of Pennsylvania Journal of International Economic Law 61.

[14] Marva Corley-Coulibaly, Ira Postolachi, and Netsanet Tesfa, 'A Multi-Faceted Typology of Labour Provisions in Trade Agreements: Overview, Methodology and Trends' (24 November 2021) <https://

The first category is made up of labour obligations comprising general, substantive, and procedural labour commitments concerning domestic labour regulations, international labour standards, and principles. Obligations under this pillar include, among others, the ratification of and implementation of ILO Fundamental Conventions. The second pillar contains mechanisms that promote compliance with labour obligations both by facilitating dialogue and cooperative activities and by addressing institutional weaknesses. One means to address institutional weakness is through the provision of technical assistance. Finally, the third pillar features dispute settlement mechanisms whose aim is to resolve issues of interpretation and non-compliance with labour obligations.

Despite their prominence nowadays, labour provisions still fall under what literature refers to as WTO-X issues because they fall outside the current WTO mandate.[15] In that context, some countries, especially developing nations, always suspect that the European Union and the United States use trade agreements as testing grounds for setting tomorrow's multilateral agenda on labour standards. It is thus no surprise that the debate on labour standards is a very sensitive and controversial topic of discussion in multilateral and regional trade policy debates. At the multilateral level, the issue is characterized by tension and antagonism between developed and developing countries. This has been the case since the early days of the General Agreement on Tariffs and Trade (GATT) and lasted until the creation of the WTO since developing countries continue to object to the linkage of WTO rules and labour rights.[16] With the creation of the WTO, some developed countries that wanted to bring the so-called 'social clauses' within the WTO legal system advocated for the resumption of the Uruguay Round discussions, which did not translate into a proper WTO mandate.

US and EU historical leadership in championing the trade and sustainability agenda continues today and is reflected in their bilateral and unilateral trade arrangements. At the launch of the Uruguay Round, the United States was concerned with the question of worker rights and their relationship with trade.[17] The United States asked ministers to 'recognize that denial of worker rights can impede the attainment of the objectives of the GATT and can lead to trade distortions, thereby increasing pressures for trade-restrictive measures'.[18] In other words, this was a

www.ilo.org/wcmsp5/groups/public/---dgreports/---inst/documents/genericdocument/wcms_829644.pdf> accessed 31 August 2023, 4.

[15] See Henrik Horn, Petros C Mavroidis, and André Sapir, 'Beyond the WTO? An Anatomy of EU and US Preferential Trade Agreements' (2010) 33(11) World Economy 1565, 1567.

[16] On the issue of social clause and international trade, see generally Adelle Blackett, 'Whither Social Clause? Human Rights, Trade Theory and Treaty Interpretation' (1999) 31(1) Columbia Human Rights Law Review 1. For an historical account of the trade–labour linkage, see Steve Charnovitz, 'The Influence of International Labour Standards on the World Trading System: A Historical Overview' (1987) 126(5) International Labour Review 565.

[17] General Agreement on Tariffs and Trade, Preparatory Committee, GATT Doc GATT PREP COM(86)W/43, 25 June 1986.

[18] ibid 1.

warning that some countries, such as the United States, might be left with no choice but to resort to trade-restrictive measures to counter the adverse effects of what the United States considered 'artificially low [labour] standards'.[19] To 'ensure that expanded trade benefits all workers in all countries', the United States proposed addressing the relationship of worker rights with GATT provisions while leaving the membership the latitude to decide which particular rights could be appropriately dealt with in the context of trade rules.[20] The Record of the discussions that took place within the Uruguay Round Preparatory Committee between 23 and 26 June 1986 already testified to the opposition to the question, some considering it too eminently political to be the subject of a commercial treaty, in particular due to the absence of criteria to be used to determine whether the workers' rights are respected.

In effect, as the Argentinian representatives ironically put it, and rightly so in our opinion, the fact that the United States had only ratified seven ILO Conventions back then, as opposed to 62 by Argentina or 115 by Spain, was not synonymous with the denial of workers' rights in the United States.[21] In other words, the United States could not be accused of violating workers' rights or not taking them into account simply because it had not yet ratified all ILO Conventions. Argentina's posture was informed by the absence of objective criteria to serve as a compass for respecting workers' rights in GATT contracting parties. Therefore, deciding who would determine when these rights are breached was crucial. The other developing countries seemed all in agreement, despite US concerns that products that appeared to derive a competitive advantage from the denial of workers' rights in the country of production might enter foreign markets. Colombia, echoing developing countries' concerns, considered that they derive their comparative advantage mainly from the 'relatively lower cost' of labour.[22] Because of the dissimilar economic situations of developed and developing countries, offering similar wages was definitely out of the question since such an attempt at harmonization would not align with the living standards in developing countries.[23]

Some of the harshest criticisms came from the Indian and Brazilian representatives, who not only censored the US approach but chastised the organization for even contemplating putting such a topic on its agenda. For Brazil, attempts to broaden the scope of the GATT are mere pretences to hide the organization's failures in its areas of competence. India agreed, saying that the tendency to 'overload

[19] ibid 3.

[20] ibid 1, 2.

[21] General Agreement on Tariffs and Trade, Preparatory Committee, Record of Discussions of 23–26 June, GATT Doc PREP COM(86) SR/8, 13 August 1986, para 44.

[22] ibid para 46.

[23] ibid para 48. The Nigerian representative also pointed out the gross exploitation of workers for purely racial reasons, which was taking place in Africa and to which he demanded close attention in view of adopting relevant GATT disciplines. Whether this question was a GATT affair remains, however, doubtful.

the GATT with problems that are foreign to it' should be halted as this was based on what its delegate described as an 'excessively liberal and loose interpretation of the preamble',[24] at the risk of 'destroying' the GATT 'as a serious institution'.[25]

While the United States appeared to be more vocal among developed nations advocating to place the subject on the agenda of the negotiations, the European Community, as it was then called, was also at the forefront of this issue. A European Parliament Resolution of 1986, at the launch of the Uruguay Round negotiations, attests to this concern. The Parliament was demanding that a new provision be negotiated within the GATT to cover fair labour standards, in line with the Havana Charter clause that never entered into force.[26] For the European Parliament, the rationale for such a demand was the same as the United States'. They considered that 'non-adherence to, and persistent violation of recognized international labour standards in certain GATT contracting parties acts as a distortion of fair competition and [a]s a major cause of pressure for greater protectionism in industrialized countries'.[27] A concrete suggestion from the European Parliament came in the form of an amendment of GATT Article XX(e) offering to extend the existing prison labour exception to cover child and forced labour as well as the right to join trade unions and engage in collective bargaining.[28] Interestingly, the European Parliament did not consider only the multilateral framework in tabling its suggestions. It also called upon the European Commission to 'introduce a social incentive clause as a means of combating underdevelopment' in the European GSP.[29] Needless to say, these are issues that now form part of EU trade agreements' sustainability chapters and incentive packages in the GSP + programmes.

The debate on labour standards at the WTO revolves around several aspects, the main legal one being whether a country can lawfully take trade actions (or sanctions) to pressure countries considered to be severely violating what is considered 'core' labour rights. The proponents of this argument contend that implementing labour standards through trade agreements would improve workers' working conditions and wages in low-income countries, thereby reducing the wage differentials between rich and poor countries. However, developing countries' position has always been that lower wages (or cheap labour and production) should be regarded as a comparative advantage. Nevertheless, except for import restrictions

[24] ibid para 50. The Preamble referred to here is the passage about improving standards of living and ensuring full employment.

[25] ibid.

[26] European Parliament, Resolution on the New Round of Multilateral Trade Negotiations within GATT, European Parliament Doc A2-87/86, Official Journal of the European Communities, C-255/78, 13 October 1986, para 65. Note that art 7 of the Havana Charter covered labour standards and required countries to take appropriate measures to eliminate unfair labour conditions within their territories.

[27] ibid para 64.

[28] See European Parliament, Report of the Committee on External Economic Relations on the Introduction of a Social Clause in the Unilateral and Multilateral Trading System, European Parliament Doc A3-0007/94 (1994) para 7.

[29] ibid para 11.

that governments may impose on products manufactured in prison (under Article XX(e) of the GATT), the unequivocal position of WTO Members has been that labour issues (or labour standards) fall outside WTO's jurisdiction—as an institution dealing with trade—and is best addressed by the more competent ILO.[30] That official posture notwithstanding, some have argued that there is an implicit social clause under GATT Article XX(a), which may permit trade restriction on the pretence that the process of producing a particular good contravenes the public morals of the importing state. These could include the non-respect of fundamental human rights and labour rights.[31]

B. A Mixed Feeling Regarding Environmental Concerns

The environmental question, while different, comes with its challenges and antagonism. Although developing countries are at the forefront of the fight against environmental degradation and climate change, they do not always agree with the measures chosen to address these challenges. Not that they do not themselves at times restrict trade for environmental goals, as the global war against plastic bags can testify,[32] but they dispute measures aiming at shifting the cost of production towards carbon-emitting countries such as the EU Emission Trading System[33] and the more recent Carbon Border Adjustment Mechanism (CBAM).[34] Simply put, the CBAM aims to subject products imported into the EU customs territory to carbon pricing equivalent to that applied to European manufacturers of the same products. The primary objective of this system is to fight carbon leakage—a phenomenon whereby the implementation of binding climate measures aimed at reducing greenhouse gas (GHG) emissions in the European Union leads to an increase in GHG emissions in other parts of the world. The US Fair, Affordable, Innovative, and Resilient Transition and Competition Act (also known as the FAIR Transition and Competition Act), a bill introduced in Congress and yet to be adopted, also

[30] See WTO, Ministerial Conference, Ministerial Declaration adopted on 13 December 1996, WTO Doc WT/MIN(96)/DEC, 18 December 1996, para 4. See also WTO, *Trading into the Future* (2nd edn, WTO 2001) 43, 51.

[31] See eg Steve Charnovitz, 'The Moral Exception in Trade Policy' (1998) 38 Virginia Journal of International Law 689, 743. See also Regis Y Simo, 'Trade and Morality: Balancing Between the Pursuit of Non-Trade Concerns and the Fear of Opening the Floodgates' (2019) 51 George Washington International Law Review 407, 441–42.

[32] See eg Regis Y Simo, 'Of Sustainable Development in Africa: Addressing the (In)Congruence of Plastic Bags Regulations with International Trade Rules' (2019) 45(1) Brooklyn Journal of International Law 241.

[33] Directive 2003/87/EC of the European Parliament and of the Council of 13 October 2003 establishing a system for greenhouse gas emission allowance trading within the Union and amending Council Directive 96/61/EC, Official Journal L 275/32, 25 October 2003.

[34] See Regulation (EU) 2023/956 of the European Parliament and of the Council of 10 May 2023 Establishing a Carbon Border Adjustment Mechanism, Official Journal L 130/52, 16 May 2023.

proposes a CBAM for goods entering the US market.[35] CBAMs therefore tackle both the origin of the goods and their production methods.

While questioning the WTO compatibility of CBAMs is reasonable,[36] what interests developing countries crucially is the CBAMs' unilateral character. Indeed, developing countries contend that piecemeal unilateral actions, regardless of their legitimate purposes,[37] should not take precedence over comprehensive multilateral solutions. The multilateral trading system considers SDT in designing and applying WTO Members' environmental laws when such rules can affect trade flows. Unilateral measures like CBAMs may sometimes counter such progress, thus justifying SDT beneficiaries' demands. In effect, the Doha Declaration is unequivocal as to the Committee on Trade and Environment's (CTE) mandate, which is tasked to give 'particular attention' to 'the effect of environmental measures on market access, especially concerning developing countries, in particular, the least-developed among them, and those situations in which the elimination or reduction of trade restrictions and distortions would benefit trade, the environment and development'.[38] Yet, unilateral measures implemented outside the multilateral oversight do not always consider their effects on developing countries' market access, thus constituting disguised restrictions to international trade.

Against this backdrop, the African Group's communication at the General Council on 13 July 2023, in which it recalled the principles guiding the development and implementation of trade-related environmental measures,[39] does not come as a surprise. The African Group lashes WTO Members over two related things. First, for the African Group, like labour issues which developing countries have argued for years are not within the WTO mandate, the CTE is being used for the same purpose because it is venturing into subjects which would, at best, feature under the CTE's any other business if not as mere experience sharing.[40] Examples of these non-mandated issues include the Fossil Fuel Subsidy Reform[41]

[35] See Bill to Amend the Internal Revenue Code of 1986 to Establish a Border Carbon Adjustment for the Importation of Certain Goods, HR 4534, 11th Congress (2021).

[36] Since CBAMs apply exclusively to imported goods, they run the risk of violating the most favoured nation clause and national treatment provisions. See eg Henrik Horn and Petros C Mavroidis, 'To B(TA) or Not to B(TA)? On the Legality and Desirability of Border Tax Adjustments from a Trade Perspective' (2011) 34(11) World Economy 1837.

[37] Standing WTO cases recognize Members' rights to pursue legitimate sustainable development objectives through unilateral trade measures. See Appellate Body Report, *United States—Import Prohibition of Certain Shrimp and Shrimp Products*, WT/DS58/AB/R, adopted 6 November 1998. See also Appellate Body Report, *United States— Import Prohibition of Certain Shrimp and Shrimp Products, Recourse to Article 21.5 of the DSU by Malaysia*, WT/DS58/AB/RW, adopted 21 November 2001.

[38] WTO, Ministerial Conference, Ministerial Declaration adopted on 14 November 2001, WTO Doc WT/MIN(01)/DEC/1, 20 November 2001, para 32.

[39] See WTO Doc WT/GC/W/894 (n 12).

[40] ibid para 2.3.

[41] See WTO, Ministerial Statement on Fossil Fuel Subsidies, Revision, WTO Doc WT/MIN(21)/9/Rev 1, 14 December 2021.

initiative, the Trade and Environmental Sustainability Structured Discussions,[42] and the Informal Dialogue on Plastics Pollution and Sustainable Plastics Trade (IDP).[43] Ironically, African countries are participating in these dialogues, such as the IDP, and even taking steps to ban plastic bags within their respective jurisdictions[44] while simultaneously opposing their full inclusion into the CTE's mandate. On a closer look, their position seems more ideologically motivated—in the spirit of refuting any new issues until the Doha Round is concluded—than resting on the rejection of the topic itself. The criticism here is not of the CTE's marginalization but that of broadening its agenda.

The African Group detects a second problem with the current trade and sustainability situation, namely the 'increasing use of unilateral measures, which are being justified as environmental measures'.[45] Not only is their WTO compatibility questioned but such measures undermine the WTO principles, such as non-discrimination and consensus, and also weaken 'multilaterally negotiated rights and obligations of countries'.[46] The African Group expresses concern that these unilateral environmental measures pursued by developed countries are being 'implemented with little consideration of their potential impact on developing countries'.[47] As mentioned earlier, such a disregard may lead to a conflict with well-established international environmental law principles such as the common but differentiated responsibilities (CBDR) principle.[48]

Therefore, like labour standards, developing countries oppose unilateral environmental protection measures such as CBAMs that did not go through the multilateral vetting process where they should be adopted by consensus, as was the Fisheries Subsidies Agreement. For this group, the only accepted mechanism to tackle sustainability is through the general exceptions that provide the scrutiny of the otherwise inconsistent unilateral measures to pass the test of GATT Article XX. It follows that, unlike their posture regarding labour standards, which they oppose frontally, arguing that it is not a topic for the WTO, the environmental question is accepted with the aforementioned caveats.

[42] See WTO, Trade and Environmental Sustainability Structured Discussions (TESSD), Ministerial Statement on Trade and Environmental Sustainability, Revision, WTO Doc WT/MIN(21)/6/Rev 2 14 December 2021.

[43] WTO, Informal Dialogue on Plastic Pollution and Environmentally Sustainable Plastics Trade (IDP), Ministerial Statement on Plastic Pollution and Environmentally Sustainable Plastics Trade, Revision, WTO Doc WT/MIN(21)/8/Rev 2, 10 December 2021.

[44] See Simo, 'Of Sustainable Development in Africa' (n 32).

[45] WTO Doc WT/GC/W/894 (n 12) para 2.5.

[46] ibid.

[47] ibid para 1.3.

[48] ibid.

III. Sustainability Obligations Through Preferential Trade

While attempts to insert a 'social clause' within the WTO failed due to a lack of consensus, labour provisions have multiplied rapidly through the back door of trade agreements and preferential trade arrangements. Apart from negotiated and agreed-upon rules in sustainability chapters, other developed countries' practice since the establishment of the GATT GSP has been to link the available benefits to the respect of core labour standards and some environmental protection commitments. Based on the premise that trade generates growth and well-being for all, developed economies such as the European Union and United States place trade at the core of their development cooperation policy. They consider trade one of the most effective tools for promoting development in that boosting trade with developing countries increases their export earnings, stimulates their industrialization, encourages them to diversify their economy, and accelerates their economic growth.[49] To achieve these objectives, granting tariff preferences is the default instrument.

According to the ILO, the number of trade agreements incorporating labour provisions grew exponentially in the last two decades, reaching over 113 in January 2022, up from 4 in 1995 when the WTO came into existence.[50] The proliferation of labour provisions goes in tandem with the expansion of their content, their scope of application, and the mechanisms for promoting and enforcing compliance with them. In addition, depending on whether it is a preferential arrangement or a bilateral/reciprocal trade agreement, developed countries generally use different means of pressure. They can choose between sanctions or boycotts of specific products from the countries no longer meeting eligibility criteria for duty-free market access, remove all preferential market access altogether, or trigger the dispute settlement clauses to force the partners, if found guilty, to respect their commitments. It follows that developed countries use two approaches in tying trade advantages to sustainability issues, notably the promotional and sanction-based techniques. For instance, the EU GSP comprises three arrangements for that purpose.[51] While the standard GSP programme allows duty-free market access to selected goods originating in developing countries or a tariff reduction for goods considered by the European Union as sensitive,[52] the special incentive GSP + arrangement rewards those countries that implement 27 international conventions

[49] On EU trade and development cooperation policy, see Lorand Bartels, 'The Trade and Development Policy of the European Union' (2007) 18(4) European Journal of International Law 715.

[50] See Corley-Coulibaly and others, 'A Multi-Faceted Typology of Labour Provisions in Trade Agreements' (n 14) 3.

[51] See Regulation (EU) No 978/2012 of the European Parliament and of the Council of 25 October 2012 applying a scheme of generalized tariff preferences and repealing Council Regulation (EC) No 732/2008, Official Journal L 303, 31 October 2012, art 1.

[52] ibid arts 4–7.

related to labour and human rights, environmental and climate protection, and good governance.[53]

In terms of monitoring and enforcement, Article 19 of the EU GSP Regulation provides that the European Union can temporarily suspend GSP benefits under the standard and GSP + arrangements if the beneficiary is guilty of 'serious and systematic violation of principles laid down' in the core UN/ILO human and labour rights conventions. It is important to note that this suspension provision does not concern only GSP + beneficiaries whose access to the incentives depends on the ratification of these conventions but extends to all GSP beneficiaries, including those under the standard GSP.[54] Moreover, the European Union does not link sanctions to non-respect of MEAs, also listed as part of the GSP + benefits, but limits the withdrawal conditions to the non-respect of UN human rights and ILO labour rights conventions.

The US adopts a similar approach to sustainability obligations in its GSP programme. While its GSP has been in place since 1974, it was ten years later, in 1984, that the labour standards conditionalities appeared for the first time.[55] The Trade and Tariff Act of 1984 established as a condition of eligibility for trade preferences that the beneficiary must have taken or is taking measures to guarantee internationally recognized workers' rights and gave the US president the power to withdraw, suspend, or limit the application of special treatment to any beneficiary that does not comply with this condition. Since then, beneficiaries' designation, exclusion, and re-admission is guided by a set of eligibility criteria, including labour rights. In the same vein, the African Growth and Opportunity Act (AGOA), under WTO law, is strictly not a GSP scheme:[56] it provides duty-free market access to goods from a selected group of African countries and also contains labour and human rights conditionalities.[57]

The common thread between the United States, the European Union, and other developed countries is that they tie the benefits of unilateral trade preferences to the respect of sustainable development standards that are also defined unilaterally and presented to beneficiaries on a take-it-or-leave-it basis. Beneficiaries cannot

[53] ibid art 9. Note that benefits under the GSP + arrangements must be expressly requested by potential beneficiaries. See ibid art 10.

[54] This is referred to as 'negative conditionality'—ie the reduction, suspension, or termination of benefits if the beneficiary violates the conditions—as opposed to 'positive conditionality' (which is the promise by a donor of a benefit if the grantee satisfies a set of conditions). See Elena Fierro, *European Union's Approach to Human Rights Conditionality in Practice* (Kluwer Law International 2003) 100–02.

[55] See Trade and Tariff Act of 1984, Public Law 98–573, 30 October 1984, ss 501–03.

[56] See Council for Trade in Goods, African Growth and Opportunity Act (AGOA as amended)—Request for a Waiver, WTO Doc G/C/W/713, 16 July 2015. In effect, WTO Members' obligations can be waived under art IX:3 of the WTO Agreement. In the case of AGOA, the United States sought and was granted a waiver of its obligations under arts I and XIII of the GATT. GSPs, on the other hand, are covered by the Enabling Clause.

[57] Trade and Development Act of 2000, Public Law 106–200, 18 May 2000, Title I (extension of certain trade benefits to sub-Saharan Africa) s 104(a)(1)–(3).

choose their level of implementation but must instead meet the standard defined by the 'donor'. Their status as developing countries is the requirement to benefit from the preferential market access, implying, in turn, that there is no consideration to their level of development in cutting those benefits when the granting countries believe that a beneficiary has ceased to meet the eligibility criteria. The inclusion and enforcement of AGOA and GSP conditionalities relating to labour, human rights, and democracy qualify these preferential trade arrangements as an instrument for the institutional and rule of law reforms in the beneficiary countries beyond their clothing as trade policy instruments.[58] One can therefore understand developing countries' refusal to link the same measures with their trade benefits at the multilateral level.

While instances of unilateral preference suspensions for non-respect of GSP conditionalities are legion and do not need recounting here,[59] triggering dispute settlement mechanisms to enforce sustainability chapters in free trade agreements is relatively more recent. Only two panels have interpreted labour standards obligations in trade agreements to date.[60] Decided cases have generated a backlash from the trade and labour community alike.[61] If the *Guatemala–Labor* panel garnered an outcry for its determination that although in breach of its commitment to enforce labour rights as the FTA requires, this violation was not in a manner affecting trade, then the *Korea–Labor* panel generated frustration for its findings that although Korea's measures were inconsistent with the freedom of association commitments under the FTA, Korea had not failed to make 'continued and sustained efforts' towards the ratification of the relevant ILO fundamental conventions. Cases that have given rise to trade and sustainable development (TSD) panel reports are on labour matters and none so far on environmental standards.

[58] See Regis Simo, 'The AGOA as Stepping Stone for USA–Africa Free Trade Agreements' (2018) 17(3) Journal of International Trade Law and Policy 115.

[59] For instance, in 2020, the European Union revoked Cambodia's duty-free market access to the European Union over human and labour rights concerns. See EU Commission, 'Cambodia Loses Duty-Free Access to the EU Market Over Human Rights Concerns' *Press Release* (12 August 2020) <https://ec.europa.eu/commission/presscorner/detail/en/IP_20_1469> accessed 31 August 2023. Questioning the European Union's double standard and policy incoherence in this regard, notably vis-à-vis Myanmar when guilty of the same sins, see Angela Pennisi di Floristella, 'The Everything But Arms (EBA) Scheme and the EU's Normative Dilemma: The Case of Myanmar's Garment Sector' (2023) Third World Quarterly 2404.

[60] See Final Report of the Panel, *In the Matter of Guatemala—Issues Relating to the Obligations Under Article 16.2.1(a) of the CAFTA-DR*, 14 June 2017; Report of the Panel of Experts, *Proceeding Constituted Under Article 13.15 of the EU–Korea Free Trade Agreement*, 20 January 2021.

[61] See Kathleen Claussen, 'Reimagining Trade-Plus Compliance: The Labor Story' (2020) 23(1) Journal of International Economic Law 25. See also Lance Compa, Eric Gottwald, and Jeffrey Vogt, 'Wrong Turn for Workers' Rights: The U.S.–Guatemala CAFTA Labor Arbitration Ruling—And What To Do About It' (International Labor Rights Forum, March 2018) <https://laborrights.org/sites/default/files/publications/Wrong%20Turn%20for%20Workers%20Rights%20-%20March%202018.pdf> accessed 31 August 2023.

Although the European Union has long resisted the implementation of legally binding clauses on labour and environmental standards in its trade agreements,[62] this forbearance is about to change drastically. In 2020, the Netherlands and France jointly called for stricter application of environmental and labour standards in EU trade agreements, saying that the activities of countries that benefit from preferential access to the EU market must be controlled.[63] The sponsors noted a 'lack of progress in compliance with TSD commitments in some partner countries multiple years after trade agreements were concluded' and exhorted the European Union to 'raise the ambition and improve the implementation of TSD Chapters.'[64] The proposal also contained, albeit not without controversy, a possibility to link tariff reduction to the implementation of sustainability commitments. In other words, France and the Netherlands were suggesting that the European Union should only abide by its other obligations under existing and future trade agreements if the other parties uphold their sustainability commitment in return. Thus, the two countries advocated for imposing higher tariffs on countries that do not respect sustainable development commitments, a suggestion that may be challenged in the case of a bilateral/regional trade agreement. This call followed the EU Commission's creation of the Chief Trade Enforcement Officer, whose role includes, inter alia, improving Brussels' ability to identify violations by third countries of the obligations they have undertaken in trade agreements with the European Union.

Given the new EU strategy, there is no doubt that enforcement through dispute mechanisms will amplify in years to come and the developing country status of the other parties to trade agreements will no longer shield them from challenges over sustainability commitments.

IV. Any Scope for Special and Differential Treatment and Sustainability Obligations?

This chapter argues that developing countries are faced with multilayered dimensions of sustainability provisions in trade, namely regional trade agreements (north–south and south–south), preferential trade arrangements, and within the multilateral trading system. While the nature of obligations is different at these levels, the common denominator is the lack of agreement or participation of

[62] See European Commission, Directorate-General for Trade, *Trade, Growth and World Affairs—Trade Policy as a Core Component of the EU's 2020 Strategy* (Publication Office 2011) COM(2010) 612, 12.

[63] See Kingdom of the Netherlands, 'Non-Paper from the Netherlands and France on Trade, Social Economic Effects and Sustainable Development' (8 May 2020) <https://www.permanentrepresentations. nl/documents/publications/2020/05/08/non-paper-from-nl-and-fr-on-trade-social-economic-effects-and-sustainable-development> accessed 31 August 2023.

[64] ibid.

developing countries in shaping some of these rules, which are now imposed on them. For lack of agreement at the WTO, where SDT provisions are their guarantee for a variable geometry in assuming commitments, sustainability matters get imposed on them through the back door of negotiated regional trade agreements or foisted as conditionalities under unilateral GSP schemes. One is therefore tempted to question whether there is or should be scope for SDT in trade and sustainability. While developing countries believe that their status should be preserved in all climate-related talks,[65] for some developed countries, climate change and environmental protection are too sensitive to warrant differentiated obligations in tackling them.[66]

In effect, WTO developing countries not only suggest that Members should refrain from unilateral trade measures for environmental protection and favour multilateral solutions within the mandate of the CTE but also that any such rules that would ensue should not negate SDT.[67] Whether measures should be included in states' unilateral climate policy to accommodate developing countries should be of concern also to developed countries as some, like the European Union, see SDT as 'the most basic principle of the international law of development'.[68] One should therefore expect that the design of climate schemes should abide by this consideration. In this vein, the European Parliament's initial recommendation was to include SDT in the EU CBAM. Indeed, in its efforts to design a 'WTO-compatible' CBAM, the European Parliament '[s]tresse[d] that Least Developed Countries and Small Island Developing States should be given special treatment to take account of their specificities and the potential negative impacts of the CBAM on their development'.[69] However, the final CBAM Regulation does not reflect this initial approach to accord SDT to LDCs but merely stipulates that their decarbonization will be financed through the revenue generated by CBAM levies.[70]

While one may argue that the European Parliament's language should be taken merely for what it is, that is, recommendations, and that it is nothing more

[65] See WTO Doc WT/GC/W/894 (n 12). See also WTO, Committee on Trade and Environment, Special Session, Communication from Argentina and Brazil—Environmental Goods and Services—Paragraph 31(iii)—Special and Differential Treatment, WTO Doc TN/TE/W/76, 30 June 2010.

[66] See eg Mary J Bortscheller, 'Equitable but Ineffective: How the Principle of Common but Differentiated Responsibilities Hobbles the Global Fight against Climate Change' (2009) 10 Sustainable Development Law and Policy 49.

[67] See WTO Doc WT/GC/W/894 (n 12). See also South African Government, Joint Statement issued at the conclusion of the 30th BASIC Ministerial Meeting on Climate Change hosted by India on 8th April 2021 (8 April 2021) <https://www.gov.za/nr/speeches/joint-statement-issued-conclusion-30th-basic-ministerial-meeting-climate-change-hosted> accessed 31 August 2023. BASIC countries include Brazil, South Africa, India, and China.

[68] Appellate Body Report, *European Communities—Conditions for the Granting of Tariff Preferences to Developing Countries*, WT/DS246/AB/R, adopted 20 April 2004, para 14 (reporting EC's submission).

[69] European Parliament resolution of 10 March 2021 towards a WTO-compatible EU carbon border adjustment mechanism (2020/2043(INI)), EP Doc P9 TA(2021)0071, Official Journal C 474/2, 24 November 2021, para 8.

[70] Regulation (EU) 2023/956, Preamble, paras (73)–(74).

than hortatory as reflected in the use of the terms 'should' in paragraph 8 of the Resolution,[71] the non-inclusion of these recommendations in the final CBAM regulation nevertheless raises questions as to its development friendliness. This is especially so since the European Parliament is fully aware that CBAM may have adverse effects on developing countries and LDCs,[72] hence its initial suggestion for a carve-out. Considering their historical and current low contributions to carbon emissions, one way to consider their fragile circumstances would be, for instance, an exemption from CBAM for relevant products originating in LDCs. This EU unilateral environmental policy, which risks jeopardizing exports from LDCs in the sectors concerned, is what the African Group denounced in their recent outing to the General Council.[73] Contrary to the EU approach to CBAM vis-à-vis LDCs,[74] the US bill specifically contains an LDC exemption.[75]

Yet, under the CBDR principle, while all countries must take their share to address common global environmental degradation, they are not equally responsible for that destruction and hence should assume differentiated responsibilities in reducing these risks.[76] The WTO Agreement also recognizes that not all of its Members are at the same level of development, hence a need for SDT. A question remains whether this SDT applies to sustainable provisions in the WTO and whether it should apply. A look at the Preamble of the WTO Agreement seems to suggest and mirror the principle of common but differentiated responsibility dear to MEAs. The relevant part reads:

> seeking both to protect and preserve the environment and to enhance the means for doing so *in a manner consistent with [WTO Members'] respective needs and concerns at different levels of economic development.*[77]

[71] EP Doc P9_TA(2021)0071 (n 69) para 8.

[72] ibid para 19.

[73] See WTO Doc WT/GC/W/894 (n 12). Studies show that Mozambique, an African LDC, exports more than half of its aluminium production to the European Union. UNCTAD, A European Border Adjustment Mechanism: Implications for Developing Countries (UNCTAD 2021) <https://unctad.org/system/files/official-document/osginf2021d2_en.pdf> accessed 31 August 2023, 10. Note also that Mozambique's aluminium constitutes over 7 per cent of total aluminium imports to the European Union.

[74] While the European Union's initial proposal also contained a recommendation to exempt LDCs from the CBA as mentioned, the US bill uses stronger language in this regard. Whether this will translate into the final law remains to be seen.

[75] HR 4534 (2021) s 9904(b). It is worth noting that instead of using the WTO criterion for LDCs, the US CBAM relies on the list of LDCs on 'the most recent Development Assistance Committee List of Official Development Assistance Recipients' published by the Organisation for Economic Co-operation and Development. This is in line with US recent practices to depart from WTO proxies for self-declared developing countries and the UN list of LDCs for trade remedies purposes, notably in countervailing duties. See eg Regis Y Simo, 'Developing Countries and Special and Differential Treatment' in Kholofelo Kugler and Franziska Sucker (eds), *International Economic Law: (Southern) African Perspectives and Priorities* (Juta 2021) 233, 259–61.

[76] See Christopher D Stone, 'Common But Differentiated Responsibilities in International Law' (2004) 98(2) American Journal of International Law 276.

[77] WTO Agreement, Preamble; Recital 1 (emphasis added).

The Paris Agreement, whose objectives the CBAMs pursue, and the WTO-covered agreements recognize SDT as core principles. The introduction of SDT in the multilateral trading system was in response to the demands of underdeveloped countries towards the international community, then engaged in eliminating trade barriers among the actors to play a similar role in establishing a mechanism through which the benefits of economic development could be shared. SDT is therefore conceived as the instrument to bring fairness and equity to the multilateral trading system. Consequently, SDT stands out as a distinctive feature of the multilateral trading system.

Bearing in mind developing countries' rebuff of labour issues at the WTO, avenues for SDT in the multilateral trading system exist and need consideration in future negotiations within the CTE's mandate. By linking WTO Members' obligations to their capacity to implement their commitments, the Trade Facilitation Agreement (TFA)[78] provides suitable guidelines in this regard. Indeed, the TFA contrasts with existing SDT provisions and contains revolutionary mechanisms that admit implementation in stages. Article 13:2 of the TFA strongly affirms this flexibility by stating that the 'extent and timing of the implementation' of its provisions by developing countries and LDCs 'shall be related to [their] implementation capacities'. Moreover, the TFA states that assistance and support will be provided to help these countries achieve the necessary capacity before any obligation to implement the Agreement duly.[79]

The TFA comprises three parts. Section II of the TFA guarantees developing countries and LDCs the possibility to implement their obligations according to three categories (A, B, and C) and each of them is requested to 'self-designate' within the provisions falling under each category.[80] In other words, the TFA allows each developing country and LDC to group all trade facilitation disciplines into three categories based on its self-assessment. The difference in categories mainly depends on the time a Member implements its obligations under the Agreement. Category A contains provisions that developing countries and LDCs designated for implementation upon entry into force of the TFA (ie on 22 February 2017), or in the case of LDCs within one year after it entered into force (ie on 22 February 2018).[81] Categories B and C represent significant reforms of SDT. Category B commitments contain provisions that a developing country or an LDC designates for implementation on a date after a transitional period following the entry into force of the TFA.[82] In Category C, one finds provisions that the Member will implement on a date after a transitional period following the Agreement's entry into force and

[78] See WTO, Protocol Amending the Marrakesh Agreement Establishing the World Trade Organization—Decision of 27 November 2014, WTO Doc WT/L/940, 28 November 2014.

[79] See ibid art 13:2.

[80] ibid art 14:2.

[81] ibid art 14:1(a).

[82] ibid art 14:1(b).

requiring the acquisition of assistance and support for capacity building.[83] These flexibilities of commitments and implementation aim at gradually incorporating these countries in a way that reflects their specific capacities, explicitly eschewing, according to commenters, 'a one-size-fits-all model'.[84] The TFA also allows developing countries to unilaterally alter certain aspects of their commitments by shifting their measures between Categories B and C.[85]

Furthermore, the TFA relieves certain measures from dispute settlement. For instance, Article 20 provides that for an implementation period of two years in the case of Category A measures for developing countries, eight years in the case of Categories B and C measures for LDCs, and six years in the case of Category A measures for LDCs, no disputes can be brought against trade facilitation measures implemented by these countries. The TFA breaks new grounds in the implementation of SDT in WTO agreements by allowing a high degree of flexibility to developing countries, mainly through a staged and tailored implementation of the measures based on individual countries' self-determination and by linking implementation to the necessary capacity. The TFA breaks with the erstwhile practice that emerged in the pre-GATT years of creating exceptions to what developed countries believed should be the default rules, rather than amending these rules to suit the demands and needs of developing countries. It would be anything but legitimate to expect that this approach, which defies 'the conventional wisdom on how deals in the WTO are meant to be done',[86] would be sustained and replicated in future trade negotiations on environmental and climate change issues. Despite these commendable features, one can only regret that the Fisheries Subsidies Agreement, which is in fact an incomplete agreement, did not reflect the standard set by the TFA since its SDT provisions are merely geared at technical assistance rather than differentiation in substantive rules.

[83] ibid art 14:1(c).

[84] Nora Neufeld, 'The Long and Winding Road: How WTO Members Finally Reached a Trade Facilitation Agreement' (2014), WTO Staff Working Paper ERSD-2014-06, 11.

[85] TFA art 19:1.

[86] Neufeld, 'The Long and Winding Road' (n 84) 3.

14

Enforcing Sustainability Obligations

Adjudication and Post-Adjudication Enforcement

Ilaria Espa

I. Introduction

Trade agreements (TAs) have gradually included increasingly ambitious labour and environment provisions in order to foster sustainable development.[1] The strength of such sustainability provisions ('sustainability obligations' or 'sustainability commitments') crucially depends on their implementation. The issue of enforcement has accordingly been at the forefront of efforts purported to ensure increased effectiveness of TAs' sustainability-related chapters.[2] Such efforts have led to two main trends: first, the increasing inclusion of fully enforceable sustainability commitments; second, the choice of different combinations of cooperative, consultative, and dispute resolution mechanisms to effectively enforce sustainability obligations.

This chapter addresses the second aspect, with a view to providing an illustration of the evolution of the methods of enforcement espoused in TAs for the purposes of ensuring the implementation of sustainability commitments.[3] It identifies

[1] For a detailed analysis of the key features (including lights and shades) of this trend, see Chapters 2–13 in this volume.

[2] While the issue has mainly been discussed in the EU context, due to peculiarities of the specialized panel of experts procedure envisaged for resolving sustainability disputes in EU TAs (see section II), enforcement has also gained prominence in the US debate with specific regard to labour provisions, particularly in the aftermath of the 2017 US–Guatemala case, described further below. The literature is vast but see, among others, M Bronkers and G Gruni, 'Taking the Enforcement of Labour Standards in the EU's Free Trade Agreements Seriously' (2019) 57 Common Market Law Review 1591; K Claussen, 'Reimagining Trade-Plus Compliance: The Labour Story' (2020) 23 Journal of International Economic Law 25; M Bronkers and G Gruni, 'Retooling the Sustainability Standards in EU Free Trade Agreements' (2021) 24 Journal of International Economic Law 25; A Nissen, 'Not *That* Assertive: The EU's Take on Enforcement of Labour Obligations in its Free Trade Agreement with South Korea' (2022) 33 European Journal of International Law 607; J Harrison and others, 'Labour Standards Provisions in EU Free Trade Agreements: Reflections on the European Commission's Reform Agenda' (2019) 18 World Trade Review 635; D Prévost and I Alexovičová, 'Mind the Compliance Gap: Managing Trustworthy Partnerships for Sustainable Development in the European Union's Free Trade Agreements' (2019) 6 International Journal of Public Law and Policy 236.; K Hradilová and O Svoboda, 'Sustainable Development Chapters in the EU Free Trade Agreements: Searching for Effectiveness' (2018) 52 Journal of World Trade 52; K Nowrot, 'Environmental Dispute Settlement Mechanisms in EU Free Trade Agreements' (2017) 20 Zeitschrift für Europarechtliche Studien 493 (2017).

[3] Cooperative mechanisms are fully covered in Chapter 9 in this volume.

Ilaria Espa, *Enforcing Sustainability Obligations* In: *The Sustainability Revolution in International Trade Agreements*. Edited by: Geraldo Vidigal and Kathleen Claussen, Oxford University Press. © Ilaria Espa 2024.
DOI: 10.1093/9780191994470.003.0014

various (combinations of) models of adjudication and post-adjudication enforcement, with a focus on the approaches emerging out of the TAs concluded by the United States and the European Union—as the 'key proponents' of sustainability provisions in TAs, on the one hand,[4] and major players in the context of the only two regional trade disputes directly concerning the enforcement of sustainability commitments that have led to reports to date, on the other hand.[5] It discusses existing and prospective challenges of adjudicating sustainability disputes in TAs and elaborates on the potential of emerging innovations experimented in most recent TAs for increasing implementation of sustainability commitments via pre-adjudication mechanisms, such as the Facility-Specific Rapid-Response Labor Mechanism (RRLM) introduced in the recent United States–Mexico–Canada Agreement (USMCA).[6] Overall, the chapter aims to address the following questions: what are the main differences and commonalities between enforcement models espoused in TAs for the purposes of ensuring effective implementation of sustainability obligations? Is there any ascertainable convergence trend among them? What do the latest developments in adjudication and post-adjudication mechanisms tell us about the effectiveness of sustainability commitments?

Against this backdrop, the chapter is organized as follows. Section II provides an overview of the different models of provisions included in TAs for the purposes of ensuring the enforcement of sustainability provisions through adjudication. Section III focuses on the post-adjudication phase and takes stock of the lessons learnt after the conclusion of the first two sustainability disputes that have arisen under TAs. Finally, section IV concludes by offering some reflections on the potential of the most recent innovations introduced in TAs with regard to

[4] L Boisson de Chazournes and J Lee, 'The European Union—Korea Free Trade Agreement Sustainable Development Proceeding: Reflections on a Ground-Breaking Dispute' (2022) 22 Journal of World Investment & Trade 329 329. This does not mean, however, that actors from different regions have not concluded TAs with sustainability provisions whose enforcement mechanisms are not worth exploring. To a large extent, however, the other models are inspired by either the US (see eg Canada) or the EU models (see eg EFTA trade agreements) models. For an analysis on emerging trends in dispute settlement models in TAs more specifically, see eg T Allee and M Elsig, 'Dispute Settlement Provisions in PTAs: New Data and New Concepts' in A Dür and M Elsig (eds), *Trade Cooperation: The Purpose, Design and Effects of Preferential Trade Agreement* (CUP 2015) 319–50. For more targeted discussions on sustainability provisions' diffusion in TAs, see, among others, J-F Morin and others, 'Kick-Starting Diffusion: Explaining the Varying Frequency of Preferential Trade Agreements' Environmental Provisions by Their Initial Conditions' (2019) 42 The World Economy 2602; J Vogt, 'The Evolution of Labour Rights and Trade—A Transatlantic Comparison and Lessons from the Transatlantic Trade and Investment Partnership' (2015) 18 Journal of International Economic Law 827.

[5] See Panel Report of the Panel of Experts Proceeding Constituted Under Article 13.15 of the EU–Korea Free Trade Agreement, 20 January 2021; Panel Report of the Panel Established Pursuant to Chapter 20 of the Dominican Republic–Central America–United States Free Trade Agreement (CAFTA–DR), *Guatemala—Issues Relating the Obligations Under Article 16.2.1(a) of the CAFTA-DR*, 14 June 2017. There are, however, many more sustainability-*related* disputes (ie disputes not arising under sustainability chapters in TAs but involving a sustainability-informed interpretation of ordinary trade provisions), as aptly noted by G Vidigal, 'Regional Trade Adjudication and the Rise of Sustainability Disputes: International Economic Law Reconfigured?: *Korea—Labor Commitments* and *Ukraine—Wood Export Bans*' (2022) 116 American Journal of International Law 567.

[6] See section IV.

(pre-)adjudication and post-adjudication enforcement for fostering the implementation of sustainability provisions.

II. Enforcing Sustainability Commitments Through Adjudication

TA provisions on the enforcement of sustainability commitments through adjudication can first be distinguished based on whether they subject such obligations to the agreements' ordinary dispute settlement mechanism or to dedicated dispute resolution procedures. In turn, this has certain implications for identifying '*who decides*'[7] whether a sustainability provision has been violated and how to determine the compliance measures to be implemented within a reasonable period of time.

The former approach has commonly been adopted in US TAs, although with significant variations across agreements concluded over the course of the last three decades.[8] The latter has constituted the standard approach espoused in EU TAs until very recently—that is, until the European Commission's so-called New Action Plan, which introduced a shift towards judicialization of sustainability provisions in 2022.[9]

A. Adjudicatory Models Relying on Ordinary Dispute Settlement

In parallel with the evolution of substantive sustainability commitments in its TAs, the United States has systemically envisaged the same dispute settlement procedures for ordinary trade obligations and sustainability commitments.[10] In the case of the European Union, apart from isolated cases,[11] a special system has long been the standard, with 'parity of dispute settlement' being just now in the making.[12]

[7] This expression is borrowed from Claussen (n 2) 30 (emphasis in original).

[8] The first US agreement containing sustainability provisions was the 1994 North American Free Trade Agreement (NAFTA), which, however, constitutes the only exception to this trend (ie labour and environment provisions were included in separate side agreements and subject to different enforcement procedures): US Congressional Research Service, 'Overview of Labour Enforcement Issues in Free Trade Agreements', 22 February 2012 2–3. The NAFTA was replaced by the USMCA on 1 July 2020.

[9] European Commission, 'The Power of Trade Partnerships: Together for Green and Just Economic Growth' COM (2022) 409 final.

[10] The only exception to this trend was the NAFTA (n 8).

[11] See L Bartels, 'Human Rights and Sustainable Development Obligations in EU Free Trade Agreements' (2013) 40 Legal Issues of Economic Integration 297, 301–11 (referring to the EU–CARICOM EPA, where labour and environmental provisions are subject to regular dispute settlement but not to trade sanctions).

[12] This expression is borrowed from A Cosbey, 'Brave New Deal? Assessing the May 10th U.S. Bipartisan Compact on Free Trade Agreements' IISD Commentary, 1 August 2007.

1. US Models

All the US TAs currently in force that include sustainability obligations on the parties ultimately subject those commitments to the same dispute settlement procedures envisaged for commercial provisions. However, different models exist with regard to both the breadth and depth of the enforcement provisions themselves and the role envisaged for the various institutions created to 'manage' sustainability provisions within dispute settlement procedures.[13]

In the case of the 2001 US–Jordan free trade agreement (US–Jordan FTA), for instance, relatively simple labour and environment provisions requiring the parties to enforce national labour and environmental laws are subject to the agreement's regular dispute settlement mechanism. Parties may thus refer a matter to a panel after the failure of mandatory consultations and in case the Joint Committee does not succeed in resolving the dispute. Importantly, the Joint Committee is composed of representatives of the parties and may include specialized experts, in addition to seeking the advice of non-governmental persons or groups.[14] There is no provision requiring specialized knowledge of labour or environment law for panellists that might be involved in sustainability disputes, however.[15] The panel is simply requested to present a report containing its findings and its determination as to whether either party has failed to carry out its obligations; in the affirmative, the panel 'may make recommendations' for the resolution of the dispute 'at the request of the Parties'; in any case, the report remains 'non-binding'.[16] It is in fact the Joint Committee that, following the presentation of the panel's report, 'shall endeavour to resolve the dispute, taking the report into account, as appropriate'.[17] Importantly, this entails further institutionalized dialogue between the parties.

Under a second, more recent model, which includes the Dominican Republic–Central America–United States Agreement (CAFTA-DR),[18] the judicialization of sustainability commitments maintains a relatively limited scope. Provisions requiring the enforcement of domestic (labour/environmental) laws remain the only sustainability obligations that are enforceable, again through standard dispute settlement procedures.[19] Requests for the establishment of a panel are conditioned

[13] Reference to 'management practices' as a valid alternative to litigating sustainability provisions is found in Claussen (n 2) 27. Cooperative mechanisms are per se discussed in Chapter 8 of this volume.

[14] Agreement between the United States and Jordan on the Establishment of a Free Trade Area, in force 17 December 2001 art 15.3.

[15] No provision is included in the Agreement on the establishment of rosters and the qualifications of the panellists either: see ibid art 17:1(c).

[16] ibid art 17.1(d).

[17] ibid art 17.2(a).

[18] The parties to the CAFTA-DR are the United States, Costa Rica, El Salvador, Guatemala, Honduras, Nicaragua, and the Dominican Republic. The other agreements following this model include the agreements concluded by the United States with Chile, Singapore, Australia, Morocco, Bahrain, and Oman: US Congressional Research Service (n 8) 3.

[19] See Dominican Republic–Central America–United States Free Trade Agreement, in force 1 March 2006, arts 16.2(a) and 17.2(a), respectively.

upon the prior activation of dedicated consultations.[20] The creation of rosters of panellists with expertise in '[labour/environmental] law or [their] enforcement, international trade or the resolution of disputes arising under international agreements' is specifically required.[21] It is also envisaged that the panel may seek information and technical advice from experts.[22] Furthermore, and similarly to the previous model, the final report of the panel[23] must contain the panel's findings of fact, its determination on nonconformity, and its recommendations to resolve the dispute, if parties have requested them.[24] Based on the report, the parties 'shall agree' on the resolution of the dispute, which 'normally shall conform with the determinations and recommendations, if any, of the panel'.[25] In case the panel determines a violation of (sustainability) obligations, the resolution of the dispute shall either consist in the elimination of nonconformity or, where appropriate, in the preparation of a 'mutually satisfactory action plan'.[26] This latter alternative is particularly relevant in case of sustainability disputes, although in the US–Guatemala case the panel ultimately concluded that, irrespective of Guatemala's failure to effectively enforce its labour laws, there was no breach of the CAFTA–DR's labour provisions, as the United States could not show that such failure occurred 'through a sustained or recurring course of action or inaction, in a manner affecting trade' as required by Article 16.2(a).[27]

After the 'May 10' political compromise,[28] the 'adjudicatory' model applies more broadly to a much wider range of sustainability provisions that have since been included in US TAs, which also importantly include parties' commitment to enshrine the core labour standards as recognized in the 1998 Declaration on Fundamental Principles and Rights at Work of the International Labour Organization (ILO) into national law as well as to enforce existing commitments arising under various multilateral environmental agreements (MEAs),[29] and the non-regression clauses—again qualified by the 'in a manner affecting trade' requirement.[30] Under this model, the same dispute settlement procedures apply to

[20] ibid arts 16.6 ('Cooperative Labour Consultations') and 17.10 ('Collaborative Environmental Consultations'). For more details, see Chapter 8 of this volume.

[21] ibid arts 16.7(2) and 17.11(2).

[22] ibid art 20.12.

[23] In this set of agreements, the panel shall also prepare an initial report based on which parties can submit written comments: ibid art 20.13.

[24] ibid art 20.13(3).

[25] ibid art 20.15(1).

[26] ibid art 20.15(2)–(3).

[27] Final Report of the Panel (n 6) paras 190–196.

[28] On 10 May 2007, the US Democratic Party and the Republicans reached a historic bipartisan compromise that led to stronger provisions in pending TAs, including on labour and environment. For more details, see Cosbey (n 12) 1.

[29] For a full discussion, see ibid. 'May 10' trade agreements include the TAs concluded by the United States with Peru, South Korea, Panama, and Colombia: Bolle (n 8) 4.

[30] See eg Free Trade Agreement between the United States of America and the Republic of Korea (US–Korea FTA), in force 15 March 2012, art 20.3(2). The same language continues to apply to the commitments to effectively enforce domestic laws (ibid art 20.3(1)(a)).

sustainability provisions as they apply to any other trade provisions, with a few notable exceptions:

(i) similar to the US–Jordan model, a panel may be established only to the extent that dedicated labour/environmental consultations have taken place without success;[31]
(ii) panellists adjudicating labour and environmental matters shall have specific expertise or experience;[32]
(iii) in the case of disputes relating to a party's alleged failure to implement its obligations under MEAs, the panels shall 'consult fully, through a mechanism that the '[Labour/Environmental Affair Council] establishes, concerning that issue with any entity authorized to address the issue under the relevant environmental agreement'.[33]

Once the final report is issued, it is again requested that the parties 'shall agree' on the resolution of the dispute, which 'shall normally conform' with the determinations and recommendations of the panel, if any. The resolution of the dispute shall comprise the elimination of the nonconformity whenever possible;[34] alternatively, parties shall enter into negotiations for the provision of mutually acceptable compensation.[35]

Finally, the recently concluded Agreement between the United States of America, the United Mexican States, and Canada (USMCA) further expands the range of sustainability provisions enforceable through standard dispute settlement procedures[36] and accordingly reinforces that institutionalized dialogue (via designated contact points),[37] monitoring mechanisms (via the Labour Council and the Environment Committee),[38] and dedicated ministerial consultations procedures are to be mandatorily completed before having recourse to dispute settlement.[39] It also contains very detailed rules on the establishment of a roster of panellists and on panel composition, including the standard rules concerning the additional qualifications for panellists adjudicating sustainability disputes.[40] Once a panel is

[31] ibid arts 19.7 and 20.9(3).
[32] ibid art 22.9(4).
[33] See eg ibid art 20.9(6)(a).
[34] ibid art 22.12(2).
[35] ibid art 22.13(1).
[36] Agreement between the United States of America, the United Mexican States, and Canada, in force 1 July 2020, chs 23 and 24. For a comment, see, among others, N Laurens and others, 'NAFTA 2.0: The Greenest Trade Agreement Ever?' (2018) 18 World Trade Review 659. Importantly, USMCA shifts the burden of proof through a rebuttable presumption that an alleged violation of sustainability obligations affects trade and investment due to the outcome of the US–Guatemala case: US Congressional Research Service, 'Labour Enforcement Issues in U.S. FTAs', 23 March 2023, 1.
[37] USMCA arts 23.15 and 24.26.
[38] ibid arts 23.17 and 24.26.
[39] ibid arts 23.17 and 24.29–32.
[40] ibid art 31.8(3).

appointed, the USMCA provides detailed guidance on the conduct of proceedings, including requirements for evidentiary submissions, hearing format, third-party participation, and the use of experts.[41] Finally, the agreement indicates processes for the release of panel reports, which shall as usual contain the findings, determinations, and recommendations for the resolution of the dispute 'if the disputing Parties have jointly requested them'.[42] As to the implementation of the final report, the chapter provides that the disputing parties 'shall endeavour to agree' on the resolution of the dispute, which can comprise 'the elimination of the non-conformity . . ., if possible, the provisions of mutually acceptable compensation, or another remedy the disputing Parties may agree'.[43]

While US models subject sustainability disputes to ordinary dispute settlement, a closer look at the rules and procedures governing dispute settlement in TAs shows that the implementation of sustainability provisions heavily relies on specialized institutional mechanisms charged to avoid disputes and ensure compliance *before* adjudication.[44] At the same time, dispute settlement involves intergovernmental dialogue and expert panels tasked with determining the existence of nonconformity and, to the extent that the parties so request, providing them recommendations so that they agree on the resolution of the dispute—similarly to the dedicated dispute settlement procedures envisaged in EU TAs.[45]

2. Emerging EU Model

The EU–New Zealand FTA is the first EU TA in which trade and sustainable development (TSD) disputes are to be handled under the regular dispute settlement chapter, but the same model was essentially replicated in the most recently concluded EU–Kenya Economic Partnership Agreement (EU–Kenya EPA).[46] Interestingly, this makes the new EU approach towards enforcement of sustainability obligations through dispute settlement arguably more 'assertive' than the US approach.[47] This is because under this new model it is envisaged that final reports contain findings on the conformity of the measure at issue with applicable covered provisions and recommendations, without any qualification (ie without leaving whether to request recommendations or not to the parties' discretion).[48] Following the release of the

[41] In the specific case of a sustainability dispute arising under art 24.22 (Conservation and Trade), panels shall seek technical advice or assistance from an entity authorized under CITES: see ibid art 24.32.

[42] ibid art 31.13(1).

[43] ibid art 31.18. Parties have 45 days to agree on the resolution of the dispute: ibid art 31.19(1).

[44] This aspect is developed further in Chapter 8 of this volume.

[45] See section III.B.

[46] See Economic Partnership between the European Union and the Republic of Kenya, signed 18 December 2023, Annex V, art 18(1).

[47] This expression is indeed used in the European Commission's New Action Plan: European Commission (n 9) 11.

[48] Free Trade Agreement between the European Union and New Zealand (EU–New Zealand FTA), in force 1 May 2024, art 26.8(b); EU–Kenya EPA art 115(3). Importantly, and similarly to the US practice, the panellists shall also be selected among labour and environmental law experts. To this end, TSD

report, furthermore, it is not just requested that parties endeavour to agree on the resolution of the dispute; rather, the party complained against 'shall take any measure necessary to comply promptly with the findings and recommendations in the final report' in order to remove the nonconformity.[49] It shall furthermore deliver a notification to the complaining party of the compliance measures it envisages to this end and, where immediate compliance is not possible, of the reasonable period of time it requires to implement such measures.[50] The parties 'shall endeavour to agree' on the length of the reasonable period of time; if this is not possible, however, the complaining party may request in writing that the original panel determines it.[51]

Importantly, recourse to dispute settlement may occur only insofar as parties have unsuccessfully engaged in consultations. Contrary to the US model(s), however, there is no dedicated ministerial consultative mechanism envisaged as a precondition for initiating the proceeding.[52]

Finally, the implementation of the compliance measure is monitored by the TSD Committee, which is assisted by the domestic advisory groups (DAGs).[53] The party complained against is, however, still requested to deliver a notification to the complaining party indicating the measures it has taken to comply by the date of expiry of the reasonable period of time.[54]

B. Quasi-Adjudicatory Models Relying on Distinct Dispute Settlement

Until the European Commission recently announced the inauguration of a new approach to enforcement of TSD provisions in its 2022 New Action Plan, sustainability commitments in EU TAs had systematically been subject to specialized dispute settlement procedures. Under this model, which is replicated quite consistently in all EU TAs concluded since the EU–Korea FTA, parties may request that a panel of (independent) experts[55] examine a matter covered under TSD chapters when disagreement on that matter has not satisfactorily been resolved through

expert lists are established by the Trade Committee: EU–New Zealand FTA art 26.6(1)(a); EU–Kenya EPA Annex V, art 18(2)–(3).

49 EU–New Zealand FTA art 26.13(1); EU–Kenya EPA art 115(4).
50 EU–New Zealand FTA art 26.13(1)–(2); EU–Kenya EPA art 115(5).
51 EU–New Zealand FTA art 26.14(1)–(2); EU–Kenya EPA art 115(6).
52 EU–New Zealand FTA art 26.3; EU–Kenya EPA art 110 and Annex V, art 17.
53 EU–New Zealand FTA art 26.13(3)(b); EU–Kenya EPA Annex V, art 18(7).
54 EU–New Zealand FTA art 26.15(1); EU–Kenya EPA art 116(1).
55 TSD chapters in EU TAs also contain specific rules aimed at identifying panellists with specific expertise and experience in trade, labour, and environmental issues and at avoiding blockages in appointments: see eg Agreement between the European Union and Japan for an Economic Partnership (EU–Japan EPA), in force 1 February 2019, art 16.18(4).

dedicated intergovernmental consultations.[56] Similarly to the US model(s), such consultations may not just occur between consulting parties but also rely on established institutional mechanisms under the TSD chapters—more specifically, the TSD Committee may be convened if a party considers that the matter requires further discussion and it shall endeavour to resolve the matter.[57] Both the consulting parties and the TSD Committee may seek expert advice from the ILO or relevant MEA bodies and DAGs.[58] Importantly, in some cases, consultations may also be triggered by communications submitted by DAGs.[59]

In contrast to the US model(s), the panel of experts are explicitly requested to make recommendations for the resolution of the matter in their report, based on their findings and determinations.[60] The report is, however, not binding, at least not in the same way as regular panel reports are for matters arising under ordinary trade chapters in EU TAs.[61] In other words, it is provided that parties 'shall discuss the appropriate action or measures to be implemented, taking into account the report and recommendations of the Panel of Experts', to resolve the matter in question.[62] In some cases, parties are given a timeframe to identify such measures (eg in the case of the EU–Canada Comprehensive Economic and Trade Agreement (CETA), parties 'shall endeavour' to do so within three months of the delivery of the final report) or the possibility to decide upon a 'mutually satisfactory action plan' if appropriate.[63] In either case, the responding party shall inform the other party and its own domestic DAG of any follow-up actions or measures with a view to increasing transparency.[64] The TSD Committee monitors implementation and stakeholders may submit observations.[65]

[56] Time frames may vary, ranging from 90 days after the delivery of a request for consultations (see eg EU–Korea FTA art 13.15(1)) to 120 days (see eg Free Trade Agreement between the European Union and the Republic of Singapore (EU–Singapore FTA), in force 21 November 2019, art 12.17(1)).

[57] The written request shall be delivered to the contact point of the other party, as the request to establish the panel in case of unsatisfactory consultations: see eg Free Trade Agreement between the European Union and the Republic of Vietnam (EU–Vietnam FTA), in force 1 August 2020, arts 13.16(4) and 13.17(1).

[58] See eg Comprehensive Economic and Trade Agreement (CETA) between Canada and the European Union and its Member States, provisionally applied 21 September 2017, arts 23.9(3)–(4) and 24.14(3)–(4).

[59] See eg FTA between the European Union and the Republic of Korea, in force 13 December 2015, art 13.14(1).

[60] See eg EU–Vietnam FTA art 13.17(6); CETA art 23.10(8); EU–Japan EPA art 16.18(2). A notable exception is the Trade and Cooperation Agreement between the European Union and the European Atomic Energy Community and the United Kingdom of Great Britain and Northern Ireland (EU–UK TCA), in force 1 May 2021,: see art 409.5.

[61] Hradilová and Svoboda (n 2); G Marín Dúran, 'Sustainable Development Chapters in EU Free Trade Agreements: Emerging Compliance Issues' 57 (2020) Common Market Law Review 1031.

[62] See eg EU–Vietnam FTA art 13.17(9); EU–Singapore FTA art 12.17.9; EU–Japan EPA art 16.18(6).

[63] CETA arts 23.10(12) and 24.15(11).

[64] See eg EU–Vietnam FTA art 13.17(9); EU–Singapore FTA art 12.17.9: EU–Japan EPA art 16.18(6).

[65] See eg EU–Singapore FTA art 12.17(9); EU–Korea FTA art 13.15(2); CETA arts 23.10(12) and 24.15(11); EU–Vietnam FTA art 12.17(9); EU–Japan EPA art 16.18(5)–(6); EU–Mexico Agreement in Principle art 27.17(8)–(9); EU–Mercosur Agreement in Principle art 14.17(11). In the case of the EU–Singapore FTA, monitoring is assigned to the Joint Board: art 12.17(9). In the case of the EU–UK TCA,

The increasingly important role of DAGs and institutional mechanisms more generally in dispute settlement proceedings has clearly emerged out of an EU–South Korea dispute regarding certain labour provisions.[66] The formal EU complaint against Korea was prompted by repeated requests submitted by the EU DAG.[67] Civil society's engagement also continued after the dispute and has admittedly been instrumental in facilitating the implementation of follow-up measures. In April 2021, three months after the release of the panel report, Korea had already ratified three of the core ILO Conventions at issue and confirmed its commitment to jointly review with the European Union its preparatory work to ratify the fourth one (ie ILO Convention 105 on the Abolition of Forced Labour).[68] In particular, during the 2021 meeting of the TSD Committee, Korea agreed to undertake a research project to identify the domestic provisions that need be to amended to avoid incompliance with ILO Convention 105, the outcome of which was then published in 2022.[69] Furthermore, during an ad hoc interim meeting of the TSD Committee in November 2021, the EU and Korea jointly assessed the implementation of the legislative amendments that Korea introduced to its Korean Trade Union Act.[70] The EU and Korea DAGs also met for the first time since 2018 to hold a Civil Society Forum.[71] Based on the latest information, the parties are determined to 'continue their exchanges in order to continue moving closer to ratification' of ILO Convention 105.[72]

C. A Comparative Analysis of Adjudicatory Models: Towards Greater Convergence?

The US and the EU approaches to sustainability disputes have traditionally been considered to be poles apart. The former has long envisaged parity of dispute settlement, with enforceable sustainability commitments subject to the same dispute settlement procedures as any other (trade) obligations. The latter has until recently relied on a specialized, formally non-binding dispute settlement procedure.

monitoring is conferred to the Trade Specialised Committee on Level Playing Field for Open and Fair Competition and Sustainable Development: EU–UK TCA art 409.17.

[66] Boisson de Chazournes and Lee (n 4) 335; Hradilová and Svoboda (n 2) 1028.

[67] For a thorough recollection of the various steps leading to the EU–Korea dispute, including a complete overview of the role played by the civil society dialogue mechanism, see Nissen (n 2) 615–28.

[68] ibid 628. The three conventions that Korea already ratified are ILO Conventions 29 (Forced Labour), 87 (Freedom of Association and Protection of the Right to Organize), and 98 (Right to Organize and Collective Bargaining).

[69] European Commission, 'Report from the Commission to the European Parliament, the Council, the European Economic and Social Committee and the Committee of the Regions on Implementation and Enforcement of EU Trade Agreements' (COM) (2022) 730 final, 23.

[70] ibid.

[71] Nissen (n 2) 628.

[72] European Commission (n 9) 23.

At a closer look, however, both approaches have more in common than what is normally acknowledged: they both establish multi-stage dispute settlement procedures involving dedicated intergovernmental dialogue and expert panels; they both contemplate close and continued coordination with various stakeholders during the proceedings;[73] and, importantly, they both lead to the release of a panel report that may include recommendations to be taken into consideration by the parties while they endeavour to agree on the resolution of the dispute.

At the same time, there still remain important differences between the two approaches even now that the European Union is switching to parity of dispute settlement. In particular, the EU–New Zealand FTA neither entails a dedicated government consultations stage involving the TSD Committee and DAGs prior to initiating the proceeding, nor does it leave parties to work out together how to resolve the dispute based on the panel's recommendations. The Agreement does, however, intensify efforts to rely on institutional mechanisms to monitor both the implementation of sustainability provisions before adjudication and the implementation of the compliance measures, to be taken by the party complained against following the release of the panel report.[74] Management practices remain, however, less sophisticated than in the US approach,[75] albeit the European Commission's New Action Plan purports to achieve significant improvements in future negotiations.[76] Nevertheless, the innovation introduced by the Commission's new approach to sustainability provisions contributed to greater convergence concerning post-adjudication enforcement through sanctions.

III. Post-Adjudication Enforcement

TA provisions on the enforcement of sustainability commitments also differ depending on whether they link compliance to 'economic consequences' (the so-called conditional approach) or rather 'provide a framework for dialogue, cooperation and/or monitoring' (the so-called promotional approach).[77] The two approaches are not necessarily antithetical, and in fact they often—and increasingly—coexist,[78] but they have long been used to identify the main difference between the US and the EU models concerning post-adjudication enforcement. The United States has generally subjected sustainability provisions to the same remedies, including potential recourse to trade sanctions, contemplated

[73] Recognizing that the approaches need not to be presented as opposed, see Boisson de Chazournes and Lee (n 4) 334–36. Guarding against the danger of 'this false dichotomy', see Harrison and others (n 2) 7.
[74] See EU–New Zealand FTA art 26.13.3.
[75] See eg Harrison and others (n 2) 7.
[76] European Commission (n 9) 8–10.
[77] ILO, *Social Dimensions of Free Trade Agreements* (ILO, 2013, rev edn 2015) 1.
[78] Harrison and others (n 2) 7.

under ordinary dispute settlement chapters—albeit with some variations across models ('hard' enforcement). The latter has until recently only envisaged dialogue and monitoring as the means for ensuring compliance with the report of the panel of experts ('soft' enforcement).[79] It is also in recent years, that is, with the EU–UK Trade and Cooperation Agreement (TCA) and, again, the EU–New Zealand FTA and the EU–Kenya EPA, that the European Union is inaugurating a model of 'hard' or, as the European Commission calls it, 'more assertive' post-adjudication enforcement.[80]

A. Conditional Approach

Under the conditional approach, non-implementation may lead to economic consequences, including the application of temporary and proportionate trade sanctions. Such an approach has long been adopted in US TAs, although not every TA provides that the same remedies envisaged for ordinary disputes be available for sustainability disputes.

In earlier models, for instance, in the case of the US–Jordan FTA, it is simply envisaged that, in those cases where the Joint Committee fails to resolve the dispute after the presentation of the panel report, the affected party 'shall be entitled to take any appropriate and commensurate measure'.[81] However, the two governments declared that they 'would not expect or intend' to resolve any potential disputes, that is, including sustainability disputes, by resorting to trade sanctions.[82]

In the CAFTA–DR model, unresolved breaches of enforceable sustainability provisions[83] grant the complaining party the right to request 'at any time' that the panel be reconvened to impose an 'annual monetary assessment' (ie a penalty) on the losing party up to USD 15 million.[84] Penalties shall be paid into a fund that is established for the purposes of increasing capacity to 'improve or enhance

[79] The expressions 'soft' and 'hard' enforcement are borrowed from Bronkers and Gruni (n 2). It should, however, be noticed that, as the authors aptly note in another paper, TSD chapters should not be interpreted to exclude the public international law rules on state responsibility, including countermeasures: M Bronkers and G Gruni, 'Retooling the Sustainability Standards in EU Free Trade Agreements' (2021) 24 Journal of International Economic Law 25, 40–44.

[80] European Commission (n 9) 11.

[81] US–Jordan FTA art 17.2(b). It is worth recalling that this possibility was contemplated irrespectively of the fact that the panel report is 'non-binding': ibid 17.1(d).

[82] Congressional Research Service (n 8) 3 (reporting on an exchange of letters between the USTR Robert Zoellick and Jordanian Ambassador Marwan Muasher).

[83] This includes both the cases where the disputing parties are unable to reach an agreement on the resolution of the dispute and those where, after having agreed, the complaining party considers that the party complained against has failed to observe the terms of the agreement: CAFTA–DR art 20.17.1(a)–(b).

[84] ibid art 20.17.(1)–(2).

labour or environmental law enforcement'.[85] In case the losing party fails to pay a monetary assessment, however, the complaining party may take 'other appropriate steps to collect the assessment or otherwise secure compliance', including via suspending tariff benefits under the Agreement.[86] This means that contrary to what is envisaged in cases of unresolved breaches of commercial provisions, trade sanctions can be avoided by the losing party by paying this agreement-sanctioned penalty.[87] In this respect, the agreement arguably prioritizes enforcement mechanisms aimed at increasing capacity to comply with sustainability obligations, which require positive actions on the part of states.

Following the 'May 10' political compromise, remedies envisaged for breaches of sustainability disputes are exactly the same as for any other trade disputes arising under TAs. As a first step, disputing parties shall enter into negotiations 'with a view to developing mutually acceptable compensation' in case they could not reach an agreement on the resolution of the dispute by 45 days after receiving the final report.[88] Failure to agree on compensation, or to observe the terms of the agreement, entitles the complaining party to suspend benefits of an equivalent effect 'at any time'.[89] Suspension of benefits cannot, however, occur if the party complained against commits to pay an annual monetary assessment of an amount to be determined through consultations with the complaining party.[90] There is therefore no pre-determined ceiling.[91] Depending on the circumstances of the case, the Joint Committee may decide that the penalty be paid into a fund that it can administer for the purposes of financing 'appropriate initiatives to facilitate trade between the Parties, including by further reducing unreasonable trade barriers or by assisting a Party in carrying out its obligations under the Agreement'.[92] This is a potentially important provision for the sake of facilitating compliance with labour and environmental obligations through capacity building. Importantly, post-'May 10' agreements also introduce the possibility for the complaining party to start compliance proceedings, which might lead to the removal of sanctions or to the interruption of the obligation to pay the monetary assessment.[93]

Finally, the USMCA proposes a less sophisticated model compared to post-'May 10' agreements. According to Article 31.19, non-implementation within 45 days from receipt of the final report entitles the complaining party to impose temporary

[85] ibid art 20.17(4). For a commentary, see Cosbey (n 12) 2. More generally, the CAFTA–DR was the first US TA to include measures specifically aimed at supporting labour capacity building: CAFTA–DR Annex 16.5.
[86] ibid art 20.17(5).
[87] For a comparison, see ibid art 20.16 (providing for compensation and suspension of benefits).
[88] ibid art 22.13(1).
[89] ibid art 22.13(2).
[90] ibid art 22.13(5).
[91] A similar model is envisaged under the Comprehensive and Progressive Agreement for Trans-Pacific Partnership, in force 18 December 2018: see art 28.20(7).
[92] USMCA art 22.13(6).
[93] ibid art 22.14.

and proportionate trade sanctions until an agreement on a resolution to the dispute is found.[94] The complaining party may, however, request to reconvene the panel should it consider that the level of benefits proposed to be suspended is manifestly excessive, or that it has eliminated the nonconformity.[95] Interestingly, a very similar approach is also espoused in the EU–UK TCA for disputes arising out of the labour and environment chapters, which basically contain non-regression and domestic enforcement clauses.[96] As per Article 410 TCA, nonconformity[97] entitles the complaining party to have recourse to the same remedies envisaged under the dispute settlement chapter for standard disputes, that is, to request consultations for temporary compensation and/or to notify its intended suspension of obligations, which shall not exceed the level equivalent to the nullification or impairment caused by the violation.[98] Standard dispute settlement provisions governing disputes with respect to the level of retaliation and compliance proceedings are also applicable.[99] These features are unique within the universe of EU TAs, which normally contain sustainability obligations in TSD chapters only. As mentioned, TSD disputes arising under EU TAs have until very recently been dealt with via a promotional approach.

B. Promotional Approach

Under the promotional approach, dialogue and cooperation—complemented by monitoring mechanisms—are the methods envisaged for ensuring compliance with the panel's reports. This has long been the approach espoused by TSD chapters in EU TAs ever since the conclusion of the EU–Korea FTA.[100] This also includes disputes arising out of the EU–UK TCA chapter on 'Other instruments for TSD'.[101]

Notwithstanding this, the European Union has started experimenting with a new approach, following the 2022 New Action Plan. The decision to subject sustainability disputes to ordinary dispute settlement in the EU–New Zealand FTA first allows extension of the compliance stage to disputes arising under the TSD chapter.[102] Importantly, however, it also means that temporary remedies are to a

[94] ibid art 31.19(1). The complaining party should prioritize retaliation in the same sector as compared to cross-retaliation: ibid art 31.19(2).

[95] ibid art 31.19(3).

[96] See EU–UK TCA chs 6 and 7.

[97] The TCA also envisages the possibility that the original panel be reconvened in case of disagreement between the parties as to the existence or the consistency of follow-up measures: art 409.18.

[98] EU–UK TCA art 410.3, making explicit reference to remedies authorized under art 749 of the Agreement.

[99] ibid art 410.2 (incorporating arts 749 and 750).

[100] Bronkers and Gruni (n 2) 37–39; Boisson de Chazournes and Lee (n 4) 342–44.

[101] See EU–UK TCA ch 8.

[102] EU–New Zealand FTA art 26.17.

certain extent applicable to sustainability disputes. The agreements envisage in particular that this might be possible in cases of serious violations of core sustainability commitments, namely the ILO fundamental principles and rights at work[103] and the Paris Agreement on climate change.[104] In the latter case, temporary remedies could be applied if the panel's final report finds that 'the Party complained against failed to refrain from any actions or omission that materially defeats the object and purpose of the Paris Agreement'.[105]

While this very stringent requirement arguably narrows down the potential scope of TSD disputes subject to remedies quite considerably, the Agreement envisages that in such cases mutually acceptable compensation and/or suspension of obligations may follow nonconformity.[106] The latter shall be proportionate, with the possibility to contest the level of retaliation before the original panel if the party complained against considers that it is not equivalent to the nullification or impairment caused by the violation.[107] Trade sanctions are therefore envisaged as a matter of last resort in cases of serious violations of core TSD commitments; for all other violations, the traditional promotional approach of the EU continues to apply.

C. Comparing Post-Adjudication Models Beyond the Hard vs Soft Enforcement Dichotomy

Post-adjudication enforcement of sustainability provisions is arguably moving beyond the traditional dichotomy between hard and soft enforcement. Models are becoming increasingly more sophisticated and nuanced, also following up on the lessons drawn from the first sustainability disputes concluded to date. The US–Guatemala case, on the one hand, showed that 'litigating the intersection of trade-plus issues and traditional concepts of trade before an adjudicatory panel may not be the best model for ensuring trading partners are meeting trade-plus standards'[108]—irrespective of the threat of sanctions that might come out of it. The EU–Korea case, on the other hand, demonstrated the importance of dialogue and cooperation and the potential of monitoring practices involving civil society for reinforcing a 'culture' of dialogue that is instrumental to facilitating compliance. At the same time, it showed that implementation requires time and that the effectiveness of implementation can, indeed, only be appreciated in the mid- to long-run.[109] In cases of serious violations of core commitments, however, we might not

[103] See ibid art 19.3(3) on 'Multilateral labour standards and agreements'.
[104] See ibid art 19.6(3) on 'Trade and climate change'.
[105] ibid art 26.16(2)(a)(ii).
[106] ibid art 26.16(1) and (3).
[107] ibid art 26.16(6).
[108] Claussen (n 2) 36–37.
[109] Boisson de Chazournes and Lee (n 4) 343–44.

be in the position to afford that luxury, especially if we want to be serious about enabling a sustainability revolution in TAs.

This is arguably why most recent TAs introduce innovations that transcend traditional boundaries between hard enforcement and soft enforcement. The EU–New Zealand FTA is the first EU TA engaging with the possibility to impose sanctions in TSD disputes, but it only envisages that they be used as a means of last resort for serious violations of core labour standards and for actions or omissions that materially defeat the object and purpose of the Paris Agreement. In other words, it endorses a more 'assertive' enforcement model that does not solely aim at deterring certain conduct but also seeks to foster more ambitious, positive actions on the part of states (eg on climate change mitigation efforts). It regrettably does not provide, however, monetary penalties as an alternative to trade sanctions with a view to creating a fund that could be used to strengthen capacity-building activities, among others.[110] The USMCA is also experimenting with new approaches for addressing sustainability disputes: the so-called RRLM in particular is a sui generis enforcement mechanism that acts at the pre-adjudication stage for the purposes of resolving fast, targeted labour disputes concerning alleged violations of the core right to collective bargaining.[111] Since the entry into force of the USMCA, the RRLM has been activated 12 times by the United States against Mexican facilities.[112]

These developments attest to the need to find new combinations of approaches for the purposes of ensuring compliance with sustainability provisions in a way that is both timely and effective but at the same time does not compromise prospects for an amicable resolution of disputes. In this perspective, hard, soft, and quasi-hard and quasi-soft enforcement models are used, but these are complemented by a whole range of management practices aimed at ensuring implementation via dialogue and close cooperation, monitoring and civil society engagement, action plans and capacity-building activities.[113] Such institutional mechanisms aim at ensuring that formal dispute settlement remains 'an *ultimum refugium* for effective implementation' of sustainability commitments, with sanctions envisaged as a matter of last resort.[114]

[110] Similarly, see Bronkers and Gruni (n 2) 45–46.

[111] USMCA Annex 31-A (between the United States and Mexico) and Annex 31-B (between Canada and Mexico).

[112] USTR 'Chapter 31 Annex A; Facility-Specific Rapid-Response Labor Mechanism' <https://ustr.gov/issue-areas/enforcement/dispute-settlement-proceedings/fta-dispute-settlement/usmca/chapter-31-annex-facility-specific-rapid-response-labor-mechanism> accessed 30 June 2023.

[113] Claussen (n 2) 33; Harrison and others (n 2) 639–42; Bronkers and Gruni (n 2) 50–51. For a discussion of these trends that also transcends that US and EU practice, see, among others, Boisson de Chazournes and Lee (n 4) 344.

[114] M Tokas, 'Highest Priority Trade Challenges Related to Climate Change: EU and Americas Economic Law Relations' (CISDL Report 2022) 75<https://www.cisdl.org/wp-content/uploads/2022/11/EU-Americas-Synthesis-Report-Nov-2022.pdf> accessed 30 June 2023.

IV. Conclusions

This chapter investigated adjudication and post-adjustment enforcement of sustainability commitments in TAs. It found that the ongoing trend of legalization of sustainability provisions is complemented with a gradual evolution towards greater—but sometimes also more creative—judicialization. This includes the recent innovations introduced by the EU since its 2022 New Action Plan (eg parity of dispute settlement, switch to trade sanctions as a means of last resort for serious violations of core sustainability commitments) but also the new RRLM inaugurated under the USMCA. While evaluating the effectiveness of these innovations may require some time, the very fact that countries are experimenting with new formats, while also searching for a different calibration between formal dispute settlement mechanisms (binding and/or non-binding) and monitoring mechanisms based on dialogue, cooperation, and best practices exchange, attests to the centrality that implementation of sustainability commitments has gained in trade negotiations and to the critical role that enforcement provisions can and shall (continue to) play to ensure the credibility of the sustainability revolution of TAs.

15

Enforcing International Sustainability Standards on International and National Platforms

Desirée LeClercq

I. Introduction

Other chapters in this volume describe how states, as trade parties, increasingly integrate international sustainability standards governing labour rights and environmental standards into their free trade agreements (FTAs). Doing so shifts the authority to interpret and enforce sustainability standards from the international standard-setting platform to state platforms. Most labour and environmental rights advocates celebrate that shift for its potential to augment non-compliance costs and thus incentivize states to adopt and respect international standards. This discussion is missing a concentrated focus on how the respective international and national platforms monitor and enforce those standards,[1] and the trade-offs between those platforms when it comes to influencing compliance.

Before explaining those trade-offs, it is first necessary to understand how this chapter treats compliance. The term has been debated extensively in the literature, and space does not permit an exhaustive recapitulation. Instead, I am interested in whether enforcement mechanisms on the international and national platforms successfully influence state and private actors to adhere to compliance demands. For instance, can those platforms influence states to implement International Labour Organization (ILO)[2] recommendations? Can they influence states to implement the provisions of laws based on *ex-ante* commitments under negotiated FTAs?

The features antecedent to influence and compliance appear straightforward but have largely been misunderstood. The common assumption in international

[1] This chapter addresses enforcement in general terms. Beyond the use of force, which this chapter does not address, the intention is to include actions by international organizations, states, and private actors to hold public and private actors accountable to international sustainability commitments.

[2] While most UN agencies are composed of states members, the ILO and its regime of international labour standards is uniquely tripartite, meaning that its members comprise workers, employers, and states.

Desirée LeClercq, *Enforcing International Sustainability Standards on International and National Platforms* In: *The Sustainability Revolution in International Trade Agreements*. Edited by: Geraldo Vidigal and Kathleen Claussen, Oxford University Press. © Desirée LeClercq 2024. DOI: 10.1093/9780191994470.003.0015

law is that public and private actors comply with rules so long as they perceive enforcement mechanisms' penalties appropriately dissuasive. For instance, critics of the ILO and designated bodies under multilateral environmental agreements (MEAs) often argue that non-binding enforcement through written and oral comments cannot influence interested state parties to adopt relatively costly worker and environmental protections. [3] Consequently, many assume that enforcement on the international platform fails to influence compliance because monitoring and enforcement lack the threat of economic sanctions. Due to the possibility of sanctions, labour and environmental advocates increasingly favour national enforcement under FTAs.

This chapter argues that by focusing almost exclusively on penalties, the mainstream discourse overlooks an additional feature of compliance: legitimacy. By 'legitimacy', I adopt Daniel Bodansky's broad conceptualization, which focuses on perceptions by regulated actors.[4] Consider, for instance, how states adopted national measures during the pandemic. While some of those measures may have been illegal, such as those that violated the international legal rights of workers to freely associate, they were nevertheless carried out under national health concerns, constituting the legitimate exercise of sovereign authority.[5] Conversely, national enforcement under FTAs may be legal under the agreements' terms yet appear illegitimate to regulated actors who perceive enforcement as protectionist.

Of course, a given enforcement platform's capacity to issue dissuasive penalties plays a significant role in compliance decision-making. However, it is not the only factor. The ways regulated actors perceive power, transparency, predictability, and fairness, perceptions that shape legitimacy, also play a substantial role.[6] This chapter assesses and compares the enforcement of sustainability standards on international and national platforms, considering penalties and perceptions of legitimacy. It concludes that each platform offers advantages yet suffers weaknesses, the latter of which may be addressed through platform complementarity and greater inclusion.

[3] This chapter is not suggesting that binding enforcement is completely missing from the international platform. Two notable exceptions are the Montreal Protocol system, which provides for the suspension of some rights, and the Kyoto Protocol, which provides for the suspension of a party's participation in the Protocol's flexibility mechanisms by denying access to the international emission allowance transaction registry.

[4] Daniel Bodansky, 'The Concept of Legitimacy in International Law' in Rüdiger Wolfrum and Volker Röben (eds), *Legitimacy in International Law* (Springer 2008) 311.

[5] ibid 311.

[6] ibid 310.

II. Enforcement on the International Platform

Under international law, states are the supreme lawmakers but struggle to manage global problems.[7] Should consumers in State A benefit from cheaper prices made by children in State B? Should workers in State A be protected from the loss of wages and decent jobs to cheaper labour regulations in State B? If environmental and climate conditions are global public goods, who should be held accountable for their deterioration?

States have responded to those multilateral issues by outsourcing the responsibility for defining, monitoring, and, in some ways, enforcing sustainability standards to the international platform, where they negotiate on a reasonably equal basis and leave supervision to neutral experts. However, states declined to likewise outsource their economic sanctions authority.[8] Thus, while international organizations and their multilateral platforms benefit from a lawful mandate and (relative) perceptions of legitimacy, they lack dissuasive penalties. This section describes labour and environmental standards and their supervisory bodies and assesses the strengths and weaknesses of those bodies through the lens of influencing compliance.

A. International Labour Standards

Unlike environmental standards, which are scattered across international and national instruments, international labour standards are centralized and managed at the ILO. The ILO's supervisory system has long been acclaimed as the cornerstone of the organization's mandate. Its reporting and monitoring procedures seek to influence compliance through neutral expertise and moral suasion.

The ILO's regular supervisory body comprises international lawyers serving in their individual capacities. It submits public reports highlighting state compliance elicited under the ILO's self-reporting process.[9] The ILO also has special supervisory procedures that can be triggered in multiple ways. First, the ILO's employers' and workers' member organizations can trigger supervision against any member state that has failed to 'secure in any respect the effective observance within its jurisdiction of any Convention to which it is a party'.[10] Second, the ILO's state members may trigger supervision against another state if both states have

[7] Edward Chuckwuemeke Okeke, *Jurisdictional Immunities of States and International Organizations* (1st edn, OUP 2018) 237; Jan Klabbers, *The Law of International Organizations* (1st edn, CUP 2015) 22–25.

[8] Daniel C Esty, *Greening the GATT: Trade, the Environment, and the Future* (Peterson Institute for International Economics 1994) 148–49.

[9] International Labour Organization, *Rules of the Game* (4th edn, ILO 2019) 107.

[10] ibid 110.

ratified the convention.[11] Third, organizations of employers and workers, even in countries that have not ratified the applicable ILO conventions, can trigger supervision under an ILO committee dedicated to freedom of association and collective bargaining.[12]

Although the ILO's Constitution provides for a tribunal to adjudicate disputes,[13] the ILO's members have failed to trigger it, leaving it moribund. Article 33 of the ILO's Constitution authorizes the organization's Governing Body to 'recommend . . . such action as it may deem wise and expedient to ensure compliance' with the recommendations of its highest supervisory body.[14] The ILO's Governing Body has twice invoked that mechanism—against Myanmar in 2000 and against Belarus in 2023. In both instances, the ILO's Governing Body invited its members to 'review . . . the relations that they may have with the Government . . . and take appropriate measures to ensure that the Government . . . cannot take advantage of such relations to perpetuate or extend the violations'.[15]

In addition to these supervisory mechanisms, some ILO instruments contain clauses authorizing member states to penalize other member states for non-compliance. For example, the ILO's Maritime Labour Convention (MLC) assigns enforcement responsibility to port state authorities. By its terms, that convention invites other port states to refuse to allow disobedient vessels to stop at their ports, access their shores to disembark, and ultimately prevent vessels from executing their delivery objectives—the costs of which are imposed directly on ship owners and, at times, on the state of origin.[16]

The ILO's supervisory system benefits from a clear legal mandate set out in the organization's Constitution. Its body of neutral experts is not linked to the states under supervision and benefits from perceived legitimacy. Those experts have nothing to gain, for instance, if the United States or China is cited for non-compliance.

Nevertheless, the organization faces several criticisms, two of which are relevant for current purposes. First, critics complain that the ILO's public reporting process, or 'name and shame' system, cannot alone entice otherwise non-compliant countries to change their behaviour.[17] Recourse to Article 33, for instance, must be adopted by the ILO's Governing Body, the organization's political organ, and thus

[11] ibid 112.
[12] ibid 114.
[13] ILO Constitution art 37.2.
[14] ibid art 33.
[15] ILO, International Labour Conference, 'Resolution concerning the measures recommended by the Governing Body under article 33 of the ILO Constitution on the subject of Belarus' (12 June 2023).
[16] See Desirée LeClercq, 'Outsourcing Enforcement' (2021) 62 Virginia Journal of International Law 271, 283–87.
[17] See Dursun Peksen and Robert Blanton, 'The Impact of ILO Conventions on Worker Rights: Are Empty Promises Worse than No Promises?' (2017) 12 Review of International Organizations 75, 77.

must be 'politically palatable' to states.[18] Even when the Governing Body achieves such consensus, as with Myanmar and Burma, penalties require states to agree to take follow-up action.[19]

Second, although the ILO's supervisory system is perceived as neutral and expert, rights advocates criticize it for excluding critical actors from formal governance mechanisms, such as members of civil society, non-governmental organizations (NGOs), and informal sectors of workers and employers that lack national and international representation.[20] As a consequence of that exclusion, the ILO's supervisory bodies fail to receive comprehensive information from those closest to implementation and who bear the brunt of non-compliance. The ILO's supervisory body's compilation of data consequently appears incomplete, which risks undermining its perceived legitimacy.

B. International Environmental Standards

States negotiate and codify most global environmental standards through MEAs. Unlike the ILO's members, MEA member states did not create a centralized supervisory system. Instead, they created a patchwork system of compliance mechanisms sewn together through resolutions and decisions.[21] Many create multilateral non-compliance procedures (NCPs) within MEAs overseen by the conference or meeting of state parties, secretariats, implementation committees, or compliance committees.[22] In the interest of brevity, this chapter refers to those bodies cumulatively as 'non-compliance bodies'.

While their details often differ, four common actors may trigger non-compliance proceedings. First, state parties may trigger NCPs under MEAs through self-reporting.[23] The self-trigger is popular because it is frequently tied to technical and financial assistance, although it has been used to adopt punitive measures.[24] Second, state parties may trigger enforcement against a fellow party,[25]

[18] Brian Langille, 'The Curious Incident of the ILO, Myanmar and Forced Labour' in Adelle Blackett and Anne Trebilcock (eds), *Research Handbook on Transnational Labour Law* (Edward Elgar 2015) 517.

[19] ibid.

[20] See eg Desirée LeClercq, 'Invisible Workers' (2022) 116 American Journal of International Law Unbound 107, 109–11.

[21] Space does not permit a comprehensive description of all MEA compliance procedures. For such a description see Tullio Treves and others (eds), *Non-Compliance Procedures and Mechanisms and the Effectiveness of International Environmental Agreements* (Springer 2009).

[22] See UN Environment Programme (UNEP), 'Compliance Mechanisms under Selected Multilateral Environmental Agreements' UNEP Report (27 May 2007) 31.

[23] See eg CITES Resolution Conference 8.4 (Rev CoP15), National laws for the implementation of the Convention, para 1.

[24] See Francesca Romanin Jacur, 'Triggering Non-Compliance Procedures' in Treves and others (n 21) 374.

[25] See eg Basel Convention on the Control of Transboundary Movements of Hazardous Wastes and Their Disposal, in force 5 May 1992, art 19.

although states rarely invoke this mechanism owing to its 'adversarial' nature.[26] Third, secretariats or other non-compliance bodies identified in the agreement may sometimes trigger enforcement. For instance, the Kyoto Protocol system establishes 'expert review teams' comprised of independent experts selected by the secretariat.[27] The Aarhus Convention similarly provides that a compliance committee consisting of independent experts may trigger compliance initiatives.[28] And the fourth, albeit rarer, trigger is third-party submissions and non-state actor participation.[29] For example, the Convention on International Trade in Endangered Species of Wild Fauna and Flora (CITES) authorizes performance monitoring by third-party NGOs.[30]

Unlike the ILO, some MEAs regulate dispute settlement through bilateral negotiation, compulsory conciliation, and voluntary arbitration.[31] CITES, for instance, authorizes state parties to bring a dispute through negotiation and, if that fails, to proceed to arbitration before the Permanent Court of Arbitration if there is mutual consent.[32] The Convention on Biological Diversity (CBD) provides that the parties should seek mediation by a third party should negotiations fail.[33]

Despite those provisions, and like the ILO's supervisory bodies, non-compliance bodies usually cannot directly impose financial sanctions on states for non-compliance. Instead, those bodies address non-compliance through technical assistance and capacity building to prevent disputes and countermeasures down the road. When those efforts fail, like the ILO's MLC, some MEAs leave penalties to state-level enforcement. CITES, for example, designates the state parties to 'enforce the provisions of the present Convention' by prohibiting trade in specific living specimens.[34] Nevertheless, state parties remain responsible for informing their customs bodies to trigger enforcement at the national level.[35]

As with the ILO's supervisory procedures, MEA procedures often benefit from perceived legitimacy but are nevertheless the brunt of longstanding criticism. Like the ILO, MEA bodies also lack dissuasive sanctions[36] and, according to

[26] Jacur (n 24) 375.

[27] Kyoto Protocol to the United Nations Framework Convention on Climate Change, in force 16 February 2005, VI.1.

[28] Aarhus Convention Decision 1/7 para 1 and Kyoto Protocol Decision 27/CMP1 para 6.

[29] See eg Convention Concerning the Protection of the World Cultural and Natural Heritage, in force 17 December 1975, Operational Guidelines 174 and 194.

[30] UNEP (n 22) 106.

[31] But see Tullio Treves, 'The Settlement of Disputes and Non-Compliance Procedures' in Treves and others (n 21) 516 (noting that MEAs are 'often more political than legal' and consequently have largely avoided adopting or triggering dispute settlement mechanisms).

[32] Convention on International Trade in Endangered Species of Wild Fauna and Flora, in force 1 July 1975, art XVII; CITES Resolution Conference 14.3 (Rev CoP18) CITES Compliance procedures, para 30.

[33] CBD, in force 19 December 1993, art XXVII.

[34] CITES, art VIII.1.

[35] PH Sand, 'Enforcing CITES: The Rise and Fall of Trade Sanctions' (2013) 22 Review of European, Comparative & International Environmental Law 251, 254.

[36] See eg Martti Koskenniemi, 'Breach of Treaty or Non-Compliance? Reflections on the Enforcement of the Montreal Protocol' (1992) 3 Yearbook of International Environmental Law 127–28.

advocates, their third-party procedures (to the extent they exist) fail to reflect the unique needs of local communities affected by climate change and environmental disasters.[37]

III. Enforcement on the State Platform

In some ways, the trajectory of sustainable development provisions in FTAs and customs legislation is an intuitive response to the criticisms displayed in section II. As the actors responsible for imposing financial penalties and sanctions and convening public consultations, the onus naturally rests on states to improve the global enforcement system. Although states could have focused their efforts on strengthening the international platforms in question—for instance, by adopting resolutions and decisions mandating international bodies to trigger sanctions directly or to include broader third-party participation—they have instead opted to reclaim the governance of sustainability standards through their FTAs and customs rules. Their actions are thus lawful and sanctions-based. Nevertheless, state enforcement procedures lack transparency, predictability, and inclusion, reducing perceived legitimacy.

A. FTAs

In the 1990s, with side agreements to the North American Free Trade Agreement (NAFTA), states began integrating the international sustainable development standards into their FTAs. Many FTAs now link compliance with labour and environmental standards to market access. Those agreements ensure that the trade parties are front-line enforcers by granting them exclusive authority to raise a complaint within dispute settlement linked to direct financial consequences. That is the case for most large-scale trade agreements, including those with the United States,[38] the European Union,[39] and

[37] See eg Carol Farbotkoa and Heather Lazrus, 'The First Climate Refugees? Contesting Global Narratives of Climate Change in Tuvalu' (2011) 22 Global Environmental Change 382, 384 (explaining how the terminology and conceptualization concerning climate change fail to reflect the identities and characteristics of local communities).

[38] See Trade Promotion Authority, Public Law 114-26, s 102(b)(10) (29 June 2015).

[39] European Commission, 'Communication From the Commission to the European Parliament, The Council, the European Economic and Social Committee and the Committee of the Regions' 2 (22 June 2022) (hereafter European Commission, '22 June Communication') (EU trade and sustainability chapters 'chapters of EU trade agreements require the effective implementation of the International Labour Organization (ILO) conventions and the Multilateral Environmental Agreements (MEAs) that each party has ratified, such as the Paris Agreement on Climate Change and the Convention on Biological Diversity').

beyond,[40] which negotiate labour and environmental standards as principal objectives.

Dispute settlement may eventually percolate up to an independent panel of experts or World Trade Organization (WTO) body—a process that could dissipate power imbalances between trade partners and introduce greater legitimacy and transparency. In the famous *Shrimp/Turtle* case, for example, the WTO Appellate Body linked such legitimacy to the lawfulness of states' unilateral measures.[41]

However, as studies on environmental[42] and labour standards[43] reveal, disputes rarely reach neutral bodies. Instead, states tend to negotiate solutions through diplomatic channels. Greg Shaffer notes that a state-to-state dispute 'permits powerful countries with large markets, such as the United States, to use their market leverage to compel foreign regulatory change, while developing countries, holding most of the world's population, wield no such clout'.[44] Without a neutral and technical intermediary, enforcement often reflects asymmetries and state-driven interpretations of global standards. Those features undermine the pluralism and the equal treatment otherwise assured on the WTO's international platform.

Weaker parties may dismiss the threat of such state-issued sanctions as illegitimate.[45] For example, in 2015, the United States withdrew trade preferences in Eswatini (formerly Swaziland) for violating international labour standards. The Eswatini government and factories dismissed US actions as imperialist and simply diverted exports to neighbouring South Africa.[46] The costs of Eswatini's repudiation have since been borne by the local workers, mainly women workers who now receive lower wages in precarious working conditions.[47]

Despite challenges to perceived legitimacy, states have begun to trigger their enforcement mechanisms vigorously. Under the United States–Mexico–Canada

[40] A significant volume of research, including other chapters in this volume, shows how countries across levels of economic development now include environmental and labour provisions in their trade agreements.

[41] *United States—Import Prohibition of Certain Shrimp and Shrimp Products*, WT/DS58/AB/R (12 October 1998) paras 173, 177.

[42] Greg Messenger, Chapter 10 in this volume.

[43] Desirée LeClercq, Raymond Robertson, and Daniel Samaan, 'Labour Provisions in Trade Agreements: Recasting the Protectionist Debate' (2023) Journal of Law, Economics, and Organization (finding that binding, sanctions-based labour provisions in FTAs had no statistically significant effects on trade flows).

[44] See Gregory Shaffer, 'Power, Governance and the WTO: A Comparative Institutional Approach' in Michael Barnett and Bud Duvall (eds), *Power in Global Governance* 139 (CUP 2005).

[45] See Daniel Peat, 'Perception and Process: Towards a Behavioural Theory of Compliance' (2022) 13 Journal of International Dispute Settlement 179, 184 (state compliance is not always rational but rather reflects 'the outcome of series of cognitive and information processing events the complexity of which mirrors—or exceeds—that which we face in daily life'); Gregory Shaffer, 'Retooling Trade Agreements for Social Inclusion' (2019) 1 University of Illinois Law Review 254 (advancing a complementary rather than coercive approach with neutral oversight).

[46] See Giovanni Pasquali and Shane Godfrey, 'Governance of Eswatini Apparel Regional Value Chains and the Implications of Covid-19' (2021) 34 European Journal of Development Resources 473, 481.

[47] ibid 381–84.

Agreement (USMCA), the United States introduced a new enforcement mechanism to penalize private facilities in Mexico directly without requiring a panel finding. The US government has invoked that mechanism numerous times since 2022, and trade partners such as the European Union and Canada are considering similar mechanisms in their agreements.[48] The United States has also increased cases under the Environmental Chapter in its agreement with Peru, and in 2019, the European Union requested a labour panel under its agreement with the Republic of Korea. Commitments to labour and environmental standards integrated into FTAs are thus becoming increasingly binding and cited to justify trade disputes and, in some cases, unilateral sanctions.

B. State-Enforced Customs Legislation

States also enforce environmental and labour standards through general customs legislation. In 2016, the United States augmented its enforcement authority under its Trade Facilitation and Trade Enforcement Act to stop shipments of goods at the US border suspected of being involved with forced labour. In June 2022, the United States adopted the Uyghur Forced Labour Prevention Act, which grants the US Customs and Border Protection (CBP) additional authority to block importing goods with ties to Xinjiang, China, under the rebuttable presumption that those goods are presumed to be made with forced labour.[49]

Not to be outdone by the United States, in September 2022, the European Commission proposed new legislation prohibiting all products made with forced labour from entering the EU market. In April 2023, the European Parliament approved an import ban into the European Union of commodities such as coffee, beef, and soy unless exporters can produce a due diligence statement and verifiable information showing that their foods were not grown on land deforested after 2020. Following the European Parliament's announcement of measures, Malaysia and Indonesia publicly accused the European Union of blocking market access to their palm oil and promised to stop exporting to the EU market.[50]

[48] The European Union chapters on sustainable development have not been linked to financial sanctions. In June 2022, however, the European Commission changed course and adopted the US approach to linking commitments to international labour and environmental standards to formal dispute settlement. See European Commission (n 39).

[49] Public Law 117-78 (2021). In Chapter 11, Maria Panezi describes 'stand-alone' sustainability provisions whereby states adopt their own standards not necessarily reflective of those integrated on the international platform. Like the environmental examples she provides, US forced labour standards in US customs legislation do not integrate ILO standards, leaving the question of whether interpretation differs across platforms.

[50] Kate Abnett, 'EU Lawmakers Back Ban on Goods Linked to Deforestation', *Reuters* (19 April 2023).

C. Implications of Increasing State-Led Enforcement

Some scholars and policymakers—typically environmentalists and labour rights activists in developed countries—applaud burgeoning state efforts to link compliance with sustainability standards to their markets and trade relationships. States are uniquely positioned to use their market access, ports and borders, sanctions procedures, and political connections to influence compliance.

Many legal realists assume that states will influence compliance by threatening sanctions and market penalties for failure to comply with international standards.[51] They also hope that the reporting mechanisms introduced in FTAs and customs legislations will strengthen local efforts to hold governments responsible, such as efforts by Peruvian citizens to hold the Peruvian government responsible for environmental standards under the US–Peru Trade Promotion Agreement[52] or local independent unions to hold the Mexican government accountable to labour reform under USMCA.

In some ways, those hopes have come to fruition—the sanctions feature has rendered positive results even without legitimacy. By leveraging market access before allowing trade agreements to enter into force, some states have successfully influenced trade partners to raise standards in other countries *ex-ante*. Forced labour customs legislation has also contributed to the international enforcement regime in the Xinjiang region, and the US government has held facilities accountable for union election interference under USMCA and has ordered facilities to award victimized workers with backpay and other financial benefits.

And yet, perceptions of illegitimacy loom large, placing into question the long-term effects of state-centric enforcement on compliance. While states declare an intention to link trade sanctions to sustainability compliance, many trigger enforcement depending 'on the economic and political interests of the enforcing state' and the costs of enforcement, not' 'obedience to international law'.[53] Consequently, observers note that trade partners like the United States and the European Union sometimes refuse to enforce sustainability standards despite evidence of non-compliance, raising significant questions concerning their selective enforcement choices.[54]

[51] See Robin Bradley Kar, 'Outsourcing, Globalization, and the Emergence of International Law' (2012) 121 Yale Law Journal Online 411, 467.

[52] See Pablo Peña, 'Could a Trade Agreement Strengthen the Enforcement of Domestic Environmental Laws? Envisioning the Impacts of the US–Peru Environmental Submissions Mechanism' (2023) Review of European, Comparative & International Environmental Law 2.

[53] See Jack L Goldsmith and Eric A Posner, *The Limits of International Law* (OUP 2005) 117.

[54] See Elliott and Freeman, *Can Labour Standards Improve Under Globalization?* (Peterson Institute for International Economics 2003) 75–76; 'Complaint on non-compliance by the Colombian and Peruvian Governments of Chapter IX, on Sustainable Development, of the Trade Agreement with the European Union', CNV International (17 May 2022).

When states serve as the arbiters of their own agreements and commercial relationships, their actions appear to reflect variables beyond or apart from technical compliance, such as unlawful market protectionism.[55] Perceptions of legitimacy, whether by grassroots actors expected to participate in monitoring or regulated governments like Eswatini, Indonesia, and Malaysia, affect their engagement and follow-through.

More recent FTAs were supposed to legitimize enforcement mechanisms by offering greater transparency and opportunities for private actor participation. USMCA provides various reporting mechanisms open to private actors to raise concerns that their governments are not complying with the agreement's commitments to respect freedom of association and collective bargaining. The US–Peru Trade Promotion Agreement created a secretariat to receive and consider submissions asserting that a party is failing to effectively enforce its environmental laws. The European Union created a 'Single Entry Point' that permits 'all EU-based stakeholders who want to lodge a complaint on market access issues or about non-compliance with commitments taken by other countries' under the FTA and preference programmes' labour and environmental chapters.[56]

In addition to new FTA monitoring channels, some trade partners have taken further steps to create advisory groups made up of non-state actors. The United States has a labour advisory committee and an environment trade policy for trade negotiations, and the European Union and the United Kingdom have Domestic Advisory Groups (DAGs), composed of business organizations, trade unions, and environmental organizations, to consult over the implementation of labour and environmental chapters.

Thus far, however, those initiatives have fallen short of their promise. Despite creating new bodies, none of the trade actors have offered transparent processes concerning their enforcement selection. They retain sole authority over when and whether to act based on consultations and information. They provide little information or explanation in that regard. For instance, although the US government has reportedly fielded over 700 calls on the USMCA hotline concerning non-compliance with labour standards in facilities in Mexico, it has acted on only one of those calls. DAG members have reported similar frustration concerning their limited influence on governments and the lack of transparency in EU monitoring and enforcement.[57] So long as the outcome of their efforts remains opaque and unpredictable, these critical interlocutors may be deterred from participating.

[55] See eg Sean Murphy, 'Taking Multinational Corporate Codes of Conduct to the Next Level' (2005) 43 Columbia Journal of Transnational Law 389, 395–96.

[56] See European Commission, 'Operating guidelines for the Single Entry Point and complaints mechanism for the enforcement of EU trade agreements and arrangements' (22 June 2022).

[57] See Deborah Martens, Diana Potjomkina, and Jan Orbie, 'Domestic Advisory Groups in EU Trade Agreements: Stuck at the Bottom or Moving up the Ladder?' (Friedrich-Ebert-Stiftung 2020).

As trade partners, states also have little incentive to enforce global standards they do not intend to respect at home. During the height of the COVID-19 pandemic in 2020, for example, states decided not to enforce the MLC's provisions requiring ports to allow foreign seafarers to disembark in their territories, citing health and transmission concerns.[58] Those states, complicit in their state-centric priorities, allowed one another to disregard the fundamental rights of global seafarers with legal impunity. They paid little attention to the ILO's supervisory comments or the joint statements and efforts across the United Nations and the International Maritime Organization denouncing port states for violating their legal obligations under the MLC.[59]

When states decide to trigger their enforcement actions, such as the slate of USMCA cases under the facility-specific mechanism, they invite legitimacy challenges unique to the national platform. If the United States targets auto facilities that compete with facilities in the United States, is it seeking to deter non-compliance for the sake of workers in Mexico? Or is it seeking justification to close its market to competitive imports? If private facilities and foreign governments perceive enforcement by more powerful partners as inevitable (if their goods pose a competitive threat) or illegitimate (market closure to eliminate competition rather than enforce standards), they may feel less compelled to obey demands.

Finally, the national platform has only opened to a small category of non-state actors: usually formal corporations, trade unions, and environmental groups. Those initiatives, driven by developed countries interested in the views of their local constituents, risk ignoring the unique challenges and constraints faced by local communities in developing countries.[60]

In sum, enforcement on the national platform reflects overarching state priorities, perceptions, and power symmetries—factors driving the creation of international platforms on global standards in the first place. By maintaining a parallel enforcement platform, states render global enforcement more political, less legitimate, and more likely to be triggered by developed countries with ample resources against developing countries eager for market access, all while excluding the voices of local communities most affected by sustainability policies. Consequential perceptions of illegitimacy, as some trade examples show, may undermine compliance abroad and enable non-compliance at home.

[58] See LeClercq, 'Outsourcing Enforcement' (n 17) 291–97.
[59] ibid.
[60] ibid; see also LeClercq, 'Invisible Workers' (n 20) 109.

IV. Advancing a Complementary Enforcement Platform

This chapter began by emphasizing dissuasive penalties and legitimacy as critical features of compliance. It assessed international and national enforcement platforms, arguing that each has unique strengths and weaknesses. The international platform lacks dissuasive penalties but mainly appears legitimate. The national platform is mandated to issue dissuasive penalties and often appears illegitimate. The best path forward, this concluding part posits, is to establish a complementary system that permits the platforms to combine their strengths and address their weaknesses.

In an ideal world, enforcement on international and national platforms would operate in unison, rather than as silos.[61] Supervisory bodies would be composed of neutral and objective experts removed from political interests to assess compliance while tolerant of legal, cultural, and economic pluralism. Local communities impacted by standards—irrespective of their formality and relationship with the state—would have access to those bodies and actively participate in monitoring compliance on the ground. Those features would bolster perceptions of legitimacy among regulated actors (public and private) and grant those actors a sense of ownership and familiarity over the rules to which they are bound.[62]

Efforts to achieve that complementarity will undoubtedly strike many as quixotic. They would require states to cede some enforcement discretion—a feat scholars have long dismissed.[63] Before explaining how states might accomplish a more effective global enforcement system, this concluding section explains why states *should* adopt such changes.

Let us begin with developed countries, which stand to benefit the most from the current enforcement system and thus have the most to lose by changing it. Those countries, notably trade actors like the United States and the European Union, have recently advanced 'worker-centric' and 'green' trade initiatives that purportedly prioritize compliance with sustainability standards throughout their supply chains. Yet, they continue administering enforcement behind closed doors and in ad hoc ways. Resulting perceptions of illegitimacy threaten to undermine the very compliance their trade policies now seek to garner. Their counterparts may dismiss their enforcement efforts as imperial, political, or protectionist. If sanctions appear inevitable or illegitimate, counterparts have fewer incentives to adopt costly improvements and regulations to avoid them. Local actors may feel less motivated to devote scarce resources to building cases if efforts to compel enforcement

[61] See eg Shaffer, 'Power' (n 44) 146–49.

[62] Abram Chayes and Antonia Handler Chayes, *The New Sovereignty: Compliance with International Regulatory Agreements* (Harvard University Press 1995) 3, 25.

[63] See eg Daniel Bodansky, *The Art and Craft of International Environmental Law* (Harvard University Press 2010) 15 (dismissing proposals to grant international institutions coercive powers because '[c]ountries are extremely reluctant to cede authority to international institutions').

action appear secondary to overarching and untransparent geopolitical priorities. Developed countries' legitimate interests in retaining discretion over their markets and customs and their interests and trade objectives have reached an impasse.

The case for developing countries is more straightforward. Current enforcement procedures are stacked against them. Powerful trade actors decide when and how to enforce compliance, including over standards they do not respect domestically.[64] Redesigning a system in which neutral and technical experts carry out legitimate enforcement protects those countries from abuse.

There are two salient steps that states should take to complement the international platform accordingly. First, they should grant bodies on the international platform the mandate to directly impose dissuasive penalties. They could do so by designing adjudicative bodies capable of addressing their state-to-state disputes and issuing sanctions.[65] To ensure the legitimacy of such an adjudicatory system, states should cede some of their enforcement discretion. Recall that some MEA committees and ILO supervisory bodies under Article 33 may authorize state countermeasures, but states alone issue such penalties and have proven reluctant to do so. States should instead adopt international regulations or decisions rendering countermeasures binding while leaving the necessary space to *reject* calls for countermeasures and maintain their trade relationships. In the latter instance, procedures should reinforce perceptions of legitimacy by requiring states to announce their decisions publicly.

Second, states should invite widespread public participation on the international platform. They could do so by ensuring that supervisory bodies and committees hold transparent hearings open to participation across all affected public and private actors. Unlike the discretionary amicus briefs procedure at the WTO,[66] new procedures should automatically accept and make public such submissions. Thus, a dispute involving alleged violations of international labour standards would include the views of the government along with representatives of the employers and workers (whether unionized or not). Disputes involving alleged environmental damages would be open to participation by the state and local communities, including indigenous communities and corporations.

Precedent suggests that if states offer local actors avenues to participate in monitoring and enforcement, those actors will use them. The Aarhus Convention stands out among sustainability instruments because it permits various non-state actors to trigger compliance procedures. Third parties have used that trigger so frequently they have rendered the Aarhus Convention 'the convention that has dealt

[64] See Desirée LeClercq, 'The Disparate Treatment of Rights in U.S. Trade Policy' (2021) 90(1) Fordham Law Review 36–40.

[65] See LeClercq, 'Outsourcing Enforcement' (n 17) 307–13.

[66] For a critique of public participation during trade disputes, see Esty, *Greening the GATT* (n 8) 211–13.

with more non-compliance cases' than other MEAs despite being such a recent agreement.[67]

There is no silver bullet when it comes to enforcement. State subjects of enforcement efforts will likely continue to decry illegitimacy or incompetence. State enforcers will likely continue to avoid diplomatic tensions. The point is not to feign optimism for solving the enforcement of sustainability standards but to move incrementally towards a governance platform capable of influencing compliance.

[67] María Cecilia Engler Palma, 'Non-Compliance Procedures: Can Regional Fisheries Management Organizations Learn from the Experience of Multilateral Environmental Agreements?' (2010) 24 Ocean Yearbook Online <https://brill.com/view/journals/ocyo/24/1/article-p185_10.xml?language=en> accessed 18 April 2024, 214–15.

16

Decentralized Enforcement of Sustainability Commitments

Rebalancing, Targeted Enforcement, and Production Requirements in Trade Agreements

Geraldo Vidigal

I. Introduction

This chapter concerns means of enforcing trade and sustainable development (TSD) commitments and objectives in trade agreements (TAs) beyond adjudication. These are means that do not require a pronouncement by an adjudicative authority but can be employed by each party directly, in what can be termed 'horizontal' or 'decentralized' enforcement. In a sense, these are the traditional means by which international commitments are enforced in treaties without specific enforcement. In these cases, enforcement measures are adopted based on a state's individual determination of what the relevant rules require from others, whether these requirements have been met, and what can be done in response to their assessment that a violation is taking place.

Decentralized enforcement can take place through international law's reciprocity mechanisms, such as countermeasures or suspension of a violated agreement, involving an *active* decision to respond to another state's unlawful conduct.[1] Another form of decentralized enforcement is mere implementation by each state, in its domestic laws and regulations, of agreed policies affecting private parties. Enforcement in which the enforcer demands compliance not from states but from producers abroad can be termed 'diagonal'.[2] Enforcement in this manner may be thought of as *passive* since it does not involve action against a state but mere domestic regulation. At the same time, enforcing sustainability requirements in production abroad requires behind-the-border verification, as well as sanctions against non-complying entities. Implementing diagonal enforcement often

[1] See Serena Forlati, 'Reactions to Non-Performance of Treaties in International Law' (2012) 25 Leiden *Journal of International Law* 759.

[2] Kathleen Claussen and Chad P Bown, 'Corporate Accountability by Treaty: The New North American Rapid Response Labor Mechanism' (2024) 118 American Journal of International Law 98, 106.

Geraldo Vidigal, *Decentralized Enforcement of Sustainability Commitments* In: *The Sustainability Revolution in International Trade Agreements*. Edited by: Geraldo Vidigal and Kathleen Claussen, Oxford University Press. © Geraldo Vidigal 2024.
DOI: 10.1093/9780191994470.003.0016

requires significant action, and may draw criticisms from other states or lead to disputes.

Mechanisms for trade-based decentralized enforcement of sustainability have been proposed from time to time. These mechanisms can be compared to trade remedies, which offer a form of consented decentralized enforcement of certain (economic) standards.[3] Trade remedies can be employed without prior resort to an international adjudicator, through a wholly domestic adjudicatory process. Another source of inspiration may be Part III of the Trade-Related Aspects of Intellectual Property Rights (TRIPS) Agreement, which provides for decentralized enforcement of intellectual property rights. Part III requires each World Trade Organization (WTO) member to establish domestic enforcement mechanisms to address violations of the intellectual property standards set out in the TRIPS Agreement, without requiring a complaint from another member. In these cases, if another state believes that an instance of decentralized enforcement is unwarranted or excessive, it falls upon the dissatisfied state to challenge it through state-to-state adjudication.

As the chapter shows, there are now meaningful—if still experimental—examples of consented decentralized enforcement of sustainability commitments in TAs.[4] Some agreements establish a right to 'active horizontal enforcement'. These provisions legitimize horizontal action by one party in response to its assessment of non-compliance by the other party, or producers within it, with sustainability commitments. Other provisions permit passive enforcement, principally as 'conditionality-based enforcement' or 'passive regulatory enforcement', limiting trade benefits under the TA to products produced under certain circumstances or legitimizing the adoption by the parties of laws and regulations imposing sustainability conditions affecting all private parties. As the chapter delves into the topic, it will be evident that these categories are not watertight.

Following this Introduction, the chapter proceeds in four parts. Section II outlines the notion of decentralized enforcement and its various forms. Section III examines provisions in international TAs that enshrine, and thereby legitimize, active or horizontal enforcement of sustainability commitments. Section IV considers provisions that enshrine the right of parties to adopt passive enforcement measures, either imposing requirements for products to receive benefits under the agreement or establishing the right of parties to adopt specific regulations. Section V concludes, considering the effects of these provisions, as well as safeguards that

[3] See eg Gregory Shaffer, 'Retooling Trade Agreements for Social Inclusion' (2019) University of Illinois Law Review 1, 35.

[4] For recent work on these, see Kathleen Claussen, 'Trade Policing', (2023) 65 Harvard International Law Journal 25; James Harrison, 'Trade Agreements and Sustainability: Exploring the Potential of Global Value Chain (GVC) Obligations' (2023) 26 Journal of International Economic Law 199–215; Tim Meyer, 'Consumption Governance: The Role of Production and Consumption in International Economic Law', Duke Law School Public Law & Legal Theory Series No 2023-39.

can be used to prevent sustainability objectives from being invoked as a pretext for protectionist or coercive action.

II. Enforcing Commitments Without Adjudication

A. Forms of Decentralized Enforcement

The term 'enforcement' in international law usually encompasses two separate legal concepts. One is what can be called 'judicial' or 'adjudicative' enforcement. In TAs, adjudication is usually associated with dispute settlement clauses or chapters, which allow an enforcing actor to request from an adjudicator an authoritative determination of the lawfulness of certain conduct under the relevant agreement. During the Uruguay Round of negotiations that led to the creation of the WTO, demands to make the rules of the future WTO 'enforceable' meant, primarily, ensuring the ability of members to resort to dispute settlement and obtain a final ruling. In *Mexico—Soft Drinks*, the Appellate Body noted that WTO obligations can be 'judicially enforced in the WTO'.[5]

The term 'enforcement' can also be used to refer to non-adjudicative or decentralized enforcement. An actor—usually a state or international organization[6]—may respond to perceived violations of a commitment not by requesting an authority to pronounce on the matter but by itself adopting certain measures. When compared to adjudication, decentralized enforcement ensures expedited response to violations of commitments, by state parties, or of standards of production, by producers.

As regards sustainability, in addition to adopting measures in response to specific wrongful conduct, a party may simply adopt sustainability policies directly affecting foreign producers. It may require a demonstration of compliance with specific production standards for products to access this party's market. Measures adopted unilaterally to enforce sustainability objectives horizontally in this manner include the production requirements adopted by the United States that led to the WTO disputes *US—Gasoline*,[7] *US—*

[5] Appellate Body Report, *Mexico—Soft Drinks*, 6 March 2006, para 42 (differentiating these obligations from obligations under the North American Free Trade Agreement [NAFTA]).

[6] International organizations can perform horizontal enforcement when they are parties to agreements on a co-equal status with states or with each other, as is the case of the European Union vis-à-vis Canada, in the Comprehensive and Economic Trade Agreement (CETA), or vis-à-vis the South African Customs Union (SACU), in the EU–Southern African Development Community Agreement (EU–SADC). By contrast, when an EU institution applies a sanctioning measure vis-à-vis an EU Member State, the EU institution operates as an authority, legally 'above' the EU Member State rather than in a horizontal relationship with it.

[7] Appellate Body Report, *United States—Standards for Reformulated and Conventional Gasoline*, 29 April 1996, WT/DS2/AB/R.

Shrimp,[8] and *US—Tuna II*.[9] They also include the more recent EU Deforestation Regulation[10] and Forced Labour Regulation,[11] or conditionalities in Generalized Systems of Preferences.[12]

B. The Purpose of Consented Decentralized Enforcement

Horizontal enforcement is generally permissible under international law as countermeasures. As the arbitral tribunal in *Air Service Agreement* put it, under international law, 'unless the contrary results from special obligations arising under particular treaties . . . each State establishes for itself its legal situation vis-à-vis other States'[13] and may adopt reciprocal measures in case it determines that another state has violated its commitments. These measures include countermeasures but also, for example, suspension of obligations under the Vienna Convention on the Law of Treaties (VCLT) in case of material breach.[14] In *Opinion 2/15*, the Court of Justice of the European Union (CJEU) referred to the VCLT to affirm that a violation of TSD commitments in agreements between the European Union and third states would permit the other party 'to terminate or suspend the [trade] liberalisation, provided for in the other provisions of the envisaged agreement'.[15]

Additionally, the prevailing interpretation of TAs permits many policies that enforce sustainability requirements passively, that is, by imposing on imported products so-called process and production method requirements. In all three aforementioned WTO disputes,[16] the basic right to adopt sustainability measures affecting foreign production was upheld. General Agreement on Tariffs and Trade (GATT) Article XX has been amply interpreted to make measures that promote sustainability objectives through product requirements justifiable, subject

[8] Appellate Body Report, *United States—Import Prohibition of Certain Shrimp and Shrimp Products*, 12 October 1998, WT/DS58/AB/R.

[9] Appellate Body Report, *United States—Measures Concerning the Importation, Marketing and Sale of Tuna and Tuna Products*, 16 May 2012, WT/DS381/AB/R.

[10] Regulation (EU) 2023/1115 of the European Parliament and of the Council of 31 May 2023 on the making available on the Union market and the export from the Union of certain commodities and products associated with deforestation and forest degradation and repealing Regulation (EU) No 995/2010 [2023] OJ L 150. See Gracia Marín Durán and Joanne Scott, 'Regulating Trade in Forest-Risk Commodities: Two Cheers for the European Union' (2022) 34 Journal of Environmental Law 245.

[11] Regulation (EU) 2023/1115 (n 10). See Marco Bronckers and Giovanni Gruni, 'Retooling the Sustainability Standards in EU Free Trade Agreements' (2021) 24 Journal of International Economic Law 25.

[12] Lorand Bartels, 'The WTO Legality of the EU's GSP+ Arrangement' (2007) 10 Journal of International Economic Law 869.

[13] *Air Service Agreement Arbitration (France v United States)* (1978) 18 RIAA 417, at 443.

[14] Vienna Convention on the Law of Treaties, in force 27 January 1980, art 60.

[15] CJEU Opinion 2/15, 17 May 2017 (ECLI:EU:C:2017:376), para 161. Arguably, this statement confuses different international legal instruments. Considering it in depth is beyond the scope of this chapter.

[16] See (n 7), (n 8), and (n 9).

to certain conditions. Under TAs modelled on the GATT—the vast majority of them—passive enforcement, even if severely trade-restrictive, is likely to be permissible, provided that it is non-discriminatory and does not involve a disguised restriction on trade.

This was confirmed, with regard to the EU–Ukraine Association Agreement (AA), by the panel in *Ukraine—Wood Export Ban*. Though considering a different matter (environmentally justified export bans), the panel based its reasoning on this WTO jurisprudence. This panel found that

> legitimate public policy goals . . . may be invoked to justify a violation of . . . the AA, provided that such measure is not applied, as specified in the chapeau of Article XX, 'in a manner which would constitute a means of arbitrary or unjustifiable discrimination between countries where the same conditions prevail or a disguised restriction on international trade'.[17]

Like this AA, many other contemporary TAs incorporate or reproduce GATT Article XX. Most of them will accordingly provide some leeway for non-discriminatory passive enforcement.

Still, adopting new trade-restrictive measures unilaterally often leads to political opposition by affected states, which believe they are unlawful, excessive, or simply abusive unilateral renegotiation of agreed terms. Even if one may ultimately argue successfully for the lawfulness of sustainability measures, a state negotiating a new TA may not find it acceptable for an agreement to include an open-ended authorization for the other party to impose new barriers to trade, unilaterally nullifying its hard-fought concessions.

The purpose of including provisions specifically permitting non-adjudicatory enforcement of TSD commitments in TAs is thus twofold. On the one hand, through these provisions, the relevant enforcement measures become legitimized by state consent, precluding a debate on whether they are violations of the trade commitments in the relevant TA (or, as developing countries sometimes see it, unilateral renegotiations of the underlying bargain by means of an exception). On the other hand, these provisions establish conditions for the adoption of these enforcement measures.

[17] Panel Report, *Ukraine—Wood Export Ban*, 11 December 2020, para 258.

III. Active Enforcement: Rebalancing, Level Playing Field, and Rapid Responses

The trend of including provisions permitting non-adjudicatory enforcement in TAs may seem contradictory. Throughout the twentieth century, much of the evolution of international trade law consisted in replacing unilateral enforcement with adjudication-mediated enforcement. At the WTO, Article 23 of the Dispute Settlement Understanding (DSU) prevents WTO members from unilaterally determining that a violation of WTO rules has taken place and acting upon this determination. WTO members may only resort to enforcement through trade-restrictive measures after a multi-stage adjudication process, whereby impartial WTO organs conclude that certain measures are unlawful, this conclusion does not lead to compliance, and the WTO authorizes a specific form and level of retaliation.[18] Although WTO retaliation is, in substance, similar to countermeasures under general international law, it is not technically a 'non-performance' of WTO obligations but part of the WTO legal framework.[19] Permitting TA parties to enforce commitments unilaterally may seem like a step back when compared to conditioning enforcement to prior adjudication and authorization.

Permitting non-adjudicatory enforcement can be justified on two grounds. The first ground is that it avoids what Rachel Brewster has termed the 'remedy gap' in WTO dispute settlement, that is, the long lag between the violation and the authorization for reciprocal non-performance.[20] This lag is likely to make post-adjudication retaliation less effective a remedy, from the perspective of actors who lose out from violations, than immediate response. Permitting immediate response would ensure that parties cannot temporarily benefit from violating their commitments. With regard to sustainability commitments, this remedy gap could be argued to be all the more concerning, since violations of at least some of these commitments can produce irreversible consequences, not only for economic operators but also for Earth's life support systems.

The second ground underlying a return to non-adjudicatory enforcement is preserving what is sometimes called the 'level playing field'. Beyond their societal objectives, sustainability commitments also aim to preserve the competitiveness of products and companies in parties that fulfil their labour and environmental commitments. Lowering (or failing to enforce) labour and environmental standards

[18] Understanding on Rules and Procedures Governing the Settlement of Disputes, in force 1 January 1995, art 22.2. See Geraldo Vidigal, 'Re-Assessing WTO Remedies: The Prospective and the Retrospective' (2013) 16 Journal of International Economic Law 505.

[19] It is beyond the scope of this chapter to compare 'suspension of concessions and other obligations' under the DSU with countermeasures under the law of responsibility, on the one hand, and reciprocal suspension of a treaty 'in part' as a response to a material breach of the treaty, as codified in VCLT art 60, on the other.

[20] Rachel Brewster, 'The Remedy Gap: Institutional Design, Retaliation, and Trade Law Enforcement' (2011) 80 George Washington Law Review 102.

may give a state's companies illegitimate competitive advantages vis-à-vis producers that abide by sustainability standards. Decentralized enforcement permits immediate responses, countering this illegitimate competitive advantage. In *Opinion 2/15*, the CJEU stated that one of the objectives of sustainability commitments is to ensure 'free trade on an equal footing', that is, without 'major disparities between the costs of producing goods and supplying services' owing to low labour and environmental standards.[21] In this regard, this form of enforcement is most justifiable when it affects the specific areas and economic actors that credibly gain from a violation of sustainability commitments.

A. Country-Wide Decentralized Enforcement—Rebalancing and Level Playing Field under the EU–UK TCA

Negotiated as part of EU–UK Trade and Co-operation Agreement (TCA), the 'Rebalancing' mechanism established by its Article 411 allows non-adjudicatory, horizontal responses to lowered sustainability standards. In TCA Article 411(1), the parties acknowledge that 'significant divergences' in the areas of 'labour and social, environmental or climate protection, or with respect to subsidy control', are 'capable of impacting trade or investment between the Parties in a manner that changes the circumstances that have formed the basis for the conclusion of this Agreement'. TCA Article 411(2) provides:

> If material impacts on trade or investment between the Parties are arising as a result of significant divergences between the Parties in the areas referred to in paragraph 1, either Party may take appropriate rebalancing measures to address the situation. Such measures shall be restricted with respect to their scope and duration to what is strictly necessary and proportionate in order to remedy the situation. Priority shall be given to such measures as will least disturb the functioning of this Agreement. A Party's assessment of those impacts shall be based on reliable evidence and not merely on conjecture or remote possibility.

Thus, resorting to rebalancing measures is permitted if: (i) there are significant divergences between the parties; (ii) as a result, material impact on trade and investment between the parties arises; and (iii) the measures adopted are appropriate to redress the situation. As regards what 'appropriate rebalancing measures' are, TCA Article 762 refers to suspension of benefits under the TCA itself—so-called 'trade retaliation'—subject to various conditions with regard to its scope and permissible level.[22]

[21] CJEU Opinion 2/15 (n 15) para 159.

[22] See, on the specific requirements, David Collins, 'Standing the Test of Time: The Level Playing Field and Rebalancing Mechanism in the UK–EU Trade and Cooperation Agreement

The TCA regulates in detail the procedure surrounding Article 411. It requires the party seeking rebalancing to notify the other party of the measures it intends to take, following which consultations between the parties must ensue. If these consultations do not yield a satisfactory outcome, the party targeted by rebalancing may request an arbitration tribunal to determine the consistency of the proposed measures with the requirements of Article 411(2) (along with, presumably, other provisions specifying what measures are 'appropriate'). In case of delay by the arbitration tribunal, the party that proposed rebalancing measures may adopt them nonetheless, but it is subject to self-judging countermeasures from the other party. A finding of inconsistency requires the 'withdrawal or adjustment of the rebalancing measures' to reflect the findings of the arbitral tribunal.[23] Upon delivery of the arbitral tribunal's award, any early adopted rebalancing measures found to be inconsistent with the TCA, as well as all countermeasures adopted to respond to this early adoption, must be withdrawn.

In short, rebalancing under the TCA is subject to both substantive and procedural requirements. These procedural requirements go beyond requiring certain conduct prior to the adoption of rebalancing measures. Once considered in their entirety, they mean that TCA rebalancing does not operate as a wholly horizontal mechanism. Instead, the party targeted by proposed rebalancing is empowered to request adjudication and obtain a ruling on the lawfulness of the proposed measures—a request that prevents the party seeking rebalancing from implementing the proposed measures pending adjudication. The horizontal enforcement based on a purely unilateral assessment (an early proposal made by the European Union) is now vestigial, remaining available provisionally, and solely in case of a delay on the part of the arbitral tribunal. Additionally, this unilateral rebalancing is subject to an equally unilateral response from the party targeted by the rebalancing measures. Ultimately, what the TCA's rebalancing mechanism creates is a reversal of the burden of bringing a dispute, perhaps (if a dispute is ever brought) with a corresponding shifting of the burden of proof.

B. Targeted Decentralized Enforcement—US–Peru Forest Governance and USMCA Rapid Response Mechanism

A second means of decentralized enforcement is targeted unilateral enforcement. Targeted unilateral enforcement replaces the blunt instrument of measures affecting

(TCA)' (2021) 12 Journal of International Dispute Settlement 617; Giulia Claudia Leonelli, 'From Extra-Territorial Leverage and Transnational Environmental Protection to Distortions of Competition: The Level Playing Field in the EU–UK Trade and Cooperation Agreement' (2021) 33 Journal of Environmental Law 611.

[23] Trade and Cooperation Agreement between the European Union and the European Atomic Energy Community and the United Kingdom of Great Britain and Northern Ireland (TCA), in force 1 May 2021, art 411.3(e), fn 65.

the trade of a non-complying state, without distinction between individual entities affected, with sanctions targeting non-complying entities. The most advanced mechanisms of this type appear in the Annex on Forest Sector Governance in the US–Peru Trade Promotion Agreement (TPA) and in the Rapid Response Mechanism (RRM) set up in the United States–Mexico–Canada Agreement (USMCA).[24] A detailed analysis of the RRM is offered in Chapter 17 of this volume.[25] For purposes of this chapter, the relevant point is that these mechanisms permit a party to act on its own interpretation that production abroad is taking place in violation of certain sustainability standards set out in the TA.

Both mechanisms involve, first and foremost, a demand from the complaining party, addressed to the party in which the sub-standard production is believed to be taking place, for an investigation on the matter. In the TPA, the mechanism applies where the United States believes that a producer or exporter of Peruvian timber products has not 'complied with applicable laws, regulations, and other measures of Peru governing the harvest of, and trade in, those products'. [26] In the USMCA, the United States or Canada may act on its belief that workers in specific facilities in Mexico are being subject to a 'Denial of Rights', in that they 'are being denied the right of free association and collective bargaining under laws necessary to fulfil the obligations of [that] Party' under the USMCA Labour Chapter.[27]

In case of non-responsiveness or of a response considered unsatisfactory, the agreements provide for different procedures. Under the TPA, following a report by Peru on the matter, the United States may directly adopt certain measures targeting the specific products or the companies involved, including 'denying entry to the shipment that was the subject of the verification' or denying entry to all products of an enterprise 'that has knowingly provided false information to Peruvian or United States officials regarding a shipment'.[28] The latter sanction has been adopted vis-à-vis two companies, in 2017[29] and 2019.[30] Peru has not objected to either application.

[24] The RRM only applies between the United States and Mexico (Annex 31-A) and between Canada and Mexico (Annex 31-B).

[25] See Chapter 17 in this volume.

[26] United States–Peru Trade Promotion Agreement, in force 1 February 2009, Annex 18.3.4, para 7.

[27] Agreement between the United States of America, the United Mexican States, and Canada, in force 1 July 2020, art 31-A.2. In principle, Mexico vis-à-vis the United States or Canada may also invoke the mechanism.

[28] TPA Annex 18.3.4, para 13(a). The same measures can be adopted if Peru does not provide a verification report. ibid para 14.

[29] USTR, 'USTR Announces Unprecedented Action to Block Illegal Timber Imports from Peru', *Press Release* (19 October 2017).

[30] USTR, 'USTR Announces Enforcement Action to Block Illegal Timber Imports from Peru', *Press Release* (26 July 2019).

The RRM involves a more complex mechanism. The complaining party must request the establishment of a 'Rapid Response Labor Panel' to adjudicate the matter.[31] If this panel finds a Denial of Rights in a 'Covered Facility', the complainant can then impose remedies, including 'suspension of preferential tariff treatment for goods manufactured at the Covered Facility or the imposition of penalties on goods manufactured at or services provided by the Covered Facility'.[32]

The RRM might seem like a regular adjudication-based enforcement mechanism. However, it includes a decentralized element, which, though formulated as optional, has become de facto the main means of enforcement of USMCA's labour component. Pursuant to USMCA Article 31-A-4(3), together with the request for an investigation, 'the complainant Party may delay final settlement of customs accounts related to entries of goods from the Covered Facility' in which it suspects Denials of Rights to be taking place.

The latter mechanism implies a de facto temporary withdrawal of USMCA preferences. As long as it is in place, in order to import into the complaining party products produced in the targeted facility, an importer may be required to post a bond equivalent to the amount of the applicable tariff. This posting must continue pending resolution of the dispute or a panel ruling, after which the bonds are either returned (in case the panel finds that the measures were unwarranted) or become part of the remedies that the complaining party can continue to apply.[33] Thus, the financial harm caused to that facility does not start after an independently verified failure to conform to USMCA standards. It starts from the unilateral determination by the complaining party that it 'has a good faith basis to believe that a Denial of Rights is occurring at a Covered Facility' and a unilateral decision to accompany its request for an investigation with a temporary suspension of USMCA preferential treatment with respect to products produced in the relevant facility.

Since its creation, the RRM has seen significant use by the United States, which has invoked it 16 times, with respect to 15 facilities, between May 2021 and September 2023. Out of these, on 12 instances (75 per cent) the US Trade Representative has compounded the request for review with a letter directing the US Secretary of the Treasury to suspend 'the liquidation for all unliquidated entries of goods from the Facility'.[34] In all cases started before 2023, this sanction was followed, over the subsequent months, by a resolution of the matter, or an agreement for a 'course of remediation'—and another letter from the US Trade Representative

[31] USMCA arts 31-A.4 and 31-A.5.

[32] USMCA art 31-A.2(2).

[33] See Chad P Bown and Kathleen Claussen, 'The Rapid Response Labor Mechanism of the US–Mexico–Canada Agreement' (forthcoming 2024) World Trade Review.

[34] Letter from United States Trade Representative to United States Secretary of Treasury, 30 January 2023 <https://ustr.gov/sites/default/files/2023-01/VU%20II%20-%20Suspension%20of%20Liquidation%20-%20for%20posting.pdf> accessed 1 September 2023.

(USTR) directing the US Secretary of Treasury to resume liquidation. In 2023, the only case in which the settlement of accounts remained suspended after three months concerned a facility for which the RRM was triggered a second time.[35] This plant has now been closed.

By contrast, only one panel has been requested under the RRM, after Mexico rejected the applicability of the mechanism to the targeted facility (the San Martín mine).[36] At the time of writing, Mexico had recently consented to allow this panel to hold a verification hearing in Mexico City.[37] The virtual lack of RRM litigation and expedited resolution of complaints suggests that more than accepting the truth of the complaint, affected facilities simply cannot afford to have their cash flow affected while they engage in a months-long international dispute settlement procedure.

Targeted unilateral enforcement may seem to be a powerful mechanism but its reach can be limited by the ability of economic operators to shift their mode of operation without addressing the underlying issue.[38] Nonetheless, when adopted between highly integrated economies and towards entities in the relatively smaller partners, which are more likely to be highly dependent on their business with the larger partner, it may lead to rapid change of behaviour. At the same time, if not tempered by adjudication, active decentralized enforcement may become difficult to distinguish from (consented) extraterritorial exercise of enforcement jurisdiction, without many of the legal safeguards that would surround this exercise in a domestic setting.

IV. Passive Enforcement: Product Conditionalities for Benefits and for Trade

What this chapter labels passive decentralized enforcement encompasses measures whose application is embedded in the ordinary operation of domestic laws and policies. Passive enforcement does not take place exceptionally, in response to specific identified instances of non-compliance with sustainability commitments or standards; instead, demonstrating compliance with sustainability standards becomes a condition for a product to be granted certain advantages or, in some cases,

[35] ibid.

[36] USTR, Letter to the Mexican Section of the USMCA Secretariat, 22 August 2023 <https://ustr.gov/sites/default/files/2023-08/US%20Request%20for%20RRM%20Panel%20-%20San%20Martin.pdf> accessed 1 December 2023.

[37] Kathleen Claussen, 'First Rapid Response Labor Panel Begins Work under USMCA' (*International Economic Law and Policy Blog*, 2023) <https://ielp.worldtradelaw.net/2023/10/first-rapid-response-labor-panel-begins-work-under-usmca.html> accessed 1 December 2023.

[38] See eg Alianza Periodística Madera Sin Rastro, 'Sanctioned Peruvian Loggers Continue Illegal Export of Amazonian Timber (Portuguese)' (*Publica*, 31 May 2023) <https://rainforestjournalismfund.org/id/node/22429> accessed 1 December 2023.

for being accepted at all in a certain market. As a matter of how these policies are conducted, this can mean imposing sustainability requirements that apply and are enforced equally vis-à-vis domestic and imported products. More controversially, it may involve applying different requirements to domestic and imported products or applying the same requirements but using different enforcement mechanisms.

In principle, applying sustainability requirements to products is permissible under international trade law, without the need for this to be specified in a treaty. In WTO dispute settlement, such measures have been found permissible in principle, including when they result in new barriers to trade or unfavourable competitive conditions for imported products.[39] In summary, the conditions set out in WTO jurisprudence for the lawfulness of trade-restrictive measures that pursue a legitimate objective are:

> (i) a demonstrable nexus between the measures being adopted and the legitimate objective, so that each measure must make an ascertainable contribution to the objective and, in some cases, make a contribution to this objective that cannot be made through a reasonably available, less trade-restrictive measure; and
>
> (ii) an application without arbitrary or unjustifiable discriminatory effects, so that any adverse effects caused by the measure on the competitive conditions of products imported from a WTO member, when compared to products of another member or domestic products, are rationally justifiable, in principle based on the same objective that justifies adopting the measure.[40]

A trade-restrictive measure that makes such a demonstrable contribution and is non-discriminatory in its application would be lawful under WTO Agreements (and TAs that reproduce the balance between trade obligations and regulatory freedom in the WTO Agreements) without the need for this to be further specified in the agreement.

Specific provisions on passive sustainability enforcement in TAs have a twofold purpose. First, they legitimize sustainability requirements in production. Compliance with these requirements can either be a condition for a product to benefit from trade preferences under the RTA or, conceivably, a condition to export specifically at-risk products to the trade partner at all. Second, these provisions specify the conditions under which trade-restrictive measures may be adopted and trade benefits may be denied. This reduces uncertainty for the parties, preventing

[39] On this see (n 7), (n 8), and (n 9).

[40] On this see Geraldo Vidigal and Ingo Venzke, 'Of False Conflicts and Real Challenges: Trade Agreements, Climate Clubs, and Border Adjustments' (2022) 116 American Journal of International Law Unbound 202; Robert Howse, Joanna Langille, and Katie Sykes, 'Pluralism in Practice: Moral Legislation and the Law of the WTO after Seal Products' (2015) 48 The George Washington International Law Review 81; Emily Lydgate, 'Is It Rational and Consistent? The WTO's Surprising Role in Shaping Domestic Public Policy' (2017) 21 Journal of International Economic Law 561; Giulia Claudia Leonelli, 'Anti-Deforestation npr-PPMs and Carbon Border Measures: Thinking About the Chapeau of Article XX GATT in Times of Climate Crisis' (2023) 26 Journal of International Economic Law 416.

resort to these measures from being perceived as 'sustainability unilateralism', and avoids difficult litigation in which trade rules can be portrayed as 'point[ing] in a different direction' from the adoption of measures to pursue sustainability objectives[41] (even when, in reality, all that trade rules require is that the measures indeed contribute to their asserted objective and do not discriminate against foreign products and producers).

A. Sustainability-Related Conditionalities

Explicit sustainability-related conditionalities have so far been included in two TAs, both conditioning the lower trade barriers in the agreement to the fulfilment of sustainability conditions in production processes. First, under the European Free Trade Association–Indonesia Comprehensive Economic Partnership (EFTA–Indonesia CEPA), the trade benefits accorded to vegetable oil—principally palm oil—are conditional upon such vegetable oil being produced sustainably. Second (and taking a broad view of 'sustainability'), under the agreed-in-principle EU–Mercosur AA, the trade benefits accorded by the European Union to eggs from Mercosur are conditional upon such eggs being produced pursuant to EU animal welfare standards.

In the EFTA–Indonesia CEPA, the sustainability-related conditionality is introduced by Article 8.10, entitled Sustainable Management of the Vegetable Oils Sector and Associated Trade. Article 8.10(a) sets out the parties' agreed sustainability objectives for the palm oil industry: 'protecting primary forests, peatlands, and related ecosystems, halting deforestation, peat drainage and fire clearing in land preparation, reducing air and water pollution, and respecting rights of local and indigenous communities and workers'. In Article 8.10(e), the parties commit to 'ensure that vegetable oils and their derivatives traded between the Parties are produced in accordance with the sustainability objectives' described in paragraph (a). Thus, parties do not only commit, under paragraph (a), to 'effectively apply laws, policies and practices' to pursue sustainability objectives in the vegetable oils sector; under subparagraph (e), they also commit to 'ensure' that all trade between them of vegetable oils and their derivatives involves products 'produced in accordance' with these sustainability objectives.

In itself, Article 8.10 appears to convey regular sustainability commitments, the enforcement of which might require resort to adjudication. The decentralized enforcement of Article 8.10 is based on an asterisk and a footnote in the Schedules of

[41] International Law Commission, 'Fragmentation of International Law: Report of the Study Group of the International Law Commission Finalized by Martti Koskenniemi' (2006) A/CN.4/L.682 and Add.1*, para 15.

Tariff Commitments of Norway, Iceland, and Switzerland (the latter being applicable to Liechtenstein). The footnote provides:

> Products of HS heading 15.11 and 15.13 imported into [relevant EFTA Member State] under the Agreement shall meet the sustainability objectives as set out in Article 8.10 (Sustainable Management of the Vegetable Oils Sector and Associated Trade) of the Agreement.[42]

CEPA tariff benefits for palm oil products are thus conditional upon the fulfilment of Article 8.10 sustainability requirements. The mechanism empowers each party, when applying its own tariff concessions, to establish means to determine whether the sustainability objectives of Article 8.10 have been met. This has been complemented by domestic laws in each EFTA Member State. For instance, under Swiss law, the products in question must be accompanied by certificates issued by the Roundtable on Sustainable Palm Oil, the International Sustainability and Carbon Certification PLUS, or the Palm Oil Innovation Group.[43] The Swiss State Secretariat for the Economy verifies regularly that these certification systems continue to meet the conditions for accurately certifying that products have been produced respecting the objectives of Article 8.10.

Significantly, Indonesia's own mandatory palm oil certification scheme (ISPO) was not accepted, with the authors of the study underlying the law stating that ISPO standards:

> compare poorly to other standards . . . The benchmark for ISPO was hence not included in this report, though we reference findings regarding ISPO from other studies and a short description. It is worth noting that ISPO is currently under review. The forthcoming version of ISPO may prove to be more relevant for the Swiss industry and could be included in a future evaluation.[44]

A similar mechanism is found in the EU–Mercosur agreed-in-principle AA regarding animal welfare standards in egg production. Animal welfare standards

[42] Comprehensive Economic Partnership Agreement between Indonesia and the EFTA States, in force 1 November 2021, *Schedule of Tariff Commitments—Iceland and Indonesia*, 14, fn *, and 5; *Schedule of Tariff Commitments—Norway and Indonesia*, 53, fn 1, and 23; *Schedule of Tariff Commitments—Switzerland and Indonesia*, 99, fn *, and 47–48. The Harmonized System headings are 15.11 ('Palm oil and its fractions, whether or not refined, but not chemically modified') and 15.13 ('Coconut (copra), palm kernel or babassu oil and fractions thereof, whether or not refined, but not chemically modified').

[43] Ordonnance sur l'importation au taux préférentiel d'huile de palme de production durable en provenance d'Indonésie, No 632.324.27, 18 August 2021 (in force 1 November 2021), art 3 <https://www.fedlex.admin.ch/eli/cc/2021/618/fr> accessed 1 December 2023.

[44] FERN, 'Using Tariffs to Incentivize Sustainable Palm Oil' (2022) fn 11 <https://www.fern.org/fileadmin/uploads/fern/Documents/2022/Fern_briefing_-_Using_tariffs_to_incentivise_sustainable_palm_oil.pdf> accessed 1 December 2023.

may be considered sustainability standards in a broad sense, in particular insofar as they prevent the development and spread of animal diseases and foodborne human diseases.[45] In the EU's Tariff Elimination Schedule, tariffs for eggs of various types, for human consumption and incubation, are to be eliminated within four years of the AA entering into force.[46] However, to benefit from this progressive tariff elimination, Mercosur eggs must be 'accompanied by a certificate of compliance with Council Directive No. 1999/74/EC or any equivalent animal welfare official standards'.[47]

Thus, as in the EFTA–Indonesia CEPA, this EU–Mercosur AA provision obviates the need for active enforcement of animal welfare standards, conditioning AA benefits to Mercosur eggs to evidence of compliance by producers with certain production standards. It is noteworthy that, in this case, the substantive standards to be applied are those set in an EU Directive, rather than standards set by an international body or especially formulated for the agreement.[48] Compliance with these standards can be verified by official certification—including, seemingly, that of Mercosur Member State governments—or by third-party certification.[49]

The provision makes it clear that the requirement applies solely to eggs exported by Mercosur Member States under the Agreement and 'does not entail requirements for all MERCOSUR egg production system'. Combined with the direct reference to an EU Council Directive, this suggests that this provision, at least as much as it aims to enhance the well-being of the animals involved in egg production, seeks to preserve a level playing field between EU and Mercosur egg producers. To prevent the elimination of tariffs from leading to a dislocation of production owing to potential lower costs of animal welfare compliance in Mercosur countries, the AA imposes on producers who seek to benefit from tariff elimination compliance with the same EU Council Directive that applies to European producers.

B. Specific Consent to Sustainability Regulation

A final means of enforcement—which one might call simply 'regulation'—does not in principle require treaty provisions. The WTO has consolidated over two decades the understanding that the imposition of requirements concerning an imported product's production methods is not, in itself, incompatible with WTO law.

[45] See Alan M Goldberg, 'Farm Animal Welfare and Human Health' (2016) 3 Current Environmental Health Reports 313; Marian Stamp Dawkins, 'Animal Welfare and Efficient Farming: Is Conflict Inevitable?' (2017) 57 Animal Production Science 201.

[46] EU–Mercosur Trade Agreement – Agreement in Principle, 1 July 2019 (not signed), Appendix 2-A-1 (Tariff Elimination Schedule for the EU), 10.

[47] EU–Mercosur Agreement in Principle, Annex-A (Tariff Elimination Schedule), para 5(1), 8.

[48] ibid. Of course, by referring to Council Directive No 1999/74/EC, the Agreement in Principle incorporates it by reference, making it the negotiated standard between the parties.

[49] ibid.

Pursuant to this jurisprudence, the WTO Agreements permit members to adopt measures to pursue sustainability objectives having a highly trade-restrictive effect, provided that the measures are applied 'in an even-handed manner' to domestic and imported products.[50] This includes measures that apply solely to imported products, such as the ban on the importation of retreaded tyres in *Brazil—Retreaded Tyres*, if there is a rationale according to which the importation of the relevant products poses an aggravated risk when compared to non-affected products (in this case, retreaded tyres were affected, but not new tyres).[51]

Despite the openness in WTO jurisprudence to such measures, they remain contentious. During the G20 meeting of 2023, for example, 17 developing countries—in Latin America, Africa, and Southeast Asia—challenged the EU Deforestation Regulation. Their Joint Letter criticized the regulation's 'one-size-fits-all' approach, its ability to contribute to halting deforestation, its 'immense costs on exporting and importing countries alike, as well as on producers and consumers', and its disproportionate impact on smallholders.[52] The following week, Mercosur responded to the European Union that it believes the EU–Mercosur AA must be 'equipped with a mechanism to rebalance trade concessions negotiated under the Agreement, should these concessions be nullified or impaired as a result of EU domestic law'.[53]

To address these matters, it seems possible for TAs to feature provisions conveying agreement between parties to specific regulations, so as to avoid contestation and litigation. Most TSD Chapters contain generic provisions in this regard, which obscure more than they clarify. The EU–Mercosur Agreement in Principle, for example, includes a provision entitled 'Right to regulate and levels of protection', which enshrines a reciprocal recognition of:

> the right of each Party to determine its sustainable development policies and priorities, to establish the levels of domestic environmental and labour protection it deems appropriate and to adopt or modify its law and policies . . . consistent with each Party's commitment to the international agreements and labour standards referred to [in the TA].[54]

[50] See (n 7), (n 8), and (n 9).

[51] Appellate Body Report, *Brazil—Measures Affecting Imports of Retreaded Tyres*, 3 December 2007, WT/DS332/AB/R.

[52] Letter to President of the European Parliament, President of the European Council, President of the European Commission and Presidency of the Council of the European Union, 7 September 2023. The letter was later submitted to the WTO Committee on Agriculture and is available as Doc G/AG/GEN/223/Rev.1 (26 September 2023).

[53] Letter from Mercosur Member States to the European Union and its Member States, 25 September 2023 (on file with author).

[54] EU–Mercosur Agreement in Principle, TSD Chapter, art 2(1).

Provisions such as this do little to clarify what is permissible regulation and enforcement. They may be read as meaning that both parties, in particular the less developed among them, may 'establish the levels' they deem appropriate for domestic environmental and labour protection, without being subject to trade restrictions by the other party. But they may, equally logically, mean that both parties, and in particular the more developed among them, may enact regulations demanding compliance, by imported products and perhaps even exporting countries as a whole, with certain production standards aimed at enforcing the regulating party's individually established levels of protection. In other words, the provision does little to resolve any specific interpretative disagreements, potentially giving rise to challenges and litigation. The panel in *Ukraine—Wood Export Ban* accorded limited, if any, interpretative value to the 'right to regulate' provision in the EU–Ukraine AA, noting that it did not establish any 'immediate and precise obligations' and, partially for this reason, did not provide either a self-standing exception or particularly relevant context for the interpretation of the regular exceptions in the agreement.[55]

In this regard, more specific provisions could be helpful in establishing, *ex ante*, specific permissible regulatory measures affecting trade between the parties, as well as specific requirements attached to the adoption and implementation of these measures.

V. Conclusion

While adding decentralized enforcement mechanisms to TAs remains uncommon, most agreements that contain these mechanisms are very recent. They demonstrate that the horizon of enforceability of sustainability commitments in international TAs is not restricted to enforcement through adjudication. Decentralized enforcement may take place through measures affecting parties, their nationals, or specific products that the enforcing party believes are failing to abide by certain sustainability requirements.

Some forms of decentralized enforcement could be lawful under general international law or conform to WTO jurisprudence on legitimate trade-restrictive regulation. Their addition to TAs has the advantage of securing consent for their use, legitimizing conduct that might be unlawful or simply clarifying the permissible conditions for, and modes of, sustainability enforcement.

Decentralized enforcement mechanisms may be powerful means for strengthening the enforcement of sustainability commitments. They avoid the challenging road of resort to adjudication under TAs and permit targeting specific products or

[55] Panel Report, *Ukraine—Wood Export Ban*, paras 250–51.

facilities in which sustainability issues arise. On the other hand, in the absence of available adjudication, they may give rise to abuse. Sustainability standards may become a pretext for, rather than the motivation behind, trade-restrictive measures, leading to TA-sanctioned protectionism, or worse, economic coercion.

For this reason, it is crucial for these mechanisms to include the possibility of adjudication, resort to which must be concretely available for those affected by consented decentralized enforcement that they deem unjustifiable. In this case, the mechanism is no longer fully decentralized: instead, its effect is to reverse the burden of resorting to adjudication, requiring the party perceived to be adopting or permitting unsustainable production in its territory to challenge the adoption by the other party of decentralized enforcement measures.

17

State and Private Accountability through the Rapid Response Labour Mechanism

Scope, Purposes, and Prospects for Effectiveness

Kevin Banks[*]

I. Introduction

Pioneering an unprecedented approach within free trade agreements (FTAs), the Rapid Response Labor Mechanism (RRLM or Mechanism), contained in the framework of the United States–Canada–Mexico Agreement (USMCA), introduces, for the first time, remedies aimed at private actors in response to labour rights denials. The inclusion of such remedies has been portrayed as a revolutionary change able to ameliorate the working conditions within the Mexican workforce.[1] The incorporation of the RRLM in USMCA played a significant role in the outstanding bipartisan support that it received in the US Congress, and led to the endorsement by the American Federation of Labour and Congress of Industrial Organizations, making it the first trade agreement to receive such support in many decades.[2] This chapter will analyse and assess the potential of the RRLM in meeting its aspirations and expectations. Firstly, the chapter will introduce the structure of obligations and understandings that can be enforced through the Mechanism and provide an overview of the procedures and remedies designed for this purpose. Secondly, it will identify the specific purposes and aims of the RRLM alongside the broader labour rights objectives of the Agreement. Finally,

[*] The author is a member of the Roster of Panelists for Chapter 31 Dispute Settlement Panels and of the Canada—Mexico List of Rapid Response Labor Panelists under the United States–Mexico–Canada Agreement. The observations in this chapter are based on a preliminary consideration of Agreement text and secondary sources, and without prejudice to any determination that the author might later make having had the benefit of submissions from the parties, if asked to serve on a panel.

[1] David A Gantz, *An Introduction to the United States–Mexico–Canada Agreement: Understanding the New NAFTA* (Edward Elgar 2021) 83. See also Kathleen Claussen, 'Reimagining Trade-Plus Compliance: The Labor Story' (2020) 23 Journal of International Economic Law 25.

[2] Gantz (n 1) 85.

Kevin Banks, *State and Private Accountability through the Rapid Response Labour Mechanism* In: *The Sustainability Revolution in International Trade Agreements*. Edited by: Geraldo Vidigal and Kathleen Claussen, Oxford University Press.
© Kevin Banks 2024. DOI: 10.1093/9780191994470.003.0017

it provides an evaluation of the RRLM's foreseeable impacts and its capability in attaining its objectives.

II. What Does the RRLM Serve to Enforce?

The RRLM is established in Annexes 31-A and 31-B of the USMCA, each entitled 'Facility-Specific Rapid Response Labor Mechanism'. The former constitutes an agreement between the United States and Mexico only, and the latter between Canada and Mexico only. Their terms are almost identical. There are no similar obligations between Canada and the United States.

A. The Nature of Enforceable Understandings

The RRLM can be invoked when a party has a 'good faith basis belief that workers at a Covered Facility are being denied the right of free association and collective bargaining under laws necessary to fulfill the obligations of the other party' under the Agreement—what the Agreement refers to as a Denial of Rights.[3] A 'Covered Facility' is essentially one that produces or supplies traded or import-competing goods services in certain priority sectors.[4] Priority sectors are those that produce manufactured goods, supply services, or involve mining.[5] In North America, facilities in these sectors tend to be owned and operated by private business organizations. The use of the passive voice to define a Denial of Rights suggests that the RRLM can be invoked regardless of which actor or actors—the state, or private actors such as the employer or a union—are responsible for it. Thus, the object of proceedings could be a single instance for which a private actor is responsible.

Remedies similarly address specific Denials of Rights, operating at the facility level. If a panel determines that there had been a Denial of Rights, the complainant party may suspend preferential tariff treatment for goods manufactured at the Covered Facility, impose penalties on goods manufactured at or services provided by the Covered Facility, or in the event of twice repeated findings of Denial of Rights, deny entry of goods produced by a Covered Facility.[6]

[3] Agreement between the United States of America, the United Mexican States, and Canada, in force 1 July 2020, arts 31-A.2 and 31-B.2.

[4] ibid arts 31-A.15 and 31-B.15. A 'Covered Facility' is defined as a facility in the territory of a party that produces goods or supplies a service traded between the parties to the annex in question, or produces goods or supplies a service that competes in the territory of a party with a good or service of the other party, and is in a priority sector. In keeping with the bilateral structure of the annexes, the term party in this context refers to the parties to the relevant annex, singly or collectively, rather than the parties to the USMCA as a whole.

[5] ibid.

[6] ibid arts 31-A.10 and 31-B.10.

The fact that the actions of private actors such as employers or unions can trigger facility-specific RRLM procedures and remedies suggests that the Mechanism aims, at least indirectly, to hold such actors accountable for committing or failing to prevent Denials of Rights, or at least to incentivize them not to do so. In any event, irrespective of whether those were the aims, these would remain the resulting effects. This represents a major innovation in labour chapter dispute settlement, one that stands to significantly improve its effectiveness.

Nonetheless, the Agreement does not expressly impose any obligations on private actors. Indeed, the annexes creating the RRLM remain resolutely international in structure, treating state signatories as parties with control over the petitions, leaving decisions to impose or remove trade remedies in their hands (subject to preconditions and review by dispute panels), and according to private actors such as facility owners no standing in RRLM proceedings.

On its face, the RRLM appears simply to be a set of procedures for resolving issues arising from petitions alleging denials of labour rights in key traded sectors. It is embedded in the dispute settlement chapter of the Agreement and does not expressly impose new obligations. It might be thought of as simply providing an additional means of enforcing the Agreement's labour obligations, which are set out in its Chapter 23.

But a closer look suggests that it may be doing more than just that. The RRLM's scope of application exceeds the scope of labour obligations set out in Chapter 23. Obligations in Chapter 23 are based on two pillars: (1) adopting and maintaining certain rights in statutes and regulations, and practices thereunder;[7] and (2) not failing to effectively enforce domestic labour laws through a sustained or recurring course of action or inaction, in a manner affecting trade or investment between the parties.[8] A single Denial of Rights would not necessarily constitute a sustained or recurring course of action or inaction by a party. The Agreement parties have defined such a course so as to exclude 'an isolated instance or case'.[9] By contrast, a Denial of Rights could be an isolated case, and need not be the result of ongoing state action or inaction. The Annex does not mandate that an RRLM panel inquire into whether a party's enforcement institutions have engaged in a course of ongoing inaction or any other type of sustained or recurring course of action or inaction.

What then are the additional understandings or commitments of state parties that the RRLM serves to enforce? How does a Denial of Rights effected by private actors engage those understandings or commitments? The text of the Agreement does not directly address these questions, and it is beyond the scope of this brief chapter to fully explore them. I will nonetheless note one possibility that merits

7 ibid art 23.3.
8 ibid art 23.5.
9 ibid art 23.5.1, fn 10.

further consideration. The stated purpose of the Mechanism is to ensure the remediation of denials of certain worker rights in priority traded sectors.[10] The creation of an international mechanism to give effect to this purpose by enabling parties to withdraw Agreement benefits in response to such denials arguably implies that ensuring such remediation within key traded sectors in their territories, regardless of whether it was due to a state failure to effectively enforce labour laws, is a condition for the full operation of the Agreement in those sectors. Such a condition might be treated as an element of a fairness framework that is a precondition for the continuation of the close economic ties enabled by the Agreement.[11] Its justifications might be grounded in awareness of systemic challenges to labour rights documented during the years of the North American Free Trade Agreement (NAFTA), which are further discussed in section C.

B. Scope of Matters that May be the Subject of an RRLM Petition

I turn to delineating the scope of rights denials that can be addressed under the RRLM.

1. Denial of the Rights of Free Association and Collective Bargaining

Ordinarily, the Mechanism is limited to remedying denials of 'the right of free association and collective bargaining under laws necessary to fulfill the obligations of the other Party under the Agreement'.[12]

a) Delineating the Right of Free Association and Collective Bargaining

The Agreement's obligations requiring laws on freedom of association and collective bargaining are found in Article 23.3. Article 23.3.1 requires, among other things, that each USMCA party adopt and maintain in its statutes, regulations, and practices thereunder 'the right of freedom of association and effective recognition of the right to collective bargaining', 'as stated in the [International Labour Organization (ILO)] Declaration on Rights at Work'.[13]

The Agreement then provides two important clarifications of the scope of this protection. First, Article 23.3 specifies, for greater certainty, that 'the right to strike is linked to the right to freedom of association, which cannot be realized without protecting the right to strike'.[14] Second, it enunciates the obligations of Mexico to

[10] ibid arts 31-A.1.2 and 31-B.1.2.

[11] For a discussion of this concept as a justification of trade-related labour agreements see Kevin Banks, 'Fit for Purpose? The Extent and Enforcement of International Trade Agreement Labor Obligations After the Guatemala-Labor Obligations Decision' (2021) 52(3) Georgetown Journal of International Law 639, 662–72.

[12] USMCA arts 31-A.1.2 and 31-B.1.2.

[13] ibid art 23.3.

[14] ibid art 23.3, fn 6.

adopt and maintain freedom of association and collective bargaining laws with additional precision. Article 23.3 identifies the obligations of Annex 23-A (Worker Representation in Collective Bargaining in Mexico) as setting out 'obligations with regard to worker representation in collective bargaining'.[15] Annex 23-A then specifies a detailed set of legal and administrative reforms to be implemented by Mexico before and following the entry into force of the Agreement.

On the other hand, Article 23.3's reference to the ILO Declaration delimits in a somewhat ambiguous way the content of the free association and collective bargaining rights that it protects. Footnote 3 to Article 23.3 adds that '[t]he obligations set out in this Article, as they relate to the ILO, refer only to the ILO Declaration on Rights at Work'.[16] The clear implication is that they do not refer to the Conventions of the ILO. The ILO Declaration does not incorporate those Conventions or obligate member states to ratify them. The rights stated in the Declaration and referenced in Article 23.3 thus do not necessarily include each of the specific rights provided by the core freedom of association Conventions of the ILO (Conventions 87 and 98), as interpreted by ILO supervisory committees.[17] But they likely include, among others, obligations to protect against acts of anti-union discrimination through means of redress that are expeditious, inexpensive, and impartial.[18]

b) Delineating 'Laws Necessary' to Fulfil Obligations under the Agreement

A claim can be brought against Mexico concerning any alleged Denial of Rights under most current Mexican labour legislation.[19] The scope of claims that can be brought concerning the United States or Canada is narrower. With respect to the United States, a claim can be brought only for an alleged Denial of Rights owed to workers under an enforced order of the National Labor Relations Board.[20] This

[15] ibid art 23.3, fn 7.

[16] This is likely due to the fact that the United States has ratified neither Convention 87 nor Convention 98, and that some aspects of its labour laws may not comply with those conventions as interpreted by ILO supervisory bodies. See Human Rights Watch, 'A Strange Case: Violations of Workers' Freedom of Association in the United States by European Multinational Corporations' (*Human Rights Watch*, 2 September 2010) <https://www.hrw.org/report/2010/09/03/strange-case/violations-workers-freedom-association-united-states-european> accessed 20 April 2024.

[17] The exact difference between rights stated in the Declaration and those provided in Conventions remains the subject of considerable debate. But that there is a difference is in my view beyond doubt. See Brian Langille, 'Can We Rely on the ILO?' (2006–07) 13 Canadian Labour and Employment Law Journal 273, 280–83.

[18] Kevin Banks, 'The Role and Promise of International Law in Canada's New Labour Law Constitutionalism' (2012) 16(2) Canadian Labour and Employment Law Journal 233, 271; Report of the Panel of Experts, *Proceedings Constituted under Article 13.15 of the EU-Korea Free Trade Agreement*, 20 January 2021, paras 139–41; Final Report of the Panel, *In the Matter of Guatemala—Issue Relating to the Obligations Under Article 16.2.1(a) of the CAFTA–DR*, 14 June 14 2017, para 427.

[19] USMCA art 31-A.3, fn 2 states that a claim can be brought against Mexico only with respect to an alleged Denial of Rights under labour legislation that complies with Annex 23-A. This indicates both that a claim that legislation does not comply with Annex 23-A would have to be brought under the regular dispute settlement provisions of Chapter 31, and that any claim denial of rights under freedom of association and collective bargaining laws that do comply with Annex 23-A can raised under RRLM procedures. Mexico has passed legislation to comply with the requirements of Annex 23-A.

[20] ibid art 31-A.3, fn 2.

limits the application of the mechanism of US federal labour law. It also effectively means that US courts, who issue decisions to enforce (or not) National Labor Relations Board orders, will determine which rights can be the subject of a Denial of Rights claim against the United States, rather than RRLM panel members directly interpreting US legislation. Similarly, a Denial of Rights claim can be brought against Canada only with respect to rights owed to workers under an enforced order of the Canada Industrial Relations Board.[21] Further, these provisions also mean in effect that Denial of Rights claims against the United States and Canada must await exhaustion of domestic procedures and remedies, whereas the Parties have stipulated no such requirement in relation to Mexico. The Mechanism thus applies asymmetrically.

2. Expanded Scope Following a Finding of Breach of Chapter 23 Obligation

Both the subject matter scope of Denial of Rights claims and the scope of application of the Mechanism expand considerably where a party is found to have breached its obligations under Article 23.3 (Labor Rights) or Article 23.5 (Enforcement of Labor Laws) by a panel established under Article 31.6.[22] In the event of such a finding, the complainant party in the case of Article 31.6 may use the RRLM 'with regard to the relevant law or laws at issue' in that dispute for two years or until the conclusion of the next joint review of the Agreement under Article 34.7, whichever is later.[23] This effectively extends the scope of the Mechanism to denials of rights beyond freedom of association and collective bargaining rights, 'in recognition of the importance of ensuring full compliance with the Labor Chapter', and of 'the commitment of the Parties to trade only in goods produced in compliance' with that Chapter.[24]

The laws potentially at issue in a finding of Article 23.3 or Article 23.5 breach include, in the case of both Article 23.3 obligations to adopt and maintain laws and Article 23.5 obligations to effectively enforce laws: laws directly related to the elimination of all forms of forced or compulsory labour, the effective abolition of child labour, prohibition on the worst forms of child labour, and the elimination of discrimination in respect of employment and occupation; and in the case of Article 23.5 obligations only: law directly related to other labour protections for children and minors, and acceptable conditions of work concerning minimum wages, hours of work, and occupational safety and health.[25] Further, the freedom of association and collective bargaining laws potentially at issue under Articles 23.3 and 23.5 may

[21] ibid art 31-B.3, fn 2. This represents an even greater narrowing, since the Canada Industrial Relations Board has jurisdiction only over federally regulated industries, which though generally national in scope employ less than 10 per cent of the Canadian workforce.

[22] ibid arts 31-A.12 and 31-B.12.

[23] ibid.

[24] ibid.

[25] ibid arts 23.3 and 23.5.

confer rights beyond those found in enforced orders or labour relations boards in Canada or the United States. Finally, Mexican laws that are not in compliance with Annex 23-A could be the subject of a panel determination under Article 31, and then subsequently of RRLM proceedings under Annexes 31-A and 31-B.

III. Enforcement and Compliance Procedures

RRLM procedures appear to have been designed to incentivize and encourage early resolution, and in the absence of such resolution, to adjudicate differences between parties and remediate Denials of Rights rapidly.

A panel must be constituted within three business days of a petition requesting its establishment.[26] It may then make its determination with or without conducting a verification process.[27] The Rules of Procedure anticipate that a panel's verification process could take the form of onsite verification, in-person or virtual review of documents, or in-person or virtual testimony, among others.[28] If the panel conducts a verification, it will have 30 days to do so.[29]

The panel is required to make a written determination of whether there has been a Denial of Rights public within 30 days of being constituted, or within 30 days of conducting a verification if it does so.[30] Panels may respond to a refusal by the owner of a Covered Facility to consent to a verification, or interference with or events or circumstances that leave the panel 'otherwise unable to conduct the verification in a manner that it believes is most appropriate to gather information relevant to the matter' by taking them into account in making determinations of whether there was a Denial of Rights.[31] A panel might, for example, in appropriate circumstances draw an inference adverse to the position of the responding party concerning the facts in connection with an alleged Denial of Rights. These provisions enable a panel to proceed expeditiously with its determination even in the absence of cooperation from local authorities or an employer or union and should serve to promote such cooperation.

[26] ibid arts 31-A.5.3 and 31-B.5.3.

[27] A petition can request either (a) the establishment of a panel to request that the respondent party allow the panel an opportunity to verify the Covered Facility's compliance with the law in question and determine whether there has been a Denial of Rights; or (b) the establishment of a panel to determine whether there has been a Denial of Rights. Presumably, a complainant party would make the latter type of request only whether the relevant facts are clear and undisputed. Even when faced with the latter type of request, a panel may at its discretion, make a verification if it considers that a verification is necessary to assist them in making their determination. The panel must also make a determination notwithstanding any refusal by the responding party to consent to a verification. See USMCA arts 31-A.5.1, 31-A.7.10, 31-B.5.1, and 31-B.7.10.

[28] ibid arts 26.11 and 27.11.

[29] ibid arts 31-A.7.7 and 31-B.7.7.

[30] ibid arts 31-A.8.1, 31-A.8.5, 31-B.8.1, and 31-B.8.5.

[31] ibid arts 31-A.7.8, 31-A.8.3, 31-B.7.8, and 31-B.8.3.

If there is a determination of Denial of Rights, the complainant party may impose remedies after providing the responding party with five business days' notice, in writing, of its intention to do so.[32] Remedies may include suspension of preferential tariff treatment of or the imposition of penalties on goods or services of the Covered Facility.[33] In cases of repeated violation, the suspension of preferential tariff treatment or the imposition of penalties could extend to the same or similar goods or services provided by another facility owned or controlled by the same persons as the Covered Facility, or to the denial of entry of such goods.[34] Importantly, immediately upon delivering its request that the respondent conduct its review at the outset of proceedings, the complainant party may delay the final settlement of customs accounts related to entries of goods from the Covered Facility in question.[35] This enables the application of any trade remedies that might eventually be authorized based on a complainant party's subsequent petition as of the date of the initial request, which in turn provides a strong disincentive for delay in resolution.

It is too early to know with any certainty how well these incentives and procedures will work, or conversely whether by permitting the imposition of trade measures ex ante they will unduly inhibit challenges to allegations made in petitions, resulting in a form of over-sanctioning. Much may depend on how quickly and fairly verification procedures operate. In any event, it is notable that the first several petitions brought forward under the Mechanism were quickly resolved in ways that appear to have made a difference on the ground to the workers whose rights were allegedly denied.[36]

IV. Reflections on the Purposes and Scope of RRLM Regulatory Regime

Having identified the salient features of the Mechanism's procedures and the obligations and understandings it enforces, it is now possible to put it into its legal, economic, and political context to reflect on its purposes. The Protocol of Amendments that added the RRLM to Chapter 31 responded directly to concerns of US legislators and the US labour movement that the labour obligations contained in Chapter 23 of the USMCA did not go far enough to address labour rights problems raised by a preferential trading relationship with Mexico.[37] During the

[32] ibid arts 31-A.9 and 31-B.9.

[33] ibid arts 31-A.10.2 and 31-B.10.2.

[34] ibid arts 31-A.10.3, 31-A.10.4, 31-B.10.3, and 31-B.10.4.

[35] ibid arts 31-A.4.3 and 31-B.4.3.

[36] See Justino De la Cruz, 'Consequences of Non-Compliance with USMCA Labor Provisions: Potential Effects on Exporting Firms' (2022) US International Trade Commission 17–18 <usitc.gov/publications/332/working_papers/consequences_of_non-compliance_of_labor_provisions_5-24-2022.pdf> accessed 12 May 2023. See also Independent Mexico Labor Expert Board, Interim Report, 20 March 2023, 12–32.

[37] See US Congressional Research Service, 'USMCA: Labor Provisions', 12 January 2023.

time of the NAFTA, serious and persistent violations of freedom of association and collective bargaining rights under Mexican and international law contributed to undermining the political acceptability of the Agreement to broad segments of electorates, particularly in the United States.[38] These rights violations, though not universal, were systemic, embedded in relatively widespread practices of corrupt unions, repressive employers, and ineffective labour law tribunals.[39] The problems of Mexican labour law enforcement extended further, affecting other fields such as occupational health and safety law.[40]

Proceedings under the previous NAFTA labour side agreement had accomplished very little to address any of these problems.[41] In an economic context of long-term stagnation or decline in US middle- and lower-middle-class incomes resulting in part from economic globalization,[42] concentrated manufacturing job losses in politically important states,[43] and perhaps modest and more widely dispersed job gains attributable to North American free trade,[44] the political salience of labour rights issues in Mexico within North American trade negotiations was predictably high. Though the USMCA contained, in Annex 23-A, a very significant set of labour law reforms that Mexico was required to enact as a precondition to its entry into force, the perception of many US legislators, and the US labour movement, was that the Agreement lacked sufficient implementation and enforcement

[38] See generally Lance Compa, 'Trump, Trade and Trabajo: Renegotiating NAFTA's Labor Accord in a Fraught Political Climate' (2019) 26(1) Indiana Journal of Global Legal Studies 263. On public opinion regarding trade policy and job losses during the Trump Administration, see Robert J Blendon, Logan S Casey, and John M Benson, 'Public Opinion and Trump's Jobs and Trade Policies' (2017) 60(3) Challenge 228. On the relationship between fairness norms and trade impacts see Banks, 'Fit for Purpose' (n 11) 662–73. On the relationship between perceived economic unfairness and the rise of populism in western countries, see Eric Protzer and Paul Summerville, *Reclaiming Populism: How Economic Fairness Can Win Back Disenchanted Voters* (Polity Press 2022). On the persistence of rights violations and the inability of the institutions of the North American Agreement on Labor Cooperation to respond effectively to them, see Kevin Banks, 'Trade, Labor and International Governance: An Inquiry into the Potential Effectiveness of the New International Labor Law' (2011) 32(45) Berkeley Journal of Employment and Labor Law 88–93, and sources cited therein.

[39] See Sandra Polaski and others, 'The USMCA: A "New Model" for Labor Governance in North America?' in Gilbert Gangé and Michèle Rioux (eds), *NAFTA 2.0: from the first NAFTA to the United States–Mexico–Canada Agreement* (Palgrave Macmillan 2022) 139. See also Michael Joseph McGuinness, 'The Landscape of Labor Law Enforcement in North America: An Examination of Mexico's Labor Regulatory Policy and Practice' (1998) 29(3) Law and Policy in International Business 365.

[40] Garrett D Brown, 'NAFTA's 10 Year Failure to Protect Mexican Workers' Health and Safety' (2004) Maquiladora Health and Safety Support Network; Linda Delp and others, 'NAFTA's Labor Side Agreement: Fading into Oblivion? An Assessment of Workplace Health & Safety Cases' (2004) UCLA Center for Labor Research and Education.

[41] Banks, 'Trade, Labor and International Governance' (n 38) 88–93.

[42] Avraham Ebenstein and others, 'Estimating the Impact of Trade and Offshoring on American Workers Using the Current Population Survey' (2014) 96(4) Review of Economics and Statistics 581.

[43] See Ann Harrison and Margaret McMillan, 'Offshoring Jobs? Multinationals and U.S. Manufacturing Employment' (2011) 93(3) The Review of Economics and Statistics 857.

[44] See US Congressional Research Service, 'NAFTA: Estimated U.S. Job 'Gains' and 'Losses' by State Over 5½ Years' (2 February 2000).

mechanisms to ensure that those reforms would be fully carried out.[45] The RRLM was the key element in a package of responses in the Protocol of Amendments designed to ensure the effectiveness of the USMCA labour rights obligations.[46]

One overall purpose of the RRLM was thus to help meet the USMCA labour chapter's objectives by remedying the most problematic Denials of Rights—those occurring in priority sectors and involving persistently violated labour rights—more effectively than was thought likely to be possible under traditional state-to-state obligation structures and dispute settlement mechanisms. It was demanded by the United States, by far the most powerful and least trade-dependent North American state, at a time it was quite possible that a new NAFTA might not pass, or might not include Mexico, unless that demand was met. In this context, the asymmetries and bilateral structure of RRLM obligations and procedures are not surprising.

USMCA Labor Chapter obligations apply to all traded goods and services, regardless of whether any failure to comply with them makes a material impression on the conditions of competition.[47] They thus appear to be ground rules and preconditions for the North American integrated economic space.[48] This is consistent with the Preamble to the USMCA's resolution to 'replace the 1994 North American Free Trade Agreement with a 21st Century, high standard new agreement to support mutually beneficial trade leading to freer, fairer markets', and with the statement of shared commitment in Chapter 23 to 'the goal of trading only in goods produced in compliance with this Chapter'.[49] This, in turn, suggests that larger purposes of labour obligations in the USMCA include establishing systemic conditions for fair competition by seeking to offset, at least in part, the economic pressures on labour standards that arise out of competitive pressures amplified by international economic integration.[50] The risk of trade remedies in response to labour rights violations can serve to align government and employer incentives with labour rights compliance. Normatively and politically, an effective set of labour obligations might in this way also establish a fairness framework as a precondition for closer economic ties, enabling members of the US and Canadian polities to tolerate concentrated costs imposed by disruptive forces of international competition, and seeking to extend greater benefits in terms of rising incomes and improved access to labour rights to Mexican workers.[51]

[45] See Isabelle Hoagland, 'Advisory Panels Cite USMCA Labor Upgrades, Need for Mexican Legislation' *Inside US Trade* (4 October 2018).

[46] See Maria Anna Corvaglia, 'Labour Rights Protection and Its Enforcement under the USMCA: Insights from a Comparative Legal Analysis' (2021) 20 *World Trade Review* 648.

[47] See Banks, 'Fit for Purpose' (n 11) 642.

[48] ibid 674–77.

[49] USMCA Preamble, art 23.2.

[50] Banks, 'Fit for Purpose' (n 11) 671–72.

[51] ibid 672–74.

This set of larger purposes helps to make sense of the RRLM's more specific, strategic ones. It accounts for the way that the Mechanism directly targets systemic labour rights problems that threatened the political legitimacy of North American free trade. Viewed in light of standard North American policy discourse on what is needed to make labour obligations effective[52]—generally understood to be enforcement mechanisms with 'teeth'—it also makes sense of the changes that the RRLM brings to standard trade dispute resolution mechanisms in order to address ways in which they are arguably maladapted to resolving labour rights issues. This can be seen in three aspects of the Mechanism.

First, the RRLM both enables a party to take up single specific instances of labour rights violations and considerably shortens timelines to resolution. This in principle makes it possible to remedy specific labour rights denials in a way that will benefit the particular workers involved. Previous trade agreement labour obligations focused on problems in legislation or enforcement that would require a political or institutional change to address and had longer and more unpredictable pathways to resolution. While such changes might well be meaningful for workers in the longer term, they would do little to remedy a breach of labour rights as normative ground rules for an integrated economic space, or the losses experienced by individual workers affected by such breaches. The RRLM thus helps to align the overall scheme of enforcement mechanisms available under the Agreement better with its larger purposes.

Second, the RRLM helps to deploy the influence of potential trade remedies more efficiently than is possible under traditional trade dispute settlement systems. As others have pointed out,[53] in state-to-state dispute settlement states often hesitate to raise allegations that another state has failed to effectively enforce laws through a sustained or recurring course of action or inaction, or that its laws fail to reflect internationally agreed upon labour rights. These are allegations of politically sensitive institutional failure that can complicate complex trade relationships. By raising the stakes in this way, traditional trade dispute resolution mechanisms reduce the likelihood that they will be used in labour cases and thus dilute the incentive effects of trade remedies. By contrast, an allegation of a Denial of Rights is more discretely focused and need not blame another state party, at least not in such a sweeping manner. Further, as is well known, trade sanctions can be a blunt instrument, potentially affecting both compliant and non-compliant employers, and creating potential trade-offs between employment and pressure for improved labour rights compliance. Trade remedies focused on non-compliant employers are better targeted. Taken together with the increased likelihood of their application, this targeting stands to enhance the incentive effects of potential trade remedies in favour of labour rights compliance.

[52] Banks, 'Trade, Labor and International Governance' (n 38) 52–56.
[53] Polaski and others 'USMCA: "A New Model"' (n 39) 142.

Finally, the RRLM's verification procedures help to address problems of proof that have arisen and are likely to continue to arise in labour rights cases.[54] They make it possible for panels to obtain information, rapidly but in a procedurally fair manner, from workers who may not be able to produce detailed written statements providing sufficient particulars to create an evidentiary record that enables a panel to determine the merits of a Denial of Rights claim on the basis of the best available information, or who may be reluctant to be identified for fear of retaliation. Further, by enabling panels to take into account refusals to cooperate or interference with verification and requiring panels to work rapidly, the RRLM creates incentives for employers and government labour law enforcement institutions to be promptly forthcoming with information. That said, the applicable Rules of Procedure provide relatively little guidance on the operation of verification proceedings. Panels need to be attentive to ensuring that proceedings are both expeditious and fair to everyone involved.

V. Foreseeable Impact and Effectiveness

Given the limits on the scope of application of the Mechanism to Canada and the United States, it is of course much less likely to be broadly effective in improving labour rights compliance in those two countries. I will focus my considerations on the main task of the RRLM, helping to reduce denials of rights in Mexico.

The main strength of the Mechanism, in terms of its likely effectiveness, is its efficiently targeted deployment of the influence of potential trade remedies in response to particular labour rights disputes. I do not agree with those who contend that the availability of trade remedies impairs the capacity of parties to deal effectively with labour rights issues under trade agreements.[55] On the contrary, I think that it is very often necessary. Denials of labour rights are among the most challenging problems faced by trade law. They are quite often the predictable consequence of institutional, economic, and political environments that include weak state enforcement capacity, endemic poverty and weak labour markets and social safety nets that leave workers economically vulnerable, weak labour movements, powerful employer political interests, and mobile and labour cost-sensitive supply chain contracting or direct investments that leave firms, workers, and governments vulnerable to being undercut by international competitors.[56] In this context, even where governments and firms are convinced of the longer-term benefits associated with labour rights compliance (such as social stability and increased productivity),

[54] For a discussion of these, see Banks 'Fit for Purpose?' (n 11) 657.

[55] For a detailed exposition see Banks, 'Trade, Labor and International Governance' (n 38) 60–97.

[56] Kevin Banks, 'Must Canada Change its Labour and Employment Laws to Compete with the United States?' (2013) 38 Queen's Law Journal 419, 433–34.

short-term pressures to compete for market share or investment on the basis of low labour costs and the ability to offer investors relatively unchecked managerial control will often prevail.[57] These conditions make it unlikely that state interests of industrialized and developing countries with respect to labour rights will converge without conditioning trade or other benefits on labour rights compliance.[58] Experience has shown that reputational harms and benefits associated with labour rights (non)compliance have little influence on state behaviour. States have acted as though there is little or no reputational consequence to failing to improve labour rights compliance.[59] There is little evidence that international dialogue, 'naming and shaming', or even international human rights adjudication, have transformed state interests around labour rights or other human rights, except in cases where states were already predisposed towards reform.[60]

On the other hand, any claims or complaints-driven enforcement regime has its own weaknesses in dealing with labour rights issues. Because those issues are embedded in complex policy environments and often challenging political economies, improving labour rights compliance tends to require sustained and strategically focused political support and programmatic institutional change.[61] Conversely, the path of institutional change will offer many opportunities for resistance to those who are not committed to it. This implies that an international regime seeking improved labour rights compliance needs a way to induce proactive cooperation between states on a sustained and strategically focused programme. By its very nature, a claims- or complaints-driven regime will tend to be ad hoc rather than strategic in its approach to raising and resolving problems. It provides no capacity to systematically monitor problems and progress, or to plan interventions. Further, experience with international labour rights complaints settlement proceedings suggests that they have tended, for predictable reasons, to generate an adversarial approach and zero-sum logic in state behaviour.[62] This in turn may overload a sanctions regime in comparison with the work that it is expected to do in inducing compliance with most other international trade law obligations.[63]

Fortunately for the prospects of the RRLM, it contains innovations and is embedded in a larger Agreement and set of supporting institutions that stand to significantly extend and complement its direct effects.

First, the better targeting of sanctions under the Mechanism stands to reduce resistance to its use. For the same reasons, I think that it is less likely that it will provoke a zero-sum, adversarial approach to dispute settlement.

[57] Banks, 'Trade, Labor and International Governance' (n 38) 67–72.
[58] ibid 72–74.
[59] ibid 85–92.
[60] ibid.
[61] ibid 97–106.
[62] ibid 113–31.
[63] ibid 131–35.

Second, by directly incentivizing non-compliant employers to comply, the RRLM stands to better align the interests of the employer community with the labour rights objectives of the Agreement, nudging the political economy of North America, or at least of Mexico, in a direction consistent with labour rights compliance.

Third, focusing on a single Denial of Rights requires less evidence than demonstrating a course of action or inaction under Article 23.5. This may encourage more workers and organizations to bring allegations forward to party governments for review, and thus potentially increase the use of the Mechanism by the parties themselves.

Fourth, and more importantly, the Mechanism operates within a strategically focused programme of international negotiation, monitoring, cooperation, and review that incentivizes and supports institutional change led by the Mexican federal government. Much of the heavy lifting in support of labour rights reform was done prior to the entry into force of the Agreement, as US negotiators pushed for and Mexican legislators enacted the most significant labour law reforms Mexico has seen in many decades.[64] Annex-23A of the Agreement made such reforms waivable preconditions for its entry into force.[65] However, some of them will take years to fully implement. In the United States, the Agreement's implementing legislation establishes the Independent Mexico Labor Expert Board to monitor and evaluate the implementation and maintenance of Mexico's labour law reforms and its compliance with its Agreement labour obligations.[66] The US and Canadian governments have committed significant multi-year funding of cooperative programming in support of them.[67] A tri-national labour council established under Article 23 must review and report publicly on the operation and effectiveness of the Chapter during the fifth year after entry into force of the agreement.[68] This report will in turn inform a review of the Agreement itself six years after it comes into effect and the parties' decision-making with respect to renewing the Agreement or allowing it to expire.[69] In this context, RRLM panel determinations stand to inform a sustained and strategically focused international effort. They do not depend for their influence solely on their moral suasion or the remedies that they may authorize.

[64] Graciela Bensusán and Kevin J Middlebrook, 'Political Change from the Outside In: U.S. Trade Leverage and Labor Rights Reform in Mexico' (2020) 60(3) Foro Internacional 985. See also Maria Curi, 'Mexican President Commits to Increased Spending on Labor Reforms Called for in USMCA' *Inside US Trade* (17 October 2019).

[65] USMCA Annex 23-A, para 3.

[66] *United States–Mexico–Canada Agreement Implementation Act*, 2020, HR 133, 116th Congress, s 731.

[67] Gantz (n 1) 84.

[68] USMCA art 23.14. Council reports must be made public unless the Council decides by consensus not to publish them.

[69] ibid art 34.7. The Agreement will expire 16 years after it comes into effect unless all parties agree to its extension.

Last but certainly not least, the nature of the labour reforms being attempted in Mexico also matters to the potential effectiveness of the Agreement's labour rights regime. Those reforms are focused on enabling Mexican workers to establish independent trade unions capable of enforcing rights at the workplace level, and forming a trade union movement capable of supporting the Agreement's labour rights aims in national politics.

VI. Conclusions

The RRLM represents a bold and promising innovation in trade agreement labour rights obligations and dispute settlement. It enables and may operate to encourage parties to address particular Denials of Rights, and to hold private actors accountable for them through facility-specific trade remedies. This is important to maintaining the basic fairness framework that the Agreement appears to set as a precondition for closer economic ties, and it stands to align private-sector incentives with the labour rights goals of the Agreement. The Mechanism's procedures are well adapted to its task. Importantly, the RRLM does not shoulder the entire burden of advancing the labour rights purposes of the Agreement. Rather, it is embedded in a strategic programme of labour reform supported by international cooperation and backed by the political contingency, at least at the point of entry into force, of the entire Agreement upon better access to labour rights in Mexico.

It is of course too early to know with any certainty what impact the RRLM will have. Whether the RRLM will contribute meaningfully to advancing the labour rights goals of the Agreement may well depend on the extent to which the Agreement's international governance structures as a whole are able to foster the ability of Mexican workers to organize independent unions who can then carry its aims forward. It may also depend of course on the extent to which the Agreement as a whole remains politically contingent on achieving those goals.

18

Sustainability Obligations in Trade Agreements

Do Exceptions and Defences Apply?

Caroline Henckels

I. Introduction

Trade agreements increasingly contain provisions on sustainability that go beyond areas traditionally regulated by trade agreements, requiring the parties to adopt and enforce measures in domestic law and policy in areas as diverse as labour standards, fishing, Indigenous rights, and marine litter. But what happens when a party believes it is justifiable not to comply with its sustainability obligations? Are these obligations, which are in many cases amenable to dispute settlement, subject to the relevant treaty's general and security exceptions and the public international law circumstances precluding wrongfulness, which both permit specific types of conduct that deviate from a government's international obligations? In other words, do General Agreement on Tariffs and Trade (GATT)[1] Article XX equivalents allow a party to deviate from obligations to stop deforestation, ratify International Labour Organization (ILO) conventions, or sanction illegal, unreported, and unregulated (IUU) fishing? Are the circumstances precluding wrongfulness applicable instead of or in addition to these exceptions, in a way we have not yet seen them applied in the trade context? What objectives could a government pursue that would allow it not to perform its obligations? Under which circumstances would it be justified for doing so?

This chapter argues that, depending always on the language of the provision being interpreted, general and security exceptions appear to be applicable to a variety of different types of sustainability obligations, just as they are to traditional obligations in trade agreements. This is the case unless the exceptions only apply to certain chapters excluding the sustainability obligations, or the sustainability obligation itself is drafted in such a way as to preclude the applicability of exceptions. However, it is also possible to argue that exceptions are implicitly only relevant to

[1] General Agreement on Tariffs and Trade (GATT), provisionally applied 1 January 1948.

Caroline Henckels, *Sustainability Obligations in Trade Agreements* In: *The Sustainability Revolution in International Trade Agreements*. Edited by: Geraldo Vidigal and Kathleen Claussen, Oxford University Press.
© Caroline Henckels 2024. DOI: 10.1093/9780191994470.003.0018

breaches of obligations with a trade dimension, based on the language of the chapeaux of general exceptions modelled on GATT Article XX. In all cases, relevant circumstances precluding wrongfulness are available to governments, but their applicability is very limited in a practical sense.

II. The Applicability of General and Security Exceptions

There are some instances where exceptions cannot be raised in dispute settlement in relation to sustainability obligations. First of all, the dispute settlement provisions in the treaty may not apply to the sustainability obligations at all.[2] Secondly, general exceptions frequently do not apply to sustainability obligations, applying, for example, only to the chapter on trade in goods.[3] Other agreements specifically provide that exceptions apply to the sustainability obligations but preclude recourse to dispute settlement.[4] Yet, other treaties' general and security exceptions contain language akin to 'Nothing in this Agreement shall be construed to prevent', suggesting that exceptions may apply to sustainability obligations.

It should be noted that parties may not need to have recourse to exceptions. Parties to disputes involving sustainability obligations have thus far tried to defend their measures according to the terms of the scope of the obligation itself (although general exceptions were not applicable to the relevant chapter of the relevant agreement). For example, in *Guatemala—Labor Commitments*,[5] in relation to a provision that provided that 'A Party shall not fail to effectively enforce its labor laws, through a sustained or recurring course of action or inaction, in a manner affecting trade between the Parties', Guatemala convinced the panel that it had not engaged in 'a sustained or recurring course of action' and that its actions were not 'in a manner affecting trade'. In *Korea—Labor Commitments*, Korea argued that

[2] See eg Comprehensive Economic and Trade Agreement (CETA) between Canada and the European Union and its Member States, provisionally applied 21 September 2017, arts 23.10 and 24.15, providing that disputes under the labour and environment chapters can only be resolved through a panel of experts procedure and are not subject to the ordinary inter-state dispute settlement mechanisms. While theoretically such a panel could apply the security exception, the findings of the panel are not binding; rather, the parties must work together to arrive at a satisfactory solution.

[3] See eg Comprehensive and Progressive Agreement for Trans-Pacific Partnership (CPTPP), in force 18 December 2018, art 29.1 (General Exceptions), CETA art 28.3 (General Exceptions), Agreement between the United States of America, the United Mexican States, and Canada (USMCA), in force 1 July 2020, art 32.1 (General Exceptions), and Dominican Republic–Central America–United States Free Trade Agreement (CAFTA-DR), in force 1 March 2006, art 21.1 (General Exceptions).

[4] The general exceptions in the Free Trade Agreement between the European Union and New Zealand (EU–New Zealand FTA), in force 1 May 2024 are specifically applicable to the animal welfare chapter, providing that 'For the purposes of . . . Chapter 6 (Animal Welfare) . . . Article XX of GATT 1994 is incorporated into and made part of this Agreement, mutatis mutandis': art 32.1(1) (General Exceptions). However, the agreement also provides that neither party shall have recourse to dispute settlement for a matter arising under the animal welfare chapter: art 6.6 (Dispute Settlement).

[5] Panel Report, *Guatemala—Issues Relating to the Obligations Under Article 16.2.1(a) of the CAFTA-DR*, 14 June 2017.

it had not failed to 'commit to respecting, promoting and realizing' fundamental labour rights or to 'make continued and sustained efforts toward ratifying' certain ILO conventions, although the panel did not agree.[6] So, there can be scope within the text of the relevant obligations for a government to argue that they should be interpreted restrictively in order to escape liability. We will see this again later when we examine certain sustainability obligations.

A. The Different Types of Sustainability Obligations

Before analysing the apparent scope of exceptions, it is necessary to discuss different types of obligations to determine to which types of obligations exceptions could apply. I will use provisions from the United States–Mexico–Canada Agreement (USMCA) as examples, but the same categorization is relevant to similarly worded provisions in other trade agreements.

1. Obligations to Which Exceptions May Apply

There are several types of sustainability obligations to which exceptions may apply.

Ordinary obligations are the most straightforward. For example, USMCA provides that 'each Party shall adopt or maintain measures . . . designed to prohibit the practice of shark finning.'[7] Here, a party would be liable simply if it failed to adopt or maintain the relevant measures and may be able to rely on exceptions to justify non-performance if the treaty so permits.

Trade-related provisions: given general exceptions' origin in GATT and GATT Article XX's reference to trade in the chapeau, the argument that exceptions apply is perhaps stronger with respect to trade-related obligations, or, in other words, where breaches can be shown to be trade-related. For example, USMCA provides that 'No Party shall fail to address violence or threats of violence against workers, directly related to exercising or attempting to exercise [labour rights] in a manner affecting trade or investment between the Parties.'[8]

Soft obligations may appear aspirational at first glance, but nevertheless might create obligations to which exceptions could apply, although this is not as clear cut as the other aforementioned categories.[9] These provisions tone down the

[6] Panel Report, *Panel of Experts Proceeding Constituted Under Article 13.15 of the EU–Korea Free Trade Agreement*, 20 January 2021. Vidigal finds this approach unconvincing: Geraldo Vidigal, 'Regional Trade Adjudication and the Rise of Sustainability Disputes: *Korea—Labor Commitments* and *Ukraine—Wood Export Bans*' (2022) 116 *American Journal of International Law* 567, 573–74.

[7] USMCA art 24.18 (2)(b) (Sustainable Fisheries Management).

[8] ibid art 23.7 (Violence Against Workers).

[9] There is precedent for treating arguably aspirational provisions as binding: in *Korea—Labor Commitments*, the panel found that 'commit' in the sense of the parties' obligation to 'commit to respecting, promoting and realising' fundamental labour rights was a legally binding obligation requiring a party to 'bind [itself] to a course of action', and that the obligation to 'make continued and sustained efforts towards ratifying' certain ILO conventions was an obligation of 'best endeavours', requiring

nature, scope, or extent of the commitment. For example, USMCA provides that the parties 'shall, to the extent possible, provide the other Parties the opportunity to comment on proposed measures that are designed to prevent trade in fisheries products derived from IUU fishing'.[10] Here, perhaps a government could be liable if it could be established that no good faith efforts to achieve the objective had been made, presumably after a reasonable efluxion of time since the conclusion of the treaty. On one hand, a government may be able to rely on an exception to justify its failure to act, but on the other hand, justification could occur instead in the context of determining whether, for example, the government had acted 'to the extent possible'; it could be argued that whether an action is 'possible' would depend on any relevant supervening events that made recourse to pursue competing policy objectives necessary or appropriate.

Largely self-judging obligations: some provisions largely give the parties leeway to determine the appropriate scope of their commitments. For example, USMCA requires each government to 'implement policies that it considers appropriate to protect workers against employment discrimination on the basis of sex'.[11] While their rulings occurred in different contexts (discussed further in relation to security exceptions, in section II.B), four World Trade Organization (WTO) panels have held that with respect to the term 'that it considers', it would be for a responding government to decide on the necessity of its actions (in two of these cases, subject to an obligation of good faith, and the other two, apparently without any scope for adjudicatory review). On one approach, if there had been no good faith attempt to implement the obligation, there would be prima facie liability, but the government may potentially be able to rely on an exception. However, again, justification may logically take place in the context of, for example, determining what measures the government 'considers appropriate' in the circumstances.

2. Obligations to Which Exceptions May Not Apply

There are other types of sustainability obligations in relation to which it appears that reliance on exceptions may be precluded.

Intra-obligation exception: some provisions provide an inbuilt exception, removing the need to have regard to general or security exceptions in relation to that issue. For example, USMCA obliges the parties to 'prohibit the killing of great whales for commercial purposes unless authorized in a multilateral treaty to which the Party is a party',[12] but this obligation 'does not apply to whaling by Indigenous peoples in accordance with a Party's law'. This would obviate the need to rely on an

something more than 'undertaking merely minimal steps or none at all' (but not 'a requirement to explore and mobilise all measures available at all times'): *Korea—Labour Commitments* [127], [227].

[10] USMCA art 24.21(3) (Illegal, Unreported, and Unregulated (IUU) Fishing).
[11] ibid art 23.9 (Discrimination in the Workplace).
[12] ibid art 24.19(2) (Conservation of Marine Species).

exception in relation to Indigenous peoples' whaling activities (but would not prevent reliance on a relevant exception for other types of commercial whaling that a party wished to pursue).

Non-derogability: where a sustainability obligation is accompanied by a non-derogation obligation, the applicability of the exception is arguably logically precluded. For example, USMCA requires that parties adopt and maintain laws and practices pertaining to certain labour rights,[13] and provides that 'no Party shall waive or otherwise derogate from . . . its statutes or regulations . . . implementing [this obligation] . . . if the waiver or derogation would be inconsistent with a right set out in that paragraph'.[14] Logically, the exception would not apply where there is no permissible derogation from these obligations. However, it could be argued that a non-derogation provision is simply a command like any other, in the sense of being a reaffirmation of the principal command itself, and it does not enjoy any special status. In this regard, it would be possible to claim an exception from both aspects of the command. But this interpretation would run contrary to the principle of effectiveness, raising the question of why the parties would include non-derogation provisions in treaties at all if they were to be interpreted in the same way as other commands. It is also arguable that non-derogation clauses are in tension with the circumstances precluding wrongfulness.

B. Interpreting Exceptions' Chapeaux: The Breadth of Exceptions' Scope

The reference to '[n]othing in this Agreement shall be construed' in the chapeaux of provisions based on GATT Articles XX and XXI raises the question of whether the phrase 'this Agreement' can be interpreted in accordance with its ordinary meaning or if it is implicitly limited to trade obligations, both as a general proposition and also where the exception is found in a trade in goods chapter. For example, the EU–Ukraine Association Agreement has a general exception phrased in this way.[15] While this provision is located in the Trade in Goods Chapter, the words 'Nothing in this Agreement' may extend the application of the clause across the Agreement. An exception for Indigenous peoples' rights[16] in USMCA

[13] ibid art 23.3.1 (Labor Rights).
[14] ibid art 23.4 (Non-Derogation).
[15] Association Agreement between the European Union and the European Atomic Energy Community and their Member States and Ukraine, provisionally applied 1 January 2016, art 36 (General Exceptions).
[16] USMCA art 32.5 (Indigenous Peoples Rights) states that 'Provided that such measures are not used as a means of arbitrary or unjustified discrimination against persons of the other Parties or as a disguised restriction on trade in goods, services, and investment, this Agreement does not preclude a Party from adopting or maintaining a measure it deems necessary to fulfill its legal obligations to indigenous peoples.'

('this Agreement does not preclude') may apply to the Labour and Environment Chapters.[17] Security exceptions commonly use the same terminology.[18]

The Appellate Body has taken a broad approach to the concept of 'this Agreement' in terms of the interoperability of provisions of the WTO agreements. This term was contained in GATT 1947 and Article XX was replicated in GATT 1994 without any modification to acknowledge that it appears in one of several related agreements. In *China—Audiovisuals*, the Appellate Body applied Article XX to China's accession protocol in certain circumstances,[19] and in *Russia—Traffic in Transit*, the panel held that GATT's security exception was applicable to Russia's accession protocol.[20] The Appellate Body has stated that whether Article XX applies to provisions of other WTO agreements is to be assessed on a case-by-case basis.[21] In another context, in *Brazil—Desiccated Coconut*, the Appellate Body found that the meaning of 'this Agreement' in Article 32.3 of the SCM Agreement[22] referred not only to the SCM Agreement but also to GATT Article VI, on the basis that the WTO agreements were 'an integrated system'.[23] Therefore, the meaning of 'this Agreement' has not been interpreted as being limited to the relevant agreement in which it appears. By implication, general and security exceptions appear to apply (always subject to the language of the provision) beyond the chapter in which they are located.

However, another reading of the cases is that in order for GATT Article XX to apply, provisions of other WTO agreements must either explicitly (eg Article 3 of the TRIMS Agreement[24] or Article 24(7) of the Agreement on Trade Facilitation) or implicitly (such as one of the paragraphs of China's accession protocol) incorporate the provision.[25] By implication, other chapters of trade agreements must

[17] This could potentially be relevant to provisions in relation to fisheries and marine mammal conservation.

[18] Eg USMCA art 32.2 (Essential Security), CETA art 28.6 (National Security), CPTPP art 29.2 (Security Exceptions).

[19] Appellate Body Report, *China: Measures Affecting Trading Rights and Distribution Services for Certain Publications and Audiovisual Entertainment Products*, 19 January 2010, WT/DS363/AB/R [229]–[233], but see Appellate Body Report, *China: Measures Related to the Exportation of Various Raw Materials*, 22 February 2012, WT/DS394/AB/R [307]; Appellate Body Report, *China: Measures Related to the Exportation of Rare Earths, Tungsten and Molybdenum*, 29 August 2014, WT/DS431/AB/R [5.74].

[20] Panel Report, *Russia: Measures Concerning Traffic in Transit*, 5 April 2019, WT/DS512/R [7.256].

[21] Appellate Body Report, *China—Measures Related to the Exportation of Rare Earths, Tungsten and Molybdenum*, 7 August 2014, WT/DS431/AB/R; WT/DS432/AB/R; WT/DS433/AB/R [5.55] and [5.74].

[22] Agreement on Subsidies and Countervailing Measures, in force 1 January 1995. See, arguing that GATT arts XX and XXI apply to the SCM Agreement, Nu Ri Jung, 'Are There "Exceptions" to the SCM Agreement? Applicability of the GATT Exceptions Vis-à-Vis the International Rules on Subsidies' (2023) 57 Journal of World Trade 457.

[23] Appellate Body, *Brazil: Measures Affecting Desiccated Coconut*, 21 February 1997, WT/DS22/AB/R 11, 16–17.

[24] Agreement on Trade-Related Investment Measures, in force 1 January 1995.

[25] See Peter Van den Bossche and Werner Zdouc, *The Law and Policy of the World Trade Organization* (5th edn, CUP 2022) 599.

explicitly (such as Article 32.1(1) of the New Zealand–United Kingdom trade agreement) or implicitly incorporate the exception. Arguably then, in order for the exception to be implicitly incorporated the obligation at issue must have some relationship with trade.[26]

Another limitation may appear from the language of the chapeaux of exceptions based on GATT Article XX. The chapeau specifically refers to trade, stating that measures must not be 'applied in a manner which would constitute a means of arbitrary or unjustifiable discrimination between countries where the same conditions prevail, or a disguised restriction on international trade'. In relation to discrimination, a measure to which the exception could apply is one that is prima facie in breach of the GATT obligations that, by definition, impact on trade. On one hand, the fact that the chapeau appears to be directed towards trade restrictions suggests that the exception only applies to deviations from sustainability obligations that impact on trade. On the other hand, the proper interpretation of the chapeau may be that a government deviating from its sustainability obligations would simply need to do so in a manner that does not unlawfully discriminate or amount to a disguised restriction on trade. One can imagine many instances of deviations from sustainability obligations (such as obligations regarding the preservation of biodiversity) that do not affect trade, at least not directly and concretely, but arguably this does not matter in order for the exception to apply—the requisite discipline on measures is found in the enumerated exceptions themselves and is restricted by the permissible policy areas and the relevant nexus requirement. What is important is that there is no unlawful discrimination or disguised restriction on trade, and if the measure has no impact on trade, all the better.

C. Which Specific Exceptions are Relevant?

Assuming that exceptions are applicable, which specific exceptions would be likely to be raised for a breach of sustainability obligations? Due to its potential breadth and the high degree of specificity of the other enumerated exceptions, the exception for public morals appears to be the most apt justification for breaches of sustainability obligations. The scope of the concept of public morals under GATT and General Agreement on Trade in[27] is broad, and in no case has a panel or the Appellate Body held that the invocation of the concept was for impermissible reasons; they have afforded WTO Members a wide measure of deference. The panel in *China—Audiovisual Products* adopted the interpretation used by the panel in *US—Gambling* and held that the term 'denotes standards of right and wrong conduct maintained by or on behalf of a community or nation'; WTO

[26] Eg USMCA art 24.4(1) (Enforcement of Environmental Laws).
[27] General Agreement on Trade in Services, in force 1 January 1995.

Members 'should be given some scope to define and apply for themselves the concepts of "public morals" . . . in their respective territories, according to their own systems and scales of values'.[28] Further, 'the content and scope of the concept of "public morals" can vary from member to member, as they are influenced by each member's prevailing social, cultural, ethical and religious values'.[29] In *EC—Seal Products*, the Appellate Body affirmed that 'Members should be given some scope to define and apply for themselves the concept of public morals according to their own systems and scales of values.'[30] Applying these tests, it noted that the 'prevention of underage gambling and the protection of pathological gamblers; restricting prohibited content in cultural goods, such as violence or pornographic content, as well as protection of Chinese culture and traditional values; protecting animal welfare; combatting money laundering; or bridging the digital divide within society and promoting social inclusion' have all been held to pertain to public morals.[31]

Exceptions for human life and health are also potentially relevant; exceptions based on GATT Article XX(b) permit the adoption of measures 'necessary to protect human . . . life or health'. One could imagine a disaster or crisis situation where it is necessary to deviate from environmental obligations in order to protect human life or health. A panel would need to examine, inter alia, 'whether the policy reflected in the measure falls within the range of policies designed to achieve the objective of or, put differently, or whether the policy objective is for the purpose of, "protect[ing] human . . . life or health"'.[32]

In relation to both morals and health, however, the measure must be 'necessary'; that is, the least restrictive means reasonably available to achieve the measure's objective. In the context of GATT, this aspect of the exception relates to trade-restrictiveness, but in the context of sustainability obligations, restrictiveness could be interpreted to relate to the objective of the obligation, so that, here, the measure must be the least restrictive on environmental standards. Whatever interpretation is adopted, the nexus requirement provides some discipline on the types of measures that may be justifiable under these exceptions.

Security exceptions may also be relevant to breaches of sustainability obligations. While some trade agreements' security exceptions mirror GATT Article XXI, restricting the concept of security to traditional security concerns[33] (perhaps most relevantly, it appears to be possible to derogate from sustainability obligations in a

[28] Panel Report, *China: Measures Affecting Trading Rights and Distribution Services for Certain Publications and Audiovisual Entertainment Products*, 19 January 2010, WT/DS363/R [7.759].

[29] ibid [7.763].

[30] Appellate Body Report, *European Communities: Measures Prohibiting the Importation and Marketing of Seal Products*, 22 May 2014, WT/DS400/AB/R and WT/DS401/AB/R [5.199].

[31] Panel Report, *United States: Tariff Measures on Certain Goods from China*, 15 September 2020, WT/DS543/R [7.118].

[32] Panel Report, *European Communities: Conditions for the Granting of Tariff Preferences to Developing Countries*, 20 April 2004, WT/DS246/R [7.198]–[7.199].

[33] Eg CETA art 28.6 (National Security).

situation of emergency in international relations), other trade agreements' security exceptions leave the concept of essential security interests undefined.[34] The potential scope of the concept of security is very broad, extending beyond traditional security concerns to include concepts such as economic security, climate security, and human security.

Other international courts and tribunals have taken a broad approach to the concept of essential security interests. In relation to treaties of friendship, commerce, and navigation, the International Court of Justice has adopted a broad approach to the concept that goes beyond the traditional approach to security, holding that it 'certainly extends beyond the concept of an armed attack and has been subject to very broad interpretations in the past', suggesting that the relevant legal test is one of reasonableness.[35] Likewise, many investment tribunals have taken a broad approach to the concept, finding that it includes economic crises.[36]

Following WTO and investment jurisprudence, a panel would determine whether the measure is directed at 'essential' security interests (including the enumerated security interests where relevant). For example, the panel in *Russia—Traffic in Transit* held that the concept of 'essential' security interests 'may generally be understood to refer to those interests relating to the quintessential functions of the state, namely, the protection of its territory and its population from external threats, and the maintenance of law and public order internally'; this would depend 'on the particular situation and perceptions of the state in question, and can be expected to vary with changing circumstances'.[37] And in *Saudi Arabia—Intellectual Property Rights*, the panel observed that 'an assessment of whether or not certain security interests are "essential" is not one that a WTO dispute settlement panel is well positioned to make'.[38]

The language 'that it considers necessary' in many treaties' security exceptions means that it is for a government to decide on the necessity of its actions for the protection of its essential security interests. As foreshadowed in section II.A.1, in the first two cases concerning security exceptions in the WTO Agreements, panels held that this was subject to an obligation of good faith,[39] but later panels appeared

[34] Eg CPTPP art 29.2(b) (Security Exceptions) and USMCA art 32.2(1)(b) (Essential Security): both provide that 'Nothing in this Agreement shall be construed to . . . preclude a Party from applying measures that it considers necessary for . . . the protection of its own essential security interests.'

[35] *Military and Paramilitary Activities in and Against Nicaragua (Nicaragua v U.S.)*, Merits (1986) ICJ Rep 14, 117, para 224.

[36] Eg *Continental Casualty v Argentine Republic*, ICSID Case No ARB/03/09, Award, 5 September 2008 [178].

[37] *Russia—Traffic in Transit* [7.124], [7.130][7.133].

[38] Panel Report, *Saudi Arabia: Measures Concerning the Protection of Intellectual Property Rights*, 16 June 2020, WT/DS567/R, fn 286.

[39] *Russia—Traffic in Transit* [7.132], [7.138]; *Saudi Arabia—Intellectual Property Rights* [7.242], [7.252], [7.285].

to implicitly take the view that this aspect of the clause was entirely self-judging.[40] Overall, security exceptions appear to give fairly broad scope for governments to act inconsistently with sustainability obligations.

III. The Applicability of the Circumstances Precluding Wrongfulness

A. Overview

If it is the case that the exceptions are not available in relation to breaches of sustainability obligations, or if a party is held to be liable after the exception has been applied, the circumstances precluding wrongfulness may play a role.[41] The International Law Commission's Draft Articles on the Responsibility of States for Internationally Wrongful Acts (ILC Articles), widely regarded as codifying customary international law, detail the six circumstances in which the wrongfulness of conduct under international law may be precluded, including, relevantly for our purposes, necessity, force majeure, and distress.

The circumstances precluding wrongfulness are general defences that can apply to *any* breach of an international obligation (except *jus cogens* norms), which would plainly include sustainability obligations. They may be invoked where a breach of an international obligation is established according to the primary rules of the particular regime, including the question of the availability of exceptions. Defences operate as secondary rules to determine whether this wrongfulness is precluded. They have not so far been applied in the trade context, but in many cases have been unsuccessfully pleaded in investorstate dispute settlement. While investment tribunals have in several instances examined the necessity defence, they have not set out a workable framework on how the circumstances precluding wrongfulness apply. While it might be argued that the circumstances precluding wrongfulness are most apposite in relation to acts rather than policies, the following analysis proceeds from the assumption that one of these defences could apply where a breach of a sustainability obligation occurs through a prevailing policy rather than a specific action. In any case, failure to observe a sustainability commitment may be due to the non-existence of a particular policy; and acts and omissions are equally government actions to which the general defences apply.

[40] Panel Reports, *United States—Certain Measures on Steel and Aluminium Products*, 9 December 2022, WT/DS544 [7.128], WT/DS552 [7.116], WT/DS556 [7.145], WT/DS564/R, [7.143]; Panel Report, *United States—Origin Marking Requirement*, 21 December 2022, WT/DS597/R [7.160].

[41] See generally Federica Paddeu, *Justification and Excuse in International Law: Concept and Theory of General Defences* (CUP 2018).

B. Necessity

A measure taken in relation to a state of necessity is a measure that is in breach of the state's international obligations but that may nonetheless be adopted by a state during a state of emergency in certain limited circumstances. It is possible to imagine a crisis situation where sustainability obligations are not observed, for example, where a party has failed to ratify relevant treaties or otherwise failed to realize labour rights or protect the environment. A state of necessity can be invoked, in theory, in relation to a broad range of circumstances ranging from the political or economic survival of a state to the continued functioning of essential services and the preservation of the environment,[42] and investment tribunals have held that severe economic crises could qualify as such an emergency.[43] However, the threshold for the successful invocation of the defence is extremely high, suggesting that it would be possible in only the rarest of cases. Article 25 of the ILC Articles provides that the defence may only be invoked to preclude the wrongfulness of an act that does not comply with a state's international obligations where, inter alia, that act is 'the only way for the State to safeguard an essential interest against a grave and imminent peril'. The ILC has also stated that 'the interest relied on must outweigh all other considerations, not merely from the point of view of the acting State but on a reasonable assessment of the competing interests, whether these are individual or collective', thereby affirming that the interest must be compelling.[44]

C. Force Majeure

Force majeure may apply to a wide range of events or circumstances on account of both naturally occurring events and human conduct, including war, insurrection, and unforeseeable natural phenomena that prevent states from observing their treaty obligations. It is possible that such an event could prevent a government from complying with sustainability obligations in its trade agreements, for example, in relation to environmental law. Under Article 23 of the ILC Articles, force majeure only applies in 'the occurrence of an irresistible force or an unforeseen event', which is 'beyond the control of the State' where there is 'material impossibility' of complying with the state's obligations. According to the ILC's Commentary, 'irresistibility' means that the government must 'not be able to avoid or oppose by its own means', while 'unforeseeability' means that the event must

[42] ILC, *Yearbook of the International Law Commission*, vol II, pt 1 (ILC 1980) 14, 19; ILC *Yearbook of the International Law Commission*, vol II, pt 2 (ILC 2001) 83.

[43] Eg *CMS Gas Transmission Company v Argentine Republic*, ICSID Case No ARB/01/08, Award, 12 May 2005 [359].

[44] ILC (n 42) 84.

be 'neither foreseen nor of an easily foreseeable kind'.[45] If the government has accepted the risk of force majeure or has induced the circumstance of force majeure, the defence will not be available. Force majeure requires an 'involuntary' act or, in other words, compulsion.[46] Where a state 'may have unwittingly contributed to the occurrence of material impossibility by something which, in hindsight, might have been done differently but which was done in good faith and did not itself make the event any less unforeseen', force majeure can still be made out; however, the government must have attempted to overcome the event or situation.[47]

D. Distress

It is conceivable that circumstances relating to danger to human life could be invoked to justify a government's breach of sustainability obligations, in reliance on the defence of distress. Pursuant to Article 24 of the ILC Articles, distress may be invoked 'if the author of the act in question has no other reasonable way, in a situation of distress, of saving the author's life or the lives of other persons entrusted to the author's care'. The state's choice to act is 'effectively nullified by the situation of peril'.[48] There are some limitations to reliance on this defence. Article 24 provides that a state cannot invoke distress where the situation is due to the conduct of the state invoking it, or 'the act in question is likely to create a comparable or greater peril'. The Commentary explains that the defence is limited to situations where the threat is to life, rather than threats to physical integrity.[49] The threat to life must relate either to the state agency's own life, or that of individuals entrusted to the state's care. In terms of the latter, there needs to be a 'special relationship' between the state and the individuals in danger.[50]

Overall, while these defences are theoretically available, they all have stringent criteria and are available in very limited circumstances. Their practical utility in the context of trade agreements seems very limited.

IV. Conclusion

It is somewhat ironic that a government might try to rely on an exception to justify failure to observe a sustainability obligation in a trade agreement, given that to date

[45] ILC, *Draft Articles on Responsibility of States for Internationally Wrongful Acts, With Commentaries* (ILC 2011) 76, para 2.
[46] ibid 76 para 1.
[47] ibid 78 para 9.
[48] ibid 78 para 1.
[49] ibid 79–80 para 6.
[50] ibid 80 para 7.

exceptions have in many cases been invoked in order to justify actions taken to achieve sustainability objectives. Reliance on exceptions to deviate from sustainability obligations has the potential to shift exceptions' jurisprudence considerably.

This chapter has argued that, subject to the language of the particular provision being invoked, general and security exceptions appear to be applicable to these obligations. Exceptions appear to be applicable to provisions that simply oblige treaty parties to engage in certain conduct directed at sustainability-related objectives, and to sustainability obligations that have a trade-related dimension. They may also be applicable to apparently soft obligations and to obligations that appear to be largely self-judging. However, they do not appear to be applicable to sustainability obligations that are explicitly non-derogable or that contain a relevant inbuilt exception.

While exceptions are often located in trade in goods chapters, they frequently contain language ('Nothing in this Agreement...') apparently extending the reach of the clause to the rest of the relevant agreement. The Appellate Body has taken a broad approach to the concept of 'this Agreement', although it is arguable that, following this jurisprudence, the relevant obligation should explicitly or implicitly incorporate the exception, such as where the obligation at issue bears some relationship with trade. Additionally, the reference to arbitrary or unjustifiable discrimination and disguised restrictions on international trade in the chapeaux of general exceptions based on GATT Article XX might be read to suggest that exceptions only apply where sustainability obligations are connected with trade, but it is also arguable that this language simply requires compliance with these provisos and does not require that the obligation is trade related.

In terms of the specific exceptions that seem relevant, the public morals exception appears to be the most apt justification, given the breadth of the concept in the WTO case law. It is also possible that exceptions for human life and health would be relevant in some circumstances. Security exceptions are also relevant, especially where the concept of 'essential security interests' is undefined in the clause, given the potentially very broad scope of the concept of security..

This chapter has also examined the role that circumstances precluding wrongfulness may play in relation to breaches of sustainability obligations. They have a role to play if exceptions are not available or have been unsuccessfully pleaded. The threshold for invoking the defence of necessity is extremely high, and is only available where, inter alia, that act is 'the only way for the State to safeguard an essential interest against a grave and imminent peril'. Force majeure is a defence that is only available where there has been an 'irresistible force' or 'unforeseen event', beyond the government's control, that has resulted in 'material impossibility' of complying with the state's obligations. Finally, the defence of distress would be relevant in certain circumstances where there is a threat to human life. These defences are as yet untested in the context of trade agreements, and their practical utility seems very limited given the strict criteria for their invocation.

PART III

SUSTAINABILITY IN TRADE AGREEMENTS AND THE FUTURE OF THE GLOBAL ECONOMY

19

Copernican Revolution or Green Protectionism?

Timothy Meyer

I. Introduction

For many years, the international trading system and environmental law seemed to move largely in parallel. Trade disputes occasionally involved environmental measures, and environmental treaties sometimes incorporated trade restrictions. But the dance between trade and the environment was in practice a chaste one.

Today, such attempts at modesty have been thrown to the wind. Contemporary trade agreements include an ever-expanding set of environmental and sustainability commitments that, if violated, can lead to the imposition of trade barriers. Likewise, the world's leading developed economies have begun rolling out green trade barriers in the form of product bans, border adjustments, and discriminatory subsidies. To those steeped in the trade liberalization of the 1990s, the rush to raise trade barriers in the name of sustainability might well look like the trade version of Sodom and Gomorrah, with nations giving in to the very protectionist impulses that the General Agreement on Tariffs and Trade (GATT) and the World Trade Organization (WTO) were designed to restrain. To those who cheered the Battle of Seattle, the picture might look more like the Summer of Love, with inherited inhibition cast aside in an effort to remake people's relationship with the world and each other.

Both of these views can be found in public commentary on trade and sustainability but neither, I argue, is right.[1] Instead, I contend that the growth of sustainable trade policies reflects two phenomena. First, it reflects the ordinary historical ebb and flow of unilateralism and multilateralism. While at some points in history multilateral institutions have taken the lead in shaping trade policy, at other times unilateralism has played a more important role. We are in the latter moment, but that does not mean that the former's time has passed. Second, like all policies, green trade policies usually pursue multiple objectives. The fact that green trade policies often have mixed motives means that assessing their effects through a

[1] Cf Yoda, 'Only a Sith deals in absolutes.' *Star Wars, Episode III: Revenge of the Sith* (2005).

Timothy Meyer, *Copernican Revolution or Green Protectionism?* In: *The Sustainability Revolution in International Trade Agreements*. Edited by: Geraldo Vidigal and Kathleen Claussen, Oxford University Press. © Timothy Meyer 2024.
DOI: 10.1093/9780191994470.003.0019

Puritan lens is a fool's errand. The quest nations are on today is not for trade policies that promote sustainability in the least trade-restrictive way possible. Instead, they are looking for policies that can generate the political support to address urgent environmental crises while still promoting economic growth.

This chapter proceeds as follows. Section II describes the growth of two different kinds of environmental measures. Section II.A describes the growth of environmental provisions within trade agreements themselves. Section II.B traces a second trend—the growth of domestic trade measures designed to address environmental problems in ways that arguably violate international trade agreements. Section III argues that, at least in the short term, this second kind of measure is likely to be more influential than trade and sustainable development (TSD) provisions in trade agreements. This influence occurs in large part by shaping subsequent multilateral negotiations, as well as the implementation and interpretation of existing multilateral provisions. Section IV argues that trade agreements and unilateral measures that raise (or authorize raising) trade barriers to tackle environmental problems are a key ingredient for addressing environmental problems and ultimately preserving the system of liberalized trade.

II. Environmental Provisions in and Under International Trade Agreements

Affirmative environmental obligations began to emerge in trade agreements shortly after the end of the Cold War. With foreign policy objectives no longer providing an overarching justification for new trade agreements, demands that trade agreements incorporate environmental commitments began to gain traction in major developed countries, especially the United States.[2] The pressure to incorporate environmental commitments into trade agreements and trade policy also corresponded to an uptick in environmental treaty making that accompanied the 1992 Earth Summit.[3]

A. Sustainability Within Trade Agreements

The North American Free Trade Agreement (NAFTA) was the first trade agreement to incorporate affirmative environmental commitments.[4] The primary text

[2] See Steve Charnovitz, 'The NAFTA Environmental Side Agreement: Implications for Environmental Cooperation, Trade Policy, and American Treaty-Making' (1994) 8 Temple International and Comparative Law Journal 257–58.

[3] See eg United Nations Framework Convention on Climate Change, in force 21 March 1994.

[4] Prior trade agreements had, to be sure, included environmental exceptions. See General Agreement on Tariffs and Trade (GATT), provisionally applied 1 January 1948, art XX(b) and (g).

of NAFTA provided that certain environmental agreements would prevail over NAFTA to the extent of any inconsistency between the two provisions.[5] Seeking to improve upon this modest rule, President Clinton, who inherited the agreement upon taking office in 1993, negotiated the so-called NAFTA 'side agreements' on labour and the environment as part of his ultimately successful push to secure approval from the US Congress.[6]

Although the NAFTA side agreements were the first of their kind, their approach was more evolutionary than revolutionary. The central obligation was to 'effectively enforce [a Party's] environmental laws and regulations through appropriate governmental action' and the dispute resolution system was distinct from, and weaker in terms of remedies than, the main NAFTA dispute system.[7] The 2001 US–Jordan Free Trade Agreement (US–Jordan FTA) revamped the textual requirements regarding the environment and moved environment provisions into the 'core' of the agreement, rather than including them in a side agreement. But the commitments remained relatively soft—not to derogate from a party's environmental rules in order to attract trade, nor to fail to effectively enforce those rules through a sustained pattern or practice in a manner affecting trade.[8]

It was not until 2007 that sustainability obligations in trade agreements showed significant progress. US President George W Bush was seeking approval of a number of trade agreements with US allies that had supported the administration's war on terror. Those agreements, however, required the approval of a Democratic Congress that insisted on more stringent environmental and labour policies. A 2007 agreement, subsequently known as the 'May 10' consensus, established a new high watermark for sustainability in trade agreements. Henceforth, US trade agreements would require compliance with a list of multilateral environmental trade agreements, in addition to the rules on enforcement and non-derogation.[9] Additionally, environmental provisions would be subject to ordinary dispute resolution alongside the agreements' commercial provisions. In 2010, the European Union followed suit, incorporating its first TSD Chapter, containing commitments

[5] North American Free Trade Agreement (NAFTA), in force 1 January 1994, art 104.

[6] North American Agreement on Environmental Cooperation (NAAEC), in force 1 January 1994; North American Agreement on Labor Cooperation, in force 1 January 1994.

[7] NAAEC art 5.1 and generally pt 5.

[8] Agreement between the United States and Jordan on the Establishment of a Free Trade Area, in force 17 December 2001, art 5. See also Kathleen Claussen, 'Reimagining Trade-Plus Compliance: The Labor Story' (2020) 23 Journal of International Economic Law 25, 32. The non-derogation and enforcement obligations in the agreements were preceded by language stating that a party 'shall strive to ensure', making the binding commitment weaker than a simple requirement to effectively enforce and not derogate from environmental laws.

[9] See eg United States–Peru Trade Promotion Agreement, in force 1 February 2009, ch 18. The non-derogation and enforcement obligations were strengthened by removing the 'shall strive to ensure' language from the US–Jordan FTA.

similar to those in the new US model, into an FTA with South Korea.[10] TSD chapters have since become a regular feature of EU trade agreements.

The United States again took the lead in pushing an expansion of sustainable development obligations. The Trans-Pacific Partnership (TPP) (now the Comprehensive and Progressive Agreement for Trans-Pacific Partnership [CPTPP]) contains commitments on managing fisheries and reducing harmful fisheries subsidies, eliminating illegal trade in flora and fauna, and protecting biodiversity, among other new obligations.[11] When it pulled out of the TPP, the United States incorporated similar commitments into the revised NAFTA (the so-called United States–Mexico–Canada Agreement, or USMCA).[12]

The expansion of environmental provisions in trade agreements is important for our purposes because modern provisions embedded in traditional trade agreements are subject to dispute resolution and violations can lead to the imposition of sanctions. The United States and the European Union differ somewhat in their approach to dispute resolution for TSD commitments. Environmental chapters of US trade agreements have been fully subject to dispute resolution since the 'May 10' agreement, meaning that unremedied violations of environmental provisions can be met by a withdrawal of commercial concessions. TSD provisions in EU trade agreements, by contrast, have historically been subject to a different dispute process from the commercial provisions. In 2022, however, the European Commission announced that it would 'extend the standard state-to-state dispute settlement compliance phase to the TSD chapter of [EU] trade agreements', making trade sanctions a possibility.[13] As Geraldo Vidigal has discussed, the decline of WTO dispute settlement has been accompanied by an increase in dispute settlement under preferential trade agreements (PTAs).[14] Eight of these FTA disputes, almost half, have been about TSD (including both labour and environmental provisions), while in a ninth the respondent raised TSD commitments as a shield.[15]

If sustainability provisions in trade agreements can lead to a rise in trade barriers, it is worth considering whether their impact might be protectionist. To spell

[10] Free Trade Agreement between the European Union and the Republic of Korea, in force 13 December 2015, ch 13. The agreement was provisionally applied from 2011 before entering into force in 2015.

[11] Trans-Pacific Partnership Agreement, signed 4 February 2016, ch 20. The CPTPP incorporates by reference the provisions of the TPP.

[12] United States–Mexico–Canada Agreement (also known as CUSMA and T-MEC), in force 1 July 2020, ch 24.

[13] European Commission, 'Commission Unveils New Approach to Trade Agreements to Promote Green and Just Growth' (22 June 2022) <https://ec.europa.eu/commission/presscorner/detail/en/ip_22_3921>.

[14] Geraldo Vidigal, 'Regional Trade Adjudication and the Rise of Sustainability Disputes: *Korea—Labor Commitments* and *Ukraine—Wood Export Bans*' (2022) 116 American Journal of International Law 567.

[15] ibid 569.

out the logic of this proposition, if TSD commitments are subject to ordinary dispute resolution and the withdrawal of concessions as a sanction for violation, then the liberalizing commitments in trade agreements are essentially conditioned on compliance with sustainability commitments. If countries are either unwilling or, especially in the case of developing countries, unable to comply with these sustainability commitments, then TSD chapters become a vehicle for at least partially cancelling concessions made in trade agreements' liberalizing chapters.

On the whole, though, TSD disputes under PTAs show no indication of leading to protectionism. As Vidigal notes, most TSD disputes have resulted in the respondent changing its behaviour to the complainant's satisfaction.[16] As a result, the suspension of concessions has yet to arise as an issue. Rather, the incorporation of TSD provisions into multilateral agreements seems to have provided the United States and the European Union the ability to use PTAs as a vehicle to negotiate improvements in the sustainability practices of their trading partners. Individual PTAs and their TSD chapters have, in other words, neither been revolutionary nor protectionist.

A new generation of sustainability-oriented agreements could change that status quo by imposing new trade barriers or more aggressively conditioning existing market access commitments on compliance with sustainability rules. These nascent agreements are primarily the work of the Biden Administration in the United States, which has focused on them to the exclusion of traditional trade liberalizing agreements. The most far-reaching of these initiatives is the Indo-Pacific Economic Framework for Prosperity (IPEF). The IPEF consists of four pillars, with the pillar on clean energy and decarbonization most directly related to sustainability. Although still in its early stages of development, the IPEF focuses on adjusting the conditions under which trade occurs between like-minded countries in order to promote a variety of values, including sustainability and fair trade.

The United States is also pursuing sector-specific sustainable trade agreements. Examples include the US–EU Global Arrangement on Sustainable Steel and Aluminum (GASSA),[17] which aims to use trade tools to address carbon intensity and overcapacity in the metals sector, and agreements with Japan and the European Union on critical minerals supply chains, which are especially important for batteries for electric vehicles.[18] These agreements are notable because sustainability goals are the main objective, and liberalizing (in the case of the critical minerals) or limiting (as in the case of US proposals for GASSA) market access is secondary. It

[16] ibid 570.

[17] Joint EU–US Statement on a Global Arrangement on Sustainable Steel and Aluminum, 31 October 2021 <https://ec.europa.eu/commission/presscorner/detail/en/ip_21_5724> accessed 1 April 2024.

[18] Agreement between the Government of the United States of America and the Government of Japan on Strengthening Critical Minerals Supply Chains, in force 28 March 2023. As of the time of writing, negotiations with the European Union on a similar agreement have not concluded.

remains too early to tell whether these kinds of agreements will become models for trade and sustainability going forward.

B. Sustainability Outside Trade Agreements

Critically, the sustainability disputes under PTAs—like the canonical WTO trade and environment disputes—have dealt with discrete products and industries. Fisheries and forestry products have been especially prominent among the environmental disputes.[19] Disputes have not raised challenges to or dealt with economy-wide measures, nor even with economic sectors that raise systemic problems for the global economy. Measures of the latter type, however, have proliferated in recent years. They have done so as unilateral measures, though, rather than via trade agreements. As such, they can be challenged under both WTO agreements and potentially PTAs.

I highlight four kinds of trade barriers here: 1) the EU Carbon Border Adjustment Mechanism (CBAM); 2) the EU Deforestation-Free Products Regulation; 3) US subsidies for renewable energy; and 4) the US ban on products made with forced labour. The EU CBAM is the first of its kind. It will require importers in key sectors of the economy—electricity, iron and steel, cement, fertilizers, aluminium, and hydrogen—to pay a duty based on the amount of carbon emitted during production.[20] The amount of the duty will be tied to the amount that European producers are charged for the same level of emissions via the EU Emissions Trading System (ETS).[21] Although scheduled to come into force provisionally in October 2023, the CBAM will not result in charges on imports until 2026.[22] The expansion of the CBAM beyond the initial sectors in the following years also seems likely.[23] While the European Union has vigorously defended the CBAM as consistent with the WTO's non-discrimination rules and justifiable under the GATT exceptions,[24] both commentators and foreign officials have expressed doubts.[25] Two concerns

[19] See Vidigal (n 14).

[20] Regulation (EU) 2023/956 of the European Parliament and of the Council of 10 May 2023 establishing a carbon border adjustment mechanism.

[21] EU Carbon Border Adjustment Mechanism <https://taxation-customs.ec.europa.eu/carbon-border-adjustment-mechanism_en#related-links> accessed 10 May 2023.

[22] ibid.

[23] See Amendments adopted by the European Parliament on 22 June 2022 on the proposal for a regulation of the European Parliament and of the Council establishing a carbon border adjustment mechanism <https://www.europarl.europa.eu/doceo/document/TA-9-2022-0248_EN.html> accessed 10 May 2023.

[24] See eg Chiara Galiffa and Ignacio Garcia Bercero, 'How WTO-Consistent Tools can Ensure the Decarbonization of Emission-Intensive Sectors' (2022) 116 American Journal of International Law Unbound 196–201.

[25] See eg Geraldo Vidigal and Ingo Venzke, 'Of False Conflicts and Real Challenges: Trade Agreements, Climate Clubs, and Border Adjustments' (2022) 116 American Journal of International Law Unbound 202–07; Ilaria Espa, 'Reconciling the Climate/Industrial Interplay of CBAMs: What Role for the WTO?' (2022) 116 American Journal of International Law Unbound 208–12; Timothy

are of particular note. First, the CBAM will exempt certain non-EU countries that have domestic emissions trading schemes tied to the ETS, a seeming violation of most-favoured nation rules.[26] Second, the CBAM will credit importers for the costs paid at home pursuant to another country's laws imposing a carbon tax, but it will not credit importers for the costs paid to comply with decarbonization regulations.[27] While in principle the latter set of costs should translate into lower emissions and thus a lower CBAM price, there is no guarantee that this crediting system will ensure treatment no less favourable as between either imports and domestic products or across importers from different countries.[28] Moreover, because these rules require countries to adopt essentially the same policy as the European Union to avoid discriminatory treatment, they may constitute unjustifiable discrimination under the chapeau of GATT Article XX and thus be ineligible for the GATT's environmental exception.[29]

The EU Deforestation-Free Product Regulation bans the import of any product from a list of covered products made on land deforested after 31 December 2020.[30] Thus, a product from land deforested in 2018 is treated differently from the same product from land deforested in 2023. The regulation builds on a similar policy embedded in the EU 2018 Renewable Energy Directive and the Commission's implementing regulations as applied to biofuels.[31] And like the biofuels policy, which Malaysia and Indonesia have challenged at the WTO, the deforestation regulation is arguably discriminatory in that it penalizes importers based on the date deforestation occurred.[32]

The US measures are no less significant. A ban on products made with forced labour should be easily justifiable under GATT exceptions, but the Uyghur Forced Labor Prevention Act creates a presumption that goods from Xinjiang province in China are made with forced labour.[33] The Inflation Reduction Act (IRA) contains $369 billion in climate-related subsidies, but the subsidies for electric vehicles in

Meyer and Todd N Tucker, 'A Pragmatic Approach to Carbon Border Measures' (2022) 21 World Trade Review 109–20.

[26] Vidigal and Venzke (n 25) 205; Espa (n 25) 212.

[27] Vidigal and Venzke (n 25) 205; Espa (n 25) 212; Meyer and Tucker (n 25) 116–17.

[28] ibid.

[29] Vidigal and Venzke (n 25) 205; Espa (n 25) 212; Meyer and Tucker (n 25) 119.

[30] Proposal for a Regulation of the European Parliament and of the Council on the making available on the Union market as well as export from the Union of certain commodities and products associated with deforestation and forest degradation and repealing Regulation (EU) No 995/2010, COM/2021/706 final, <https://eur-lex.europa.eu/legal-content/EN/TXT/?uri = CELEX%3A52021PC0706> accessed 10 May 2023.

[31] Directive (EU) 2018/2001 of the European Parliament and of the Council of 11 December 2018 on the promotion of the use of energy from renewable sources, art 26.2; Commission Delegated Regulation (EU) C(2019) 2005/1013409 supplementing Directive (EU) 2018/2001 (13 March 2019).

[32] Carolyn Fischer and Timothy Meyer, 'Baptists and Bootleggers in the Biodiesel Trade: *EU—Biodiesel (Indonesia)*' (2020) 19 World Trade Review 297–315.

[33] Public Law 117–78, ss 3.

particular contain local content requirements (LCR).[34] Canada and Mexico are 'local' in regard to final assembly of the vehicle and battery components, as are countries with free trade agreements with the United States with regard to critical minerals, but that still excludes economies like the European Union, Japan, and China.[35] Indeed, the discussed critical minerals agreements are designed to allow US allies that do not have a free trade agreement with the United States to qualify.[36]

Finally, climate clubs offer the possibility of minilateralism in sustainable trade policy. As such, they may be coercive to non-members, just as unilateral measures are, although cooperative with respect to members.[37] Although climate club proposals are trendy, to date relatively little progress has been made on concrete arrangements.[38] Perhaps the most advanced proposal is the 2021 GASSA, discussed in section II.A. That arrangement dropped the US Trump-era national security tariffs on steel and aluminium and the EU's retaliatory tariffs. It also called for the US and EU to negotiate an arrangement on decarbonizing the steel and aluminium sectors and addressing overcapacity in the sector by October 2023.[39] Although some have called for GASSA to take the form of a common external tariff on dirty steel or an outright ban on the import of dirty steel, the two governments have so far not announced any more specifics.

III. Leading Through Unilateralism

While environmental considerations have thus made their way into the trade realm, trade agreements are not leading the way. Instead, unilateral measures like the EU CBAM and Deforestation-Free Products Regulation, as well as the measures in the US IRA, are more important in terms of both their economy-wide effects and spurring future action. This section argues that, while unilateral measures have been more important than trade agreements in pushing a green trade agenda, the rise of unilateral measures does not reflect a turn to protectionism as much as a recalibration of the terms of the liberalized multilateral order.

[34] William Alan Reinsch, Apeksha Chauhan, and Elizabeth Duncan, *An Electric Debate: Local Content Requirements and Trade Considerations* (Center for Strategic and International Studies 12 October 2022).

[35] Public Law 117–69, ss 13401.

[36] See Kathleen Claussen, 'What is a Free Trade Agreement Anyway?' (*International Economic Law and Policy Blog*, 3 January 2023) <https://ielp.worldtradelaw.net/2023/01/what-is-a-free-trade-agreement-anyway.html> accessed 10 April 2024.

[37] Michael Mehling and others, 'The Form and Substance of International Cooperation on Border Carbon Adjustments' (2022) 116 American Journal of International Law Unbound 213–18.

[38] Makane Moise Mbengue and Elena Cima, '"Clubbing in the Club": Could Climate-Related Trade Arrangements Set the Pace for Future Climate Cooperation?' (2022) 116 American Journal of International Law Unbound 219–24.

[39] Ana Swanson, 'U.S. Proposes Green Steel Club that Would Levy Tariffs on Outliers' *New York Times* (New York, 7 December 2022).

A. The Causes of the Turn to Unilateralism

The relative importance of unilateral measures is driven in part by the slow pace of negotiations in both trade and environmental institutions over the last quarter century. In the trade space, the story is an often-told one. The Doha Round of trade negotiations, launched in 2001, has been declared dead so many times that the alliterative phrase now elicits groans. The WTO has struggled to address even seemingly small-bore environmental problems. Indeed, it was only in 2022, after 20 years of negotiations, that WTO Members managed to conclude an agreement aimed at curbing environmentally harmful fisheries subsidies.[40] Efforts to rein in more systemically important environmentally harmful subsidies, like those for fossil fuels, have failed to gain traction.[41] As is well known, negotiating activity largely shifted to PTAs. But, while PTAs increased economic integration faster than WTO negotiations would have and have been the site of advances in trade and sustainability, they have continued to move more slowly than many would like in comprehensively integrating environmental considerations.

With the WTO negotiating function largely paralysed, the WTO's Appellate Body (AB) had become the primary means through which WTO rules, as applied, became more environmentally friendly. Although it never moved as fast as critics would have liked, over two decades the AB interpreted WTO rules in ways that made it easier for states to impose trade-restrictive environmental and health measures without inviting WTO-sanctioned retaliation.[42] But even later AB decisions focused on more permissive interpretations of WTO exceptions, rather than incorporating regulatory purpose into non-discrimination rules.[43] And the defenestration by the United States of the AB ultimately eliminated the AB's role in integrating sustainability considerations into WTO law.

The result is a multilateral trading system that has helped dramatically reduce barriers to trade globally, raising millions out of poverty and lowering the costs of goods and services globally, while also making it easier for states to consume products produced in countries with poor environmental standards. The WTO system does not have any affirmative obligations that lead countries to offset the risk that the consumption enabled by trade liberalization will fuel poor environmental practices. Instead, the WTO operates through a norm-exception framework,

[40] Agreement on Fisheries Subsidies, Draft Ministerial Decision of 17 June 2022, WT/MIN(22)/W/22.

[41] Former WTO Director-General Pascal Lamy has called the failure to address fossil fuel subsidies a 'missed opportunity'. See Pascal Lamy, Energy Policies and the WTO (WTO 2013) <https://www.wto.org/english/news_e/sppl_e/sppl279_e.htm> accessed 10 May 2023).

[42] Appellate Body Report, *United States—Import Prohibition of Certain Shrimp and Shrimp Products*, WT/DS58/AB/R (adopted 6 November 1998); Appellate Body Report, *Brazil—Measures Affecting Imports of Retreaded Tyres*, WT/DS332/AB/R (adopted 17 December 2007).

[43] See generally Timothy Meyer, 'The Political Economy of WTO Exceptions' (2022) 99 Washington University Law Review 1299.

in which the affirmative obligations encourage liberalized trade and a system of exceptions is designed to enable, within limits, unilateral action to address non-economic public policy concerns.[44]

Environmental agreements have offered no more fertile ground. Treaties like the Montreal and Kyoto Protocols have long contained, or the parties have interpreted them to authorize, trade-restrictive measures as penalties for violation or non-participation.[45] Other 'environmental' treaties, like the Convention on International Trade in Endangered Species and the so-called Chemicals Conventions, might just as easily be thought of as sectoral trade agreements. But, despite the innovation in environmental treaties, large-scale institutions like the Conference of the Parties to the UN Framework Convention on Climate Change have struggled to significantly change state behaviour with regard to climate change and related environmental problems like deforestation, habitat loss, and biodiversity loss.

B. The Push-and-Pull of Unilateralism and Multilateralism

The slow pace of progress, especially on the more economically significant issues like climate change and deforestation, has pushed states with large internal markets increasingly towards unilateral action. This turn to unilateralism reflects a historically recurring push-and-pull between unilateral and multilateral initiatives. Significantly, moments of increased unilateralism often herald a reorientation of the multilateral system, rather than the demise of it. The most familiar such turn in the trade world is the increased unilateralism the United States displayed during the 1980s. The United States used Section 301 of the Trade Act of 1974 to conduct a number of unilateral investigations of trade agreement violations. This US unilateralism played an important role in inducing other nations to agree to the automatic adoption of dispute resolution reports in the WTO's revamped dispute settlement mechanism.[46] An equally well-known example is the US imposition of seafood bans for products caught in a manner that creates excessive risks of harm to other forms of marine life.[47] The US Congress first authorized such a measure in the 1972 Marine Mammal Protection Act,[48] most famously used to ban tuna

[44] GATT art XX; see also Meyer 'Political Economy' (n 43), Julian Arato, Kathleen Claussen, and J Benton Heath, 'The Perils of Pandemic Exceptionalism' (2020) 114 American Journal of International Law 627.

[45] See Scott Barrett, 'The Strategy of Trade Sanctions in International Environmental Agreements' (1997) 19 Resource and Energy Economics 345.

[46] C O'Neal Taylor, 'The Limits of Economic Power: Section 301 and the World Trade Organization Dispute Settlement System' (1997) 30 Vanderbilt Journal of Transnational Law 209.

[47] *Shrimp–Turtle*; see Panel Report, *United States—Restrictions on Imports of Tuna*, DS21/R-39S/155, 3 September 1991 (not adopted).

[48] Public Law 92–522.

imports to protect dolphins, and then later authorized essentially the same kind of mechanism to ban some shrimp imports in order to protect sea turtles.[49] The persistent use of such mechanisms by the United States, even in the face of adverse action by GATT panels, eventually helped persuade the AB to excuse such measures under some circumstances pursuant to GATT Article XX.[50]

These historical instances of unilateralism provide strong evidence that multilateralism works best when it is not the only option. Given international law's consent requirement for new treaties, and the consensus rule by which institutions like the WTO operate, changes in multilateral institutions frequently need to make every state at least as well off as they would have been without the change.[51] Worse, states may hold up cooperation in the hopes of extracting even further concessions.[52] WTO Members' inability to make significant progress is a testament to these dynamics.

Unilateralism gives states the possibility of removing the multilateral status quo as an option. At least certain of the EU institutions have been explicit about this goal in the context of the CBAM.[53] If a state is committed to its unilateral course, that becomes the new status quo from which negotiations proceed. Those negotiations may occur within the shadow of multilateral institutions and rules. But such unilateral measures provide otherwise intransigent nations a reason to reconsider their behaviour and/or their legal position.[54] Unilateral action can also provide the basis for negotiation among smaller groups of nations. As noted in section III.A , the turn towards PTAs is widely understood to be in part a product of negotiating paralysis at the WTO.

Unilateral action can influence multilateralism through two tracks: the negotiation of trade agreements and their implementation and interpretation. Unilateral and minilateral action has set the table for the spread of sustainability provisions into larger agreements. Disciplines on fisheries subsidies provide an example. WTO Members began negotiations on curbing fisheries subsidies in 2001 and did not conclude negotiations until 2022. During much of that time, members made little progress and it seemed that negotiations might fail entirely. Shifting to negotiations among the 12 members of the TPP showed that disciplines on fisheries subsidies within trade agreements were achievable.

[49] Public Law 101–62 ss 609.

[50] Appellate Body Report, *Import Prohibition of Certain Shrimp and Shrimp Products*, Recourse to Article 21.5 of the DSU, WT/DS58/AB/RW (adopted 21 November 2001).

[51] Andrew T Guzman, 'Against Consent' (2012) 52 Virginia Journal of International Law 747.

[52] Timothy Meyer, 'Power, Exit Costs, and Renegotiation in International Economic Law' (2010) 51 Harvard International Law Journal 379.

[53] European Parliament Briefing, EU Carbon Border Adjustment Mechanism: Implications for Climate and Competitiveness <https://www.europarl.europa.eu/RegData/etudes/BRIE/2022/698889/EPRS_BRI(2022)698889_EN.pdf> accessed 10 May 2023 ('the [CBAM] could also encourage partner countries to adopt carbon pricing that tests the prediction of a Brussels effect').

[54] Meyer 'Power' (n 52).

The likely spread of CBAMs is another important example. Although the exact nature of that expansion remains unclear, the EU CBAM has served as a catalyst for other nations to begin seriously considering how they might design their own CBAMs.[55] The spread of CBAMs is also likely to create a significant administrative barrier to trade, as importers serving multiple markets have to comply with different systems of CBAM-related paperwork. The resulting administrative costs will put pressure on nations to harmonize their CBAMs, either through climate club-like structures that harmonize CBAMs at the border or through crediting systems and mutual recognition. The GASSA is an early effort at negotiating over these issues on a trans-Atlantic basis, with the possibility of expansion to include other nations going forward.

Apart from influencing negotiations, unilateral and minilateral actions can also influence implementation, especially through dispute resolution and the resulting case law. The clearest example of this phenomenon is the US implementation and defence of import bans based on domestic regulations aimed at protecting species like dolphins and sea turtles. A commitment to a certain type of measure, combined with consistent advocacy for its legality, ultimately succeeded in influencing how the AB interpreted GATT Article XX.

The European Union appears to be aiming for a similar approach with a suite of sustainability measures, including its trade remedies on biodiesel made from soy and palm oil, its deforestation measures, and its CBAM. Unlike the United States, which has expressed scepticism about WTO dispute settlement, the European Union has continued to participate in dispute settlement and advocate for the legality of its measures. Oftentimes, this has resulted in losses. The European Union has lost two trade remedy disputes over biodiesel made from soy and palm, with another pending.[56] EU persistence in defending the CBAM as non-discriminatory and non-coercive (in the sense used under the chapeau of Article XX) when many commentators view the measure as both under existing WTO precedents, is best understood as a bid to change the interpretation of GATT rules from within. Whereas the United States has become the leading agitator for wholesale change, the EU approach would change the interpretation of trade rules sub rosa.

The contrast in styles between the two trading powers leads to conflict between them, and among commentators has sometimes led to the (wrong) impression that the European Union does not use sustainable trade policies to advance domestic economic objectives. The difference between the US and EU approaches is

[55] See eg Shiho Takezawa, 'Japan Mulls Carbon Border Tax for Polluters, Nikkei Says' *Bloomberg Tax* (10 February 2021); Charlie Pinkerton, 'The Budget Sets the Stage for Carbon Tariffs' *iPolitics* (20 April 2021).

[56] Panel Report, *European Union—Antidumping Measures on Biodiesel from Indonesia*, WT/DS480/R, 25 January 2018; Appellate Body Report, *European Union—Anti-Dumping Measures on Biodiesel from Argentina*, WT/DS473/AB/R (adopted 26 October 2016); see also Request for Consultations, *European Union—Countervailing Duties on Imports of Biodiesel from Indonesia*, WT/DS618/1.

at least as much about tactics as it is about strategy. While the United States has, for the time being, given up on common law-like changes to how WTO rules are interpreted, the European Union remains committed both to the law-like features of the global trading system and to pushing WTO adjudicators to change how those rules are interpreted to give states more space to pursue sustainable trade policy under trade agreements.

The current US and EU attitudes towards multilateralism aside, the fact remains that unilateralism and multilateralism are connected. The one often stimulates activity in the other, either by way of reaction or incorporation. One question going forward is how the turn to economy-wide trade barriers will impact the multilateral trading system. While some fear that the rise of 'protectionism' generally, including green protectionism, may put the global trading system under undue stress, it seems likely that the multilateral system will adjust, either through renegotiation that provides clearer space for unilateral TSD policies or even requires such policies, as proposals for the GASSA contemplate, or through the implementation of existing rules.

IV. Do Green Trade Barriers Support Green Objectives?

The emergence of green trade barriers, primarily through unilateral action, raises at least one additional question: Do 'green trade barriers'—defined as trade barriers that aim to limit trade in products that are produced in environmentally harmful ways—promote better environmental practices and sustainability more generally?[57] This question could come up in the context of TSD provisions in trade agreements if states eventually begin sanctioning each other for violations, but it is significant already because of the increasing prominence of unilateral measures.

Developing countries have long worried that incorporating environmental policies into trade agreements and national trade policies is simply a smokescreen for protecting uncompetitive domestic markets in developed countries. The US subsidies for renewable energy in the IRA, the EU CBAM, and the Deforestation-Free Products Regulation have all been subject to these criticisms. Moreover, both economies have a history of losing WTO disputes over similar programmes, the United States in the context of LCRs for renewable energy and the European Union for its efforts to protect its domestic biodiesel market from subsidized overseas competition that also happens to come from deforested land.

Debate over whether green trade barriers promote green objectives are often really debates about how to compare counterfactuals. Two inapposite comparisons are worth highlighting. First, some critics of green trade barriers have argued

[57] Espa (n 25).

that trade liberalization would better promote sustainability than trade barriers.[58] These critics argue that proponents of sustainability in trade agreements should spend their energy on initiatives like the Environmental Goods Agreement (EGA), rather than on contentious unilateral measures that reduce trade.

Increased trade in environmentally friendly products might, indeed, promote green objectives. Allowing faster technological diffusion and making environmental goods cheap can lead to the expanded use of green products and could allow developing countries to largely skip fossil fuel-driven technologies in their quest for growth. But, for the most part, liberalizing trade in environmental goods is not a policy that is in competition with the kinds of unilateral TSD measures that nations have imposed. Environmental goods are largely, although not entirely, distinct from the industrial and agricultural inputs that are the subject of most unilateral TSD measures. The latter tend to target core industrial and agricultural products that serve as inputs into the larger economy, like steel, aluminium, cement, fertilizers, and timber. The most environmentally beneficial products, by contrast, are more likely to be finished products, like solar panels, wind towers, or energy efficient appliances. Eliminating tariffs on solar panels does not limit nations' ability to impose carbon border adjustments on steel products or seek a trade agreement on the reduction or elimination of fossil fuel subsidies.

To the extent that these two approaches are competitive, it is mostly over scarce diplomatic and political capital. Multiple large-scale agreements seem unlikely given the pace of multilateral trade negotiations in recent years. Given limited diplomatic and political resources, imposing green trade barriers via unilateral measures seems to offer more environmental benefits than reducing barriers on environmental goods. Many environmental goods are already subject to low tariffs in most countries, while industrial inputs like steel threaten to consume much of the world's remaining carbon budget. Moreover, negotiations over the EGA have been stalled for years. Reducing trade remedies on goods like solar cells might do more to promote trade in those products but would require nations to agree on how to regulate industrial policy measures. Agreement on green subsidy rules might be possible among a subset of WTO Members, but a truly multilateral agreement would be difficult given Chinese state intervention in the solar sector. With agreement on liberalization seeming out of reach and the significant returns to decarbonizing more traditional industrial sectors, limited diplomatic capital is better spent on achievable green trade barriers that incentivize decarbonization.

The second comparison often drawn is between a green trade barrier that contains a discriminatory or coercive component and an identical policy without the discriminatory or coercive component. The argument is that reducing discrimination or coercion will improve the measure's ability to achieve its green objectives.

[58] See eg Simon Lester and K William Watson, 'Free Trade in Environmental Goods: The Trade Remedy Problem' (*Cato Inst Free Trade Bulletin* 19 August 2013).

Discrimination, the argument goes, is inefficient. Introducing inefficiencies into government policies designed to promote the growth of a green economy, and in particular a green industrial sector, will only slow the growth of the field, distort innovation, and artificially prolong the business life of inefficient import-competing producers.

The problem with this comparison is that it ignores politics. Discriminatory conditions like LCRs or measures that contain some degree of protection for domestic producers, as the EU's deforestation measures do, make it easier to build political coalitions for green policies. Environmental policies, after all, are often public goods—pursuing them imposes concentrated costs while creating diffuse benefits. Because the benefits are diffuse, political support for the policies does not match the benefits created. As a result, the policy is undersupplied relative to the benefits it creates.

For example, decarbonizing the steel sector creates significant environmental benefits, as steel production is highly energy-intensive and still involves the burning of coal—the dirtiest fossil fuel—in some places. But decarbonization also imposes costs for producers that invest in decarbonization and their consumers who may face higher prices. Consumers and producers thus may lobby the government to continue to allow the burning of coal to produce steel. These groups typically consist of companies that are well organized, have access to government, and thus have the ability to influence policy outcomes. Citizens who benefit from cleaner air and tackling climate change, on the other hand, are likely to be poorly organized and less well-resourced in terms of obtaining political influence. Because climate change is not their business, in other words, it does not incentivize organization and investment by those who benefit from regulating it on the same scale as businesses that oppose regulation. Nevertheless, the diffuse benefits of decarbonizing the steel sector for these citizens outweigh the costs to participants in the steel industry itself.

Scholars of political economy have long understood that the solution to this problem is to provide private benefits to those who support public goods.[59] Some degree of protection for domestic production serves this function. It creates advocates for green policies by providing concrete economic benefits to those that support, for example, the consumption of biofuels or subsidies for renewable energy.[60] Absent these benefits, green policies might not exist at all. In the context of the steel example, using recycled steel and electricity drawn from renewable sources can significantly cut carbon emissions. A CBAM or similar measure offers protection to domestic industries willing to invest in cleaner production. They can invest in

[59] Mancur Olson, *The Logic of Collective Action: Public Goods and the Theory of Groups* (Harvard University Press 1965).

[60] Timothy Meyer, 'How Local Discrimination Can Promote Global Public Goods' (2015) 95 Boston University Law Review 1935; Lise Johnson, *Space for Local Content Policies and Strategies: A Crucial Time to Revisit an Old Debate* (Columbia Center on Sustainable Development 2015).

green production without fear of being undercut by cheap, dirty imports. The offer of protection from those imports thus converts domestic industry to both an investor in green technology and a political advocate for policies that support green production. Indeed, the EU CBAM is critical precisely because it offers protection to EU industries, which will in turn allow the EU to eliminate free emissions allowances with its domestic ETS, thereby raising the price of carbon within the EU.

LCRs attached to subsidies, such as those in the US IRA, are another common method to achieve this conversion. In the case of environmental law, LCRs provide financial benefits to industries that both reduce their environmental impact and also provide political lobbying and support for government subsidization of a green economy. Recent fights over the implementation of the local content rules in the IRA, with US Senators arguing that watering down those rules is inconsistent with their support for the legislation in the first place, indicate just how important this political support was to the passage of the measure.[61] Moreover, recent research into the effectiveness of LCRs in generating local economic benefits has refuted the argument—often made in the context of trade disputes—that LCRs cannot achieve their objectives. Instead, studies find that LCRs can effectively promote local economic growth when certain preconditions are satisfied.[62]

Put differently, the realistic counterfactual comparison is almost never between a policy with a discriminatory or coercive condition and an identical policy without such a condition. The comparison is much more often going to be between a government policy with a discriminatory or coercive condition and a watered-down policy that might even then fail to obtain sufficient political support to pass. Mixed motive policies are, in other words, hardier political policies than pure policies that seek to achieve only a single goal.[63]

Of course, the reality that some degree of protection may be necessary to ensure political support for green trade policies does not mean that any trade barrier should be allowed. The key is to find—either through negotiation or the development of case law—an approach that allows governments the space to engage in politics that advance ambitious and politically realistic green trade policies, while at the same time preventing protectionism from becoming the sole objective. The leadership of the US and the EU, in their different ways, have created multiple fora in which nations can attempt to develop one or more approaches to address this problem. The answer(s), though, will not be technical ones, even if they are presented as such by specialists making arguments about legal texts. Rather, they will

[61] Kat Lucero, 'Senators Say Green Energy Domestic Content Rules Lack Teeth' *Law360* (15 May 2023).

[62] UE Hansen and others, 'The Effects of Local Content Requirements in Auction Schemes for Renewable Energy in Developing Countries: A Literature Review' (2020) 127 Renewable & Sustainable Energy Review 109843; F Scheifele, M Brauning, and B Probst, 'The Impact of Local Content Requirements on the Development of Export Competitiveness in Solar and Wind Technologies' (2022) 168 Renewable & Sustainable Energy Review 112831.

[63] Meyer (n 43).

be political compromises that attract sufficient support to provide a stable balance between nations' environmental, economic, and political objectives.

V. Conclusion

So, is the expansion of green trade policy, and in particular green trade barriers, a revolution or a return to protectionism? Like most such dichotomies, it is neither. Rather, the emergence of green trade policy reflects the standard mix of unilateralism and multilateralism that has driven the evolution of the global trading system for decades. Our current moment is one in which unilateral and minilateral initiatives seem to be playing a more important role than multilateral initiatives. But history teaches us that those unilateral initiatives are more likely to reshape the multilateral system—a system that is itself already changing to incorporate green objectives—than they are to destroy it.

20

The Role of 'Development' in Sustainable Development in Trade Agreements

James J Nedumpara

I. Introduction

Modern-day trade agreements are all-encompassing. They transcend traditional market access issues and often touch upon various topics, some rather remotely connected to trade. In recent times, in addition to labour and environment, a number of trade agreements include disciplines on issues such as anti-corruption, gender, animal welfare, and sustainable food systems, for example.[1]

The efforts to incorporate 'non-trade concerns' in trade agreements have a long history.[2] Of late, apart from core labour or environment concerns, other non-trade concerns such as climate change, clean energy, fisheries conservation, rural development, good corporate governance, and special provisions for Indigenous people have been constantly pushing for acceptance in trade agreements.[3] Non-trade concerns are often addressed in the trade and sustainable development (TSD) chapters of trade agreements, but it is also not uncommon to find stand-alone sustainability chapters in trade agreements with binding dispute settlement aimed at addressing such concerns.[4] For instance, the TSD chapters concluded by developed nations such as Canada, the European Union, and the United States include dispute settlement provisions with or without sanctions or countermeasures.

The concept of sustainable development has received particular salience and impetus ever since the adoption of the 17 Sustainable Development Goals (SDGs)

[1] Aaditya Mattoo, Nadia Rocha, and Michela Ruta, *Handbook of Deep Trade Agreements* (World Bank Group 2020) 3–5.

[2] Inclusion of sustainable development provisions was first conceptualized in the North American Free Trade Agreement in 1994. See Paul R Baker, *Handbook on Negotiating Sustainable Development Provisions in Preferential Trade Agreements* (United Nations 2018) 9–10.

[3] ibid.

[4] The agreements in the new generation of EU trade agreements contain specific provisions and even dedicated chapters on mandatory obligations for labour rights promotion and environmental sustainability. The EU–Korea FTA, for instance, contained binding dispute settlement provisions; this was used by the European Union to raise a dispute against Korea for its failure to fulfil its labour rights obligations. See Nicolás Brando, Brecht Lein, and Axel Marx, 'The Protection of Labour Rights in Trade Agreements: The Case of the EU-Columbia Agreement' (2016) 50 Journal of World Trade 587.

James J Nedumpara, *The Role of 'Development' in Sustainable Development in Trade Agreements* In: *The Sustainability Revolution in International Trade Agreements.* Edited by: Geraldo Vidigal and Kathleen Claussen, Oxford University Press.
© James J Nedumpara 2024. DOI: 10.1093/9780191994470.003.0020

by the UN General Assembly in 2015.[5] The SDGs are designed to be a 'shared blueprint for peace and prosperity for people and the planet, now and for the future'.[6] The UN 2030 Agenda and the 17 SDGs, the Paris Agreement on Climate Change, and other multilateral agreements for the protection of the environment and labour standards form the core of sustainability provisions. The SDGs represent a set of comprehensive, human-oriented, integrated, and transformative goals and targets to achieve sustainable development by 2030.[7] Importantly, the SDGs are premised on the principle of 'leaving no one behind' in the development path.[8]

While there is widespread commitment to achieve SDGs, the reference to SDGs in trade agreements is still contentious. There are several fundamental questions, of which a critical question is the role of 'economic development' in 'sustainable development'. In this context, the first three SDGs clearly capture and reflect the developmental concerns of low-income economies, for example, no poverty, zero hunger, good health, and well-being. The very essence of development, specifically economic development, lies in eradicating poverty and hunger and ensuring basic amenities for all by providing a decent standard of life.[9] Other questions also arise. How do the leading trading nations accommodate the often-competing non-instrumental values inherent in sustainable development? Are the TSD chapters disproportionately focused on addressing negative externalities or non-economic objectives of trade without adequately addressing the developmental needs and aspirations of the trading partners? These questions demand answers, especially given the longstanding concern that trade and sustainability provisions are unduly burdensome on developing countries because those provisions may saddle developing countries with responsibilities without offering commensurate developmental assistance and supportive measures.[10]

While the focus of the TSD chapters is to require trading partners to adopt progressive standards and approaches and to discourage regressive policies in relation to non-trade concerns, the pattern and nature of the trade and sustainability obligations are unmistakably familiar and predictable. A mapping of the trade and sustainability chapters of the recent trade agreements clearly indicates that the template of the TSD obligations is set, standardized, and exported widely across jurisdictions, mostly by advanced countries. The very possibility of accommodating

[5] UNGA Res 70/1 (25 September 2015), Transforming Our World: The 2030 Agenda for Sustainable Development <https://documents-dds-ny.un.org/doc/UNDOC/GEN/N15/291/89/PDF/N1529189.pdf?OpenElement> accessed 1 May 2023.

[6] 'The 17 Goals, History' (Sustainable Development, UN Economic and Social Council) <https://sdgs.un.org/goals> accessed 1 May 2023.

[7] UNGA Res 70A/1 (n 5).

[8] ibid.

[9] The Brundtland Commission Report also notes that 'a world in which poverty is endemic will never be free from ecological or other catastrophes'. See GH Brundtland, 'Our Common Future: Report of the World Commission on Environment and Development. Geneva' (1987) UN Doc A/42/427.

[10] Cosimo Beverelli, Jürgen Kurtz, and Damian Raess, *International Trade, Investment and the Sustainable Development Goals* (CUP 2020) 111–14.

pluralist notions of sustainability or proposing alternative approaches and models, or even replacing the use of certain words or phrases, looks forlorn.[11] Arguably, it is the similarity, the repetitiveness, and often the rigidity of some of the TSD provisions that apparently leave limited room for negotiation manoeuvre that makes sustainability in trade agreements an agenda of the Global North.

The focus of the chapter is to briefly examine the elements of TSD in recent free trade agreements (FTAs) and how those elements address the core concept of development. The chapter seeks to address the larger question of whether the concept of 'economic development' has lost its place in the discussion on 'sustainable development' and how various sustainability concerns can best be reconciled with trade priorities.

II. The Meaning Of 'Development'

The concept of 'development' remains a hugely controversial and debated topic in international economic and legal scholarship.[12] According to some development scholars, the focus of development should be economic growth.[13] The two standard terms to define 'development' are gross domestic product (GDP) and gross national product. Both these concepts focus on the wealth created through the production of goods and services. In other words, these concepts capture economic value creation fostered by domestic production, trade openness, and access to markets.

A. The Role of Economic Development

Economic development is the central pillar of the concept of development.[14] Most developing countries went through long years of hardships and struggle focusing on the bottom of the value chain, destined to languish as 'hewers of wood and drawers of water'.[15] First of all, the developing world only had the ability for low-value manufacturing and commodities, whose potential to affect positive terms of

[11] To provide certain examples, TSD chapters in most of the advanced country FTAs contain provisions relating to 'affirmation and effective implementation of international instruments', 'non-derogation', 'effective enforcement', and 'ratification of certain fundamental instruments or conventions' through a 'sustained and recurring course of action or inaction', and thematic provisions on similar lines.

[12] Leila Choukroune and James J Nedumpara, *International Economic Law: Text, Cases and Materials* (CUP 2021) 683–710.

[13] ibid 687.

[14] Brundtland Report (n 9).

[15] Michael J Trebilcock and Robert Howse, *The Regulation of International Trade* (Routledge 1995) 382; Gary Gereffi and Olga Memedovic, *The Global Apparel Value Chain: What Prospects for Upgrading by Developing Countries* (UNIDO 2003) 3–6.

trade was limited. In addition, in the absence of meaningful export market opportunities, constrained by high tariffs and quota restrictions especially in areas like textiles and agriculture, developing countries had to struggle with perennially weak foreign trade and persisting balance of payment concerns. The economic development of several low-income countries depended on their ability to access the developed country markets and therefore it was realized that special provisions are required under trade agreements to advance their interests.

In many ways, Article XVIII and Part IV of the General Agreement on Tariffs and Trade (GATT) as well as the 1979 Enabling Clause[16] emphasized the primacy of economic development, specifically the contribution of trade, in improving the standards of living. These provisions highlight the importance of 'less than full reciprocity' in relation to trade liberalization and the need for additional flexibilities such as economic assistance and infant industry protection. In particular, the Enabling Clause emphasized measures consistent with the 'development, financial and trade needs' of developing countries. The World Trade Organization (WTO) Appellate Body noted in the landmark *EC—Tariff Preferences* that '[t]he very purpose of special and differential treatment (SDT) permitted under the Enabling Clause is to foster economic development of developing countries'.[17] The importance of economic development is also echoed in the UN SDGs. It is important in this context to recall Goal 8 of the SDGs that focuses on inclusive and sustainable economic growth, employment, and decent work for all. These goals have continuing relevance for several least developed countries (LDCs) and developing economies that continue to struggle from weak economic recovery and labour market fallouts in the backdrop of multiple crises including the COVID-19 pandemic.[18]

Economic development can also lead to poverty alleviation, a key SDG. According to the World Bank, without a significant reduction in inequality, especially in countries with high poverty and inequality, the world would not be able to meet its goal of ending extreme poverty.[19] In other words, inequality can be addressed only if there are better economic opportunities and greater redistribution of wealth. The GATT 1947 in particular acknowledged the importance of securing a share for developing countries in international trade commensurate with their needs for economic development.[20] It is established beyond doubt that integration

[16] Differential and More Favourable Treatment, Reciprocity and Fuller Participation of Developing Countries (28 November 1979), GATT BISD L/4903 (26th Supp) 203–05.

[17] WTO, European Communities: Conditions for the Granting of Tariff Preferences to Developing Countries—Appellate Body Report (7 April 2004) WT/DS246/AB/R 164.

[18] United Nations Department of Economic and Social Affairs, 'The Sustainable Development Goals Report 2022' (7 July 2022) <https://unstats.un.org/sdgs/report/2022/The-Sustainable-Development-Goals-Report-2022.pdf> accessed 1 May 2023.

[19] World Bank, 'Inequality and Shared Prosperity' <https://www.worldbank.org/en/topic/isp/overview≥ accessed 1 May 2023.

[20] Article XXXVIII, General Agreement on Tariffs and Trade (1947) 55 UNTS 194.

of global markets through trade openness is one of the best means to ending poverty.[21] Developing and low-income countries need sustained growth fuelled by trade to create economic opportunities including employment opportunities.

B. The Role of Social Development

Economic development in the sense of GDP growth will not, in itself, ensure the well-being of the individual or the society. The concept of development gradually recognized the importance of social development. The concept of social development embraces the idea of the state ensuring adequate and sufficient opportunities for individuals to realize their potential, capabilities, and most importantly, dignity.[22] Social development could also be based on the idea of justice, social inclusion, and greater participation of stakeholders in mainstream activities that were once traditionally reserved only for a few. In other words, social development recognizes the importance of bringing up individuals and societies who are confined to the margins. On the whole, social development is a comprehensive process that aims at the 'constant improvement of the well-being of the entire population and of all individuals on the basis of their active, free and meaningful participation in development'. Notably, the recent focus on women's empowerment and mainstreaming gender, minorities, and indigenous people in trade agreements is based on this worthy objective.

Among the various dimensions of sustainable development, social development receives the least attention in trade agreements. While social development remains important, trade agreements have inherent limitations in furthering this objective. Trade agreements are primarily aimed at guaranteeing market access, ensuring adequate conditions for fair competition, and regulatory harmonization. As a general observation, social development provisions in trade agreements are usually exhortative and are couched in the nature of best endeavour provisions.

C. The Need for Environmental Protection

Along with economic development and social development, the protection and preservation of the environment occupies an important role, especially when Planet Earth is in peril. In many ways, pursuing the first two goals could lead to greater stress on the existing natural resources. The world population has nearly

[21] Marcus Bartley Johns and others, 'The Role of Trade in Ending Poverty' (World Bank Group 2015) <http://documents.worldbank.org/curated/en/726971467989468997/The-role-of-trade-in-ending-poverty> accessed 1 May 2023.

[22] Amartya Sen, 'The Idea of Justice' (2005) 6(2) Journal of Human Development 151–66.

doubled in the last 50 years. The steady demands on natural resources, including fossil fuel-based energy resources and raw materials, have seriously challenged the concept of sustainability. It has also led to the exhaustion of critical natural resources including the disappearance of evergreen forests, advancing deforestation, displacement and loss of habitat for rare species of fauna and flora, and irreparable damage to the environment. The worst of all crises is the climate crisis.[23] Life can be sustained only in a narrow temperature zone and the impacts of global warming—demonstrated in the nature of glacial melting, unseasonal rains and changing weather patterns, flash floods and cloudbursts, sea surges, and land erosion—are too alarming for anyone to ignore. In addition, man-made disasters including war and political conflicts have only compounded the misery.

The good thing, however, is that all these concerns are now more frequently discussed and debated than ever before, although the global response does not necessarily measure up to the gravity of the crisis. The concept of sustainable development is also about the prudent management of the world's resources, namely, the reduction of our dependence on precious resources, the quest for finding alternative and less environmentally harmful sources of energy and investing in clean technologies. As recognized by the Brundtland Commission as early as 1987, the concept of sustainable development emphasizes 'meeting the needs of the present without compromising the needs of the future generations to meet their own needs'.[24] This is broadly the concept of intergenerational equity.[25] Sustainability is also about making hard choices in our lifetime to preserve our resources at least in the same manner or roughly to the same extent that we inherited them. As Robert Solow noted, sustainability is in essence a moral obligation that we are supposed to have for future generations—essentially, a form of trusteeship.[26] However, there is another dimension of developmental equity. One of the often-repeated complaints is that climate crisis mitigation and adaptation obligations are not based on equity and that rich countries frequently advocate measures that dramatically differ from the paths that they had adopted to become rich. For example, import substitution industrialization, buying local provisions, and production subsidies were often highlighted as bad public policy instruments and have been either prohibited or disciplined in various trade agreements including the WTO agreements, but there is a growing trend to use these measures, even in highly developed economies, to gain competitive advantage in new age industries such as renewable energy and

[23] Amartya Sen, 'Sustainable Development and Our Responsibilities' (2010) <https://www.unipol.it/sites/corporate/files/document_attachments/sen_2010_eng_ugf_01-01-2010_en.pdf> accessed 1 May 2023.

[24] Brundtland Report (n 9) para 27.

[25] Lynda M Collins, 'Revisiting the Doctrine of Intergenerational Equity in Global Environmental Governance' (2007) 30(1) Dalhousie LJ 79 (noting that it validates the right of an individual to have an adequate quality of life during her life in an inter-temporal world community).

[26] Robert M Solow, 'Sustainability: An Economist's Perspective' in Robert N Stavins (ed), *Economics of the Environment* (4th edn, WW Norton 2000) 505–13.

electric vehicles.[27] To quote the familiar expression of Ha Joon-Chang, some of the sustainability obligations in international trade agreements literally amount to 'kicking away the ladder'[28] and create obstacles for the developing world to adopt heterodox policies for meeting their developmental aspirations. Necessarily, there will be significant economic and social costs involved in conforming to a number of sustainability goals, especially in relation to adopting higher environmental, labour, and other social standards. Late industrializers, especially developing countries, will possibly find at least some of the decarbonization targets and fossil fuel subsidy reforms impacting their economic growth prospects.[29] In addition, with the current levels of economic endowments or technological prowess, it is feared that most developing countries will be unable to meet the constantly evolving sustainability standards so as to remain competitive in several key product segments in international markets. In other words, the developed versus developing divide is likely to accentuate in the trade and sustainability debate.

It is natural that there are diversities of views on the meaning of 'development' itself. The dominant theories in the 1950s and 1960s assumed that there were predefined stages through which a state must progress in order to achieve economic development.[30] According to theories that fall within the category of 'capital fundamentalism', developing countries needed capital formation to accelerate economic growth. Most developing countries focused on traditional subsistence agriculture and needed investment and technology to transform from agrarian economies to modern, mechanized, and industrialized economies. Later on, it was realized that investment in certain economic sectors alone will not ensure growth. Specially targeted programmes, including investments in infrastructure and education, urban planning, and developing legal systems and institutions, were essential to achieve economic growth.

While the need to protect the environment and preserve the fragile planet is a goal shared by countries irrespective of their development status, the existing narratives do not often do justice to the concept of sustainable development. Most proponents of strong TSD provisions are more concerned about the so-called 'race to the bottom'—a possibility that countries could reduce environmental, labour, or other compliance requirements to gain competitive advantage in the field of trade and investment. The basic assumption is that high environmental and labour standards can drive up the cost of production, leading producers to

[27] Editorial, 'American Green Subsidies are Causing Headaches in Europe', *The Economist* (Europe, 1 December 2022) <https://www.economist.com/europe/2022/12/01/americas-green-subsidies-are-causing-headaches-in-europe> accessed 1 May 2023.

[28] Chang H-J, *Kicking Away the Ladder: Development Strategy in Historical Perspective* (Anthem Press 2002).

[29] McKinsey & Company, 'The Net-Zero Transition: What it Would Cost, What it Would Bring' (2023) <https://www.mckinsey.com/capabilities/sustainability/our-insights/how-the-net-zero-transition-would-play-out-in-countries-and-regions> accessed 30 September 2023.

[30] WW Rostom, *The Stages of Economic Growth: A Non-Communist Manifesto* (CUP 1960) ch 1.

shift production facilities to countries with lower regulatory costs. There is an underlying resentment that free trade and open markets have led to some of the advanced countries losing their comparative advantage in manufacturing goods and the only way to level the playing field is to introduce sustainability standards, including the controversial 'process and production methods' requirements.[31] In light of this, there is a clear focus on using trade agreements as a 'carrot and stick'. If manufacturing sites, production facilities, or services firms in the partner countries pay wages lower than fair wages or use certain methods of production with comparatively higher energy or emissions intensity, there is a clear intent to target such practices through TSD provisions. The resentment in developing economies towards undertaking TSD obligations is also because these provisions appear to them as a double-edged sword—forcing them to bring down tariff and non-tariff barriers in environmental goods and services (where their industries are at a nascent stage) on the one hand while limiting the comparative advantages that they naturally command, by setting higher labour and environment standards, on the other.[32]

It is often not clear whether the TSD provisions are aimed at addressing genuine sustainability concerns or at neutralizing the comparative advantages. At least the origins of the trade and sustainability debate are steeped in the controversy regarding unfair competitive advantage.[33] In a number of FTAs, such provisions are included to mollify special interest groups.[34] If the text of TSD chapters explicitly provides for neutralizing the comparative advantage of the FTA partner on account of low-cost labour, it is natural to assume that such provisions are not per se addressed at sustainability. On the other hand, there are concerns that such sustainability requirements would completely alter the existing paradigms of comparative advantage to the detriment of developing countries. It will also be difficult to negate the criticism that the concept of sustainable development is introduced as a mask for protectionism or to slow down the progress of developing countries in climbing up the ladder and posing an economic challenge to developed countries in the long run.[35] On the other hand, if the proponents of TSD provisions

[31] Steve Charnovitz, 'The Law of Environmental PPMs in the WTO: Debunking the Myth of Illegality' (2002) 27 Yale Journal of International Law 59.

[32] For instance, the USMCA sets minimum wage rate in the automobile sector for the industries of Mexico and Canada as well. See Office of the United States Trade Representative, 'Report to Congress on the Operation of the United States–Mexico–Canada Agreement with respect to Trade in Automotive Goods' (1 July 2022).

[33] WTO, Singapore Ministerial Declaration (18 December 1996) Doc WT/MIN(96)/DEC/W, 4; see also Jagdhish Bhagwati, 'Trade Liberalization and "Fair Trade" Demands: Addressing the Environmental and Labour Standards Issues' (1995) 18 World Economy 745.

[34] US Congressional Research Service, 'Labor Enforcement Issues in U.S. FTAs', 18 December 2020; US Congressional Research Service, 'Worker Rights Provisions in Free Trade Agreements (FTAs)', 25 October 2023.

[35] Maria Garcia and Annick Masselot, 'EU–Asia Free Trade Agreements as Tools for Social Norm/Legislation Transfer' (2015) 13 Asia Europe Journal 241, 246.

are able to convince their developing country FTA partners that enforcing TSD provisions is advantageous, at least in the long run, to developing country partners assuming enforcement obligations, the resistance would be much less. There are several areas where developed countries can onboard the developing countries to co-sponsor the trade and sustainability agenda through cooperative mechanisms. The cooperative mechanisms will be particularly helpful in areas such as combating ecological challenges like air pollution, ocean conservation, solid waste disposal and management, water management and purification, and ensuring safe health conditions and workers' welfare, for example. This approach holds true with respect to the participation of civil society in domestic advisory groups in relation to the enforcement of sustainability provisions. While civil society engagement can bring in democratic accountability, developing countries often fear that powerful civil society groups within and outside their territories can create narratives and whip up societal backlash leading to political instability. Although this is not a typical development issue, it is an area where most developing countries share the same concerns and views.

Section III will focus on some of the provisions of the TSD chapters of FTAs to explore the question of how sustainability and development considerations can be managed.

III. Balancing Sustainability and Development Considerations

Non-trade concerns figure rhetorically in the trade policy agenda of most upper-income-level countries. For years, the European Union predicated the grant of unilateral trade preferences on meeting non-trade concerns such as labour and environmental policies in their partner countries. The Treaty of Lisbon explicitly calls for trade and investment policy to support and promote EU values and standards relating to a number of non-economic objectives such as human rights, labour rights, the environment, and sustainable development.[36] Even in the United States, the Generalized System of Preferences (GSP) incorporates criteria relating to workers' rights, child labour, and forced labour in determining GSP (in)eligibility.[37] In other words, meeting the sustainability obligations is a condition precedent for preferential market access, especially in upper-income countries.

[36] For instance, art 2(5) of the Treaty on the Functioning of the European Union, 2008/C 115/01 states '[i]n its relations with the wider world, the Union shall uphold and promote its values and interests and contribute to the protection of its citizens. It shall contribute to peace, security, the sustainable development of the Earth.'

[37] 'Other Bases for Ineligibility' 19 US Code, s 2462 (b)(2); see Gene Grossman and Alan O Sykes, 'A Preference for Development: The Law and Economics of GSP' in George A Bermann and Petros C Mavroidis (eds), *WTO Law and Developing Countries* (CUP 2010) 255, 257–58.

While there is a certain element of reciprocity in exchanging market access commitments in trade agreements, the inclusion of sustainability obligations is often not the outcome of shared consent. While North–North trading partners have relatively little discomfort in agreeing to these provisions, sustainability provisions often prove contentious in North–South preferential trade agreements, barring certain exceptions. Developing countries and other economies in transition find it onerous to enforce higher standards of sustainability standards and often grudgingly agree to sustainability provisions.

The stated purpose of many TSD chapters is to seek the integration of sustainable development priorities in the trade and investment policies of the parties. Most TSD chapters negotiated in recent times introduce a range of obligations including a long preamble that refers to a multitude of international labour and environment conventions and principles.[38] The TSD obligations broadly fall into four different categories: (i) obligations related to existing international commitments; (ii) obligations related to existing domestic legislation; (iii) aspirational provisions related to higher levels of protection; and (iv) monitoring mechanism for existing domestic legislation. At a broader level, the TSD provisions directly or indirectly establish 'linkages', that is, by either conditioning or limiting benefits arising under the trade agreement to the adoption or pursuit of certain policies or commitments at the domestic or international level.

The first group of obligations is to 'effectively implement' the international obligations that the parties have already undertaken and to ratify the international obligations that the parties have not ratified.[39] The latter is especially true for International Labour Organization (ILO) core conventions.[40] The obligations to ratify relate to core ILO conventions covering: the freedom of association; recognition of the right to collective bargaining; prohibition of child labour and forced/compulsory labour; the elimination of discrimination in respect of employment and occupation; and occupational health and safety.[41] In addition, TSD chapters often contain an obligation to respect, promote, and realize fundamental principles of the ILO Declaration of Rights at Work,[42] even if a party has not ratified the convention that outlines the principles.[43] The reference to the ILO Declaration on Social Justice for Fair Globalization 2008, is also invariably present in labour chapters.[44] When it comes to the environment, the TSD chapters often refer

[38] See Free Trade Agreement between the European Union and the Republic of Korea, in force 13 December 2015, art 13.1.
[39] ibid.
[40] ibid.
[41] ibid.
[42] ILO, Declaration on Fundamental Principles and Rights at Work (Declaration on Fundamental Rights) (18 June 1998).
[43] ibid.
[44] See Agreement between the United States of America, the United Mexican States, and Canada, in force 1 July 2020, art 23.2.

to Agenda 21 and the Rio Declaration on Environment and Development, the Johannesburg Declaration on Sustainable Development, and the Johannesburg Plan of Implementation on Sustainable Development, 2002.[45] On the whole, the approach is to transform several soft obligations undertaken by the parties in various international fora into hard obligations, which are enforceable under the trade agreement.[46]

The elevation of soft commitments into hard obligations through the 'effective implementation' clause has major implications, especially for developing countries. Most developing countries participated in a range of international treaties with the understanding that the commitments or engagements that they had made were aspirational in nature and were not directly enforceable. At least, it is inconceivable to imagine that countries considered the possibility of any monetary penalty for breach of obligations under multilateral environmental or labour agreements. It is evident that most developing countries agreed to conditional enforceability at best. Also, most of the multilateral environmental or labour conventions do not specify a prescribed method or timeline for meeting the sustainability goals. A prominent example is the Paris Agreement where the meeting of Nationally Determined Contributions (NDCs) is not a legally binding obligation, and the agreement has left it up to the parties to establish national frameworks for meeting their targets.[47] However, reaffirming a commitment to effectively implement the United Nations Framework Convention on Climate Change (UNFCCC) or the Paris Agreement in the TSD chapters may have the effect of rendering certain commitments in such treaties directly enforceable through the trade agreement. In most cases, the TSD provisions, by specifically linking the commitments under other international conventions to the trade agreement, seek to hasten or expedite the process of meeting the SDGs. Cross linkages in trade agreements to obligations in other environments or labour agreements or conventions can upend the carefully calibrated balance achieved multilaterally. In addition, there will be systematic monitoring of compliance with sustainability obligations within the framework of the trade agreement, often with little regard to the parties' specific circumstances, needs, and capabilities. In a nutshell, elevating soft commitments into hard obligations through the TSD provisions is itself an economic cost to most countries, especially developing countries.

In addition, the concept of SDT is missing either partially or wholly from modern trade agreements. This is a significant departure from the practice under

[45] See eg art X.1 of the EU proposal to Australia on Trade and Sustainable Development, 17 June 2022 <https://circabc.europa.eu/ui/group/09242a36-a438-40fd-a7af-fe32e36cbd0e/library/39e0b420-4f11-4b57-8eef-7818a251b811/details> accessed 1 May 2023.

[46] See Canada–Republic of Korea Free Trade Agreement, in force 1 January 2015, Annex 18-E; FTA between the United States of America and the Republic of Korea, in force 15 March 2012.

[47] Christina Voigt, 'The Paris Agreement: What is the Standard of Conduct for Parties?' (2016) 26 QIL Zoom in 17, 19–20.

the WTO where SDT has a firm and solid presence.[48] In addition, obligations in multilateral climate agreements generally incorporate the concept of common but differentiated responsibilities and respective capabilities (CBDR-RC).[49] The objective is to consider the differing national priorities, capacities, and levels of development of the countries assuming obligations. The incorporation of CBDR-RC in some of the environmental agreements is a triumph of the collective positions taken by developing nations over time.[50] By remaining silent or indifferent to SDT provisions, the TSD provisions in trade agreements can be considered as whittling down some of the hard-fought victories that the developing countries had achieved in other areas of international cooperation. When developing countries individually negotiate treaties that are driven by reciprocal considerations with developed countries, it is not easy to seek the same kind of acceptance for SDT provisions. Oftentimes, the sustainability commitments are placed on the parties without any differentiation based on the levels of development. SDT treatment is generally amplified when developing countries negotiate collectively and as a group. It is important to recall that at the WTO, in the initial phase of the Doha Round negotiations, the developing countries fiercely opposed the inclusion of the so-called Singapore issues—a set of issues which had clear linkages with trade such as investment and competition—and ensured that such issues were removed from the negotiating agenda. Surprisingly, a number of developing countries negotiated disciplines relating to trade-plus provisions in FTAs with developed country partners. At least there is a clear empirical pattern that SDT provisions matter significantly less when developing countries negotiate trade and sustainability provisions as part of FTAs.

A bulk of the developing countries join FTAs for improved market access in key export destinations. In other words, developing countries broadly appreciate the importance of market access in key developed country markets. However, the liberalization of tariffs alone will not ensure market access. For example, under the WTO, most of the LDCs are entitled to receive duty-free quota-free access to almost 97 per cent of the products.[51] However, not all the LDCs have been able to derive meaningful market access due to a lack of export competitiveness, supply side constraints, and other factors. Similarly, strong TSD provisions have the potential of depriving the developing country partners of the expected market access unless

[48] John Whalley, 'Special and Differential Treatment in the Millennium Round' (1999) 22 The World Economy 1064.

[49] UNFCCC, in force 21 March 1994, Preamble and art 3; United Nations Conference on the Human Environment, Stockholm, 5–16 June 1972, 11 ILM 1416 (1972), UNTS 11, Principle 11. See also Stellina Jolly and Abhishek Dev, 'Principle of CBDRC: Its Implementation and Interpretation through NDCS in the Context of Sustainable Development' (2021) 11 Washington Journal of Environmental Law and Policy 310.

[50] Kyoto Protocol to the United Nations Framework Convention on Climate Change, in force 16 February 2005, Annex B, art 10. See also Jolly and Dev (n 49).

[51] WTO, 'Duty-Free and Quota-Free Access for Least-Developed Countries', Ministerial Decision (7 December 2013) WT/L/919.

targeted and effective supportive measures are provided under the trade agreements. In other words, for TSD provisions to be meaningful, the trade agreements need to provide a robust framework for the industries in the partner countries to access low-carbon technologies including climate finance and other facilitative measures.

A. Sustainability and Preserving Development Space

For developing countries, achieving development on their own terms may be a priority. In this regard, the right to development would entail the right to be able to pursue policies that foster economic development without restrictions and conditions.

At the same time, given the challenges that the world faces today, even developing countries can ill-afford to follow the same or similar unsustainable policies that the developed countries had pursued in the past to achieve economic progress. In particular, there is a need to focus on climate mitigation and adaptation measures including lesser dependence on fossil fuel-based energy resources. However, accelerated climate mitigation and adaptation is possible only if developing countries receive the new technology or other resources. Furthermore, there should be a recognition that given the significant differences in the developmental levels and historical emissions of countries, meaningful outcomes in multilateral environmental agreements such as the Paris Agreement have been made possible only on the basis of a tailor-made approach—for example, by including differential treatment provisions in favour of developing economies.[52] The TSD chapters in trade agreements need to necessarily incorporate sufficient flexibilities.

Most developing governments consider social clauses including non-trade concerns as an anti-development agenda promoted by the Global North. Historically speaking, social clauses also have a neocolonial element to them.[53] At the same time, several developing countries have agreed to or continue to engage in negotiations for including sustainability provisions because of the fear of missing out from major export markets or otherwise getting marginalized in international economic relations.[54] What is required is a collective sense of decision-making acknowledging that 'we're in this together'. If there is an effort to treat non-trade concerns as the organizing principle of how trade should take place in the future, we may see an inevitable clash of interests—a clash that could undermine global efforts to find coordinated solutions to the common challenges of the planet.

[52] S Maljean-Dubois and L Rajamani, *Implementation of International Environmental Law* (Brill 2011); Lavanya Rajamani, *Differential Treatment in International Environmental Law* (OUP 2006).

[53] Aleydis Nissen, 'Not That Assertive: The EU's Take on Enforcement of Labour Obligations in its Free Trade Agreement with Korea' (2023) 33 European Journal of International Law 607.

[54] RE Baldwin, 'The Causes of Regionalism' (1997) 20 World Economy 865.

While sustainability deserves special concern and focus, any effort to remove once and for all the policy flexibility to pursue pro-development policies could slow down collective actions for protecting the global commons. An example is the recent WTO Agreement on Fisheries Subsidies.[55] The Agreement introduced disciplines, including prohibitions on subsidies to illegal, unreported, and unregulated (IUU) fishing and overfished stocks as well as to fishing or fishing-related activities in unregulated high seas. While there is no doubt that IUU fishing depletes fisheries stocks, destroys marine habitats, and puts at risk fishing-based livelihood activities, several WTO Members were unwilling to assume obligations in relation to subsidies that lead to overcapacity and overfishing (OCOF). In particular, fleshing out the elements of appropriate and effective SDT consistent with SDG Target 14.6 proved difficult and elusive. The disagreements surrounding the SDT provisions on OCOF were the key reason why a more comprehensive agreement on fisheries subsidies was not achieved during the 12th Ministerial Conference of the WTO.[56]

Finally, equity and greater concern for the needs of developing countries ought to be at the heart of the sustainability discussion in trade agreements. There should be a greater focus on concerns such as poverty and hunger eradication, which at present are confined to mere political statements in fora such as the G20. As stated earlier, the first two SDGs also lay down the key concerns of developing countries, which should be given utmost priority and recognized as a standalone element in trade agreements. Developing countries are beset by their own unique challenges in terms of growing population, resource constraints, poor access to technology, climate challenges, lack of adequate healthcare, and so on, and do not have the ability to undertake enhanced sustainable development obligations without hurting their economic development goals. Most modern trade agreements do not envisage meaningful supportive or cooperative approaches to assist the developing country partners in their specific needs and requirements, including the assumption of trade-related sustainability obligations. Importantly, most trade agreements do not adequately address the constraints faced by developing countries in integrating with global production networks and accessing global markets. In this context, sustainability considerations should ideally promote inclusive trade aimed at overall economic growth with access to technology solutions, wherever feasible.

[55] Agreement on Fisheries Subsidies, done at Geneva on 17 June 2022, WT/MIN (22)/33 and WT/L/1144.

[56] Mukesh Bhatnagar, 'A Good Catch at the WTO' *The Hindu Business Line* (7 July 2022).

IV. Conclusion

Sustainable development is a universal concept. There is widespread recognition of the SDGs and the need to meet them by 2030, or even earlier. With the increasing threat of climate change, major economies have been committing to achieving carbon neutrality in the long run (for some, by 2050). While governments are increasingly adopting pro-environment policies, with special emphasis on renewable and newer forms of energy, integration of such concerns within trade agreements raises a unique set of challenges, as highlighted in this chapter. The same is true with labour standards. The current perception that TSD provisions in trade agreements are coercive tools to enforce non-trade values or targeted instruments in nullifying the cost advantage of developing economies is unlikely to serve the sustainability cause.

Social clauses in international trade have a unique history, which was always steeped in a divide between the developed and the developing. Meeting SDGs requires a careful, inclusive, and calibrated approach. Compliance with sustainability provisions requires an inner and grounded sense of compliance that cannot be achieved through unilateral approaches or with the use of sanctions or monetary compensation. In other words, sustainable development requires softer approaches, suited to different economies' specific circumstances and abilities (including resource constraints), and can include supportive measures such as building physical and social infrastructure, transfer of technology, building rule of law institutions, and creating a civil society with greater sustainability awareness.

In other words, enforcing sustainability standards without allowing the developing countries to bridge the development gap is unlikely to yield the desired results. While government intervention to prevent market failures is desirable, unlimited state funding for the industries of the future such as green industries can trigger protectionist considerations. On a disappointing note, not all TSD chapters of trade agreements afford sufficient consideration for the notion of economic development. For TSD provisions to flourish, a development-friendly approach tempered with equity is essential.

21

Interactions Between Free Trade Agreements' Sustainability Provisions and WTO Law

Yuka Fukunaga

I. Introduction

Sustainability provisions proliferate in free trade agreements (FTAs) recently adopted by developed countries, particularly the United States and the European Union. Issues covered by these provisions range from environmental issues, such as climate change and fisheries, to social issues, such as labour standards and gender equality.[1] While the majority of FTA sustainability provisions remain 'defensive', in the sense that they allow sustainability policies as an exception to trade rules, the number of 'offensive' sustainability provisions included in FTAs that set sustainable development as a primary goal and use trade as a tool to achieve it is increasing.[2] Both are expected to contribute to efforts to achieve the UN Sustainable Development Goals (SDGs).[3]

Nevertheless, sustainability provisions in FTAs cannot be sufficient in themselves to achieve the SDGs and need to be supplemented by multilateral or plurilateral trade and sustainability instruments, given the need for collective effort on a global scale. In fact, several initiatives have been undertaken in the World Trade Organization (WTO) to multilateralize FTA sustainability provisions. For example, the recent adoption of the Agreement on Fisheries Subsidies (AFS) marked the first positive step towards the multilateralization of FTA sustainability provisions on fisheries management. Moreover, the recently launched Trade and

[1] JB Velut and others, 'Comparative Analysis of Trade and Sustainable Development Provisions in Free Trade Agreements' Trade Policy Hub, LSE Consulting (February 2022) 48–65, 67–96 <https://www.lse.ac.uk/business/consulting/reports/comparative-analysis-of-tsd-provisions-for-identification-of-best-practices> accessed 12 April 2024.

[2] Dominique Blümer and others, 'Environmental Provisions in Trade Agreements: Defending regulatory space or pursuing offensive interests?' (2020) 29 Environmental Politics 866, 875–76. See also Daniel C Esty, *Greening the GATT: Trade, Environment, and the Future* (Peterson Institute for International Economics 1994) 3.

[3] Resolution adopted by the General Assembly on 25 September 2015, 70/1. Transforming Our World: The 2030 Agenda for Sustainable Development, A/RES/70/1 (21 October 2015).

Yuka Fukunaga, *Interactions Between Free Trade Agreements' Sustainability Provisions and WTO Law* In: *The Sustainability Revolution in International Trade Agreements*. Edited by: Geraldo Vidigal and Kathleen Claussen, Oxford University Press.
© Yuka Fukunaga 2024. DOI: 10.1093/9780191994470.003.0021

Environmental Sustainability Structured Discussions (TESSD) address many environmental sustainability issues that are covered in FTAs. While the TESSD is a forum for dialogue and does not seek to adopt binding rules, it could pave the way for negotiations on multilateral or plurilateral sustainability obligations in the WTO.

Some WTO Members question the suitability of the WTO as a trade organization to host discussions and negotiations on sustainability. However, the Preamble to the Marrakesh Agreement Establishing the World Trade Organization (Marrakesh Agreement) explicitly recognizes the importance of sustainable development in the multilateral trading order. In addition, Article XX of the General Agreement on Tariffs and Trade (GATT) has played a central role in reconciling WTO Members' sustainability policies with WTO rules. While neither Article XX of the GATT nor any other WTO provision, except the Preamble to the Marrakesh Agreement, uses the terms 'sustainable development' or 'sustainability', the WTO Agreements have been interpreted and applied in an evolutionary manner in dispute settlement to accommodate sustainability concerns of WTO Members. Some of the interpretative developments of the WTO Agreements have been reflected in FTA sustainability provisions.

This chapter examines interactions between FTA sustainability provisions and WTO sustainability developments. While FTA sustainability provisions cover broad issues, including the environment and labour rights, the chapter focuses on environmental sustainability because WTO sustainability developments are most advanced on environmental issues.[4] The interactions occur in both directions. On the one hand, innovative sustainability provisions agreed upon in FTA negotiations may be later incorporated into WTO law. Although there are only a few successful cases of incorporation so far, they show that FTAs can potentially be regarded as laboratories[5] for multilateral or plurilateral trade and sustainability provisions. The other often underestimated form of interactions happens when WTO dispute settlement practice regarding sustainable development, which has evolved over time, is codified, and is further developed in FTAs.

[4] In the WTO Singapore Ministerial Declaration adopted in December 1996, the WTO Members renewed their 'commitment to the observance of internationally recognized core labour standards' and affirmed their belief that 'economic growth and development fostered by increased trade and further trade liberalization contribute to the promotion of' labour standards. WTO Ministerial Conference, Singapore Ministerial Declaration: Adopted on 13 December 1996, WT/MIN(96)/DEC (18 December 1996) para 4. However, unlike trade and environment, the Declaration did not lead to structured discussions on labour issues. It should be noted though that the Informal Working Group on Trade and Gender (IWG) was established in September 2020, following the Buenos Aires Declaration on Trade and Women's Economic Empowerment, endorsed by 120 WTO Members and 7 observers. The IWG was created to discuss women's participation in international trade and other relevant issues. WTO Interim Report Following the Buenos Aires Joint Declaration on Trade and Women's Economic Empowerment: Revision, WT/L/1095/Rev 1 (25 September 2020).

[5] Lorand Bartels and Federico Ortino, 'Introduction' in Lorand Bartels and Federico Ortino (eds), *Regional Trade Agreements and the WTO Legal System* (OUP 2006) 2.

This chapter begins with a brief review of the jurisprudence developed by WTO panels and the Appellate Body, with a focus on the evolutionary interpretation of Article XX of GATT (section II). It then examines FTA sustainability provisions and argues that some 'defensive' sustainability provisions reflect WTO dispute settlement practice while other 'offensive' sustainability provisions that do not exist in the WTO have been invented in some FTAs (section III). It further discusses how these FTA 'defensive' and 'offensive' sustainability provisions promoted relevant initiatives in the WTO and whether they can constitute building blocks for multilateral or plurilateral sustainability provisions (section IV). It concludes with an assessment (section V).

II. Jurisprudence in WTO Dispute Settlement

A. Overview

A close linkage between trade and sustainability was already implicitly recognized in the Havana Charter for an International Trade Organization,[6] although sustainable development did not exist even as a concept, let alone a principle, at the time of its signing in March 1948. The most notable example of the linkage appeared in Article 7 of the Havana Charter, which provided that 'all countries have a common interest in the achievement and maintenance of fair labour standards related to productivity'. While the Havana Charter never entered into force and the linkage between trade and labour standards is not fully incorporated even in the WTO, its general exception clause, which allowed Member States to take measures relating to environmental sustainability, such as the conservation of exhaustible natural resources, made its way into GATT.

The WTO Agreements, adopted in 1994, two years after the adoption of the Rio Declaration on Environment and Development, took a step further by explicitly acknowledging in Paragraph 1 of the Preamble to the Marrakesh Agreement the need 'to protect and preserve the environment', 'while allowing for the optimal use of the world's resources in accordance with the objective of sustainable development'. Similarly, Paragraph 6 of the Preamble to the Agreement on Technical Barriers to Trade confirms the WTO Members' recognition that 'no country should be prevented from taking measures . . . for the protection of human, animal or plant life or health, of the environment'.

These preambulatory provisions in the WTO Agreements recognizing the importance of sustainability do not transform the WTO into an organization for

[6] United Nations Conference on Trade and Employment, Final Act and Related Documents, UN Doc E/Conf 2/78 (1948) 3.

sustainability. The primary objective of the WTO remains trade liberalization, and sustainability is given a secondary status, often as an exception to trade rules. Measures relating to sustainability are allowed only to the extent that they are designed and applied in accordance with the requirements of the WTO Agreements so that they do not undermine trade liberalization.

Nevertheless, the evolutionary interpretation and application of the WTO Agreements in WTO dispute settlement has succeeded in making WTO law more sustainable than it may appear on the surface.

B. Evolutionary Interpretation

The meaning of a treaty may change over time from when it is concluded. Evolutionary interpretation is a method to interpret a treaty in light of factual and normative developments after the conclusion of the treaty in order to ensure that the treaty remains effective in its object and purpose.[7] This subsection briefly reviews a few cases regarding Article XX of GATT as an example of the evolutionary interpretation of WTO Agreements to incorporate environmental sustainability into WTO law.

The first WTO dispute relating to environmental sustainability was *US—Gasoline*. In this case, a panel found that the US Gasoline Rule setting standards for gasoline quality to reduce air pollution violated Article III:4 of GATT because the Rule accorded less favourable treatment to imported gasoline than to domestic gasoline,[8] and was not justified by Article XX of GATT.[9] The Appellate Body upheld the panel's findings.[10] Nevertheless, the panel's findings that 'clean air' is an 'exhaustible natural resource' in the sense of Article XX(g) of GATT clarified that measures to reduce the depletion of clean air could be justified as long as the conditions in Article XX(g) were met.[11]

In addition, as is well known, the observation made by the Appellate Body in this case that GATT 'is not to be read in clinical isolation from public international law'[12] was critical in confirming the close relationship between WTO law and non-WTO law relating to sustainability. The Appellate Body also noted that the Preamble to the Marrakesh Agreement contains a 'specific

[7] See eg Richard K Gardiner, *Treaty Interpretation* (2nd edn, OUP 2015) 292–95; Isabelle Van Damme, 'Understanding the Choice for Evolutionary Interpretation' in Georges Abi-Saab and others (eds), *Evolutionary Interpretation and International Law* (Hart 2020) 295–98.

[8] Panel Report, *United States—Standards for Reformulated and Conventional Gasoline*, WT/DS2/R, 29 January 1996 paras 6.5–6.16.

[9] ibid paras 6.20–6.41.

[10] Appellate Body Report, *United States—Standards for Reformulated and Conventional Gasoline*, WT/DS2/AB/R, 29 April 1996 13–29.

[11] Panel Report, *US—Gasoline* para 6.37. This issue was not appealed. Appellate Body Report, *US—Gasoline* 11–12.

[12] ibid 17.

acknowledgement' of the 'importance of coordinating policies on trade and the environment', and unequivocally stated that 'WTO Members have a large measure of autonomy to determine their own policies on the environment (including its relationship with trade), their environmental objectives and the environmental legislation they enact and implement'.[13] These statements affirm that the WTO Agreements should be interpreted in conformity with non-WTO environmental agreements.

In *US—Shrimp*, another WTO dispute concerning the US unilateral measures relating to environmental sustainability, the Appellate Body put its words into action by considering non-WTO multilateral environmental agreements (MEAs) in interpreting Article XX of GATT.[14]

In this case, the panel found that the US import ban on shrimp from certain WTO Members to protect sea turtles violated Article XI:1 of GATT and could not be justified by Article XX(g) of GATT. The United States appealed the panel's finding on Article XX(g). The Appellate Body acknowledged that sea turtles were an 'exhaustible natural resource' within the meaning of Paragraph (g) of Article XX, given that all seven recognized species of sea turtles were listed in Appendix 1 of the Convention on International Trade in Endangered Species of Wild Fauna and Flora (CITES) as among the most endangered species.[15] The Appellate Body also noted that Paragraph 1 of the Preamble to the Marrakesh Agreement 'must add colour, texture and shading to our interpretation of the' WTO Agreements, including Article XX of GATT.[16]

In the end, the Appellate Body concluded that the US measure was not justified by Article XX(g) of GATT because the measure was applied in a manner that constitutes arbitrary and unjustifiable discrimination between countries where the same conditions prevail, contrary to the requirements of the chapeau of Article XX.[17] However, three years later, having acknowledged that the United States had taken measures to implement the recommendations by the Dispute Settlement Body (DSB), the Appellate Body found that the application of the US measure met the requirements of Article XX of GATT and that therefore the measure was justified by the provision.[18]

These cases show that, although the text of Article XX of GATT does not explicitly mention environmental sustainability or biodiversity, it has evolved through

[13] ibid 29–30.

[14] See Chapter 13 in this volume.

[15] Appellate Body Report, *United States—Import Prohibition of Certain Shrimp and Shrimp Products*, WT/DS58/AB/R, 12 October 1998 para 132. The Appellate Body also took into account the Rio Declaration on Environment and Development and Agenda 21 to insist that environmental measures should be based on international consensus rather than taken unilaterally. ibid para 168.

[16] ibid paras 152–55.

[17] ibid para 187.

[18] Appellate Body Report, *United States—Import Prohibition of Certain Shrimp and Shrimp Products*, Recourse to Article 21.5 of the DSU by Malaysia, WT/DS58/AB/RW, 22 October 2001, para 154.

interpretation in light of the development of international law on environmental sustainability. In terms of the interpretation of a treaty in the light of another treaty, Article 31(3)(c) of the Vienna Convention on the Law of Treaties (VCLT) provides for the so-called principle of 'systemic integration', which requires that 'any relevant rules of international law applicable in the relations between the parties' *shall* be taken into account in the interpretation of a treaty.[19] The scope of the 'relevant rules of international law' that *shall* be taken into account under this provision may be limited because they have to be applicable to all WTO Members or at least to the parties to a dispute at hand.

However, this does not prevent panels and the Appellate Body from taking into account other rules of international law in the interpretation of the WTO Agreements as context if these rules are 'informative'.[20] In this regard, there is a presumption among international judges that treaty interpretation should avoid or mitigate conflict with other treaties.[21] In fact, panels and the Appellate Body have interpreted WTO Agreements in light of non-WTO international instruments.[22] Moreover, the fact that the importance of environmental sustainability is growing 'adds colour, texture and shading' to the interpretation of WTO Agreements. In some cases, panels and the Appellate Body interpreted and applied Article XX of GATT in a flexible manner to accommodate environmental measures taken by WTO Members, by taking into account sustainable development as an 'object and purpose' of the provision.[23]

As discussed in section III, the evolutionary interpretation of the WTO Agreements in light of environmental sustainability has been reflected in some recently adopted FTAs.

[19] Campbell McLachlan, 'The Principle of Systemic Integration and Article 31(3)(c) of the Vienna Convention' (2005) 54 International and Comparative Law Quarterly 279.

[20] Cf Panel Reports, *European Communities—Measures Affecting the Approval and Marketing of Biotech Products*, WT/DS291/R, WT/DS292/R, WT/DS293/R, 29 September 2006, paras 7.92–7.94.

[21] Fragmentation of International Law: Difficulties Arising from the Diversification and Expansion of International Law, Document A/CN 4/L 682 and Add 1, Report of the Study Group of the International Law Commission, finalized by Mr Martti Koskenniemi, para 37.

[22] See eg Panel Reports, *Australia—Certain Measures Concerning Trademarks, Geographical Indications and Other Plain Packaging Requirements Applicable to Tobacco Products and Packaging*, WT/DS435/R, WT/DS441/R, WT/DS458/R, WT/DS467/R, 28 June 2018, paras 7.412–7.417; Panel Report, *United States—Measures Affecting the Production and Sale of Clove Cigarettes*, WT/DS406/R, 2 September 2011, paras 7.414–7.415; Appellate Body Report, *European Communities—Regime for the Importation, Sale and Distribution of Bananas*, WT/DS27/AB/R, 9 September 1997, para 167.

[23] Marie-Claire Cordonier Segger, *Crafting Trade and Investment Accords for Sustainable Development: Athena's Treaties* (OUP 2021) 129–40.

III. Sustainability Provisions in FTAs

A. Overview

FTAs recently adopted by developed countries often contain provisions recognizing the need to enhance mutual supportiveness between trade and the environment, and to promote environmental sustainability.

For example, the parties to the Comprehensive and Progressive Agreement for Trans-Pacific Partnership (CPTPP) recognize 'the importance of mutually supportive trade and environmental policies and practices to improve environmental protection in the furtherance of sustainable development'[24] and commit to furthering 'the aims of sustainable development, including through mutually supportive trade and environmental policies and practices'.[25] Similarly, the Environment Chapter of the United States–Mexico–Canada Agreement (USMCA), also referred to as CUSMA or T-MEC, provides that the objectives of the Chapter 'are to promote mutually supportive trade and environmental policies and practices; promote high levels of environmental protection and effective enforcement of environmental laws; and enhance the capacities of the Parties to address trade-related environmental issues, including through cooperation, in the furtherance of sustainable development'.[26] The need to ensure and enhance mutual supportiveness between trade and the environment is also recognized in other recently agreed FTAs, such as the Comprehensive Economic and Trade Agreement between Canada and the EU (CETA),[27] the Free Trade Agreement Between the United Kingdom and Australia (UK–Australia FTA),[28] the Trade and Cooperation Agreement between the European Union and the United Kingdom (EU–UK TCA)[29] and the European Union and New Zealand FTA (EU–NZ FTA).[30]

The environmental sustainability provisions included in these FTAs can be categorized into two types. The first is the 'defensive' type. Exception clauses, which allow the parties to adopt environmental sustainability measures as long as certain

[24] Comprehensive and Progressive Agreement for Trans-Pacific Partnership (CPTPP), in force 18 December 2018 art 20.3.1.

[25] ibid Preamble.

[26] Agreement between the United States of America, the United Mexican States, and Canada (USMCA), in force 1 July 2020, art 24.2.2.

[27] Comprehensive Economic and Trade Agreement between Canada and the European Union and its Member States (CETA), provisionally applied 21 September 2017, art 24.4.1.

[28] Free Trade Agreement between Australia and the United Kingdom of Great Britain and Northern Ireland (UK–Australia FTA), in force 31 May 2023, art 22.4.2.

[29] Trade and Cooperation Agreement between the European Union and the European Atomic Energy Community and the United Kingdom of Great Britain and Northern Ireland (EU–UK TCA), in force 1 May 2021, art 400.1.

[30] Free Trade Agreement between the European Union and New Zealand (EU–NZ FTA), in force 1 May 2024 art X.5.1.

conditions are met, can be categorized into this type. The first type of provision not only incorporates Article XX of GATT but also reflects the interpretative development in WTO dispute settlement. The second is the 'offensive' type, which sets environmental sustainability as a primary goal and uses trade as a tool to achieve it. The second type of environmental sustainability provisions cannot be found in WTO law but may be incorporated into WTO law in the future.

The following two subsections discuss these two types respectively.

B. 'Defensive' Environmental Sustainability Provisions

It is common for FTAs to incorporate Article XX of GATT and make part of it mutatis mutandis. In addition, some FTAs add clarification regarding the meaning of Article XX, partly building upon WTO dispute settlement practice. For example, Article 32.1.3 of the USMCA adopts the WTO dispute settlement findings on Article XX(g) of GATT in *US—Shrimp* that the provision applies to measures relating to the conservation of *living* and non-living exhaustible natural resources.[31] It also provides that the 'measures necessary to protect human, animal, or plant life or health' provided in Article XX(b) include *environmental* measures.[32] Moreover, Article 24.19 explicitly regards sea turtles, along with sharks, seabirds, and marine mammals as animals whose long-term conservation the parties shall promote.[33] In relation to the panel's findings in *US—Gasoline* that 'clean air' is an 'exhaustible natural resource',[34] Article 24.11.1 of the USMCA explicitly recognizes that air pollution is a 'serious threat to public health, ecosystem integrity, and sustainable development and contributes to other environmental problems'.[35]

The Appellate Body's endorsement that trade rules do not interfere with the parties' right to regulate environmental matters is also reflected in many FTAs. For example, in the CPTPP, the parties recognize 'the sovereign right of each Party to establish its own levels of domestic environmental protection and its own environmental priorities, and to establish, adopt or modify its environmental laws and policies accordingly'[36] and 'that each Party retains the right to exercise discretion and to make decisions regarding' a wide range of environmental regulatory matters.[37] Similar provisions are included in other FTAs.[38]

[31] See also CPTPP art 29.1.2; UK–Australia FTA art 31.1.2; EU–UK TCA art 412.3(b); EU–NZ FTA ch X, art X.1.3(b); CETA art 28.3.1.

[32] See also CPTPP, art 29.1.2; UK–Australia FTA art 31.1.2; EU–UK TCA art 412.3(a); EU–NZ FTA ch X, art X.1.3(a); CETA, art 28.3.1.

[33] See also CPTPP art 20.16.4; UK–Australia FTA art 22.12.4; EU–NZ FTA ch XX, art X:10.3(c).

[34] See n 11.

[35] See also UK–Australia FTA art 22.9.1.

[36] CPTPP art 20.3.2.

[37] ibid art 20.3.5.

[38] See eg USMCA art 24.3.1; UK–Australia FTA art 22.3.2; EU–NZ FTA ch XX, art X.2.1; CETA art 24.3; EU–UK TCA art 391.1.

In some FTAs, the parties affirm their commitment to implement and comply with the MEAs to which they are party.[39] Occasionally, FTAs refer to specific MEAs, such as CITES,[40] the Montreal Protocol on Substances that Deplete the Ozone Layer,[41] the UN Framework Convention on Climate Change,[42] and the Paris Agreement.[43] A few FTAs confirm that measures taken to comply with MEAs can be justified by a general exception clause. For example, under Article 24.4 of CETA, the parties acknowledge their right to use a general exception clause in relation to measures taken pursuant to MEAs to which they are party. Moreover, Article 400.4 of the EU–UK FTA provides that measures adopted or enforced to implement MEAs may be justified under the exception clause.[44] Article 412.3(c) of the EU–UK FTA goes as far as to specifically mention the parties' understanding that measures taken to implement MEAs can fall under Article XX(b) or Article XX(g) of GATT.[45]

These provisions ensure that the exception clause in the FTAs is interpreted and applied in accordance with relevant MEAs and that the FTAs do not interfere with the parties' right to take measures to implement these agreements. This does not mean that measures that are otherwise inconsistent with an FTA can be justified by the relevant MEAs. Similar to WTO panels and the Appellate Body, an FTA panel reviews measures at issue by interpreting and applying the rules of the relevant FTA, and a justification of measures otherwise inconsistent with FTA rules has to be made based on exception clauses provided in the FTA. Nevertheless, when an FTA explicitly confirms the parties' obligation to imply a specific MEA, that MEA has to be taken into account either as the 'object and purpose' or as the 'context' in the sense of Article 31.1 of the VCLT. Thus, the defensive environmental sustainability provisions of FTAs embody the principle of systemic integration in the sense that FTAs are required to be interpreted in light of MEAs.

In reality, it is unlikely that a dispute concerning environmental measures taken to implement an MEA will be brought to an FTA panel. However, the proliferation of the defensive provisions can have implications for WTO dispute settlement as will be discussed in section IV.B.

[39] See eg CPTPP art 20.4.1; USMCA art 24.8.4; CETA art 24.4; EU–UK TCA art 400.2: EU–NZ FTA ch XX, art X.5.2; UK–Australia FTA art 22.4.1. See Chapter 2 in this volume.

[40] See eg CPTPP art 20.17.2; USMCA art 24.8.4(a); UK–Australia FTA art 22.16.2; EU–UK TCA art 402.1; EU–NZ FTA ch XX, art X.8.1.

[41] See eg USMCA art 24.8.4(b); UK–Australia FTA art 22.8.1; EU–UK TCA art 437; EU–NZ FTA ch XX, art X.6.5.

[42] See eg UK–Australia FTA art 22.5.1; EU–UK TCA art 764.1; EU–NZ FTA ch XX, art X.6.5.

[43] See eg UK–Australia FTA art 22.5.1; EU–UK TCA art 764.1; EU–NZ FTA ch XX, art X.6.5.

[44] See also EU–NZ FTA ch XX, art X.5.4.

[45] See also ibid ch X, art X.1.3(c).

C. 'Offensive' Environmental Sustainability Provisions

FTAs recently adopted by developed countries often include 'offensive' environmental sustainability provisions that set environmental sustainability as a primary goal and use trade as a tool to achieve it. These provisions cover a wide range of subjects. This subsection discusses the following subjects that can potentially be incorporated into WTO law: trade in goods and services; subsidies; and circular economy.

1. Trade in Environmental Goods and Services

FTAs often explicitly recognize the importance of trade liberalization in environmental goods and services. For example, Articles 22.6.1 and 22.6.2 of the UK–Australia FTA provide that the parties recognize the 'importance of trade and investment in environmental goods and services as a means of improving environmental and economic performance, contributing to clean growth, and addressing global environmental challenges', and agree to 'facilitate and promote, as appropriate, trade and investment in environmental goods and services'. Trade liberalization commitments include not only tariffs but also non-tariff barriers.[46] Similar provisions are included in other FTAs.[47]

The European Union has recently unveiled its new position that it will prioritize market access for environmental goods and services, particularly in the area of renewable energy and energy efficiency.[48] This position has materialized in the EU–NZ FTA negotiations, where the parties have eliminated customs duties on environmental goods.[49] Moreover, the parties are required to 'promote and facilitate' trade in environmental goods and services by, for example, awareness-raising actions, information and public education campaigns, and reference to relevant international standards.[50]

One of the challenges in the trade liberalization of environmental goods and services is to define the scope of environmental goods and services. In this regard, a few FTAs specifically provide that trade in goods and services related to combat climate change be facilitated. For example, the EU–NZ FTA provides a non-exhaustive list of products that contribute to mitigating climate change by more efficient use of energy and dissemination of renewable technologies[51] as well as environmental services and manufacturing activities.[52] Article 401.2.(c) of the

[46] UK–Australia FTA art 22.6.3.

[47] See eg CETA art 24.9.1; USMCA art 24.24; CPTPP art 20.18; EU–UK TCA art 400.5(b).

[48] Communication from the Commission to the European Parliament, the Council, the European Economic and Social Committee and the Committee of the Regions: The power of trade partnerships: together for green and just economic growth, Brussels, 22 June 2022, COM(2022) 409 final.

[49] EU–NZ FTA ch XX, art X.11.2.

[50] ibid ch XX, art X.11.4.

[51] ibid ch XX, Annex X10A.

[52] ibid ch XX, Annex X10B.

EU–UK TCA requires the parties to 'facilitate the removal of obstacles to trade and investment in goods and services of particular relevance for climate change mitigation and adaptation, such as renewable energy, energy efficient products and services'. Article 24.9 of CETA requires the parties to 'pay special attention to facilitating the removal of obstacles to trade or investment in goods and services of particular relevance for climate change mitigation and in particular trade or investment in renewable energy goods and related services'.

In September 2019, Costa Rica, Fiji, Iceland, New Zealand, Norway, and Switzerland launched negotiations of an Agreement on Climate Change, Trade and Sustainability (ACCTS), one of the primary objectives of which is to eliminate tariffs on environmental goods and to adopt binding liberalization commitments for environmental services.[53] If agreed, this would be the first agreement to use trade liberalization to take action on climate change and the environment.

These FTA provisions may not immediately lead to multilateral trade liberalization of environmental goods and services but at least complement stalled negotiations in the WTO.

2. Subsidies

FTAs often recognize the importance of sustainable fisheries management.[54] As part of the implementation of such management, some FTAs explicitly prohibit certain fisheries subsidies. For example, Article 20.16.5 of the CPTPP prohibits subsidies to any fishing vessel engaged in illegal, unreported, and unregulated (IUU) fishing as well as subsidies for 'fishing that negatively affect fish stocks that are in an overfished condition'. A similar provision is included in other FTAs, such as the USMCA[55] and the UK–Australia FTA.[56]

A few FTAs, concluded before the adoption of the AFS, anticipate the development of additional disciplines on fisheries subsidies in the WTO. For example, Article 24.20.10 of the USMCA provides that the 'Parties shall work in the WTO towards strengthening international rules on the provision of subsidies to the fisheries sector and enhancing transparency of fisheries subsidies'. CETA does not prohibit fisheries subsidies in any form, but Article 7.4.1(b) recognizes the parties' shared understanding that they will work jointly to reach an agreement to 'help develop a global, multilateral resolution to fisheries subsidies'. Similarly, while the EU–NZ FTA does not prohibit any fisheries subsidies, it provides the parties' acknowledgement of the need for action to end practices relating to fisheries

[53] New Zealand Ministry of Foreign Affairs and Trade, Agreement on Climate Change, Trade and Sustainability (ACCTS) negotiations <https://www.mfat.govt.nz/en/trade/free-trade-agreements/trade-and-climate/agreement-on-climate-change-trade-and-sustainability-accts-negotiations/> accessed 12 April 2024.

[54] See eg USMCA art 24.18.1; Australia–UK FTA art 22.12.3; CPTPP art 20.16.3.

[55] USMCA art 24.20.1.

[56] UK–Australia FTA art 22.12.5.

subsidies that contribute to overcapacity and overfishing[57] and requires the parties to 'work together to strengthen their cooperation on trade-related aspects of fishery and aquaculture policies and measures, bilaterally regionally and in international fora, as appropriate, including in the WTO'.[58] These provisions helped build a shared understanding among FTA parties and laid the groundwork for the adoption of the AFS.

In addition to fisheries subsidies, fossil fuel subsidies may cause social and environmental externalities by distorting trade in renewable energy products and thus need to be disciplined by FTA sustainability provisions. No FTA prohibits harmful fossil fuel subsidies. However, in the EU–NZ FTA, the parties recognize that 'fossil fuel subsidies can distort markets, disadvantage renewable and clean energy, and be inconsistent with the goals of the Paris Agreement', and reaffirm their commitment to work to reform and progressively reduce fossil fuel subsidies.[59] Moreover, ACCTS, currently under negotiation, seeks to adopt disciplines to eliminate harmful fossil fuel subsidies.[60]

3. Circular Economy

The UK–Australia FTA has an innovative provision that recognizes the 'importance of a transition towards a circular economy and the role that waste avoidance and greater resource efficiency can play in reducing pressure on the natural environment, improving resource security, and reducing other associated negative environmental effects arising from the use of materials throughout their lifecycle', and also recognizes the 'role that trade can play in achieving these goals through trade in second-hand goods, end-of-life products, secondary materials, processed waste, as well as trade in related services'.[61] More specifically, it provides that the areas of cooperation between the parties related to the transition to a circular economy include technological innovation related to sustainable plastic packaging and sustainable use of plastics.[62] The parties further acknowledge the 'importance of taking action to prevent and reduce marine litter, including plastics and microplastics, in order to preserve marine and coastal ecosystems, prevent the loss of biodiversity, and mitigate marine litter's costs and impacts',[63] and promise to 'cooperate to address matters of mutual interest with respect to combatting marine litter'.[64]

While no FTAs have an equivalent provision, the EU–NZ FTA provides that cooperation between the parties on trade-related aspects of environmental

[57] EU–NZ FTA ch XX, art X.10.2.
[58] ibid ch XX, art X.10.7.
[59] ibid ch XX, art X.7.2.
[60] NZ Ministry of Foreign Affairs and Trade (n 49).
[61] UK–Australia FTA art 22.7.1.
[62] ibid art 22.7.3.
[63] ibid art 22.11.1.
[64] ibid art 22.11.3.

policies and measures may include 'sharing information on policies and practices to encourage the shift to a circular economy' and 'promoting, including by removing obstacles to trade and investment, initiatives that contribute to a circular economy'.[65] A similar provision is included in the EU–UK TCA.[66]

Although these provisions do not impose a specific obligation on the parties to act, they could work as laboratories for new ideas that can be incorporated into WTO law in the future.

IV. Incorporation into WTO Law?

A. Overview

The importance of environmental sustainability has already been recognized by the WTO Members and acknowledged in WTO instruments. The Preamble to the Marrakesh Agreement attests to the fact that such recognition existed from the establishment of the WTO. The Doha Ministerial Declaration reaffirms the members' 'commitment to the objective of sustainable development' and endorses mutual supportiveness between the aim of 'upholding and safeguarding an open and non-discriminatory multilateral trading system' and that of 'acting for the protection of the environment and the promotion of sustainable development'.[67] However, such recognition did not result in any binding commitments by the WTO Members until recently.

The efforts to ensure mutual supportiveness between trade and environmental sustainability intensified after the TESSD was launched in November 2020, when 50 WTO Members expressed their 'intention to collaborate, prioritize and advance discussions on trade and environmental sustainability' to 'complement and support the work of the Committee on Trade and Environment (CTE) and other relevant WTO Committees and Bodies'.[68] The first meeting of the TESSD was held on 5 March 2021.[69] In a Ministerial Statement on Trade and Environmental Sustainability adopted in December 2021, the participating members agreed to launch discussions on, among others, trade-related measures that contribute to climate and environmental goals and commitments, trade in environmental goods

[65] EU–NZ FTA ch XX, art X.5.5(a).

[66] EU–UK TCA art 400.5(a).

[67] Ministerial Declaration adopted on 14 November 2001, WT/MIN(01)/DEC/1, 20 November 2001.

[68] Communication on Trade and Environmental Sustainability, WT/CTE/W/249, 17 November 2020.

[69] WTO Trade and Environmental Sustainability Structured Discussions: Meeting Held on 5 March 2021: Informal summary by the Coordinators, INF/TE/SSD/R/1, 15 March 2021.

and services, subsidies, and the circular economy.[70] The discussions on these subjects are partly inspired by the development of the offensive and defensive FTA sustainability provisions. As of today, 74 WTO Members are participating in the TESSD, co-coordinated by Canada and Costa Rica.

While it is premature to predict what these discussions will bring and whether they will succeed in multilateralizing or plurilateralizing FTA sustainability provisions, the road ahead is undoubtedly full of challenges that make interactions difficult particularly with respect to 'offensive' ones.

One of the greatest challenges is perhaps the divide between developed and developing WTO Members. 'Offensive' sustainability provisions have been developed in FTAs that were adopted between developed countries. Developing countries are generally reluctant to undertake broader and deeper obligations in trade agreements and are also concerned that sustainability objectives can be used as a pretext to take protectionist measures.[71]

Another challenge is differences among developed members. While developed countries have shared interest in the promotion of sustainability, their approaches to it in FTAs are not identical. They may find it difficult to find common ground in the efforts to multilateralize or plurilateralize FTA 'offensive' sustainability provisions.[72]

There may also be a claim that environmental sustainability should be addressed elsewhere and should not be given priority in the WTO.[73] While it is neither accurate nor appropriate to regard the WTO as an organization dealing exclusively with trade matters,[74] its existing rules and institutions were primarily designed to ensure an open, fair, and non-discriminatory trading environment. The increasing importance of environmental sustainability in the WTO does not transform the trade organization into an environmental organization.

The following subsections review multilateral and plurilateral initiatives on environmental sustainability in the WTO and discuss whether and how FTA environmental sustainability provisions have influenced and could continue to influence them.

[70] Trade and Environmental Sustainability Structured Discussions (TESSD) Ministerial Statement on Trade and Environmental Sustainability: Revision, WT/MIN(21)/6/Rev 2, 14 December 2021.

[71] Peter Draper, Nkululeko Khumalo, and Faith Tigere, 'Sustainability Provisions in Regional Trade Agreements: Can they be Multilateralised?' RTA Exchange: Overview Paper (July 2017) 30–31 <https://www.tralac.org/images/docs/11916/sustainability-provisions-in-rtas-can-they-be-multilateralised-rta-exchange-overview-paper-july-2017.pdf> accessed 12 April 2024.

[72] Sophie Meunier and Kalypso Nicolaïdis, 'The European Union as a Conflicted Trade Power,' (2006) 13 Journal of European Public Policy 906, 911–12.

[73] Brett Fortnam, 'At Reform Retreat, WTO Members Stick to Well-Established Positions' (*Inside Trade* 11 November 2022).

[74] See section II.A.

B. 'Defensive' Environmental Sustainability

Trade-related measures taken to protect the environment have provoked several trade disputes, including high-profile ones, as discussed in section II. As the need to address environmental problems, particularly climate change, becomes more urgent, more WTO Members will take trade-related measures to combat climate change, which will provoke more trade disputes. Some WTO Members in particular have raised a concern that a Carbon Border Adjustment Mechanism (CBAM), proposed by the European Union,[75] may be inconsistent with Articles I and III of GATT[76] and not justified by Article XX, although the European Union maintains that the CBAM is carefully designed to ensure its WTO compatibility.[77]

In order to ensure that trade rules do not prevent WTO Members from taking climate measures, such as a carbon border adjustment measure, it may be ideal to amend the WTO Agreements. Alternatively, the WTO Members may agree on a climate waiver to exempt certain climate measures from the WTO obligations for a limited period of time.[78] However, an amendment or a waiver requires consensus of the WTO Members, which is extremely difficult given the current divergence of views among them.

This does not mean that trade-related climate measures cannot be taken under the current WTO law. As highlighted in section II.B, WTO Agreements, particularly Article XX of GATT, have been interpreted in an evolutionary manner to accommodate environmental measures taken by WTO Members. Evolutionary interpretation enables the interpretation of Article XX of GATT to reflect the fact that the increasing number of FTAs insist on mutual supportiveness between trade and environmental sustainability and require the parties to comply with their international commitments regarding climate change as part of the object and purpose and the context of the provision. In other words, the development of FTA environmental sustainability provisions can be seen as informative evidence regarding at least some WTO Members' intent as to the meaning of Article XX.

There is a potential issue of whether a trade-related climate measure taken based on an FTA 'offensive' sustainability provision can be justified by Article XX of GATT when such measure is applied in a discriminatory manner against non-FTA WTO Members. For example, a mutual recognition scheme of circular products

[75] European Commission, Proposal for a Regulation of the European Parliament and of the Council Establishing a Carbon Border Adjustment Mechanism, COM (2021) 564 final, 14 July 2021.

[76] Ilaria Espa, 'Reconciling the Climate/Industrial Interplay of CBAMs: What Role for the WTO?' (2022) 116 American Journal of International Law Unbound 202–03, 208.

[77] Chiara Galiffa and Ignacio Garcia Bercero, 'How WTO-Consistent Tools can Ensure the Decarbonization of Emission-Intensive Industrial Sectors' (2022) 116 American Journal of International Law Unbound 196, 198–99; Michael A Mehling and others, 'Designing Border Carbon Adjustments for Enhanced Climate Action' (2019) 113 American Journal of International Law 432, at 465–70.

[78] James Bacchus, *Trade Links: New Rules for a New World* (OUP 2022) 187–96.

between FTA parties could have a restrictive impact on trade with non-FTA parties. The question comes down to whether the discriminatory application is arbitrary or unjustifiable contrary to the chapeau of Article XX.[79] It has to be answered on a case-by-case basis in the light of the circumstances of a specific case, but the fact that a measure is taken based on an FTA can be considered to suggest the absence of arbitrariness or the justifiability of the measure.[80]

C. 'Offensive' Environmental Sustainability Provisions

The incorporation of 'offensive' environmental sustainability provisions into the WTO is more difficult for the reasons stated in the beginning of this section. However, they have stimulated discussions on mutual supportiveness in the WTO, which may lead to tangible outcomes in the future.

1. Trade in Environmental Goods and Services

Trade liberalization in environmental goods and services is one of the priorities in the TESSD, but it is not a new agenda in the WTO.

The multilateral negotiations on trade liberalization in environmental goods and services date back to 2002, when the Special Session of the Committee on Trade and Environment commenced its work.[81] In 2014, the plurilateral negotiations on the Environmental Goods Agreement was also launched.[82] Both initiatives failed to produce any results. One of the principal reasons for this failure was the absence of the agreed identification of environmental goods and services.[83]

It may be expected that the development of FTA sustainability provisions will help break the deadlock, but FTAs are no more successful than multilateral or plurilateral negotiations in identifying environmental goods and services. While some FTAs recognize the importance of trade liberalization in environmental goods and services generally, most fail to identify the scope of environmental goods and services. The EU–NZ FTA is exceptional in identifying products that

[79] Appellate Body Report, *US—Shrimp* para 187.

[80] Conversely, if a measure is applied in a discriminatory manner and not based on an FTA, the discriminatory application may be considered as arbitrary or unjustifiable. ibid paras 169–73.

[81] Summary Report on the First Meeting of the Committee on Trade and Environment Special Session: 22 March 2002: Note by the Secretariat, TN/TE/R/1, 19 April 2002. The multilateral negotiations on trade liberalization in services had started in 2000 as part of the build-in agenda pursuant to Article XIX of the General Agreement on Trade in Services (GATS). Council for Trade in Services Special Session: Report of the Meeting Held on 26 May 2000: Note by the Secretariat, S/CSS/M/3, 26 June 2000, para 148.

[82] WTO, Environmental Goods Agreement <https://www.wto.org/english/tratop_e/envir_e/ega_e.htm> accessed 12 April 2024.

[83] Trade and Environmental Sustainability Structured Discussions (TESSD): Experiences in the Promotion and Facilitation of Environmental Goods and Services: Note by the Secretariat, INF/TE/SSD/W/18, 23 March 2022, paras 2.18–2.25.

contribute to mitigate climate change. ACCTS may become another example if it is successfully concluded.

Considering the limited success in trade liberalization in goods and services even under FTAs, it is probably premature to expect WTO Members to launch negotiations on trade in environmental goods and services. Nevertheless, the continued FTA negotiations as well as the exchange of information on these could help WTO Members identify tariff and non-tariff barriers to trade in environmental goods and services.

2. Subsidies

The multilateral negotiations on fisheries subsidies reached a small but significant milestone by adopting the AFS at the 12th Ministerial Conference in June 2022,[84] which prohibits subsidies to 'a vessel or operator engaged in IUU fishing or fishing related activities in support of IUU fishing'[85] or 'for fishing or fishing related activities regarding an overfished stock'.[86] Although not explicitly mentioned, the AFS was adopted with a view to achieving Goals 14.4[87] and 14.6[88] of the UN SDGs concerning the conservation and sustainable use of the oceans, seas, and marine resources for sustainable development. In addition, the adoption of the AFS was facilitated by the development of international regulations on IUU fishing.

While the AFS successfully incorporates some of the disciplines on fisheries subsidies in FTAs, as discussed in section II.C, the failure of the WTO Members to agree to prohibit subsidies that contribute to overcapacity and overfishing reflects the lack of FTA disciplines on these subsidies. The difficulty of adopting such disciplines even in FTAs implies the difficulties of future multilateral negotiations in the WTO. Nevertheless, when adopting the AFS, the WTO Members agreed to continue negotiations to 'achieve a comprehensive agreement on fisheries subsidies, including through further disciplines on certain forms of fisheries subsidies that contribute to overcapacity and overfishing'.[89] The continued efforts in the WTO could produce outcomes in either multilateral or regional negotiations.

[84] Agreement on Fisheries Subsidies, Ministerial Decision of 17 June 2022, WT/MIN(22)/33, WT/L/1144, 22 June 2022.

[85] ibid art 3.1.

[86] ibid art 4.1.

[87] 'By 2020, effectively regulate harvesting and end overfishing, illegal, unreported and unregulated fishing and destructive fishing practices and implement science-based management plans, in order to restore fish stocks in the shortest time feasible, at least to levels that can produce maximum sustainable yield as determined by their biological characteristics.'

[88] 'By 2020, prohibit certain forms of fisheries subsidies which contribute to overcapacity and overfishing, eliminate subsidies that contribute to illegal, unreported and unregulated fishing and refrain from introducing new such subsidies, recognizing that appropriate and effective special and differential treatment for developing and least developed countries should be an integral part of the World Trade Organization fisheries subsidies negotiation.' Footnote 16 to this paragraph states: 'Taking into account ongoing World Trade Organization negotiations, the Doha Development Agenda and the Hong Kong ministerial mandate.'

[89] Ministerial Decision on AFS (n 84) 1.

Another category of subsidies that may require disciplines is fossil fuel subsidies. In this regard, while no FTAs prohibit fossil fuel subsidies, Chapter XX, Article X.7 of the EU–NZ FTA requires the parties to 'work together and encourage the other WTO Members to advance the reform and pursue new fossil fuel subsidy disciplines in the WTO'.

In fact, 45 WTO Members, including the European Union, New Zealand, and the other ACCTS parties, issued a ministerial statement on fossil fuel subsidies in December 2021.[90] The sponsor members 'seek the rationalization and phase out of inefficient fossil fuel subsidies' while taking 'fully into account the specific needs and conditions of developing countries'.[91] The first meeting of the work plan of the Fossil Fuel Subsidy Reform initiative held in October 2022 was focused on the exchange of information and improvement of transparency, but the initiative aims at 'achieving ambitious and effective multilateral disciplines' on inefficient fossil fuel subsidies.[92]

However, unlike IUU fishing, there is no international instrument that prohibits the use of fossil fuel subsidies. Glasgow Climate Pact, adopted in 2021, merely requires the parties to the Paris Agreement to accelerate efforts towards the 'phase-out of inefficient fossil fuel subsidies'.[93] Considering that disciplines of FTAs and other international instruments on fossil fuel subsidies are limited, the likelihood of WTO Members agreeing on new rules on fossil fuel subsidies is extremely slim.

3. Circular Economy

Trade-related aspects of the plastic pollution have been discussed in the CTE since 1995, but the discussion has intensified since the Informal Dialogue on Plastic Pollution and Environmentally Sustainable Plastics Trade (IDP) was launched in July 2021 to 'explore how improved trade cooperation, within the rules and mechanisms of the WTO, could contribute to domestic, regional and global efforts to reduce plastics pollution and transition to a more circular and environmentally sustainable global plastics economy'.[94] In the Ministerial Statement on Plastic Pollution and Environmentally Sustainable Plastics Trade, the members

[90] Ministerial Statement on Fossil Fuel Subsidies: Revision, WT/MIN(21)/9/Rev 1, 14 December 2021.

[91] ibid para 8.

[92] WTO, First meeting on fossil fuel subsidy reform held at WTO in follow-up to MC12 (*WTO News* 3 October 2022) <https://www.wto.org/english/news_e/news22_e/ffsr_03oct22_e.htm> accessed 12 April 2024.

[93] Report of the Conference of the Parties serving as the meeting of the Parties to the Paris Agreement on its third session, held in Glasgow from 31 October to 13 November 2021, Addendum: Part two: Action taken by the Conference of the Parties serving as the meeting of the Parties to the Paris Agreement at its third session, FCCC/PA/CMA/2021/10/Add.1.

[94] WTO Informal Dialogue on Plastics Pollution and Environmentally Sustainable Plastics Trade: Communication from Australia, Barbados, Cabo Verde, Canada, Central African Republic, China, Costa Rica, Ecuador, Fiji, The Gambia, Jamaica, Kazakhstan, Morocco, New Zealand, Switzerland, Thailand, and United Kingdom: Revision, WT/CTE/W/250/Rev 1, 26 July 2021.

participating in the IDP reached a further shared understanding to intensify their work on areas of common interest by exchanging information and sharing experiences.[95]

The dialogue and exchange of information involve other relevant international organizations, such as the UN Environment Programme and the World Customs Organization, as well as stakeholders.[96] As in the case of FTA provisions on circular economy, the dialogue is not meant to produce binding commitments. However, given the importance of promoting a circular economy on a global scale, the dialogue in the multilateral settings is expected to enhance transparency.

V. Conclusion

This chapter discusses how FTA sustainability provisions and WTO law interact and potentially cross-fertilize each other.

In terms of 'defensive' sustainability provisions, Article XX of GATT has been interpreted and applied in an evolutionary manner in WTO dispute settlement, which has then been incorporated into FTAs and further developed with the clarification of the relationship between trade rules and MEAs. The clarified 'defensive' provisions in FTAs can be taken into account as the context in the interpretation of Article XX in future WTO disputes concerning measures to promote sustainability.

'Offensive' sustainability provisions have been developed principally in FTAs. Nevertheless, most are voluntary in the sense that the FTA parties are simply encouraged to cooperate in promoting mutual supportiveness between trade and sustainability by, for example, liberalizing trade in environmental goods and services, adopting disciplines on fisheries and fossil fuel subsidies, and exchanging information on the circular economy. The development of the FTA 'offensive' provisions has provoked dialogues and discussions in the WTO, which will not result in any binding rules in the near future but is expected to facilitate the shared understanding of the need for mutual supportiveness between trade and sustainability among the WTO Members.

[95] WTO Informal Dialogue on Plastic Pollution and Environmentally Sustainable Plastics Trade (IDP): Ministerial Statement on Plastic Pollution And Environmentally Sustainable Plastics Trade: Revision, WT/MIN(21)/8/Rev 2, 10 December 2021, para 1.

[96] See eg Dialogue on Plastics Pollution and Environmentally Sustainable Plastics Trade: Pre-Plenary Meeting Held on 19–20 September 2022: Aide Memoire by the Facilitators, INF/TE/IDP/R/7, 5 October 2022.

22

Sustainability Meets Trade

Assessing Trade Agreements' New Endeavour to Incorporate Sustainability Issues

Jaemin Lee

I. Introduction

In recent years, trade agreements have begun conducting various new experiments. They are expanding their scope of coverage to new areas. Some of them concern novel issues that the global community has not dealt with before such as digital trade and cross-border data flow. Others concern existing issues that have not been covered by conventional free trade agreements (FTAs) such as labour, environment, human rights, competition, and small and medium enterprises. Among the various issues falling in the second category, labour and environment were taken up by some states early on under the title of 'sustainable development', 'sustainable trade', 'sustainability', or other similar variations. Its meaning came from the notion that trade liberalization sought in a trade agreement needs to be balanced with comparable undertakings in labour and environment in order for the 'liberalization' objective to remain 'sustainable'. As such, stand-alone chapters on sustainability have started to emerge. Over the years, these chapters have now become one of the core components of modern trade agreements.

The 'sustainability' incorporation initiative and the adoption of separate chapters for this cause have turned out to be an important achievement. They have expanded the scope of trade agreements beyond market liberalization and ensured a level playing field in trade by harmonizing labour and environmental standards among different countries. Most importantly, this development has achieved what other international organizations and treaties have arguably been encountering difficulties with, thereby contributing to the fulfilment of their objectives and ultimately spreading the rule of law in these critical areas of global concern.

At the same time, the new endeavour has also posed challenges and raised problems of various sorts. It has further pushed the envelope of trade agreements already struggling with various conventional trade topics at a time when protectionism and unilateralism are on the rise. It has also brought into trade agreements issues that are not fully elaborated or fine-tuned in underlying treaties and agreements covering sustainability issues such as labour and environment. It has further

Jaemin Lee, *Sustainability Meets Trade* In: *The Sustainability Revolution in International Trade Agreements*.
Edited by: Geraldo Vidigal and Kathleen Claussen, Oxford University Press. © Jaemin Lee 2024.
DOI: 10.1093/9780191994470.003.0022

exposed trade agreements to yet another uncharted territory filled with controversial and sensitive subjects. The question now for sustainability issues in trade agreements therefore is how to amplify their contribution and overcome attendant challenges.

This chapter is structured as follows. Section II analyses the contributions and limitations of the sustainability initiative in trade agreements. It then conducts an overall assessment and concludes that the current development to incorporate sustainability issues into trade agreements is indeed a welcome move. Section III then suggests a future course of action so as to expedite and streamline the new incorporation. Finally, section IV concludes.

II. Assessment of the Sustainability Issues in Trade Agreements—Contributions and Limitations

The incorporation of sustainability issues in a trade agreement is not a recent phenomenon; the North American Free Trade Agreement opened the door as early as 1992. Over the years, however, sustainability issues have evolved in subsequent trade agreements. They have come to cover not only trade-related aspects of sustainability to ensure a level playing field but also other critical issues of global concern. While the former function has always been a fundamental objective of sustainability issues in trade agreements, it is the latter newly introduced function that constitutes a notable change in recent trade agreements.

This novel attempt has elevated trade agreements to serve as a new legal vehicle to achieve a variety of critical objectives in the global community extending beyond trade liberalization and market opening. Most importantly, these 'enhanced' sustainability-equipped trade agreements have made contracting parties alert to their obligations in other treaties and agreements that originally regulate these issues involving sustainability. In doing so, they have lent critical assistance to the international organizations in charge of those treaties and agreements comprising underlying obligations. They have also provided a suite of dispute settlement proceedings to resolve disputes relating to underlying obligations and enforce such obligations.

Noteworthy contributions notwithstanding, 'enhanced' sustainability endeavours have also exposed some inherent limitations of this experimentation. For instance, ambiguous texts and insufficient logistical arrangements have rendered the administration of sustainability chapters a challenging task. Additionally, despite a strong linkage in substantive matters, cooperation and coordination with relevant international organizations have not been necessarily optimal.

A. Contributions

Contributions of the sustainability incorporation schemes may be classified as follows: (i) fostering the rule of law; (ii) ensuring a level playing field; (iii) expanding the scope of trade agreements; (iv) facilitating fulfilment of legal obligations of other treaties; and (v) harmonizing laws and regulations.

1. Fostering Rule of Law

The most important contribution of the sustainability incorporation project is the global spread and permeation of the rule of law in critical areas of global concern. Labour, environment, human rights, and corporate social responsibility are all important tasks, being handled by international organizations and various legal instruments. These organizations and instruments, however, have not featured reliable dispute settlement or enforcement mechanisms, making their authority and relevant legal obligations largely abstract and remote. The incorporation of these issues into trade agreements has changed this traditional shortcoming: sustainability issues are now capable of being reviewed and enforced through the dispute settlement mechanism of trade agreements. This process has fostered the rule of law at a global level. Due to the new trade agreements with sustainability chapters, states now feel pressure to abide by their existing legal obligations, established in other treaties and agreements, more faithfully and promptly than before.

Different sustainability chapters adopt different formulas. However, the specific formulas these chapters adopt are not particularly significant. To varying degrees, they arguably contribute to strengthening the rule of law in one way or another. Sometimes even with a narrow and limited scope, sustainability chapters nonetheless can contribute to fostering the rule of law.

For instance, the sustainability-related chapters under the United States–Mexico–Canada Agreement (USMCA) introduce a facility-specific labour dispute settlement proceeding.[1] Its Chapter 31 Annex A on Facility-Specific Rapid-Response Labour Mechanism applies to specific manufacturing facilities in Mexico where bilateral trade implication is clear and robust.[2] This scheme of USMCA shows the traditional US approach to sustainability issues where the 'trade-related' trigger is underscored. Only the facilities that may affect US trade interests directly are arguably listed for special dispute settlement mechanisms

[1] The USMCA does not have a sustainability chapter, but it has a Labour Chapter, an Environment Chapter, and a Rapid Response Labor Mechanism in the Dispute Settlement Chapter; Office of the United States Trade Representative, 'Chapter 31 Annex A; Facility-Specific Rapid-Response Labor Mechanism' <https://ustr.gov/issue-areas/enforcement/dispute-settlement-proceedings/fta-dispute-settlement/usmca/chapter-31-annex-facility-specific-rapid-response-labor-mechanism> accessed 15 April 2024; Geraldo Vidigal, 'Regional Trade Adjudication and the Rise of Sustainability Disputes: *Korea–Labor Commitments* and *Ukraine–Wood Export Bans*', International Decisions (2022) 116(3) American Journal of International Law 569.

[2] ibid 570.

under sustainability chapters. While the dispute settlement proceeding of the USMCA Sustainability Chapter has quite a narrow scope, it still stands to advance the rule of law within the stipulated narrow scope.

Similarly, it can be argued that a sustainability chapter—if it exists in a stand-alone format separate from other chapters of a trade agreement—is interpreted and applied independent of other chapters and provisions of the trade agreement. Under the circumstances, it may be said that such a stand-alone chapter, in and of itself, does not affect bilateral trade or trade obligations under other chapters of trade agreements, setting the tone for the separateness and independence of the sustainability chapter. For instance, *Ukraine—Export Prohibitions on Wood Products* clarifies the independent and limited nature of the scope of sustainability chapters.[3] While the panel underscored the significance of the sustainability chapter of the trade agreement at issue, it reached a conclusion that the chapter is not intended to exert any consequences for the parties' trade obligations.[4] While the decision is highly fact-specific and a different panel may reach a different conclusion in the future, here again, one could posit that the narrow reading of the scope notwithstanding, sustainability chapters still help advance the rule of law within the limited scope.

2. Ensuring a Level Playing Field

Secondly, sustainability chapters have helped ensure a level playing field in global trade. Fast globalization has further increased the benefit of taking advantage of low labour, environmental, or human rights obligations. These benefits are not properly captured or regulated by existing provisions of conventional trade agreements, where the focus is placed on the final product or service as opposed to the process or societal circumstances surrounding the life cycles of the product or service. Sustainability chapters stand to address this loophole in conventional trade agreements. They play the role of mitigating unfair competition in the market flowing from the wide disparity in labour, environment, and other critical societal values.[5]

This understanding of the contribution of sustainability chapters is not necessarily linked to the ongoing debates on whether sustainability chapters should be confined to trade-related aspects or applied more broadly. In both instances, the inclusion of sustainability chapters may affect the behaviour of contracting parties in a direction desired by relevant international legal instruments, which would then

[3] Integrated Executive Summary of the European Union, to the Arbitration Panel established pursuant to Article 306 of the Association Agreement between the European Union and the European Atomic Energy and their Member States and Ukraine in the dispute Ukraine–Export Prohibitions on Wood Products (Brussels, 7 October 2020) <https://circabc.europa.eu/rest/download/f827aca5-9de0-42ac-99ca-a1f3a4b15bdd> accessed 15 April 2024.

[4] Vidigal (n 1) 577.

[5] Kateřina Hradilová and Ondřej Svoboda, (2018) 52(6) 'Sustainable Development Chapters in the EU Free Trade Agreements: Searching for Effectiveness' Journal of World Trade 1021.

lead to changes in measures, which would in turn affect the trade they conduct. In this process, the playing field is going to be levelled over time.[6] Accordingly, sustainability chapters help introduce fairer trade between contracting parties.

3. Expanding the Scope of Trade Agreements

From the perspective of a trade agreement, one noteworthy contribution of the sustainability chapter is that it has expanded the scope of the agreements. Conventional subjects of trade agreements such as tariff reductions, customs classifications, and trade remedies are still important today, but subjects that affect the trade interest of a state have become far wider and broader than before. Without addressing these issues thoroughly, a trade agreement could not be said to offer a reliable balancing scale of competing trade interests of contracting parties. At the same time, trade agreements are not merely trade-specific instruments but may rather operate as a legal vehicle to address issues of mutual or global concern. In a sense, trade agreements might be understood as a global 'public good'. On both counts, the expansion of the scope and coverage of trade agreements is a welcome move. The new endeavour seen in the Indo-Pacific Economic Framework for Prosperity negotiations seems to present both aspects of the expansive scope of a trade agreement well.

This being the case, trade agreements' incorporation of such subjects as environmental conservation, labour rights, indigenous peoples' rights, and gender equality through sustainability chapters[7] would help ensure the legitimacy and relevance of trade agreements in the fast-changing global trade and economic landscapes. Enhanced legitimacy and relevance of trade agreements may also help strengthen stakeholders' confidence in the global trading regime and multilateralism.

4. Facilitating Fulfilment of Legal Obligations in Other Treaties

Another critical contribution of the sustainability endeavour relates to the facilitation for the fulfilment of the legal obligation in other treaties and agreements such as International Labour Organization (ILO) conventions and related instruments for labour issues, and multilateral environmental agreements for environmental issues.[8] Needless to say, these other treaties and agreements all pursue critical objectives in diverse areas of international concern. More often than not, these other instruments are not so well equipped with procedural tools to explore outstanding issues and resolve disputes. Sustainability chapters with their dialogue, consultation, mediation, and arbitration schemes provide platforms for states to address this chronic problem. Whether binding or non-binding, these diverse procedural

[6] Vidigal (n 1) 577.

[7] ibid 568.

[8] Anna-Alexandra Marhold, 'Externalising Europe's Energy Policy in EU Free Trade Agreements: A Cognitive Dissonance between Promoting Sustainable Development and Ensuring Security of Supply?' (2019) 3(1) Europe and the World: A Law Review 7.

platforms respectively impose pressure, though with varying degrees and nature, on states so that they are either incentivized or forced to fulfil their relevant obligation.

In that respect, it would be fair to say that sustainability chapters' procedural features are filling the loophole of these other legal instruments. Increased attention and alertness to these instruments ensure that international organizations carry out their mandates more efficiently and faithfully than before. The increasing support for various treaties, agreements, and international organizations is a critical contribution of the sustainability chapters.

5. Harmonizing Laws and Regulations

Sustainability chapters have also advanced the harmonization of domestic laws and regulations of contracting parties in the areas covered by the chapters. Sustainability issues are usually heavily interrelated and interlocked with domestic implementation through laws and regulations and their effective enforcement. Ongoing dialogue between contracting parties featured in sustainability chapters enhances the harmonization of domestic laws and regulation and enforcement schemes. Contracting parties can compare experiences, exchange views, and iron out differences through the various vehicles contained in sustainability chapters.

In the *Republic of Korea—Compliance with Obligations under Article 13.4(3) of the EU—Korea* FTA case (*Korea—Labour Commitments*),[9] the panel opined that the sustainability chapter of the FTA constitutes one of the core components of the agreement.[10] The obligation to respect the principle of freedom of association of workers and the obligation to make continued and sustained efforts towards ratifying the fundamental conventions of the ILO were both stipulated in Article 13.4.3. of the sustainability chapter of the FTA.[11] In this proceeding, Korea was of the view that these commitments would only be violated if infringements upon labour rights or environmental conservation were proven to be 'trade-related.'[12] The panel, however, interpreted the scope of the provision differently. The provision does explicitly limit the chapter's commitments to 'trade-related aspects' of labour

[9] Report of the Panel of Experts, *Panel of Experts Proceeding Constituted Under Article 13.15 of the EU–Korea Free Trade Agreement*, 20 January 2021; ;Panel of Experts Proceeding Constituted under Article 13.15 of the EU–Korea Free Trade Agreement, 'Republic of Korea—Compliance with Obligations under Article 13.4(3) of the EU–Korea FTA', Oral Statement by the European Union (1 October 2020) <https://circabc.europa.eu/ui/group/09242a36-a438-40fd-a7af-fe32e36cbd0e/library/a3a556dd-f15b-4e3d-869b-6e793896d96a/details> accessed 15 April 2024. It should be noted that the author participated in the panel proceeding as one of the three panellists.

[10] Vidigal (n 1) 568; Panel of Experts Proceeding Constituted Under Article 13.15 of the EU–Korea FTA Report (n 9) para 95; Investment Treaty News, 'The "Trade-Related" Conundrum of the EU–Korea FTA Expert Panel: Are FTAs a Novel Forum to Enforce Sustainable Development Goals?' (7 October 2021) <https://www.iisd.org/itn/en/2021/10/07/the-trade-related-conundrum-of-the-eu-korea-fta-expert-panel-are-ftas-a-novel-forum-to-enforce-sustainable-development-goals/> accessed 15 April 2024.

[11] Vidigal (n 1) 573.

[12] Report of the Panel of Experts (n 9) paras 55, 61.

and environmental issues, but this provision is qualified with the proviso '[e]xcept as otherwise provided'. In other words, if there are issues that are otherwise provided in a chapter, they fall under the scope of that chapter even if they are not directly 'trade-related'.

Furthermore, in this respect, the panel held that, unlike other provisions in the sustainability chapter, Article 13.4.3 requires the parties to incorporate certain principles 'in their laws and practices' rather than referring solely and narrowly to trade.[13] Thus, the reference to 'laws and practices' of contracting parties was found to be a triggering point for determining the scope of the chapter to be extended beyond trade. This case therefore indicates the essential role of sustainability chapters as a catalyst for the harmonization of domestic laws and regulations in areas of sustainability. Moreover, the case arguably indicates that this harmonization can be achieved even without a binding dispute settlement mechanism: that is, 'naming and shaming' can do the trick if pursued systematically with evidence and results on record as stipulated in the sustainability chapter.[14]

B. Limitations

The short experience of the sustainability chapters in trade agreements has also presented inherent limitations. The significant contributions of sustainability chapters should be viewed together with these limitations. The predominant limitations of sustainability chapters identified are: (i) exposing trade agreements to controversial subjects; (ii) insufficient cooperation with other international organizations; (iii) logistical burdens and limited resources; (iv) textual ambiguity; and (v) enforcement of decisions from dispute settlement proceedings.

1. Exposing Trade Agreements to Controversial Subjects

With the weakening of multilateralism and the authority of the World Trade Organization (WTO), trade agreements are arguably thinly stretched and struggle with their own trust deficit. Under these circumstances, the expansion of the scope of trade agreements into sustainability issues may place an additional burden on them. It should be noted that sustainability issues are controversial in and of themselves as much as they are important because they touch upon the sovereignty of a state.

For instance, the panel's rationale in *Korea–Labour Commitments* is sometimes subject to critical review.[15] In interpreting Article 13.4.3 of the FTA between the

[13] Vidigal (n 1) 573–74.

[14] María J García, 'Sanctioning Capacity in Trade and Sustainability Chapters in EU Trade Agreements: The EU-Korea Case' (2022) 10 Politics and Governance 64.

[15] Vidigal (n 1) 574.

European Union and the Republic of Korea, which provides that '[t]he Parties will make continued and sustained efforts towards ratifying the fundamental ILO Conventions as well as other Conventions that are classified as "up-to-date" by the ILO', the panel found an intrinsic connection between sustainability commitments on the one hand and the parties' agreement to trade liberalization on the other hand.[16] As such, the panel's view was that the European Union as the complainant was not required to demonstrate the connection between the breach of sustainability commitment and impact on international trade.[17] The panel's reading of the provision has been judged to be excessively broad, making trade-related components in the text inutile. This conclusion of the panel seems inevitable given the language in the text stating 'unless otherwise provided in this chapter'. That said, this rationale of the panel potentially opens the door to the FTA for all matters relating to fundamental ILO conventions.

As for certain issues covered in sustainability chapters, tension exists between developing and developed states. It is usually the developed states that demand sustainability chapters in trade agreements.[18] Developing states tend to be more cautious and conservative when it comes to the incorporation of sustainability issues into trade agreements out of concern over possible infringement on national sovereignty.[19] For example, the European Union's continued effort to advance sustainability issues through trade agreements is not enthusiastically shared by all its counterparts. Nor do the officials in all of the EU counterpart governments seem to be apprised of the role and expectation of the sustainability chapters in their trade agreements with the European Union. Obviously, there seems to be a gap in the level of understanding between the European Union and its trade partners as far as sustainability chapters are concerned.[20]

These gaps show the controversial nature of sustainability issues in trade agreements. The inclusion process may be smooth, but sustainability chapters might trigger heated debates and acute confrontations once disputes arise. Thus, one could argue that inclusion may not tell much unless and until actual disputes arise and sustainability chapters are actually mobilized. Mindful of this possibility, exposing trade agreements to a series of controversial matters bordering on national sovereignty may continue to operate as a burden for such agreements. Domestic

[16] ibid.

[17] ibid.

[18] Kevin Banks, 'Fit for Purpose? The Extent and Enforcement of International Trade Agreement Labor Obligations After the Guatemala—Labor Obligations Decision' (2021) 52 Georgetown Journal of International Law, 667; Aleydis Nissen, 'Not That Assertive: The EU's Take on Enforcement of Labour Obligations in Its Free Trade Agreement with South Korea' (2022) 33(2) European Journal of International Law 610–11.

[19] Banks (n 18) 670; Nissen (n 18) 628; James Harrison, 'The Labour Rights Agenda in Free Trade Agreements' (2019) 20 Journal of World Investment & Trade 724.

[20] James Harrison and others, 'Governing Labour Standards through Free Trade Agreements: Limits of the European Union's Trade and Sustainable Development Chapters' (2019) 57 Journal of Common Market Studies 270–72.

constituents' negative views towards trade agreements in some countries may grow further.

2. Insufficient Cooperation with International Organizations

The administration of sustainability chapters so far has also brought to the fore the insufficient or weak cooperation and coordination between contracting parties of trade agreements and relevant international organizations. While trade agreements' contracting parties (or their secretariats) are not international organizations themselves, they, either individually or collectively, should communicate and interact with relevant international organizations with regard to sustainability issues contained in their trade agreements. This is because the aforementioned organizations are where sustainability issues first emerged and progressed. Proper operation and administration of sustainability chapters would be challenging, if not entirely impossible, without close interaction with specialized international organizations, as these organizations are the masters of the underlying legal instruments now being referred to in sustainability chapters. And yet, the interaction between contracting parties and these organizations seems to have been either sporadic or flimsy. This poses a serious challenge to the success of the sustainability chapters.

As for international organizations, they appear to realize the opportunity that recent sustainability projects offer and take advantage of it. For instance, various ILO conventions and declarations are frequently mentioned in sustainability chapters of numerous trade agreements.[21] Knowing this, the ILO has been publishing reports reflecting this new phenomenon and expecting sustainability chapters to function as potential institutional arrangements to facilitate dialogue among different interest groups, both domestic and foreign.[22] The ILO is of the view that sustainability chapters provide a forum to address labour issues in new regulatory settings such as in the corporate social responsibility context.[23] It goes as far as to discuss other proposals for trade sanctions in the context of dispute settlement proceedings in the sustainability chapters.[24] There does not seem to be any concrete evidence that the plans and desires of the ILO have prompted meaningful

[21] European Parliament, 'Labour Rights in EU Trade Agreements: Towards Stronger Enforcement', European Parliamentary Research Service (2022) 4; US Congressional Research Service, 'Worker Provisions in Free Trade Agreements (FTAs)' (25 October 2023) 1.

[22] ILO, 'Labour Provisions in G7 Trade Agreements: A Comparative Perspective' (ILO 2019) 3–4.

[23] ibid 27.

[24] ILO, 'Promoting and Enforcing Compliance with Labour Provisions in Trade Agreements: Comparative Analysis of Canada, European Union and United States Approached and Practices' (ILO 2023); Leanne Roncolato and Mark Anner, 'Trade Union Rights, Democracy and Trade: An Industry-level Approach' Employment Policy Dept Seminar (October 2022) <https://www.ilo.org/wcmsp5/groups/public/---ed_emp/documents/presentation/wcms_857705.pdf> accessed 15 April 2024; European Parliament, 'Resolution on the Outcome of the Commission's Review of the 15-Point Action Plan on Trade and Sustainable Development' (June 2022) <https://oeil.secure.europarl.europa.eu/oeil/popups/summary.do?id=1719134&t=d&l=en> accessed 15 April 2024.

responses to the contracting parties of trade agreements. Nor has there been any specific interaction between the ILO and the contracting parties with regard to interpretation or enforcement of ILO instruments. Situations with other international organizations do not appear to be that much different.

Insufficient or weak cooperation and coordination with international organizations in charge of underlying instruments and legal obligations arising from them portray a serious limitation for achieving the objectives of sustainability chapters. Sustainability issues could not be adequately understood and properly administered in the absence of joint effort of the contracting parties of trade agreements at issue and relevant international organizations.

3. Logistical Burden and Limited Resources

The addition of new proceedings to a trade agreement increases the logistical burden. The burden increases further if multiple proceedings are introduced simultaneously. This is the situation with respect to sustainability chapters: many new proceedings are introduced concurrently spanning dialogue, consultation, mediation, and arbitration, while engaging diverse interest groups. From the contracting parties' perspective, this translates to significant human and financial resources needing to be mobilized on an ongoing basis. Handling logistical burdens is yet another challenge for states with regard to sustainability chapters.

Logistical burdens also pose a challenge to civil society and non-governmental organizations (NGOs) that play an important role in sustainability chapters.[25] They need financial and human resources to participate in the process of sustainability chapters in a meaningful manner. Proceedings carried out under the current sustainability chapters do not seem to reflect the active participation of civil society. It would be important therefore for the contracting parties to contemplate specific ways to address the logistical burdens both for the governments and civil society.

4. Textual Ambiguity

The text of sustainability chapters often lacks clarity and specific obligations, making it challenging for contracting parties to confront each other when disputes arise. The general objective and direction are arguably clear-cut, but the terms and phrases in specific provisions are sometimes ambiguous and vague. Several proceedings undertaken by contracting parties under sustainability chapters appear to have spent significant time on clarifying the meaning of key provisions of sustainability chapters where the contracting parties sometimes present a sharply divided view. Having contrasting views can harm a sustainability project where contracting parties commit to exert joint efforts to cope with societal challenges.

[25] Harrison and others (n 20).

Ambiguity and vagueness seem inevitable, of course, given that the sustainability project is a novel attempt: it certainly requires a learning curve as with anything. That said, however, mindful of the fact that sustainability issues are by nature controversial because of their close nexus to national sovereignty, states should make more efforts during the negotiation of a trade agreement to include clearer and more accurate language in the text of the chapter. Textual ambiguities impose a serious limitation on the proper operation and administration of the sustainability chapters.

5. Enforcement of Decisions from Dispute Settlement Proceedings

Having a weak enforcement mechanism is another important limitation of sustainability chapters. It is true that sustainability chapters include various proceedings, both binding and non-binding. In any event, there should be mechanisms to enforce the decisions from these proceedings. In the absence of enforcement, these proceedings may turn out to be a 'paper tiger'.[26]

Legally binding proceedings such as arbitration will lead to a binding decision that is subject to enforcement. The enforcement mechanism should be designed to ensure compliance. For instance, monetary assessment or compensation together with a legislative action requirement subject to a mandatory deadline may be effective in ensuring compliance. Legally non-binding proceedings should also explore a way to ensure the implementation of the agreed outcome. For instance, the disputing parties may reduce their agreement to writing and commit to implementing it. The written agreement as such may provide a legal tool to enforce the agreed outcome. In other words, the proceeding is non-binding but the outcome of the proceeding can be designed to be binding.

The texts of the sustainability chapters and the proceedings carried out under them so far have not paid much attention to enforcement. This has arguably lowered the level of expectations and therefore reduced the potential of sustainability chapters. Consequently, it has become an important limitation for these chapters. Contracting parties should be more creative when they contemplate enforcement. After all, several proceedings in sustainability chapters are regarded as lex specialis designed to apply to disputes arising from the chapters only.[27] Sometimes these disputes are even carved out from those subject to the general dispute settlement mechanism of a trade agreement.[28] This scheme of independence

[26] Marco Bronckers and Giovanni Gruni, 'Retooling the Sustainability Standards in EU Free Trade Agreements' (2021) 24 Journal of International Economic Law 37; Denise Prevost and Iveta Alexovicova, 'Mind the Compliance Gap: Managing Trustworthy Partnerships for Sustainable Developments in the European Union's Free Trade Agreement' (2019) 6(3) International Journal of Public Law and Policy 249.

[27] Bronckers and Gruni (n 26) 40; see also Prevost and Alexovicova (n 26) 254.

[28] Katerina Hradilova and Ondrej Svoboda, 'Sustainable Development Chapters in the EU Free Trade Agreements: Searching for Effectiveness' (2018) 52 Journal of World Trade 1023; James Harrison and others, 'Labour Standards Provisions in EU Free Trade Agreements: Reflections on the European Commission's Reform Agenda' (2019) 18 World Trade Review 643; Prevost and Alexovicova (n 26) 241.

arguably supports the view that parties can and should be more creative when they design proceedings and administer them in practice.

Well-drafted substantive provisions may not achieve their objectives when an enforcement mechanism is lacking.[29] Nonetheless, states have focused on the drafting of substantive provisions and paid less attention to the subsequent enforcement scheme. The disparity appears to place a critical limitation on the current sustainability chapters.

C. Overall Assessment

Trade agreements' absorption and diffusion of sustainability issues have brought about significant contributions to the trade agreements themselves and their contracting parties by addressing critical items that affect trade and/or underpin the new global regime. It also contributes to fulfilling the noble causes of other treaties and international agreements that regulate these issues. At the same time, sustainability chapters have also encountered various limitations and problems. Ambiguous texts, lack of liaison with other international organizations, logistical burdens, and insufficient enforcement are examples of such limitations and problems. Thus, contributions and limitations should be weighted together to determine the overall performance of sustainability chapters.

Contributions are arguably already tangible and specific—they are being felt in domestic planes and state-to-state relations. Contributions are also being realized by interest groups and civil society, both domestic and foreign. Considering how sustainability chapters' contributions have evolved and grown, it would be a fair assessment to say that they will continue to evolve and grow over time. On the other hand, limitations and problems are closely linked to the lack of experience and practice. Consider ambiguity in texts, lack of logistical support, cooperation with other international organizations, or insufficient enforcement. They are all important limitations and problems. However, their negative impact will be mitigated and reduced over time with the accumulation of relevant experience and practice.

Since contributions continue to increase while limitations continue to decrease as time passes by, one would argue that the overall scorecard of the sustainability project is positive and promising at this point. The endeavour is moving in the right direction and should continue to stay on course.

[29] Stefanie Schacherer and Tensin Studer, 'Trade and Sustainable Development Chapters in EU FTAs: Adapting Enforcement Methods to the Purposes?' (*CIL Dialogues: An International Law Blog*) <https://cil.nus.edu.sg/blogs/trade-and-sustainable-development-chapters-in-eu-ftas-adapting-enforcement-methods-to-the-purposes-by-stefanie-schacherer-and-tensin-studer/> accessed 15 April 2024.

III. Future Tasks for Sustainability in Trade Agreements—What Needs to be Done?

The recent development to absorb and accommodate sustainability issues into trade agreements is indeed a welcome move in many respects. These issues are closely intertwined with trade interests of contracting parties of trade agreements. Environment and labour matters offer good examples. If a trade agreement fails to address these issues, it would effectively create a sizeable loophole in regulating trade between the contracting parties. The increasing absorption and diffusion of sustainability by trade agreements is therefore said to be a step in the right direction for the sake of the agreements themselves. In addition, and more importantly, the merger and acquisition have brought sustainability issues into the jurisdictional folds of various dispute settlement proceedings of trade agreements, be it binding or non-binding, thereby prompting contracting parties to pay more attention to these issues and take concrete action to implement relevant obligations.

There remain important tasks for the global community to complete the merger and acquisition and achieve the stated objective. The ultimate success of the sustainability endeavour hinges on how we handle these tasks going forward.

Then what needs to be done to improve the sustainability chapters in future trade agreements? The sustainability chapters in the existing trade agreements are already established and they are to be interpreted and applied as they are written down. Little room for manoeuvre, if any, would be found here. Future trade agreements, however, can be more carefully thought through and tightly drafted.

A. Clarifying the Objectives of Sustainability Chapters

The most important thing in a prospective trade agreement, with regard to a sustainability chapter, is to clarify its objective. Does it purport to address trade-related aspects of labour or environment, or enhance the overall standard of labour or environment? Or does it aim to achieve both? Preferably, both should consider the increasing importance of the subject. In any event, the objective should be set forth up front in a clear manner, so that contracting parties are on the same page.

In this regard, the relationship between the trade agreement at issue, on the one hand, and the relevant treaties and international agreements, on the other hand, need to be clearly stipulated in the text of the chapter. Whether these outside treaties are merely referred to as reference points or whether they now become part of the corpus of obligations of the trade agreements is not entirely clear, which frequently leads to controversies and debates between contracting parties. Equally unclear in this respect would be the status of the discussions and negotiations in relevant international organizations. The relationship between the discussions in these other international organizations and those in the trade agreement at issue (including various committees and sub-committees) is anything but clear-cut. These critical issues are closely interlinked with the objective of a sustainability chapter. It would prove beneficial to stipulate these matters using clear language in the texts of future trade agreements. As chapters in a trade agreement usually do not contain a preamble, the first article of a sustainability chapter may elaborate in a detailed fashion the basic objectives.

Clearer language of course helps contracting parties avoid disputes over the meaning of the text of the sustainability chapter in a trade agreement, and instead focus on achieving the basic goal of the chapter, that is, enhancing labour and environmental standards and promoting compliance with relevant international legal obligations. Explicitly stipulated objectives will provide important guidance in interpreting various provisions of the sustainability chapter.[30] More importantly, clearer language will also help expedite and tighten domestic implementation. Ambiguous terms tend to be exploited by government officials for a delay or refusal of otherwise necessary implementation. Explicit stipulation will be able to handle this rampant phenomenon and initiate a two-way interaction between international obligations, on the one hand, and domestic legislation with strong enforcement, on the other hand.[31]

In addition, clearer language for the objective of the chapter also facilitates diverse consultation and dispute-settlement mechanisms embedded in the chapter. It is particularly critical for the successful operation of non-binding proceedings such as labour–environmental dialogue, expert group consultation, or mediation. These proceedings could gain further traction from the general public and interest groups once the objective of the chapter is clear enough such that a party complained against has difficulty hiding behind the legal shield of ambiguity and abstractness of the objective of the whole chapter. The purported effect of 'naming and shaming' in a sustainability chapter, which is one of the key components of the chapter, would only work if these conditions were met.[32]

[30] See Vienna Convention on the Law of Treaties, art 31, para 1 (underscoring 'context' as one of the elements of general rules of treaty interpretation).

[31] Julien Chaisse, 'FDI and Sustainable Development in the EU–China Investment Treaty: Neither High nor Low, Just Realistic Expectations' (Columbia Center on Sustainable Investment 2022) 2; see also Marco Bronckers, 'The EU's Inconsistent Approach towards Sustainability Treaties: Due Diligence Legislation v. Trade Policy' (*EJIL:Talk!* 9 November 2022) <https://www.ejiltalk.org/the-eus-inconsistent-approach-towards-sustainability-treaties-due-diligence-legislation-v-trade-policy/> accessed 15 April 2024.

[32] Maria Garcia, 'Sanctioning Capacity in Trade and Sustainability Chapters in EU Trade Agreements: The EU–Korea Case' (2022) 10(1) Politics and Governance 65.

B. Exploring Creative Methods to Induce Implementation and Compliance

The success of sustainability chapters in future trade agreements also depends on the width and depth of creativity of contracting parties in exploring novel methods to induce implementation and compliance. Existing chapters already include diverse schemes and proceedings. They include labour–environment consultation, labour–environment dialogue with experts, ministerial consultation, mediation, joint committee referral, and arbitration. At this point, it is not entirely clear how effective these schemes and proceedings are respectively. Over time, with the accumulation of experience and through trial and error, each of them can be evaluated, which may then lead to an amendment of the chapters and introduction of different schemes and proceedings.

For example, states might want to explore the possibility of commissioning status reports for individual contracting parties on a regular basis in which carefully chosen experts review and evaluate relevant measures of the parties. The report may then be circulated between the contracting parties and disclosed to the general public, and possibly submitted to relevant international organizations such as the WTO, the ILO, the Organisation for Economic Co-operation and Development, and the Secretariat of the United Nations Framework Convention on Climate Change. The scheme would be analogous to the Trade Policy Review Mechanism of the WTO Agreements. The purpose is to give objective meaning to the status of individual contracting parties, going beyond the two-way discussion between the two contracting parties, so that a deviating party can face the further pressure of naming and shaming.

Similarly, sanctions also need outside-the-box thinking. Unlike other chapters, sustainability chapters in some recent trade agreements are already experimenting with financial penalties.[33] While there are many practical and logistical challenges to administering financial penalties,[34] in terms of effectiveness they are likely to stand out. Mindful of this, future trade agreements might want to elaborate on provisions for financial penalties, setting forth key elements in advance. For instance, calculation methodology, payment scale, and spending schedule are to be stipulated in the text of a sustainability chapter.

In a similar vein, a more targeted measure can be contemplated as well. An example would be to target a corporation found to have violated labour or environmental laws and regulations of a contracting party with possible restrictions on the

[33] See eg Dominican Republic–Central America–United States Free Trade Agreement, in force 1 March 2006, ch 20 (Dispute Settlement), art 20.17 (Non-Implementation in Certain Disputes), para 1.

[34] Bronckers and Gruni (n 26) 45; there are penalty fees and sanctions in FTAs drafted by the United States and Canada. Velut and others (n 2) 28, 98; however, some scholars opined that as seen from the examples of US and Canada FTAs, the availability of sanctions does not mean that this tool is actually used to improve compliance. Prevost and Alexovicova (n 26) 242; European Parliament (n 21) 11.

shipment, customs clearance, or market circulation of the product manufactured by the corporation.[35] The restriction may target multiple corporations at the same time if similar violations occur in them, or a particular industry where the violation has become an industry-wide phenomenon.

Given the inherent nature of sustainability chapters, 'best effort' provisions sometimes seem inevitable and appropriate. At the same time, however, 'best effort' provisions need not be carved in stone and instead should evolve over time in a phased manner. Thus, they may become substantive obligations with time (ie ten years after the entry into force of the agreement).[36] In addition, if at all possible, 'best effort' provisions should not be adopted for procedural matters. Contracting parties would also benefit from a prospective provision that stipulates more objective and quantifiable standards to evaluate the existence of 'best effort'.

C. Cooperation and Coordination with Other International Organizations

A two-way interaction between international organizations and contracting parties (or a relevant entity, if any, such as a committee) of trade agreements is critical for the success of both. One cannot stand without the other. That said, current trade agreements are relatively silent on this point. Future trade agreements should pay more attention here and introduce detailed provisions to ensure cooperation and coordination.

Most importantly, trade agreements and their contracting parties do not usually adopt global standards on labour or the environment; instead, such standards are often established by international organizations in the respective fields. Thus, their continued effort to adopt, fine-tune and improve standards is essential for the interpretation and application of a sustainability chapter in the first place. These standards also play a crucial role in the interpretation and application of exception clauses in trade agreements such as general exceptions and essential security exceptions,[37] and other chapters of trade agreements such as the technical barriers to trade chapters and the sanitary and phytosanitary measures chapters.

In this regard, provisions should be introduced to ensure closer cooperation and coordination with the ILO for labour issues.[38] Regular dialogues with the ILO

[35] Bronckers and Gruni (n 26) 49; Hradilova and Svoboda (n 28) 1040; Harrison and others (n 28) 648.

[36] Chaisse (n 31) 2.

[37] Csongor István Nagy, 'Trade Interests and Extraterritorial Value Considerations in New-Generation Free Trade Agreements: The Psychology of Redirection' (2020) 19 Journal of International Business and Law 17.

[38] Hradilova and Svoboda (n 28) 1040.

should be sought, and the ILO should remain apprised of the development of sustainability chapters.

Furthermore, engaging with international organizations is important to administer and operate various elements and proceedings of a sustainability chapter. Views and advice from international organizations will lend crucial help in fulfilling the tasks laid out in sustainability chapters. Maintaining long-term relationships while handling differences and disputes and carrying out capacity-building projects would demand tight choreography with international organizations.[39] Diverse societal interest groups and NGOs would also benefit from increased communication with international organizations because they also participate in robust discussions with these international organizations.[40] International organizations may perform the role of an intermediary or liaison if necessary. They could even perform a balancing role when a conflict intensifies.

With the spread of sustainability chapters, international organizations can take up the task of monitoring. They can receive status reports submitted by contracting parties regularly according to the provisions in sustainability chapters, prepare their reports including evaluation, and disseminate them among their members together with contracting parties of trade agreements at issue.[41]

Finally, the rising attention to the supply chain at present further underscores the importance of addressing labour and environmental issues at each leg and segment of a lengthy supply chain of a core product (such as semiconductors). As constituent states and their private entities pertaining to a particular supply chain may be subject to different trade agreements, fragmentation in sustainability chapters even in the same supply chain may well take place going forward.[42] Proper engagement of international organizations would also contribute to mitigating legal and practical complexities flowing from such circumstances.

[39] Trade and Sustainable Development (TSD) Chapters in EU Free Trade Agreements (FTAs), Non-Paper of the Commission Services, Brussels (2017) <http://trade.ec.europa.eu/doclib/docs/2017/july/tradoc_155686.pdf> accessed 15 April 2024, 9; Marc Jütten, 'Trade and Sustainable Development in EU Free Trade Agreements', European Parliamentary Research Service (November 2023) <https://www.europarl.europa.eu/RegData/etudes/BRIE/2023/754613/EPRS_BRI(2023)754613_EN.pdf> accessed 15 April 2024; Prevost and Alexovicova (n 26) 242.

[40] Harrison and others (n 28) 347, 643–34; Bronckers and Gruni (n 26) 34; Hradilova and Svoboda (n 28) 1029; Marslev and Staritz, 'Towards a Stronger EU Approach on the Trade–Labor Nexus? The EU–Vietnam Free Trade Agreement, Social Struggles and Labor Reforms in Vietnam' (2022) Review of International Political Economy 19; Prevost and Alexovicova (n 26) 247–48.

[41] Nicolás Brando and others, 'The Protection of Labour Rights in Trade Agreements: The Case of the EU–Colombia Agreement' (2016) 50 Journal of World Trade 604; Harrison and others (n 28) 644; Prevost and Alexovicova (n 26) 245–47; European Parliament (n 21) 8–9.

[42] Mirela Barbu and others, 'The Trade-Labour Nexus: Global Value Chains and Labour Provisions in European Union Free Trade Agreements' (2018) 9(3) Global Labour Journal 275.

IV. Concluding Thoughts—Upgrading Trade Agreements with 'Sustainability' Components

Increasingly, sustainability issues have become an important component of new trade agreements. At a time when trade agreements are expected to delve into ways to ensure a genuine level playing field and perform the role of a legal vehicle to apply critical global norms, this can indeed be said to be a welcome move. It is true that as a new component of a trade agreement, sustainability issues are raising various concerns and novel challenges. The accumulation of experience and practice, however, will enable these concerns and challenges to be dealt with properly. Through negotiation and interpretation of the text of sustainability issues in new trade agreements, further clarity will be secured going forward.

The sustainability initiative represents the continuing effort to upgrade trade agreements so that they can cater to the demands of contracting parties and diverse interest groups. Such upgrades will help increase the legitimacy and relevance of trade agreements at this crucial point in time. More attention needs to be paid to the sustainability initiative in trade agreements.

23

From Neoliberalism to Ordoliberalism, and Beyond

Sustainability and Trade Governance

Frank J Garcia and Mario R Osorio Hernández

I. Introduction

The future of the world economic order is unclear. Concerns about government failure, trade liberalization, investment protection, the free movement of capital, and monetary independence have been displaced by concerns about market failure, climate change, national security, economic resilience, and the role of the US dollar in the global economy. These changes have come about as the world grapples with an impending environmental crisis, the aftermath of a global pandemic, the consequences of the invasion of Ukraine, the return of high inflation and high interest rates amid the rise of inequality, and geopolitical tensions intensifying across the globe. Dissatisfaction with the Bretton Woods institutions, the multilateral trading system, and, more generally, with global economic governance is at an all-time high. How did we get here, and what should a programme of sustainable global economic ordering fit for the twenty-first century look like?

In this chapter, we explore this question by turning our attention to economic ideologies and their role in leading the world down the current path, as well as their potential and limits for charting a new and more sustainable future for humanity. Analysing the crisis at this level opens the possibility of considering a post-neoliberal, even post-globalization, ideological shift towards an alternative, more sustainable view of state–market relations at the global level. The alternative we consider here draws on the European 'ordoliberal' approach to market regulation, which views an egalitarian, voluntarist, and competitive market as a public good to be secured through law, and foregrounds economic stability and social welfare over pure free-market efficiency. Reconceptualizing the trading system through an ordoliberal perspective thus helps us imagine a transnational socio-legal framework within which to embed the contemporary post-neoliberal global economy, towards traditional ordoliberal goals of crisis-free markets that promote both voluntary agreements and competition among equals on the inter-state and private

Frank J Garcia and Mario R Osorio Hernández, *From Neoliberalism to Ordoliberalism, and Beyond* In: *The Sustainability Revolution in International Trade Agreements.* Edited by: Geraldo Vidigal and Kathleen Claussen, Oxford University Press.
© Frank J Garcia and Mario R Osorio Hernández 2024. DOI: 10.1093/9780191994470.003.0023

levels, and embed profit maximization within a broader vision of social good than simply profit maximization.

Foregrounding neoliberalism and ordoliberalism as contending frameworks for constructing and understanding international economic law also allows us to consider the role of ideology, and its limits, in the contemporary legal and institutional imaginary. The act of playing up neoliberalism, ordoliberalism, or any other universal 'ism' and making it the guiding framework of economic governance tends to engender a way of thinking about state–market relations that takes as a given what in fact needs to be studied and explained. Ways of thinking that stem from an ideational, institutional, or policy core obviate all or part of the *politics* of economic ordering, politics which ought to be a primary object of inquiry, not something that is minimized or presupposed. At the end of this chapter therefore we argue for mainstreaming ways of thinking that proceed from ideational, institutional, and policy variation and for replacing a one-size-fits-all approach with a mindset of experimentation around a fluid notion of state–market relations. A truly sustainable system of global economic governance is one in which the values of pluralism and democracy are in fruitful dialogue at the core.

II. Neoliberalism and the Sustainability Crisis

A. Neoliberalism and Its Ideational, Institutional, and Policy Core

Neoliberalism is at once an ideology of capitalism, a political process (including the institutions that make up that process), and a set of policy prescriptions.[1] In effect, popular accounts within economics, law, history, and sociology have presented neoliberalism as an ideological creed and epistemological ethos,[2] a class project,[3] and an economic programme at the centre of which are a set of defined policies.[4] As an ideology, neoliberalism is typically associated with free markets, individualism, limited government intervention, and other ideas that seek

[1] Bob Jessop, 'Ordoliberalism and Neoliberalization: Governing through Order or Disorder' (2019) 45 Critical Sociology 967; Wendy Larner, 'Review of A Brief History of Neoliberalism' (2006) 82 Journal of Economic Geography 449.

[2] See eg Nicolás M Perrone, *Investment Treaties and the Legal Imagination: How Foreign Investors Play by Their Own Rules* (OUP 2021); Quinn Slobodian, *Globalists: The End of Empire and the Birth of Neoliberalism* (Harvard University Press 2018); Andrew TF Lang, *World Trade Law after Neoliberalism: Reimagining the Global Economic Order* (OUP 2011); Yves Dezalay and Bryant G Garth, *The Internationalization of Palace Wars: Lawyers, Economists, and the Contest to Transform Latin American States* (University of Chicago Press 2002).

[3] See eg David Harvey, *A Brief History of Neoliberalism* (OUP 2005).

[4] See eg Gary Gerstle, *The Rise and Fall of the Neoliberal Order: America and the World in the Free Market Era* (OUP 2022); David Held, *Global Covenant: The Social Democratic Alternative to the Washington Consensus* (Polity Press 2004).

to promote the productive operation of a capitalist market economy by minimizing the role of government regulation and intervention in order to maximize capitalism's disruptive capabilities. As a political process, Harvey characterizes it as a project to re-establish conditions for the accumulation of capital and the restoration of the power of economic elites.[5] Institutions that consistently accompany this process include the law of contracts and property, and, for purposes of trade governance, the law and institutions of the World Trade Organization (WTO) (at least on some accounts).

In terms of domestic policies, neoliberalism habitually supports economic rules that further the free movement of goods, services, capital, and people; deregulation; the reduction of government spending; and the protection of private property and of the corporate form. At the core of neoliberalism are policies closely associated with Reaganism and Thatcherism that emphasize reducing the role of government in the economy through privatization, reducing economic regulations that restrict business activity, and reducing taxes, on the grounds that this set of policies will best favour growth and employment in the long term.[6]

Internationally, neoliberalism is most closely associated with the Washington Consensus, a set of policies sold to developing economies in particular, and the global economy in general, through the work of national governments and the Bretton Woods institutions (the World Bank and the International Monetary Fund), both headquartered in Washington, DC (hence the name). The Washington Consensus also emphasizes reducing the role of the government in the domestic economies of borrowing countries, through privatization and reduced public spending; and liberalizing rules restricting trade and foreign investment in order to open the economy to more competition and investment.[7]

B. How Neoliberalism Has Transformed the World Economic Order and Undermined Sustainability

This process of neoliberalization accelerated with the creation of the WTO in 1994 and the concomitant acceleration of neoliberal US bilateral and regional trade policies. It has been argued, though not unequivocally, that the creation of the WTO in 1994 represented, among other things, a shift away from the embedded liberalism of the General Agreement on Tariffs and Trade (GATT) and towards a neoliberal global economic framework, with decisive results.[8] Bilateral and regional

[5] Harvey (n 3) 19.

[6] ibid 22–26.

[7] Indeed, Harvey argues that it was through the structural adjustment process that neoliberalism was first forced on developing countries, with the assistance of domestic elites. See Larner (n 1).

[8] Quinn Slobodian has gone as far as to say that the creation of the WTO was the 'crowning victory' of the neoliberal project, although that view has been challenged. See Ernst-Ulrich Petersmann and

trade agreements have also been used as a means to impose a neoliberal trade agenda, under conditions maximizing negotiating leverage.[9]

Neoliberalism, with its effects on the trade regime and on the global economy, is at the heart of the sustainability crisis. Neoliberalism is inherently unsustainable because it is a disruptive strategy that unbinds institutional and regulatory constraints on the free market in the naïve belief that the free market will consequently attain its own self-regulated growth.[10] Insofar as that belief proved unfounded, the crisis period between the high-water mark of neoliberalism (the 1990s) and the global financial crisis (its public death knell) illustrates that a global economic order built on neoliberal principles is unlikely to be sustainable, as it consists of a set of dismantled national and international frameworks, within which a financialized capitalism moves freely from profit-taking to profit-taking opportunity while ignoring social costs.

Under embedded liberalism, a sustainable balance was struck at the level of global economic affairs through international economic law. Not only was the maintenance of stable currencies, external financial positions, and national balances of payments prioritized, but the interests of a wide array of competing groups, ranging from export-oriented producers (through enhanced market access) to importers (through lower tariff barriers) to import-competing industries (through trade remedies), were protected and furthered through GATT law.[11]

In contrast, under neoliberalism, there has been a disproportionate concentration of power, with the interests of large corporations, multinationals, and well-organized export-oriented groups lopsidedly favoured. Through trade law, intellectual property protections were conferred to multinationals seeking to sell their products in foreign markets, with the promise that these protections would spur innovation in economies where those rules were not as expansive. Moreover, a slew of new non-tariff barriers was made visible and rolled back in further enhancing export-oriented producers' access to markets, but with no equivalent consideration (such as non-tariff trade remedies) given to import-competing groups. Through international investment law, global investors were afforded one-sided legal protections, under the rationale that domestic investors would always wield excessive domestic power. Through domestic and international finance and

Armin Steinbach, 'Neo-Liberalism, State-Capitalism and Ordo-Liberalism: "Institutional Economics" and "Constitutional Choices" in Multilevel Trade Regulation' (2021) 22 Journal of World Investment & Trade 1.

[9] Frank J Garcia, *Consent and Trade: Trading Freely in a Global Market* (CUP 2019).

[10] Jessop (n 1) 972.

[11] We qualify this as primarily for OECD countries, since developing countries were not in the original embedded liberalism compromise, and most have not succeeded in entering into it or benefiting by it. MK Lewis, 'The Embedded Liberalism Compromise in the Making of the GATT and Uruguay Round Agreements' in Moon and Toohey (eds), *The Future of International Economic Integration: The Embedded Liberalism Compromise Revisited* (CUP 2018) 14, 19.

monetary law, not only were currencies minted in previously inconceivable contexts and locations (eg Eurodollars and Quantitative Easing-derived money) but those groups that were given access to new money were often the most powerful and vested global investors. Through domestic and international tax law, sizeable loopholes were opened for multinational and other sophisticated corporations, allowing the most global and well-organized groups to conduct their business while paying little to no tax at all. Finally, in antitrust/competition law, regulatory approaches allowing corporations to attain dominance and monopolize markets spread through organizations such as the Organization for Economic Cooperation and Development (OECD) and the International Competition Network, reaching jurisdictions of many nations.

For all of these reasons, the neoliberal model has not served the majority of interests, nor, in terms of successful growth and development, worked for the vast majority of countries.[12] Instead, a globalized neoliberalism has contributed to a global economy in which economic growth is put in competition against social welfare and environmental protection. Workers, marginalized and underrepresented populations, and groups who lack the sufficient organization and power continue to be exploited abroad and increasingly at home, and inequality continues to increase dramatically both globally and domestically.

Moreover, the global financial crisis of 2007–08 and the current politico-economic crisis in developed countries have both demonstrated, among many things, that the line between domestic and international policy is also unsustainable in a globalized economy. Increased downward pressure on wages and social welfare benefits in OECD countries has led to increased job insecurity and long-term stagnation in terms of real incomes for most working people. In other words, developed countries cannot have neoliberalism abroad and social welfare capitalism at home.

In summary, when we look at the regulatory framework for global trade, at both the multilateral and regional levels, we can see with the benefit of hindsight that the system took a sharp turn away from the embedded liberalism of the early GATT period, beginning with the structural adjustment policies of the 1980s and accelerating with the creation of the WTO in the 1990s. This shift has been more pronounced in the exercise of US economic dominance through free trade agreement (FTA) negotiations, and less pronounced in EU regional trade policy, but has nevertheless characterized both the multilateral and regional trading regimes. All of this has upset the delicate balance between what is good for capital and what is

[12] See eg Roser Manzanera-Ruiz and others, 'Prologue: Neoliberalism or Neoliberalisms? Ideology, Governmentality and Real-World "Experiments"' in Roser Manzanera-Ruiz and others (eds), *Neoliberalism and Unequal Development: Alternatives and Transitions in Europe, Latin America and Sub-Saharan Africa* (Routledge 2022) (cataloguing neoliberalism's many development failures across multiple regions).

good for everyone else, with serious consequences for both democracy and overall global well-being.

III. Ordoliberalism: Towards a More Sustainable Trade Regime?

A. Ordoliberalism and Its Ideational, Institutional, and Policy Core

Ordoliberalism can also be thought of as an ideology, a political process (and its institutions), and a set of policy prescriptions, all at once. Indeed, popular accounts within economics, law, history, and sociology have presented ordoliberalism as an ideological creed and epistemological ethos,[13] and as a series of orders with distinct structural features and formal principles.[14]

In contrast to neoliberalism, and despite some shared history and a shared commitment to market principles, ordoliberalism constitutes an economic ideology centred on sustainability rather than disruption. As an ideology, ordoliberalism seeks the productive operation of a capitalist market economy by establishing a strong legal/political framework to correct market failures and ensure overall social welfare.

At the core of ordoliberalism are the ideas of a competitive market economy, the rule of law, an ordered society, and individual freedom. In their ordoliberal form, these ideas hinge on the concept of a 'strong state',[15] and are typically traced back to the first phase (1948–66) of the German 'social market economy', as policy in Germany during this period was heavily influenced by ordoliberal thinking.[16] Scholars, however, are often careful to set the concept of the 'social market economy' apart from that of the 'welfare state'. While ordoliberal and welfare-based approaches come together in their rejection of the laissez faire liberalist style of

[13] See eg Slobodian (n 2); Josef Hien and Christian Joerges, *Ordoliberalism, Law and the Rule of Economics* (Bloomsbury Publishing 2017).

[14] See eg Ernst-Ulrich Petersmann, *International Economic Law in the 21st Century: Constitutional Pluralism and Multilevel Governance of Interdependent Public Goods* (Hart 2012); Viktor Vanberg, *The Constitution of Markets: Essays in Political Economy* (Routledge-Cavendish 2001).

[15] Christian Joerges and Josef Hien, 'Dead Man Walking? Current European Interest in the Ordoliberal Tradition' (2018) 24 European Law Journal 142, 147; Christian Joerges, 'The Science of Private Law and the Nation-State' in Francis Snyder (ed), *The Europeanisation of Law: The Legal Effects of European Integration* (Hart Publishing 2000) 56–57; Hagen Schulz-Forberg, 'Laying the Groundwork: The Semantics of Neoliberalism in the 1930s' in Niklas Olsen and Hagen Schulz-Forberg (eds), *Re-inventing Western Civilisation: Transnational Reconstructions of Liberalism in Europe in the Twentieth Century* (Cambridge Scholars Publishing 2014) 13, 29–35.

[16] Harald Hagemann, 'Ordoliberalism, the Social-Market Economy, and Keynesianism in Germany, 1945–1974' in Roger E Backhouse and others (eds), *Liberalism and the Welfare State: Economists and Arguments for the Welfare State* (Oxford Academic 2017); Anna E Jurczuk and Piotr Pysz, 'Market and State in Socio-Economic Order: A Brief Review of Theories' (Working Paper, Institute of Economic Research Working Papers, Institute of Economic Research 2018) 16.

self-regulating markets, ordoliberalism singularly takes off from the view that the market is an unstable human creation that is competitive only by virtue of a strong legal foundation. This view is compounded by the ordoliberal preoccupation with sheltering the market from disruptive political forces, forces that, during the rise of the German 'social market economy', were keenly exemplified by the highly cartelized economy of the Weimar Republic. Accordingly, robust legal or constitutional orders, rather than politics, are to ordoliberalism the central mechanisms through which competition in the market ought to be secured.[17]

The fundamental institution of ordoliberalism is the 'economic constitution'. The contours of that constitutional framework can be described with reference to two basic principles: the principle of *coordination* of economic activities within a framework of general rules and the principle of *subordination* of the market within a centralized administrative system. The element of design and agency is key—although the founders of ordoliberalism recognized the evolutionary and anarchic development of the market order, they also insisted that economic orders are subject to human design and can be improved by intentional reform.[18]

The economic constitution as an institution, as it happens, also takes inspiration from the concept of a 'strong state'. As per ordoliberalism, a genuine market economy can only materialize through a competitive environment that is sustained by a strong legal framework. Ordoliberalism, hence, is predicated on the need and desirability of government action through law and regulation.[19] Likewise, while the ordoliberal model was originally conceived in the context of the national (German) economy, its legal or 'constitutional' dimension need not solely be embodied in the order of the national. Economic law and regulation supporting a competitive market economy should ideally materialize at the local, national, regional, and international levels. Therefore, in today's interconnected world, the ordoliberal model is structurally interlocked with the concept of 'multilevel governance'. In the trade field, for example, Petersmann has written extensively about how the 'economic constitution' of the WTO is situated at the top of a multilevel governance structure.[20]

[17] Vanberg, *The Constitution of Markets* (n 14).

[18] Viktor J Vanberg, 'The Freiburg School: Walter Eucken and Ordoliberalism' (Working Paper, Freiburg Discussion Papers on Constitutional Economics, Walter Eucken Institute V 2004) 8.

[19] Viktor J Vanberg, 'Ordoliberalism, Ordnungspolitik, and the Reason of Rules Special Issue, Part I: German Ordoliberalism' (2015) 2 European Review of International Studies 27, 28–31.

[20] Petersmann and Steinbach (n 8); Ernst-Ulrich Petersmann, 'Between "Member-Driven Governance" and "Judicialization": Constitutional and Judicial Dilemmas in the World Trading System' in Chang-fa Lo and others (eds), *The Appellate Body of the WTO and Its Reform* (Springer 2020); Petersmann, *International Economic Law in the 21st Century* (n 14); Petersmann, 'Multilevel Trade Governance in the WTO Requires Multilevel Constitutionalism' in Christian Joerges and Ernst-Ulrich Petersmann (eds), *Constitutionalism, Multilevel Trade Governance and International Economic Law*, vol 12 (Studies in International Trade Law, Hart Publishing 2011); Ernst-Ulrich Petersmann, *Constitutional Functions and Constitutional Problems of International Economic Law: International and Domestic Foreign Trade Law and Foreign Trade Policy in the United States, the European Community and Switzerland* (Westview Press 1991).

With regards to policies, ordoliberalism is commonly associated with the free movement of goods, services, capital, and people; fiscal discipline; and the protection of private property and of the corporate form. Policies that effectively help mimic the theoretical outcome of a perfectly competitive market can generally be thought of as being under the aegis of the ordoliberal model.

In summary, although they share a common history, neoliberalism and ordoliberalism thus differ fundamentally in two key respects. First, in terms of priority or emphasis, neoliberalism foregrounds the reduction of the government's role in the market economy, whereas ordoliberalism foregrounds the role of government in structuring the framework for a market economy and embedding it into a well-ordered society. In this sense, according to Vanberg, the key contribution of ordoliberal theory has been to highlight the constructed—and constitutional—dimension of the liberal economic paradigm.[21] Second, and related to the first, is the fundamental structural impulse of ordoliberalism, namely that the market order ought to be a constitutional order, that is, defined by an institutional framework and subject to constitutional choices.[22] It is this embedded quality of the market, as an order rooted in an economic constitution, which brings us into conversation with Polanyi's historic study of embedded and dis-embedded markets, and to Ruggie's application of this to the trading system through the notion of embedded liberalism.[23]

B. What Ordoliberal Economic Governance Would Look Like and What Its Sustainability Virtues and Flaws Are

At first glance, neoliberalism and ordoliberalism would seem to have a great deal in common in terms of the economic order they would create. Many of their ideas, institutions, and policies appear as if they were cut from the same cloth. However, in several important respects, these two 'isms' differ, and so too would their respective economic orders. Most importantly, in terms of sustainability, they could not be more different: neoliberalism seeks to profit from crises and may well foment them, whereas ordoliberalism aims to reduce crisis tendencies and create an ordered society.[24]

[21] In highlighting this, Vanberg points explicitly to the work of James Buchanan, and implicitly yet unequivocally towards the work of Ernst-Ulrich Petersmann. See Vanberg, 'The Freiburg School' (n 18) 18.

[22] ibid 5.

[23] Ordoliberals have effectively sought to associate themselves with the likes of Polanyi (and Keynes). See Ernst-Ulrich Petersmann, 'Globalists: The End of Empire and the Birth of Neoliberalism. Book Review' (2018) 21 Journal of International Economic Law 915, 915; Hagen Schulz-Forberg, 'Embedded Early Neoliberalism: Transnational Origins of the Agenda of Liberalism Reconsidered' in Dieter Plehwe and others (eds), *Nine Lives of Neoliberalism* (Verso Books 2020) 194–95.

[24] Jessop (n 1) 968.

At the level of ideas, ordoliberalism is predicated on the basis that government intervention is necessary to ensure and support a competitive market economy. Neoliberalism, in contrast, is purposefully skewed against government intervention, a bias that often hinges on the association of freedom with the private domain and coercion with the public sphere.

Furthermore, at the level of policies and institutions, ordoliberalism generally holds that a robust system of legal rules is essential for promoting a level playing field for producers, protecting consumers, and averting market failure. If, as per the ordoliberal ethos, these legal rules are enshrined in an economic constitution, all the better. Neoliberalism, conversely, typically prescribes a hands-off approach to economic ordering, embracing deregulation and actions that prevent government failure. Law and regulation, under the neoliberal ideal, is by and large suspect.

At a very basic dimension, these differences between neoliberalism and ordoliberalism seem to suggest that, in a world where the direction and conduct of economic governance are informed by the latter, rather than the former, there should be more economic regulation and government intervention. However, more regulation and intervention do not, on their own, implicate a more sustainable governance model. Rather, it is ordoliberalism's emphasis on the delivery of social goods through a strong legal framework that makes the ordoliberal model a more promising paradigm for the sustainable governance of trade and contrasts starkly with neoliberalism's rejection of that same legal framework.

One could put the contrast thusly: while neoliberalism seeks to organize society around free markets, ordoliberalism seeks a constitutional foundation for both a free economy *and* a free society.[25] Essentially, this comes down to differing views of the market and its role in a well-ordered society. Petersmann, an architect of ordoliberalism in post-war trade, characterizes it this way:

> ordoliberalism perceive[s] markets as legal constructs of reasonable citizens, who cannot maximize their general consumer welfare without legal limitation of market failures, governance failures and constitutional failures.[26]

Fundamentally, an ordoliberal global trading order would need to constitutionalize trade and its institutions, around a specific vision of how markets can be regulated to best protect public goods and enhance social welfare, instead of how regulation can best protect the market itself from government intervention. This means foregrounding social welfare *through* constitutionally framed free markets *and* the social welfare state, rather than the idea of a free market *as* social welfare, that is, as itself both the ordering principle and the ethical desideratum. This must be done at the constitutional level, as norms for core economic policy. Ordoliberal

[25] Vanberg, 'The Freiburg School' (n 18) 1.
[26] Petersmann and Steinbach (n 8) 2.

scholars remind us that if we want to improve economic outcomes, and hence social outcomes more broadly, this comes about by changing the economic constitution, not by specific policy interventions into the economy.[27]

Thus, the guiding inquiry for ordoliberals goes beyond simply the regulation of markets, into 'the constitutional foundations of a functional and humane socio-economic-political order'.[28] The term 'ordo' in ordoliberalism conveys more than just functional order; it signifies an order that is 'desirable for the human beings who inhabit it'.[29] This order will not spontaneously evolve—it has to be consciously shaped, and it is not achieved by simply ensuring that markets operate as freely as possible with as little government intervention as possible. Rather, it must be achieved through understanding the essential role that 'constitutional' economic policy—the inter-related functioning of an intentionally designed set of economic and commercial rules such as tax, labour, commercial law, trade, investment, bankruptcy, and so on—plays in creating a desirable market order. With this understanding in mind, the necessary reforms can be implemented to continuously maintain and improve the functioning of this market society.

In this way, ordoliberal economic governance can be seen as a quest to develop and implement Adam Smith's basic intuitions about markets, by creating an economic constitution under which economic actors promote the common interest by pursuing their own, but within a larger framework that ensures other values are pursued as well.[30] As Amartya Sen has pointed out, there is a difference between Smith's account of the reasons that people seek to trade, and his account of the range of motivations that enter into the stability and success of trade, and markets generally, over time.[31] For the former, Smith argues (in perhaps his most famous language) that simple self-interest is sufficient reason to seek trade:

> It is not from the benevolence of the butcher, the brewer, or the baker that we expect our dinner, but from their regard to their own interest. We address ourselves, not to their humanity but to their self-love.[32]

However, and this is the key to the distinction, this simple self-interest is not, in Smith's view, sufficient to ensure the success of trade or markets over time, nor their contribution to the larger goals of a market society. Instead, markets require a number of values and motivations to succeed over time, including trust and confidence that market bargains will be enforced, that they are mutually beneficial, and

[27] Vanberg, 'The Freiburg School' (n 18) 8–9.
[28] ibid 7 (citing Eucken).
[29] ibid.
[30] ibid 7–8.
[31] Amartya Sen, 'Adam Smith and Economic Development' in Ryan Hanley (ed) *Adam Smith: His Life, Thought and Legacy* (Princeton University Press 2016) 296–97.
[32] Adam Smith, *The Wealth of Nations* (WN I.ii.2).

that they take place in a framework designed to take into account inequalities in market power that threaten equality and freedom.[33]

The essential contrast to neoliberalism is that, while for neoliberals this market potential is optimized by minimizing governmental regulation so the market's own internal logic can deliver social goods, for ordoliberals it is *the internal logic of the economic constitution*—which embraces both the logic of markets and the needs of a thriving social order—that delivers social goods through the appropriately constituted market regime. To put it another way, the free-market order is not simply the market order one would find if the government were absent, that is, a natural phenomenon, but is instead a political-cultural product based on a constitutional order that requires continuous cultivation for its proper functioning.[34]

The normative benchmark for this economic constitution is a market in which private actors meet as legal equals and engage in voluntary exchanges and contracts.[35] Put another way, at the heart of a functioning market we find respect for consent and consensual exchange.[36] A key move made by ordoliberals is to upload this commitment to freedom and consent into the constitutional-formation level and not confine it to the private-actor market level.[37] Thus, at the level of both market regulation and the creation of the economic constitution (which for the global economy means international economic law), there must be voluntary exchanges and voluntary agreements.

The policy imperative that flows from ordoliberal principles is to continuously understand and implement whatever changes are necessary in the regulatory framework to uphold competition and voluntary exchange in the face of anti-competitive, rent-seeking interests. This means maintaining a clear prohibition against private interests using their freedom of contract at the sub-constitutional level to contract around the fundamental rules of the game set by the state at the constitutional level.[38]

At its most fundamental level, ordoliberalism requires us to reform and re-establish the economic constitution, around both economic principles that will help mimic the results of a perfectly competitive market *and* a clear understanding

[33] Thus, Smith's curious and provocative maxim about regulation and capture: 'When the regulation, therefore, is in favour of the workmen, it is always just and equitable, but it is sometimes otherwise when in favour of the masters' (WN I.x.c.61). See generally Sen (n 31).

[34] Vanberg, 'The Freiburg School' (n 18) 9.

[35] ibid 10.

[36] Ordoliberalism thus embodies a voluntarist account of trade relations. See Garcia (n 9).

[37] Vanberg finds this ordoliberal principle highlighted and further developed in the work of James Buchanan. See Vanberg, 'The Freiburg School' (n 18) 18–19; similarly, Garcia argues that a respect for consensual exchange is necessary not simply at the market level, thereby letting trade be trade and not coercion or predation; but must also be active at the level of the public rule-setting, which in trade involves the negotiation of the rules at the international level, both in the WTO and bilaterally. See Garcia (n 9).

[38] This leads naturally to concern over two fundamental elements of contemporary economic behaviour of great interest to the global market as well: the creation of cartels, and the efforts of the business community to self-regulate. See Vanberg, 'The Freiburg School' (n 18) 10–11.

that trade rules and trade governance are constitutional matters that require a strong 'supranational' order. At the private-actor-market level, this means that trade rules must ensure that the international spill-over of key trade-related economic policies such as subsidies, quotas, and tariff rates is restrained or at a minimum kept in check, and that the use of more subtle mechanisms such as food security or cultural protection does not become a pretence for legitimizing rent-seeking interests. Further, at both the public constitutional-formation level and the private-actor market level, the trade rules themselves, that is, the supranational economic constitution, must be negotiated with respect for, and enable the attainment of, free and voluntary agreements.

In terms of constitutional formation, reform at both the multilateral and regional levels is indispensable for an ordoliberal global trade regime to emerge. Multilaterally, although the trading system is often touted as a 'rule-based', consent-driven system (especially as exemplified by the post-GATT WTO), there are powerful accounts that describe its formation as more the product of a 'power-based' than 'rule-based' negotiation. For example, scholars have documented how developing countries were strong-armed into accepting the Uruguay Round Agreements as a result of the combined US–EU approach of negotiating all agreements as a 'single undertaking' and of bringing an end to the 1947 GATT, while in tandem replacing it with a legally distinct yet substantially identical 1994 GATT.[39] The combined tactics of a take-it-or-leave-it outcome and removing developing countries' best alternative to a negotiated agreement (ie of cutting them off from access to American and European markets in the terms provided for under the GATT) allowed developed countries to get much of what they sought during the Uruguay Round.[40] Regionally, the lack of free and voluntary bargaining is even more pronounced, as can be seen in a number of highly asymmetric US bilateral and regional trade agreements.[41] In the hypothetical of an ordoliberal trade regime, this means that a new approach to trade bargaining is required, such that the rules that are ultimately arrived at are more genuinely the product of equal, voluntary bargaining between countries.

In terms of private-market actors, an ordoliberal trade regime ought to mean that trade rules provide the basis upon which free and voluntary bargaining occurs among economic actors, independent of their differing interests, provided those interests are not anti-competitive, rent-seeking interests. However, important aspects of both multilateral and regional trade cooperation have elevated to the level of the 'economic constitution' rules that overwhelmingly benefit anti-competitive interests. For example, in the area of intellectual property rights, WTO

[39] John H Barton and others, *The Evolution of the Trade Regime: Politics, Law, and Economics of the GATT and the WTO* (Princeton University Press 2008) 94–105.

[40] ibid.

[41] Regional and bilateral trade rules are rife with asymmetric treaty problems undermining consent-based exchange and overall social welfare. See Garcia (n 9).

and FTA rules openly provide for, and extend monopoly protections to, export-oriented, developed-country firms. Although such rules were first brought into the trade regime on the grounds that they would spur innovation in countries where intellectual property rules were not as expansive, in reality, these rules have not been shown to bring about a significant increase in the supply of innovation either targeted specifically to developing-country markets or more globally.[42] Instead, as in standard textbook cases, they have served to spread the costs of research and development and transfer rents from developing-country to developed-country consumers.[43]

Relatedly and as a final point, notwithstanding the potential for a more sustainable form of global economic governance through an ordoliberal framework, it is important to note that ordoliberal thinkers have very openly espoused trade rules that are quite at odds with the aim of making all non-rent-seeking private actors legal equals and enabling their voluntary exchanges. Effectively, there is one private-actor group that ordoliberals consistently repudiate and for whom they preclude any legal treatment that would have them treated as equals in the trade governance sphere: import-competing producers.[44] The distinctive ordoliberal bias against the import-competing industry is based on the notion that producers within this group yield disproportionate political power and thus participate in the market on a rent-seeking basis. The fact is, however, that export-oriented firms are also prone to anti-competitive behaviour and they are more likely to be in a rent-seeking position today.[45] As a result, ordoliberalism has never truly lived up to its own standards, and it would need to be structurally recast were it ever to serve as the intellectual foundation upon which a sustainable global trade regime is built.

IV. Beyond the 'Isms'

The ordoliberal vantage point puts into perspective the failures of neoliberalism as a sustainable economic governance paradigm and makes it possible to imagine an alternative framework for the ordering of international economic affairs that is more sustainable. However, one final obstacle must be overcome before the path for a sustainable alternative to neoliberalism is cleared. Despite ordoliberalism's

[42] Cassandra Mehlig Sweet and Dalibor Sacha Eterovic Maggio, 'Do Stronger Intellectual Property Rights Increase Innovation?' (2015) 66 World Development 665, 671–74.

[43] Kenneth A Reinert, *An Introduction to International Economics: New Perspectives on the World Economy* (CUP 2021) 157.

[44] See eg Jan Tumlir, *Protectionism: Trade Policy in Democratic Societies* (American Enterprise Institute for Public Policy Research 1985).

[45] Dani Rodrik, 'What Do Trade Agreements Really Do?' (2018) 32 Journal of Economic Perspectives 73, 82–87; Michael Blanga-Gubbay and others, 'Lobbying for Globalization' (Discussion Paper, CEPR Press 11 April 2020) 15ff; Iain Osgood and others, 'The Charmed Life of Superstar Exporters: Survey Evidence on Firms and Trade Policy' (2016) 79 Journal of Politics 133, 147–48.

potential to chart a new and more sustainable course for global economic governance, this framework, as much as neoliberalism, involves processes and a way of thinking about state–market relations that are not without limitations. Neoliberalism and ordoliberalism, and other universal 'isms' that are conventionally read as proceeding from an ideational, institutional, and policy core, are all caught up in a paradigm about state–market relations that inculcates the propagation of a single optimal set of ideas, institutions, and policies that presupposes the politics of economic ordering, or reduces it to a point where it is partial and inherently skewed, or so negligible that it negates what needs to be studied and explained the most. Indeed, as noted previously by other commentators, the central defining characteristic of these 'isms' is their hostility to politics.[46]

In order for global economic governance to be enduring and sustainable, the paradigm about an optimal set of ideas, institutions, and policies characteristic of the universal 'isms', needs to be replaced with a view of state–market relations that proceeds first from ideational, institutional, and policy variation. This alternative way of thinking entails a rejection of one-size-fits-all approaches to economic ordering that radically opens up the legal and institutional imagination to the descriptive and normative merits of an understanding of the connection between global economic governance and sustainability that proceeds from the fluidity of state–market relations.

This new paradigm offers at least three concrete advantages over the alternatives. First, it provides a more accurate account of the relationship between the market and the state observable across the world. It avoids the oversimplifications that the 'isms' incur in portraying the heterogeneity of institutional models visible throughout the globe and in minimizing or negating the role of economic governance in the production of institutional diversity. Second, it turns the centre of attention away from focusing on an ideology as a determining descriptive and normative force in economic relations and towards prioritizing the motley of governance projects and the myriad, often conflicting, intellectual and material interests of the groups that give shape to and are affected by, the different conceivable configurations of state–market relations. Finally, it contributes to overcoming the false binaries of coercion and noncoercion of legal regulation that are at the heart of approaches to the law that centre on 'policy space' or 'regulatory autonomy', which have been unsuccessful and not conducive to a more sustainable model of international economic ordering.

The first step towards a truly sustainable framework of global economic governance is to transcend ways of thinking that proceed from false dichotomies between intervention and non-intervention, politics and anti-politics (neoliberalism, ordoliberalism, and other similar and/or conceivable universal 'isms'). Any

[46] William Davies, *The Limits of Neoliberalism: Authority, Sovereignty and the Logic of Competition* (SAGE 2014) 4.

framework of global economic governance that is driven by a 'sustainability' imperative ought to first come to terms with the insurmountable fact of a social world in which varying types of state–market relations and different forms of statecraft must exist and learn to coexist as well as with the desirability of enabling a mindset of legal and institutional experimentation and processes for the continual emergence and re-emergence of entrepreneurial statecraft.

Sustainability is at the heart of this alternative paradigm, not in the form of an ideational, institutional, and policy core capable of withstanding the test of time, but as a function of an enduring process of pluralistic and democratic contestation. With the vantage point of institutional variation, it is possible to envision an organizing framework for global economic affairs in which its most desirable features are those that allow for the recurrent bargaining of the competing interests of society. Rather than an optimal set of policies and institutions determined by a unique combination of interests at a specific moment in time (a thing), sustainability can be understood as the production of diverse institutional formations, continually and with a view to allowing different combinations of interests to arrive at different social and economic distributions at different moments in time (a process).[47] In the context of trade governance, such understanding would mean upholding the multilateral trading system's commitment to pluralism and to preserving the ability of members to organize their internal economic and political structures as they see fit.[48]

Moreover, it would mean that the reconstitution of the state in relation to the market, and the practice of statecraft (with democratic politics at the helm), are constantly bolstered in a way that allows for the intrinsic diversity of national institutional forms to be embraced. Rather than placing any insurmountable limits to the forms that state–market relations can take, a sustainable trade governance model under this alternative paradigm would involve supporting processes for the reconciliation of, and the democratic bargaining around, the cross-border effects of countries' economic policies.

Finally, a sustainable trade governance model compatible with this new understanding would presuppose the creation of domestic and international mechanisms that enable all those involved in, and affected by, trade, from exporters and importers to import-competing producers, to workers, communities, and the whole range of groups that have been underrepresented or not represented at all in international trade policy formation processes, to democratically determine how they extract a share of the surplus from the gains from trade. One of the least

[47] See Jamie Peck and Nik Theodore, 'Reanimating Neoliberalism: Process Geographies of Neoliberalisation' (2012) 20 Social Anthropology 177, 183 (especially their concern that a 'core' of neoliberalism can never really be determined).

[48] Robert Howse and Joanna Langille, 'Continuity and Change in the World Trade Organization: Pluralism Past, Present, and Future' (2023) 117 American Journal of International Law 1, 16.

sustainable features of the current world trade governance model is that it has been built almost entirely around the interests of the most powerful and best-organized producers, to the exclusion of the many groups that have traditionally exerted less influence and power within markets.[49]

V. Conclusion

A sustainable understanding of state–market relations generally, and of trade governance in particular, ought to have, in our view, some basic features. First, it should not be built around disruption and crises, as neoliberalism is. A framework that foments one crisis after another and rewards the few who profit from them, as it condemns or forestalls the advancement of the many who were either at a disadvantage to begin with or could not find the way to make the disruptions work to their advantage, is far from sustainable.

Second, a sustainable understanding should comport with a model that not only serves the interests of the most powerful and well-organized groups but also the interests of the groups who have traditionally lacked power in, and access to, markets. In the trade governance sphere, despite their hostility towards import-competing groups, ordoliberals and neoliberals have routinely sided with the interests of multinational corporations and large export-oriented producers. Moreover, both 'isms' have regularly neglected the interests of workers, minorities, marginalized peoples, and other underrepresented groups. In order to ensure that a particular governance model is serving the interests of all, the economic rules, structures, and transactions it promotes and facilitates must respect consent, and the model itself must be constantly and continually subject to contestation. In this sense, a sustainable approach must also provide a mechanism for meeting present needs, but without compromising the ability of future generations—as underrepresented groups—to meet theirs.

Finally, a sustainable understanding of state–market relations should cohere with a reality in which there is a variegated relationship between the market and the state. Not only is it more accurate, and therefore descriptively desirable, to foster an understanding of governance that recognizes the varying types of state–market relations observable around the world, but it is also more sustainable, normatively, to encourage ways of thinking that proceed from the recognition that

[49] Blanga-Gubbay and others (n 45); Timothy Meyer and Frank Garcia, 'Restoring Trade's Social Contract' (2018) 116 Michigan Law Review Online 78; Rodrik (n 45) 82–87; Iain Osgood, 'The Breakdown of Industrial Opposition to Trade Firms, Product Variety, and Reciprocal Liberalization' (2017) 69 World Politics 184, 193–203; Osgood and others (n 45) 135–38, 147–48; Thierry Mayer and Gianmarco IP Ottaviano, 'The Happy Few: The Internationalisation of European Firms: New Facts Based on Firm-Level Evidence' (2008) 43 Intereconomics 135, 137–43; Paul Krugman, 'The Move Toward Free Trade Zones' (1991) 76 Economic Review 5, 16–17.

institutional variation is the norm and that different forms of statecraft must co-exist. This understanding, in turn, enables a mindset of legal and institutional experimentation and processes that provide the impetus to constantly and continually re-evaluate and reimagine the governance programmes in place, and, by way of politics and democratic processes, keep it in check whenever it is only serving the interests of a few.

Trade relations have been burdened by predatory and anti-competitive practices that have been mislabelled as 'trade', and enshrined in existing bilateral and multilateral 'trade' rules. Moreover, trade governance has been plagued by a democratic deficit. While most countries have, to some extent, been able to determine the nature of their participation in the prevailing global programme for trade, the processes for the formation of trade policy have been far from pluralistic or democratic. Most interests have been and continue to be grossly underrepresented or not represented at all in trade deals.[50] This dynamic has, in our view, played a significant role in fomenting the sustainability crisis of our time. Accordingly, any solution with sustainable trade governance top of mind must have consent, pluralism, and democracy at its core.

[50] 'LOADED: Corporate Interests Dominate the Official U.S. Government Trade Advisory System' (Rethink Trade, American Economic Liberties Project 30 March 2023).

24
The Road Ahead

Kathleen Claussen and Geraldo Vidigal

I. The Work That Remains

The contributors to this volume have studied deeply the legal, political, and economic effects of the incorporation of sustainability provisions as standard elements in trade agreements, recent advances surrounding such provisions, and the future outlook for trade agreements as sustainability tools. Their nuanced perspectives on the environmental, social, and development trends of the last decade have demonstrated the challenges of this momentous undertaking by policymakers and civil society advocates. But, as these contributions demonstrate, a research agenda investigating and analysing sustainability provisions in trade agreements has only just begun.

The work in understanding and reimagining sustainability provisions in trade agreements going forward has multiple dimensions. One dimension concerns navigating diverging views on the goals and the content of these provisions. Despite the proliferation of sustainability commitments in trade agreements, states and stakeholders remain divided as to which sustainability priorities and objectives are most important, and precisely what commitments and mechanisms can most aptly pursue them. Even among the strongest proponents of these provisions, instruments vary, sometimes at cross purposes. In their contributions to this volume, Maria Panezi and Emily Lydgate have both demonstrated how language in US trade agreements concerning environmental sustainability differs from those promoted by the European Union and by New Zealand. The United States was a first mover on environmental provisions but its recent agreements do not address climate change concerns in a meaningful way. In contrast, the European Union and New Zealand have sought advanced provisions that either seek to enforce decarbonization requirements in the case of the European Union or that seek cooperation on environmental regulation in the case of New Zealand. Alongside these regional and bilateral initiatives, governments have not achieved consensus on how to link trade agreements to multilateral environmental agreements, as Greg Messenger has noted. Similarly, Giovanni Gruni has underscored how labour chapters have converged in their references to International Labour Organization (ILO) standards but remain divergent in their enforcement mechanisms. Amrita Bahri, James

Kathleen Claussen and Geraldo Vidigal, *The Road Ahead* In: *The Sustainability Revolution in International Trade Agreements*. Edited by: Geraldo Vidigal and Kathleen Claussen, Oxford University Press. © Kathleen Claussen and Geraldo Vidigal 2024.
DOI: 10.1093/9780191994470.003.0024

Harrison, Risa Schwartz, and Carrie Stoddart-Smith each has shown that gender, Indigenous rights, disability, and animal welfare are among the themes that have found their way into modern agreements, albeit unevenly and with mixed results.

Moreover, the authors featured in this volume have highlighted how, even where there may have been convergence in sustainability provisions among trade agreements, those provisions have come to the fore as a consequence of diverse motivations. Frank Garcia and Mario Osorio Hernández have highlighted just some of the tensions in this story, as have Anne van Aaken and Joel Trachtman.

Still, not even a robust edited volume such as this could fully investigate the multiple motives and complex drivers in the sustainability revolution. Just as we stressed in our introduction, revolutions come in many sizes and shapes. They can also be amorphous and subject to debate. Observers have found their multiple causes difficult to evaluate even with the benefit of historical record. Here, in a story that remains very much unfinished, any elaboration of the diverse reasons for states' consideration of sustainability in their trade agreements would be necessarily incomplete. Some espouse domestic economic correctives—the 'level the playing field' rationale—and moral or existential justifications at once, while others appear to adopt these principles as a matter of diplomacy, or simply with the ultimate goal of securing greater market access, where the other party conditions the signature of an agreement upon such an agenda.

A second dimension of the work ahead concerns reconciling environmental and social priorities in the sustainability agenda with common notions of 'development'. Some advocates have embraced environmental and social objectives as part of sustainable development, whereas others seek to maintain the distinction among these ideas. Sonia Rolland has captured this tension in her chapter, offering different pathways for articulating the relationship between development, international economic law, and sustainability. The social aspect also emerges regarding the diminished role that pre-sustainability 'development'—meaning economic enrichment of the poorer countries—retains in present conceptions of 'sustainable development'. James Nedumpara has advanced these themes, examining whether trade and sustainable development chapters have the purpose or effect of undermining the notion of 'economic development' within the broader context of sustainable development. Regis Simo in turn has explored the role of special and differential treatment at the multilateral, regional, and unilateral levels of trade governance and sustainability provisions. Together, the contributors to the volume have drawn attention not only to the synergies but also the remaining departures between the trade agreement discourse and the sustainable development agenda. Trade agreement negotiators have not widely embraced a notion of development as part of their work programme. Rolland and Nedumpara have both identified the reasons for these frictions, as well as the challenges that remain to reconcile them. In some circumstances, trade law and policy appear to rebuff the incorporation of explicit development norms. Some observers have publicly expressed concern that to proceed otherwise would risk undermining trade agreements' relative independence and success, while others openly query whether the trade agreement agenda prioritizes some communities' environmental and social sustainability needs over others. In a case study of small island developing states (SIDS), Jan Yves Remy and Sanvid Tuljapurkar have examined whether environmental sustainability is a space in which SIDS have enhanced authority given their vulnerability with rising global temperatures.

Finally, a third dimension of future work involves the emergent focus on private actors and supply chains in international trade agreements. Though enforcement mechanisms differ across models from several regions, experimental and innovative tools increasingly involve private actors directly. Kevin Banks has described the USMCA (Agreement between the United States, the United Mexican States, and Canada) Rapid Response Mechanism as one such example, which, like the annex on forestry in the US–Peru Trade Promotion Agreement, allows the governments to target private firms and individual facilities with penalties if the governments identify violations of, respectively, labour and environmental law. The newly negotiated Indo-Pacific Economic Framework for Prosperity (IPEF) continues that trend in its Supply Chain Pillar. IPEF is the first agreement of its kind in its express attention to reconfiguring supply chains, and part of that effort includes soft commitments for private actors when it comes to labour law. Not as stringent or punitive as the USMCA Rapid Response Mechanism, the IPEF Supply Chain Pillar nevertheless seeks to follow in its steps somewhat, only using more carrots than sticks.

The European Union likewise has undertaken to pursue corporate wrongs, but less through trade agreements and more through legislation, such as in its efforts regarding corporate due diligence, forced labour, and deforestation. Those initiatives may create pressure for negotiators to find a place for those themes in future trade agreements. Both Ilaria Espa and Desirée LeClercq have studied these enforcement innovations and challenges that the new initiatives pose. A handful of them require involvement by external organizations, while others operate in-house. And, while governments design these alternative dispute resolution and compliance tools, corporate actors are modifying their practices in response. Much work remains to be done in uncovering and understanding their preferences and responses, and what those mean for upcoming deals.

Timothy Meyer and Jaemin Lee are among the contributors to this volume that have sorted through the multifaceted debates to evaluate the revolution. Questioning the motivations and aspirations of these new provisions, both Meyer and Lee foresee challenges in the formulation of trade policies that promote sustainability in the least trade-restrictive way possible. Likewise, Yuka Fukunaga has undertaken to reconcile these revolutionary provisions with the work of the World Trade Organization (WTO). At a time when the global trading system has come under increased scrutiny, the sustainability revolution in trade agreements is the result of a push by governments to new outlets and novel avenues to achieve loosely related regulatory aims. No longer does this work rely on extraordinary defences laid out in WTO law, as Caroline Henckels has explained; rather, sustainability provisions have increasingly made their way from exception to mainstream.

II. Trade Agreements of the Future

The trade agreements of yesterday and even of today are likely to differ substantially from those of tomorrow. Already that shift has begun with the rise of new forms of agreements that seek to address individual topics or sectors. This volume has focused almost exclusively on free trade agreements (FTAs) or what some would call traditional trade agreements. These are agreements that seek to reduce barriers to trade between their parties, usually through tariff reduction. The General Agreement on Tariffs and Trade (GATT) specifically accounts for these agreements, insofar as they create free trade areas within the meaning of Article XXIV. Most of the agreements discussed in this volume easily meet the GATT's qualifications. Their purpose is trade liberalization and, to the extent they cover sustainability commitments, those are secondary to their emphasis on reducing barriers to trade. Some states appear to be putting the brakes on traditional FTAs, however. The United States, in particular, has negotiated only one such agreement since 2011. The US Biden Administration has made clear that it does not intend to conclude any such agreements in the near term. Doubts linger about the future of the South American trade bloc, Mercosur, in light of years of backsliding towards protectionism—and those are just two.

New agreements now under negotiation and some recently completed, however, are 'next-generation' trade agreements with different scope and shape. While much ink has been spilled on this de-FTAization, other agreements are becoming increasingly important trade tools. Some of these agreements may adjust tariff rates, but more often they address non-tariff barriers, or even barriers to 'new trade', which has extended to different fields and operates under different assumptions than the trade for which the GATT was designed. Though WTO rules may of course be applied to these agreements by a panel called upon to do so, none of the WTO's conceptual boxes was designed for them.

This incongruity can be seen in digital trade, with certain states having negotiated specialized deals to cover only digital trade and transfers of data, or in agreements to allow movement of persons or recognition of professional qualifications. These nonstandard trade-related agreements often surround and support a broader agreement with sustainability provisions, and sometimes shroud them, but they also stand alone. They lack a common vocabulary. They are often shorter, more targeted, and often bilateral. Consider the negotiations towards a Global Arrangement on Sustainable Steel and Aluminum (GASSA) underway between the United States and the European Union. Though the decarbonization objective is shared by most other states and enshrined in various multilateral agreements, the GASSA itself is being negotiated bilaterally and, as proposed, would lay down common rules for trade in the steel and aluminium sectors, aimed both at 'address[ing] carbon intensity', limiting the carbon dioxide emissions of steel and aluminium in all types of production, and at 'restor[ing] market-oriented conditions' on the international steel markets.[1]

There are fewer such agreements in the social sustainability and sustainable development areas, although at least one commentator has considered the revised USMCA to be a labour agreement more than a trade agreement given the focus on labour over market access in the 2019 revision.[2] Some of these non-FTA agreements receive less attention as compared to traditional FTAs, but many are critical to regulating twenty-first century transnational commerce—and they are growing in importance and interest.

A category of agreement increasingly coming under scrutiny is those without enforcement mechanisms that emphasize cooperation or soft commitments, especially as regards the regulation of transnational production chains. We mentioned already the IPEF, an initiative by the United States with 13 partners. The IPEF has four broad pillars covering many sectors of trade and investment, as well as topics such as labour and environment, much like a traditional FTA, without, however, attaching these provisions to market access commitments. The United States is also pursuing a similar agreement with partners throughout the Western Hemisphere in its Americas Partnership for Economic Prosperity. At the same time, companies operating in a legal environment with significant sustainability regulations may see ensuring consistency of requirements, and their clear and efficient application, as more relevant than a tariff reduction from 2 per cent to 0.

A final example of these next-generation agreements are so-called critical minerals agreements. Spurred largely by the US Inflation Reduction Act of 2022, states are now negotiating agreements that ensure their reciprocal trade in critical minerals, particularly those used for batteries in electric vehicles but also those used for semiconductors generally, and in defence. These agreements focus almost exclusively on critical minerals and their sustainable extraction without any reduction in trade barriers.

Some of the underestimation of these sorts of agreements results from their domestic administration and narrow international cooperation. Another cause is their rather quiet negotiation and conclusion. In some government systems, and in contrast with FTAs, these sorts of agreements do not require extensive political approval; nor do they affect multiple broad constituencies. A third factor in their underappreciation is confusion about their categorization or contribution to the

[1] US–EU Joint Statement, *Steel & Aluminium*, 31 October 2021.

[2] Ricardo Ramírez Hernández, 'T-MEC: Me acabo de enterar' (*El Universal* 16 December 2019).

trade law system. Policymakers have referred to these often-short trade agreements as 'mini' or 'skinny' trade deals to distinguish them from FTAs. But that does not mean they are insignificant. The United States alone is party to more than 1200 such agreements that control the cross-border movement of hundreds of goods and services into and out of the United States. Few of these are reported to or discussed within the WTO. The institutional infrastructure of China's Belt and Road Initiative is also comprised of agreements related to trade, but they too do not fit the 'traditional' mould. Certain arrangements on the African continent are neither FTAs nor customs unions nor mini deals in the US sense; and Latin American countries have, under the umbrella of the Latin American Integration Association, entered into hundreds of sector-specific agreements among themselves, ranging from auto parts to natural gas. While we do not have global statistics on just how many such arrangements states have agreed, preliminary investigations suggest that there are many thousands with more to come. These trade agreements are the sites of cutting-edge advances in cross-border foreign commerce in the 2020s.

Finally, as hinted above, the strength of next-generation trade agreements lies not only in their text but also in their implementation. In some instances, states have embedded these sustainability tools in their domestic administrative state, empowering their trade bureaucracies to undertake still greater regulatory action beyond the language of the agreement. For example, the USMCA Implementation Act provides extensive funding as well as additional staff positions to the relevant US agencies to pursue sustainability objectives. Labour and environmental attachés are now active in US embassies in Mexico to monitor and oversee engagement with the Mexican government pursuant to the Labour, Environment, and Dispute Settlement Chapters. Thus, whether in statute, regulation, or appropriation, states are expanding the reach of their agreements, particularly with respect to sustainability chapters.

III. The Road Ahead

This volume has begun the work of unearthing the sustainability revolution in trade agreements, building on the studies of those who have highlighted elements of this turn. The road ahead for sustainability provisions in trade agreements is to some degree unknowable. Just as revolutions sometimes spur counter-revolutions, there are forces working against this turn, economically and legally. Continued demand for provisions of this kind suggests to us that attention to these issues is likely to increase, while the forms and designs of the agreements that further these aims continue to evolve.

Index

For the benefit of digital users, indexed terms that span two pages (e.g., 52–53) may, on occasion, appear on only one of those pages.

Tables are indicated by an italic *t* following the page number.

The manufacturer's authorised representative in the EU for product safety is Oxford University Press España S.A. of el Parque Empresarial San Fernando de Henares, Avenida de Castilla, 2 – 28830 Madrid (www.oup.es/en or product.safety@oup.com). OUP España S.A. also acts as importer into Spain of products made by the manufacturer.

www.ingramcontent.com/pod-product-compliance
Lightning Source LLC
LaVergne TN
LVHW011904200926
848484LV00002B/526
9780198886884